# garde manger

3rd edition

The Art and Craft of the Cold Kitchen

# garde manger

The Culinary Institute of America

BICENTENNIAL
1807
WILEY
2007
BICENTENNIAL

John Wiley and Sons, Inc.

Published by John Wiley & Sons, Inc., Hoboken, New Jersey
Published simultaneously in Canada

Cover and interior design by Vertigo Design, New York City
Photo on page 578 by Dennis Gottlieb
Wiley Bicentennial Logo: Richard J. Pacifico

**_Library of Congress Cataloging-in-Publication Data:_**

Garde manger : the art and craft of the cold kitchen / The Culinary Institute of America. — 3rd ed.
p. cm.
Includes bibliographical references and index.
ISBN 978-0-470-05590-8 (cloth); ISBN 978-0-470-22873-9 (cloth; custom)
1. Cookery (Cold dishes) 2. Quantity cookery. I. Culinary Institute of America.
TX830.G37 2007
641.7'9-dc22
2007001280

Printed in the United States of America

10 9 8 7 6 5 4 3 2 1

# The Culinary Institute of America

Finally, for their tireless efforts during every stage of the production of this book, we would especially like to thank Chef Olivier Andreini C.M.C., David Barillaro, Chef Corky Clark, Chef Richard Gabriel, Chef Michael Garnero, Chef Lynne Gigliotti, Chef Tom Kief, Chef John Kowalski, Chef Pierre LeBlanc, Chef Hubert Martini, Chef Michael Pardus, Chef Henry Rapp , Chef John Reilly, Chef Michael Skibitcky, Taliaferro Organic Farms, Chef Daniel Turgeon, and Paul Wigsten. This book would not have been possible without their keen insight, vast knowledge, and continuous devotion.

# Contents

# Recipe Contents

## 2 Cold Sauces and Cold Soups

### Vinaigrettes

### Dairy-based and egg-based dressings

### Salsas

### Coulis, purées, and other sauces

## Soups

# 3   Salads

## Green salads

## Vegetable salads

## Potato salads; pasta, grain, and legume salads; and fruit salads

## Composed salads and warm salads

# 4 Sandwiches

## Hot sandwiches

## Cold sandwiches

## Tea sandwiches and crostini

# 5 Cured and Smoked Foods

## Cured foods

# 6  Sausage

## 7 Terrines, Pâtés, Galantines, and Roulades

### Pâtés en croute

### Galantines and roulades

## 8 Cheese

### Soft fresh cheese

## 9 Appetizers and Hors d'oeuvre

## 10 Condiments, Crackers, and Pickles

### Mustards

### Ketchups

### Chutneys

# 12 Basic Recipes

# Preface

In writing the third edition of *Garde Manger: The Art and Craft of the Cold Kitchen,* we have drawn widely from within the contemporary practice of garde manger, putting those skills and techniques into words, pictures, and recipes and gathering them into a single volume. This book is geared to meet the needs of students and seasoned practitioners alike, giving not only the basics of technique but also the sound principles that result in the highest quality foods. We have introduced new sections in virtually every chapter to encompass subjects ranging from espumas to fermented sausage and expanded the book to include more information on ice carving and the proliferation of the artisan American cheese maker.

The book begins with a basic overview of the history of the garde manger and the charcuterie. An understanding of how garde manger has moved from its origins to become the vibrant and exciting work it is today is especially relevant when you intend to make this work your career. Today's garde manger has a wide range of career options, some harking directly back to the traditional methods for preparing sausages, pâtès, and cheeses. Others look to more contemporary ways and may find their ultimate career path in banquets, catering, or event management. Throughout this book, the work of the garde manger is explored with an eye toward basic methods, safe food handling techniques and procedures, and cutting-edge approaches to combining flavors, colors, and textures in the foods prepared on the cold side of kitchens in restaurants, hotels, banquet halls, and specialty food producers.

Beginning with cold sauces and soups, both traditional and newer adaptations of cold emulsions sauces (such as vinaigrettes and mayonnaise) and cold soups are explained and illustrated. The recipes were selected not only to give a practical means of putting those techniques to use but also to provide recipes for a cross section of cold sauces and soups found on menus worldwide.

Cold sauces and soups are followed by salads. The salad chapter contains an extensive identification section and discusses the proper selection of ingredients and their care, as well as fundamental rules for preparing and presenting salads. Often, the care and handling of salad greens, herbs, and other salad components is the first assignment given to novice kitchen workers, regardless of whether they have their eyes set on the goal of becoming a line cook on the hot side or pursuing a career dedicated to all that the cold side encompasses.

Sandwiches were not always the popular menu item that they are today. However, an increasing interest in healthful, satisfying, and unusual fare has prompted the garde manger to look beyond deli and diner specialties to embrace a variety of breads, fillings, and garnishes that make sandwich making more intriguing and challenging. Methods and practical advice for preparing sandwiches for an à la carte menu as well as for teas and receptions are provided. Recipes from classics to less widely known sandwiches drawn from the global scene are also included.

Sausages, pâtès, terrines, and cured and smoked foods were once the province of professionals known as charcutières. The foods produced by the charcutières of days gone by are still familiar to us—from classic andouille sausage and sugar-cured bacon to gravalax and duck confit. These foods are appreciated today for their satisfying flavors and textures. Chefs are finding that a thorough understanding of the hows and whys of curing and preserving meats, fish, and poultry is indispensable in the quest for healthier, lighter, and more contemporary approaches to these ancient practices. It is in these foods and their safe, wholesome preparation that the cold kitchen most clearly retains its original intent and purpose.

Cheeses have always had a place in the cold kitchen. Like other cured and preserved foods, cheeses are a time-honored practical solution to the problem of keeping a constant supply of wholesome, nutritious foods on hand throughout the year. They are also the showcase for the talents and originality of their producers. Local and artisan cheeses are once more in the limelight, and the garde manger is faced with the challenge of learning to select, maintain, and present these complex and fascinating foods to an increasingly sophisticated audience. This chapter reviews the basics of cheesemaking, defines and describes various cheese families, and provides guidelines for putting together a cheese selection. In addition, the basics of preparing fresh cheeses as well as special preparations featuring those cheeses are included.

Hors d'oeuvre and appetizers represent an opportunity for the garde manger to pull together all the various skills and preparations of the entire discipline in a high-impact way. Just as hors d'oeuvre set the tone for a reception or banquet, so can a well-executed appetizer selection on a menu set the tone for the entire dining experience. There are a few classic standards to guide you in preparing and presenting appetizers and hors d'oeuvre. Many of the elements of these composed dishes are typically drawn from the chapters that precede this one. A perfect cold sauce provides the counterpoint to a plated appetizer. A flourish of baby greens offers texture and color contrast to a luxurious slice of smoked salmon or pâtè and so forth.

Relishes, compotes, pickles, chutneys, mustards, ketchups, and crackers provide the little something that takes the presentation from run-of-the-mill to memorable. These finishing touches, offered as condiments and garnishes to bring out all the flavors and textures of a dish, are gathered together in a chapter that explores another time honored realm of the cold kitchen: garnishing.

In the in-depth chapter about buffet presentation, you will find information about developing the concept or theme for a buffet, establishing prices and controlling costs, using basic design principles for platter layout, and contemporary solutions to setting up a buffet to maximize flow, interactivity, and international flavors and themes, as well as management concerns for buffets.

The book concludes with a chapter containing a variety of basic preparations, from stocks and aspics to marinades and spice rubs. The glossary provides thumbnail descriptions of a wide range of cooking terms and tools.

The instructions, photographs, and recipes in this book are meant to help you, whatever your current challenge may be. Perhaps you will choose to use them as a resource and teaching tool. You may want to use them as a foundation that you can modify to your particular needs by adjusting the seasoning and garnishes to create signature dishes, or scaling recipes up or down to match your production needs. One thing is certain: the continued appreciation on the part of the diners and chefs everywhere for the foods that are prepared by today's garde manger makes this one of the most fascinating and exciting areas of the professional culinary arts.

*objectives*

- Trace the origin of the garde manger

- Describe the growth of the guilds

- Explain the origin of restaurants and the role of the garde manger

- Compare and contrast the garde manger of past and present

- Understand the role of a garde manger as a businessperson and the skills required to practice this profession

# The professional garde manger

The term *garde manger* was originally used to identify a storage area. Preserved foods such as hams, sausages, and cheeses were held there. Cold foods were prepared and arranged for banquets there as well. Over time, garde manger has evolved to mean more than just a storage area or larder. It also indicates the station in a professional kitchen responsible for preparing cold foods, the cooks and chefs who prepare these cold foods, as well as an area of specialization in professional culinary arts. Members of today's garde manger share in a long culinary and social tradition, one which stretches back to well before the dawn of recorded history.

# The European garde manger tradition

As our ancestors became herdsmen and farmers, they developed the practical skills necessary to ensure a relatively steady food supply. This meant learning not only to domesticate animals and raise crops, but also how to preserve those foods. The first preserved fish were most likely produced by accident. Fish were "brined" in sea water and left to dry on the shore, where they either fermented or dried. Meats were hung off the ground and near the fire. This kept them out of the reach of scavenging animals and insects. The smoky bath surrounding them darkened, flavored, dried and preserved the meats and kept them from spoiling.

Records of various **curing** methods have been tracked back as far as 3000 B.C.E., when it is believed the Sumerians salted meats as a way to preserve this valuable but perishable food. Historical evidence shows that the Chinese and the Greeks had been producing and consuming salted fish for many years before passing their knowledge on to the Romans. In 63 B.C.E., the Greek writer Strabo detailed the importance of fish-salting centers in Spain and the existence of salt producers in the Crimea. Salt cod, made in the same basic way as Strabo described, is still an important food in cuisines around the world.

Food **preservation** skills and the necessary ingredients, including salt, sugar, and spices, were greatly valued. Cities such as modern-day Rome and Salzburg were founded near a ready source of salt. As the Romans extended their empire, they conquered lands rich in a variety of resources, including foodstuffs. They brought with them their own recipes and formulas for a variety of preserved meats, fish, cheeses, wines, and cordials. As is the way of all such invasions, the invaders brought their taste for familiar foods from home. But the culinary exchange was never in one direction. The conquering forces also learned to appreciate the local specialties. The Gauls, in what became France, were credited as highly successful hog domesticators and became renowned for

FIG 1-1    *An example of a historical garde manger kitchen*

their preserved hams and bacon. These products were regularly sent from Gaul to Rome and served at the Romans' legendary banquets. After the fall of the Roman Empire, the great houses of the Church and the nobility throughout Europe kept alive both local food traditions and those learned from the invaders.

Into the 12th century, approximately 80 to 90 percent of the world's population still fell into a category known as **rural peasants.** These peasants worked the nobles' lands to raise crops and farm animals. One of the most important activities of the year occurred at the end of the growing season. Vegetables, fruits, and grains were harvested and preserved by drying or by placing them into cold storage, along with pickles, jellies, and cheeses. Cows, sheep, and other animals were butchered and the meat preserved by a variety of means: pickled, salted, brined, cured, dried, packed in fat, or smoked. Once the foods had been prepared, they could be held in storage.

The right to collect and keep these foods, as well as to trade and tax them, was a visible symbol of power, wealth, and rank. During the Middle Ages, this privilege belonged to the kings, lords, dukes, and other nobility, as well as the monasteries and convents of the Catholic church. The castles and manor houses of the nobility each had an area devoted to food storage. It was typically located in an area below ground level to keep the foods cool. Garde manger (literally **"keep to eat"**) was the term used to identify this storage area. It is still used to indicate a larder or pantry—a place for cold food storage. The member of the household staff known as the **officier de bouche,** or steward, was responsible for managing this storeroom, dispensing foods as necessary.

# The growth of the guilds

Some of these special items, such as hams and cheeses, became part of the commerce and trade between towns and states. They were included as dowries and tributes, along with livestock, buildings, servants, and jewels, as well as being used as a kind of currency to acquire other goods. Eventually, rules were established governing how merchants prepared and sold these goods and services to prevent monopolies and pricing abuses. The work itself was clearly defined and assigned to various groups known as **guilds.** The guilds developed training systems for their members, taking them from an apprenticeship to the journeyman stage and finally conferring the status of master. Each individual guild was granted a charter, giving them some specific rights.

By the end of the 16th century, there were approximately two dozen guilds dedicated specifically to food. They fell into two groups—those that provided raw materials and those that provided prepared foods. For example, the guild that prepared and sold cooked items made from the pig was referred to as ***charcuterie,*** derived from French root words meaning "cooked flesh." This guild kept the practical work of preserving meats alive and thriving, making bacons, hams, sausages, and pâtés.

There were numerous strategies to get around restrictions imposed on any given guild, and the charcutières were no exception. One of their tactics led to the development of terrines: Charcutières were not permitted to sell foods baked in pastries. Making and selling **pâté** en croûte, forcemeat loaves baked in pastry, would not have been allowed according to a strict reading of the charcutière's charter. Rather than stop making pâté en croûte, the charcutières baked the forcemeat in an earthenware mold instead of pastry—and so pâtés en terrine were created.

# Restaurants and the role of the garde manger

The more essential the food, the more closely it was regulated. The more lucrative a guild's activities, the more likely it was that one guild might be tempted to infringe on another. Each guild fought to protect its individual rights. There were several cases brought before judges to determine if one guild's activities had crossed the line into the work of another's.

One such case had a profound impact on the work of today's garde manger. In 1765, **Monsieur Boulanger,** a tavern-keeper, was brought to court for selling a hot dish, which he referred to as a *restorante* (restorative). Traditionally, the right to sell hot prepared foods like this restorative had been the exclusive privilege of another guild. The judge ruled that M. Boulanger had not broken any law, and so the first restaurant was born. Others quickly followed this new type of venture.

When the **French Revolution** began in 1789, the upheaval in noble households was enormous. Noblemen left France to escape the guillotine, leaving their household staffs to look out for themselves. The garde manger, as well as chefs and cooks, were household employees, and as such did not have a formal guild of their own. These workers found their way into restaurants in increasing numbers throughout Europe and the British Isles.

At first, there was no widely recognized structure for kitchen workers. There were no established duties or areas of specialization. It took several years before a serious attempt was made to organize the kitchen workers. Eventually, the **brigade system,** recorded by Auguste Escoffier, detailed a logical chain of command that brought order to the unruly working arrangements of his day. We still use the brigade system, and refer to the various "stations" in the kitchen with the names assigned by Escoffier: saucier, rôtisseur, pâtissier, and garde manger.

When the guild system was officially abolished in **1791,** some members of the charcutière guild also joined the ranks of restaurant and hotel kitchen garde manger staffs. Others continued to operate their businesses as before. The charcutière and the garde manger have always been closely linked, since they are both founded on cold preserved foods. When the term garde manger is used today, it is often understood to include the work of the charcutière as well.

# Today's garde manger

The garde manger, recast in a restaurant setting, has retained its traditions of preparing a variety of preserved and cold foods. It has also expanded its scope to include appetizers, hors d'ouevre, salads, sandwiches, and the accompanying cold sauces and condiments. Garde manger is involved in à la carte service as well as banquets, receptions, and buffets.

The techniques required to prepare pâtés, terrines, sausages, and fresh cheeses are the particular domain of the garde manger. However, becoming a skilled garde manger also means learning a broad base of culinary skills, those directly related to handling basic cold food preparations as well as those required to prepare hot foods: roasting, poaching, simmering, and sautéing meats, fish, poultry, vegetables, grains, and legumes.

It is precisely because the skills and responsibilities are so broad that many of today's most highly regarded chefs got their start in the garde manger as apprentices or *commis*. In addition, recent years have seen a rebirth of the more traditional practices of charcuterie and cheese-making by purveyors with retail shops and wholesale businesses. Handcrafted foods such as country-style hams, sausages, pâtés, and fresh and aged cheeses are increasingly available to both the restaurant chef and the home cook.

## Establishments

Hotels, full-service restaurants, and private clubs that offer à la carte menus may have one or more people working exclusively in the area of garde manger, though the specific name of this area varies from place to place. Some operations refer to it as the pantry, others may call it the salad station, still others the "cold side," and so on. The specific duties of this station can include cold sauces and soups, salads, hors d'oeuvre, and canapés.

This station may, in some kitchens, supply other stations with sauces, condiments, and garnishes. The garde manger in some operations shapes and portions meats, poultry, and fish, adding marinades or stuffings as appropriate.

During à la carte service, the garde manger typically plates salads and cold appetizers, and may also be responsible for plating desserts. The breakfast, lunch, and brunch menus

FIG 1-2 | *Contemporary garde manger kitchen*

often rely heavily upon the garde manger as well, especially for fruit, cereal, and egg dishes.

Cooks and chefs working in banquet and catering operations practice all the same basic cooking skills as the garde manger in an à la carte restaurant. However, the approach to work is slightly different. This work is so stimulating and challenging that many professionals choose it as a lifelong career path. Here, where the goal is to produce and serve flavorful, attractive food to large numbers of individuals simultaneously, you learn to use the special equipment and cooking techniques of volume production. The chef develops not only a menu, but also all the planning necessary to come up with scaled recipes, accurate and timely orders for food and other items, and food costs. Presentation is often a significant component of banquets and receptions. Decor, appropriate and effective garnishes for plates, platters, and other food displays, and concerns for food quality and customer safety are considered. The nature of large events often involves a certain level of risk, and always calls for the ability to think under pressure and come up with a creative solution to a crisis. To learn more about the development and management of a buffet, read Chapter 11, Buffet Presentation.

Delicatessens, charcuteries, and shops selling prepared foods of all types offer yet more options for the professional garde manger. Some operations feature handcrafted foods, such as cheeses or sausage. Their goods may be sold through a retail shop or exclusively to those in the restaurant trade. Large companies, including hotel and restaurant chains and food manufacturers, look to those with strong skills in garde manger to undertake projects such as the development of a new line of sauces or condiments, spice rubs or salad blends.

## Types of work

Both employers and schools recognize that formal education on its own is not enough to assure excellence, however. Garde manger is a practical art. To succeed, you need to work. Whether you work for yourself or for someone else, you must make choices about your work carefully. It is tempting to make a decision based on salary, location, or some similar immediately tangible consideration. However, if you consider each job as an investment in your future, it is far easier to evaluate the long-lasting rewards.

Making wise career choices is complicated, so take the time to evaluate any career move. Develop your own plan for the future as specifically as you can to create a framework so that you can determine the type of establishment and the type of work that will set you up to secure the next level in your career.

Look for work environments where each person has a stake in getting things done correctly. When every person has the opportunity to help make decisions and has the tools they need to perform at their best, everyone succeeds. If you want to do a job well, you need to know the quality standards. Objective evaluations, constructive criticism, and additional training are part of any good working situation.

## Entry level

Work at the entry level includes cleaning and cutting produce, making vinaigrettes and compound butters, and following simple standard recipes under supervision. It is important to ask questions and follow advice, watch carefully what goes on around you, and supplement what you see and hear by reading. Taste foods that are both familiar and unfamiliar to you and keep accurate notes and records. Begin compiling a foundation of knowledge by assembling a library of books and subscriptions, as well as important contact numbers and URLs. Learn the necessary skills to handle special equipment safely and efficiently. Slicers, mixers, grinders, blenders, food processors, thermometers, smokers, sausage stuffers, and salometers are just a few of the specialized pieces of equipment used in the garde manger and smokehouse.

## Advanced level

As your skills improve, you move from entry-level positions into positions of more responsibility. You take on more advanced and challenging work, and your title may advance to lead or executive chef. At this level you have more responsibility for conceiving new menu items, recording standard recipes, costing, and developing and maintaining a budget. You will train kitchen and dining-room staff in the proper presentation of the new and standard menu items. You are responsible for keeping food costs down and improving quality in all areas of your work.

Banquet and buffet chefs develop menus—both standard and custom—and go through a process of scaling and costing each menu item. Staffing and scheduling responsibilities for the banquet chef include maintaining and training a relatively large pool of talent, often working directly with the dining-room manager. Some special aspects of this work include coordinating with other service providers, such as florists, musicians, and photographers.

Entrepreneurs develop handcrafted specialty items that are produced on both the small and large scale. Their work focuses more on the development of a product or line of products for sale. They must be concerned with a variety of regulations, certifications, and inspections in order to be sure that foods prepared for sale meet all the necessary legal requirements. Food quality and cost remain as important as ever, and additional business concerns accrue. To grow a company from something that used to be small and local into something large, some key factors that should be focused on in order to sell and distribute items include consistency, timeliness, packaging, labeling, and general appeal.

# The practice of a profession

Any profession has a great many sides and the culinary vocation is no different. A culinary professional is an artist, a businessperson, a scientist, and a cultural explorer, among other attributes. Acquiring the skills and knowledge necessary to succeed in this profession is a lifelong journey.

## Education and training

Employers today look for both experience and education when they hire at virtually all levels higher than entry level. At the most prestigious shops, even entry-level positions may demand a degree or some sort of formal training. Employees look for jobs that offer the opportunity to use the skills and education they already possess and, at the same time, to learn new skills.

## Formal education

The increasing emphasis on a formal education goes hand in hand with the emergence of a number of programs dedicated exclusively to the culinary arts. Employers rely upon the general and specific skills of the craft taught by these schools to establish a common ground of ability. This saves them hours of on-the-job training. The demand for graduates continues to grow each year, and so has the number of programs specializing in the culinary arts. The best education couples hands-on practice with coursework devoted to product and equipment knowledge. In addition, a well-rounded program provides study in important aspects of culinary arts as a business: customer service, math, food and menu costing, and team-building skills.

Programs that are recognized in the industry attract high-quality instructors and offer opportunities for students to network, join clubs and organizations, compete, and do advanced studies in an area of specialization. Their graduates receive plenty of hands-on experience and develop confidence and control in all areas of culinary arts. Industry leaders look to graduates of those programs to staff their companies because they bring with them a solid foundation.

Even garde manger chefs who already have achieved significant success in their careers take advantage of the many opportunities offered through continuing education. Classes that are tailored to a specific topic give professionals exposure to new techniques and methods and new equipment and ingredients.

## Food knowledge

The ingredients that the garde manger uses on a daily basis run the gamut from the mundane and utilitarian, such as calves' heads and pigs' feet, to the priceless and exotic: saffron, foie gras, caviar, and truffles.

When you know what an ingredient looks like, tastes like, and acts like, you can use that knowledge to be more creative, more adaptable, and more efficient. At first, you may rely solely upon the recipe or formula to tell you what to use. As long as everything required by the recipe is on hand, things should work out. Take the extra minute or two required to really examine the ingredient and make note of what it looks like, how it smells or feels, its shape, and its color.

Classes, workshops, or demonstrations that offer comparison tastings are excellent learning opportunities. You can also arrange your own blind tastings. This information is invaluable, whether your responsibility is using ingredients appropriately or buying them to maintain quality and profit.

Beyond knowing the color, taste, and cost of an ingredient, however, today's garde manger typically find themselves facing an increasing number of special concerns about the manner in which foods are grown, harvested, and processed. A safe and wholesome food supply is a growing concern of both the public and the profession. Topics such as sustainable agriculture, bioengineering, genetically modified organisms (GMOs), organics, and the support of local and regional growers all factor into the decisions you and your business must make.

## Equipment knowledge

It is true that the foods made by the garde manger and charcuterie are not beyond the technical skill of any good cook, and many individuals enjoy making their own sausages, bacon, or smoked trout. However, acquiring the tools and ingredients, as well as the skills required to use them, can be time-consuming and somewhat expensive. You need not only the correct equipment and ingredients, but also the appropriate storage space—one you can keep at the correct temperature and humidity—to produce some items. In addition to working with knives, pots, and pans, the garde manger must be well-versed in the use of equipment such as meat slicers and grinders, food processors, smokehouses, brining tubs and salometers, and, for some practitioners, ice-carving tools.

Learn to use important business tools; computers, the Internet, budgets, accounting systems, and inventory control systems all play a role. Many organizations, from the largest chains to the smallest one-person catering company, rely upon software systems that allow them to efficiently administer a number of areas: inventory, purchases, losses, sales, profits, food costs, customer complaints, reservations, payroll, schedules, and budgets. If you are not using a system capable of tracking all this information and more, you cannot be as effective as you need to be.

## Communications skills

A well-written resumé can sell you to a potential employer. Your own mission statement, if properly worded, keeps you on track and helps you make the best possible career moves. A precise and specific plan for an event can keep it on track and on budget. A thorough and fair interview can unearth the perfect employee or business partner. Each of these activities demands good communication skills. Today's garde manger must communicate using a wider variety of media than ever before, from written memos and letters, to e-mails and reports, to video-conferencing and interactive learning. A good education program addresses the general and specific communications needs of its students and offers courses, workshops, and tutoring or labs in a wide range of communication skills.

## Continuing education

Your education and your experience combine to form the most important source for your personal professional development. Every career choice or move that you make is part of your lifelong education. If you have a long-term plan, you can choose jobs that give you the opportunity to learn new skills and take on greater responsibility as you advance toward your goals.

Keeping current with basic skills and new trends is a lifelong task. Once initial training has been completed, **continuing education** is equally important, as the industry is constantly evolving.

Evaluate your career, both as it is right now and as you would like it to be in the future, and then take the appropriate steps to keep on top of the latest information in the areas in which you are most interested. Attend classes and workshops, hone your skills in specialized areas, keep up with new ingredients or equipment, learn new management strategies, or strengthen your skills in team-building, writing and communication, marketing, and promotion.

Some of the courses or seminars you attend can earn you credits (CEUs, or continuing education units). They may be necessary to achieve certain certifications or advancements. Continuing education and professional development programs are available through a wide range of colleges and universities, in both a traditional and a distance-learning environment.

Not all continuing education occurs in a classroom or over an Internet hookup. Magazines, television programming, newsletters, Web sites, government publications, and books are all excellent sources. Directed travel programs can open up a completely new way of seeing the profession by exposing you to a new cuisine, a new part of the world, a new ingredient, or a new contact.

## Networking

The old saying that it's "who you know" has a great deal of truth. The group of professionals you know is called a **network.** A solid network is an indispensable tool for the professional and should include members of your industry from as many areas as possible. Knowing someone in a niche not obviously related to your own can turn up unexpected opportunities.

Creating a professional network is a task that should be taken seriously. Working with other professionals to share information and knowledge is an important avenue of growth, both professional and personal. Networks can be formal or informal. The way to begin is simply to introduce yourself to others in your field. Have business cards with you when you go out to other restaurants or to trade shows. Write letters to individuals whose work you have seen and admired.

Join professional organizations to expand your network. Well-run groups typically have a variety of meetings and forums to allow members to come in contact with each other. Take advantage of local and national meetings and conventions to learn more about your profession.

When you make a good contact, follow up with a phone call or a note. The communication that you develop with your peers will keep your own work fresh and contemporary, and an established network makes it much easier for you to find a new job or an employee.

## Competition

Contests and **competitions** offer you a chance to really stretch yourself. Professional magazines, journals, newsletters, and Web sites have information about contests on the local, national, and international level. Whenever you submit your work to the scrutiny of a panel of judges, you learn. Critical review provides you a means to keep improving in a way that your daily production work never can. Practice, research, and the stress of competition exercises your professional muscles, the same way that competing in a sporting event strengthens an athlete. Even if you are not entered in the competition, attend the judging if you can so that you can benefit from the experience.

# The garde manger as businessperson

## *Managing physical assets*

**Physical assets** are the equipment and supplies needed to do business. In the case of a restaurant, these might include food and beverage inventory, tables, chairs, linens, china, flatware, glassware, computers and point-of-sale systems, cash registers, kitchen equipment, cleaning supplies, and ware-washing machines. When we talk about managing physical assets, we are considering how anything that you must purchase affects your ability to do business well.

The first step in bringing the expenses associated with your physical assets under control is to know what your expenses actually are. Then you can begin the process of making the adjustments and instituting the control systems that will keep your organization operating at maximum efficiency.

One of the biggest expenses for any restaurant will always be food and beverage costs. You or your purchasing agent will have to work hard to develop and sustain a good purchasing system. Because each operation has different needs, there are no hard-and-fast rules, just principles that you will apply to your own situation. Maintaining quality is of course the highest priority.

## *Managing time*

It may seem that no matter how hard you work or how much planning you do, the days aren't long enough. Learning new skills, so that you can make the best possible use of the time you have, certainly ought to be an ongoing part of your career development. If you look over your operation, you will see where time is wasted. In most operations, the top five time-wasters are: (1) no clear priorities for tasks, (2) poor staff training, (3) poor communication, (4) poor organization, and (5) missing or inadequate tools to accomplish tasks. To combat these time-wasters, use the following strategies:

### Invest time in reviewing daily operations

Consider the way you, your coworkers, and your staff spend the day. Does everyone have a basic understanding of which tasks are most important? Do they know when to begin a particular task in order to bring it to completion on time? It can be an eye-opening experience to take a hard look at where the workday goes. Once you see that you and your staff need to walk too far to gather basic items or that the person who washes the dishes is sitting idle for the first two hours of the shift, you can take steps to rectify the problem. You can try to reorganize storage space. You may decide to train the dishwasher to do some prep work, or you can rewrite the schedule so that the shift begins two hours later. Until you are objective about what needs to be done and in what order, you can't begin the process of saving time.

### Invest time in training others

If you expect someone to do a job properly, take enough time to explain the task carefully. Walk yourself and your staff through the jobs that must be done, and be sure that everyone understands how to do the work, where to find necessary items, how far each person's responsibility extends, and what to do in case a question or emergency comes up. Give your staff the quality standards they need to evaluate the job and determine if they have done what was requested, in the appropriate fashion, and on time. If you don't invest this time up front, you may find yourself squandering precious time following your workers around, picking up the slack, and handling work that shouldn't be taking up your day.

### Learn to communicate clearly

Whether you are training a new employee, introducing a new menu item, or ordering a piece of equipment, clear **communication** is important. Be specific, use the most concise language you can, and be as brief as possible without leaving out necessary information. If tasks are handled by a number of people, be sure to write each task out, from the first step to the last. Encourage people to ask questions if they don't understand you. If you need help learning communication skills, consider taking a workshop or seminar to strengthen any weak areas.

### Take steps to create an orderly work environment

If you have to dig through five shelves to find the lid to the storage container you just put the stock in, you haven't been using your time wisely. Planning work areas carefully, thinking about all the tools, ingredients, and equipment you need for preparation and throughout service, and grouping like activities together are all techniques that can help you organize your work better. Poor placement of large and small tools is a great time waster. Use adequate, easy-to-access storage space for common items such as whips, spoons, ladles, and tongs. Electrical outlets for small equipment ought to be within reach of everyone. While you may be forced to work within the limits of your existing floor plan, be on the lookout for products or storage strategies that can turn a bad arrangement into one that works smoothly.

### Purchase, replace, and maintain all necessary tools

A well-equipped kitchen will have enough of all the tools necessary to prepare every item on the menu. If you can't purchase new equipment, then think about restructuring the menu to even out the workload. If you can't remove a menu item, then invest in the tools you need to prevent a slow-down during service.

## Managing information

The garde manger is part of the much larger world. Read about all areas that might affect your career and your industry: business and economics, arts and entertainment, society and politics. Popular culture has a curious way of influencing your work. Your customers and clients do not live in a vacuum and neither should you.

There are numerous print or on-line sources devoted to the specifics of new or unusual ingredients, unfamiliar dishes or equipment, and more. Information gathering can become a full-time task on its own. To make use of the information available, you must be able to analyze and evaluate carefully to sift out the important material from useless data and use all sorts of media and technology effectively.

Learn more about the profession's history, not just because it is interesting, but because it gives relevance and ballast to the decisions you make.

# Managing people

Restaurant operations rely directly on the work and dedication of a number of people, from executives and administrators to line cooks, wait staff, and maintenance and cleaning staff. No matter how large or small your staff may be, the ability to engage all your workers in a team effort is one of the major factors in determining whether you will succeed or not.

Most people prefer to work in an environment where everyone can make a distinct and measurable contribution. The first task in creating such an environment is a properly written job description. Training is another key component. To do a job well, the employee needs to know the quality standards and have those standards consistently reinforced with clear, objective evaluations, feedback, constructive criticism, and, when necessary, additional training or disciplinary measures.

Everyone has the right to work in an environment that is free from physical hazards. This means that, as an employer, you must provide a work space that is well lit, properly ventilated, and free from obvious dangers, such as improperly maintained equipment. Employees must have access to potable water and bathroom facilities. Beyond this bare minimum, you may offer a locker room, a laundry facility that provides clean uniforms and aprons, or other such amenities.

Workers' compensation, unemployment insurance, and disability insurance are also your responsibility. You are required to make all legal deductions from an employee's paycheck and to report all earnings properly to state and federal agencies. Liability insurance (to cover any harm to your facility, employees, or guests) must be kept up-to-date and at adequate levels.

Employers may choose to offer additional forms of assistance as part of an employee benefits package. Life insurance, medical and dental insurance, assistance with such things as dependent care, adult literacy training, and enrollment in and support for those enrolled in substance-abuse programs are examples of the support an employer can provide for employees.

# Key qualities of a professional

Every member of a profession is responsible for the profession's image. Those who have made the greatest impact in their fields know that the cardinal virtues of the culinary profession are an open and inquiring mind, an appreciation of and dedication to quality wherever it is found, and a sense of responsibility. Success also depends on several character traits, some of which are inherent, some of which are diligently cultivated throughout a career. These include:

### A commitment to service
The food service industry is predicated on service; therefore, a culinary professional should never lose sight of what that word implies. Good service includes (but is not limited to) providing quality food that is properly and safely cooked, appropriately seasoned, and attractively presented in a pleasant environment—in short, making the customer happy. The degree to which an operation can offer satisfaction in these areas is the degree to which it will succeed in providing good (and, ideally, excellent) service. The customer must always come first.

## A sense of responsibility

A culinary professional's responsibility is fourfold: to him- or herself, to coworkers, to the restaurant, and to the guest. This should include respecting not just the customer and his or her needs but also staff, food, equipment, and the facility itself. Waste, recklessness, disregard for others, and misuse or abuse of any commodity are unacceptable. Abusive language, harassment, ethnic slurs, and profanity do not have a place in the professional kitchen. When employees feel that their needs are given due consideration, their self-esteem will increase and their attitude toward the establishment will improve; both will increase productivity and reduce absenteeism.

## Judgment

Although it is not easy to learn, good judgment is a prerequisite for becoming a professional. An ability to judge what is right and appropriate is acquired throughout a lifetime of experience. Good judgment is never completely mastered; rather, it is a goal toward which one should continually strive.

# 2

*objectives*

- Gain an understanding of and be able to identify cold emulsion sauces

- Recognize the basic vinaigrette preparation

- Learn to prepare and repair mayonnaise sauces

- Begin to classify dairy-based sauces, salsas, coulis and purées, and miscellaneous sauces

- Be able to explain the preparation of coating sauces including the use of gelatin

- Describe a variety of cold soups such as vegetable and fruit soups, cream-style soups, and clear cold soups

# Cold sauces and cold soups

Sauces and soups are among the first true tests of a chef's skill. For the garde manger, the ability to produce perfectly balanced vinaigrettes, subtly flavored and creamy mayonnaise sauces, and cold soups of all varieties is a skill that should be constantly honed throughout a career.

# Cold sauces

The successful pairing of a sauce with any food demonstrates an understanding of the food and an ability to judge and evaluate a dish's flavors, textures, and colors. Evaluating why some combinations work well while others are less successful offers valuable lessons in composing a dish. What does the sauce bring to the dish? How does it function in the total composition? How does it taste? Sauces are not just an afterthought. They add **flavor, color, texture, sheen,** and **moisture** to a dish. In the cold kitchen, the chef's sauce repertoire includes:

- Cold emulsion sauces: vinaigrettes and mayonnaise
- Dairy-based sauces
- Salsas
- Coulis and purées
- Coating sauces
- Miscellaneous cold sauces such as horseradish and mignonette

## *Cold emulsion sauces*

Vinaigrettes and mayonnaise are made by combining two ingredients that would not otherwise blend into a homogeneous mixture. In order to understand how these sauces are prepared, we will first discuss what an **emulsion** is and how it is formed.

An emulsion consists of two phases, the **dispersed phase** and the **continuous phase.** When making vinaigrette, for example, the dispersed phase is the oil, meaning that the oil has been handled in such a way that it is broken up into very small droplets. Each oil droplet is suspended throughout the continuous phase, in this case the vinegar (see Fig 2-1).

**Temporary emulsions,** such as vinaigrettes, form quickly and require only the mechanical action of whipping, shaking, or stirring (see Fig 2-2). To make an emulsion stable enough to keep the oil in suspension, additional ingredients known as **emulsifiers** are necessary (see Fig 2-3). The emulsifiers used to make cold sauces include egg yolks, mustard, and glace de viande. Starches such as those in garlic or modified starches such as cornstarch or arrowroot are also used. These emulsifiers are able to attract and hold both the oil and liquid in suspension so that the mixture does not separate into its two phases. In some instances, the molecules of the emulsifiers surround the molecules in the dispersed phase and prevent them from joining back together again.

**Stable emulsions,** such as mayonnaise, are made by very carefully controlling the rate at which the oil is added to the egg yolks. Egg yolks provide both the liquid that holds the oil droplets in suspension and a special emulsifier known as **lecithin.** The oil is added very gradually at first so that the droplets can be made extremely fine. The more oil that is added to the yolks, the thicker the sauce will become. If the oil is added too rapidly, the emulsion cannot start to form properly. And if the emulsion becomes too thick early in the mixing process, the full amount of oil cannot be added, unless the sauce is thinned with a little water or an acid, such as vinegar or lemon juice.

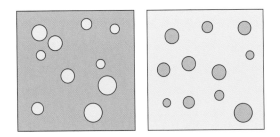

FIG 2-1  *An oil-in-water emulsion (left) disperses oil droplets in water, while a water-in-oil emulsion (right) disperses water droplets in oil. Examples of an oil-in-water emulsion include mayonnaise and vinaigrette while an example of a water-in-oil emulsion is butter.*

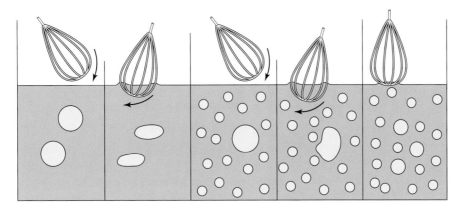

FIG 2-2 *Temporary emulsions are created through mechanical agitation, which breaks molecules up into smaller sizes and disperses them throughout the continuous phase; if left to sit, however, the emulsion's lack of stabilizer will cause it to separate eventually.*

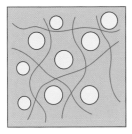

FIG 2-3 *Emulsifiers stabilize an emulsion by creating a network, usually of proteins or starch, that keeps the dispersed molecules from coming into contact with each other and combining into larger molecules, which would break the emulsion.*

## Vinaigrettes

Vinaigrettes are closely associated with green salads, but they are also used in other applications: as a marinade for grilled or broiled foods, and to dress salads made from pastas and vegetables. It is interesting to note that while **oil** is the largest component by volume and weight of a vinaigrette, the sauce is most often named for the **acid**—red wine vinaigrette, balsamic vinaigrette, lemon vinaigrette, and tomato vinaigrette. The flavor of the acid dominates that of the oil. When an oil has a distinctive enough flavor, however, the vinaigrette may be called by the oil's name.

### Making a basic vinaigrette

The challenge of making a good vinaigrette lies in achieving what chefs refer to as **"balance,"** a point at which the acidity of the vinegar or juice is tempered, but not dominated, by the richness of the oil.

Many chefs know the **standard vinaigrette ratio** of 3 parts oil to 1 part acid. This works well as a starting point, but it is important to taste and evaluate the vinaigrette whenever a change is made in the type of oil, acid, or specific flavoring ingredients. Some vinaigrette formulas may call for either a quantity of water to dilute very acidic vinegars, or a bit of sugar to soften the acidity instead of additional oil.

A basic vinaigrette is a temporary emulsion, made by blending the measured ingredients until they form a homogenous sauce. The sauce remains an emulsion for only a short time, quickly separating back into oil and vinegar. To keep the sauce well-balanced each time it is used, stir or whisk the vinaigrette each time it is served.

The best way to check for flavor and balance in a vinaigrette is to dip a piece of lettuce into it, shake off the excess, and then evaluate the taste of the sauce on the lettuce.

### Making an emulsified vinaigrette

The ratio for an **emulsified vinaigrette** is the same as for a basic vinaigrette. To make these sauces, egg yolks, mustard, garlic, fruit or vegetable purées, or glace de viande are included in the formula, both to add flavor and to help stabilize the sauce.

1.  **Combine the vinegar and all of the seasoning ingredients.** Add the salt, pepper, herbs, mustard, or other ingredients to the vinegar to be sure that they are evenly dispersed throughout the sauce (see Fig 2-4a). Note: Fresh herbs give vinaigrettes a wonderful flavor and color. However, if they are added too far in advance, the vinegar can start to discolor their fresh green color and begin to break down their lively flavors. When preparing a large batch of vinaigrette intended to last through several service periods, it may be preferable to add the fresh herbs to the sauce just before service begins.

2.  **Add the oil gradually.** Slowly add a few droplets of oil at a time into the bowl, whisking constantly. Once the emulsion has started to form, pour or ladle the oil in a fine stream while whisking the sauce (see Fig 2-4b). Another way to create a stable vinaigrette is to use a blender, immersion blender, standing mixer with a whip, or food processor. Vinaigrettes made this way can hold their emulsion longer than those that are simply whipped together.

3.  **Add any garnish and check the seasonings at this point.** Fresh or dried fruits and vegetables, crumbled cheese, or other garnishes can be added, if desired. Review the previous section for information about how to check the seasoning and serve this sauce.

**FIG 2-4A** *Begin the vinaigrette by incorporating the emulsifier, in this case mustard, into the vinegar base.*

**FIG 2-4B** *Whisking steadily, stream the oil into the vinegar base until fully incorporated.*

**Reduced-fat vinaigrettes**

The total amount of oil in a vinaigrette can be greatly reduced by replacing up to two-thirds of the oil with a lightly thickened stock or juice. Add enough diluted arrowroot or other modified starch to simmering stock or juice so that it will mimic the consistency of a salad oil once cooled.

Purées of fruits and vegetables can also be used in place of part of a vinaigrette's oil. Naturally thick purées such as tomato or red pepper purées may not need to be thickened further. Tomato Vinaigrette (page 33) is one such vinaigrette.

Store **reduced-fat vinaigrettes** as you would basic or emulsified vinaigrettes and follow the appropriate steps for recombining and adjusting seasoning before service.

## Mayonnaise

Mayonnaise and dressings made with mayonnaise as a base can be used to dress salads, as a dip or spread, and to produce a **coating sauce,** such as Mayonnaise Collée (page 597). This sauce is made by combining egg yolks with oil so that a stable emulsion forms. Unlike vinaigrettes, this cold sauce should not break as it sits. Mayonnaise is a sauce that requires skill and finesse to prepare correctly. It also requires careful handling to avoid contamination.

1. **Select and prepare the ingredients for the mayonnaise.** Classic recipes for mayonnaise-style dressing call for 6 to 8 fl oz / 180 to 240 mL oil to each egg yolk. To avoid any possible food-borne illness (such as salmonella), professional chefs should use **pasteurized egg yolks.** Since mayonnaise is often intended as a base sauce that can be used for a variety of purposes, it is usually best to choose an oil that does not have a pronounced flavor of its own. There are exceptions to this general rule. For example, a mayonnaise made with extra-virgin olive oil or a nut oil would be appropriate to serve as a dip with a platter of grilled vegetables or crudité. Various acids may be used to prepare a mayonnaise, including lemon juice, wine, or cider vinegars. The **acid** is used both to give the sauce flavor and, along with water, to adjust its consistency.

2. **Blend the yolks with a bit of water.** Whisk the yolks and water together to loosen the eggs and make it easier for them to absorb the oil. You may also wish to include lemon juice or vinegar or mustard at this point, if your formula calls for those ingredients.

3. **Add the oil a little at a time, whisking in the oil completely.** It is important to proceed cautiously when the oil is first being added (see Fig 2-5a). The oil must be whipped into the egg yolks so that it is broken up into very fine droplets. This stage is where the emulsion first starts to form. If the oil is added too quickly, the droplets will be too large to blend into the yolks, and the sauce will appear broken. Adding the oil slowly allows eggs to absorb the oil properly, and the sauce will start to thicken. Once about one-fourth to one-third of the oil has been properly blended into the egg mixture, you may start to increase the amount you add. When preparing a mayonnaise in a mixer, add the oil in a thin stream as the machine runs. It is still true that the oil should be added more slowly at the beginning than at the end.

4. **Adjust the thickness and flavor of the sauce by adding a bit more acid or water as you incorporate the oil.** Additional lemon juice, vinegar, or a little water is added once the eggs have absorbed enough of the oil to become very thick. If this step is neglected, the sauce will become too thick to absorb any more oil. Continue adding oil until the amount specified in the recipe has been added. A finished mayonnaise should be thick enough to hold soft peaks

| FIG 2-5A | *During the beginning stages of the emulsion, the oil must be added slowly and steadily to properly disperse the fat in the liquid.* |

| FIG 2-5B | *When finished, the mayonnaise should be thick and hold a soft peak.* |

(see Fig 2-5b). However, depending upon its intended use, you may wish to thin the sauce with additional water to make it more pourable.

5.  Add any additional flavoring or garnish ingredients at the point indicated in the recipe. **Aïoli** (page 36), a garlic-flavored mayonnaise, calls for a good quantity of garlic to be included from the earliest stages of mixing. Other ingredients, such as vegetable purées or pastes, fresh herbs, chopped pickles, and so forth may be blended into the sauce once the oil is fully incorporated. Green Mayonnaise (Sauce Vert) (page 36) and Rémoulade Sauce (page 38) are two such variations.

### When mayonnaise breaks

Mayonnaise and similarly prepared emulsified dressings may break for a number of reasons: the oil was added too rapidly for the egg yolk to absorb it, the sauce was allowed to become too thick, or the sauce became either too cold or too warm as it was being prepared.

A **broken mayonnaise** can be corrected as follows:

1.  Beat a pasteurized egg yolk until foamy.

2.  Gradually incorporate the broken mayonnaise, whisking constantly. The mayonnaise should recombine into a homogenous sauce. Be sure to taste and season it appropriately before serving.

**Storing mayonnaise**

Mayonnaise should be kept refrigerated at all times once it is prepared. Transfer it to a storage container, cover it carefully, and label it with a date. Before using mayonnaise that has been stored, stir it gently and check the seasoning carefully. If the sauce needs to be thinned, add a bit of water.

# Dairy-based sauces

**Dairy-based sauces** are used as salad dressings or dips. They are made from soft cheeses such as quark, mascarpone, and cream cheese; cultured milks such as sour cream, crème fraîche, or buttermilk; cream; or low- or reduced-fat versions of ricotta, sour cream, or cottage cheese. These dressings are generally white or ivory, so they can take on the color of purées or coulis of herbs, fruits, or vegetables.

Some typical additions to dairy-based dressings include cheeses (especially blue cheese, parmesan, or feta), fresh lemon, black pepper, and minced or puréed herbs. Diced, minced, or grated vegetables, pickles, capers, or olives add texture as well as flavor.

Creamy sauces can be prepared in a range of textures, from a relatively stiff sauce to serve as a dip or spread, to a pourable sauce that easily dresses a green salad. For a very light, almost mousse-like texture, whipped cream can be folded into the sauce at the last moment.

# Salsas

**Salsas** are typically made from uncooked fruits or vegetables. They often include an acid, such as citrus juice, vinegar, or wine, to add a sharp flavor. Spices, chiles, and herbs are sometimes added to these sauces to give them a potent flavor and a higher-than-average level of "heat."

Sauces made from vegetables and fruits have become increasingly popular. Both fresh (or raw) and cooked versions of salsas, **chutneys, relishes,** and **compotes** are found in cuisines from Mexico to India. While there will always be distinctions made by aficionados about when the term salsa is correctly used—versus chutney, relish, or even compote—in practical terms, the differences between them have more to do with their country or cuisine of origin than a difference in preparation method. The recipes for a variety of chutneys, relishes, and compotes can be found in Chapter 10.

# Coulis and purées

The classical definition of a **coulis,** written by Escoffier in *Le Guide Culinaire,* states that a coulis is the "well reduced, highly concentrated essential flavours of a food, in either purée or liquid form."

In the modern cold kitchen, coulis are made by puréeing raw or cooked fruits or vegetables to a saucelike consistency. The term **purée** may frequently be used interchangeably with coulis. The texture of these sauces can range from very light and smooth to coarse. They may be served "as is," or they may be adjusted by adding stocks, wines, infusions, oils, or cream.

Coulis or purées may begin to weep a clear liquid as they sit. To prevent this, bring the sauce to a simmer and add a small amount of diluted arrowroot or cornstarch. This is a helpful practice whenever advance plating is required, as might be the case for a banquet or reception.

# Coating sauces: chaud-froid and aspic gelée

Although these sauces are not as popular as they once were, they still have several applications for the garde manger. They can be used to coat canapés and other hors d'oeuvres, to prepare platters for display and service, and to coat various timbales and other appetizers.

**Chaud-froids** are made by adding **gelatin** to a warm sauce, such as demi-glace, béchamel, or velouté. Techniques for working with gelatin are illustrated on page 23. The term chaud-froid means "hot and cold," a name that reflects the way in which the sauce is prepared for use. It is warmed over a hot water bath to the point at which it flows easily. Next, it is cooled over an ice water bath to the point at which the gelatin has thickened and the sauce starts to cling to the sides of the bowl. The sauce is then used to coat a variety of items from platters to ballotines. A quickly prepared substitute for chaud-froid, known as a **Mayonnaise Collée** (page 597), is made by thickening mayonnaise and/or sour cream with an appropriate amount of gelatin to produce a coating consistency.

Clear coating sauces, known as **aspic gelée** or simply aspics, are made by clarifying stocks, juices, or essences and adding enough gelatin to achieve the desired strength (see Table 2.1). After making the aspic gelée, temper the mixture by stirring it constantly over an ice bath with a rubber spatula to cool it to the proper temperature (see Fig 2-6a). Once it just begins to thicken, ladle or pour the aspic over the desired application. Aspic gelée is one of the more versatile coating sauces used in garde manger. It can be used to seal a platter, giving it an almost mirror-like finish (see Fig 2-6b). Items such as herb leaves, grape slices, or vegetables cut into a variety of shapes can be inlaid into the aspic gelée before it congeals to add to the presentation of the platter. Aspic can be cut into shapes and used as a flavorful, decorative garnish (see Fig 2-6c). It is also utilized frequently to seal an edible item, such as pâté en croûte, both after it is baked to fill in the air gaps and after it is sliced (see Fig 2-6d).

## table 2.1 — Ratios for aspic gelée

| Ratio per gallon | Ratio per pint | Gel Strength | Possible Uses |
|---|---|---|---|
| 2 oz / 57 g | ¼ oz / 7 g | Delicate gel | When slicing is not required. Individual portion of meat, vegetable, or fish bound by gelatin. Jellied consommés. |
| 4 oz / 113 g | ½ oz / 14 g | Coating gel | Edible chaud-froid. Coating individual items. |
| 6 to 8 oz / 170 to 227 g | 1 oz / 28 g | Sliceable gel | When product is to be sliced. Filling pâté en croûte, head cheese. |
| 10 to 12 oz / 284 to 340 g | 1¼ to 1½ oz / 35 to 43 g | Firm gel | Coating platters with underlayment for food show or competition. |
| 16 oz / 454 g | 2 oz / 57 g | Mousse strength | When product must retain shape after unmolding. Production of a mousse. |

**FIG 2-6A** *Before using aspic, it must be cooled slightly over an ice water bath to thicken the solution.*

**FIG 2-6B** *Two layers of aspic can be used to seal a garnish into a platter, preparing it for presentation.*

**FIG 2-6C** *If cast and allowed to set, aspic can be portioned into an edible garnish.*

**FIG 2-6D** *Edible items, such as these pâté en croûte slices, can be sealed with aspic solution before serving, giving them a glossy sheen.*

| FIG 2-7A | *Before use, powdered gelatin must be bloomed in cold water* | FIG 2-7B | *Powdered gelatin is properly bloomed once all of the granules have absorbed the liquid, causing them to swell and become translucent.* |

## Working with powdered gelatin

In order to achieve the correct results when preparing aspic or any other item including gelatin, you must be able to handle gelatin properly and incorporate it correctly. Ratios for producing aspic gelée in a variety of strengths can be found in Table 2.1 (page 22).

1. **Weigh the gelatin carefully.** Granulated or powdered gelatin, gelatin sheets (see information below), or instant gelatin can be used interchangeably.

2. **Add the gelatin to a cool liquid.** Sprinkle the gelatin powder evenly over a cool liquid (see Fig 2-7a). If the liquid is warm or hot, the gelatin cannot soften properly before melting. Scattering the gelatin over the liquid's surface prevents the gelatin from forming clumps.

3. **Bloom the gelatin.** As the gelatin absorbs the liquid, each granule becomes enlarged; this is known as **blooming** (see Fig 2-7b).

4. **Melt the gelatin enough to dissolve the granules.** Bloomed gelatin (or gelatin solution) can be dissolved in one of two ways: add it directly to a warm liquid (at about 100 to 110°F / 38 to 43°C), or warm the mixture over a hot water bath. As the softened gelatin warms, the mixture will clear and become liquid enough to pour easily. Combine the gelatin thoroughly with the base liquid to be sure that it gels evenly.

   Note: In some kitchens, chefs prefer to have some of this bloomed softened gelatin on hand at all times, and refer to it as a **gelatin solution**. This mixture can be held for several weeks, and used as required to prepare aspics or other jellied sauces or soups.

5. **Test the gelatin strength.** To test the strength of both aspics and reduced stocks, chill a plate in the freezer. Ladle a small amount of the aspic or reduced stock on the plate, and chill under refrigeration until it gels. Adjust the strength by rewarming the aspic and then adding more gelatin or more base liquid as necessary.

## Working with sheet gelatin

Another form of gelatin that is becoming readily available to professional kitchens is sheet gelatin. After extraction and drying, the gelatin is formed into thin sheets which you place in large volumes of cool water to bloom. Sheet gelatin is sold in different bloom strengths, or gauges, but as there is no universal standard of identification, the strengths of different gauges may vary depending on the manufacturer. One advantage of sheet gelatin is that it introduces less air into the base and so the finished product is somewhat clearer than one that uses powdered gelatin. The process for using sheet gelatin is similar to that for powdered gelatin in that you must first bloom and then melt the gelatin. Place the sheets in a large volume of water (see Fig 2-8a). When sheet gelatin is fully bloomed, it should soften dramatically (see Fig 2-8b). The sheet gelatin can then be added directly to the base and melted as opposed to powdered gelatin, which must be bloomed in a measured amount of water before it is melted.

FIG 2-8A  *Before use, bloom sheet gelatin in enough cold water to completely submerge it.*

FIG 2-8B  *Once properly bloomed, sheet gelatin becomes hydrated and takes on a more plastic consistency.*

## Miscellaneous sauces

In addition to the sauces discussed above, the garde manger may be called on to prepare some special sauces that do not necessarily fit into a single category. Cocktail, Cumberland, Oxford, mint, and horseradish sauces are among the basic repertoire of the cold kitchen. Dipping sauces, such as those served with satay and tempura, are also considered cold sauces. Consult specific recipes for information about preparing and serving these sauces.

# Cold soups

Soups prepared by the garde manger are served chilled. They are found as first-course offerings, as appetizer courses, hors d'oeuvre, or desserts. They may be presented in a variety of ways—in chilled stemware, traditional soup plates or cups, or in tiny tasting portions served at stand-up receptions. Cold soups refresh the palate, regardless of what point in the meal they are served. They can be rich and suave, as in the case of cream-based soups, or bold and robust. Whenever you intend to serve any food chilled, be sure to taste it carefully at the correct service temperature. Remember to allow soups sufficient time to develop their flavor; some soups are at their best and ready to serve as soon as they are prepared. Other soups will develop a more complex and satisfying flavor if they are allowed to mellow (under refrigeration) for several hours or overnight.

Cold soups may be prepared in one of three ways, depending on their type. Vegetable or fruit soups are made by puréeing or chopping fruits and vegetables finely enough to form a souplike consistency; cream soups are made from a thickened base such as a velouté, béchamel, or a potato purée; and clear soups are made by clarifying and fortifying a rich broth and, if desired, thickening the base with a little gelatin.

## Vegetable and fruit soups

Cold vegetable and fruit soups are popular hot-weather offerings around the world. Many cuisines have special cold soups that feature a seasonal food, such as cherries, melons, tomatoes, peppers, and cucumbers. You will find an interesting range of soups in the following pages, as well as some unique garnishing and presentation ideas.

Vegetable or fruit soups range in texture from the appealingly coarse texture of a gazpacho to the velvety smoothness of a chilled melon soup. A broth or juice is often added to the fruits or vegetables to loosen the purée enough to create a good soup consistency. Other ingredients, such as cream, milk, buttermilk, garnish items, or granités, may also be included in the soup for additional interest.

# Cream-style soups

Cold cream soups should have the same velvety smooth texture as any hot cream soup. Taste and evaluate the flavor carefully, and give equal attention to the texture and consistency. Cold soups may thicken as they cool, so be certain that you have adjusted the consistency to make a soup that is creamy but not stiff. Good cold soups should not leave your mouth feeling coated with fat, so keep the amount of cream in good proportion to the other ingredients.

**Vichyssoise** is a classic example of a **cream-style soup.** It is made by preparing a purée of potato and leek. Other cold soups are made by preparing a cream-style or velouté soup. They are typically finished by adding chilled cream, yogurt, or crème fraîche. The Chilled Edamame Soup on page 67 is a good example.

# Clear cold soups

Clear soups must have a deep and satisfying flavor in order to be successful. The body of the soup can be adjusted by adding gelatin, if you prefer to serve it jellied. (To review the information about working with gelatin, read pages 24–25 earlier in this chapter.) Not all clear soups are jellied, however, and some of the recipes included here are based on a delicious broth garnished or left plain according to your intended presentation.

**Clear cold soups** require a rich, full-bodied, clarified broth or juice. Infusions, essences, or well-strained purées are often used to create the special character of the soup. Traditional clear cold soups, such as **jellied consommés,** are made by adding enough bloomed and dissolved gelatin to the soup to make it gel. Jellied clear soups should barely hold their shape, and should melt in the mouth instantly.

# Basic Red Wine Vinaigrette

YIELD: *32 fl oz / 960 mL*

8 fl oz / 240 mL red wine vinegar

2 tsp / 10 g mustard (optional)

2 shallots, minced

16 fl oz / 480 mL mild olive oil or canola oil

8 fl oz / 240 mL extra virgin olive oil or canola oil

2 tsp / 8 g sugar (optional)

2 tsp / 6 g salt, or as needed

½ tsp / 1 g coarse-ground black pepper, or as needed

3 tbsp / 9 g minced herbs, such as chives, parsley, tarragon (optional)

1. Combine the vinegar, mustard, if desired, and shallots.

2. Whisk in the oil gradually.

3. Season with sugar, salt, and pepper. Add the fresh herbs, if desired.

*Chef's note*  *This vinaigrette can easily be adapted for a variety of situations by substituting a different flavored vinegar or oil for the red wine vinegar or canola oil.*


# Balsamic Vinaigrette

YIELD: *32 fl oz / 960 mL*

4 fl oz / 120 mL red wine vinegar

4 fl oz / 120 mL balsamic vinegar

2 tsp / 10 g mustard (optional)

16 fl oz / 480 mL mild olive oil or canola oil

8 fl oz / 240 mL extra virgin olive oil or canola oil

2 tsp / 6 g salt

½ tsp / 1 g ground black pepper

3 tbsp / 9 g minced herbs, such as chives, parsley, tarragon (optional)

1. Combine the vinegars and mustard, if desired.

2. Whisk in the oil gradually.

3. Season with salt and pepper. Add the fresh herbs if desired.

*Variation*  *Port Balsamic Vinaigrette: Substitute 2 fl oz / 60 mL ruby port and 2 fl oz / 60 mL Ficklin Port for the red wine vinegar.*

# Truffle Vinaigrette

YIELD: *32 fl oz / 960 mL*

12 fl oz / 360 mL red wine vinegar

4 fl oz / 120 mL balsamic vinegar

2 fl oz / 60 mL water

2 tsp / 10 g Dijon mustard

2 shallots, minced

9 fl oz / 270 mL mild olive oil

5 fl oz / 150 mL extra-virgin olive oil

1½ fl oz / 45 mL truffle oil

2 tsp / 8 g sugar

2 tsp / 6 g salt

½ tsp / 1 g ground black pepper

1 black or white truffle, chopped (optional)

1. Mix together vinegars, water, mustard, and shallots.

2. Whisk in the oils gradually.

3. Season with sugar, salt, and pepper. Add the truffles just before serving if desired.

*Chef's note* *Truffle oil is very potent and this vinaigrette should be tasted frequently as it is made so that the amount of truffle oil can be adjusted as needed.*

# Vinaigrette Gourmande

YIELD: *32 fl oz / 960 mL*

4 fl oz / 120 mL sherry vinegar

3 fl oz / 90 mL lemon juice

2 tsp / 6 g salt

½ tsp / 1 g coarse-ground black pepper

16 fl oz / 480 mL olive oil

10 fl oz / 300 mL extra-virgin olive oil

1 oz / 28 g minced Fines Herbes (page 590)

1. Combine vinegar and lemon juice with salt and pepper.

2. Whisk in the oils gradually.

3. Add the herbs; adjust seasoning with salt and pepper, if necessary.

*Variation* *Walnut and Red Wine Vinaigrette: Substitute walnut oil for the vegetable oil and red wine vinegar for the sherry vinegar. Substitute parsley and chives for Fines Herbes (page 590).*

# Lemon Parsley Vinaigrette

YIELD: *32 fl oz / 960 mL*

6 fl oz / 180 mL lemon juice

2 fl oz / 60 mL Champagne vinegar

1 oz / 28 g Dijon mustard

½ oz / 14 g minced garlic

1¼ oz / 35 g minced shallots

Salt, as needed

Coarse-ground black pepper, as needed

1 tbsp / 6 g fennel seeds, crushed

1½ tsp / 3 g red pepper flakes

8 fl oz / 240 mL olive oil

4 fl oz / 120 mL  extra-virgin olive oil

1 oz / 28 g chopped flat-leaf parsley leaves

½ oz / 14 g chopped oregano

1. Combine the lemon juice, vinegar, mustard, garlic, shallots, salt, pepper, fennel seeds, and red pepper flakes.

2. Whisk in the oil and reserve.

3. Whisk in the parsley and oregano just before service. Adjust seasoning with salt and pepper, if necessary.

*Chef's note*  *This versatile dressing can be used not only on green salads, but also as a dressing for grain or legume salads. The spices can also be adapted to suit a variety of regional flavor profiles.*

# Apple Cider Vinaigrette

YIELD: *32 fl oz / 960 mL*

16 fl oz / 480 mL apple cider

6 fl oz / 180 mL cider vinegar

1 Granny Smith apple, peeled, cored and cut into brunoise

16 fl oz / 480 mL vegetable oil

8 fl oz / 240 mL  extra-virgin olive oil

2 tbsp / 6 g chopped tarragon leaves

2 tsp / 6 g salt

¼ tsp / 0.50 g ground white pepper

½ tsp / 2 g sugar

1. Reduce the cider in a small saucepan over medium high heat to 6 fl oz / 180 mL. Combine the cider reduction, the vinegar, and the brunoise apple.

2. Whisk in the oil gradually.

3. Add the tarragon and season with salt, pepper, and sugar.

*Chef's note*  *Use hard cider to replace the apple cider for a deeper, more complex flavor in the finished dressing.*

# Curry Vinaigrette

YIELD: *32 fl oz / 960 mL*

6 fl oz / 180 mL cider vinegar

4 fl oz / 120 mL orange juice

2 fl oz / 60 mL lemon juice

1½ oz / 43 g honey

1 oz / 28 g minced ginger

1 oz / 28 g minced lemongrass

18 fl oz / 540 mL Curry-Infused Oil (page 546)

2 tsp / 6 g salt

2 tsp / 4 g coarse-ground black pepper

1. Combine the vinegar, orange and lemon juices, honey, ginger, and lemongrass.

2. Whisk in the curry oil gradually.

3. Adjust seasoning with salt and pepper.

*Presentation idea*  Substitute this dressing for the dressing used on the Roasted Beet Salad on page 102.

# Mustard-Walnut Vinaigrette

YIELD: *32 fl oz / 960 mL*

8 fl oz / 240 mL Champagne vinegar

2 oz / 57 g spicy brown mustard

½ oz / 14 g sugar

4 shallots, minced

20 fl oz / 600 mL mild olive oil

4 fl oz / 120 mL walnut oil

½ oz / 14 g chopped dill

½ oz / 14 g chopped flat-leaf parsley leaves

2 tbsp / 6 g minced chives

Salt, as needed

Coarse-ground black pepper, as needed

1. Combine the vinegar, mustard, sugar, and shallots.

2. Whisk in the oils gradually.

3. Add the herbs and season with salt and pepper.

*Variation*  Hazelnut-Oregano Vinaigrette: Substitute hazelnut oil for the walnut oil. Replace the dill and parsley with 1 oz / 28 g chopped fresh oregano. Eliminate the chives, if desired.

# Chipotle-Sherry Vinaigrette

YIELD: *32 fl oz / 960 mL*

7 fl oz / 210 mL sherry vinegar

1 fl oz / 30 mL lime juice

4 chipotles in adobo sauce, minced

2 shallots, minced

2 garlic cloves, minced

16 fl oz / 480 mL pure olive oil

8 fl oz / 240 mL  extra-virgin olive oil

1 oz / 28 g chopped Fines Herbes (page 590)

1 fl oz / 30 mL maple syrup

1 tsp / 3 g salt

½ tsp / 1 g coarse-ground black pepper

1. Combine the vinegar, lime juice, chipotles, shallots, and garlic.

2. Whisk in the oil gradually.

3. Add the Fines Herbes just before service, and season with maple syrup, salt, and pepper.

*Chef's note*  *Chipotles in adobo sauce are dried, smoked jalapeño chiles that are typically packed into a red sauce made up of ground chiles, vinegar, and herbs. Adjust the amount used in the vinaigrette depending on the level of spiciness and the brand that you prefer.*

# Roasted Shallot Vinaigrette

YIELD: *32 fl oz / 960 mL*

8 shallots

4 garlic heads

18 fl oz / 540 mL extra-virgin olive oil

3 fl oz / 90 mL balsamic vinegar

2 tsp / 2 g chopped rosemary

2 tsp / 2 g chopped thyme

1 fl oz / 30 mL honey

2 tsp / 6 g salt

1 tsp / 2 g cracked black pepper

1. Peel the shallots and garlic and remove the cores. Place them in a small ovenproof saucepan and completely submerge them with the oil. Cover the pan with foil and place in a 350°F / 149°C oven for 2 hours, or until both the shallots and the garlic are extremely tender, almost to the point of falling apart, and light golden.

2. Remove the pan from the oven and allow the mixture to cool to room temperature. Separate the shallots and garlic from the oil and reserve both.

3. Place the vinegar, herbs, honey, shallots, and garlic in a blender and blend on high until smooth. With the blender on low, slowly drizzle in the reserved oil, then season with salt and pepper. Reserve until needed.

*Presentation idea*  *Try this dressing as a substitute for the balsamic vinaigrette in the Marinated Roasted Pepper Salad (page 103).*

# Tomato Vinaigrette

YIELD: *32 fl oz / 960 mL*

| | |
|---|---|
| 1 lb / 454 g ripe tomatoes, seeded | 2 fl oz / 60 mL lemon juice |
| 1 oz / 28 g minced shallots | 2 fl oz / 60 mL lime juice |
| 4 fl oz / 120 mL red wine vinegar | 2 tbsp / 6 g chopped basil |
| 1 oz / 28 g egg yolks | 1 tbsp / 3 g chopped tarragon leaves |
| 5 fl oz / 150 mL mild olive oil | 2 tsp / 6 g salt |
| 3 fl oz / 90 mL extra-virgin olive oil | 1 tsp / 2 g ground white pepper |

1. Purée the tomatoes, shallots, vinegar, and egg yolks in a blender or food processor. Add the olive oil slowly with the blender running to form a thick sauce.

2. Add the juices and herbs, and season with salt and pepper.

*Variation* Fire-Roasted Tomato Vinaigrette: Char the tomatoes over an open flame and allow them to cool before puréeing them. Season the vinaigrette with Tabasco sauce as needed.

*Presentation idea* This nontraditional juice-based vinaigrette may be served with vegetable terrines or the Poached Salmon and Lemon Terrine on page 336.

# Beet Vinaigrette

YIELD: *32 fl oz / 960 mL*

| | |
|---|---|
| 2 lb / 907 g beets | 1¾ oz / 50 g chopped dill |
| 12 fl oz / 360 mL cider vinegar | 2 tsp / 6 g salt |
| 6 fl oz / 180 mL extra-virgin olive oil | 1 tsp / 2 g coarse-ground black pepper |

1. Simmer the beets in acidulated water until tender. When the beets are cool enough to handle, peel and chop.

2. Place the beets and vinegar in a blender and purée until smooth. Whisk in the oil and season with the dill, salt, and pepper.

*Chef's notes* For more intense color and flavor, use a juicer to juice the raw beets. Combine the juice and vinegar, whisk in the oil, and season with dill, salt, and pepper.

Acidulated water is made by combining 1 gal / 3.84 L water with 1 fl oz / 30 mL lemon juice or vinegar.

# Tangerine-Pineapple Vinaigrette

YIELD: *32 fl oz / 960 mL*

10 fl oz / 300 mL tangerine juice

5½ fl oz / 165 mL pineapple juice

1 fl oz / 30 mL lemon juice

2 tsp / 10 mL balsamic vinegar

2 tsp / 10 g prepared Creole mustard

10 fl oz / 300 mL vegetable oil

5½ fl oz / 165 mL olive oil

2 tsp / 6 g salt

½ tsp / 1 g coarse-ground black pepper

1. Combine the juices, vinegar, and mustard.

2. Whisk in the oils gradually.

3. Season with salt and pepper.

*Variations*  *Orange (or Blood Orange) Vinaigrette: Substitute 16 fl oz / 480 mL orange (or blood orange) juice for the tangerine and pineapple juice. Reduce lemon juice to 1 tbsp / 15 mL.*

*Lemon Vinaigrette: Substitute 12 fl oz / 360 mL lemon juice and 8 fl oz / 240 mL water for the tangerine and pineapple juice. Eliminate the mustard.*

# Grapefruit Emulsion

YIELD: *32 fl oz / 960 mL*

30 fl oz / 900 mL grapefruit juice

4 fl oz / 120 mL olive oil

2 fl oz / 60 mL extra virgin olive oil

½ oz / 14 g grapefruit zest, finely grated, with no pith, blanched and shocked 2 to 3 times

1. Combine the grapefruit juice, olive oil, and zest in a blender. Blend on high speed until emulsified, 2 minutes on high speed. Strain the oil through cheesecloth into a clean container.

2. Serve immediately, or cover and refrigerate until needed. Blend briefly to reemulsify before service if necessary.

*Presentation idea*  *In addition to the Lobster Salad (page 140), try this emulsion as a dressing for a spinach salad with citrus segments or use it to add a layer of flavor as an accompaniment for crab cakes.*

# Almond-Fig Vinaigrette

**YIELD:** *32 fl oz / 960 mL*

4 fl oz / 120 mL balsamic vinegar

4 fl oz / 120 mL red wine, such as Zinfandel or Merlot

4 shallots, minced

4 oz / 113 g roasted and chopped almonds

Salt, as needed

Ground black pepper, as needed

12 fl oz / 360 mL almond oil

16 fl oz / 480 mL olive oil

5¼ oz / 149 g chopped dried figs

2 fl oz / 60 mL lemon juice

Tabasco sauce, as needed

1. Combine the vinegar, wine, shallots, almonds, salt, and pepper. Gradually whisk in the oils.

2. Stir in the chopped figs and adjust seasoning with lemon juice, Tabasco sauce, salt, and pepper.

3. Serve immediately or cover and refrigerate until needed.

*Presentation idea*  Dress a simple green salad with this fruity, slightly spicy vinaigrette and serve it with the Goat Cheese and Sweet Onion Crostini (page 179).


# Guava-Curry Vinaigrette

*Makes 32 fl oz / 960 mL*

4 oz / 113 g guava paste

8 fl oz / 240 mL red wine vinegar

2 tbsp / 12 g curry powder

4 fl oz / 120 mL lime juice

1 Scotch Bonnet chile, seeded, minced

Salt, as needed

Ground pepper, as needed

16 fl oz / 480 mL olive oil

8 fl oz / 240 ml extra-virgin olive oil

3 tbsp / 9 g chopped cilantro leaves

1. Combine the guava paste, vinegar, and curry powder in a small saucepan and warm slightly until the guava paste is melted. Allow the mixture to cool.

2. Combine the guava mixture with lime juice, chile, salt, and pepper. Gradually whisk in the oil.

3. Stir in the cilantro and adjust the seasoning with salt and pepper, if necessary.

4. Serve immediately or cover and refrigerate until needed.

*Chef's note*  Most any variety of chile may be substituted for the Scotch Bonnet to achieve a vinaigrette that is less spicy.

# Basic Mayonnaise

YIELD: *32 fl oz / 960 mL*

3 oz / 85 g egg yolks

1 fl oz / 30 mL white vinegar

1 fl oz / 30 mL water

2¼ tsp / 4 g dry mustard

24 fl oz / 720 mL vegetable oil

2¼ tsp / 7 g kosher salt

½ tsp / 1 g ground white pepper, or as needed

1 fl oz / 30 mL lemon juice, or as needed

1. Whisk the yolks, vinegar, water, and mustard until slightly foamy.

2. Add the oil gradually in a thin stream, whisking constantly, until all the oil is incorporated and the mayonnaise is thick.

3. Season with salt, pepper, and lemon juice, as needed. Refrigerate immediately.

*Variation*   *Green Mayonnaise (Sauce Vert): Finely chop 1 oz / 28 g cooked spinach. Squeeze it in a cheesecloth to extract the juice. Add the juice to the finished mayonnaise. Add other chopped herbs as needed, such as parsley, basil, chives, or dill.*


# Aïoli (Garlic Mayonnaise)

YIELD: *32 fl oz / 960 mL*

6 oz / 170 g pasteurized egg yolks

1 tbsp / 10 g garlic paste

24 fl oz / 720 mL vegetable oil

8 fl oz / 240 mL extra-virgin olive oil

1½ tsp / 7.50 mL red wine vinegar

2 tsp / 10 mL lemon juice

Salt, as needed

Prepare as for Basic Mayonnaise (above), adding the garlic to the egg yolk mixture. Cover and refrigerate immediately.

*Variations*   *Rouille: Reduce 6 oz / 170 g Red Pepper Coulis (page 55) to about 4 oz / 113 g. Add cayenne as needed. This sauce should have noticeable heat.*

*Saffron Aïoli: Infuse ½ tsp / 1 g lightly crushed saffron threads in 1 fl oz / 30 mL boiling water. Add this infusion to eggs along with the garlic paste.*

CLOCKWISE FROM TOP: *Aïoli, Tapenade (page 53), Guacamole (page 51)*

# Rémoulade Sauce

YIELD: *32 fl oz / 960 mL*

24 fl oz / 720 mL Basic Mayonnaise (page 36)

2 oz / 57 g capers, drained, rinsed, and chopped

2 oz / 57 g chopped cornichons

3 tbsp / 9 g chopped chives

3 tbsp / 9 g chopped chervil

3 tbsp / 9 g chopped tarragon leaves

1 tbsp / 15 g Dijon mustard

1 tsp / 5 g anchovy paste

Salt, as needed

Worcestershire sauce, as needed

2 to 3 dashes Tabasco sauce

Combine all ingredients thoroughly. Adjust seasonings as needed. Cover and refrigerate immediately.

*Chef's note*  *Rémoulade sauce is a classic accompaniment for a variety of seafood dishes such as crab cakes, shrimp, grilled salmon, cold meats, or the Oyster and Shrimp Po'boy (page 154).*

# Russian Dressing

YIELD: *32 fl oz / 960 mL*

20 fl oz / 600 mL Basic Mayonnaise (page 36)

7 fl oz / 210 mL prepared chili sauce

2 oz / 57 g prepared horseradish

1 tbsp / 15 mL Worcestershire sauce

2 tsp / 6 g salt

1 tsp / 2 g ground black pepper

Combine all ingredients thoroughly. Adjust seasoning as needed. Cover and refrigerate immediately.

*Variation*  *Thousand Island Dressing: Add 4 oz / 113 g pickle relish and 2 oz / 57 g chopped hard-cooked egg to Russian Dressing.*

# Green Goddess Dressing

YIELD: *32 fl oz / 960 mL*

24 fl oz / 720 mL Basic Mayonnaise (page 36)

2 fl oz / 60 mL tarragon vinegar

1 oz / 28 g chopped flat-leaf parsley leaves

4 tsp / 4 g chopped chives

3 tbsp / 9 g chopped tarragon leaves

2 tsp / 6 g salt

1 tsp / 5 g anchovy paste (1 or 2 fillets)

1 tsp / 2 g coarse cracked black pepper

1. Combine all ingredients thoroughly. Adjust seasoning as needed. This dressing may be puréed in a food processor if desired.

2. Cover and refrigerate immediately.

*Chef's note*  If tarragon vinegar is unavailable, substitute white wine vinegar and add 2 tbsp / 6 g additional chopped fresh tarragon.


# Creole Honey-Mustard Sauce

YIELD: *32 fl oz / 960 mL*

1 oz / 28 g minced shallots

¾ oz / 21 g crushed green peppercorns (brine-packed)

1 tbsp / 15 mL vegetable oil

6 fl oz / 180 mL dry white wine

1 tbsp / 6 g cracked black pepper

2 oz / 57 g Dijon mustard

6 oz / 170 g Creole mustard

8 fl oz / 240 mL Basic Mayonnaise (page 36)

8½ fl oz / 255 mL sour cream

1½ oz / 43 g honey

Kosher salt, as needed

1. Sweat the shallots and peppercorns in oil; do not brown.

2. Add the white wine and reduce until the wine has almost completely evaporated. Cool.

3. Add the remaining ingredients; mix well and check seasoning. Cover and refrigerate immediately.

*Presentation idea*  Try this sauce as the spread for the Soft-Shell Crab Sandwich on page 154.

# Creamy Black Pepper Dressing

YIELD: *32 fl oz / 960 mL*

| | |
|---|---|
| 2 fl oz / 60 mL lemon juice | 1 tbsp / 10 g salt |
| 3 oz / 85 g egg yolks | 12 fl oz / 360 mL olive oil |
| 1 oz / 28 g Dijon mustard | 12 fl oz / 360 mL vegetable oil |
| ½ oz / 14 g anchovy paste (3 or 4 fillets) | 2½ oz / 71 g grated Parmesan |
| 2 tsp / 6 g minced garlic | 1 tbsp / 6 g coarse-ground black pepper |

1. Whisk together the lemon juice, eggs, mustard, anchovy paste, garlic, and salt.

2. Add the oils gradually, whisking constantly.

3. Add remaining ingredients and mix well. Cover and refrigerate immediately.

*Chef's note* *Try this dressing for a spicy alternative to the traditional Caesar dressing on a Caesar salad.*


# Roquefort Dressing

YIELD: *32 fl oz / 960 mL*

| | |
|---|---|
| 6 oz / 170 g crumbled Roquefort cheese | 2 tsp / 10 mL Worcestershire sauce |
| 16 fl oz / 480 mL Mayonnaise (page 36) | 2 tsp / 6 g salt |
| 4½ fl oz / 135 mL sour cream | 1 tsp / 2 g ground black pepper |
| 6 fl oz / 180 mL buttermilk, or as needed | 1 tbsp / 3 g chopped flat-leaf parsley |
| 1 tbsp / 15 mL lemon juice | |

1. Mix Roquefort, mayonnaise, sour cream, and buttermilk well.

2. Season with lemon juice, Worcestershire sauce, salt, pepper, and parsley. To thin, add more buttermilk. Adjust seasoning as needed. Refrigerate immediately.

*Chef's note* *For a thicker sauce to use as a dip, add half of the cheese and purée the dressing until smooth. Fold in remaining crumbled cheese.*

# Ranch Dressing (Reduced-Fat)

YIELD: *32 fl oz / 960 mL*

| | |
|---|---|
| 12 oz / 340 g part-skim ricotta cheese | ½ oz / 14 g Dijon mustard |
| 8 fl oz / 240 mL nonfat yogurt | ½ tsp / 1 g celery seed |
| 12 fl oz / 360 mL buttermilk | 1 tbsp / 10 g kosher salt |
| 1 fl oz / 30 mL lemon juice | 1 tsp / 2 g ground black pepper |
| 1 fl oz / 30 mL red wine vinegar | 2 tbsp / 30 mL Worcestershire sauce |
| 1 tsp / 3 g minced garlic | 2 tsp / 2 g chopped flat-leaf parsley leaves |
| 1 oz / 28 g minced shallots | 1 tsp / 1 g chopped chives |

1. Combine the cheese, yogurt, buttermilk, lemon juice, vinegar, garlic, shallots, mustard, celery seed, salt, pepper, and Worcestershire sauce. Purée in food processor until smooth.

2. Mix in the parsley and chives and adjust seasoning. Cover and refrigerate immediately.

*Chef's note*  This versatile dressing can be used as a flavorful dip for a vegetable crudité as well as a dressing on greens for a sandwich or a wrap.


# Maytag Blue Cheese Dressing (Reduced-Fat)

YIELD: *32 fl oz / 960 mL*

| | |
|---|---|
| 3½ oz / 99 g Maytag blue cheese | ½ tsp / 2 g Roasted Garlic (page 606) |
| 12 oz / 340 g part-skim ricotta cheese | 2 tsp / 6 g kosher salt |
| 12 fl oz / 360 mL buttermilk | 2 tbsp / 6 g chopped chives |
| 2 fl oz / 60 mL cider vinegar | 1½ tsp / 3 g cracked black pepper |
| 1 tbsp / 15 mL Worcestershire sauce | |

1. Combine all ingredients except chives and pepper and purée in food processor until smooth. Stir in chives and pepper.

2. Serve immediately or cover and refrigerate until needed.

*Chef's note*  This dressing can be made with other blue-veined cheeses such as Roquefort, Danish Blue, or Gorgonzola.

# Yogurt Cucumber Sauce

YIELD: *32 fl oz / 960 mL*

| | |
|---|---|
| 32 fl oz / 960 mL yogurt | 1 garlic clove, crushed |
| 1 fl oz / 30 mL lemon juice | 8 oz / 227 g cucumber, peeled, seeded and cut into ¼-in / 6-mm dice |
| 2 tsp / 6 g salt | |

1. Combine the yogurt, lemon juice, and salt until smooth and well blended. Place mixture in a bowl and add the garlic clove. Fold in the diced cucumber.

2. Cover and refrigerate for at least 1 hour and up to 24 hours before use. Remove the garlic clove before serving. Adjust seasoning with salt and additional lemon juice as desired.

*Chef's note*  *To create a thicker sauce, drain the yogurt overnight through cheesecloth before combining with the remaining ingredients.*


# Tahini Sauce

YIELD: *32 fl oz / 960 mL*

| | |
|---|---|
| 32 fl oz / 960 mL yogurt | 3 fl oz / 90 mL lemon juice |
| 4 oz / 113 g tahini | 2 tsp / 6 g salt |

Place all ingredients in the bowl of a food processor fitted with a blade attachment. Pulse until the mixture is smooth and homogenous. Adjust seasoning with salt. Cover and refrigerate immediately.

*Chef's note*  *Tahini is paste made from ground sesame seeds that can be used to flavor sauces, hummus, falafel, or baba ghanoush.*

# Salsa Verde

YIELD: *32 fl oz / 960 mL*

1 lb 8 oz / 680 g fresh tomatillos, husked and washed

4 serranos, stemmed and seeded

¾ oz / 21 g chopped cilantro

12 oz / 340 g chopped onions

2 garlic cloves, roughly chopped

½ oz / 14 g lard

24 fl oz / 720 mL Chicken Stock (page 592)

Salt, as needed

1. Boil the tomatillos and serranos in salted water to cover until tender, 10 to 15 minutes. Drain.

2. Place the tomatillos and serranos in a blender along with the cilantro, onions, and garlic. Process until almost smooth.

3. Heat the lard in a medium skillet over medium-high heat. When the skillet is hot, pour in the purée and stir constantly until the purée is darker and thicker, 4 to 5 minutes. Add the stock, bring the sauce to a boil, reduce the heat to medium, and simmer until thick enough to coat a spoon, about 20 minutes. Season with salt.

4. Serve immediately, or it may be rapidly cooled, covered, and refrigerated until needed.

*Chef's note*  To make a vegetarian salsa verde, substitute vegetable oil for the lard and water or vegetable stock for the chicken stock.

# Mango-Lime Salsa

YIELD: *32 fl oz / 960 mL*

1 lb / 454 g small-dice mango

3 oz / 85 g small-dice red onion

2 tsp / 10 g minced jalapeños (or as needed)

2 fl oz / 60 mL lime juice

2 fl oz / 60 mL extra-virgin olive oil

3 tbsp / 9 g chopped basil

2 tsp / 6 g finely chopped lime zest, without pith

Salt, as needed

Coarse-ground black pepper, as needed

1. Combine all ingredients.

2. Allow to sit under refrigeration 1 hour before serving. Adjust seasoning with salt, pepper, or lime juice, if necessary.

*Presentation idea*  Serve this salsa alongside the Salsa Fresca (page 44) and the Papaya and Black Bean Salsa (page 44) and pair it with a variety of chips and crisps (pages 541–544)

# Salsa Fresca

YIELD: *32 fl oz / 960 mL*

1 lb 1½ oz / 496 g seeded and diced tomatoes

3¼ oz / 92 g minced onion

2¾ oz / 78 g diced green pepper

2 garlic cloves, minced

1 tbsp / 3 g chopped cilantro

1 tsp / 1 g chopped oregano

2 fl oz / 60 mL lime juice

1 jalapeño, minced

1 fl oz / 30 mL olive oil

¼ tsp / 0.50 g ground black pepper

2 tsp / 6 g salt

Combine all ingredients and adjust seasoning. Cover and refrigerate immediately.

*Presentation ideas*  Try this salsa with the Pork Piccadillo Empanadas on page 464.

# Papaya and Black Bean Salsa

YIELD: *32 fl oz / 960 mL*

6½ oz / 184 g cooked black beans

1 papaya cut into small dice

5¼ oz / 149 g small-dice red pepper

3¼ oz / 92 g small-dice red onion

2 jalapeños, seeded and minced

3 tbsp / 9 g chopped cilantro leaves

2 tsp / 2 g dried Mexican oregano

2 tbsp / 18 g minced fresh ginger

2 fl oz / 60 mL olive oil

2 fl oz / 60 mL lime juice

1 tsp / 2 g coarse-ground black pepper

2 tsp / 6 g salt

Combine all ingredients and adjust seasoning. Serve immediately or cover and refrigerate until needed.

*Chef's note*  The papaya in this recipe must be ripe in order to provide the appropriate texture and sweetness to the salsa.

*Use a reamer to extract the freshest juice possible from the limes.*

# Chipotle Pico de Gallo

YIELD: *32 fl oz / 960 mL*

1 lb 2 oz / 510 g plum tomatoes, chopped, seeded

3 oz / 85 g red onion, chopped

2 fl oz / 60 mL lime juice

1½ tsp / 4.50 g garlic, minced to a paste

¼ oz / 7 g chipotle in adobo, mashed to a paste

Salt, as needed

Pepper, as needed

1 oz / 28 g cilantro leaves, chopped

1. Combine the tomatoes, onion, lime juice, garlic, and chipotle. Adjust seasoning with salt and pepper.

2. Cover and refrigerate at least 4 and up to 24 hours before serving.

3. Fold the cilantro into the pico de gallo just before serving.

*Chef's note*   *If desired, try folding some chopped avocado or cucumber into the salsa to cut some of the heat from the chipotle peppers.*


# Grapefruit Salsa

YIELD: *32 fl oz / 960 mL*

2 fl oz / 60 mL olive oil

1 tbsp / 3 g chopped cilantro

4 oz / 113 g finely diced red onions, rinsed

¼ to ½ tsp / 0.75 to 1.50 g seeded and minced Scotch Bonnet chile

2 tsp / 2 g chopped flat-leaf parsley

4 Ruby Red grapefruits, segmented

Salt, as needed

1. Combine the oil, cilantro, onions, Scotch bonnet, and parsley and mix well.

2. Just before service, add the grapefruit. Season with salt.

3. Serve immediately, or cover and refrigerate until needed.

*Variation*   *If a slightly sweeter salsa is desired, substitute orange segments for half of the grapefruit segments.*

# Smoked Poblano Salsa

YIELD: *32 fl oz / 960 mL*

| | |
|---|---|
| 6 poblanos chiles | 3 fl oz / 90 mL lime juice |
| 12 oz / 340 g tomatillos, husked and hulled | Salt, as needed |
| 2 tbsp / 30 mL olive oil | Coarse-ground black pepper, as needed |
| 1½ yellow onions, minced | 3 tbsp / 9 g coarsely chopped cilantro |
| ¼ oz / 7 g garlic cloves, minced | 3 tbsp / 9 g coarsely chopped oregano |
| 3 tbsp / 45 mL rice wine vinegar | 1½ fl oz / 45 mL extra-virgin olive oil |
| 3 jalapeños, seeded and minced | |

1. Char the poblanos over an open fire on all sides, 3 to 4 minutes. Cover with plastic wrap and let stand for half an hour. When cool, peel and remove the seeds. Leave the chiles in large pieces at this point.

2. Cold smoke the poblanos at 70°F / 21°C using two hotel pans, a half roasting rack, and hickory chips until lightly smoked, about 30 minutes. Cut into small dice.

3. Wash the tomatillos and cut them in half. Toss the tomatillos with 1 tbsp / 15 mL olive oil. Grill the tomatillos over medium-high heat until they have definite grill marks and are tender, about 3 to 5 minutes. They should not be mushy. Roughly chop the tomatillos into small dice and reserve.

4. Heat 1 tbsp / 15 mL olive oil over medium heat and add onions and garlic. Cook gently for 2 to 3 minutes or until the onions are translucent and the raw flavor of the garlic is gone.

5. Deglaze pan with rice wine vinegar and remove from heat. Chill.

6. Combine the onion mixture with the tomatillos, diced poblanos, jalapeños, lime juice, salt, pepper, cilantro, oregano, and extra-virgin olive oil. Mix well and adjust seasonings, if necessary. Cover and refrigerate, if necessary, but this sauce is best served the day it is made.

*Presentation idea* This can be used as a sauce for raw oysters instead of or in addition to the traditional mignonette sauce.

# Pickled Ginger Salsa

YIELD: *32 fl oz / 960 mL*

6 fl oz / 180 mL pickled ginger, minced

8 fl oz / 240 mL jicama, peeled and minced

8 fl oz / 240 mL peeled, seeded, and minced cucumber

8 fl oz / 240 mL minced red onion

2 fl oz / 60 mL rice wine vinegar

2 fl oz / 60 mL mirin (sweet rice wine)

4 fl oz / 120 mL lime juice

2 fl oz / 60 mL pure olive oil

4 tsp / 20 mL Tabasco sauce

Salt, as needed

Black pepper, as needed

Combine all of the ingredients. Mix well and adjust seasoning with salt and pepper as needed. Cover and refrigerate until needed.

*Chef's note*  This salsa is better when prepared with freshly pickled ginger, but it can be made with prepared pickled ginger.

# Pesto

YIELD: *32 fl oz / 960 mL*

5 oz / 142 g toasted pine nuts

1 oz / 28 g minced garlic

12 oz / 340 g basil leaves

7 oz / 198 g grated Parmesan

12 fl oz / 360 mL olive oil

2 tsp / 6 g salt

2 tsp / 4 g ground black pepper

1. Combine the pine nuts, garlic, basil, and Parmesan in a food processor fitted with the metal chopping blade. Process to blend.

2. Add the olive oil with the processor running and process until smooth. Adjust seasoning with salt and pepper. Cover and refrigerate until needed.

*Presentation idea*  Try this pesto instead of the aïoli as the spread on the Grilled Chicken Sandwich with Pancetta and Arugula on Focaccia (page xxx).

# Mint Pesto Sauce

YIELD: *32 fl oz / 960 mL*

2½ oz / 71 g mint leaves, loosely packed

1¾ oz / 50 g chopped parsley, loosely packed

3 oz / 85 g grated Parmesan

3¾ oz / 106 g extra-virgin olive oil

2¼ oz / 64 g pine nuts or walnuts

1 fl oz / 30 mL lemon juice

4 garlic cloves, chopped

½ tsp / 1.50 g salt, and as needed

¼ tsp / 0.50 g ground black pepper

4¼ fl oz / 128 mL sour cream

1. In a food processor or blender, combine mint, parsley, Parmesan, olive oil, pine nuts, lemon juice, garlic, salt, and pepper.

2. Process until a coarse paste forms. Add sour cream and mix until blended.

3. Serve immediately or cover and refrigerate until needed.

*Presentation idea* Serve the mint pesto with the Lamb Brochettes on page 461.


# Sun-Dried Tomato Pesto

YIELD: *32 fl oz / 960 mL*

1 oz / 28 g basil leaves, tightly packed

6 oz / 170 g sun-dried tomatoes in oil, drained, chopped

6 garlic cloves

2 oz / 57 g grated Parmesan

2 oz / 57 g toasted pine nuts

12 fl oz / 360 mL olive oil

Salt, as needed

Ground black pepper, as needed

1. Combine the basil, tomatoes, garlic, Parmesan, and pine nuts in a food processor and pulse until the ingredients are evenly chopped.

2. With the processor running, add the olive oil and purée to an even-textured paste. Adjust seasoning as needed with salt and pepper.

*Presentation idea* In addition to being popular as a pasta sauce, this pesto can also be added to softened butter to make a spread for canapés.

# Cocktail Sauce

YIELD: *32 fl oz / 960 mL*

1 lb ¾ oz / 475 g prepared chili sauce

1 lb ¾ oz / 475 g prepared ketchup

2 fl oz / 60 mL lemon juice

1 oz / 28 g sugar

2 tsp / 10 mL Tabasco sauce

2 tsp / 10 mL Worcestershire sauce

2¼ oz / 64 g prepared horseradish

1. Combine all ingredients thoroughly.

2. Serve immediately or cover and refrigerate until needed. Stir the sauce and adjust seasoning if necessary before serving.

*Chef's note*  This sauce is classically used as an accompaniment for shrimp cocktail.


# Asian-Style Dipping Sauce

YIELD: *32 fl oz / 960 mL*

16 fl oz / 480 mL soy sauce

8 fl oz / 240 mL white vinegar

8 fl oz / 240 mL water

4 garlic cloves, minced

4 green onions, minced

1 oz / 28 g minced ginger

2 tsp / 4 g dry mustard

1 tsp / 5 g hot bean paste

3 oz / 85 g honey

1. Combine all ingredients thoroughly.

2. Serve immediately, or cover and refrigerate until needed. Stir the dressing and adjust seasoning if necessary before serving.

*Presentation idea*  Serve this dipping sauce with the Chinese Skewered Bites (page 468) or Beef Negimaki (page 458).

# Peanut Sauce

YIELD: *32 fl oz / 960 mL*

| | |
|---|---|
| 1 lb / 454 g peanut butter | 8 fl oz / 240 mL lime juice |
| 1½ oz / 43 g jalapeño, seeded and minced | 8 fl oz / 240 mL soy sauce |
| 2 oz / 57 g garlic, minced | 8 fl oz / 240 mL peanut oil |
| 1 oz / 28 g sugar | 8 fl oz / 240 mL water |
| ¼ tsp / 0.50 g cayenne | 1 oz / 28 g cilantro leaves, chopped |

1. Combine all the ingredients except the cilantro in a small saucepan. Heat over medium heat, stirring frequently, until the sauce comes to a boil.

2. Reduce the heat to low and simmer for 2 to 3 minutes. Adjust the consistency with water. Remove from heat and stir in the cilantro.

*Presentation idea*  Serve warm with Beef Saté (page 462) and garnish with chopped, toasted peanuts.


# Guacamole

YIELD: *32 fl oz / 960 mL*

| | |
|---|---|
| 10 avocados, halved, pitted, and peeled | 3 tbsp / 9 g chopped cilantro |
| 2 fl oz / 60 mL lime juice | 1 tsp / 5 mL Tabasco sauce |
| 7 oz / 198 g diced tomato (optional) | Salt, as needed |
| 1 jalapeño, seeded and minced (optional) | Ground black pepper, as needed |
| 1 bunch green onions, sliced | |

1. Push avocados through a medium-coarse screen or coarsely chop.

2. Combine all ingredients thoroughly. Taste for seasoning and adjust with lime juice and salt and pepper.

3. Cover tightly and refrigerate until needed. It is best to make guacamole the same day it is to be served.

See photo on page 37.

*Chef's note*  The original Aztec name for the avocado, the primary ingredient in guacamole, was ahuacatl.

# Roasted Eggplant Dip with Mint (Baba Ghanoush)

YIELD: *32 fl oz / 960 mL*

4 lb / 1.81 kg eggplants, cut in half

Salt, as needed

Ground black pepper, as needed

2 fl oz / 60 mL olive oil

3 shallots, minced

3 fl oz / 90 mL lemon juice

4 oz / 113 g tahini

1 oz / 28 g chopped flat-leaf parsley leaves

½ oz / 14 g chopped mint

2 garlic cloves, minced

Harissa Sauce (page 533), as needed

1. Season the eggplant with salt and pepper and lightly coat the cut faces with some of the olive oil. Roast cut side down on a sheet pan in a preheated 375°F / 190°C oven until soft, about 30 to 40 minutes. Cool to room temperature; scoop out flesh and discard seeds.

2. While the eggplant is roasting, macerate the shallots in the lemon juice with ¼ tsp / 0.75 g salt.

3. Combine the roasted eggplant with the olive oil, macerated shallots, tahini, and parsley.

4. Season with mint, garlic, salt, pepper, and harissa sauce. Chop the dip rough by hand or purée smooth.

*Chef's note*  This dip is traditionally served with pita or flatbread and can be topped with a drizzle of olive oil and sea salt.

# Hummus

YIELD: *32 fl oz / 960 mL*

1 lb 8 oz / 680 g cooked chickpeas, drained

4 oz / 113 g tahini

1½ fl oz / 45 mL lemon juice, or as needed

2 fl oz / 60 mL extra-virgin olive oil

4 garlic cloves, minced, or as needed

1 tbsp / 10 g salt

Ground black pepper, as needed

Combine all ingredients. Purée in food processor (in batches if necessary), adding water to thin if needed. Adjust seasoning with lemon juice and garlic. Cover and refrigerate until needed.

*Chef's note*  Hummus can be passed through a drum sieve for a very smooth texture.

# Tapenade

YIELD: *32 fl oz / 960 mL*

12 oz / 340 g Niçoise olives, pitted

8 oz / 227 g black olives, pitted

4 oz / 113 g salt-packed anchovy fillets, rinsed and dried

3 oz / 85 g capers, rinsed

2 oz / 57 g minced garlic

Ground pepper, as needed

Lemon juice, as needed

Extra-virgin olive oil, as needed

Chopped herbs, such as oregano or basil, as needed

1. In food processor, combine the olives, anchovies, capers, garlic, and pepper. Incorporate the lemon juice and oil slowly. Blend until chunky and easily spread. Do not over mix; the tapenade should have texture and identifiable bits of olive.

2. Adjust seasoning and finish with herbs. Cover and refrigerate until needed.

See photo on page 37.

*Chef's note*  This spread hails from Provence, France, and can be used as a spread for sandwiches, as a dip, or as part of a stuffing for meats.

# Muhammara

YIELD: *32 fl oz / 960 mL*

1 lb 8 oz / 680 g red peppers

1½ oz / 43 g coarse-ground walnuts

½ oz / 14 g fresh white bread crumbs

2 fl oz / 60 mL lemon juice

1 oz / 28 g pomegranate molasses

¼ tsp / 1 g prepared red chili paste

Salt, as needed

1 tbsp / 15 mL olive oil

¼ tsp / 0.50 g ground cumin

1. Roast the peppers, then peel, seed, and set aside to drain in a colander.

2. Process the walnuts and bread crumbs until finely ground. Add the peppers, lemon juice, and pomegranate molasses; purée until smooth and creamy. Add the chili paste and salt as needed. Cover and refrigerate at least overnight before serving.

3. When ready to serve, decorate with a drizzle of olive oil and a light dusting of cumin.

*Chef's note*  This spicy-hot sauce made with peppers, walnuts, and pomegranate molasses, originated in Aleppo in Syria. Pomegranate molasses is produced by cooking ripe pomegranates and sugar to a thick, jam-like consistency. Muhammara is best when made 4 to 5 days in advance, covered, and refrigerated, to allow the flavor to develop fully.

# Hazelnut Romesco Sauce

YIELD: *32 fl oz / 960 mL*

| | |
|---|---|
| 4 ancho chiles | ¾ oz / 21 g Spanish paprika |
| 4 Marinated Roasted Peppers (page 103) | ½ tsp / 1 g cayenne |
| 10 fl oz / 300 mL olive oil | 4 oz / 113 g tomato paste |
| 6 garlic cloves, minced | 1 lb / 454 g ground hazelnuts |
| 2 fl oz / 60 mL red wine vinegar | Salt, as needed |

1. Put the ancho chiles in a small saucepan and cover with water. Bring to a boil, then turn off the heat and let steep for 20 minutes.

2. Add marinated roasted peppers and ancho chiles to the olive oil, garlic, vinegar, paprika, cayenne, tomato paste, and hazelnuts, and purée to a smooth consistency. Allow to rest overnight to develop full flavor. Adjust seasoning with salt before serving.

*Chef's notes* *Hazelnut Romesco Sauce should be made the day before needed.*

*This rich and flavorful sauce can be used with a variety of foods, including fish, lamb chops, and such vegetables as beets, potatoes, asparagus, green beans, and green onions.*


# Garlic and Parsley Compound Butter

YIELD: *1 lb / 454 g*

| | |
|---|---|
| 1 oz / 28 g garlic, roughly chopped | 1 tsp / 3 g salt |
| 1½ bunches parsley, without stems | 1 lb / 454 g butter, cold, cut into small dice |

1. Place the garlic, parsley, and salt in a food processor fitted with a blade attachment and pulse until evenly minced and mixture is well blended.

2. Combine the garlic-parsley mixture and the butter in a mixer fitted with a paddle attachment. Blend on medium speed until butter is softened and mixture is well blended and light green in color.

3. Compound butter may be placed in a ramekin or shaped into a log. Cover or wrap and refrigerate or freeze until needed.

*Chef's note* *Compound butters can be made by combining any number of herbs, spices, pastes, zests, or diced vegetables or nuts. They can be either sweet or savory and used as a spread on a sandwich or canapé or to top meats, poultry, fish, or vegetables.*

# Red Pepper Coulis

YIELD: *32 fl oz / 960 mL*

4 to 4 lb 8 oz / 1.81 to 2.04 kg red peppers, diced

2 oz / 57 g minced shallots

4 fl oz / 120 mL olive oil

12 fl oz / 360 mL dry white wine

12 fl oz / 360 mL Chicken Stock (page 592)

Salt, as needed

1. Sauté the peppers and shallots in the olive oil until they are tender.

2. Deglaze with white wine.

3. Add the stock and reduce to approximately half the original volume.

4. Place the mixture in a food processor and purée until smooth. Season with salt.

*Variation* Roasted Red Pepper Coulis: Roast, peel, and seed the peppers before preparing the coulis.


# Huckleberry Sauce

YIELD: *32 fl oz / 960 mL*

9 oz / 255 g sugar

6 fl oz / 180 mL water

12 fl oz / 360 mL balsamic vinegar

2 lb 7 oz / 1.1 kg huckleberries

½ oz / 14 g minced ginger

½ oz / 14 g grated orange zest

24 fl oz / 720 mL Sauternes

1. Combine the sugar and water in a small sauce pot and simmer gently until the sugar turns brown. Wash down the sides of the pot frequently with a pastry brush dampened in water; add the vinegar and reduce by one-fourth.

2. Add the remaining ingredients and simmer until a syrupy consistency is achieved. Strain and press through a fine mesh strainer. Cover and refrigerate.

*Chef's note* This sauce uses a gastrique, which is a reduction of caramelized sugar and vinegar, to achieve a rich, flavorful fruit sauce that is not too sweet and that pairs well with roasted and grilled meat, poultry, and fish.

# Apricot-Ancho Barbecue Sauce

YIELD: *32 fl oz / 960 mL*

| | |
|---|---|
| 6 oz / 170 g bacon, diced | 6 oz / 170 g dark brown sugar |
| 6 oz / 170 g onion, diced | 2 ancho chiles, diced |
| 1 garlic clove, minced | 1 tsp / 2 g paprika |
| 4 oz / 113 g dried apricots | 1 tsp / 2 g dry mustard |
| 7 oz / 198 g ketchup | 1 tsp / 5 mL Tabasco sauce |
| 2 fl oz / 60 mL malt vinegar | 1 tsp / 2 g cayenne |
| 2 fl oz / 60 mL orange juice | |

1. Sauté the bacon until almost crisp. Add the onions and sauté until browned. Add the garlic and sauté another minute.

2. Add remaining ingredients. Simmer until the apricots are soft.

3. Purée in a blender; reheat and adjust seasoning as needed with salt and pepper.

*Chef's note*   *This barbecue sauce can be used cold or warm and can be stored, covered and refrigerated, up to 1 week.*

# Southwestern Barbecue Sauce

YIELD: *32 fl oz / 960 mL*

2 fl oz / 60 mL vegetable oil

4 oz / 113 g onions, finely diced

1 tbsp / 9 g garlic, minced to a paste

1 tbsp / 6 g dry mustard

1 oz / 28 g dark chili powder

2 tbsp / 12 g ground cumin

2 tbsp / 12 g ground coriander

1 tbsp / 6 g dried Mexican oregano

2 chipotles in adobo sauce

1 lb 8 oz / 680 g plum tomatoes, seeded and coarsely chopped

10 oz / 284 g ketchup

4 fl oz / 120 mL Chicken Stock (page 592)

1 oz / 28 g molasses

1 fl oz / 30 mL sherry vinegar

1 fl oz / 30 mL Worcestershire sauce

1. Heat the oil in a saucepan over medium high heat. Add the onions and sauté, stirring from time to time, until lightly caramelized and tender, 5 to 6 minutes. Add the garlic and sauté until aromatic, about 1 minute.

2. Add the mustard, chili powder, cumin, coriander, and oregano and sauté briefly.

3. Add the chipotles, tomatoes, ketchup, stock, molasses, vinegar, and Worcestershire. Bring to a simmer over medium heat. Adjust the heat as necessary and simmer until flavorful, 1 hour. Stir and skim the sauce as it simmers. Strain.

4. The sauce is ready to use at this point or it may be cooled, covered and refrigerated, for up to 1 week.

# Aspic Gelée

YIELD: *32 fl oz / 960 mL*

CLARIFICATION

| | |
|---|---|
| 4 oz / 113 g Mirepoix (page 586) | 3 fl oz / 960 mL stock (see Chef's Note) |
| 12 oz / 340 g ground beef | ¼ standard Sachet d'Épices (page 587) |
| 3 egg whites, beaten | ¼ tsp / 1 g kosher salt |
| 3 oz / 85 g tomato concassé (see page 607) | Ground white pepper, as needed |
| | Gelatin powder (see Table 2-1, page 22), as needed |

1. Mix the ingredients for the clarification and blend with the stock. Mix well.

2. Bring the mixture to a slow simmer, stirring frequently until raft forms.

3. Add the sachet d'épices and simmer until the appropriate flavor and clarity are achieved, about 45 minutes. Baste raft occasionally.

4. Strain the consommé; adjust the seasoning with salt and pepper as needed.

5. Soften the gelatin in cold water, then melt over simmering water. Add to the clarified stock. Cover and refrigerate until needed. Warm as necessary for use.

*Chef's note*   *Choose an appropriate stock, depending upon the intended use. For example, if the aspic is to be used to coat a seafood item, prepare a lobster stock and use ground fish for the clarification.*

*Variation*   *Ruby Port Gelée: Replace half of the stock with ruby port.*


# Chaud-Froid Sauce

YIELD: *32 fl oz / 960 mL*

| | |
|---|---|
| 16 fl oz / 480 mL Velouté (page 595) | 4 fl oz / 120 mL heavy cream |
| 12 fl oz / 360 mL Aspic Gelée, warmed to 110°F / 43°C (above) | 2 tsp / 6 g salt |
| | ¼ tsp / 0.50 g ground white pepper |

1. Bring the velouté to a simmer and combine with aspic.

2. Add the cream, salt, and pepper. Strain into a bowl set over an ice bath.

3. Cool to coating consistency and use as required.

*Chef's note*   *Béchamel may be substituted for the Velouté.*

# Gazpacho Andalusia

YIELD: *1 gal / 3.84 L or 20 servings (6 fl oz / 180 mL each)*

| | |
|---|---|
| 1 lb 8 oz / 680 g tomatoes, cored, diced | 4 garlic cloves, mashed |
| 1 lb 4 oz / 567 g cucumbers, peeled, diced | ½ tsp / 2.5 g minced jalapeño |
| 10 oz / 284 g green peppers, seeded, diced | 2½ fl oz / 75 mL olive oil |
| 10 oz / 284 g red peppers, seeded, diced | 3 fl oz / 90 mL white wine vinegar |
| 1 lb / 454 g onions, sliced | 2 tsp / 6 g salt |
| 1 lb 4 oz / 567 g crustless white bread, diced | 1 tsp / 2.25 g ground black pepper |
| 24 fl oz / 720 mL tomato juice | 4 oz / 113 g Garlic-Flavored Croutons (page 613) |
| 2 fl oz / 60 mL tomato purée | |

1. Reserve about 1 fl oz / 30 mL each of the tomatoes, cucumbers, peppers, and onions for garnish.

2. Soak the bread cubes in the tomato juice.

3. Purée the soaked bread with the diced vegetables, tomato purée, garlic, jalapeño, olive oil, and vinegar.

4. Adjust seasoning with salt and pepper; cover and refrigerate until needed.

5. Serve with garnish of diced vegetables and croutons on the side.

*Presentation idea*  For an hors d'oeuvre presentation, portion the soup into shot glasses and serve the garnishes buffet style on the side.

# Chilled Cucumber Soup with Dill, Leeks, and Shrimp

YIELD: *1 gal/ 3.84 L or 20 servings (6 fl oz/ 180 mL each)*

1 lb 4 oz / 567 g shrimp (26/30 count)

64 fl oz / 1.92 L Shellfish Stock (page 593)

SOUP BASE

1 lb / 454 g diced yellow onion

1 lb / 454 g diced celery

2 oz / 57 g butter

6 lb / 2.72 kg cucumbers, peeled, seeded, and diced

1 oz / 28 g arrowroot

1 lb 9½ oz / 723 g sour cream

8 fl oz / 240 mL heavy cream

1 bunch dill, chopped

½ oz / 14 g salt

1 tsp / 2.25 g ground white pepper

Tabasco sauce, as needed

6 fl oz / 180 mL lemon juice, as needed

GARNISH

2 cucumbers, peeled, seeded, and finely diced

4 oz / 113 g leeks, julienned and fried until crisp

¼ bunch dill sprigs

1. Poach the shrimp in the stock. Cut in half lengthwise and reserve for garnish. Reserve the stock.

2. Sauté the onions and celery in the butter until translucent.

3. Add the cucumbers and reserved stock and simmer 30 minutes.

4. Purée in a blender and strain through a sieve. Thicken with arrowroot. Bring back to a boil. Remove and cool to 40°F / 4°C.

5. To finish the soup, blend 16 fl oz / 480 mL soup base with the sour cream, heavy cream, and dill. Add this to the remaining soup base. Season with salt, pepper, Tabasco, and lemon juice.

6. Garnish individual servings of the soup with the reserved shrimp, diced cucumbers, fried leeks, and dill sprigs.

*Presentation ideas* Top the soup with a brunoise of tomato concassé, chiffonade of mint leaves, and a drizzle of Curry Oil (page 546).

Top the cucumber soup with 1 tsp of faux caviar (recipe follows).

# Faux Caviar

YIELD: *10 servings*

| | |
|---|---|
| 16 fl oz / 480 mL base liquid (such as wine or fruit or vegetable juices) | ¼ tsp / 1 g baking soda |
| 1 tsp / 5 mL sodium alginate | 1 tsp / 5 mL calcium chloride |

1. Blend ½ of base liquid with sodium alginate in blender until completely dissolved.

2. Heat to 190°F / 88°C, then remove from the heat and add remaining base liquid. Stir in baking soda.

3. Strain through fine mesh strainer and place the mixture over an ice bath until cool and all bubbles have subsided.

4. Dissolve calcium chloride in 1 qt / 960 mL water and bring solution to a simmer in a medium saucepan.

5. Fill syringe with base mixture and add mixture one drop at a time into barely shimmering calcium chloride solution. Cook pearls for thirty seconds, strain, and cool in ice bath. Serve immediately.

*Chef's note* For the Chilled Cucumber Soup garnish on page 14, the base liquid used was cucumber juice.

# Cold Roasted Tomato and Basil Soup

YIELD: *1 gal / 3.84 L or 20 servings (6 fl oz / 180 mL each)*

4 oz / 113 g minced garlic

1 fl oz / 30 mL olive oil

1 lb / 454 g celery, chopped

1 lb 8 oz / 680 g onions, chopped

4¾ oz / 135 g leeks, white part only, chopped

3 lb / 1.36 kg Roasted Plum Tomatoes (page 607)

64 fl oz / 1.92 L Vegetable Stock (page 593) or Tomato Water (see step 1, page 74)

4 oz / 113 g basil

2 bay leaves

1 tsp / 3 g salt

¼ tsp / 0.50 g ground black pepper

GARNISH

1 lb / 454 g yellow tomatoes, diced

1 oz / 28 g basil chiffonade

1. Lightly sauté garlic in oil.

2. Add celery, onions, and leeks, and continue to sauté until fragrant.

3. Add tomatoes, stock, basil, and bay leaves. Simmer 40 minutes or until vegetables are tender.

4. Remove the bay leaves and purée the soup in a blender; season with salt and pepper. Cover and refrigerate until needed.

6. Adjust seasoning before service if necessary. Garnish with yellow tomatoes and basil.

*Chef's note* *You can pan-smoke the tomatoes instead of roasting them to give the soup a deeper, richer flavor.*

# Cold Carrot Soup

YIELD: *1 gal/ 3.84 L or 20 servings (6 fl oz/ 180 mL each)*

| | |
|---|---|
| 1 oz / 28 g minced shallots | 2 fl oz / 60 mL white wine |
| 2 garlic cloves, minced | ½ tsp / 1 g ground cardamom |
| ¾ oz / 21 g minced ginger, or as needed | 32 fl oz / 960 mL orange juice |
| 4 oz / 113 g minced onion | 7 fl oz / 210 mL yogurt |
| 1½ oz / 43 g butter | 16 fl oz / 480 mL carrot juice |
| 3 lb 8 oz / 1.59 kg carrots, thinly sliced | ½ oz / 14 g salt, or as needed |
| 80 fl oz / 2.4 L Vegetable Stock (page 593) | |

1. Sauté shallots, garlic, ginger, and onion in the butter.

2. Add carrots, stock, wine, cardamom, and orange juice; simmer for 30 minutes or until carrots are tender.

3. Place the mixture in a food processor and purée to a smooth texture; chill.

4. Finish with yogurt. Thin with carrot juice. Cover and refrigerate until needed. Adjust seasoning with salt before service.

*Chef's note*  *Soup can be garnished with dollop of whipped cream, chives, and carrot chips. Fried ginger chips also make a spicy garnish.*

# Vichyssoise

YIELD: *1 gal / 3.84 L or 20 servings (6 fl oz / 180 mL each)*

1 lb 4 oz / 567 g leeks, white part only, finely chopped

1 onion, minced

1½ fl oz / 45 mL vegetable oil

1 sachet containing 4 whole cloves, 4 parsley stems, 3 peppercorns, 1 bay leaf

2 lb 8 oz / 1.13 kg diced potatoes

80 fl oz / 2.4 L Chicken Stock (page 592)

24 fl oz / 720 mL half-and-half, chilled

1 bunch chives, snipped

2 tsp / 6 g salt

¼ tsp / 0.50 g ground white pepper

1. Sweat the leeks and onion in the oil until tender and translucent.

2. Add the sachet, potatoes, and stock. Bring to a full boil, then reduce heat and simmer until the potatoes begin to fall apart.

3. Remove and discard the sachet. Purée the soup. Cool rapidly. Cover and refrigerate until needed.

4. To finish the soup for service, add cold half-and-half to the soup, fold in the chives, and adjust seasoning as needed with salt and pepper.

*Variation*   Chilled Potato-Herb Soup with Lobster: Substitute the following garnish for the chives: 1 lb / 454 g medium dice cooked lobster, 2 oz / 57 g chopped chives, ½ oz / 14 g chopped tarragon leaves, 2 oz / 57 g chopped chervil, ½ oz / 14 g chopped parsley leaves.

# Chilled Edamame Soup

YIELD: *1 gal / 3.84 L or 20 servings (6 fl oz / 180 mL each)*

2 lb 4 oz / 1.02 kg edamame beans, pods removed

1½ fl oz / 45 mL vegetable oil

9 oz / 255 g leeks, mostly white part, small dice

9 oz / 255 g Spanish onions, minced

12 oz / 340 g green leaf lettuce, shredded

72 fl oz / 2.16 L vegetable stock

1½ Sachet d'Épices (page 587)

Salt, as needed

White pepper, as needed

6 fl oz / 180 mL mirin

3½ fl oz / 105 mL crème fraîche

20 chervil pluches

1. Reserve 60 of the edamame beans for garnish.

2. For soup, heat a 1 gal 64 fl oz / 5.76 L sauce pot over medium heat and add vegetable oil.

3. Sweat leeks and onions until almost translucent, 4 to 5 minutes.

4. Add edamame beans and shredded lettuce and continue to sweat until the lettuce wilts and the ingredients combine, 2 to 4 minutes.

5. Add the stock and sachet; bring to boil and then reduce the heat to bring the mixture to a simmer. Move the pot halfway off the burner to create a convection simmer.

6. Simmer until beans are tender, about 15 to 20 minutes.

7. Season with salt and white pepper.

8. Puree the mixture with the mirin in a blender and pass through a fine tamis.

9. Chill completely. Cover and refrigerate until needed. Serve in chilled cups.

10. Garnish with 1 tbsp / 5 mL crème fraîche, 3 edamame beans, and a chervil pluche.

*Chef's note* *Edamame can usually be found frozen if fresh is not available.*

# Fresh Spring Pea Purée with Mint

YIELD: *1 gal/ 3.84 L or 20 servings (6 fl oz/ 180 mL each)*

8 oz / 227 g minced leeks

8 oz / 227 g minced onions

1 fl oz / 30 mL vegetable oil

14 oz / 397 g shredded green leaf lettuce

2 lb 12 oz / 1.25 kg fresh peas

80 fl oz / 2.4 L Vegetable Stock (page 593)

1 sachet containing 6 each chervil and parsley stems and 6 white peppercorns

10 to 12 fl oz / 300 to 360 mL light cream or half-and-half

1 tbsp / 9 g salt

¼ tsp / 0.50 g ground white pepper

2 tbsp / 6 g fine mint chiffonade (or 20 chervil pluches)

1. Sauté leeks and onions in oil.

2. Add lettuce and peas and smother briefly.

3. Add stock and sachet; bring to a boil.

4. Reduce heat and simmer until all ingredients are very tender.

5. Remove and discard sachet. Purée mixture in a blender until smooth. Cover and refrigerate until needed.

6. To finish for service, add chilled cream to cold soup. Adjust seasoning as needed with salt and pepper. Fold in mint chiffonade, or garnish each serving with a chervil pluche.

*Chef's note* *This soup has a delicate texture and flavor, making it suitable for elegant menus in the spring and summer. Cook the soup just until the peas are tender for the freshest green color in the finished soup.*

# Chilled Cantaloupe Melon and Champagne Soup

YIELD: *1 gal/ 3.84 L or 20 servings (6 fl oz/ 180 mL each)*

LIME GRANITÉ

64 fl oz / 1.92 L white wine (Chardonnay)

2 lb / 907 g sugar

8 fl oz / 240 mL lime juice

2 fl oz / 60 mL Midori liquor

1 oz / 28 g lime zest

SOUP

2 cantaloupe melons, diced

12 to 16 fl oz / 360 to 480 g orange juice

2½ oz / 71 g cornstarch

8 fl oz / 240 mL good-quality Champagne

3 fl oz / 90 mL lemon juice

96 fl oz / 2.88 L sparkling water

2 oz / 57 g grated orange zest

2 oz / 57 g grated lemon zest

10 oz / 284 g sugar, or as needed

1 lb 8 oz / 680 g small melon balls (for garnish)

1. For the granité: Combine all the ingredients in a shallow pan and freeze for 3 hours, stirring every 30 minutes with a fork until a slushy consistency is created. Reserve until needed.

2. For the soup: Purée the diced melon and fresh orange juice in a blender on medium high speed until smooth and refrigerate.

3. Make a cornstarch slurry with the cornstarch and ½ fl oz / 15 mL Champagne.

4. Bring lemon juice, sparkling water, and orange and lemon zests to a boil in a small saucepan and thicken with cornstarch slurry, then chill. Refrigerate until cool and the mixture has thickened.

5. Add melon puree and adjust seasoning with sugar and lemon.

6. Add remaining Champagne to the mixture.

7. Serve 8 oz / 240 mL soup with 2 oz / 57 g lime granité in a soup bowl 10 in/25 cm in diameter. Garnish with melon balls.

*Chef's note*   *This soup is a refreshing alternative on those hot summer days. It may be too sweet as a main course, but makes for a great appetizer or finish to a meal.*

# Chilled Morello Cherry Soup

YIELD: *1 gal / 3.84 L or 20 servings (6 fl oz / 180 mL each)*

2 lb 5 oz / 1.05 kg pitted Morello cherries

36 fl oz / 1.08 L water

5 to 6 cloves

1½ cinnamon sticks

8 fl oz / 240 mL dry red wine

1½ lemons, juiced and strained

8 fl oz / 240 mL superfine sugar

Pinch salt

1½ tbsp / 13.5 g arrowroot

2¾ fl oz / 83 mL light cream

1. Wash the cherries and place them in a 64 fl oz / 1.92 L stockpot with their own juices and the water.

2. Make a sachet with the cloves and cinnamon sticks and place it in the stockpot.

3. Add the red wine, strained lemon juice, sugar, and salt to the soup.

4. Simmer the soup over medium heat until the cherries are tender, about 15 to 30 minutes.

5. Remove about half of the cherries from the pot and reserve them for garnish on the finished soup.

6. Remove the sachet from the pot and discard it.

7. Purée the remaining soup in a blender until smooth.

8. Return the soup to the pot. Make an arrowroot slurry using the cream and lié the soup with it.

9. Cool the soup and stir in the reserved cherries.

*Chef's note* *Morello cherries are a variety of sour cherry with dark red skin and flesh that are difficult to find fresh. They can generally be found frozen, and their sour nature makes them ideal for cooking but not necessarily for eating raw.*

# Caribbean Coconut and Pineapple Bisque

YIELD: *1 gal/ 3.84 L or 20 servings (6 fl oz/ 180 mL each)*

48 fl oz / 1.44 L coconut milk

32 fl oz / 960 mL milk

16 fl oz / 480 mL light cream or half-and-half

LIAISON

16 fl oz / 480 mL half-and-half

6 egg yolks

¾ oz / 21 g arrowroot

48 fl oz / 1.44 L pineapple juice

4 fl oz / 120 mL Simple Syrup (page 606), or as needed

1 fl oz / 30 mL lime juice, or as needed

13 oz / 369 g diced pineapple

2 fl oz / 60 mL light rum

1. Bring the coconut milk, milk, and cream or half-and-half to a simmer.

2. Combine the liaison ingredients and temper into the soup base. Continue to cook over low heat until thickened, about 4 to 5 minutes. Chill thoroughly.

3. Add pineapple juice, then adjust flavor with simple syrup and lime juice.

4. Macerate the pineapple in the rum and garnish the soup at service.

*Presentation idea*   *Garnish with Plantain Chips (page 541) that have been fried or baked. Serve in a glass dish on shaved ice with a skewer of pineapple chunks alternating with sliced bananas rolled in toasted coconut.*

*Chef's note*   *Rum may be reduced or omitted as desired.*

# Chilled Clear Borscht

YIELD: *1 gal / 3.84 L, or 20 servings (6 fl oz / 180 mL each)*

8 lb / 3.63 kg raw beets, peeled and grated or chopped

1 gal 32 fl oz / 4.8 L White Duck Stock (page 592)

2½ fl oz / 75 mL red wine vinegar

½ oz / 14 g sugar

32 fl oz / 960 mL sweet white wine, such as Riesling

2 tbsp / 18 g kosher salt

1 tsp / 0.50 g ground white pepper

GARNISH

8 oz / 227 g cooked beets, julienned

4 oz / 113 g radishes, julienned

¼ bunch dill sprigs

1. Simmer the beets gently in the stock and vinegar for one hour.

2. Strain through doubled cheesecloth or a paper coffee filter; add sugar, wine, salt, and pepper as needed. Chill.

3. Garnish with julienned beets, radishes, and dill sprigs at service.

*Presentation idea*  Garnish the soup with 4 oz / 113 g julienned smoked duck or smoked ham.

# Chilled Tomato Saffron Soup with Shellfish

YIELD: *1 gal/ 3.84 L, or 20 servings (6 fl oz/ 180 mL each)*

9 lb / 4.08 kg tomatoes

¾ tsp / 2.25 g salt

96 fl oz / 2.88 L Shellfish Stock (page 593)

¾ tsp / 0.50 g saffron, crushed

1 oz / 28 g orange zest and juice

9 fl oz / 270 mL orange juice

¼ tsp / 0.50 g ground black pepper

GARNISH

8 oz / 227 g diced cooked lobster meat

8 oz / 227 g diced cooked scallops

2 oz / 57 g cantaloupe, scooped into pea-sized balls

2 oz / 57 g honeydew, scooped into pea-sized balls

3 oz / 85 g diced yellow tomato

3 oz / 85 g diced red tomato

3 tbsp / 9 g fine basil chiffonade

½ oz / 14 g fine mint chiffonade

1. Chop the tomatoes, salt well, and hang in cheesecloth overnight. Reserve the collected tomato water.

2. Combine stock with saffron, orange juice, and zest; bring to a simmer. Season with salt and pepper and strain through several layers of cheesecloth. Add the reserved tomato water and chill thoroughly.

3. Garnish with lobster, scallops, melon balls, tomatoes, basil, and mint.

*Chef's notes* *Prepare the Shellfish Stock on page 593 using lobster shells. Be sure that the stock is very clear. If necessary, clarify it following the method outlined in the basic stock recipe.*

*Add 1 oz / 28 g gelatin solution (pages 24–25) along with the tomato water in step 2 for a lightly jellied version of this soup.*

# Fresh Infusion of Vegetables

YIELD: *1 gal / 3.84 L, or 20 servings (6 fl oz / 180 mL each)*

3 lb / 1.36 kg red tomatoes, quartered

INFUSION

2 lb / 907 g leeks, white and light green parts, sliced

10 oz / 284 g sliced celeriac

5 oz / 142 g minced shallots

3 oz / 85 g minced parsley

1 oz / 28 g minced chives

1 gal / 3.84 L water, as needed

3 garlic cloves, minced

2 thyme sprigs

1 bay leaf

½ oz / 14 g salt

1½ tsp / 3 g ground black pepper

GARNISH

4 oz / 113 g baby carrots, sliced on bias

4 oz / 113 g petits pois, blanched

4 oz / 113 g fresh favas, shelled and cooked

4 oz / 113 g asparagus tips, parcooked

4 oz / 113 g tomatoes, peeled, seeded, and cut into diamond shapes

20 chervil pluches

1. Make a tomato broth by combining the tomatoes with 24 fl oz / 720 mL water. Simmer gently for 30 minutes, then strain through a fine sieve or cheesecloth. Chill thoroughly.

2. Make the vegetable infusion by simmering the ingredients in 96 fl oz / 2.88 L water, covered, for 1 hour. Add a little water to bring it back to its original level, return briefly to a boil, remove from heat, and allow to cool. Strain through a fine sieve or cheesecloth. Chill thoroughly.

3. Mix the tomato broth and the vegetable infusion; adjust seasoning.

4. Toss the garnish vegetables together. At service, garnish each serving with 1 oz / 28 g mixed vegetables and a chervil pluche.

*Chef's note* *Traditional French country boasts a wealth of soups and stews that feature tender and succulent vegetables straight from the garden. Here, baby carrots, petits pois, fresh fava beans, and asparagus tips are presented in a subtly flavored and satisfying vegetable infusion based on leeks and celeriac.*

# 3

- Recognize and discuss the place of salad in culinary history

- Identify specific salad greens in categories such as mild greens, spicy greens, bitter greens or chicories, prepared mixes of greens, and herbs and flowers

- Describe how to care for salad greens

- Explain how to dress and garnish the salad

- Understand the role of side salads

- Formulate a description of composed salads

# Salads

**Salads** appear on the menu in so many different guises and are embraced by today's garde manger with such enthusiasm that one might imagine salads were invented by this generation of chefs. In fact, salads have played a key role throughout culinary history. Fresh concoctions of seasoned herbs and lettuces, known as **herba salata,** were enjoyed by the ancient Greeks and Romans alike. According to legend, the Greek philosopher Aristoxenus was so obsessed with freshness that while the lettuce was still growing he would sprinkle it with vinegar and honey the night before he planned to prepare a salad. We are indebted to the Romans for our very word *salad*, deriving as it does from their word for salt.

he early European settlers of America also valued salad greens. Thomas Jefferson recorded that the markets of his day supplied the cook with a variety of lettuces, endive, sorrel, corn salad (mâche), and cress. After a long absence from the market, the greens Jefferson favored are again appearing in salads served as appetizers, entrées, accompaniments to other items, or as intermezzos. This chapter will discuss three major salad categories:

- Green salads
- Side salads, made from vegetables, potatoes, grains, pastas, legumes, and fruits
- Composed salads

## Green salads

By selecting the appropriate greens and pairing them with properly chosen **dressings,** a wide range of salads suitable to several different menu needs can be created, from a delicate salad of butterhead with a light lemon vinaigrette served as a first course to an appetizer salad of bitter greens, walnuts, and blue cheese with a sherry vinaigrette.

### *Salad greens*

Commercially prepared salad blends are now available, but chefs can also create their own by combining lettuces from within one category or by selecting from among two or more categories. The greens that are selected will determine the character of the salad. Today's garde manger can choose from:

- Mild greens
- Spicy greens
- Bitter greens or chicories
- Prepared mixes of greens
- Herbs and flowers
- Micro greens

### *Mild greens*

One of the biggest categories of **mild greens** is lettuce. Each of the thousands of lettuce varieties can be classified into one of the following categories: leaf, butterhead, or crisphead (see Fig 3-1). Select lettuce that is crisp, never wilted or bruised. Lettuce should only be washed in cold water, cut, or torn when it is ready to serve. Store lettuce in the refrigerator, covered loosely with damp absorbent paper towels and plastic wrap or a lid. As with most greens, it is very important to thoroughly wash lettuce, as dirt and grit tend to hide between the leaves. Never submerge lettuce in water for an extended amount of time, and be sure that it is dried well after washing (a salad spinner is great for this). The following table covers several varieties of lettuce.

**FIG 3-1** MILD GREENS, CLOCKWISE FROM TOP: *green leaf, red leaf, romaine, Boston, iceberg*

*table 3.1*

## Mild Greens

| Type | Description | Common Culinary Uses |
|---|---|---|
| **BUTTERHEAD** | | |
| *Bibb* | Smaller than Boston; loosely formed heads; soft, very tender leaves; vibrant green color; mild, sweet, delicate flavor | In salads; braised |
| *Boston* | Loosely formed heads; soft, very tender leaves; vibrant green color; mild, sweet, delicate flavor | In salads; braised |
| **CRISPHEAD** | | |
| *Iceberg* | Tight heading lettuce with pale green leaves; very mild flavor | In salads (shredded or served as a wedge) |
| *Romaine/cos* | Long, cylindrical head; outer leaves are ribbed; dark green leaves, becoming lighter on the interior; outer leaves are slightly bitter, inner leaves are mild and sweet. The name Cos derives from the Greek island of the same name, where some believe this lettuce to have originated. | In salads, especially Caesar Salad; braised |
| **LEAF** | Baby varieties are often included in special salad blends. | |
| *Green or red leaf* | May be green or red-tipped; loose heading lettuce; tender, crisp leaves; mild flavor, becoming bitter with age. | In salads |
| *Oak leaf* | Scalloping on leaves; loose heading lettuce; tender, crisp leaves; nutty flavor | In salads |

In addition to the lettuces described above, the mild greens also include mâche (a.k.a. corn salad or lamb's lettuce), some of the spicy greens when they are still young or immature, and baby varieties of various cooking greens and cabbages.

## Bitter greens and chicories

**Bitter salad greens** are those that are tender enough to be eaten in salads, but that may also be sautéed, steamed, grilled, or braised. There are many varieties that fit into this category, from green, leafy **watercress** to crimson heads of **radicchio** (see Fig 3-2). Selection criteria and handling practices for bitter salad greens are similar to those for lettuce. **Chicories** are heading-style or loose-leaf greens characterized by a distinctive bittersweet flavor. When young, they may be used in salads. More mature chicories are considered cooking greens. The following table covers several varieties of bitter salad greens and chicories.

FIG 3-2 BITTER GREENS, CLOCKWISE FROM TOP: *escarole, frisée, arugula, watercress, mâche, radicchio, Belgian endive (center)*

table 3.2

## Bitter Greens and Chicories

| Type | Description | Common Culinary Uses |
| --- | --- | --- |
| *Arugula / rocket* | Tender leaves; rounded "teeth" on the ends of the leaves; vibrant green color; peppery flavor | In salads, pesto, and soups; sautéed |
| *Belgian endive* | Tight, oblong head; white leaves with yellowish-green or red at tips; crisp leaves; mildly bitter flavor | In salads; grilled; roasted; and braised |
| *Curly endive* | Narrow leaves with deeply ridged edges; assertive flavor and texture. When very young it may be sold as frisée. | In salads |
| *Dandelion, beet, and collard greens* | Distinctly bitter varieties have dark green, long, narrow leaves, some with white or red ribs. If they are over-mature, they may give salads an unpleasant flavor. Beet greens have a tendency to bleed when combined with a dressing. | In salads; sautéed; braised |
| *Escarole* | Large heads of greenish-yellow, slightly crumpled leaves are succulent and slightly nutty. Slightly less bitter in flavor than frisée or chicory. | In salads and soups; sautéed |
| *Frisée* | Thin, curly leaves; white with yellowish-green tips; mildly bitter flavor | In salads and lettuce mixes such as mesclun |
| *Mâche / lamb's lettuce* | Loose bunches; thin, rounded leaves; dark green; very tender; nutty flavor | In salads; steamed |
| *Radicchio* | Round or oblong heads; firm, deep red to purple leaves, white veining; bitter flavor | In salads; grilled; sautéed; baked; braised |
| *Tat-soi* | Flat black cabbage with round leaves that form an open rosette; faint but pleasant cabbagelike taste; used in its very young stages. | In salads, sandwiches, and soups; as a garnish |
| *Treviso radicchio* | Resembles an elongated loose Belgian endive with red streaks or tips; succulent texture; flavor similar to heading radicchio | In salads and soups |
| *Watercress* | One of the oldest known leafy greens consumed. Small, scalloped leaves; dark green color; crisp texture; mustard-like, peppery flavor | In salads, soups, and sandwiches |

# Spicy greens

**Spicy greens** have a distinct pepperiness or assertive flavor, but are still delicate enough to eat in salads (see Fig 3-3). The younger they are, the less spicy they will be. Some spicy greens are:

**FIG 3-3** SPICY GREENS, CLOCKWISE FROM TOP: *mizuna, curly cress, tat soi, mustard greens, watercress*

table 3.3

## Spicy Greens

| Type | Description | Common Culinary Uses |
|------|-------------|----------------------|
| *Amaranth* | Spinach-like in flavor; varies in color from green to purple to red; blooms from late spring to early fall | In salads; stir-fried; sautéed |
| *Arugula (a.k.a. rocket or roquette)* | Taste ranges from mild and nutty to peppery and pungent; when leaves are small and narrow, the arugula usually has a more pronounced pepper flavor. | In salads; sautéed; in sauces; baked (on pizza); pesto |
| *Mizuna* | A Japanese mustard, mizuna has a mildly spicy flavor. Choose crisp green leaves and avoid those that are brown or wilted. | In salads; sandwiches; soups |
| *Mustard greens* | The leaves of the mustard plant provide a pungent, peppery green; they can have a crumpled or flat texture. | In salads; soups |
| *Watercress* | One of the oldest known leafy greens consumed. Small, scalloped leaves; dark green, crisp leaves; mustard-like peppery flavor | In salads; soups; sandwiches |

# Prepared mixes of greens

The market also provides a number of specialty items for salad making. Among the most popular of these items are convenient, prewashed and trimmed mixes of greens (see Fig 3-4). Their ready availability and ease of use have made them very popular, even to the point of indiscriminate use. The three most commonly available mixes are:

FIG 3-4 ONE EXAMPLE OF MESCLUN MIX, LEFT COLUMN, FROM TOP TO BOTTOM: *prizehead lettuce, red giant mustard greens, rouge d'hiver;* MIDDLE COLUMN, FROM TOP TO BOTTOM: *red salad bowl lettuce, baby fern leaf dill, chervil;* RIGHT COLUMN, FROM TOP TO BOTTOM: *green salad bowl lettuce, hon tsai tai, Detroit red beet greens;* BOTTOM: *These greens are combined to form mesclun mix.*

table 3.4

## Prepared Mixes of Greens

| Type | Description | Common Culinary Uses |
|------|-------------|----------------------|
| *Mesclun mix* | Often found in combination with herbs or flowers; commercially available mesclun mixes may contain blends of various mild, sweet, and peppery greens, with or without a flower or herb component. | In salads, sandwiches |
| *Oriental mix (OMX)* | A combination of some or all of the following: tat-soi, lola rosa, red oak, arugula, beet greens, Swiss chard, sorrel, amaranth, dill, purslane, mizuna, red mustard, bok choy, red shiso, red fire, sierra, and shungi ku. | In salads |
| *Baby mix (BMX)* | A generic term for mixes of very young leaves of several varieties, colors, and textures, this is sold both in heads and prewashed leaves. A typical combination may include lola rosa, tango, baby red oak, baby romaine, and baby green oak. | In salads; garnishing plates |

# *Herbs*

**Herbs** are the leaves of aromatic plants and are used primarily to add flavor to foods (see Fig 3-5). Aroma is a good indicator of quality in both fresh and dried herbs; a weak or stale aroma indicates old and less potent herbs. Fresh herbs may also be judged by appearance. They should have good color (usually green), healthy-looking leaves and stems, and no wilting, brown spots, sunburn, or pest damage. Herbs can range from pungent to lightly fragrant, and they can add a wonderful accent to a special dish (see Fig 3-6). Some varieties of herbs may also be used in salads. Herbs that have a naturally tender texture or soft leaves—young basil, chives, small mint leaves, pluches of chervil or flat-leaf parsley—are the ones to choose for salads. The following table covers a selection of herb varieties.

table 3.5

## Herbs

| Type | Description | Common Culinary Uses |
|------|-------------|----------------------|
| *Basil* | Small to large oval, pointed leaves; green color (though purple varieties are available); delicate leaves; pungent, licorice-like flavor; varieties include Opal, Lemon, and Thai Basil | Flavoring for sauces, dressings, infused oils and vinegars; pesto sauce; popular in Mediterranean cuisine. Also available dried. |
| *Bay leaf / laurel leaf* | Smooth, oval leaves; green color; aromatic | Flavoring for soups, stews, stocks, sauces, and grain dishes. Most commonly available dried. |
| *Chervil* | Small, curly leaves; green color; delicate texture; anise flavor | Component of "fines herbes," garnish. Also available dried. |

| | | |
|---|---|---|
| *Chives* | Long, thin; bright green color; mild onion flavor | Flavoring for salads and cream cheese; garnish; component of "fines herbes." |
| *Cilantro / chinese parsley / coriander* | Similar leaf shape to flat-leaf parsley; green color; delicate leaves; fresh, clean flavor | Flavoring for salsa and uncooked sauces; popular in Asian, Caribbean, and Latin American cuisines. |
| *Dill* | Long, feather-like leaves; green color; distinct flavor | Flavoring for salads, sauces, stews, braises; popular in Central and Eastern European cuisines. Also available dried. |
| *Marjoram* | Small oval leaves; pale green color; mild flavor, similar to oregano | Flavoring for lamb and vegetable dishes; popular in Greek, Italian, and Mexican cuisines. Commonly available dried. |
| *Mint* | Pointed, textured leaves; pale green to bright green color; leaf size and strength of flavor vary with type. Varieties include Peppermint, Spearmint, and Chocolate Mint | Flavoring sweet dishes, sauces, and beverages; garnish for desserts, mint jelly is a common accompaniment to lamb. |
| *Oregano / wild marjoram* | Small oval leaves; pale green color; pungent flavor; Mexican and Mediterranean varieties are available. | Flavoring for tomato-based dishes, popular in Mediterranean and Mexican cuisines. |
| *Parsley* | Curly or flat leaves; pointed, scalloped edges; bright green color; clean tasting. Flat-leaf parsley is also known as Italian parsley. | Flavoring for sauces, stocks, soups, dressings, and other dishes; component of "fines herbes," garnish; stems are used in bouquet garni and sachet d'épices. Commonly available dried. |
| *Rosemary* | Pine needle–shaped leaves, woody stem; grayish, deep green color; strong pine aroma and flavor | Flavoring for grilled goods (lamb) and marinades; popular in Mediterranean cuisine; branch-like stems are used as skewers. Commonly available dried. |
| *Sage* | Thin, oval, velvety leaves; grayish-green color; musty flavor; varieties include Pineapple sage | Flavoring for stuffing, sausage, and stews. Commonly available dried, both crumbled and ground. |
| *Savory* | Oblong leaves; dark green; soft, fuzzy texture | Flavoring for pâtés, stuffing; used to make poultry seasoning. Commonly available dried. |
| *Tarragon* | Thin, pointed leaves; dark green color; delicate texture; anise flavor | Flavoring for Béarnaise sauce and other dishes; component of "fines herbes." Commonly available dried. |
| *Thyme* | Very small leaves; woody stem; deep green color; varieties include Garden thyme and Wild thyme | Flavoring for soups, stocks, sauces, stews, braises, and roasted items; used in bouquet garni and sachet d'épices. Commonly available dried. |

**FIG 3-5** HERBS, CLOCKWISE FROM
TOP LEFT: *curly parsley; flat-leaf parsley, purple basil, mint, basil, chervil, sorrel, cilantro, Thai basil (center)*

**FIG 3-6** AROMATIC HERBS,
TOP ROW, FROM LEFT TO
RIGHT: *chives, rosemary, curry leaves;* SECOND
ROW, FROM LEFT TO RIGHT:
*lemongrass, tarragon, lemon thyme, sage, oregano;* BOTTOM ROW,
FROM LEFT TO RIGHT:
*thyme, dill, marjoram*

# Flowers

Flowers can turn an ordinary salad into something quite unique and beautiful, as long as they are not overused. And not only should they not be overused, but it is also important to note the size and flavor of the flower. Taste the flower to see how strongly it is flavored. If it is pungent, it may be necessary to use only a few petals rather than the whole flower. Edible flowers are normally divided into two groups: garden flowers and herb flowers (see Fig 3-7).

**FIG 3-7** EDIBLE FLOWERS, CLOCKWISE FROM TOP: *dianthus, snap dragons, marigolds, pansies, calendula, bachelor's buttons, popcorn shoots (center)*

## table 3.6 | Flowers

| Type | Description | Common Culinary Uses |
|---|---|---|
| **GARDEN FLOWERS** | | |
| *Bachelor's buttons* | Bright violet, silky petals with 4 to 5 crown-like points at the end of each petal; petals radiate like spokes on a wheel from a center disc of florets | In salads and tea; as a garnish |
| *Carnation* | Flower with somewhat densely packed frilly-edged petals; a wide variety of colors. Carnations have a spicy aroma and are indigenous to the Mediterranean. | In salads; as a garnish |
| *Dianthus* | Genus of flowers that includes the species carnations. Typically have frilly edged petals and can range in color from white to yellow to purple. | In salads; candied; pickled |
| *Johnny jump-ups* | Small flowers that are purple, blue, yellow, or white. Predecessor of the modern pansy. | In salads; as a garnish |

| | | |
|---|---|---|
| *Marigolds / calendula* | Small flower with bright petals ranging from pale yellow to gold to orange; slightly spicy aroma | In salads; as a garnish |
| *Nasturtiums* | Delicate, intensely colored flower with rounded petals and a funnel-shaped back; slight peppery flavor akin to watercress | In salads; as a garnish |
| *Pansies* | Member of the violet family; the flower is asymmetrical with four fan-shaped petals (two on each side) and one lobe-shaped petal at the bottom of the flower that points down. Flowers are usually multicolored. | In salads; candied |
| *Popcorn shoots* | Creamy yellow 3- to 4-in / 7.5- to 10-cm thin shoot with 3 to 4 ovular petals; slightly sweet flavor | In salads and desserts; as a garnish |
| *Roses* | Colors range from white to yellow to red, and the tips of the petals can be tinged with a variety of colors; slightly sweet flavor and a strong aroma. Trim the bitter white base off of the petal. | In salads, stuffings, desserts, syrups, tea, and confectionery |
| *Snap dragons* | The flower resembles the open mouth of a dragon and is generally white, yellow, red, orange, or crimson. | In salads; as a garnish |
| *Violets* | Genus of flowers that include pansies. Colors can range from purple to yellow to white and cream. Flavor is slightly sweet and wintergreen. | In salads, stuffings, and desserts; candied |

**HERB FLOWERS**

| | | |
|---|---|---|
| *Anise hyssop* | Fuzzy, mauve, finger-sized flowers with slight anise flavor | In salads |
| *Chive* | Flowers are a pink-lavender color and bloom in June. They have a mild onion flavor. | In salads, egg dishes, vegetable preparations, soups, sauces/compound butter; as a garnish |
| *Lavender* | Small purple flowers with a very floral aroma and slight citrus flavor | In salads, desserts, confectionery, sauces, and compound butters, jellies, bread; as a garnish |
| *Mustard* | Small bright yellow flower with pungent flavor | In salads, sauces, sautés; as a garnish |
| *Oregano* | Small white and red flowers with a relatively strong flavor | In salads, sauces, sautés; as a garnish |
| *Rosemary* | White, pink, purple, or blue flowers | In salads, sauces; as a garnish |
| *Sage* | Purple flowers with a fairly pungent flavor of sage | In salads, stuffings; as a garnish |
| *Thyme* | Tiny flowers with thyme flavor | In salads, compound butters; with fruit |

# Micro greens

Micro greens are seedlings of various herbs, greens, and vegetables (see Fig 3-8). They have been cultivated for many years but their popularity has recently grown rapidly. As a result, they have become much more affordable and the number of varieties available has increased. Most micro greens are grown hydroponically in plug flats and are snipped as they grow. It is possible for someone to grow their own micro greens but the plug flats are difficult to seed (typically, they are done by machine), so they are generally purchased.

Their flavors are similar to their fully grown counterparts but milder. These are usually too expensive to be used as the primary mix for a salad but they can be used as part of a salad mix or of a composed salad as well as a garnish. Their high price stems from the growing process being labor-intensive; however, a small amount goes a long way, especially when they are used as a garnish. They are typically not cooked and, sometimes, not even washed because they are grown in extremely clean, enclosed environments that are free of pesticides. Since they are grown in greenhouses, they are available year round. They generally last for up to a week, but it is best to use them within three days.

Examples of micro greens are listed below.

FIG 3-8  MICRO GREENS, LEFT COLUMN, FROM TOP TO BOTTOM: *pink orach, red garnet amaranth, beet tops;* MIDDLE COLUMN, FROM TO TO BOTTOM: *red mustard, celery; cilantro, arugula;* RIGHT COLUMN, FROM TOP TO BOTTOM: *pea shoots, radish, red cabbage*

table 3.7

## Micro greens

| Type | Description | Common Culinary Uses |
|---|---|---|
| *Arugula* | Sharp, slightly spicy flavor and light green color | In salads; as a garnish |
| *Beet top / bull's blood* | Green leaves with pink underside and veining; light beet flavor | In salads; as a garnish |
| *Celery* | Tiny, slightly frilly bright green leaves with a mild celery flavor | In salads; as a garnish |
| *Cilantro* | Elongated bright green leaves and a flavor similar to fully grown cilantro | In salads; as a garnish |
| *Mustard* | Tangy flavor; green and red mustard micro greens available. Red mustard has light green leaves with purply red tinges. | In salads; as a garnish |
| *Pea shoot* | Light green shoot with mild grassy flavor | In salads; as a garnish |
| *Purple or pink orach* | Purple and pink stems or leaves with arrowhead-shaped leaves and a mild spinach flavor | In salads; as a garnish |
| *Radish* | Available in varieties such as daikon and purple radish. Can have white stem and green leaves or purple leaves | In salads; as a garnish |
| *Red garnet amaranth* | Striking fuschia stems with small light green leaves and a light spinach flavor | In salads; as a garnish |
| *Red cabbage* | Dark green leaves with purple veins and a light cabbage aroma and flavor | In salads; as a garnish |

# Caring for salad greens

Nothing is worse than a gritty salad. Careful and thorough washing of salad greens is integral to providing high quality in both the look and palatability of the salad greens when you serve them. Salad greens should be kept properly chilled from the time they arrive until they are ready to be plated. The following guidelines should also be observed when handling salad greens.

1. **Wash greens thoroughly in plenty of cool water to remove all traces of dirt and sand.** Sturdy greens may be able to hold up to a spray, but delicate greens, herbs, and flowers should be gently plunged into and lifted out of the water repeatedly to remove dirt or sand. The water should be changed as often as necessary until there are absolutely no traces of dirt, grit, or sand in the rinsing water.

2. **Dry greens completely.** Salad dressings cling best to well-dried greens. In addition, greens that are carefully dried before they are stored will last longer. Spinners are the most effective tools to use, either large-scale electric spinners for volume salad making, or hand baskets. Spinners should be cleaned and sanitized carefully after each use.

3. **Store cleaned greens in tubs or other containers.** They should not be stacked too deep, as their own weight could bruise the leaves. They should be loosely wrapped or covered with dampened toweling and plastic wrap or a lid to prevent them from wilting rapidly (see Fig 3-9). Once greens have been cleaned, they should be used in a day or two.

4. **Cut or tear the lettuce into bite-sized pieces.** Traditional salad-making manuals have always called for lettuces to be torn to avoid discoloring, bruising, or crushing the leaf. This also provides a natural look to the final greens. Today's knives are not likely to discolor the leaves and there is no reason to believe that properly sharpened knives could bruise the lettuce more than tearing. This is still a matter of personal style and preference, of course.

FIG 3-9     *Once washed and dried, lettuces and greens should be covered with a damp towel and refrigerated to prevent rapid wilting.*

## Dressing the salad

Place the greens (about 2 oz / 57 g, or 6 fl oz / 180 mL, per serving) in a bowl and ladle a serving of salad dressing over them (1 to 1½ fl oz / 30 to 45 mL per serving). Use a lifting motion to toss the greens and dressing. Tongs, spoons, or, where appropriate, gloved hands can all be used to toss the salad. Each piece of lettuce should be coated completely but lightly with the dressing. There should be just enough dressing for the greens; if the dressing pools on the plate, there is too much.

Vinaigrette recipes can be found on pages 28–35 and include the following options: Basic Red Wine Vinaigrette, Truffle Vinaigrette, Apple Cider Vinaigrette, Curry Vinaigrette, Chipotle-Sherry Vinaigrette, or Mustard-Walnut Vinaigrette. Two reduced-fat vinaigrettes, Tomato Vinaigrette and Beet Vinaigrette, can be found on page 33.

Creamy-style salad dressings can be used successfully with green salads. Recipes for these dressings can be found on pages 36–40 and include Russian Dressing, Green Goddess Dressing, Creamy Black Pepper Dressing, and Rouquefort Dressing. Two reduced-fat dressings, Maytag Blue Cheese Dressing and Ranch Dressing, can be found on page 41.

## Garnishing the salad

Choose from a variety of vegetable **garnishes** according to the season and your desired presentation: slices or wedges of tomatoes, cucumbers, carrots, radishes, jícama, mushrooms (raw or marinated), olives, peppers, and so forth. In addition to these vegetable garnishes, the chef may also opt to use more unusual garnishes: raw or very lightly blanched asparagus, green peas or beans, pea shoots, sprouts of all sorts. These ingredients may either be tossed along with the greens as they are being dressed, or marinated separately in a little vinaigrette and used to top the salad.

Adding a crisp component to the salad gives another level of interest, in terms of both flavor and texture. There are several included in the recipes throughout the book, such as the following: Assorted Vegetable Chips, page 541; Pepper Jack and Oregano Crackers, page 542; Cheddar and Walnut Icebox Crackers, page 544; Toasted Almonds, page 513, or a Parmesan Crisp, page 612.

Breads and breadsticks can be served with simple green salads to make them more interesting and satisfying as well: Foccacia or Grissini, page 602. Sliced peasant-style breads can be served along with the salad, spread with a bit of Tapenade, page 53, or drizzled with one of the flavored oils found on pages 546–548.

# Side salads

## Vegetable salads

Vegetables for **vegetable salads** are prepared as required by the specific recipes. Some are simply rinsed and trimmed; others may need to be peeled, seeded, and cut to the appropriate shape. Some vegetables may require an initial blanching to set colors and textures, while others must be fully cooked.

If the salad is to be served raw, the prepared vegetables are simply combined with a vinaigrette or other dressing and allowed to rest long enough for the flavors to "marry." When the vegetables are partially or fully cooked, there are two options for applying the dressing. In the first option, the vegetables are drained and combined with the dressing while they are still warm, for faster flavor absorption. This works well for root vegetables such as carrots, beets, and parsnips, as well as leeks, onions, and potatoes. Some vegetables (especially green vegetables like broccoli or green beans) may discolor if they are combined with an acid in advance; in that case, the vegetables should be refreshed and chilled before being added to the dressing. In either case, the vegetables should be thoroughly drained and blotted dry to avoid watering down the dressing.

## Potato salads

Potatoes should be cooked completely, but not overcooked. Waxy potatoes (Yukon golds or Finnish) hold their shape better after cooking than starchy potatoes (Russets or baking potatoes).

The classic "American" potato salad is a creamy salad, typically dressed with mayonnaise. Other **potato salads** enjoyed around the world are often dressed with a vinaigrette. In some traditional European-style recipes, the dressing may be based on bacon fat, olive oil, stock, or a combination of these ingredients. The key to success with this style of potato salad is to combine the potatoes and dressing while the potatoes are still warm. The dressing is typically brought to a simmer before the potatoes are added, for the best finished flavor.

## Pasta and grain salads

Grains and pastas for salads should be fully cooked, but care should be taken to avoid overcooking. Grains and pasta will still be able to absorb some of the liquid in the dressing, and can quickly become soggy.

If a **pasta or grain salad** is held for later service, be especially careful to check it for seasoning before it is served, because these salads have a tendency to go flat as they sit. Salt and pepper are important seasonings, of course, but others, such as vinegars, herbs, or citrus juices, can give a brighter flavor.

## Legume salads

Dried beans should be cooked until they are tender to the bite and allowed to cool in their own cooking liquid. The center should be soft and creamy, and it is even possible that the skins may break open slightly. If a salad is made from a variety of dried beans, it is important that beans with different cooking times be cooked separately to the correct doneness.

Unlike grains and pastas, which might become too soft as they sit in a dressing, beans will not soften any further. In fact, the acid in salad dressings will make the beans tougher, even if they are fully cooked. Bean salads, therefore, should not be dressed and allowed to rest for extended periods. If the salad is used within four hours of preparation, however, there is little significant texture change.

## Fruit salads

Fruits have a variety of characteristics, making some **fruit salads** fairly sturdy, while others lose quality very rapidly. Fruits that turn brown (apples, pears, and bananas) can be treated with fruit juice to keep them from oxidizing, as long as the flavor of the juice doesn't compete with the other ingredients in the salad. Dilute acidic juices, such as lime, with water.

Mixed fruit salads that include highly perishable fruits can be produced for volume operations by preparing the base from the least perishable fruits such as cantaloupe, honeydew, or pineapple. More perishable items, such as raspberries, strawberries, or bananas, can then be combined with smaller batches or individual servings at the last moment, or they can be added as a garnish.

Fresh herbs such as mint, tarragon, basil, or lemon thyme may be added to fruit salads as a garnish. Experiment to determine which herbs work best with the fruits selected for the salad.

# Composed salads

**Composed salads** are made by carefully arranging items on a plate, rather than tossing them together. A "main item," such as grilled chicken or shrimp, a serving of cheese or grilled vegetables, and so forth, is often set on a bed of greens. The salad is garnished and dressed. Some composed salads feature foods that have contrasting colors, **flavors, texture,** heights, and temperatures (see Fig 3-10). Others are based on a single motif that holds the plate's elements together.

Although there are no specific rules governing the requirements for a composed salad, the following principles should be kept in mind:

- Consider how well each of the elements combine. Contrasting flavors are intriguing. Conflicting flavors are a disaster.
- Repetition of a color or flavor can be successful if it contributes to the overall dish. But generally, too much of a good thing is simply too much.

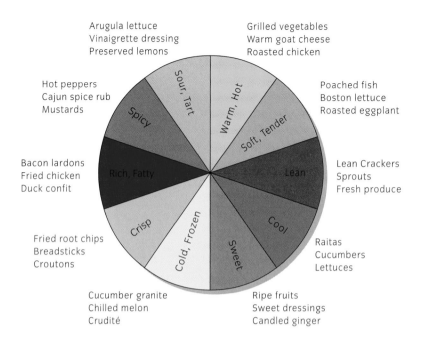

Arugula lettuce
Vinaigrette dressing
Preserved lemons

Grilled vegetables
Warm goat cheese
Roasted chicken

Hot peppers
Cajun spice rub
Mustards

Poached fish
Boston lettuce
Roasted eggplant

Bacon lardons
Fried chicken
Duck confit

Lean Crackers
Sprouts
Fresh produce

Fried root chips
Breadsticks
Croutons

Raitas
Cucumbers
Lettuces

Cucumber granite
Chilled melon
Crudité

Ripe fruits
Sweet dressings
Candled ginger

FIG 3-10 *A balance of flavors and textures should be considered when preparing a composed salad.*

- All of the components on the plate should be capable of standing alone; however, the composition should be such that each part is enhanced by being in combination with the others. This produces a more intriguing eating experience than when one of the components is eaten alone.
- **Components** should be arranged in such a way that the textures and colors of the foods are most attractive to the eye. The appearance of the plate should be given careful thought.

# Warm salads

**Warm salads,** known in French as ***salades tièdes,*** are made by tossing the salad ingredients in a warm dressing, working over moderate to low heat. The salad should be just warmed through. Another approach is to use a chilled crisp salad as the bed for a hot main item, such as grilled meat or fish.

# Parson's Garden Salad

YIELD: *10 appetizer servings*

| | |
|---|---|
| 5 oz / 142 g mâche | GARNISH |
| 5 oz / 142 g frisée | 16 fl oz / 480 mL olive oil |
| 5 oz / 142 g red treviso radicchio | 2 garlic cloves, crushed |
| 5 oz / 142 g watercress leaves | 8 whole black peppercorns |
| 6½ oz / 184 g soybean sprouts, blanched and chilled | 8½ oz / 241 g julienne carrots |
| 6 oz / 170 g shelled peas, blanched and chilled | 6 oz / 170 g julienne celeriac |
| 2 tbsp / 6 g chopped chives | Salt, as needed |
| 2 tbsp / 6 g chopped parsley | 10 fl oz / 300 mL Vinaigrette Gourmande (page 29) |
| | 5 oz / 142 g slab bacon, cut into medium dice, cooked crisp |
| | 30 quail eggs, poached (see Chef's Notes) |

1. Clean and thoroughly dry all the lettuces. Combine all mixed greens. Portion as necessary for single servings or larger batch salads. Refrigerate until ready to serve.

2. Up to 2 hours before service, heat the oil, garlic, and peppercorns to 325°F / 163°C. Add the carrots and celeriac and fry slowly until very crisp. Drain on absorbent paper towels and hold warm. Season with salt, if desired.

3. Salad Assembly: Just before serving, whisk the vinaigrette vigorously and reseason. For each serving, toss 2 oz / 57 g mixed greens with 1 fl oz / 30 mL vinaigrette. Arrange on chilled plates; top with bacon and fried vegetables. Add 3 warm poached quail eggs. Serve immediately.

*Chef's note* To poach quail eggs, combine 32 fl oz / 960 mL white table wine, 32 fl oz / 960 mL water, and a pinch of salt. Bring to 200°F / 93°C. Carefully crack eggs into cups and add to poaching liquid. Reduce heat to 170°F / 77°C and cook until eggs are set, 2 to 3 minutes. Remove with a perforated spoon and blot dry before adding to salads. Refrigerate until ready to serve.

# Spring Herb Salad

YIELD: *10 appetizer or side salad servings*

### MIXED GREENS

10 oz / 284 g baby arugula

5 oz / 142 g mizuna

5 oz / 142 g baby tat-soi

½ head radicchio, cut into chiffonade

1 bunch flat-leaf parsley, leaves only

2 bunches chervil, separated into pluches

1 bunch chives, sliced ½ in / 1 cm long

10 fl oz / 300 mL Truffle Vinaigrette (page 29)

Shaved truffle, as needed (optional)

Salt, as needed

Coarse-ground black pepper, as needed

1. Clean and thoroughly dry the mixed greens. Portion as necessary for single servings or larger batch salads. Refrigerate until ready to serve.

2. Salad Assembly: Just before serving, whisk the vinaigrette vigorously and reseason. For each serving, toss 2 oz / 57 g mixed greens with 1 fl oz / 30 mL vinaigrette. Arrange on chilled plates, top with shaved truffles if desired, and season with salt and pepper. Serve immediately.

*Chef's note* *Other herbs, such as dill, fennel, and tarragon, may be used in place of or in addition to the herbs listed.*

# Watermelon and Red Onion Salad with Watercress

YIELD: *10 servings*

4 bunches watercress

2 red onions, sliced paper thin

2 fl oz / 60 mL white wine vinegar

Salt, as needed

Cracked black pepper, as needed

4 fl oz / 120 mL vegetable oil

1 lb 10½ oz / 751 g seeded and cubed watermelon

½ oz / 14 g toasted pine nuts (optional)

1. Trim the stems of the watercress. Rinse the watercress and dry thoroughly. Refrigerate until ready to assemble the salad.

2. Place the sliced onions in ice water and allow them to soak for at least 2 hours and up to 24 hours in advance.

3. Combine the vinegar, salt, and pepper. Gradually whisk in the oil. Adjust seasoning with additional salt and pepper if necessary.

4. Salad Assembly: For each serving, toss 1½ oz / 43 g of the watercress with ½ fl oz / 15 mL of the dressing. Lift the watercress from the bowl, allowing the dressing to drain back into the bowl. Arrange on a chilled salad plate. Add the watermelon to the bowl and toss or roll until coated with the remaining dressing. Place the watermelon on top of the watercress. Garnish with a few slices of drained red onion, and ½ tsp / 2 g pine nuts if desired. Top with a few turns of freshly ground pepper.

*Presentation idea* *For a more mildly flavored salad, substitute baby spinach leaves for the watercress.*

# Georgia Peanut Salad

**YIELD:** *10 servings*

**DRESSING**

3 garlic cloves, minced

1 tbsp / 3 g finely chopped tarragon

1 tbsp / 3 g finely chopped chives

1 tbsp / 3 g finely chopped parsley

½ tsp / 1 g ground black pepper

1 oz / 28 g brown sugar

3 oz / 85 g malt vinegar

6 fl oz / 180 mL peanut oil

2 fl oz / 60 mL salad oil

1 oz / 28 g peanut butter

¼ tsp / 0.75 g salt

3 splashes Tabasco

**SALAD**

5 oz / 142 g multigrain bread

1½ fl oz / 45 mL olive oil

½ tsp / 1 g garlic, finely minced (about ½ medium clove)

½ tsp / 1.5 g salt

¼ tsp / 0.50 g ground black pepper

12½ oz / 354 g baby greens

10 oz / 284 g peanuts, toasted

10 oz / 284 g red seedless grapes, halved

1. Combine dressing ingredients thoroughly and adjust seasoning if necessary. Reserve separately.

2. Cut small cubes from the multigrain bread.

3. Toss the bread with the olive oil, garlic, salt, and pepper.

4. Toast in a 325°F / 175°C oven for 10 to 15 minutes, turning the croutons once, or until golden brown.

5. For each serving, toss 1¼ oz / 35 g greens with approximately 1 fl oz / 30 mL of the dressing. Arrange the mixed greens on a salad plate. Garnish with croutons, toasted peanuts, and grapes.

*Presentation idea*  *Top the salad with grilled chicken to create a delicious light lunch out of this salad.*

# Greek Salad with Feta Cheese and Whole Wheat Pita

YIELD: *10 servings*

| | |
|---|---|
| 10 oz / 284 g Kalamata olives | 1 lb 4 oz / 567 g cherry tomatoes, halved |
| 16 fl oz / 480 mL Lemon-Parsley Vinaigrette (page 30) | 10 oz / 284 g yellow peppers, cut into julienne |
| 2 lb 4 oz / 1.02 kg romaine lettuce | 10 oz / 284 g red onions, peeled, sliced ⅛ in / 3 mm thick |
| 10 whole wheat pitas, cut into 8 wedges each | 15 oz / 425 g feta cheese, crumbled |
| 1 lb 4 oz / 567 g seedless cucumbers, peeled, sliced ⅛ in / 3 mm thick | |

1. Drain the olives and mix with 4 fl oz / 120 mL of the vinaigrette and allow to marinate overnight.

2. Clean the romaine lettuce and partially remove about a third of the stem. Wash and spin-dry.

3. Just before serving, whisk the vinaigrette vigorously and reseason. Toss 3½ oz / 99 g of the romaine lettuce with 1 fl oz / 30 mL of the vinaigrette for each serving.

4. Arrange the wedges of one pita around the rim of a chilled plate. Place the dressed romaine lettuce in the center of the plate and top with 2 oz / 57 g sliced cucumber, 2 oz / 57 g tomatoes, 1 oz / 28 g peppers, onions, and olives, and 1½ oz / 43 g feta cheese.

*Presentation idea*  Serve each salad with two Stuffed Grape Leaves (page 477), as pictured here.

# Caesar Salad

YIELD: *10 appetizer servings*

1 lb 4 oz / 567 g romaine lettuce

12 oz / 340 g Garlic-Flavored or Plain Croutons (page 613)

DRESSING

1 tbsp / 9 g minced garlic

5 anchovy fillets

¾ tsp / 2.25 g salt, or as needed

½ tsp / 1 g ground black pepper, or as needed

2 fl oz / 60 mL egg (whole or yolk only)

2 fl oz / 60 mL lemon juice, or as needed

10 fl oz / 300 mL extra-virgin olive oil

6 oz / 170 g finely grated Parmesan, or as needed

1. Separate the romaine into leaves. Clean and dry thoroughly. Tear or cut into pieces if necessary. Refrigerate until ready to serve.

2. Prepare croutons and hold at room temperature until ready to serve.

3. To prepare the dressing, mash together the garlic, anchovy fillets, salt, and pepper in a bowl to form a relatively smooth paste. Add the egg and the lemon juice and blend well. Gradually add the olive oil, whisking as it is added to form a thick emulsion. Stir in the Parmesan. Adjust seasoning with salt and pepper if necessary.

4. For each serving, combine 2 oz / 57 g greens with 1 fl oz / 30 mL dressing, tossing gently until evenly coated. Garnish with a few croutons.

*Presentation idea* Keep the leaves whole and lightly dress them with the Caesar dressing. Garnish the plate with croutons and shaved curls of Parmesan cheese over the top of the salad.

*Chef's note* According to culinary lore, this salad was created by Caesar Cardini in 1924 at his restaurant in Tijuana, Mexico. Today, Caesar salads may be served as a salad buffet item, a plated first course, or a main course salad garnished with seafood, sliced grilled chicken, or duck breast.

# Baby Spinach, Avocado, and Grapefruit Salad

YIELD: *10 servings*

1½ avocados, peeled, pitted, and sliced

3 grapefruit, cut into suprêmes

1 lb / 454 g baby spinach

5 fl oz / 150 mL Balsamic Vinaigrette
(page 28)

Salt, as needed

Ground black pepper, as needed

1. For each serving, combine 1¼ oz / 35 g avocado with 1½ oz / 43 g grapefruit segments (about 3).

2. Toss 1½ oz / 43 g spinach with 1 tbsp / 15 mL vinaigrette for each serving. Season with salt and pepper as needed.

3. Arrange the spinach on chilled plates. Top it with the avocados and grapefruit. Serve immediately.

*Chef's note*  To add a crunchy texture to the plate, top the finished salad with a few toasted pecans or pine nuts.


# Roasted Beet Salad

YIELD: *10 servings*

4 beets, greens trimmed to 1 in / 3 cm
(about 2 lb / 907 g)

Salt, as needed

DRESSING

1¼ fl oz / 37.50 mL extra-virgin olive oil

1 tbsp / 15 mL red wine vinegar

1 tbsp / 15 mL lemon juice

Pinch cayenne

1. Preheat the oven to 375°F / 191°C. Arrange the beets in a 2-in / 5-cm half hotel pan; add water just to cover the bottom of the pan. Season with salt. Cover with foil and roast until fork-tender, approximately one hour depending on size.

2. While the beets are roasting, combine dressing ingredients.

3. Trim the beets, slip off the skin, and slice into ¼-in / 6-mm rounds. The slices should also be halved or quartered as needed to provide a uniform size. Add to the dressing while still warm.

4. Let rest at room temperature for at least 30 minutes before serving or cooling for storage.

*Presentation ideas*  Use red or golden beets for this salad.

The beets are roasted in this recipe, but they could also be boiled or steamed.

For a special presentation, alternate the sliced beets with orange slices, but be sure to assemble this at the last minute or the beets will bleed onto the oranges.

# Marinated Roasted Pepper Salad

YIELD: *10 servings*

8 oz / 227 g roasted red peppers, peeled and seeded

8 oz / 227 g roasted green peppers, peeled and seeded

8 oz / 227 g roasted yellow peppers, peeled and seeded

4¾ oz / 135 g tomatoes, peeled and seeded

1 oz / 28 g golden raisins

1½ fl oz / 45 mL dry sherry

DRESSING

6⅔ fl oz / 200 mL Balsamic Vinaigrette (page 28)

4 oz / 113 g red onions, cut into julienne

2 oz / 57 g black olives, cut into strips (20 each)

½ oz / 14 g chopped cilantro leaves

½ jalapeño, minced

1 garlic clove, minced

GARNISH

¾ oz / 21 g Parmesan

¾ oz / 21 g toasted pine nuts

1. Cut the roasted peppers into ½-in / 1-cm strips. Cut the tomatoes into ½-in / 1-cm strips. Plump the raisins in the sherry.

2. Combine the dressing ingredients and pour over the peppers, tomatoes, and drained raisins.

3. Toss to combine. Let the salad rest at room temperature for 30 to 45 minutes before serving at room temperature, or refrigerate for later service.

4. Salad Assembly: Just before serving, shave Parmesan curls over each serving and top with toasted pine nuts.

*Variations*  *Marinated Roasted Peppers: Omit the tomatoes and plumped raisins. Dress with a plain Balsamic Vinaigrette, omitting olives, onions, cilantro, jalapeño, and garlic. Use as required in other recipes (see Roasted Chicken Sandwich, page 168).*

*Marinated Peppers and Mushrooms: Prepare Marinated Peppers, adding 8 oz / 227 g julienned shiitake or white mushrooms to the pepper and tomato mixture.*

# Hearts of Artichoke Salad

YIELD: *10 servings*

10 artichokes or 30 baby artichokes

2 lemons, halved

DRESSING

9 fl oz / 270 mL olive oil

3 fl oz / 90 mL balsamic vinegar

Salt, as needed

Ground white pepper, as needed

½ bunch flat-leaf parsley, leaves only

6½ oz / 184 g Kalamata olives, pitted (30 each)

1 red onion, sliced into thin rings or julienne

4 lb / 1.81 kg plum tomatoes, peeled, seeded, and quartered

1. Cut the ends off the artichokes and trim off the outer leaves (see Fig 3-13a). Scoop out the chokes (see Fig 3-13b). Quarter each heart and rub with the halved lemons. Hold in acidulated water.

2. Simmer the artichoke hearts in a cuisson (see Chef's Note) until tender, about 8 to 12 minutes. Drain and let dry on absorbent paper towels while preparing the dressing.

3. Whisk together the dressing ingredients. Add the artichoke hearts, olives, onions, and tomatoes.

4. Let rest at room temperature for at least 30 minutes before serving or cooling for storage.

*Chef's note* *To prepare a cuisson, combine 1 gal / 3.84 L water with 2 fl oz / 60 mL lemon juice, 4 whole cloves, 1 bouquet garni (page 586), and 2 tsp / 6 g salt. Bring all ingredients to a simmer.*

**FIG 3-13A** *To clean an artichoke, cut off the ends at the widest point and trim off the tough outer leaves.*

**FIG 3-13B** *Once the bottom of the artichoke has been trimmed, scoop out the thistly choke from the center.*

# Haricots Verts with Prosciutto and Gruyère

YIELD: *10 servings*

| | |
|---|---|
| 1 lb 4 oz / 567 g haricots verts | 1 tbsp / 15 mL white wine vinegar |
| 5 oz / 142 g prosciutto | ½ tsp / 1.5 g salt |
| 5 oz / 142 g Gruyère | ¼ tsp / 0.50 g ground white pepper |
| DRESSING | ½ oz / 14 g minced shallots |
| 1 fl oz / 30 mL lemon juice, or as needed | 3 fl oz / 90 mL vegetable oil |

1. Trim the haricots verts and rinse. Cut the prosciutto and Gruyère into fine julienne.

2. Combine the lemon juice, vinegar, salt, pepper, and shallots. Gradually whisk in the oil to make a dressing.

3. Blanch the haricots verts in salted boiling water until barely tender to the bite. Refresh in cold water. Drain and blot dry.

4. Add the haricots verts, proscuitto, and Gruyère to the dressing. Toss to combine and let rest at room temperature for at least 30 minutes before serving or storing.

*Chef's note*    *This salad could be featured as a side salad for a pâté, terrine, or galantine. Or it could be served on its own or as part of a salad "sampler" appetizer plate. If haricots verts are unavailable, this salad is equally good prepared with regular green beans, asparagus, or leeks.*

*Variation*    *Haricots Verts with Walnut and Red Wine Vinaigrette (page 29): Paul Bocuse, the famous chef of Lyons, France, combines 12 oz / 340 g haricots verts, 8 oz / 227 g sliced white mushrooms, a few slivers of truffles, and a dressing made with walnut oil and Beaujolais wine vinegar for a simple but elegant salad.*

# Shaved Fennel and Parmesan Salad

YIELD: *10 servings*

1 lb 4 oz / 567 g fennel bulbs (about 2 large bulbs)

4 to 6 fl oz / 120 to 180 mL extra-virgin olive oil

2 fl oz / 60 mL lemon juice

Salt, as needed

Pepper, as needed

½ oz / 14 g chopped flat-leaf parsley leaves

10 oz / 284 g raw cèpes, sliced thin (optional)

GARNISH

3 oz / 85 g Parmesan

½ to 1 fl oz / 15 to 30 mL white truffle oil or hazelnut oil

1. Trim, core, and shave the fennel very thin using a knife or mandolin.

2. Combine the olive oil, lemon juice, salt, and pepper thoroughly. Add the fennel, parsley, and sliced cèpes, if using; toss to coat evenly.

3. Serve immediately or refrigerate until needed.

4. Salad Assembly: For each serving, arrange 2½ oz / 71 g salad on a chilled plate. Shave some Parmesan over the salad and drizzle with a little truffle or hazelnut oil.

*Variations*    *Fennel and Persimmon Salad: Prepare the salad through step 3. Garnish with shaved fuyu persimmon and finish with a few drops of balsamic vinegar.*

*Artichoke and Fennel Salad: Replace half the fennel with cooked artichoke hearts (see page 609 for cooking instructions). Dress and finish as above.*

*Grilled Fennel Salad: Slice the fennel ¼ in / 6 mm thick, brush with a little of the dressing, and grill until tender. Cool the fennel before combining with the remaining dressing in step 2.*

# Coleslaw

YIELD: *10 servings*

1 lb 2 oz / 510 g green cabbage, cut into chiffonade

5¼ oz / 149 g red cabbage, cut into chiffonade

1¾ oz / 50 g carrots, cut into julienne

1¾ oz / 50 g red and yellow peppers, cut into julienne

1¾ oz / 50 g red onions, cut into julienne

DRESSING

½ oz / 14 g sugar

2 tsp / 4 g dry mustard

1 tsp / 2 g celery seed

3⅓ fl oz / 100 mL Basic Mayonnaise (page 36)

3⅓ fl oz / 100 mL sour cream

1 fl oz / 30 mL cider vinegar

2 tsp / 11 g prepared horseradish (optional)

1 tsp / 5 g mild brown mustard

Salt, as needed

Ground white pepper, as needed

Tabasco sauce, as needed

1. Combine the cabbages, carrots, peppers, and onions. Reserve.

2. Stir together the sugar, mustard, and celery seed to work out lumps. Add the remaining dressing ingredients and stir to combine.

3. Fold the cabbages, carrots, peppers, and onions into the dressing. Serve immediately or cover and refrigerate until serving.

*Chef's note*  *A mixture of cabbages, peppers, carrots, and onions makes a colorful variation on the classic coleslaw. For a more traditional slaw, omit the peppers and onions.*

# Roasted Corn and Tomato Salad

YIELD: *10 servings*

DRESSING

5⅓ fl oz / 160 mL olive oil

4 fl oz / 120 mL white wine vinegar

1½ tsp / 5 g roasted garlic paste

1 tsp / 3 g salt

½ tsp / 1 g coarse-ground black pepper

1 lb 4 oz / 567 g roasted corn kernels (see Chef's Note)

1 lb 1 oz / 482 g tomato concassé

¾ oz / 21 g sliced green onions

1 tbsp / 3 g chopped cilantro

1 tbsp / 3 g chopped flat-leaf parsley

1. Blend the oil, vinegar, and garlic paste. Season with salt and pepper.

2. Add the corn, tomato concassé, green onions, and herbs. Toss to coat evenly. Adjust seasoning, if necessary Serve immediately or cover and refrigerate until serving.

*Chef's note* *To roast corn, cut the kernels off of the cob, toss with olive oil, salt, and pepper, and spread in a single layer on a sheet pan. Roast in a 350°F / 177°C oven until the some of the moisture has evaporated from the kernels and they have turned a dark golden color with light brown tinges.*

# Marinated Tomato Salad

YIELD: *10 servings*

4 oz / 113 g minced red onions

2 garlic cloves, minced

2 fl oz / 60 mL sherry wine vinegar

4 fl oz / 120 mL extra-virgin olive oil

1 bunch flat-leaf parsley, chiffonade

2 bunches opal basil, chiffonade

1 lb 13 oz / 822 g peeled, seeded, and diced heirloom tomatoes

1 lb 9 oz / 709 g halved currant tomatoes

Salt, as needed

Ground black pepper, as needed

1. Combine the onions, garlic, and sherry vinegar and allow to macerate for 15 minutes.

2. Drizzle in the olive oil then stir in the parsley and opal basil.

3. Add the tomatoes and marinate for 1 hour under refrigeration.

4. Season with salt and pepper and serve immediately or refrigerate until needed.

# Celeriac and Tart Apple Salad

YIELD: *10 servings*

| | |
|---|---|
| 2 lb / 907 g celeriac | ½ oz / 14 g sugar |
| DRESSING | Salt, as needed |
| 3 fl oz / 90 mL crème fraîche (page 382) | Ground black pepper, as needed |
| 3 fl oz / 90 mL Basic Mayonnaise (page 36) | |
| 1 oz / 28 g Dijon mustard | 3 Granny Smith apples |
| 1 fl oz / 30 mL apple cider vinegar | |

1. Cut away the outer rind of the celeriac and cut into allumettes, about 1½ in / 4 cm long. Hold in a blanc (see Chef's Notes) to prevent discoloring.

2. Combine the dressing ingredients by whisking thoroughly.

3. Rinse the celeriac, and boil until tender in acidulated water. Refresh in cold water and drain on absorbent paper towels.

4. Peel and cut the apples into allumettes. Fold the apples and the celeriac into the dressing. Adjust seasoning with salt and pepper if necessary.

5. Serve immediately or cover and refrigerate until serving.

*Chef's notes*    *Both celeriac and apples will oxidize when exposed to air. This turns their creamy white flesh an unappetizing brown color. Although acidulated water containing lemon juice is often used to keep apples from browning, it might give the apples a strong lemon taste. We prefer to use apple juice combined with a few drops of apple cider vinegar. The acid in the juice and the vinegar will keep the apples from browning, and they add another "apple" flavor dimension.*

*To prepare the blanc, whisk together 32 fl oz / 960 mL water with 2 oz / 57 g all-purpose flour and 1 fl oz / 30 mL lemon juice.*

*For the acidulated water to blanch the celeriac, add 1 tbsp / 15 mL lemon juice to each quart of water.*

# Mushroom Salad with Celery and Tuscan Pecorino

YIELD: *10 servings*

3 fl oz / 90 mL lemon juice

1 tsp / 3 g lemon zest

6 fl oz / 180 mL extra-virgin olive oil

2 tsp / 6 g kosher salt, plus as needed

¼ tsp / 0.50 g ground black pepper, plus as needed

7½ oz / 213 g celery ribs

10 oz / 284 g white mushrooms, cleaned

10 oz / 284 g crimini mushrooms, cleaned

1¼ oz / 35 g celery leaves

2½ oz / 71 g arugula

1½ oz / 43 g green onion, sliced thin

2 tbsp / 6 g flat-leaf parsley chiffonade

2 tbsp / 6 g mint chiffonade

5 oz / 142 g Tuscan Pecorino, shaved

1. Whisk together the lemon juice and zest. Slowly drizzle in the olive oil, whisking constantly. Season as needed with salt and pepper. Set aside.

2. Slice celery ribs on the bias, about ⅛ in / 3 mm thick. Slice mushrooms ⅛ in / 3 mm thick.

3. Combine the mushrooms, celery, celery leaves, arugula, onion, and parsley in a bowl.

4. Whisk the lemon vinaigrette to recombine and adjust seasoning with salt, if necessary. Add 8 fl oz / 240 mL to the salad. Toss well to combine and season as needed with salt and pepper.

5. For each serving, place 8 fl oz / 240 mL salad in center of a ring mold in the center of a plate.

6. Remove the ring mold and garnish with ½ oz / 14 g shaved Tuscan Pecorino cheese.

7. Drizzle some of the remaining vinaigrette around salad on the plate. Grind a bit of fresh pepper over the salad before serving.

*Chef's note*  *Mushrooms such as porcinis, chanterelles, or morels may be substituted for some or all of the mushrooms in this salad.*

# Polish Cucumber Salad (Mizeria Ze Śmietaną)

YIELD: *10 servings*

3 European cucumbers

1½ tsp / 4.5 g salt

⅛ bunch dill, rinsed and chopped

4 fl oz / 120 mL sour cream

1½ tsp / 7 mL vinegar, white or champagne

⅛ tsp / 0.25 g ground black pepper

1. Peel the cucumbers, slice them in half lengthwise, and seed them.

2. Thinly slice the cleaned cucumbers and place in a bowl. Sprinkle them with 1 tsp / 3 g salt and allow them to rest for 1 hour at room temperature.

3. Rinse and drain the cucumbers.

4. Add the dill, sour cream, and vinegar to the cucumbers and mix well to combine.

5. Season with the remaining salt and pepper.

6. Drain any excess moisture from the salad. There should be just enough dressing to coat the cucumbers.

*Chef's note*  *Serve this cucumber salad as an accompaniment for a green salad and smoked fish.*

# Mediterranean Potato Salad

YIELD: *10 servings*

2 lb 8 oz / 1.13 kg waxy potatoes (such as Yellow Finn or Yukon Gold)

DRESSING

7 fl oz / 210 mL extra-virgin olive oil

3 fl oz / 90 mL red wine vinegar

1 fl oz / 30 mL balsamic vinegar

1 oz / 28 g coarsely chopped flat-leaf parsley leaves

1½ oz / 43 g chopped capers

½ oz / 14 g chopped anchovy fillets

1 tsp / 3 g minced garlic

1 tsp / 3 g salt

¼ tsp / 0.50 g ground white pepper

1. Simmer the potatoes in salted water until just cooked through.

2. While the potatoes are cooking, mix the dressing ingredients.

3. Drain the potatoes and dry briefly to remove any excess moisture. Peel and dice while still very hot and place in a bowl.

4. Whisk dressing to recombine and pour over the potatoes. Let rest at room temperature for at least 30 minutes before serving or cooling for storage.

*Chef's note*   *This salad can be served either warm or cold. If the salad is to be served warm or at room temperature, it should be made just prior to service and held no longer than 3 hours. If the salad is to be held or served cold, cool it to room temperature once the potato salad has been assembled.*

*Variation*   *Mediterranean Potato Salad with Mussels: This salad makes an interesting addition to a seafood buffet or antipasti and is a creative way to feature mussels. Steam or poach mussels until just cooked through. If the salad is being served warm, poach the seafood just before serving and fold into the salad while still warm. For a cold presentation, steam or poach the mussels, chill well, and add to the cooled salad. Store as described above. Other shellfish, such as clams, can be used as well.*

# German Potato Salad

YIELD: *10 servings*

2 lb 4 oz / 1.02 kg waxy potatoes (such as Yellow Finn or Yukon Gold)

DRESSING

2 oz / 57 g diced bacon

20 fl oz / 600 mL Chicken Stock (page 592)

2 fl oz / 60 mL white wine vinegar

4 oz / 113 g diced onions

1 tsp / 3 g salt, or as needed

1 tsp / 4 g sugar, or as needed

Ground white pepper, as needed

2 fl oz / 60 mL vegetable oil

1 oz / 28 g mild brown mustard

½ bunch chives, snipped

1. Cook the potatoes in simmering salted water until just tender. Drain and dry. While the potatoes are still hot, remove the peels and slice the potatoes ⅓ in / 8 mm thick.

2. While the potatoes are cooking, prepare the dressing: Render the bacon, remove it from the pan with a slotted spoon, and keep it warm.

3. Bring the chicken stock, vinegar, onions, salt, sugar, and pepper to a boil.

4. Combine the oil, rendered bacon fat, and mustard with the warm potatoes. Pour over the onions and then add the boiling stock-vinegar mixture. Add the rendered bacon and chives; toss the salad gently.

5. The salad may be served warm or at room temperature.

*Chef's note* It is important to use waxy potatoes for this salad so that the warm salad will retain its structure when served.

# Tabbouleh Salad

YIELD: *10 servings*

| | |
|---|---|
| 1 lb / 454 g bulgur | DRESSING |
| 2½ oz / 71 g chopped flat-leaf parsley leaves | 8 fl oz / 240 mL extra-virgin olive oil |
| 14 oz / 397 g diced tomatoes | 4 fl oz / 120 mL lemon juice |
| 1 oz / 28 g finely sliced green onions, white part only | Salt, as needed |
| ½ oz / 14 g chopped mint | Ground black pepper, as needed |

1. Place the bulgur in a bowl and cover with warm water. Soak for 30 minutes and drain well.

2. In a large mixing bowl, combine the bulgur with the parsley, tomatoes, green onions, and mint.

3. Whisk together the dressing ingredients, pour over the salad, and toss to coat evenly. Serve immediately or cover and refrigerate until serving.

*Chef's note* *This recipe offers a faithful rendition of a salad that, according to many authorities, is more a parsley salad with some bulgur than a bulgur salad with a little parsley!*


# Israeli Couscous and Heirloom Grains

YIELD: *10 servings*

| | |
|---|---|
| 2 oz / 57 g kamut rice blend | 3½ oz / 99 g medium-dice savoy cabbage |
| 3¾ oz / 106 g green lentils | 1½ oz / 43 g green onion, thinly cut on bias |
| 5½ oz / 156 g Israeli couscous | 8 fl oz / 240 mL Lemon-Parsley Vinaigrette (page 30) |
| 9½ oz / 269 g seedless cucumber, cut into small dice | |

1. Cook the kamut blend and green lentils separately and allow them to cool to room temperature.

2. Cook the Israeli couscous and allow it to cool to room temperature.

3. Mix the cooled grains together in a large bowl. Add the cucumber, cabbage, and green onion to the grains and mix to combine.

4. Fold in the vinaigrette.

5. Serve about 6 fl oz / 80 mL (4½ oz / 128 g) per person, or refrigerate until needed.

*Chef's note* *Israeli couscous is a large granular pasta and should be cooked briefly in a large pot of boiling water, as you would cook pasta. It may be necessary to shock the couscous to help it cool to room temperature.*

# Lentil and Walnut Salad

YIELD: *10 servings*

10⅔ oz / 302 g French lentils

1 carrot, cut into brunoise, blanched

⅔ stalk celery, peeled, cut into brunoise, blanched

⅓ leek, white part only, cut into small dice, blanched

5⅓ oz / 151 g toasted walnuts, skins removed

3⅓ fl oz / 100 mL Mustard–Walnut Vinaigrette (page 31)

1. Simmer the lentils in water until they are tender. Refresh in cold water and drain well. Drain, rinse until cold, and drain well again.

2. Combine the lentils, carrots, celery, leek, and walnuts. Refrigerate until ready to serve.

3. Salad Assembly: Up to 4 hours before serving, combine the lentil mixture with the vinaigrette. Serve at room temperature or chilled. Adjust seasoning before serving, if necessary.

*Chef's note* Legumes will toughen if they are left in contact with an acid, such as this vinaigrette, for extended periods. As with all bean salads, this salad is best when prepared and consumed on the same day.

# Mixed Bean and Grain Salad

YIELD: *10 servings*

6 oz / 170 g chickpeas (garbanzos), soaked overnight

6 oz / 170 g green lentils

3 oz / 85 g acini de pepe pasta

6 oz / 170 g bulgur

DRESSING

5⅓ fl oz / 160 mL Hazelnut–Oregano Vinaigrette (page 31)

3 sun-dried tomatoes, minced

Salt, as needed

Coarse-ground black pepper, as needed

1. Cook the chickpeas, lentils, and pasta separately in salted water. Refresh in cold water and drain well. Combine gently in a bowl.

2. Place the bulgur in a bowl and cover with warm water. Soak for 30 minutes and drain well. Combine with the chickpea mixture.

3. Whisk together the dressing ingredients, pour over the salad, and toss to coat evenly. Serve immediately, or cover and refrigerate until ready to serve.

*Presentation idea* Serve the salad with skewers of grilled lamb and red and yellow peppers.

*Mixed Bean and Grain Salad*

# Fattoush (Eastern Mediterranean Bread Salad)

YIELD: *10 to 12 servings*

6 pitas

1½ fl oz / 45 mL extra-virgin olive oil

Salt, as needed

Ground black pepper, as needed

DRESSING

2 fl oz / 60 mL lemon juice

1 tbsp / 15 mL white wine vinegar

1 tbsp / 15 g ground sumac

2 garlic cloves, minced

4 fl oz / 120 mL extra-virgin olive oil

Salt, as needed

Ground black pepper, as needed

2 tbsp / 6 g chopped thyme

½ tsp / 1 g cayenne

2 tsp / 8 g sugar

VEGETABLES

1 bunch green onions, chopped

1 oz / 28 g chopped flat-leaf parsley leaves

6 plum tomatoes, seeded and cut into medium dice

1 seedless cucumber, peeled and cut into medium dice

8 oz / 227 g radishes, brunoise or sliced thin

1 yellow pepper, seeded and cut into small dice

1. Cut the pita bread into small wedges. Toss with the oil, salt, and black pepper. Bake on a sheet pan in a 300°F / 149°C oven for about 15 minutes, turning halfway through the baking. The pita should be crisp, but not crumbly.

2. Combine dressing ingredients thoroughly and adjust seasoning if necessary. Reserve separately.

3. Salad Assembly: Combine the vegetables with the dressing and toss until coated. Fold in the pita bread. Adjust seasoning with salt and pepper. If the salad is too dry, sprinkle with a little water to moisten.

*Chef's note* *Sumac is a favored seasoning in Syrian, Lebanese, and other Middle Eastern cuisines. It is made from the berries of the sumac tree and has a tart, slightly bitter flavor.*

# Fall Panzanella Salad (Roasted Vegetable and Bread Salad)

YIELD: *10 servings*

2 lb 4 oz / 1.02 kg butternut squash, peeled and cut into medium dice

2 fl oz / 60 mL olive oil

½ oz / 14 g salt

2 tsp / 4 g ground black pepper

8 oz / 227 g dried cranberries

14 oz / 397 g sourdough bread

4 oz / 113 g walnuts, toasted and roughly chopped

¼ oz / 7 g sage chiffonade

16 fl oz / 480 mL Roasted Shallot Vinaigrette (page 32)

1. Preheat the grill to medium.

2. Lightly coat the diced squash with some of the olive oil and season with salt and pepper. Spread the squash out on a parchment-lined sheet pan and bake in a 350°F / 177°C oven for about 30 minutes until tender, yet still holding its shape. Allow to cool to room temperature.

3. Rehydrate the cranberries in hot water for 5 to 10 minutes; discard water.

4. Cut the sourdough down the center lengthwise and brush the insides very lightly with the remaining olive oil. Lay the bread cut side down on the grill to dry out and get marks. Rotate the bread halfway through to get crosshatch marks, if desired. Cool and cut the bread into a large dice. If needed, bake the cubes in the oven to dry further. The cubes should be crisp on the outside but still slightly tender and chewy on the inside. They should not be completely dried out like croutons.

5. Once the squash and bread are cool, combine all of the ingredients and vinaigrette and fold VERY GENTLY to keep the shape of the squash. (NOTE: The amount of dressing may vary depending on the bread used.)

6. Taste and adjust seasoning as needed with the remaining salt and pepper.

*Chef's note*  *This salad is best if made the day before serving and is a thrifty way to use bread that has become too dry for slicing and eating. The squash can be roasted and the bread can be grilled ahead of time before tossing the salad ingredients together.*

# Couscous Salad with Curried Vegetables

YIELD: *10 servings*

| | |
|---|---|
| 1 lb 8 oz / 680 g asparagus, trimmed and cut on the bias 2 in / 5 cm long | 1 lb 8 oz / 680 g dry couscous |
| 12 oz / 340 g cauliflower florets | 1 cinnamon stick |
| 12 oz / 340 g fennel, julienned | 1 oz / 28 g flat-leaf parsley leaves, whole or chiffonade |
| 6 oz / 170 g cooked chickpeas, drained and rinsed | 3 oz / 85 g slivered almonds, toasted |
| 8 fl oz / 240 mL Curry Vinaigrette (page 31) | 2 oz / 57 g dry currants, plumped in warm water |
| Salt, as needed | 1 lb / 454 g grape or cherry tomatoes |
| Ground black pepper, as needed | 1 fl oz / 30 mL Harissa Sauce (page 533) |

1. Steam or boil the vegetables separately until tender; drain well. Combine the vegetables and the chickpeas with the vinaigrette while the vegetables are still hot. Season with salt and pepper. Cover and refrigerate for at least 2 and up to 12 hours.

2. Steam the couscous with the cinnamon stick until hot, fluffy, and tender. Fluff the couscous to break up any lumps and fold in the parsley, almonds, and currants. Taste and season with salt and pepper. Top with the marinated vegetables and tomatoes. Drizzle a few drops of harissa sauce on the salad.

*Chef's note* *Quartered artichoke bottoms or hearts can be included with the vegetables as they marinate.*

# Soba Noodle Salad

YIELD: *10 servings*

| | |
|---|---|
| 1 lb 4 oz / 567 g soba noodles | ½ tsp / 1 g red pepper flakes |
| 2 tbsp / 30 mL rice vinegar | 6 oz / 170 g carrots, cut into fine julienne |
| 4 fl oz / 120 mL tamari | 4 oz / 113 g green onions, thinly sliced on the bias |
| 1½ tsp / 7 g light miso | |
| 4 fl oz / 120 mL sesame oil | Salt, as needed |
| ¾ oz / 21 g sesame seeds, unhulled | Ground black pepper, as needed |

1. Cook the noodles in boiling salted water until al dente. Rinse with cold water, drain, and dry.

2. To prepare the dressing, stir together the rice vinegar, tamari, and miso. Whisk in the sesame oil, sesame seeds, and red pepper flakes.

3. Toss the carrots and green onions in the dressing.

4. Pour the dressing over the pasta; toss, and adjust seasoning with salt and pepper.

*Chef's note* *Soba noodles are made from buckwheat and wheat flours and have a brownish-gray color when cooked.*

Soba Noodle Salad

# Black Bean Salad

YIELD: *10 servings*

| | |
|---|---|
| 8 oz / 227 g dried black beans | 2 fl oz / 60 mL olive oil |
| 7 oz / 198 g white rice | 2 tsp / 6 g salt, plus as needed |
| 4 oz / 113 g diced red peppers | 1 fl oz / 30 mL lime juice |
| 5 oz / 142 g diced onions | 1 tbsp / 9 g chopped cilantro |
| 1 tbsp / 9 g minced garlic | 8 oz / 227 g queso blanco, crumbled |

1. Soak the black beans overnight and discard soaking water.

2. Place the soaked beans in medium saucepan and cover with fresh cold water. Bring to a boil, cover, and cook over medium-high heat until tender, 1½ to 2 hours. As the beans are cooking, watch the liquid level and add water as needed to prevent scorching. When beans are fully cooked, drain well and cool slightly.

3. Cook the white rice in abundant rapidly boiling salted water just until tender, about 10 minutes for white medium-grain rice, then drain well and cool slightly.

4. Sauté the red pepper, onion, and garlic in 1 fl oz / 30 mL olive oil. Season lightly with salt and cool slightly.

5. Fold the red pepper mixture into the cooked and cooled beans.

6. Make a vinaigrette using the remaining olive oil, lime juice, cilantro, and salt. Pour over bean mixture and gently fold, coating the salad.

7. Gently fold in the rice.

8. Gently fold the crumbled queso blanco into the salad. Adjust seasoning with salt. Cool completely; cover and refrigerate until serving.

*Chef's note*  Queso blanco is a fresh, soft, white cheese that is originally from Mexico, and it is very simple to make fresh (see page 380).

# Corona Bean Salad with Basil

YIELD: *10 servings*

1 lb / 454 g corona beans, sorted, rinsed, and soaked 12 to 24 hours in advance (see page 122)

2 fl oz / 60 mL olive oil

3 oz / 85 g carrot, peeled and left whole

3 oz / 85 g celery, halved

¼ oz / 7 g garlic cloves, crushed

1½ rosemary sprigs

1½ thyme sprigs

½ bay leaf

2 oz / 57 g pancetta (optional)

3½ oz / 99 g red onions, fine julienne or small dice

Salt, as needed

2½ oz / 71 g celery hearts (including leaves), chopped

½ oz / 14 g lemon zest chiffonade, blanched

2 tbsp / 6 g flat-leaf parsley leaves

2 tbsp / 6 g basil chiffonade

¼ oz / 7 g garlic cloves, thinly sliced

2 fl oz / 60 mL extra-virgin olive oil

1½ tsp / 7 mL white balsamic vinegar

Ground black pepper, as needed

1. Combine the beans, oil, carrot, celery halves, crushed garlic, rosemary, thyme, and bay leaf (and pancetta, if desired) in a saucepot. Add enough fresh cold water to cover the mixture by 4 in / 10 cm and bring to a full boil. Reduce the heat to a simmer and cook the beans until tender, 60 to 90 minutes. Stir occasionally to prevent scorching and add more water as necessary to keep the beans covered by about 2 in / 5 cm.

2. Add salt to season the beans. Remove and discard the celery, carrot, garlic, and herbs. Cool in the cooking liquid. Cover and keep refrigerated until ready to prepare the salad.

3. Drain the beans. Combine the red onion, celery hearts, lemon zest, parsley, basil, and garlic slices. Drizzle with the extra-virgin olive oil and vinegar, season with 1 tsp / 3 g salt and ¼ tsp / 0.50 g pepper, toss to combine, and set aside.

4. Add the drained beans and toss to combine. Taste and season with salt and pepper. Cover the salad and allow to rest for at least 30 minutes and up to 3 hours before serving.

*Variation*   *Red Borlotti Bean Salad with Rosemary: Substitute red borlotti beans for the corona beans, adjusting the cooking time as necessary. Replace the basil chiffonade with 2 tsp / 2 g minced rosemary leaves.*

# Waldorf Salad

YIELD: *10 servings*

2 Red Delicious apples

2 Golden Delicious apples

2 Granny Smith apples

4 oz / 113 g red grapes

DRESSING

3 fl oz / 90 mL Basic Mayonnaise (page 36)

3 fl oz / 90 mL sour cream

½ tsp / 1.50 g salt

¼ tsp / 0.50 g ground black pepper

Lemon juice, as needed

⅓ stalk celery, peeled, cut into medium dice

1½ oz / 43 g roughly chopped toasted walnuts

1. Cut the apples into medium dice. Cut the grapes in half.

2. Mix together all the dressing ingredients and season as needed. Fold in apples, celery, and walnuts.

3. Serve immediately or cover and refrigerate for up to 8 hours. This salad should be made the same day it is to be served.

*Chef's note*  Peeling the celery removes the tough fibers and gives this salad additional refinement. Choose the most tender celery from the heart whenever possible. If the only celery available is very large and bitter, simply omit it from the salad.


# Ambrosia Salad

YIELD: *10 servings*

2⅔ fl oz / 80 mL whipping cream

½ oz / 14 g sugar, or as needed

4 oranges, segmented

⅓ pineapple, peeled, cored, and cubed

10¾ oz / 308 g bananas, sliced

5¾ oz / 163 g green grapes, halved

2¾ oz / 78 g unsweetened coconut flakes, toasted

1. Whip the cream to soft peaks and add sugar as needed.

2. Fold the oranges, pineapple, bananas, and grapes into the whipped cream.

3. Cover and refrigerate at least 30 minutes before serving.

4. Salad Assembly: Garnish each serving with toasted coconut.

*Presentation ideas*  Serve this salad with turkey or chicken sandwiches, grilled or smoked shrimp or scallops, or to accompany hearty game or pork pâtés. This salad offers a refreshing counterpoint of sweetness and texture.

*Chef's note*  Make this and other fruit salads only when fruits are ripe and full-flavored. This salad should be made just prior to service and should not be held overnight.

# Thai-Style Green Papaya Salad

YIELD: *10 servings*

| | |
|---|---|
| 8 garlic cloves, roughly chopped | 2 lb 8 oz / 1.13 kg green papaya julienne |
| 3 Thai chiles, roughly chopped | 4 oz / 113 g carrot julienne |
| ½ oz / 14 g dried shrimp, chopped | 4 oz / 113 g toasted peanuts, roughly chopped |
| 2 fl oz / 60 mL tamarind pulp | 10 cherry tomatoes, halved |
| 2 fl oz / 60 mL lime juice | 10 green cabbage leaves |
| 3 fl oz / 90 mL fish sauce | 2 lb 8 oz / 1.2 kg steamed sticky rice |
| 1½ oz / 43 g palm sugar | |
| 8 oz / 227 g long beans, cut into 1½-in / 4-cm lengths | |

1. Combine the garlic, chiles, and dried shrimp.

2. Add the tamarind, lime juice, fish sauce, and sugar. Stir to mix, then add the long beans. Pound the mixture a few times to bruise the beans. Add the papaya, carrots, and peanuts.

3. Stir in the tomato halves and bruise lightly. Adjust seasoning with lime juice, fish sauce, and palm sugar, if necessary.

4. Serve the salad in a cabbage leaf with the steamed sticky rice on the side.

*Chef's note*   The papaya should not be fully ripe for this preparation.

# Grilled Pineapple, Jícama, Red Onion, and Grapefruit Salad

YIELD: *10 servings*

1 pineapple, peeled and cored

8 oz / 227 g red onion, sliced

8 oz / 227 g jicama, cut into julienne

1½ fl oz / 45 mL vegetable oil

¾ fl oz / 22.5 mL white wine vinegar

1 tbsp / 11 g minced shallot

Pinch ground cumin

1¼ oz / 35 g cilantro chiffonade

2 red grapefruit, cut into suprêmes

1. Slice the pineapple into ¼-in / 6-mm-thick rounds and grill each side for 1 to 2 minutes, or until the slices have grill marks and the pineapple begins to become translucent. Core and quarter the grilled pineapple slices and reserve.

2. Combine the red onion and jicama, and toss together.

3. Whisk together the vegetable oil, white wine vinegar, shallot, and cumin. Pour the dressing over the salad mixture and toss to coat evenly.

4. For each serving, place about 1¼ oz / 35 g (about 10 pieces) of pineapple on a salad plate and arrange 2½ oz / 71 g of the salad mixture on top and garnish with cilantro and suprêmes of grapefruit.

*Chef's note*   To cut some of the bitter, piquant flavor from the sliced red onions, soak them in ice water for 20 minutes and drain well before using in the salad.

# Salad of Crab and Avocado

YIELD: *10 servings*

1 lb / 454 g red peppers

1 lb / 454 g yellow peppers

2 fl oz / 60 mL olive oil

1 tsp / 3 g salt

1 tsp / 2 g ground black pepper

10 oz / 284 g tomato concassé

1½ oz / 43 g red onion, finely chopped

1 tbsp / 9 g minced garlic

1 tbsp / 9 g chopped cilantro leaves

1 jalapeño, seeded, finely diced

10 oz / 284 g avocado, ripe, cut into ¼-in / 6-mm dice

1 fl oz / 30 mL lime juice

1 lb 4 oz / 567 g crabmeat, picked over

4 oz / 120 mL crème fraîche

Paprika, as needed

10 cilantro sprigs

1. Rub each pepper with about 1 fl oz / 30 mL olive oil.

2. Roast the peppers on a rack in a 375° to 400°F / 191° to 204°C oven until the skin becomes loose, about 35 to 45 minutes. Do not allow the peppers to gain color. Remove the skin and the seeds from the peppers.

3. Cool the peppers and purée them separately in a food processor, and pass each through a fine-mesh strainer. Season each with approximately ½ tsp / 1.5 g salt and a pinch of pepper and put into squeeze bottles.

4. One hour before molding, mix the tomato, onion, garlic, chopped cilantro, and jalapeño to form a salsa.

5. Combine the avocado, lime juice, ½ tsp / 1.5 g salt, and a pinch of pepper.

6. In a 2½-in / 6-cm-diameter by 1¼-in /3-cm-high ring mold, layer 1½ oz / 43 g avocado mixture, 1½ oz / 43 g tomato salsa, and 3 oz /85 g crabmeat. Press each layer into the mold gently and make sure that the last layer is pressed firmly into the ring mold.

7. Spoon approximately 1 tbsp / 15 mL crème fraîche on top of the crab and smooth it even with the rim of the ring mold, using a small offset spatula.

8. Lightly dust the crème fraîche with paprika.

9. Transfer the filled ring to the center of a plate 8 in / 20 cm in diameter and carefully lift off the ring mold. Place a cilantro sprig on top of the crème fraîche.

10. Use the squeeze bottles to create two concentric circles of sauce around the crab salad.

*Presentation idea* Layer the salsa, avocado, and crab in a clear glass and top with the crème fraîche and cilantro, if desired.

# Baked Goat Cheese with Garden Lettuces, Roasted Figs, Pears, and Toasted Almonds

YIELD: *10 appetizer servings*

1 lb 4 oz / 567 g Marinated Goat Cheese (page 382)

8 oz / 227 g dry bread crumbs

10 roasted figs (see Chef's Note), halved

1 lb 4 oz / 567 g mesclun lettuce mix

2 pears, cored and sliced into thin wedges

15 fl oz / 450 mL Balsamic Vinaigrette (page 28)

Salt, as needed

Ground black pepper, as needed

2½ oz / 71 g Toasted Almonds (page 513)

1. Drain the marinated goat cheese of excess oil. Gently dip the goat cheese into the bread crumbs and place on sheet pans. Refrigerate at least 2 hours and up to overnight.

2. Salad Assembly: For each serving, bake 2 rounds of cheese in a 450°F / 232°C oven until lightly browned, about 10 minutes. Let the cheese cool while grilling the figs. Lightly grill figs to heat. Toss 3 oz / 85 g mesclun and 3 to 4 pear slices with 1 fl oz / 30 mL vinaigrette; season with salt and pepper. Mound on a chilled plate. Top with goat cheese rounds, figs, and a few almonds.

*Chef's note* *To roast figs for this salad, remove the top portion of the stem. Season with salt and pepper, and put into a 2-in / 5-cm-deep hotel pan. Add enough chicken stock to cover the figs halfway. Add a bay leaf and thyme sprig. Cover and roast at 350°F / 177°C until tender and plump, about 20 minutes. Warm skin side down on a grill just before service, if desired.*

# Avocado, Tomato, and Corn Salad with Aged Cheddar and Chipotle-Sherry Vinaigrette

YIELD: *10 entrée servings*

3 red beefsteak tomatoes, sliced thin

3 yellow beefsteak tomatoes, sliced thin

5¼ oz / 149 g cherry tomatoes, halved lengthwise

5 oz / 142 g pear tomatoes, halved lengthwise

5 oz / 142 g currant tomatoes

5 ears corn on the cob

1 lb 4 oz / 567 g mesclun lettuce mix, rinsed and dried

15 fl oz / 450 mL Chipotle-Sherry Vinaigrette (page 32)

5 ripe avocados, peeled, pitted, and sliced or diced at assembly

10 oz / 284 g aged Vermont cheddar, crumbled

1 red onion, thinly sliced and separated into rings

Coarse-ground black pepper, as needed

1. Portion the tomatoes for each salad as follows: 2 slices each red and yellow tomatoes, 1½ oz / 43 g combined cherry, pear, and currant tomatoes.

2. Roast the corn (see page 610) and cut the kernels away; you will use about ½ ear per salad.

3. Salad Assembly: For each serving, toss 2 oz / 57 g mesclun with 1 fl oz / 30 mL vinaigrette. Mound on a chilled plate. Slice or dice half an avocado and scatter over salad. Top with tomatoes, corn, cheddar, and red onion. Drizzle with an additional tablespoon of vinaigrette. Grind black pepper over salad. Serve immediately.

*Chef's notes*  This salad features one of Vermont's famous culinary resources, aged Cheddar cheese, along with a variety of ripe tomatoes. It makes an excellent appetizer salad or a meatless main course for lunch menus.

# Buffalo Chicken Salad

YIELD: *10 entrée servings*

2 lb 8 oz / 1.13 kg chicken wings, tips removed, disjointed

8 oz / 227 g flour (seasoned with salt and pepper) as needed for dredging

HOT SAUCE

8 fl oz / 240 mL Frank's Hot Sauce

1 oz / 28 g butter

Tabasco sauce, as needed

Ground cayenne, as needed

Lemon juice, as needed

1 lb 4 oz / 567 g mixed greens, washed, dried, and chilled

10 fl oz / 300 mL Basic Red Wine Vinaigrette (page 28)

½ bunch celery, cut into 4-in / 10-cm allumettes

12 oz / 340 g carrots, cut into 4-in / 10-cm allumettes

1 seedless cucumber, peeled and sliced

20 Celeriac Crisps (page 544) (optional)

15 fl oz / 450 mL Roquefort Dressing (page 40)

1. Dredge the chicken wings in flour and deep fry in 350°F / 177°C oil until golden brown and crisp, about 12 minutes. Drain well.

2. Simmer the ingredients for the hot sauce. Pour over the warm chicken wings; hold in the sauce.

3. Salad Assembly: For each serving, warm 4 oz / 113 g chicken wings, if necessary. Toss 2 oz / 57 g mixed greens with 1 fl oz / 30 mL vinaigrette. Arrange the mixed greens in a soup plate or salad bowl and top with the wings. Garnish with the celery, carrots, cucumbers, and celeriac chips. Serve with 3 fl oz / 45 mL Roquefort Dressing.

*Chef's note*  This salad is a variation on the popular appetizer Buffalo Chicken Wings, created in 1964 at the Anchor Bar in Buffalo, New York, by owner Teressa Bellissimo.

# Cobb Salad

YIELD: *10 servings*

5 chicken breasts, on the bone

Salt, as needed

Ground black pepper, as needed

20 bacon slices

1 lb 4 oz / 567 g romaine lettuce, washed, dried, and torn into pieces

10 fl oz / 300 mL Basic Red Wine Vinaigrette (page 28)

10 oz / 284 g medium-dice tomatoes

10 oz / 284 g crumbled blue cheese

3 avocados, peeled, pitted, and cut into medium dice at assembly

5 green onions, thinly sliced on the bias

1. Season the chicken with salt and pepper and roast chicken breasts to an internal temperature of 165°F / 74°C. Cool and remove from bone. Cut meat into ⅓-in / 8-mm dice.

2. Bake, broil, or griddle the bacon until crisp. Drain on absorbent paper towels; crumble and keep warm.

3. Salad Assembly: For each serving, toss 2 oz / 57 g romaine with 2 tbsp / 30 mL vinaigrette. Mound on a plate, and top with 4 oz / 113 g chicken, 1¼ oz / 35 g diced tomato, 1 oz / 28 g blue cheese, 2 oz / 57 g avocado, ¼ oz / 7 g green onions, and 2 bacon strips, crumbled.

*Chef's notes*   *If you use a spice rub on the chicken before roasting, you may opt to leave the skin on for additional flavor in the salad. Hot-smoked or smoke-roasted chicken breasts would also be good choices.*

*Cobb Salad was created at the Brown Derby Restaurant in Hollywood, California. Various interpretations may call for either chicken or turkey. The garnish suggestions here are typical, but some versions have included watercress, celery, Cheddar cheese, hard-cooked eggs, black olives, and alfalfa sprouts.*

# Shrimp and Bean Salad

YIELD: *10 servings*

2 lb 8 oz / 1.13 kg shrimp, peeled and deveined

1 tsp / 3 g sea salt

Ground black pepper, as needed

4 fl oz / 120 mL extra-virgin olive oil

½ oz / 14 g garlic, minced to a paste

3 tbsp / 9 g minced oregano leaves

3 tbsp / 9 g minced fresh mint leaves

Red pepper flakes, as needed

1 lb 4 oz / 567 g Red Borlotti Salad with Rosemary (page 123)

8 oz / 227 g Oreganata Crumb Mixture (recipe follows)

10 lemon wedges

1. Slightly butterfly the shrimp. Place in hotel pan, laid out flat. Season with 1 tsp / 3 g salt and a little pepper.

2. Combine the olive oil, garlic, oregano, mint, and red pepper. Spoon over the shrimp, coating them lightly. Marinate at least 30 minutes and up to 2 hours before broiling.

3. For each serving, mound 3 oz / 85 g bean salad on a plate. Remove 3 oz / 85 g shrimp from the marinade, draining well. Place on a sizzler platter and top with ¾ oz / 21 g Oreganata Crumb mixture. Broil until the shrimp are fully cooked and the crumbs are golden brown, about 3 minutes. Arrange the shrimp on the salad and season with a squeeze of fresh lemon juice. Serve immediately.

# Oreganata Crumb Mixture

YIELD: *10 oz / 284 g*

7 oz / 198 g dry bread crumbs

2 oz / 85 g grated Parmesan

3 tbsp / 9 g minced oregano leaves

3 tbsp / 9 g minced flat-leaf parsley leaves

1 tbsp / 3 g minced mint leaves

1 tbsp / 9 g finely grated lemon zest

Salt and ground black pepper, as needed

⅛ tsp / 0.25 g red pepper flakes

2 fl oz / 60 mL extra-virgin olive oil, or as needed to moisten

1. Blend the bread crumbs, Parmesan, oregano, parsley, mint, lemon zest, salt, and pepper.

2. Use a fork or wooden spoon to work in enough olive oil to moisten the mixture; the mixture should look like coarse grains of sand.

# Corona Bean Salad with Grilled Baby Octopus

YIELD: *10 servings*

| | |
|---|---|
| 1 tbsp / 15 mL olive oil | ½ oz / 14 g rosemary leaves |
| 2 oz / 57 g onions, cut into medium dice | 2 garlic cloves, crushed |
| 2 oz / 57 g carrots, cut into medium dice | Salt, as needed |
| 1 oz / 28 g celery, cut into medium dice | Ground black pepper, as needed |
| 3 whole garlic cloves, crushed | |
| 2 lb / 907 g baby octopus, cleaned and cut into portions | 2 lb / 907 g Corona Bean Salad with Basil (page 123) |
| 4 fl oz / 120 mL dry white wine | 20 lemon wedges |
| 12 fl oz / 360 mL water | 2½ oz / 71 g flat-leaf parsley, leaves only |
| 8 fl oz / 240 mL tomato juice | 1 oz / 28 g fennel fronds |
| 4 thyme sprigs | 5 oz / 142 g frisée, white heart only |
| 2 rosemary sprigs | 2 oz / 57 g celery heart leaves |
| 2 bay leaves | Basil Oil (page 546), as needed |
| ½ tsp / 1.5 g salt | Extra-virgin olive oil, as needed |
| ¼ tsp / 0.50 g ground black pepper | Sea salt, as needed |
| MARINADE | Ground black pepper, as needed |
| 4 fl oz / 120 mL olive oil | |
| ½ oz / 14 g thyme leaves | |

1. For the octopus: Heat the olive oil in a saucepot over medium heat. Add the onion, carrot, and celery; sweat, stirring occasionally, until tender and translucent, 5 minutes. Add the garlic and sweat until aromatic. Add the octopus and continue to cook, turning the octopus until it is stiff on all sides, 2 to 3 minutes.

2. Add the white wine, stirring to deglaze the pan, and continue to simmer until wine is reduced to one-third its original volume. Add the water, tomato juice, thyme, rosemary, bay leaves, ½ tsp / 1.5 g salt, and ¼ tsp / 0.50 g pepper, or as needed. Braise the octopus over very low heat, uncovered, until tender, about 1 hour. Remove and discard the bay leaves and herb sprigs. Cool and reserve the octopus in the braising liquid until ready to grill.

3. For the marinade: Combine the oil, thyme, rosemary, and garlic. Add salt and pepper as needed and reserve.

4. Salad Assembly. For each serving, mound 3 oz / 85 g of the bean salad on a plate. Remove 3 oz / 85 g octopus from the braising liquid, draining well. Brush or roll the octopus in the marinade and grill over a hot fire until marked and very hot, 1 to 2 minutes per side. Arrange the grilled octopus on the salad and season with a squeeze of fresh lemon juice. Garnish the plate with an additional lemon wedge, parsley, fennel fronds, frisée, and celery hearts. Drizzle with a little basil oil and extra-virgin olive oil. Scatter with sea salt and freshly ground pepper. Serve.

*Chef's notes* *If baby octopus is unavailable, substitute squid for the octopus. Other seafood and shellfish can be substituted, such as shrimp or scallops, but they should be cooked quickly and not braised.*

**Me**

# Lobster Salad with Grapefruit Emulsion and Tarragon Oil

YIELD: *10 servings*

LOBSTER SALAD

4 gal / 15.36 L water

16 fl oz / 480 mL white wine vinegar

5 oz / 142 g kosher salt

5 lobsters, 1 lb 8 oz / 680 g each

1 lb 8 oz / 680 g butter, melted

2 tsp / 6 g minced shallots

½ oz / 14 g celeriac, small diced

1 oz / 28 g avocado, small diced

1 tbsp / 15 mL lemon juice

1 oz / 28 g butter, softened

1½ oz / 43 g mayonnaise

Salt, as needed

Ground black pepper, as needed

GARNISH

20 fl oz / 600 mL Grapefruit Emulsion (page 34)

2 fl oz / 60 mL Tarragon Oil (page 548)

20 fried lotus-root chips or fried wonton skins

10 chives, cut on the bias into 1-in / 2-cm lengths

¾ cup / 180 mL micro celery sprouts, washed

1. Combine the water, vinegar, and salt in a pot and bring to a boil over high heat.

2. Place the lobsters in a 4-in / 10-cm hotel pan and pour the water mixture over the lobsters. Steep them for 5 to 8 minutes, just long enough to set the lobster meat so you can take it out of the shell.

3. Transfer the lobsters to a cutting board; remove the tails, claws, and knuckle meat. Discard the shells or reserve for other kitchen applications.

4. Place the lobster meat in the melted butter (the butter should just cover the lobster) and gently simmer until the meat is just cooked through, about 10 minutes. Take care not to overcook it.

5. Reserve the claw meat in a whole piece. Cut the tail and knuckle meat into a small dice and reserve.

6. In a bowl, combine the reserved tail and knuckle meat with the shallots, celeriac, avocado, lemon juice, butter, and mayonnaise and mix well.

7. Season and set aside in the refrigerator.

8. For each serving, place a 2-in / 5-cm ring mold in the center of a soup bowl 8 in / 20 cm in diameter. Fill the ring to the top with salad, using about ⅓ cup / 80 mL.

9. Remove the mold and top the salad with a lobster claw.

10. Spoon 2 fl oz / 60 mL grapefruit emulsion around the dish and drizzle with 1 to 2 tsp / 5 to 10 mL tarragon oil.

11. Place a lotus root chip or fried wonton chip on top. Garnish with 2 to 3 chive pieces and 1 tbsp / 15 mL micro celery sprouts.

*Presentation idea*   *This salad can be converted into hors d'oeuvre by presenting the salad in a porcelain spoon. Assemble as above by layering the grapefruit emulsion and the tarragon oil, the lobster salad, a piece of the lobster claw, and then the garnish.*

# Wilted Spinach Salad with Warm Bacon Vinaigrette

YIELD: *10 servings*

8 oz / 227 g bacon, cut into small dice

1½ oz / 43 g minced shallots

2 tsp / 6 g minced garlic

4 oz / 113 g brown sugar

3 fl oz / 90 mL cider vinegar

5 to 6 fl oz / 150 to 180 mL vegetable oil

Salt, as needed

Cracked black peppercorns, as needed

1 lb 8 oz / 680 g spinach

5 hard-cooked eggs, small dice

6 oz / 170 g mushrooms, cleaned and sliced

3 oz / 85 g thinly sliced red onion

4 oz / 113 g Croutons (page 613)

1. To make the vinaigrette, render the bacon over medium low heat. When the bacon is crisp, remove it from the pan, drain on absorbent paper towels, and reserve.

2. Add the shallots and garlic to the bacon fat and sweat until soft. Stir in the brown sugar. Remove the pan from the heat. Whisk in the vinegar and oil. Season with salt and pepper as needed.

3. Toss the spinach with the eggs, mushrooms, onions, croutons, and bacon. Add the warm vinaigrette, toss once, and serve immediately.

*Chef's note*  It is imperative not to dress the salad too early or the spinach will wilt significantly.

# Southern Fried Chicken Salad

YIELD: *10 entrée servings*

2 lb / 907 g chicken breasts (about 7)

8 fl oz / 240 mL buttermilk

5 heads butterhead lettuce (such as Boston, Bibb, or Kentucky Limestone)

30 cherry tomatoes

2 Vidalia onions

4 oz / 113 g flour, seasoned with black pepper and salt as needed

12 fl oz / 360 mL peanut oil

3¾ oz / 106 g white mushrooms, cleaned and sliced

1½ oz / 43 g capers, drained

¾ oz / 21 g minced shallots

2½ fl oz / 75 mL white wine vinegar

2¾ oz / 78 g Dijon mustard

1¼ oz / 35 g chopped tarragon

1. Trim chicken breasts and cut into ½-oz / 14-g strips. Pour buttermilk over chicken, cover, and refrigerate until ready to assemble the salad.

2. Separate the lettuce into leaves; wash and dry. Core and quarter the tomatoes. Slice the Vidalia onions thinly and separate into rings. Cover and refrigerate ingredients separately.

3. Salad Assembly: For each serving, remove 6 pieces of chicken from the buttermilk and dredge in the seasoned flour. Pan-fry in 1½ fl oz / 45 mL peanut oil. Remove and drain on absorbent paper towels while finishing the dressing.

4. Add 2½ oz / 71 g sliced mushrooms to the peanut oil along with 1 tsp / 9 g capers and ½ tsp / 1.5 g shallots; sauté until the mushrooms are tender. Add 1 tbsp / 15 mL vinegar and 1½ tsp / 8 g mustard. Heat through, remove from heat, and stir in 1 tbsp / 3 g tarragon.

5. Arrange 2 oz / 57 g lettuce on a chilled plate. Top with the chicken, tomato, and Vidalia onion. Pour the warm sauce over the salad and serve immediately.

*Chef's note*   *Be sure to have the mise en place portioned out properly for each serving so that both the chicken and the dressing can be served warm with this salad.*

# Smoked Duck and Malfatti Salad with Roasted Shallot Vinaigrette

YIELD: *10 entrée servings*

8 oz / 227 g Malfatti Pasta (page xxx)

1 lb 4 oz / 567 g mixed bitter greens (such as arugula, frisée, and radicchio), washed and dried

10 oz / 284 g chanterelles, halved or quartered if necessary

2 to 3 fl oz / 60 to 90 mL olive oil, as needed

1 lb / 454 g Smoked Duck Breast (page 218), cut into strips across the grain

15 fl oz / 450 mL Roasted Shallot Vinaigrette (page 32)

Salt, as needed

Ground black pepper, as needed

3 oz / 85 g shaved Parmesan

1. Cook the pasta in boiling salted water until al dente. Refresh in cold water; drain and dry. Toss with oil if cooked in advance.

2. Wash and dry the greens; tear or cut into bite-sized pieces. Refrigerate until needed.

3. Salad Assembly: For each serving, sauté 1 oz / 28 g mushrooms in 2 tsp / 10 mL olive oil until tender. Add about 2 oz / 57 g cooked pasta and 1½ oz / 43 g duck. Toss over high heat until hot. Add 2 oz / 57 g mixed greens and 1 oz / 28 g vinaigrette to the pan. Toss briskly and mound on a warm plate once the ingredients are just warmed through. Drizzle with an additional ½ fl oz / 15 mL dressing. Season with salt and pepper and garnish with shaved Parmesan and some of the shallots from the dressing. Serve while still warm.

*Chef's notes* *This salad is best made in a nonstick pan in small batches at the very last minute before being served. Be certain to distribute shallots evenly over the salad.*

*Malfatti means something that is poorly made or irregularly shaped, so when making the pasta for this salad, exact dimensions are not important. This warm salad combines several flavors and textures that may appear to be unusual, but when this salad is executed properly, it is hard to find a more pleasing dish.*

# Warm Salad of Hearty Greens, Blood Oranges, and Tangerine-Pineapple Vinaigrette

YIELD: *10 servings*

6 1/2 oz / 194 g frisée, washed and dried

6 1/2 oz / 194 g radicchio, washed and dried

4 1/2 oz / 128 g arugula, washed and dried

5 oz / 142 g baby spinach, washed and dried

1 cup / 240 mL Tangerine-Pineapple Vinaigrette, warm (page 34)

1 lb 9 oz / 709 g blood oranges, cut into supremes

5 oz / 142 g slivered almonds, toasted

1 pomegranate, seeds removed

1. Tear or cut greens into bite-sized pieces. Combine all of the greens and refrigerate until needed.

2. For each serving: Toss 2¼ oz / 64 g mixed greens with 4½ tsp / 45 mL warm vinaigrette and place in the center of a warm plate. Garnish with 5 to 6 blood orange supremes, ½ oz / 14 g of the almonds, and a few pomegranate seeds.

4

- Define various types of sandwiches

- Identify a number of international sandwiches

- Identify appropriate breads, spreads, fillings, and garnishes for sandwiches depending on the occasion

- Recognize the appropriate presentation style of sandwiches

# Sandwiches

**Sandwiches** have been part of virtually all cuisines since well before any written records were kept, though they have not always been called sandwiches. The honor of naming this favorite luncheon item goes to the infamous gambler **John Montague,** the fourth Earl of Sandwich. According to legend, this gentleman refused to leave the gaming tables because he didn't want to break his winning streak. He asked that some bread filled with meat be brought to him, and the rage for sandwiches was on.

**L**ouis P. De Gouy published *Sandwich Manual for Professionals* in 1940. His approach to the assembly of sandwiches, based upon his work as the chef at New York's famous Waldorf-Astoria Hotel, detailed hundreds of sandwiches organized into specific categories. This classic work has stood the test of time and is still a valuable resource of practical information and inspiration.

Sandwiches can range from delicate finger and tea sandwiches served on doilies to *pan bagnat,* traditionally served wrapped in plain paper from stalls in the open markets of southern France. It may be an elegant bite-sized morsel of foie gras served on toasted brioche as an *amuse-gueule* or a grilled Reuben on rye, served with potato salad and a pickle. We can select from diverse culinary traditions, from Scandinavian *smørrebrod* to American regional favorites like the po'boy to Italian bruschetta and panini to Mexican tacos and burritos. What unifies the concept of the sandwich in all instances is a tasty filling served on or in bread or a similar wrapper.

In this chapter you will learn about handling and preparing ingredients to make the following styles:

- Cold sandwiches
- Hot sandwiches, including grilled sandwiches
- Finger and tea sandwiches

**Cold sandwiches** include standard deli-style versions made from sliced meats or mayonnaise-dressed salads. Club sandwiches, also known as **triple-decker sandwiches,** could be included in this category as well.

**Hot sandwiches** may feature a hot filling, such as hamburgers or pastrami. Others are grilled, such as a Reuben sandwich. In some cases, a hot filling is mounded on the bread and the sandwich is topped with a hot sauce (Barbecued Pulled Pork Sandwich, page 156, for example).

**Finger and tea sandwiches** are delicate items made on fine-grained bread, trimmed of their crusts and precisely cut into shapes and sizes that can be eaten in about two average bites.

## Sandwich elements

The garde manger may be called upon to prepare sandwiches for receptions and teas, for lunch and bistro menus, for special appetizers, and for picnics. In order to produce high-quality sandwiches, it is important to understand how basic filling, cutting, and holding techniques contribute to the overall quality of sandwiches.

### *Breads*

**Breads** for making sandwiches run a fairly wide gamut, including many ethnic specialties. Sliced white and wheat Pullman loaves are used to make many cold sandwiches. The tight crumb of a Pullman makes it a good choice for delicate tea and finger sandwiches, since they must be sliced thinly without crumbling. Whole-grain and peasant-style breads are not always as easy to slice thinly.

Specific breads, buns, rolls, and wrappers are used to make specific sandwiches. The characteristics of the bread and how they will fit in with the fillings should be considered. Bread should be firm enough and thick enough to hold the filling, but not so thick that the sandwich is too dry to enjoy.

Most bread can be sliced in advance of sandwich preparation as long as it is carefully covered to prevent drying. Some sandwiches call for toasted bread, which should be done immediately before assembling the sandwich.

Bread choices include:

- Pullman loaves of white, wheat, or rye
- Peasant-style breads such as sourdough, baguettes, and other artisan breads
- Flatbreads including focaccia, pita, ciabatta, and lavash
- Rolls, including hard, soft, and Kaiser rolls
- Wrappers such as crêpes, rice paper, and egg roll wrappers
- Flour and corn tortillas

FIG 4-1 | *An established workflow eases and streamlines the assembly of sandwiches.*

## Spreads

Many sandwiches call for a **spread** that is applied directly to the bread. This element acts as a barrier to keep the bread from getting soggy. Spreads also add moisture to the sandwich and help it to hold together as it is held and eaten. Some sandwich fillings may include a "spread" directly in the filling mixture (for example, a mayonnaise-dressed tuna salad), so there is no need to add a separate one when assembling the sandwich.

Spreads can be very simple and subtly flavored, or they may themselves bring a special flavor and texture to the sandwich. The following list of spread options includes some classic choices, as well as some that may not immediately spring to mind as sandwich spreads.

- Mayonnaise (plain or flavored, such as aïoli or rouille) or creamy salad dressings
- Plain or compound butters
- Mustard or ketchup
- Spreadable cheeses, such as ricotta, cream cheese, or mascarpone
- Tahini, olive, or herb spreads (hummus, tapenade, or pesto, for example)
- Nut butters
- Jelly, jam, compotes, chutneys, or other fruit preserves
- Mashed avocado or guacamole
- Oils or vinaigrettes

## Fillings

Sandwich **fillings** may be cold or hot, substantial or minimal. In all cases, they are the focus of the sandwich. It is as important to roast and slice turkey properly for club sandwiches as it is to be certain that the watercress for tea sandwiches is perfectly fresh and completely rinsed and dried.

The filling should determine how all the other elements of the sandwich are selected and prepared. Choices for fillings include:

- Sliced roasted or simmered meats (beef, corned beef, pastrami, turkey, ham, pâtés, and sausages)
- Sliced cheeses
- Grilled, roasted, or fresh vegetables
- Grilled, pan-fried, or broiled burgers, sausages, fish, or poultry
- Salads of meats, poultry, eggs, fish, and/or vegetables

## Garnishes

Lettuce, slices of tomato or cheese, onion slices, or sprouts can be used to garnish many sandwiches. These **garnishes** become part of the sandwich's overall structure.

When sandwiches are plated, a variety of side garnishes may also be included:

- Green or side salads
- Lettuces and sprouts
- Sliced fresh vegetables
- Pickles spears or olives
- Dips, spreads, or relishes
- Sliced fruits

# Presentation styles

A sandwich constructed with a top and a bottom slice of bread is known as a **closed sandwich.** **Club sandwiches** are closed sandwiches that have a third slice of bread. Still other sandwiches have only one slice of bread, acting as a base; these are **open-faced sandwiches.**

Finger and tea sandwiches (as well as canapé bases; see page 396) are cut into special shapes. To prepare them, the loaf of bread is sliced lengthwise so that the greatest possible surface area is available. The bread is coated with a spread, filled, garnished if desired, then closed if desired, and the crust is removed. The sandwich is then cut to shape and served at once.

**Straight-edged shapes** give the best yield with the lowest food cost. These shapes are created by cutting with a sandwich knife or bread knife into squares, rectangles, diamonds, or triangles (see Fig 4-2). Cutters in various shapes may be used to cut rounds, ovals, and other special shapes. The yield is generally lower when preparing these shapes, making them slightly more expensive to produce but a more interesting presentation.

Time should be taken to cut shapes in an exacting and uniform fashion so that they will look their best when set in straight rows on platters or arranged on plates. It is best to cut tea sandwiches as close to service as possible. If these sandwiches must be prepared ahead of time, they can be held for a few hours, covered in airtight containers.

# Sandwiches around the globe

Sandwiches are an approachable meal that has been adopted by nearly every country worldwide. Each country features its own regional ingredients for the breads, spreads, fillings, and garnishes in their sandwiches. French sandwiches include classics such as the Croque Monsieur (a grilled cheese sandwich with gruyere, ham, and mustard, on page 153), Croque Madame (a Croque Monsieur with an egg on top, page 153), and tartines, which are open-faced sandwiches that can be topped with any variety of fillings and garnishes. These are similar to the Italian crostini or crostone, which feature a slice of toasted bread that can feature a wide variety of toppings as well. Other Italian sandwiches that have gained popularity are panini. These closed sandwiches are grilled in a panini press, which uses two grill plates to grill the top and the bottom slices of bread simultaneously. The result is a hot, crispy, delicious sandwich. The Italian version of the tea sandwich is called tremezzini. It features white bread with a tight crumb and a variety of fillings. It is usually cut into 4 triangles and served at a café.

In Germany, slices of pumpernickel are buttered and filled with any of their regional cured meats and sausages. Spain's version of a canapé or crostini is a montadito. This sandwich involves topping a slice of toasted bread with a filling, usually comprised of meat, and is often served as a tapa. One sandwich that features an interesting combination of flavors and influences is the Bahn Saigon (page 168), a Vietnamese specialty. It uses a French baguette for the bread and a cinnamon paté and green papaya salad for the filling. All of the layers create a fantastic combination of sweet, salty, and spicy flavors and a variety of textures. Many of these sandwiches have become popular in the United States as people's desire to broaden their horizons and their palates expands.

**FIG 4-2**  *Sandwiches can be finished in a variety of shapes.*

# Chicken Burger

YIELD: *10 sandwiches*

2 tbsp / 20 g minced shallot (1 large)

1 fl oz / 30 mL vegetable oil

1 lb 8 oz / 680 g fresh white mushrooms, minced

3 fl oz / 90 mL dry white wine

½ tsp / 1.5 g salt, or as needed

¼ tsp / 0.50 g ground black pepper, or as needed

2 lb 8 oz / 1.13 kg ground chicken

4 oz / 113 g dry bread crumbs

2 tsp / 2 g chopped fresh herbs (such as chives, oregano, and basil)

½ tsp / 0.75 g chopped fresh rosemary

½ tsp / 0.50 g poultry seasoning, or as needed

5 oz / 142 g provolone cheese (10 slices)

10 soft sandwich rolls, split and toasted

10 fl oz / 300 mL Tomato Ketchup (page 525)

1. Sauté the shallots in the oil over moderate heat. Increase the heat, add the mushrooms, and sauté until all the moisture has cooked off. Add the wine and continue to sauté until dry, as for duxelles.

2. Season as needed with salt and pepper. Remove from heat and chill thoroughly.

3. Combine the chicken with the bread crumbs, mushroom mixture, herbs, salt, pepper, and poultry seasoning.

4. Make a test as for forcemeat. Adjust seasoning as necessary.

5. Form the chicken mixture into patties, about 4½ oz / 128 g each.

6. Sauté or griddle the patties until browned on both sides.

7. Transfer to a sheet pan or sizzler platter. Top each patty with a slice of provolone. Finish cooking the patties in a moderate (350°F / 177°C to 375°F / 191°C) oven to an internal temperature of 165°F / 74°C.

8. Sandwich Assembly: For each sandwich, place a patty on a roll, top with about 1 fl oz / 30 mL of tomato ketchup, and serve at once.

*Chef's note* If ground chicken is unavailable, substitute an equal amount of ground turkey.

# Croque Monsieur

YIELD: *10 sandwiches*

20 slices Pullman bread (about 1 loaf)

10 oz / 284 g Dijon mustard (optional)

8 oz / 227 g Gruyére cheese (10 thin slices)

1 lb 4 oz / 567 g boiled ham (10 slices)

8 oz / 227 g Muenster cheese (10 thin slices)

4 oz / 113 g soft butter

1. To assemble the sandwiches for griddling, spread one side of the bread slices with mustard if using.

2. On 10 of the bread slices, layer one slice each of Gruyère, ham, and Muenster over the mustard.

3. Top the sandwiches with the remaining bread slices.

4. Griddle both sides of the sandwiches on a lightly buttered 325°F / 163° C griddle until the bread is golden, the cheese is melted, and the sandwich is heated through.

5. Cut the sandwiches on the diagonal and serve immediately.

*Variations*   *Croque Madame: Some recipes simply add a fried egg to the Croque Monsieur. In the United States and England, the ham is usually replaced with sliced chicken breast. Use Emmentaler instead of Gruyère. Grill as directed.*

*Monte Cristo: Dip any of the variations in beaten egg and grill as you would French toast.*

# Oyster and Shrimp Po'boy

YIELD: *10 sandwiches*

Oil for deep frying, as needed

20 shrimp (16/20 count), peeled and deveined

30 oysters, shucked and drained

1 tsp / 3 g salt

¼ tsp / 0.50 g ground white pepper

Pinch cayenne

4 oz / 113 g all-purpose flour, or as needed for breading

2 eggs

1 fl oz / 30 mL milk or water (beaten with 2 eggs for eggwash)

5 oz / 142 g cornmeal, or as needed for breading

10 baguettes or hero rolls, split lengthwise

12 fl oz / 360 mL Rémoulade Sauce (page 38)

1 head green leaf lettuce, shredded

3 tomatoes (cut into 20 slices)

2 red onions (cut into 20 slices)

3 lemons (optional)

1. Preheat oil for deep frying to 350°F / 175°C.

2. Season the seafood with the spices. Dip the shrimp and oysters into the flour, then the egg wash, and then the cornmeal.

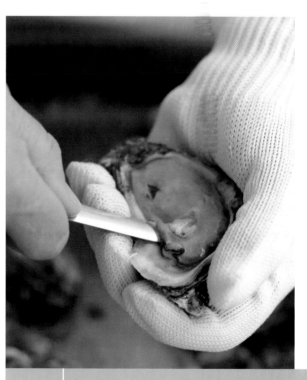

FIG 4-3A  *Wear a wire mesh glove and hold the oyster so that the hinged side is facing outward. Work the tip of an oyster knife into the hinge holding the upper and lower shells together and twist it to break open the hinge.*

FIG 4-3B  *Once the oyster is open, slide the knife over the inside of the top and bottom shells to release the oyster from the shell.*

3. Deep-fry the breaded shrimp and oysters in batches until golden and cooked through. Drain on absorbent paper towels and keep warm.

4. Sandwich Assembly: For each sandwich, spread each side of a baguette with 1 tbsp / 15 mL rémoulade sauce. Fill the baguette with lettuce, tomato, and onion. Top with 2 shrimp and 3 oysters. Top the seafood with another teaspoon of rémoulade sauce, or serve with additional sauce on the side. Close the sandwich and serve at once with either sauce or lemon wedges on the side.

*Chef's note*  *The po'boy is a specialty of New Orleans. Like heroes, submarines, hoagies, and grinders, the po'boy can contain almost any ingredient, although seafood seems to be one of the most popular fillings.*

# Soft-Shell Crab Sandwich with Rémoulade Sauce

YIELD: *10 sandwiches*

8 oz / 227 g all-purpose flour

1 tbsp / 8 g Old Bay seasoning

1 tbsp / 6 g ground dry mustard

2 tsp / 6 g salt

¼ tsp / 0.50 g cayenne

32 fl oz / 960 mL peanut oil, or as needed

10 jumbo soft-shell crabs, cleaned (page 614)

16 fl oz / 480 mL milk

10 soft sandwich rolls, split

16 fl oz / 480 mL Rémoulade Sauce (page 40)

20 lettuce leaves, shredded for garnish

2 lemons, cut into wedges

1. Combine flour, Old Bay, mustard, salt, and cayenne.

2. Heat 1 in / 2 cm peanut oil in a rondeau to 375°F / 190°C.

3. Sandwich Assembly: For each sandwich, dip a crab into the milk and dredge it in the seasoned flour. Pan fry the crab in the hot peanut oil until golden on both sides, 4 to 5 minutes total cooking time. Drain on absorbent paper towels.

4. Toast a roll and spread with 1 to 2 tbsp / 15 to 30 mL rémoulade sauce. Layer it with lettuce. Top with the crab, and close the sandwich with the top of the bun. Serve immediately with lemon wedges.

*Chef's note*  *The soft-shelled crabs may also be breaded using the standard breading procedure and deep-fried before assembling the sandwiches.*

# Barbecued Pulled Pork Sandwich

YIELD: *10 sandwiches*

2 lb 8 oz / 1.13 kg Barbecued Pork Butt (page 226)

12 fl oz / 360 mL Barbecue Sauce (recipe follows)

10 Kaiser rolls

1. Pull the meat off the pork butt and shred it. Remove and discard excess fat.

2. Simmer the shredded pork meat with the barbecue sauce for about 15 minutes.

3. Split the Kaiser rolls and grill or toast.

4. Sandwich Assembly: For each sandwich, mound approximately 4 to 5 oz / 113 to 142 g barbecued pork on the roll and serve immediately.

*Presentation idea*  Accompany the sandwich with Coleslaw (page 107) and Assorted Vegetable Chips (page 541).


# Barbecue Sauce

YIELD: *approximately 1 gal / 3.84 L*

2 fl oz / 60 mL vegetable oil

2 lb / 907 g minced onions

7 garlic cloves, chopped (about 2 tbsp)

10 ancho chiles, chopped, stems and seeds removed

3 dry chipotle chiles, coarsely chopped

3 ripe mangoes, peeled, seeded, and chopped

64 fl oz / 1.92 L ketchup

16 fl oz / 480 mL hoisin sauce

32 fl oz / 960 mL Chicken Stock (page 592)

8 fl oz / 240 mL bourbon

8 fl oz / 240 mL cider vinegar

4 oz / 113 g brown sugar

4 fl oz / 120 mL Worcestershire sauce

4 fl oz / 120 mL lemon juice

2 tsp / 4 g ground black pepper

1. Heat the vegetable oil in a large saucepan; add the onions and caramelize. Add the garlic and cook until the raw aroma is gone.

2. Add the remaining ingredients and simmer for one hour.

3. Purée in a blender until smooth and reserve until needed. Adjust consistency with water as necessary.

# Reuben Sandwich

YIELD: *10 sandwiches*

6 oz / 170 g soft butter

20 slices rye bread

15 oz / 425 g Swiss cheese, sliced thin

3 lb 8 oz / 1.59 kg corned beef brisket, sliced thin

1 lb 8 oz / 680 g Braised Sauerkraut (recipe follows)

5 fl oz / 150 mL Russian Dressing (page 38)

1. Butter each slice of bread. Lay slices butter-side down on a sheet pan, and top with a slice of Swiss cheese.

2. Place 2 oz / 57 g beef on each bread slice. Top 10 sandwich halves with 2 oz / 57 g sauerkraut, adding a tablespoon of Russian dressing if desired.

3. Preheat a sandwich griddle or frying pan to medium heat.

4. For each sandwich, transfer two sandwich halves (one with, one without sauerkraut) and griddle, butter-side down, until golden brown and the cheese is melted.

5. Invert the sandwich half without sauerkraut on top of the half with sauerkraut.

6. The sandwich may be placed in a 350°F / 177°C oven to heat through if needed. Cut sandwich diagonally in half and serve.

*Presentation idea* Mini open-faced versions of this sandwich make great hors d'oeuvre.

# Braised Sauerkraut

YIELD: *1 lb 8 oz / 680 g*

6 oz / 170 g minced onions

1 fl oz / 30 mL bacon, goose, or chicken fat

1 lb 8 oz / 680 g prepared sauerkraut, rinsed and drained

1 oz / 28 g sugar

8 fl oz / 240 mL Chicken Stock (page 592)

4 fl oz / 120 mL white wine (optional)

Salt, as needed

Ground white pepper, as needed

1. Sauté the onion in the fat over low heat until tender and translucent. Add the sauerkraut, sugar, stock, wine, salt, and pepper.

2. Simmer until most of the liquid has been absorbed by the sauerkraut, 30 to 40 minutes.

3. Adjust seasoning if necessary.

4. Serve immediately or cover and refrigerate.

# Eggplant and Prosciutto Panini

YIELD: *10 sandwiches*

| | |
|---|---|
| 8¾ oz / 248 g Ricotta Cheese (page 378) | 10 Italian hard rolls |
| 2 tsp / 2 g chopped basil leaves | 5 fl oz / 150 mL oil from marinated eggplant |
| 1 tsp / 2 g coarse-ground black pepper | 20 oz / 567 g Marinated Eggplant Filling (recipe follows) |
| 1 tsp / 1 g chopped fresh oregano | |
| 1 tsp / 1 g chopped flat-leaf parsley | 1 lb 4 oz / 567 g prosciutto, sliced thin |
| ½ tsp / 1.5 g salt | |

1. In a bowl, combine ricotta cheese, basil, black pepper, oregano, parsley, and salt. Mix well. Cover and refrigerate overnight.

2. Sandwich Assembly: For each sandwich, split a roll lengthwise and brush the inside with oil from the marinated eggplant. Spread 1 oz / 28 g herbed ricotta mixture on one half of the roll and top with 2 oz / 57 g each eggplant and prosciutto. Top with the other half of the roll.

3. Grill each sandwich, under a panini press if possible, until the bread is marked and the filling warmed through.

*Variation*  Portobello mushrooms may be substituted in the Marinated Eggplant Filling and then topped with arugula before grilling to create a hearty variation for this sandwich.


# Marinated Eggplant Filling

YIELD: *approximately 1 lb / 454 g*

| | |
|---|---|
| 1 lb / 454 g Italian eggplant | 2 tbsp / 6 g dried oregano |
| 1 tbsp / 10 g salt | 1 tbsp / 2.5 g dried basil |
| 16 fl oz / 480 mL extra-virgin olive oil | 1 tbsp / 6 g coarse-ground black pepper |
| 3 garlic cloves, crushed | Pinch crushed red pepper flakes |
| 1½ fl oz / 45 mL red wine vinegar | |

1. Cut the eggplant into slices ⅛ in / 3 mm thick. Layer slices in a colander, salting each layer liberally. Let sit at room temperature 1 hour.

2. Rinse off bitter liquid and blot slices dry with absorbent paper towels.

3. Mix remaining ingredients.

4. Toss eggplant slices in marinade; cover and refrigerate for 3 to 4 days. Stir every day.

*Chef's note*  The eggplant in this recipe is not cooked, so it needs approximately 3 days to marinate. This allows the eggplant to completely denature and take on an almost-cooked texture and flavor.

The eggplant is ready when the flesh has become relatively translucent and no longer tastes raw.

# Falafel in Pita Pockets

YIELD: *10 sandwiches*

| | |
|---|---|
| 1 lb / 454 g dried chickpeas | 1 tbsp / 10 g salt |
| 8½ oz / 241 g onion, roughly chopped | 16 fl oz / 480 mL vegetable oil |
| 1 tbsp / 9 g minced garlic | 5 pitas, halved |
| ½ bunch cilantro, large stems removed | 10 oz / 284 g shredded lettuce |
| 1 tbsp / 6 g ground coriander | 10 oz / 284 g chopped plum tomatoes, drained (optional) |
| 4 tsp / 8 g ground cumin | |
| ½ tsp / 1 g cayenne | 20 fl oz / 600 mL Tahini Sauce (page 42) |

1. Sort dried chickpeas and remove any stones. Rinse and drain. Cover with fresh cold water and soak overnight and up to 24 hours. Drain. Rinse with fresh water and drain again thoroughly.

2. Place the chickpeas in a food processor fitted with a blade attachment and process until finely ground. Process in batches as necessary. Remove and place in a large bowl.

3. Place the onion, garlic, cilantro, coriander, cumin, cayenne, and salt in the food processor and pulse until the onion, cilantro, and garlic are evenly minced and well blended with the spices. Stir the onion mixture into the ground chickpeas.

4. Form 30 small patties, approximately 1¼ oz / 35 g each, about 1½ in / 4 cm in diameter.

5. Heat half of the olive oil in a large frying pan until very hot, but not to the smoking point. Gently lay half of the patties in the hot oil. Fry, browning the first side, about 5 minutes. Lower the heat to medium-low, flip patties and cook slowly to cook the chickpea mixture all the way through. Remove to a rack or sheet pan lined with absorbent paper towels, drain, and keep warm. Repeat with the remaining oil and chickpea mixture.

6. Heat a pita half and make a pocket in it.

7. Sandwich Assembly: Put 1 oz / 28 g lettuce in the pita, add 3 falafel patties and 1 oz / 28 g tomatoes, if using, and top with 2 fl oz / 60 mL tahini sauce. Serve immediately.

# Duck Confit with Apples and Brie on a Baguette

YIELD: *10 sandwiches*

6 oz / 170 g duck fat (from confit), or as needed

12 oz / 340 g onion, julienne

1 lb / 454 g Granny Smith apples, peeled, small dice (about 3 each)

Salt, as needed

Ground black pepper, as needed

½ oz / 14 g Dijon mustard

1½ fl oz / 45 mL white wine vinegar

3 fl oz / 90 mL olive oil

2 lb / 907 g Duck Confit, shredded meat (see page 230)

10 oz / 284 g frisée lettuce, cleaned

2 baguettes, 20 in / 51 cm each, cut into 4-in / 10-cm lengths and split

1 lb 14 oz / 850 g Brie, sliced into 1 oz / 28 g slices

1. Heat 1 oz / 28 g duck fat in a large skillet over high heat. Add the onions and apple and sauté, stirring frequently, until pale golden, about 10 minutes. Season as needed with salt and pepper. Cool and reserve.

2. Whisk together the mustard and vinegar. Slowly drizzle in the olive oil, whisking constantly. Season with salt and pepper. Set aside. (Before using, whisk to recombine.)

3. To assemble each sandwich, heat ½ oz / 14 g duck fat in a medium sauté pan. Add 3½ oz / 99 g duck meat and 2 oz / 57 g onion mixture and toss to coat in the fat and heat through, about one minute.

4. Remove the pan from the heat and add 1 tbsp / 15 mL vinaigrette and 1 oz / 28 g frisee. Toss to combine ingredients in the pan and immediately spoon onto a split baguette.

5. Top the mixture with three 1 oz / 28 g slices Brie. Place the sandwich in a 450°F / 232°C oven to crisp the bread and melt cheese, about 2 minutes. Serve immediately.

# Grilled Chicken Sandwich with Pancetta and Arugula on Focaccia

YIELD: *10 sandwiches*

2½ fl oz / 75 mL olive oil

2½ oz / 71 g garlic, sliced

1 tbsp / 3 g thyme

3 tbsp / 12 g lemon zest (from 2 lemons)

Salt, as needed

Ground black pepper, as needed

10 boneless chicken breasts (4 oz / 113 g each)

30 slices Pancetta (page 227), ⅛ in / 3 mm thick

20 slices Focaccia (page 602)

10 fl oz / 300 mL Aïoli (page 36)

6 oz / 170 g arugula, washed and dried (1 to 2 bunches)

1. Combine the oil, garlic, thyme, lemon zest, salt, and pepper.

2. Pound the chicken breasts to an even thickness and marinate in the oil mixture, covered and refrigerated overnight.

3. Preheat the grill, and the oven to 350°F / 177°C. Lay the pancetta out on a sheet pan and place in the oven until crisp.

4. Sandwich Assembly: For each sandwich, lightly brush two slices of bread with the olive oil mixture and grill over moderate heat until golden and crispy on the outside but soft on the inside. Reserve. Grill a chicken breast until cooked through.

5. Spread some aïoli on the grilled bread. Place a few leaves of arugula, 3 slices of crispy pancetta, and the chicken breast on one side of the bread. Top with the other slice of bread, slice diagonally, and serve immediately.

*Presentation idea*  In the summer, serve with Marinated Tomatoes (page 108) and in the winter with Celeriac and Tart Apple Salad (page 109).

# Vegetable Burger

YIELD: *10 sandwiches*

1 lb 8 oz / 680 g carrots, peeled

4 oz / 113 g celery

4 oz / 113 g onions, peeled

½ red pepper

½ green pepper

8 oz / 227 g fresh white mushrooms, chopped

4 oz / 113 g walnuts, ground

4 oz / 113 g green onions, chopped fine

2 eggs

Sesame oil, as needed

Soy sauce, as needed

Tabasco sauce, as needed

Ground ginger, as needed

Salt, as needed

Ground black pepper, as needed

1 oz / 28 g matzo meal, or as needed

2½ oz / 71 g cornflake crumbs, or as needed

Oil for frying, as needed

10 soft hamburger rolls

5 fl oz / 150 mL Yogurt Sauce (see Chef's Note)

3½ oz / 99 g alfalfa sprouts

1. Preheat oven to 350°F / 177°C. Grind carrots, celery, onions, and peppers through a ½-in / 1-cm die, and press out any excess liquid. Add mushrooms, walnuts, green onions, eggs, sesame oil, soy sauce, Tabasco sauce, ginger, salt, and pepper. Mix well.

2. Add enough matzo meal to firm up and bind the mixture.

3. Form a small test patty, coat in cornflake crumbs, and pan-fry. Adjust seasoning as necessary.

4. Form the remaining mixture into 10 patties of equal size. Roll in cornflakes to coat.

5. Sandwich Assembly: For each sandwich, pan fry both sides of one vegetable burger, and finish in the oven until cooked thoroughly. Split and toast a bun; spread with sauce. Top with the vegetable burger and alfalfa sprouts. Serve immediately.

*Chef's note*  *To make the Yogurt Sauce, add 4 fl oz / 120 mL juice of 2 lemons and 2 tsp / 6 g finely minced garlic to 32 fl oz / 960 mL plain yogurt. Season with salt and pepper. You can also use the Yogurt Cucumber Sauce on page 42.*

# Turkey Club Sandwich

YIELD: *10 sandwiches*

30 slices white Pullman bread

8 fl oz / 240 mL Basic Mayonnaise (page 36)

20 green leaf lettuce leaves, washed and dried

2 lb 8 oz / 1.13 kg roast turkey breast, sliced thin

4 tomatoes, cut into 20 slices

15 strips Basic Bacon (page 222), cut in half, cooked

1. Sandwich Assembly: For each sandwich, toast 3 pieces of toast and spread with mayonnaise. Top one piece of toast with a lettuce leaf and 2 oz / 57 g turkey. Cover with a second piece of toast.

2. Top with 1 lettuce leaf, 2 tomato slices, and 3 half strips of bacon. Top with remaining toast, secure with 4 club frill picks, and cut into four triangles.

*Chef's note* If desired, substitute 20 oz / 567 g thinly sliced smoked ham for half of the turkey.

# New England Lobster Roll

YIELD: *10 sandwiches*

3 Maine lobsters (1 lb 8 oz / 680 g each), cooked (page 614)

6 oz / 170 g celery (3 to 4 stalks), cut into small dice

10 fl oz / 300 mL Basic Mayonnaise (page 36)

1 tbsp / 15 g Dijon mustard

2 tsp / 10 mL lemon juice

Pinch salt

Pinch ground white pepper

10 frankfurter rolls

1. Remove lobster meat from the shells and dice into ½-in / 1-cm pieces.

2. Combine lobster meat, celery, mayonnaise, mustard, lemon juice, salt, and white pepper in a mixing bowl. Adjust seasoning if necessary.

3. Sandwich Assembly: For each sandwich, open a roll and toast on a griddle until golden brown. Fill with some of the lobster salad and serve immediately.

# Pan Bagnat

YIELD: *10 sandwiches*

DRESSING

3 fl oz / 90 mL red wine vinegar

½ oz / 14 g chopped basil leaves (about 1 bunch)

1½ oz / 43 g rough-chopped flat-leaf parsley (about ¾ bunch)

4 anchovy fillets

1 jalapeño, roasted, peeled, seeded, and chopped fine

8 fl oz / 240 mL extra-virgin olive oil

10 hard rolls

1 lb / 454 g Tuna Confit (page 229) or drained oil-packed tuna, flaked

10 oz / 284 g tomato concassé (5 plum tomatoes)

15 oz / 425 g Marinated Roasted Peppers (page 103)

3 oz / 85 g rough-chopped pitted black olives

1 cucumber, peeled, seeded, and chopped

2½ oz / 71 g minced red onion

2 hard-cooked eggs, chopped

1 oz / 28 g capers

4 tsp / 12 g minced garlic (4 cloves)

Salt, as needed

Ground black pepper, as needed

1. Purée the vinegar, basil, parsley, anchovies, and jalapeño in a blender. With blender running, slowly pour in oil to emulsify.

2. Cut rolls in half lengthwise, and scoop out insides, leaving a shell ½ in / 1 cm thick.

3. Crumble the removed bread and combine it with the tuna, tomatoes, peppers, olives, cucumber, onion, eggs, capers, and garlic. Add enough dressing to moisten and bind the filling. Season as needed with salt and pepper.

4. Sandwich Assembly: For each sandwich, brush a roll with some of the remaining dressing. Fill the roll with 5 oz / 142 g of the filling, and firmly press the sandwich closed. Wrap each sandwich tightly with deli paper. Let sandwiches rest at room temperature at least 1 hour before serving.

*Chef's note*   *This tasty sandwich is built on excellent fresh, crusty bread. Without that key element, this recipe will produce only an ordinary sandwich.*

# Roast Beef on a Roll

YIELD: *10 sandwiches*

10 sandwich rolls, 5 to 6 in / 12½ to 15 cm in diameter

6 oz / 170 g Aïolli Sauce (page 36)

1 lb 8 oz / 680 g red leaf lettuce, cleaned and trimmed

2 lb 4 oz / 1.02 kg roast beef, rare, sliced thin

10 oz / 284 g Pickled Red Onions, drained (page 536)

1. Split each roll in half and spread ½ oz / 14 g Aiolli sauce inside.

2. Place 2 oz / 57 g lettuce on each roll.

3. Layer 1¾ oz / 50 g roast beef on top of lettuce, place 1 oz / 28 g pickled onion over beef, and top onion with another 1¾ oz / 50 g beef. Top final layer of beef with another 2 oz / 57 g lettuce and top with other half of roll. It is best if these sandwiches are made right before serving. Wrap them very gently in parchment paper rather than plastic wrap.

# Roasted Chicken and Peppers on Olive Bread

YIELD: *10 sandwiches*

2 lb 8 oz / 1.13 kg roasted chicken meat (from 2 chickens, about 3 lb / 1.36 kg each)

1 lb 4 oz / 567 g Marinated Peppers and Mushrooms (page 103)

1 lb 1½ oz / 496 g Whole Milk Ricotta Cheese (page 378)

2 oz / 57 g Mascarpone (page 377)

1 oz / 28 g grated Parmesan

Ground white pepper, as needed

20 slices olive bread

2⅔ fl oz / 80 mL Basic Herb Oil (page 546), made with rosemary

1. Shred the chicken meat into ¼ in / 6 mm pieces. Stir it into the peppers and mushrooms. Adjust seasoning as needed.

2. Mix together the ricotta, mascarpone, and Parmesan. Season with white pepper.

3. Sandwich Assembly: For each sandwich, brush 2 slices of bread with herb oil and grill on both sides until toasted. Spread about 1 oz / 28 g cheese mixture on one slice of bread. Mound 5 oz / 142 g chicken salad over the cheese spread and top with the second slice of bread. Cut the sandwich diagonally and serve immediately.

*Presentation idea* Accompany this sandwich with a salad of tossed baby greens, fresh mozzarella cubes, diced tomato, and Basic Red Wine Vinaigrette (page 28).

# Bahn Saigon (Saigon Subs)

YIELD: *10 sandwiches*

### VIETNAMESE CINNAMON PÂTÉ

¾ oz / 21 g cornstarch

5 oz / 142 g fish sauce

2½ oz / 71 g lemongrass, white parts only, minced

3¾ oz / 106 g galangal, peeled and minced

¾ oz / 21 g sugar

4 tsp / 8 g freshly ground black pepper

4 tsp / 8 g ground cinnamon

2½ fl oz / 75 mL light soy sauce

2 lb 8 oz / 1.13 kg pork shoulder, ground through a ½-in / 1-cm die

### GREEN PAPAYA SALAD

1 lb 10 oz / 737 g green papayas, fine julienne

7½ oz / 205 g peanuts, toasted and coarsely chopped

6 fl oz / 180 mL lime juice

2½ oz / 71 g coconut, grated

3¾ oz / 106 g palm sugar

1¼ oz / 35 g cilantro, chiffonade

1 oz / 28 g green jalapeños, julienne

1 oz / 28 g red jalapeños, julienne

3 baguettes, cut into 6-in / 15-cm lengths

8 oz / 227 g butter, melted

1. For the pâté: Combine the cornstarch, fish sauce, lemongrass, galangal, sugar, pepper, cinnamon, and soy sauce with 1 tbsp / 15 mL water to make a marinade.

2. Toss the spice mixture with the ground pork. Cover and refrigerate 1 hour.

3. Grease a terrine mold or loaf pan 4 in / 10 cm deep. Bring 32 fl oz / 960 mL water to a boil.

4. Add 1 fl oz / 30 mL ice cold water to the meat and mix thoroughly. Spoon the mixture into the greased mold and spread in an even layer.

5. Place the mold in a baking pan in a 350°F / 177°C oven. Pour water into the baking pan until it comes halfway up the mold. Be careful not to get any water into the mold with the meat.

6. Bake until meat reaches an internal temperature of 150°F / 66°C, 20 to 25 minutes.

7. Remove the mold from the water bath and cool to room temperature. Wrap the mold in plastic wrap and refrigerate overnight.

8. For the salad: Combine all of the ingredients and marinate for 30 minutes to blend the flavors.

9. Sandwich Assembly: Cut the baguettes in half lengthwise across the meridian and brush the insides of the baguettes with melted butter.

10. On a griddle, toast the baguettes, buttered side down, over medium high heat until golden brown, about 2 minutes.

11. Slice the pâté into pieces ¼ in / 6 mm thick. Place 5 oz / 142 g pâté on one half of each baguette and 3 oz / 85 g salad on the other side. Put the two halves together, secure with toothpicks, and slice in half on the diagonal. Serve immediately.

# Muffuletta

YIELD: *12 sandwiches*

6 oz / 170 g picholine olives, pitted and chopped

8 oz / 227 g Kalamata olives, pitted

4 fl oz / 120 mL extra-virgin olive oil

3 oz / 85 g flat-leaf parsley, chopped

5 oz / 142 g piquillo peppers, roasted, chopped

2 anchovy fillets

1 tbsp / 15 mL red wine vinegar

1 tbsp / 15 mL lemon juice

1 tsp / 1 g dried oregano

2 focaccia, 1 lb 8 oz / 680 g each

20 romaine lettuce leaves trimmed, cleaned and left whole (about 10 oz / 284 g)

12 oz / 340 g mortadella, sliced thin

12 oz / 340 g provolone cheese, sliced thin

12 oz / 340 g soppressata, sliced thin

1. Combine olives, olive oil, parsley, peppers, anchovies, vinegar, lemon juice, and oregano in the bowl of a food processor fitted with a blade attachment. Pulse until combined and homogenous. Cover and refrigerate for several hours before using.

2. Cut loaves in half lengthwise. Hollow out top and bottom of loaf slightly to make room for filling. Line hollows with romaine leaves. Spread olive mixture evenly over romaine on both sides.

3. Place mortadella over olive spread, cheese over mortadella, and soppressata over the cheese. Top with other half of bread, which is already lined with lettuce and olive spread. Cut loaf into 6 wedges and serve each wedge as one serving.

# Mediterranean Salad Sandwich

YIELD: *10 sandwiches*

| | |
|---|---|
| 10 pitas, 6 in / 15 cm in diameter | 1 fl oz / 30 mL lemon juice |
| 10 oz / 284 g mesclun mix, chopped | ½ tsp / 1.5 g sea salt |
| 4 oz / 113 g red onion, sliced thin | ¼ tsp / 0.50 g ground black pepper |
| 10 oz / 284 g seedless cucumber, diced | 10 oz / 284 g feta cheese, crumbled |
| 10 oz / 284 g tomato, diced | 5 oz / 142 g Kalamata olives, whole pitted |
| 2 fl oz / 60 mL extra-virgin olive oil | 15 oz / 425 g Hummus (page 52) |

1. Warm the pitas slightly in a 300°F / 149°C oven for 10 minutes or individually in a dry pan over medium heat, 3 to 4 minutes. Hold under a clean dampened linen towel, so that they stay moist and pliable.

2. Place the salad greens, onion, cucumber, and tomato in a large bowl. Season with olive oil, lemon juice, salt, and black pepper. Toss gently. Add the feta cheese and olives and toss to combine.

3. Cut off the top quarter of the pita so that it creates a large pocket. Spread 1½ oz / 43 g hummus inside one side of the pita. Place about 8 fl oz / 240 mL of the seasoned salad inside the pita.

# Shrimp Open-Faced Sandwich

YIELD: *30 open-faced sandwiches*

| | |
|---|---|
| 30 shrimp (26/30 count), cooked, peeled, and deveined | 30 slices baguette, cut on the bias into slices ¼ in / 6 mm thick |
| 6 fl oz / 180 mL Green Mayonnaise (page 36) | 30 mâche sprigs |
| | 10 radishes, sliced |

1. Slice the shrimp in half lengthwise.

2. Sandwich Assembly: Spread 1 tsp / 5 mL green mayonnaise on each bread slice. Top with one shrimp, halved. Garnish with a sprig of mâche, 2 radish slices, and a small dollop of green mayonnaise.

# Curried Chicken Salad Open-Faced Sandwich

**YIELD:** *30 open-faced sandwiches*

1 lb / 454 g cooked chicken meat, cut into small dice

4 oz / 113 g celery, cut into small dice

12 fl oz / 360 mL Basic Mayonnaise (page 36)

2 tbsp / 12 g curry powder

Salt, as needed

Ground white pepper, as needed

1 head Bibb or Boston lettuce, washed and dried

4 oz / 113 g butter, whipped

30 slices baguette, cut on the bias, ¼ in / 6 mm thick

8 oz / 227 g cashews, toasted

2 Red Delicious apples, peeled, cored, and sliced thin

1. Combine chicken, celery, mayonnaise, and curry powder; mix well. Season as needed with salt and pepper.

2. Cut the lettuce leaves to fit the bread slices.

3. Sandwich Assembly: Spread butter on the bread slices. Top with a piece of lettuce and 1½ oz / 43 g chicken salad. Garnish with a cashew and 2 apple slices. Serve immediately.

# Bruschetta with Oven-Roasted Tomatoes and Fontina

YIELD: *30 sandwiches*

| | |
|---|---|
| 1 baguette, 15 in / 38 cm long | ¾ tsp / 1.5 g ground black pepper |
| 4½ fl oz / 135 mL olive oil | 1½ fl oz / 45 mL balsamic vinegar |
| 15 plum tomatoes | 2 tsp / 2 g chopped marjoram |
| 2 tsp / 6 g salt | 15 oz / 425 g Fontina, grated |

1. Cut the baguette on the bias into slices ¼ in / 6 mm thick. Brush the sliced bread with olive oil and toast in a 375°F / 191°C oven for about 10 minutes or until crisp and lightly golden along the edges.

2. Blanch and peel the tomatoes.

3. Slice the tomatoes in half lengthwise and scoop out seeds. Place the tomatoes cut side up on wire rack and place the rack on a parchment-lined sheet pan.

4. Season the tomatoes with salt and pepper, drizzle with olive oil and vinegar, and finish by sprinkling with the chopped marjoram. Turn the tomatoes cut side down on the rack. Season the opposite side with salt, pepper and a small drizzle of olive oil.

5. Roast the tomatoes in a 325°F / 163°C oven until moisture in the tomatoes is reduced by half, about 1 hour.

6. Top each toast with ½ oz / 14 g of grated Fontina.

7. Top cheese with a tomato and heat in a 375°F / 191°C oven until the cheese has melted and begun to brown, 7 to 10 minutes.

# Fig and Walnut Bruschetta

YIELD: *30 pieces*

| | |
|---|---|
| 4 oz / 113 g figs, dried, stems removed, flesh small diced | 1 tbsp / 15 mL brandy or cognac |
| 1¼ oz / 35 g walnut halves, shelled | Freshly ground black pepper, as needed |
| 10 to 12 oil-packed anchovy fillets, drained | 1 baguette cut into 30 slices, ½ in / 1 cm thick |
| 4 garlic cloves | ¾ fl oz / 23 mL olive oil |
| Kosher salt, as needed (amount will vary depending on anchovies) | 2½ oz / 71 g Parmiggiano-Reggiano or manchego shavings (24 shavings, ½ to ¾ in / 1 to 1.5 cm) |
| 2½ fl oz / 75 mL extra-virgin olive oil | |

1. Place the figs, walnuts, anchovies, garlic, and ¼ tsp / 1.25 g salt in a food processor. Pulse until finely chopped.

2. Add the olive oil, brandy or cognac, and pepper to the food processor in a stream and pulse until a coarse paste is formed.

3. Cover and refrigerate until needed. The spread may need to be taken out of the refrigerator for 15 to 30 minutes to soften before using.

4. Preheat a grill to medium high.

5. Lightly brush the bread slices on both sides with olive oil. Grill the bread evenly on both sides until grill marks are achieved, about 1 to 2 minutes.

6. Spread ½ oz / 14 g fig and walnut mixture evenly over each piece of the grilled bread and top with two cheese shavings. Serve immediately.

*Presentation idea*  Garnish the platter with ripe fig halves and toasted walnuts.

# Mussel Crostini

YIELD: *30 crostini*

| | |
|---|---|
| 1 baguette, 15 in / 38 cm long | 3 oz / 85 g shallots, minced |
| 7½ oz / 213 g Garlic Butter, softened (page 54) | ¾ fl oz / 23 mL olive oil |
| 7½ fl oz / 225 mL white wine | 7½ oz / 205 g tomato concassé |
| 7½ fl oz / 225 mL water | Sherry vinegar, as needed |
| 3 tbsp / 27 g minced garlic | Salt, as needed |
| 1½ dried bay leaves | Ground black pepper, as needed |
| 90 mussels, cleaned & de-bearded (about 5 lb / 2.27 kg) | 1½ tbsp / 4.5 g chopped flat-leaf parsley |

1. Slice the baguette on the bias into 30 slices ¼ in / 6 mm thick. Brush each slice with softened garlic butter and toast in a 400°F / 205°C oven 10 to 12 minutes.

2. Combine the wine, water, garlic, and bay leaves in a large pot and bring to a simmer.

3. Add the mussels, cover, and cook over high heat for 5 minutes or just until the mussels open.

4. Remove the mussels and cool. Reduce the cuisson by three-fourths and reserve.

5. Sauté the shallots in olive oil until translucent, 3 to 4 minutes. Add the tomatoes and reduced cuisson and cook for 3 minutes, or until the mixture simmers and the aroma of the mussels is apparent from the reduction. Allow to cool completely.

6. Remove the mussels from the shells. Just before serving, add the vinegar, salt, pepper, and parsley, and adjust seasoning as needed.

7. Place three mussels on each crostini. Garnish each with ¼ oz / 7 g tomato mixture.

*Variation*   Scallop Crostini: Replace the Garlic and Parsley Butter with Saffron Aïoli and replace the mussels with 90 poached bay scallops (about 12 oz / 340 g).

FROM TOP TO BOTTOM: *Mussel Crostini (page 176), Lobster and Prosciutto Crostini (page 178), Goat Cheese and Sweet Onion Crostini (page 179).*

# Lobster and Prosciutto Crostini

YIELD: *30 crostini*

| | |
|---|---|
| 1 baguette, 15 in / 38 cm long | 30 sage leaves |
| 7½ oz / 213 g Garlic Butter, softened (page 54) | 8 oz / 227 g goat cheese |
| | 8 oz / 227 g prosciutto, thinly sliced |
| Olive oil, as needed, for frying | 8 oz / 227 g cooked lobster meat |

1. Slice the baguette on the bias into 30 slices ¼ in / 6 mm thick. Brush each slice with softened garlic butter and toast in a 400°F / 204°C oven until slightly browned on the edges, 10 to 12 minutes.

2. Heat 1 in / 3 cm olive oil in a small sauté pan. Lay the sage leaves in the oil and lightly fry for 2 to 3 minutes. Remove and drain on paper toweling. Hold at room temperature until needed.

3. Spread ¼ oz / 7 g goat cheese on each of the toasted baguette slices. Place ¼ oz / 7 g thinly sliced prosciutto on top of the cheese and top with ¼ oz / 7 g lobster meat. Garnish each with a fried sage leaf.

*Chef's note*  The prosciutto will not hold long at room temperature.

# Goat Cheese and Sweet Onion Crostini

YIELD: *30 crostini*

1 baguette, 15 in / 38 cm long

7½ oz / 213 g Garlic Butter, softened (page 54)

1 lb 5 oz / 595 g white onions, small

1½ oz / 43 g sun-dried tomatoes, chopped

Olive oil, as needed, for sautéing

1 tbsp / 9 g garlic, chopped

1½ tbsp / 18 g sugar

1 fl oz / 30 mL red wine vinegar

Salt, as needed

Ground black pepper, as needed

8 oz / 227 g goat cheese

1. Slice the baguette on the bias into 10 slices ¼ in / 6 mm thick. Brush each slice with softened garlic butter and toast in a 400°F / 204° oven for 10 to 12 minutes until crisp and lightly browned around the edges.

2. Roast the onions in a 350°F / 191°C oven until tender, 1½ to 2 hours. Allow to cool to room temperature, then peel and cut into medium dice and reserve.

3. To prepare the relish, sweat the sun-dried tomatoes in a little olive oil over medium heat until slightly tender, about 10 minutes. Stir the mixture with a wooden spoon to prevent breaking up the ingredients. Add the garlic and onions and continue to cook over low heat for 12 to 15 minutes, or until the ingredients are warm and the flavors have blended together.

4. Add the sugar and red wine vinegar, and season as needed with salt and pepper.

5. Spread ¼ oz / 7 g goat cheese on each baguette slice and top with ¾ oz / 21 g onion/sun-dried tomato mixture, and serve.

# Egg Salad Tea Sandwich

YIELD: *32 tea sandwiches*

10 hard-cooked eggs, chopped

2 oz / 57 g chopped celery

½ oz / 14 g green onions, thinly sliced

1 fl oz / 30 mL cider vinegar

6 fl oz / 180 mL Basic Mayonnaise (page 36)

Salt, as needed

Ground white pepper, as needed

16 slices pumpernickel bread, crusts removed

1. Combine the eggs, celery, mayonnaise, green onions, and vinegar. Add salt and pepper as needed; mix well.

2. Sandwich Assembly: Spread the egg salad over half of the bread slices. Top with the remaining bread slices and slice each sandwich into 4 smaller square tea sandwiches.

# Smoked Salmon Tea Sandwich

YIELD: *32 tea sandwiches*

6½ fl oz / 195 mL crème fraîche

6¾ tsp / 6.75 g chopped chives

16 slices seedless rye bread, ¼ in / 6 mm thick

12 oz / 340 g Smoked Salmon (page 208), cut into thin slices

1. Combine the crème fraîche and chives.

2. Sandwich Assembly: Spread each slice of bread with the crème fraîche. Lay salmon slices over half of the bread slices and top each with the remaining bread. Using a cutter 1½ in / 4 cm in diameter, cut 4 rounds from each sandwich.

*Smoked Salmon Tea Sandwich*

# Watercress Tea Sandwich

YIELD: *30 tea sandwiches*

4¼ oz / 128 mL crème fraîche

20 slices white Pullman bread, ¼ in / 6 mm thick, crusts removed

3 bunches watercress

Sandwich Assembly: Spread a thin layer of crème fraîche on one side of the bread slices. Place sprigs of watercress over half of the bread slices. Top with remaining bread and slice each sandwich into 3 smaller rectangular tea sandwiches.

# Cucumber Tea Sandwich

YIELD: *32 tea sandwiches*

6½ fl oz / 195 mL crème fraîche

6¾ tsp / 6.75 g chopped dill

16 slices white Pullman bread, ¼ in / 6 mm thick, crusts removed

3 seedless cucumbers, peeled, cut into ⅛ in / 3 mm slices

1. Combine the crème fraîche and dill.

2. Sandwich Assembly: Spread one side of each bread slice with the dilled crème fraîche. Layer the cucumber slices over half of the bread slices. Top with the remaining bread and slice each sandwich into 4 smaller triangular tea sandwiches.

# Marinated Salmon with Fennel, Capers, and Crème Fraîche on Pumpernickel Bread

YIELD: *32 tea sandwiches*

8 fl oz / 240 mL crème fraîche

16 slices pumpernickel bread

1 lb / 454 g fennel bulb, sliced paper thin on mandoline

10 oz / 284 g Gravlax salmon (page 203) (8 to 10 slices)

2¼ oz / 64 g capers, roughly chopped

4 to 6 oz / 113 to 170 g red onion, sliced paper thin on mandoline

1. Spread a thin layer of crème fraîche (approximately ½ fl oz / 15 mL per slice) on one side of each slice of bread.

2. Top half of the bread slices with the fennel, gravlax, capers, and red onions.

3. Top with another slice of slice of bread.

4. Remove the crusts and cut sandwiches to desired shape.


# Avocado, Brie, Sprouts, and Country Bacon on Croissant

YIELD: *30 sandwiches*

30 mini croissants

8 fl oz / 240 mL mayonnaise

3 tbsp / 7 g chives, finely minced

3 Haas avocadoes, sliced into wedges ⅛ in / 3 mm thick

12 oz / 340 g Brie, cut into slices ¼ in / 6 mm thick

12 oz / 340 g applewood smoked bacon, cooked, drained, and cut in half

8 oz / 227 g micro sprouts

1. Slice the croissants in half across the meridian.

2. Combine the mayonnaise and the chives.

3. Spread each side of the croissant with ½ tsp / 3 mL chive mayonnaise.

4. Place 2 wedges of avocado, 1 to 2 slices of Brie, 1 slice of bacon, and a pinch of microsprouts on top of the bottom half of each croissant. Place the top half of each croissant on top of the sandwiches.

# Cucumber, Watercress, and Brie with Apricot Chutney on Walnut Bread

YIELD: *32 tea sandwiches*

APRICOT CHUTNEY

8 oz / 227 g red onion, sliced paper thin on a mandoline

4 tbsp / 43 g minced ginger

2 oz / 57 g butter

8 fl oz / 240 mL verjus (grape juice vinegar)

6 oz / 170 g honey

16 fl oz / 480 mL orange juice

2 tbsp / 6 g orange zest

32 fl oz / 960 mL water

1 fl oz / 30 mL lemon juice

2 tsp / 2 g lemon zest

½ tsp / 1 g ground cloves

½ tsp / 1 g ground cardamom

½ tsp / 1 g ground cinnamon

2 tbsp / 28 g green peppercorns

1 lb / 454 g dried apricots, cut into brunoise

SANDWICH

4 oz / 113 g unsalted butter, room temperature

1 lb / 454 g Brie (rind optional)

10 oz / 284 g Granny Smith apple, peeled, cored, and quartered

16 fl oz / 480 mL orange juice

10 oz / 284 g seedless cucumber, peeled, cut into quarters, and finely sliced lengthwise

12 oz / 340 g watercress, washed, leaves only

16 slices walnut bread or other bread with fairly dense crumb

1. For the chutney: Sweat onions and ginger in the butter in a 32-fl oz / 960-mL saucepot over medium heat until translucent, about 2 minutes.

2. Add remaining ingredients and bring to boil over high heat.

3. Reduce the heat and simmer for 20 minutes or until apricots are tender and the chutney has a consistency to similar to a marmalade or relish.

4. Cover and refrigerate until needed.

5. Whip butter using the paddle attachment of an electric mixer on medium speed until light and fluffy, 4 to 5 minutes.

6. Finely cut brie into slices ⅛ in / 3 mm thick.

7. Cut the apples into slices ¹⁄₁₆ in / 1.5 mm thick. Reserve apples in orange juice to prevent oxidation. Drain the apples before use.

8. Spread thin layer of butter on one side of half of the bread slices.

9. Top the butter with the cucumber, apples, watercress, and brie.

10. Spread a thin layer of chutney on one side of the remaining slices of bread. Top the sandwiches with the second slice of bread.

11. Remove the crust from the sandwiches and cut them into desired shape.

*Chef's note* *The apricot chutney may be made up to a week in advance.*

FROM BACK TO FRONT: *Marinated Salmon with Fennel, Capers, and Crème Fraîche on Pumpernickel Bread (page 183), Avocado, Brie, Sprouts, and Country Bacon on Croissant (page 183), Scrambled Eggs and Sevruga Caviar on Brioche (page 187), Chicken, Celery, and Sun-Dried Tomato Butter on Rye Bread (page 186) (left). Cucumber, Watercress, and Brie with Apricot Chutney on Walnut Bread (right, page 184)*

# Chicken, Celery, and Sun-dried Tomato Butter on Rye Bread

YIELD: *32 tea sandwiches*

### SUN-DRIED TOMATO BUTTER

8 oz / 227 g unsalted butter, room temperature

4 oz / 113 g oil-packed sun-dried tomatoes, drained and cut into brunoise

1 tbsp / 15 mL lemon juice

6 basil leaves, chiffonade

Salt, as needed

Black pepper, as needed

### SANDWICH

4 chicken breasts, boneless and skinless (approximately 6 to 8 oz / 170 to 227 g each)

Salt, as needed

Fresh ground black pepper, as needed

6 thyme sprigs, finely minced

1 fl oz / 30 mL olive oil

4 celery ribs, peeled

16 slices rye bread

1. For the sun-dried tomato butter: Whip butter using the paddle attachment of an electric mixer on medium speed until light and fluffy, 4 to 5 minutes.

2. Fold in sun-dried tomatoes, lemon juice, and basil. Adjust seasoning with salt and black pepper.

3. Season the chicken breasts with salt, pepper, and thyme.

4. Sear chicken on medium high heat in the olive oil until it is golden brown in color on both sides, but still raw in the middle. Finish in oven at 350°F / 177°C until internal temperature reaches 165°F / 74°C, 8 to 10 minutes. Allow to cool.

5. Thinly slice chicken on a bias into slices ⅛ in / 3 mm thick.

6. Wash and peel the celery and thinly slice lengthwise on mandoline. Cut the celery into pieces 3½ to 4 in / 9 to 10 cm in length.

7. Spread thin layer of prepared butter on one side of each slice of bread.

8. Top half of the sandwich slices with celery and chicken. Top with the remaining slices of bread.

9. Remove the crust from the sandwiches and cut them into desired shape.

# Scrambled Eggs and Sevruga Caviar on Brioche

YIELD: *32 tea sandwiches*

8 oz / 227 g butter, room temperature

16 slices brioche loaf, ¼ in / 6 mm thick

6 eggs

2 fl oz / 60 mL heavy cream

Salt, as needed

White pepper, as needed

2 oz / 57 g butter

2 oz / 57 g sevruga caviar

2 oz / 57 g chives, thinly sliced

1. Whip room-temperature butter using the paddle attachment of an electric mixer on medium speed until light and fluffy, about 4 to 5 minutes.

2. Toast brioche in a 350°F / 177°F oven until golden brown, 6 to 8 minutes.

3. Whisk together the eggs and heavy cream and season with salt and pepper.

4. Spread a thin layer of prepared butter on one side of each slice of brioche.

5. Heat a nonstick pan 8 in / 20 cm in diameter over medium heat and add the butter. Scramble the eggs, gently forming soft curds. Divide scrambled eggs evenly among 8 buttered slices of brioche.

6. Top the eggs with caviar and chives and then with the other half of buttered bread slices.

7. Remove the crust from the sandwiches and cut them into desired shape.

*Presentation idea*  Remove the head from a brioche a tête or hollow out a similarly shaped brioche. Spread the butter on the inside of the hollow and place the scrambled eggs inside. Top with caviar and chives.

**5**

# Cured and smoked foods

The first preserved foods were most likely produced by accident. In fishing communities, fish were "brined" in sea water and left on the shore to either ferment or dry. Hunting communities and tribes hung meats near the fire to keep them away from scavenging animals, where they became smoked and dried. Salted, dried, or smoked foods added much-needed proteins and minerals to a diet that could otherwise have been woefully inadequate to keep body and soul together.

Preserved foods differ from fresh in various ways. They are saltier and drier, and have sharper flavors. All of these attributes stem from the judicious application of some key ingredients: salt, curing agents, sweeteners, and spices.

Food preservation techniques from the most ancient to the most high-tech are all intended to control the effects of a wide range of microbes, eliminating some and encouraging the growth of others. This is accomplished by controlling the food's water content, temperature, acidity levels, and exposure to oxygen.

Today's garde manger may be less responsible for ensuring a steady source of food intended to last throughout the year, but the practical craft and science of preserving foods remains important, if only because we have learned to savor and enjoy hams, bacons, gravlax, confits, and rillettes. These same techniques are used to produce sausages (Chapter 6) and cheeses (Chapter 8).

This chapter explains the ingredients, methods, and processes for these preservation techniques:

- Curing and brining
- Smoking
- Drying
- Preserving in fat

# The ingredients for preserving foods

## *Salt*

The basic ingredient used by the garde manger to preserve foods is **salt.** This common seasoning, found in virtually every kitchen and on every table, meant the difference between life and death to our ancestors, and it is still important to us from both a physiological and a culinary point of view. Salt changes foods, by drawing out water, blood, and other impurities. In so doing, it preserves them, making them less susceptible to spoilage and rot. The basic processes in which salt plays an important role are:

- Osmosis
- Dehydration
- Fermentation
- Denaturing proteins

### Osmosis

**Osmosis** happens without human intervention all the time, but to make use of osmosis for preserving foods, it is helpful to have a basic idea of how the process occurs. A simple definition states that osmosis is the movement of a solvent (typically water) through a semipermeable membrane (the cell walls) in order to equalize the concentration of a solute (typically salt) on both sides of the membrane. In other words, when you apply salt to a piece of meat, the fluids inside the cell travel across the cell membrane in an effort to dilute the salt on the other side of the membrane. Once there is more fluid outside the cell than in, the fluids return to the cell's interior, taking with them the dissolved salt. Getting the salt inside the cell, where it can kill off harmful pathogens, is the essence of salt-curing foods.

### Dehydration

The presence of **"free" water** is one of the indicators of a food's relative susceptibility to spoilage through microbial action. In order to keep foods safe and appealing to eat for long periods of time, it is important to remove as much excess water as possible. Applying salt to foods can dry them effectively, since the salt tends to attract the free water, making it unavailable to microbes. Exposure to air or heat for controlled periods allows the water to evaporate, reducing the overall volume and weight of the food.

### Fermentation

Substances known as enzymes feed on the compounds found in energy-rich foods, such as meats and grains. They ferment the food by breaking down the compounds in these foods into gases and organic compounds. The gases may be trapped, producing an effervescent quality in beverages, holes in cheeses, or the light texture of yeast-raised breads; or they may simply disperse, leaving behind organic acid, as occurs when preparing sauerkraut or other pickles.

By increasing the acid levels in the food, enzymes also help to preserve foods, since most harmful pathogens can only thrive when the levels of acids are within a specific **pH level range**. Of course, a higher acid level means that the food's flavor is changed, as well, making it sharper and tarter.

Left unchecked, the process of **fermentation** would completely break down the food. Salt is important to act as a control on this process, since it affects how much water is available to the enzymes. Like bacteria and other microbes, enzymes cannot live without water. Salt "uses up" the water and thereby prevents fermentation from getting out of hand.

### Denaturing proteins

Whenever you preserve foods, you will inevitably change the structure of the proteins found in the food. This change, known as **"denaturing"** the protein, involves the application of heat, acids, alkalis, or ultraviolet radiation. Simply put, the strands that make up the protein are encouraged to lengthen or coil, open or close, recombine or dissolve in such a way that foods that were once soft may become firm. Smooth foods may become grainy. Translucent foods may become cloudy. Firm foods may soften and even become liquid. Examples of these changes include preparing a seviche from raw fish, blooming gelatin, and cooking meats.

## Curing salts: nitrates and nitrites

For thousands of years humans have been eating meat cured with unrefined salt, and those meats took on a deep reddish color. The reason for the color change was discovered at the turn of the twentieth century, when German scientists unlocked the mystery of how **nitrates** and **nitrites**—compounds already present in unrefined salts—cause cured meats to redden. **Saltpeter,** or potassium nitrate, the first curing agent to be identified as such, does not produce consistent results; the color of the meat did not always set properly and the amount of residual nitrates was unpredictable. And in fact, the use of saltpeter has been limited since 1975, when it was banned as a curing agent in commercially prepared cured meats.

Nitrates ($NO_3$) take longer to break down in cured foods than nitrites. For that reason, foods that undergo lengthy curing and drying periods must include the correct level of nitrates. Nitrites ($NO_2$) break down faster, making them appropriate for use in any cured item that will later be fully cooked.

## The nitrosamine controversy

Today, we know that sodium nitrate and sodium nitrite are important elements in keeping meats safe from botulism infection. But we also know that when nitrates and nitrites break down in the presence of extreme heat (specifically, when bacon is cooked), potentially dangerous substances known as **nitrosamines** may form in the food.

The presence of nitrosamines in cured products has been a concern since 1956, when they were discovered to be carcinogenic. The amount of nitrosamine in any individual, like his or her cholesterol level, is influenced not only by the foods he or she eats but also by the amount of nitrosamine produced by the salivary glands and in the intestinal tracts.

Although more than 700 substances have been tested as possible nitrate replacements, none has been identified as effective. Nitrites do pose some serious health threats when they form nitrosamines. There is little doubt that without nitrites, however, deaths from botulism would increase significantly and pose a more serious risk than the dangers associated with nitrosamines. The use of nitrates and nitrites is closely regulated.

| *table 5.1* | USDA regulations for recommended nitrite/nitrate levels in various meats | |
| --- | --- | --- |
| Product | Ingoing Nitrite Level (ppm)* | Ingoing Nitrate Level (ppm)* |
| *Bacon, pumped* | 120 (with 550 ppm ascorbate or erythrobate) | None |
| *Bacon, immersion cured* | 200 (2 lb / 907 g to 100 gal / 384 L brine) | None |
| *Cooked sausage* | 156 (¼ oz / 7 g to 100 lb / 45.36 kg meat) | None |
| *Dry and semi-dry sausage* | 625 (1 oz / 28 g to 100 lb / 45.36 kg meat dry cured) | 1719 (2¾ oz / 80 g to 100 lb / 45.36 kg meat) |
| *Dry-cured meats* | 156 (¼ oz / 7 g to 100 lb / 45.36 kg meat) | 2188 (2 lb / 907 g to 100 gal / 384 L brine at 10% pump) |

* parts per million

## Tinted cure mix, pink cure, and prague powder I

A blend of agents, also known simply as **"TCM"** or "Insta-cure #1," combines 94 percent sodium chloride (salt) and 6 percent sodium nitrite. It is tinted pink (by adding FD&C#3) to make it easily identifiable and thus help avoid its accidental use. When used at the recommended ratio of 4 oz / 113 g TCM to each 100 lb / 45.36 kg meat (or 4% of the total weight of meat), the meat is treated with only 6.84 g of pure nitrite, or slightly less than ¼ oz.

## Prague powder II

**Prague Powder II,** or Insta-cure #2, contains salt, sodium nitrite, sodium nitrate, and pink coloring. It is used to make dry and dry-fermented products. The longer curing and drying periods require the presence of the nitrate in order to cure the meats safely.

## Cure accelerators: sodium erythorbate and ascorbate

Both sodium erythorbate and ascorbate are **cure accelerators** and work together with the nitrite to enhance color development and flavor retention in cured foods. They have also been shown to inhibit nitrosamine formation in cooked bacon. Since the 1950s federal regulations have permitted a measured amount of either ascorbic acid, sodium ascorbate, or sodium erythorbate to be included in commercially prepared cured meat.

These cure accelerators do have some of the same reddening effects as nitrites and nitrates, though the effect is temporary. More importantly, they cannot be used to substitute for nitrites or nitrates when those ingredients are called for in order to properly preserve or cure foods.

# Seasoning and flavoring ingredients

Salt-cured foods have a harsh flavor unless some additional ingredients are added to the cure. Sugar and other sweeteners, spices, aromatics, and wines have all been used over time to create regional adaptations of hams, bacons, and preserved fish and poultry.

## Sugar (sweetener)

**Sweeteners**—including dextrose, sugar, corn syrup, honey, and maple syrup—can be used interchangeably in most recipes. Some sweeteners have very distinct flavors, so be certain the one you choose will add the taste you intend. Dextrose is often called for in cures because it has the same ability to mellow the harsh salt and increase moisture as other sweeteners, without adding an extremely sweet flavor of its own. Sweeteners can:

- Help overcome the harshness of the salt in the cure
- Balance the overall flavor palette
- Counteract bitterness in liver products
- Help stabilize color in cured meats
- Increase water retention (moisture) in finished products
- Provide a good nutrient source for fermentation

## Spices and herbs

A variety of **spices and herbs** are used in curing and brining processes to enhance a product's flavor and give it a particular character. Traditionally many of the sweet spices have been used, such as cinnamon, allspice, nutmeg, mace, and cardamom. These spices and spice blends are still used in many classic recipes.

In addition, ingredients such as dry and fresh chiles, infusions or essences, wines, fruit juices, or vinegars can be incorporated to give a contemporary appeal to cured meats, fish, and poultry. When you change a classic seasoning mix, make several tests to determine the best combinations and levels of intensity before putting anything new on your menu.

# Cures and brines

*Cure* is the generic term used to indicate brines, pickling or corning solutions, or dry cures. When salt, in the form of a dry cure or brine, is applied to a food, the food is referred to as **cured, brined, pickled, or corned.** The term "corned" is less familiar now, but derives from the fact that the grains of salt used to cure meats and other foods were likened to cereal grains, or corn, because of their size and shape. Salt brines may also be known as pickles; this is true whether or not vinegar is added to the brine.

Although unrefined salt or sea water were most likely the original cures or brines, we have learned more over time about how the individual components of cures and brines work. Refined and purified salts, sugar, and curing ingredients (nitrates and nitrites) have made it possible to regulate the process more accurately. This means we can now produce high-quality, wholesome products with the best texture and taste.

FIG 5-1 · *Dry cures are applied thoroughly and evenly to items in order to ensure proper curing.*

## Dry cures

A **dry cure** can be as simple as salt alone, but more often the cure is a mixture of salt, a sweetener of some sort, flavorings, and, if indicated or desired, a commercially or individually prepared curing blend. (Brand names of some commercially prepared curing mixes include tinted curing mix, commonly referred to as Insta-cure #1 or TCM, and Insta-cure #2 or Prague Powder II.) This mixture is then packed or rubbed over the surface of the food. It may be necessary to wear gloves as you apply the dry cure, as the salt might dehydrate your skin (see Fig 5-1).

Keeping the foods in direct contact with the cure helps to ensure an evenly preserved product. Some may be wrapped in cheesecloth or food-grade paper; others may be packed in bins or curing tubs with cure scattered around them and in between layers. They should be turned or rotated periodically as they cure. This process is known as **overhauling.** Larger items such as hams may be rubbed repeatedly with some additional cure mixture over a period of days. (See Table 5.2 for a chart of dry curing times.) If there is an exposed bone in the item, it is important to rub the cure around and over the exposed area to cure it properly.

table 5.2

## Dry cure time for meats

| Item to be cured | Approximate curing time |
|---|---|
| ¼ in / 6 mm thick, approximate | 1 to 2 hours |
| 1 in / 2.5 cm thick, approximate (lean meat) | 3 to 8 hours |
| 1½ in / 4 cm thick pork belly | 7 to 10 days |
| Ham, bone-in (15 to 18 lb / 6.80 to 8.16 kg) | 40 to 45 days |

# Brines

When a dry cure is dissolved in water, it is known as a **wet cure,** or a **brine.** As you make the brine, you may opt to use hot water, or even to bring the brine to a simmer to infuse it with spices or other aromatics. However, the brine must be thoroughly chilled before you use it to cure foods. This technique is used primarily for moisture retention but can also add some flavor to the foods that are brined.

The brine may be applied in two different ways, depending upon the size and composition of the food you are brining. For small items such as quail, chicken breasts, or ham hocks, it is usually enough to submerge the food in the brine, a process sometimes referred to as **brine-soaking** (see Fig 5-2a). These foods are placed in enough brine to completely cover the food, topped with a

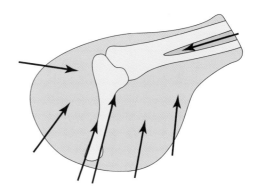

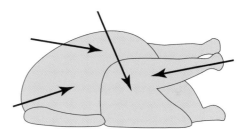

**FIG 5-2A** *When brining, completely submerge the meat, in this case quail, in the brine and weigh it down to maintain submersion.*

FIG 5-2B *When injecting brine, the areas noted by the arrows indicate points of injection that will ensure thorough brining.*

Brine pump with needle properly stored

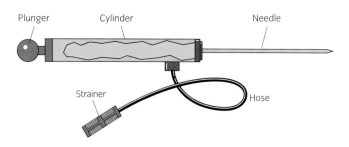

Plunger      Cylinder                    Needle

Strainer                      Hose

FIG 5-2C  *A continuous-feed brine pump, both collapsed for storage (top) and properly assembled for use (bottom).*

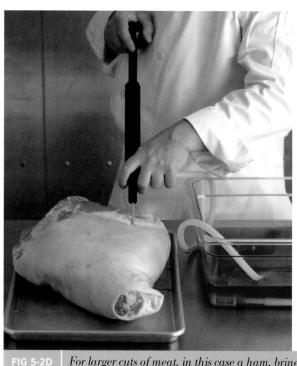

FIG 5-2D  *For larger cuts of meat, in this case a ham, brine is injected using a syringe-like pump to ensure complete and even brining in a shorter amount of time.*

weight to keep them submerged as they cure, and allowed to rest in the solution for the required number of days (consult specific recipes for information).

Larger items, such as turkeys or hams, are **injected** with brine to ensure that the brine penetrates completely and evenly in a shorter period of time (see Fig 5-2b). An amount of brine equivalent to 10 percent of the item's weight is injected into the meat. A turkey breast weighing 12 lb / 5.44 kg, for example, requires 1 lb 3 oz / 539 g brine. Once the brine is injected, the product is generally submerged in a brine bath throughout the curing period. See Table 5.3 for a chart of brining times.

A number of tools are used to inject brine. **Syringe** and **continuous-feed pumps** are the most popular tools for small operations (see Figs 5-2c and 5-2d).

Commercial operations use a variety of high-production systems. In some, vacuum pressure is used to force brine into the meat. Another process, known as **artery pumping,** was first introduced by a New Zealand undertaker named Kramlich in 1973. In this method, brine is injected through the arterial system. **Stitch pumps** inject brine by inserting a single needle into the meat at specific points. **Multiple needle pumps** rapidly inject meats through a large number of evenly spaced offset needles.

Recently, the basic formula for brine has changed because the purpose of brining has evolved. In recent years, meat has begun to be bred leaner to address health concerns throughout the country. Brines are now used primarily to add moisture and flavor to meat rather than to preserve it for long periods of time. Brines are also now commonly made without TCM or other curing agents because meats are not brined for very long and they are cooked very soon after they are brined. The omission of TCM in the brines reduces the risk of nitrosamines (see above) and makes for a more natural brine. See the basic formula for brine below. This can be adapted for a variety of meats and flavor profiles by adding spices or changing the type of sweetener. The possibilities are nearly endless. Also, the size of the meat determines how long it stays in the brine: e.g. turkey is brined for 36 hours, pork loin for 24 hours, chicken for 12 to 24 hours depending on the size, and duck breast for 12 hours.

*Brine formula for moisture and flavor (makes 5 gal/ 19.20 L)*

- 4 gal / 19.2 L water
- 1 lb / 454 g salt
- 1 lb / 454 g sugar
- 1 gal / 3.84 L ice

Heat 1 gal / 3.84 L water; add the salt, sugar, and flavorings. Dissolve the salt and sugar. Add 3 gal / 11.92 L cold water and 1 gal / 3.84 L ice to chill the brine.

| *table 5.3* | Brining Time for Meats | | |
|---|---|---|---|
| Item | Not Pumped | Pumped (10% of Weight) | |
| *Chicken or duck breast* | 24 to 36 hours | Not recommended | |
| *Chicken, whole* | 24 to 36 hours | 12 to 16 hours | |
| *Pork butt or loin (boneless)* | 5 to 6 days | 2½ to 3 days | |
| *Turkey, whole*, 10 to 12 lb / 4.54 to 5.44 kg | 5 to 6 days | 3 days | |
| *Corned brisket* | 7 to 8 days | 3 to 5 days | |
| *Ham boneless* | 6 days | 4 days | |
| *Ham, bone-in* | 20 to 24 days | 6 to 7 days | |

# Smoke

Smoke has been intentionally applied to foods since it was first recognized that holding meats and other provisions off the ground near the smoky fires did more than dry them more quickly or prevent animals from getting to them. The hanging foods, treated to a smokebath, took on new and enticing flavors.

Today we enjoy smoked foods for their special flavors. By manipulating the smoking process, it is possible to create a range of products, both traditional and nontraditional. Besides such perennial favorites as smoked salmon, hams, bacon, and sausages, many unique smoked products are being featured on contemporary menus: smoked chicken salad, smoked tomato broth, even smoked cheeses, fruits, and vegetables.

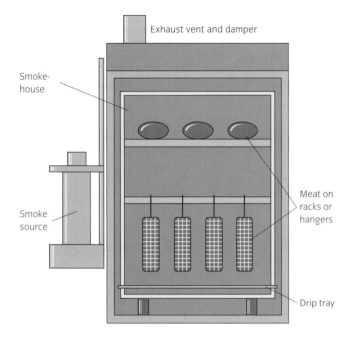

Exhaust vent and damper

Smoke-
house

Smoke
source

Meat on
racks or
hangers

Drip tray

FIG 5-3 *Smokers will vary in style and construction but will always utilize a smoke source, smoke chamber, and mechanisms for circulation and ventilation.*

Several types of **smokers** are available. The basic features shared by each type of smoker are a smoke source, a smoke chamber where the food is exposed, circulation, and ventilation (see Fig 5-3).

**Hardwoods** such as hickory, oak, cherry, walnut, chestnut, apple, alder, mesquite, and wood from citrus trees, are good choices for smoking. They produce a rich, aromatic smoke with proportionately few of the particles that make smoked foods taste sooty or bitter. Soft woods, such as pine, burn hot and fast with too much tar, making them unsuitable for smoking foods.

In addition to various hardwoods, other flammable materials can be used. Teas, herb stems, whole spices, grapevine clippings, corn husks, fruit peels (such as orange and apple), and peanut shells can be added to the smoker to give a special flavor. A special smoking mixture is used to prepare Asian-Style Tea-Smoked Duck Breast (page 219).

FIG 5-4A *A properly formed pellicle should make foods tacky and give their surface a glossy appearance.*

FIG 5-4B *The pellicle allows the smoke to adhere to foods during the smoking process.*

Wood for smoking can be purchased in chunks, chips, or sawdust. If you use a wood-burning oven to create smoke-roasted specialties, you can use larger pieces of wood, available for purchase by the bundle, truckload, or cord. Make the effort to purchase woods from a reputable source. You should be certain that the wood is free of contaminants such as oil or chemicals. Never use **pressure-treated wood** under any circumstances—it is deadly poisonous.

## Pellicle formation

Before cured foods are smoked, they should be allowed to **air-dry** long enough to form a tacky skin, known as a **pellicle.** The pellicle plays a key role in producing excellent smoked items. It acts as a kind of protective barrier for the food, and also plays an important role in capturing the smoke's flavor and color.

Most foods can be properly dried by placing them on racks or by hanging them on hooks or sticks. It is important that air be able to flow around all sides. They should be air-dried uncovered, in the refrigerator or a cool room. To encourage pellicle formation, you can place the foods so that a fan blows air over them. The exterior of the item must be sufficiently dry if the smoke is to adhere (see Figs 5-4a and 5-4b).

## Cold smoking

Some of the basic criteria used to determine which foods are suitable for **cold smoking** include the type and duration of the cure and whether or not the food will be air-dried after smoking. Smithfield hams, for example, are allowed to cold smoke for one week; after that, they are air-dried for six months to a year. But cold smoking need not be reserved just for hams that will be air-dried or salmon that has been rendered safe by virtue of the salt-cure. It can also be used to prepare foods that will be cooked by another means before they are served.

Cold smoking can be used as a flavor enhancer for items such as pork chops, beef steaks, chicken breasts, or scallops. The item can be cold smoked for a short period of time, just enough to give a touch of flavor. They are ready to be finished to order by such cooking methods as grilling, sautéing, baking, or roasting, or they may be hot smoked to the appropriate doneness for an even deeper smoked flavor.

Cheeses, vegetables, and fruits can be cold smoked for an extra, unique flavor. Typically a very small measure of smoke is best for these foods, just enough to produce a subtle change in the food's color and flavor.

**Smokehouse** temperatures for cold smoking should be maintained below 100°F / 38°C. (Some processors keep their smokehouses below 40°F / 4°C to keep foods safely out of the danger zone.) In this temperature range, foods take on a rich smoky flavor, develop a deep mahogany color, and tend to retain a relatively moist texture. They are not cooked as a result of the smoking process, however.

Keeping the smokehouse temperature below 100°F / 38°C prevents the protein structure of meats, fish, or poultry from denaturing. At higher temperatures, proteins change and take on a more crumbly texture. The difference is easy to imagine: think of the difference in texture between smoked and baked salmon fillets.

## Hot smoking

**Hot smoking** exposes foods to smoke and heat in a controlled environment. Although we often reheat or cook foods that have been hot smoked, they are typically safe to eat without any further cooking. Hams and ham hocks are fully cooked once they have been properly smoked.

Hot smoking occurs within the range of 165°F / 74°C to 185°F / 85°C. Within this temperature range, foods are fully cooked, moist, and flavorful. If the smoker is allowed to get hotter than 185°F / 85°C, smoked foods will shrink excessively, buckle, or even split. Smoking at high temperatures will also reduce the yield, since both moisture and fat will be "cooked" away.

FIG 5-5A    *In lieu of a smoker or smokehouse, a pan-smoker can be used to achieve the same effect, in this case using whole ducks.*

## Smoke-roasting

**Smoke-roasting** refers to any process that has the attributes of both roasting and smoking. This smoking method is sometimes referred to as **barbecuing** or **pit-roasting**. It may be done in a smoke-roaster, closed wood-fired oven or barbecue pit, any smoker that can reach above 250°F / 121°C, or in a conventional oven (one you don't mind having smoky all the time) by placing a pan filled with hardwood chips on the floor of the oven so that the chips can smolder and produce a smokebath.

## Pan-smoking

It is possible to produce smoked foods even if you don't have a smoker or smokehouse (see Fig 5-5a). **Pan-smoking** is a simple and inexpensive method to give a smoke-enhanced flavor to foods in a relatively quick time. Pan-smoking requires two disposable aluminum pans, a rack, and some sawdust (see Fig 5-5b). The drawback of pan-smoking is that it is hard to control the smoke and products tend to get a flavor that is too intense and may be bitter.

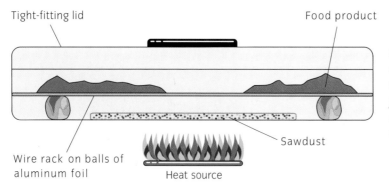

Tight-fitting lid

Food product

Wire rack on balls of aluminum foil

Heat source

Sawdust

FIG 5-5B  *A pan smoker can be easily assembled using two pans, a rack, sawdust or wood chips, and a heat source.*

# Drying

In addition to drying items before they are smoked to form a pellicle, you may also need to air-dry certain items in lieu of or in addition to smoking them (see Fig 5-6).

**Air-drying** requires a careful balance of **temperature** and **humidity** control. It is important to place foods in an area where you can monitor both temperature and humidity, since dried hams may take weeks, months, or more to cure and dry properly. Be sure to learn and follow all the safe food-handling precautions for foods that undergo extended drying periods.

Several world-famous hams, including Serrano ham from Spain, Smithfield ham from the United States, and prosciutto crudo di Parma from Italy, are cured, cold smoked, and then dried for an extended period, making them safe to store at room temperature and eat without further cooking. Other products, including Roman-Style Air-Dried Beef (page 228), Bresaola, and Beef Jerky (page 213), are also preserved by drying.

**FIG 5-6**   AIR-DRIED MEATS, FROM LEFT TO RIGHT: *soppresatta, brasaola, coppa, prosciutto*

# Preserving in fat: confits and rillettes

**Confits** and **rillettes** are classic methods of preserving foods. To prepare a confit of poultry or other small game animals such as rabbit and hare, the legs and other portions of the bird or animal are cured and then gently simmered in rendered fat, ideally fat from the animal itself. After this long cooking process is complete, the pieces are packed in crocks and completely covered with the fat. The fat acts as a seal, preventing the meat from being exposed to the air, which would turn it **rancid.** Traditionally, the meat was salted for 2 to 3 days so that the meat could be stored in the fat for up to 4 months. Now that the confit process is used as a cooking method and the meat is not necessarily stored for such long periods, the curing time for the meat can be cut dramatically. For most cuts of meat, one day of curing time is sufficient. After the meat is cooked and stored in the fat, it is important to allow the meat to age in the fat for one week before serving. This allows the proteins in the meat to soften slightly and create a more tender product.

Duck or goose confit is a traditional component of cassoulet and other long-simmered dishes based on beans. Today's chef has adapted this traditional dish to suit contemporary tastes. You will find confit prepared not only from ducks, geese, and rabbits, but also made from tuna (page 229) or red onions (page 531), which are allowed to stew gently in butter or oil to a rich, jamlike consistency.

Rillettes are made by stewing boned meats in broth or fat with vegetables and aromatics. The thoroughly cooked meat is blended with fat to form a paste. This mixture is typically stored in crocks or pots, covered with a layer of fat to act as a seal, and served with bread or as a topping or filling for canapés and profiteroles.

# Gravlax

YIELD: *2 lb 12 oz / 1.25 kg; 12 to 14 servings*

1 salmon fillet, skin on (approximately 3 lb / 1.36 kg)

2 fl oz / 60 mL lemon juice

1 fl oz / 30 mL aquavit or gin (optional)

CURE MIX

6 oz / 170 g salt

3 to 6 oz / 85 to 170 g sugar (see Chef's Note)

½ oz / 14 g cracked black pepper

¾ oz / 21 g coarsely chopped fresh dill

1. Remove the pin bones from the salmon and score the skin. Center it skin side down on a large piece of cheesecloth. Brush the lemon juice (and aquavit or gin, if desired) over the salmon.

2. Mix the cure ingredients and pack evenly over the salmon. (The layer should be slightly thinner where the fillet tapers to the tail.) Cover with chopped dill.

3. Wrap the salmon loosely in the cheesecloth and place it in a perforated hotel pan set in a regular hotel pan. Top with a second hotel pan, and press with a 2-lb / 907-g weight.

4. Refrigerate the salmon for 3 days to cure. After the third day, gently scrape off the cure. Slice and serve the salmon immediately, or it may be wrapped and refrigerated for up to 5 days.

*Chef's note* *Ratios of salt to sugar may range from two parts salt to one part sugar, to equal parts of each, or up to relatively sweet cures made with one part salt to one and a half to two parts sugar. Adding more sugar to any dry cure lends a moister texture and a sweeter flavor.*

*Variation* *Southwestern-Style Gravlax: Proceed as for Gravlax, substituting lime juice for the lemon juice and 1 fl oz / 30 mL tequila for the aquavit or gin. Replace the dill with a equal amount of chopped fresh cilantro. This version can be served with Papaya and Black Bean Salsa (page 44).*

# Norwegian Beet and Horseradish Cure

YIELD: *2 lb 12 oz / 1.25 kg; 12 to 14 servings*

| | |
|---|---|
| 1 salmon fillet, skin on (approximately 3 lb / 1.36 kg) | 1 lb / 454 g grated fresh horseradish |
| | 6 oz / 170 g sugar |
| CURE MIX | 6 oz / 170 g salt |
| 12 oz / 340 g finely chopped or grated raw beets | ½ oz / 14 g cracked black pepper |

1. Remove the pin bones from the salmon and score the skin. Center it skin side down on a large piece of cheesecloth or plastic wrap.

2. Mix the cure ingredients and pack evenly over the salmon. (The layer should be slightly thinner where the fillet tapers to the tail.)

3. Wrap the salmon loosely in the cheesecloth or plastic wrap and place it in a hotel pan.

4. Refrigerate for 3 days to cure. After the third day, gently scrape off the cure.

5. Slice and serve the gravlax immediately, or it may be wrapped and refrigerated for up to 1 week.

*Chef's note*  *This is a vibrant, magenta-colored, spicy version of basic smoked salmon with a sweet-hot flavor. Try it as an alternative for smoked salmon served with traditional accompaniments.*

# Pastrami-Cured Salmon

YIELD: *2 lb 12 oz / 1.25 kg; 12 to 14 servings*

1 salmon fillet, skin on (approximately 3 lb / 1.36 kg)

2 fl oz / 60 mL lemon juice

CURE MIX

6 oz / 170 g salt

3 to 6 oz / 85 to 170 g granulated sugar

½ oz / 14 g cracked black pepper

4 oz / 113 g minced shallots

3 fl oz / 90 mL molasses

½ tsp / 1 g cayenne

5 crushed bay leaves

2 tsp / 4 g crushed coriander seed

2 tsp / 4 g paprika

2 tsp / 4 g ground black pepper

1 bunch cilantro, coarsely chopped

1 bunch parsley, coarsely chopped

1. Remove the pin bones from the salmon and score the skin. Center it skin side down on a large piece of cheesecloth. Brush with lemon juice.

2. Mix the cure ingredients and pack evenly over the salmon. Combine the cilantro, parsley, and shallots; pack evenly over the salmon.

3. Wrap the salmon loosely in the cheesecloth and place it in a hotel pan. Refrigerate for 3 days to cure. After the third day, gently scrape off the cure.

4. Bring the molasses, cayenne, and bay leaves to a simmer; remove from heat and cool. Brush evenly over the salmon. Blend the coriander, paprika, and black pepper. Press evenly over the salmon.

5. Refrigerate uncovered for at least 12 hours before serving. The salmon may be wrapped and refrigerated for up to 1 week.

*Chef's note*  *The salmon pairs very well with spices that are typically used for pastrami and the molasses imparts a slight sweetness to the fish. Cold smoke the cured salmon to create a more intense flavor.*

# Corned Beef

YIELD: *16 to 18 lb / 7.25 to 8.16 kg cooked corned beef*

4 briskets (10 to 12 lb / 4.54 to 5.44 kg each)

CORNED BEEF BRINE

3 gal / 11.52 L cold water

2 lb / 907 g salt

10 oz / 284 g corn syrup

7 oz / 198 g tinted curing mix (TCM)

6 garlic cloves, minced to a fine paste

½ oz / 14 g pickling spices

1. Trim the fat cover on the briskets to ¼ in / 6 mm.

2. Combine the water, salt, corn syrup, and TCM. Mix well to dissolve completely.

3. Combine 16 fl oz / 480 mL brine mixture with the garlic and spices in a blender and process until evenly blended. Add to the remaining brine.

4. Weigh each brisket individually and inject brine equal to 10 percent of its weight evenly throughout the brisket.

5. Place the briskets in a deep plastic or stainless-steel container and add enough brine to submerge them. Cover with plastic wrap to keep them completely below the surface. Refrigerate for 4 to 5 days to cure.

6. Rinse the briskets in slightly warm water and drain thoroughly. Refrigerate 24 hours.

7. Place the briskets in a deep pot. Cover them with cool water and bring the water to a simmer. Continue to cook the brisket until fork-tender, about 3 hours.

FIG 5-7A · *The "grain" is a visible network of protein strands that run from one end of cuts of meat to the other.*

FIG 5-7B · *All meats should be thinly sliced against the grain to break this network apart, providing a more palatable end product.*

8. Remove the brisket from the cooking liquid. Trim excess fat. Carve or slice for hot or warm service (see Figs 5-7a and 5-7b, and Chef's Note) immediately, or cool the brisket, wrap, and refrigerate for up to 2 weeks.

*Chef's note*   *To rewarm cold corned beef for slicing warm, steam until heated through and slice on a machine or hand carve.*

*Variation*   *Pastrami: Pastrami may be prepared from either the brisket or plate of beef. Trim exterior fat to ¼ in / 6 mm. Prepare a brisket as directed for the Corned Beef through step 5, but do not split. Mix 2 oz / 57 g each cracked coriander seed and black peppercorns, and coat the brisket with the mixture. Cold smoke at 100°F / 38°C for 2 hours, then hot smoke at 185°F / 85°C for 8 hours. The pastrami can be simmered as directed in steps 7 and 8 above, or it may be slow roasted at 300°F / 149°F to an internal temperature of 150°F / 66°C.*

# Smoked Shrimp

**YIELD:** *3 lb 8 oz / 1.59 kg*

| | |
|---|---|
| 5 lb / 2.27 kg shrimp | ½ tsp / 1 g garlic powder |
| BASIC SEAFOOD BRINE | ½ tsp / 1 g onion powder |
| 3½ oz / 99 g salt | 1 tbsp / 15 mL lemon juice |
| 2¼ oz / 64 g sugar | 64 fl oz / 1.92 L hot water |

1. Peel and devein the shrimp. Place in a plastic or stainless-steel container.

2. Stir together the salt, sugar, garlic and onion powders, and lemon juice. Add the hot water and stir until the dry ingredients are dissolved. Cool.

3. Pour enough brine over the shrimp to completely submerge them. Use a plate or plastic wrap to keep them completely below the surface. Cure at room temperature for 30 minutes.

4. Remove the shrimp from the brine; rinse and blot dry. Cold smoke below 100°F / 38°C for 45 minutes to an hour.

5. Grill, sauté, poach, stew in a sauce, or prepare the shrimp according to other needs immediately, or they may be wrapped and refrigerated for up to 1 week.

*Chef's notes*   *To prepare the shrimp for smoking, completely remove the shells, the tail section, and the veins. Even though it has been a standard practice to leave the tails on, removing them is more easily accomplished during kitchen preparation than by your guest. It is safer too, since there is no chance that someone might accidentally swallow a bit of shell.*

*This brine can be doubled or tripled and used according to need. It can be covered and refrigerated for up to 2 weeks. If preferred, the seafood may be pan-smoked to an internal temperature of 145°F / 63°C, for about 6 to 8 minutes, and served hot, warm, or cold. This brine is also suitable for mussels, oysters, and eel.*

*Variation*   *Smoked Scallops: 4 lb / 1.81 kg scallops may be substituted for the shrimp. The tough muscle tab should be removed before smoking.*

# Smoked Salmon

YIELD: *2 lb 12 oz / 1.25 kg; 12 to 14 servings*

| | |
|---|---|
| 1 salmon fillet, skin on (about 3 lb / 1.36 kg) | ¾ tsp / 1.50 g ground cloves |
| DRY CURE | ¾ tsp / 1.50 g ground or crushed bay leaf |
| 8 oz / 227 g salt | ¾ tsp / 1.50 g ground mace |
| 4 oz / 113 g sugar | ¾ tsp / 1.50 g ground allspice |
| 2 tsp / 4 g onion powder | ⅛ tsp / 0.60 g tinted curing mix (TCM) (optional) |

1. Remove the pin bones from the salmon and score the skin.

2. Mix the cure ingredients thoroughly and sprinkle some of the dry cure over a large piece of cheesecloth. Center the salmon skin side down on the cheesecloth and pack the remaining cure evenly over the salmon. (The layer should be slightly thinner where the fillet tapers to the tail.) (See Fig 5-8a)

3. Wrap the salmon loosely in the cheesecloth and place it in a hotel pan (see Fig 5-8b).

4. Refrigerate the salmon 12 to 24 hours to cure. Gently rinse off the cure with room-temperature water and blot dry.

5. Refrigerate, uncovered, on a rack overnight to air-dry and form a pellicle (see Fig 5-8c).

6. Cold smoke at 100°F / 38°C or less for 4 to 6 hours.

7. Slice and serve the smoked salmon immediately, or it may be wrapped and refrigerated for up to 1 week (see Fig 5-8d).

*Presentation ideas* Smoked salmon is an ideal carving item for a buffet or reception and can be served on brioche or pumpernickel croutons with a dollop of crème fraîche (page 382). Traditional accompaniments include capers, finely chopped onions, hard-cooked eggs, and parsley.

Basic Mayonnaise (page 36) or sour cream–based sauces flavored with caviar, mustard, or horseradish are often served with smoked salmon.

*Chef's notes* The dry cure can be doubled or tripled, if desired. Store, tightly covered, in a cool, dry area until ready to use.

For additional flavor dimensions, brush salmon with a liquor such as brandy, vodka, or tequila before it is air-dried.

Trim or end pieces can be used for rillettes, mousse, or cream cheese–based spreads for canapés, tea sandwiches, or bagels.

FIG 5-8A | *Apply the cure evenly over the salmon, packing it slightly thinner where the fillet tapers to the tail.*

FIG 5-8B | *Wrap the salmon in the cheesecloth and allow it to cure under refrigeration.*

FIG 5-8C | *Once air-dried in the refrigerator, a pellicle will form on the surface of the fillet.*

FIG 5-8D | *After it is smoked, slice the salmon into paper-thin pieces with a slicing knife.*

*Cured and smoked foods*     **209**

# Southwest-Style Smoked Salmon

YIELD: *2 lb 12 oz / 1.25 kg; 12 to 14 servings*

1 salmon fillet, skin on (about 3 lb / 1.36 kg)

SOUTHWEST-STYLE DRY CURE

8 oz / 227 g salt

3 oz / 85 g brown sugar

1 tbsp / 6 g dry mustard

2 tsp / 4 g ground cumin

2 tbsp / 12 g dried oregano leaves

½ tsp / 1 g ground allspice

½ tsp / 1 g ground ginger

½ tsp / 1 g ground nutmeg

½ oz / 14 g mild red chili powder

¼ oz / 7 g paprika

2 tsp / 4 g ground white pepper

1 oz / 28 g chopped cilantro

2 tsp / 4 g onion powder

1 tsp / 2 g garlic powder

½ tsp / 1 g cayenne

¼ tsp / 1.25 g tinted curing mix (TCM) (optional)

2 fl oz / 60 mL tequila

1. Prepare the salmon and apply the cure as in step through 4 for Smoked Salmon (page 208).

2. Brush the salmon with tequila before air-drying and smoking (Steps 5 and 6).

*Presentation idea*  This can be used as a pizza garnish with Lime-Flavored Crème Fraîche (page 382) or tossed with pasta. As an hors d'oeuvre, it can be served on tiny corn pancakes with cilantro cream.

# Swiss-Style Smoked Salmon

YIELD: *2 lb 12 oz / 1.25 kg; 12 to 14 servings*

1 salmon fillet, skin on (approximately 3 lb / 1.36 kg)

DRY CURE

8 oz / 227 g salt

4 oz / 113 g sugar

½ oz / 14 g coarse black pepper

1 bunch dill, coarsely chopped

1 lemon, cut into five slices

1 orange, cut into five slices

32 fl oz / 960 mL white wine, or as needed

32 fl oz / 960 mL milk, or as needed

1. Remove the pin bones from the salmon and score the skin.

2. Mix the salt, sugar, and pepper thoroughly and sprinkle some of the dry cure over a large piece of cheesecloth. Center the salmon skin side down on the cheesecloth and pack the remaining cure evenly over the salmon. (The layer should be slightly thinner where the fillet tapers to the tail.) Cover the salmon with a layer of chopped dill. Lay alternating slices of lemon and orange over the dill.

3. Wrap the salmon loosely in the cheesecloth and place it in a hotel pan.

4. Refrigerate the salmon 24 hours to cure. Gently wipe off the cure and return the salmon to a clean container. Add enough cold white wine to completely cover the fillet. Refrigerate overnight.

5. Remove the salmon from white wine. Add enough cold milk to completely cover the fillet. Refrigerate overnight.

6. Remove the salmon from the milk and air-dry uncovered on a rack, refrigerated for at least 8 and up to 14 hours to air-dry and form a pellicle.

7. Cold smoke below 100°F / 38°C for 4 to 6 hours.

8. Slice and serve the smoked salmon immediately. or it may be wrapped and refrigerated for up to 1 week.

*Presentation idea* *Smoked salmon should be sliced as thin as possible, as needed. This version can be used in the same manner as the basic version.*

# Smoked Honey-Cured Quail

YIELD: *24 quail*

| | |
|---|---|
| 24 sage leaves | 8 oz / 227 g salt |
| 24 thyme sprigs | 6 oz / 170 g honey |
| Cracked or coarse-ground black pepper, as needed | 4 oz / 113 g dark brown sugar |
| | 2⅓ oz / 65 g tinted curing mix (TCM) |
| 24 quails (3½ oz / 99 g each), glove-boned (see Chef's Notes) | 2 tsp / 4 g onion powder |
| | 1 tsp / 2 g garlic powder |
| HONEY BRINE | 1½ oz / 43 g pickling spice |
| 1 gal / 3.84 L water | |

1. Put 1 sage leaf, 1 thyme sprig, and a pinch of pepper into the cavity of each quail. Tie the quail legs together with string to maintain shape. Place in a deep plastic or stainless-steel container.

2. Combine the brine ingredients.

3. Pour enough brine over the quail to submerge them. Use a plate or plastic wrap to keep them completely below the surface and cure under refrigeration for 8 hours or overnight. Rinse the quail and blot dry. Refrigerate uncovered overnight to air-dry and form a pellicle.

4. Cold smoke the quail at 100°F / 38°C for 3 hours.

5. Grill, sauté, or roast the quail to an internal temperature of 165°F / 74°C, or wrap and refrigerate for 7 to 10 days.

*Presentation idea* Honey-smoked quail can be used in salads, appetizers, or entrées.

*Chef's notes* Glove-boned quail have the backbone, rib cage, and keel bone removed.

These quail are flavored with a hint of honey, although they are not distinctly sweet. The quail are cold-smoked, so it is important to fully cook them by roasting, sautéing, or grilling before service.

# Beef Jerky

YIELD: *12 oz / 340 g*

3 lb / 1.36 kg top round beef

JERKY CURE

½ oz / 14 g salt

1 tsp / 2.75 g tinted curing mix (TCM)

1 tsp / 2 g onion powder

1 tsp / 2 g garlic powder

1 tsp / 2 g ground black pepper

2 fl oz / 60 mL dark soy sauce

2 fl oz / 60 mL Worcestershire sauce

1. Cut the beef across the grain into thin strips, ¼ by 2 by 8 in /6 mm by 5 cm by 40 cm.

2. Combine with the cure ingredients and refrigerate 24 hours to cure.

3. Place the meat on lightly oiled racks and cold smoke for 2 hours at 100°F / 38°C; continue to dry at 80°F / 27°C for 24 hours. Store in an airtight container for up to 2 weeks.

*Chef's note*   *Buffalo, venison, or other red game meat can be used instead of the beef. Most lean cuts, such as leg cuts, are appropriate.*

# Chile-Rubbed Tenderloin

YIELD: *3 lb 8 oz / 1.59 kg*

CHILE PASTE

2 oz / 57 g dried ancho chiles

1½ tbsp / 9 g ground cumin, toasted

1½ tsp / 4 g minced garlic

½ tsp / 1 g chili powder

Pinch cayenne pepper

Salt, as needed

4 lb / 1.81 kg beef tenderloin, trimmed

Vegetable oil, as needed

1. To prepare the chile paste: Remove the seeds and stems from the chiles and put them in a bowl. Pour enough hot water over them to barely cover. Soak until the chiles are soft, about 30 minutes. Alternatively, toast the chiles on a flattop until soft. Using a slotted spoon, transfer the chiles to a blender or food processor. Add the cumin, garlic, chili powder, cayenne and salt. Purée to a smooth paste, adding some of the soaking liquid from the chiles if necessary to adjust the consistency; it should spread over the beef evenly.

2. Trim the tenderloin and tie to even the shape of the meat. Rub the chile paste evenly over all surfaces of the beef. Refrigerate at least 4 and up to 24 hours to marinate.

3. Prepare a smoker and set the beef on a rack in the smoker. Cold smoke at 80°F / 26°C until flavored, no more than 2 hours. Any more time in the smoker might cause botulism to occur.

4. Remove the beef from the smoker. Sear the tenderloin in very hot oil over high heat until browned, turning to color all sides. Transfer to a rack in a roasting pan and roast at 350°F / 177°C to an internal temperature of 130°F / 54°C for medium rare, about 40 minutes.

5. Let the tenderloin rest for at least 10 minutes before untying and slicing. The meat will slice more easily for use on platters, canapés, and similar cold presentations if it is refrigerated at least 4 and up to 24 hours before slicing and serving.

*Chef's note* *For use with canapés, bruschetta, sandwiches, composed salads, portioned as appropriate. Also appropriate for use at carving/action station, buffet line.*

# Hot-Smoked Rainbow Trout

YIELD: *30 whole trout (6½ oz / 184 g each after smoking)*

30 rainbow trout, pan-dressed (8 oz / 227 g each)

BRINE

2 gal / 7.68 L water

2 lb 8 oz / 1.13 kg salt

4 oz / 113 g dark brown sugar

1½ tsp / 3 g garlic powder

1 tbsp / 6 g onion powder

1½ oz / 43 g pickling spice

3 oz / 85 g honey

1. Place the trout in a deep plastic or stainless-steel container.

2. Combine the brine ingredients.

3. Pour enough brine over the trout to submerge them. Use a plate or plastic wrap to keep them completely below the surface. Refrigerate the trout for 8 hours to cure.

4. Rinse the trout in slightly warm water and soak in fresh water for 10 minutes. Blot them dry with absorbent paper towels.

5. Hot smoke at 215°F / 102°C to an internal temperature of 145°F / 64°C, or about 2 hours.

6. Cool the trout completely before serving. Smoked trout can be covered and refrigerated for up to 2 weeks.

*Presentation idea*  *Fish should be filleted and boned and served 1 fillet per serving. Smoked trout fillets can be served whole as a cold appetizer with Swedish Mustard Sauce (page 525), or can be flaked into bite-sized pieces for tea sandwiches or canapés with a Horseradish Butter (page 597).*

# Citrus-Scented Hot Smoked Sturgeon

YIELD: *4 lb 8 oz / 2.04 kg; 24 to 30 servings*

1 sturgeon fillet, skin on (approximately 5 lb / 2.27 kg)

CITRUS DRY CURE

1 lb / 454 g salt

10 oz / 284 g light brown sugar

1½ oz / 43 g minced lime zest

1½ oz / 43 g minced lemon zest

1. Remove the pin bones from the sturgeon and score the skin.

2. Mix the cure ingredients thoroughly and sprinkle some of the dry cure over a large piece of cheesecloth. Center the sturgeon skin side down on the cheesecloth and pack the remaining cure evenly over the sturgeon. (The layer should be slightly thinner where the fillet tapers to the tail.)

3. Wrap the sturgeon loosely in the cheesecloth and place it in a hotel pan.

4. Refrigerate the sturgeon overnight to cure. Gently rinse off the cure with room-temperature water and blot dry.

5. Refrigerate uncovered on a rack overnight to air-dry and form a pellicle.

6. Hot smoke at 160°F / 71°C to an internal temperature of 145°F / 63°C, or about 1 hour.

7. Slice and serve the smoked sturgeon immediately, or it may be wrapped and refrigerated for up to 1 week.

*Chef's note* *This sturgeon tastes great served warm right out of the smoker or at room temperature as a component of an appetizer or hors d'oeuvre. Sturgeon can be sliced thin and served warm or cold.*

# Smoked Turkey Breast

YIELD: *7 lb / 3.18 kg usable meat*

2 turkey breasts, bone-in (12 lb / 5.44 kg each)

BASIC POULTRY BRINE

1 lb 8 oz / 680 g salt

12 oz / 340 g dextrose, honey, or white or light brown sugar

1 tbsp / 6 g garlic powder (optional)

1½ tbsp / 7 g onion powder (optional)

7 oz / 198 g tinted curing mix (TCM)

3 gal / 11.52 L warm water

1. Trim any excess fat from the turkey.

2. Stir together the salt, sugar, garlic and onion powders, if desired, and TCM. Add the water and stir until the dry ingredients are dissolved. Cool this brine completely.

3. Weigh the turkey breasts individually and pump 10 percent of the weight in brine evenly throughout each breast.

4. Place the breasts in a deep plastic or stainless-steel container. Pour enough brine over the turkey breasts to submerge them. Use a plate or plastic wrap to keep them completely below the surface. Brine, refrigerated, 2 to 3 days.

5. Remove the turkey from the brine, rinse with room-temperature water, and blot dry. Refrigerate, uncovered, overnight to air-dry and form a pellicle.

6. Hot smoke at 185°F / 85°C to an internal temperature of 165°F / 75°C, or about 4 hours.

7. Cool the turkey completely before serving. Smoked turkey breast can be covered and refrigerated for up to 2 weeks.

*Chef's note*  Instead of hot smoking, you can opt to pan-smoke the turkey breast for approximately 1 hour and finish roasting the turkey in a 275°F / 135°C oven to an internal temperature of 165°F / 75°C, or about 30 minutes.

*Presentation idea*  Smoked turkey makes a great presentation on a buffet, especially if it is sliced to order in front of guests. It can also be sliced and arranged on a buffet platter with Cranberry Relish (page 529). Slice it for sandwiches or cube the meat for smoked turkey salad or Cobb Salad (page 134).

*Variation*  Bourbon-Smoked Turkey Breast: Prepare the Smoked Turkey Breast as directed above, pan–smoking the turkey for 1 hour as directed in the Chef's note. Bring to a simmer: 8 fl oz / 240 mL bourbon, 4 fl oz / 120 mL pure maple syrup, and 2 oz / 57 g brown sugar. Keep warm. Brush the turkey with this glaze 2 or 3 times during the final 30 minutes of roasting.

# Smoked Duck

YIELD: *6 ducks*

6 Pekin or Long Island ducks
(4 to 6 lb / 1.81 to 2.72 kg each)

DUCK BRINE

12 fl oz / 360 mL Madeira

6 bay leaves

1½ tsp / 1.5 g thyme leaves

1½ tsp / 1.5 g juniper berries

1½ tsp / 1.5 g chopped sage

3 gal / 11.25 L Basic Poultry Brine (page 217)

1. Trim excess fat from the ducks.

2. Combine Madeira, herbs, and spices with the basic brine.

3. Weigh each duck individually and inject with brine equal to 10 percent of its weight. Place in a deep plastic or stainless-steel container. Pour enough brine over the ducks to submerge them. Use a plate or plastic wrap to keep them completely below the surface. Refrigerate the ducks for 12 hours to cure.

4. Rinse the ducks in room-temperature water and soak in fresh water for 1 hour; blot dry. Refrigerate uncovered for at least 8 hours or overnight to air-dry and form a pellicle.

5. Hot smoke at 185°F / 85°C to an internal temperature of 165°F / 75°C, or about 4½ to 5 hours.

6. Cool the ducks completely before serving. Smoked ducks can be covered and refrigerated for up to 2 weeks.

*Presentation ideas* Smoked duck can be used in numerous dishes, including hors d'oeuvre, salads, and main courses. It is featured in the Smoked Duck Malfatti Salad with Roasted Shallot Vinaigrette (page 144), Foie Gras Roulade with Roasted Beet Salad and Smoked Duck Breast (page 436), and Smoked Breast of Duck Niçoise Style (page 422).

# Asian-Style Tea-Smoked Moulard Duck Breasts

YIELD: *6 breasts*

6 boneless Moulard duck breasts (3 lb 8 oz / 1.59 kg per double breast)

1 recipe Basic Poulty Brine (page 217)

SMOKING MIXTURE

1½ oz / 43 g black tea leaves

4 oz / 113 g light brown sugar

1¾ oz / 50 g dry jasmine rice

1 tbsp / 6 g Szechwan peppercorns

2 whole cinnamon sticks, crushed

¼ oz / 7 g orange zest

1. Submerge the duck breast in the brine and refrigerate for 12 hours to cure. Rinse and dry the breasts.

2. Combine the smoking mixture in the bottom of a disposable roasting pan. Set a rack over the smoking mixture, place the cured breasts on the rack, and cover the pan tightly with a second roasting pan. Smoke for 8 minutes.

3. Roast in a 275°F / 135°C oven to an internal temperature of 145°F / 63°C, or about 30 to 40 minutes.

4. Cool the ducks completely before serving. Smoked duck breasts can be covered and refrigerated for up to 2 weeks.

*Presentation idea* This style of duck can be served as part of an Asian-style appetizer platter, or served with Soba Noodle Salad (page 120).

*Chef's note* The skin can be slowly rendered in a sauté pan with a few drops of water to help give a crispier finished product. For a lower-fat version, remove skin completely before smoking and reserve. Lay the reserved skin over the top during the final roasting to keep the duck from drying out.

# Smoked Ham Hocks

YIELD: *35 lb / 15.88 kg*

| | |
|---|---|
| 45 lb / 20.41 kg ham hocks | 2 lb / 907 g salt |
| BASIC MEAT BRINE | 1 lb / 454 g corn syrup |
| 3 gal / 11.52 L cold water | 7 oz / 198 g tinted curing mix (TCM) |

1. Place the ham hocks in a deep plastic or stainless-steel container.

2. Combine the brine ingredients and mix until dissolved.

3. Pour enough brine over the ham hocks to submerge them. Use a plate or plastic wrap to keep them completely below the surface. Refrigerate the ham hocks for 3 days to cure.

4. Rinse the ham hocks in cool water and soak in fresh water for 1 hour; drain. Refrigerate, uncovered, overnight to air-dry and form a pellicle.

5. Hot smoke at 185°F / 85°C to an internal temperature of 150°F / 65°C, or about 4 hours.

6. Cool the ham hocks completely before storing. Smoked ham hocks can be covered and refrigerated for up to 6 weeks.

*Chef's note*  *Smoked ham hocks are a staple in many kitchens and are a concentrated source of flavor for stews, soups, beans, braised greens, and sauerkraut.*

# Smoked Pork Loin

YIELD: *16 lb / 7.26 kg*

| | |
|---|---|
| 3 boneless pork loins (about 7 lb / 3.18 kg each) | 1 recipe Basic Meat Brine (page 195) |

1. Cut the roasts in half if desired; tie or net them.

2. Weigh each pork loin roast individually and inject with brine equal to 10 percent of its weight. Place the roasts in a plastic or stainless-steel container.

3. Pour enough brine over the pork loin roasts to submerge them. Use a plate or plastic wrap to keep them completely below the surface. Refrigerate the pork loin for 3 days to cure.

4. Rinse the pork loin roasts in slightly warm water and soak in fresh water for 1 hour; blot dry. Refrigerate uncovered for at least 16 hours to air-dry and form a pellicle.

5. Hot smoke at 185°F / 85°C to an internal temperature of 155°F / 68°C, or about 4 hours, or until the meat gets slightly pink from the nitrite.

6. Slice and serve the pork loins immediately, or they can be covered and refrigerated for up to 2 weeks.

*Presentation idea*  Carve the smoked pork loin to order at a buffet station and offer it with an assortment of chutneys and relishes (see pages 526–531). It is also excellent in sandwiches and salads. Edible trim can be added to pâtés, terrines, soups, and stews.

*Variation*  Canadian Bacon: Trim the roasts down to the eye muscle. Cut the roasts in half if desired and tie or net them. Pump with brine and cure, submerged in brine, for 2 days. Smoke and store as for smoked pork loin.

# Kassler Ribchen

YIELD: *2 roasts*

| | |
|---|---|
| 2 center-cut pork loins, with 10 to 11 rib bones (about 8 lb / 3.63 kg each) | 1 recipe Basic Meat Brine (page 195) |

1. Weigh each pork loin individually and inject with brine equal to 10 percent of its weight. Place the loins in a plastic or stainless-steel container.

2. Pour enough brine over the pork loins to submerge them. Use a plate or plastic wrap to keep them completely below the surface. Refrigerate the pork loins for 3 to 4 days to cure.

3. Rinse the pork loins in cool water and soak in fresh water for 1 hour; blot dry. Refrigerate for 16 hours to air-dry and form a pellicle.

4. Hot smoke at 185°F / 85°C to an internal temperature of 150°F / 65°C, or about 5 hours.

5. Roast the loins whole or slice into individual chops for grilling, sautéing, or use in other preparations immediately, or they can be covered and refrigerated for up to 2 weeks.

*Chef's note*  The German city of Kassel is famous for its smoked pork products. This specialty is made from the prized pork loin cut. It is one of the main components of choucroute garni, *the famous dish of smoked meats and sauerkraut enjoyed throughout Germany and Alsace.*


# Basic Bacon

YIELD: *18 lb / 9.16 kg*

| | |
|---|---|
| 2 fresh pork bellies, skin on (10 lb / 4.54 kg each) | 5½ oz / 156 g sugar |
| | 1.6 oz / 45 g tinted curing mix (TCM) |
| BASIC DRY CURE | |
| 8 oz / 227 g salt | |

1. Weigh the pork bellies and adjust the basic cure as necessary, using a ratio of 8 oz / 227 g dry cure for every 10 lb / 4.54 kg fresh belly.

2. Mix the cure ingredients thoroughly.

3. Rub the cure mix over the bellies, making sure to cover all areas. Stack skin side down in plastic or stainless-steel tubs.

4. Refrigerate for 7 to 10 days to cure, overhauling them every other day (see Fig 5-9a).

5. Rinse the bellies in slightly warm water. Soak in fresh water for 30 minutes and blot dry. Hang them on hooks and refrigerate 18 hours to air-dry and form a pellicle.

6. Hot smoke at 185°F / 85°C to reach an internal temperature of 155°F / 68°C, or about 3½ hours; cool. Remove rind (see Fig 5-9b).

7. Slice or cut the bacon immediately as required for baking, sautéing, or griddling, or for use as a flavoring in other dishes, or it may be wrapped and refrigerated for up to 2 weeks.

*Chef's notes*   *Bacon is an example of a fully cooked smoked item that first undergoes a conventional dry curing method, based upon a standard ratio of 2 parts salt to 1 part sugar.*

*For the most accurate results, weigh the fresh pork bellies and then determine how much of the cure mixture you will need. A cured belly will lose 7 to 8 percent of its water volume throughout curing and smoking.*

*Variations*   *Honey-Cured Bacon: Substitute 1 lb 8 oz / 680 g honey for the white sugar in Basic Dry Cure (above).*

*Brown Sugar–Cured Bacon: Substitute brown sugar for the white sugar in Basic Dry Cure (above), and adjust salt-to-sugar ratio to 10 parts salt to 8 parts sugar.*

*Maple-Cured Bacon: Substitute maple sugar for the granulated sugar and reduce salt amount to 7 oz / 198 g.*

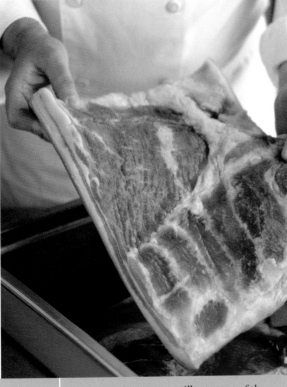

**FIG 5-9A**   *During curing, water will seep out of the pork belly, slightly firming its texture.*

**FIG 5-9B**   *Once smoked, the bacon shrinks slightly and takes on a darker color.*

# Tasso (Cajun-Style Smoked Pork)

YIELD: *about 4 lb 8 oz / 2.04 kg*

1 pork butt (about 5 lb / 2.27 kg)

4 oz / 113 g Basic Dry Cure (page 194)

SEASONING MIX

½ oz / 14 g ground white pepper

1½ tbsp / 9 g cayenne

½ oz / 14 g ground marjoram

½ oz / 14 g ground allspice

1. Cut the pork across the grain into slices 1 in / 3 cm thick.

2. Press the pork slices into the dry cure; cure for 3 hours at room temperature.

3. Rinse off the cure in cool water, drain the meat well, and blot dry.

4. Combine the ingredients for the seasoning mix, dredge the meat in it on all sides, and refrigerate, uncovered, overnight to air-dry and form a pellicle.

5. Hot smoke at 185°F / 85°C to an internal temperature of 155°F / 68°C, or about 2¼ hours or until the color sets.

6. Use the tasso immediately, or it may be wrapped and refrigerated for up to 2 weeks.

*Chef's note*  Tasso is a spicy cured and smoked pork product used primarily as a flavoring ingredient in Cajun dishes, such as gumbo and jambalaya.

# Smoked Whole Ham

YIELD: *1 smoked ham*

1 fresh ham (pork leg roast, bone-in, about 20 lb / 9.07 kg)

1 recipe Basic Meat Brine (page 195)

1. Trim the ham, leaving 6 in / 15 cm skin around the shank. Remove the aitchbone and weigh the ham; inject with brine equal to 10 percent of its weight at the injection points on page 195. Place the ham in a plastic or stainless-steel container.

2. Pour enough brine over the ham to submerge it. Use a plate or plastic wrap to keep it completely below the surface. Refrigerate the ham for 7 days to cure.

3. Rinse the ham in cool water and soak in fresh water for at least 1 hour or overnight; blot dry. Refrigerate, uncovered, for 16 hours to air-dry and form a pellicle.

4. Hot smoke at 185°F / 85°C to an internal temperature of 150°F / 65°C, or about 12 hours.

5. Slice the ham for cold preparations, or reheat, slice, and serve hot immediately, or cover and refrigerate up to 2 weeks.

*Presentation idea*  *Smoked hams can be used in any number of ways. They can be carved on buffet lines hot, or wrapped in a brioche dough and baked for a more elegant presentation. Use smoked ham in any pâté or terrine recipes that call for ham, either as a liner or an internal garnish. The trim can be used in a variety of sandwiches and salads or used to flavor pasta dishes or soups.*

# Smoke-Roasted Sirloin of Beef

YIELD: *3 lb / 1.36 kg*

| | |
|---|---|
| 3 lb 4 oz / 1.47 kg strip loin roast, oven-ready, tail removed | 1 tbsp / 3 g chopped rosemary |
| | 1 tbsp / 3 g chopped thyme |
| HERB MIXTURE | 2 tsp / 6 g salt |
| 3 garlic cloves, minced | 1 tbsp / 6 g ground black pepper |

1. Trim the fat cover to ⅛ in / 3 mm; remove backstrap. Tie the roast to give it a uniform shape.

2. Combine the ingredients for the herb mixture and spread evenly over the beef. Refrigerate uncovered overnight.

3. Smoke-roast at 185°F / 85°C to final internal temperature of 140°F / 60°C, or about 3½ to 4 hours.

4. Smoke-roasting enhances the flavor of the meat and gives it chargrilled flavor. It can be served as an entrée or it can be cooled and sliced as a buffet item.

*Chef's note*  *This dish can be pan-smoked, if desired. Review the information about a pan-smoking setup on page 200. Pan-smoke the beef for 20 to 30 minutes. Remove from the pan-smoker and finish roasting at 275°F / 135°C and remove at an internal temperature of 130°F / 55°C to reach a final temperature of 140°F / 60°C. Since this preparation does not actually cure the meat, it should be used within 3 to 4 days.*

# Carolina Barbecued Pork Butt

**YIELD:** *8 to 9 lb / 3.63 to 4.08 kg pulled meat*

2 pork butt (5 to 6 lb / 2.27 to 2.72 kg each)

BARBECUE DRY RUB

2 oz / 57 g sweet paprika

1 oz / 28 g chili powder

2 tbsp / 18 g salt

1 tbsp / 6 g ground cumin

1 oz / 28 g sugar

1 tbsp / 6 g dry mustard

2 tsp / 4 g black pepper

2 tbsp / 6 g dried thyme

2 tbsp / 6 g dried oregano

1 tsp / 2 g cayenne pepper

1. Trim the pork butts of excess fat, leaving approximately ⅟₁₆ in / 1.50 mm fat on the meat. Score the remaining fat in a criss-cross pattern to allow spices to penetrate.

2. Combine the dry rub ingredients and rub well over all surfaces of the pork. Refrigerate overnight. Place on roasting racks.

3. Hot smoke at 185°F / 85°C to an internal temperature of 155°F / 68°C, 2 to 3 hours.

4. Pull meat off the pork bone and shred by hand. Remove any excess fat.

5. Use the pork as needed immediately, or it may be cooled, wrapped, and refrigerated for up to 7 days.

*Chef's note* *The barbecue rub given here can be used for other cuts of pork, including spareribs, loin roasts, or cottage butts.*

# Pancetta

YIELD: *18 lb / 9.16 kg*

| | |
|---|---|
| 2 fresh pork bellies, skin on (10 lb / 4.54 kg each) | 2 oz / 57 g juniper berries, crushed |
| | 8 bay leaves, crushed |
| PANCETTA DRY CURE | 2 tsp / 4 g grated nutmeg |
| 1 lb / 454 g salt | 2 tbsp / 6 g thyme leaves |
| 4 oz / 113 g brown sugar | 8 garlic cloves, mashed |
| 4 oz / 113 g cracked black pepper | 1 oz / 28 g tinted curing mix (TCM) |

1. Weigh the pork bellies and adjust the basic cure as necessary, using a ratio of 8 oz / 227 g dry cure for every 10 lb / 4.54 kg fresh belly.

2. Combine the cure ingredients in a bowl and mix well.

3. Cure the bellies as for Basic Bacon (page 222) through step 4.

4. Rinse the bellies in cool water. Remove the skin.

5. Roll up into a cylinder and tie tightly if desired (see Fig 5-10a). Hang the pancetta and allow to air-dry for 2 to 3 weeks in a dry, cool area.

6. Slice the pancetta as desired for sautéing or other preparations immediately (see Fig 5-10b) or it may wrapped well and refrigerated for 2 to 3 weeks.

*Chef's note* Pancetta can be prepared in a natural shape, known as a *stresa, or it may be rolled into a cylinder and tied before air-drying, referred to as an* arrotola.

FIG 5-10A  *Secure the pancetta by tying it with butcher's twine to maintain the shape.*

FIG 5-10B  *Once given time to air-dry, pancetta can be prepared and served as desired.*

# Roman-Style Air-Dried Beef

YIELD: *4 lb / 1.81 kg*

5½ lb / 2.49 kg beef eye round or top round

MARINADE

96 fl oz / 2.88 L dry red wine, or as needed to cover beef

4 oz / 113 g salt

1 tbsp / 6 g cracked black pepper

1 tsp / 2 g red pepper flakes

2 bay leaves

1 sprig rosemary

1 oz / 28 g Prague Powder #2 or Insta-cure #2

7 garlic cloves, mashed to a paste

1. Trim the beef and place it in a deep hotel pan or other suitable container.

2. Combine the marinade ingredients.

3. Pour enough marinade over the beef to submerge it. Use a plate or plastic wrap to keep it completely below the surface. Refrigerate the beef for 8 days to cure. Turn the beef at least once a day as it cures.

4. Remove the beef from the marinade, blot dry, wrap in clean cheesecloth, and hang to dry in a cool, dry room for 4 to 5 days.

5. To serve the beef, thinly slice it immediately, or wrap and refrigerate until needed. (Consult local health authorities if you have any concern about food safety and the service of this item to your guests.)

*Presentation idea*  This air-dried beef makes a great component of an antipasto or it can be served alone with crusty bread and good olive oil.

# Tuna Confit

YIELD: *1 lb / 454 g*

2 tbsp / 18 g salt

1 lb 8 oz / 680 g tuna (steak, belly strip, or good-sized trimmings)

HERB OIL

4 oz / 113 g sliced yellow onion

4 garlic cloves, quartered lengthwise

1 fennel bulb, sliced thin

1 serrano, split lengthwise, seeded (optional)

4 basil stems, bruised

4 thyme sprigs, bruised

4 bay leaves, crushed

1 tsp / 2 g black peppercorns

24 to 32 fl oz / 720 to 960 mL mild olive oil

1. Salt the fish liberally so there is a visible coating of salt on the surface. Small pieces should rest, refrigerated, for 1 hour; large pieces should be refrigerated overnight.

2. Put onion, garlic, fennel, serrano, basil, thyme, bay leaves, peppercorns, and olive oil into a 64 fl oz / 1.92 mL saucepan and bring to 180°F / 82°C for 20 to 30 minutes.

3. Add the salted fish and gently poach it in the oil. Watch the fish carefully; when it is barely pink in the center, remove from the oil. Adjust seasoning.

4. Cool the oil, strain if desired, and pour over the fish. Serve immediately, or refrigerate.

*Presentation idea*  Use tuna confit on antipasto plates and in composed salads. It may also be eaten cold as a spread on toasted bread or crackers, or as canapés.

*Chef's note*  This is best if served immediately. It may be covered and refrigerated for several days, but the delicate texture will be affected. The herbed oil mixture can be kept refrigerated for up to a week and used to flavor salads, for cooking, or to prepare more tuna confit.

# Duck Confit

YIELD: *3 lb / 1.36 kg*

| | |
|---|---|
| 5 to 6 lb / 2.27 to 2.72 kg Moulard duck legs | 1 tsp / 2 g ground thyme |
| CONFIT CURE MIX | 2 garlic cloves, minced (optional) |
| 2 to 3 oz / 57 to 85 g kosher salt | 10 black peppercorns |
| 2 oz / 57 g light brown sugar | 72 fl oz / 1.92 L duck fat |
| 1 tbsp / 3 g Quatre Epices (page 588) | |

1. Disjoint the duck and trim the excess fat from the legs. Reserve any trim for stock or a similar use (see Fig 5-11a).

2. Combine the cure mix ingredients; rub the duck pieces well with the cure mixture.

3. Place the duck in a stainless-steel pan, cover, and press with a weight. Refrigerate the duck for 1 to 2 days to cure.

4. On the third day, rinse any remaining cure from duck pieces and blot dry (see Fig 5-11b).

5. Bring the duck fat to a simmer; add the duck pieces and simmer for 3 hours, or until fork tender (see Fig 5-11c).

6. Allow the duck confit to cool to room temperature in the duck fat. Cover the duck and refrigerate in the fat. Remove it from the fat as needed and use as directed in other recipes (see Fig 5-11d).

*Chef's note*    *The duck fat for this recipe can be the fat reserved from ducks, including the fatty skin, or you can purchase duck fat. Be sure to properly strain the duck fat so that it can be reused to make a second batch of confit.*

**FIG 5-11A** *Trim the excess fat from the duck leg and reserve it for later use.*

**FIG 5-11B** *Once the duck has cured under refrigeration, rinse off the excess cure and blot the leg dry.*

**FIG 5-11C** *The leg is finished simmering when it is fork tender when tested.*

**FIG 5-11D** *Cool and store the finished legs in the fat they were simmered in until ready for use.*

# Pork Rillettes

YIELD: *about 5 lb / 2.27 kg*

5 lb / 2.27 kg pork butt, very fatty, cubed

1 lb / 454 g Mirepoix, large dice (page 586)

1 Standard Sachet d'Épices (page 587)

96 fl oz / 2.88 L White Beef Stock, as needed (page 592)

2 tbsp / 18 g salt, or to taste

2 tsp / 4 g ground black pepper, or to taste

1. Place the pork, mirepoix, and sachet in a heavy saucepan. Add stock almost to cover.

2. Simmer, covered, very slowly on the stove, or braise in a 350°F / 150°C oven until meat is cooked and very tender, at least 2 hours.

3. Lift out the pork, reserving stock and rendered fat. Discard the mirepoix and sachet. Let the meat cool slightly.

4. Transfer the meat to a chilled mixer bowl. Add the salt and pepper. Mix on low speed until meat breaks into pieces. Test for appropriate seasoning and consistency. Adjust consistency by adding back some of the fat and stock (consistency should be spreadable, not runny or dry). Make any adjustments before filling the mold.

5. Divide the rillettes among earthenware molds no larger than 32 fl oz / 960 mL. Ladle some reserved fat over them and allow to cool before serving. (The fat can be scored for a decorative effect.) Rillettes can be refrigerated for 2 to 3 weeks.

*Variations*     *Smoked Chicken Rillettes: Substitute 3 lb / 1.36 kg cured, cold-smoked chicken leg meat and 2 lb / 907 g pork butt for the pork.*

*Duck Rillettes: Substitute duck meat for the pork and add a small sprig of rosemary to the sachet.*

**6**

# Sausage

The word *sausage* comes from the Latin word *salsus,* meaning "salted," and it was in ancient Rome and Greece that some of the earliest sausages were created—from just about everything available. In the ninth century B.C.E., Homer wrote about his famous hero Odysseus consuming sausages during his historic journey, and the ancient Egyptians were producing their own form of sausage by 641 C.E.

*L*ucanica sausages, produced in a part of Italy known today as Basilicata, traveled with the conquering Romans into ancient France and whetted the Gauls' appetites for this versatile and useful food. These same long, nonsegmented, spicy smoked sausages are still eaten today, and have found a place in other cuisines as well. They are known in Portugal and Brazil as *linguica,* in Spain as *longaniza,* and in Greece as *loukanika.*

By the Middle Ages, regional forms of sausage had begun to evolve into definite and unique forms all over Europe. Spices and herbs changed from region to region, as did the choice to smoke or dry the sausage, or leave it fresh. Grains and potatoes were often added to extend expensive or scarce meat supplies, and some devout Christians made sausage from fish to enjoy on meatless fasting days. Even the variety of wood used to smoke sausages and other foods changed from area to area and gave subtle flavor characteristics.

Nearby cultures further influenced this important foodstuff. French- and German-influenced cuisines feature blood sausages, the addition of apples, and traditional "sweet" spices such as mace, allspice, and coriander. The sausages of the Mediterranean are more likely to be made from either pork or lamb, and are flavored with fennel, rosemary, and oregano.

# Sausage ingredients

**Sausages** are made by grinding raw meats along with salt and spices. This mixture is then stuffed into the natural or synthetic casings. The original "containers" were formed from intestines, stomachs, and other animal parts. In fact, the Italian word for sausages, **insacatta,** literally means "encased."

## *Main ingredient*

The sausages in this chapter are made with pork, veal, beef, lamb, venison, pheasant, chicken, and turkey. Traditionally, sausages have been made from the tougher cuts of meat from the leg or shoulder. The more exercised the muscle, the more highly developed the flavor. Any tendency toward toughness is eliminated by grinding the meat.

Meats for sausages should be trimmed, if necessary, and diced or cut into strips. When pork liver is called for in a sausage recipe, cut it into cubes before grinding. The seasonings or cure mix are tossed together with the meat before grinding.

### Certified pork

Pork sausages that undergo lengthy smoking or drying procedures but aren't cooked must be made with **certified pork,** which has been treated in a way that destroys the pathogens responsible for **trichinosis.** You can purchase certified pork or prepare it yourself.

*table 6.1* Certified Pork Temperatures and Freezing Times

| Minimum temperature | Minimum freezing and holding time |
| --- | --- |
| 5°F / −15°C | 20 days |
| −10°F / −23°C | 12 days |
| −20°F / −29°C | 6 days |

Pack pork in containers to a depth of 6 in / 15 cm.

## Fat

**Fat** is an integral part of any delicious sausage. Today we are accustomed to foods with a reduced percentage of fat; this is true of our hamburgers and chops as well as our pâtés and sausages. While the percentage of fat considered appropriate for a **forcemeat** might have been as high as 50 percent in earlier formulations, today an average of 25 to 30 percent is generally preferred (see Fig 6-1).

Reducing the amount of fat in a formula any further does require some additional understanding of the role each ingredient plays in a forcemeat, as well as a careful analysis of the reduced-fat version to be sure that it will fulfill your expectations as well as those of your guests.

Although all types of animal fat have been used at one time or another to produce a specialty product, you will find that most contemporary forcemeat recipes call for pork fat (jowl fat or fatback) or heavy cream.

**FIG 6-1** *For optimal texture in prepared sausages, use an approximate ratio of 70% meat to 30% fat, by weight.*

## Seasonings and cure mixes

The sausages in this chapter can be successfully prepared using ordinary table salt, but you can substitute other salts, such as kosher or sea salt. Be sure to weigh salt, since different salts have differing volume to weight relationships.

Sausages that are dried or cold-smoked must include either nitrate or a nitrite-nitrate combination in order to fully and safely cure the sausage. One such curing blend is available for purchase under the brand name of Prague Powder II. Hot-smoked sausages and fresh sausages do not require nitrite.

Sugar, dextrose, honey, and various syrups are added to the curing mixture to mellow the sausage's flavor and make the finished product moister. For more information about the role of sweeteners and curing agents, see page 241.

## Spices

**Spices** are added to sausages as whole toasted seeds, ground, or in special blends, such as quatre épices and pâté spice. To get the most from your spices, purchase them whole whenever reasonable. Toast them in a dry pan or in the oven, and grind them just before you are ready to use them. Or, if you prefer, make larger batches of spice blends, and store them in airtight cans or jars, away from heat, light, and moisture.

Spice blend recipes can be found in Chapter 12.

## Herbs

Sausage formulas often call for dried **herbs.** They should be handled in the same way as dried spices. When fresh herbs are necessary, be sure to rinse and dry them well before chopping. You may substitute fresh herbs for dried herbs, but the taste will be different and you must taste the sample carefully. As a general rule, you will need about two to three times more fresh herbs compared to dried herbs.

## Aromatics

Many types of **aromatic** ingredients may be included in sausage recipes, including vegetables (especially the onion family, mushrooms, and celery), wines, and citrus zests.

Vegetables, though they may be left raw for some special formulas, are most often cooked. The cooking method and the degree of cooking has an impact on the finished flavor of the dish. Onions are generally cooked, but those cooked just until translucent and limp have a decidedly different flavor than onions that have been slowly caramelized to a deep mahogany color. Be sure to allow any cooked ingredient to cool completely before incorporating it into the sausage.

Additional aromatic flavorings and seasonings added to sausages include prepared sauces (such as Tabasco and Worcestershire), powdered onions and garlic, and stock. Highly acidic ingredients such as wines or vinegars should be added with care; too much can give the finished sausage a grainy texture.

# Equipment selection, care, and use

**Electric meat grinders, food processors, choppers, mixers,** and **sausage stuffers** have all but replaced the hand tools once used to make sausages and other forcemeats. These tools are certainly great for saving time and labor, but even more important, they produce sausages of superior quality to those made by the laborious process the original charcuterie and garde manger chefs knew (see Fig 6-2).

**FIG 6-2**  *The parts of a meat grinder, from left to right: grinder housing or grinder body, worm, blade, different size plates, collar.*

Use the following guidelines:

1. **Make sure the equipment is in excellent condition.** Evaluate any machinery you use in the kitchen and consider its functionality and safety as part of a standard checklist. Are the blades sharp? Are all the safety features fully functional? Are the cords and plugs in good repair?

2. **Make sure the equipment is scrupulously clean before setting to work.** Every part of the equipment must be thoroughly cleaned and sanitized between uses. **Cross contamination** is a serious problem, especially for foods as highly processed and handled as sausages.

3. **Chill any part of the machine that comes into direct contact with the sausage ingredients.** Place parts in the freezer or refrigerator, or chill equipment rapidly by placing it in a sink or container of ice water (see Fig 6-3a). Remember that if your sausage mixture becomes warm during production, you may need to cool both the mixture and the equipment before continuing.

4. **Choose the right tool for the job.** Do not overload your equipment. If you do not have equipment large enough to handle bulk recipes, then break the formula down into batches that your equipment can handle without straining.

5. **Assemble the grinder correctly; novices often make the mistake of improperly setting up the blade and die assembly.** Be certain that the blade is sitting flush against the die (see Fig 6-3b). This cuts the food neatly, rather than tearing or shredding it. Make sure the power is disconnected before assembling or disassembling the grinder.

**FIG 6-3A** *Before grinding any meat, submerge all pieces of equipment that will come in direct contact with the meat in ice water to thoroughly chill them.*

**FIG 6-3B** *Insert the blade of the grinder with the flat side facing the die so that the meat is properly ground.*

FIG 6-4 *Progressively ground meats, from top to bottom: coarse die, medium-coarse die, small die.*

## Progressive grinding

Some sausages and other forcemeat recipes require that the meat and/or fat be ground through a succession of increasingly smaller plates. This is known as progressive grinding. The plates used for progressive grinding usually consist of the ⅜ in / 9 mm plate, the ¼ in / 6 mm plate, and the ⅛ in / 3 mm plate (see Fig 6-4).Progressive grinding gives a fine, even texture to the forcemeat and makes it easier for the grinder to process the meat down to a fine grind. The meat and/or fat should be near 28° to 30°F / –2 to –1°C so that the meat grinds properly. It may be necessary to chill the meat and/or fat between each plate when they are progressively ground.

## Basic grind sausages

Sausages produced using the basic grind method have a medium to coarse texture. When left loose they are referred to as **bulk sausages.** Each of the following sausage types is made with the basic grind method:

- **Fresh sausages** are raw sausages that are typically pan-fried, broiled, grilled, baked, or braised before serving.
- **Cooked sausages** are poached or steamed after they are shaped; they may be sliced and served cold or prepared by grilling, baking, or pan frying.
- **Smoked and dried sausages** are cold or hot smoked, then allowed to air-dry in a curing room to the desired texture; they may be prepared for service in the same way as cooked sausages.

Sausages that are not fully cooked during smoking or are not fully dried must be fully cooked before serving. When smoking sausages until they are fully cooked, sometimes it is advantageous to gradually raise the temperatures of the smokehouse while smoking. Start by smoking the sausages in a 120°F / 49°C environment for 2 hours, then raise the temperature to 130°F / 54°C for 2 hours before finishing the hot smoking process at 180°F / 82°C.

1.  **Grind chilled and diced meats, as well as other ingredients as required by recipe, to the desired texture.** Meats should ideally be between 28°F and 30°F / –2°C and –1°C when it is ground. Meat or other foods should be cut into a size and shape that fits the feed tube. You should not have to force foods through the tube with a tamper. When they are correctly cut, the worm will pull them evenly along without requiring you to exert undue pressure. If you have cut your food properly and it is still sticking to the sides of the feed tube, you may need to "coax" the pieces along.

If you discover that the products are not flowing smoothly through the grinder, stop immediately. This is a sign that the meat is being squeezed and torn, rather than cut cleanly. Disassemble the grinder unit, remove any obstructions, and reassemble the grinder properly.

2. **Mix the ground sausage meat(s) on the first speed for 1 minute, then on second speed for 15 to 30 seconds, or until it become homogenous.** Once the sausage is properly ground, it should be mixed just long enough to evenly distribute the fat and lean components, as well as the spices and other seasonings. The process of mixing also continues to draw out the myosin water-soluble proteins responsible for the finished texture of the sausage. Do not allow the finished forcemeat to sit for more than a few minutes after grinding and mixing or the forcemeat will not fill the casings properly and will have too many air pockets under the surface of the casing.

Mixing may be done by hand with a wooden spoon. An ice bath under the mixing bowl helps keep the sausage properly chilled as you work. Add any liquids gradually, making sure that they are very cold when added.

If you are using an electric mixer, be certain that the parts that come into contact with the sausage are properly chilled. Do not overload the bowl; it is more efficient in both the short and the long run to work in smaller batches. Overloading the machine could cause an uneven mix, as well as unnecessary friction that will overheat the sausage. Depending upon the quantity of forcemeat being mixed, total mixing time should be about one to three minutes. The sausage is properly mixed when the ingredients become more homogenous. Look for a tacky appearance and a slightly sticky texture.

3. **The sausage mixture is now ready to test,** garnish, and shape (pages 246–251).

# Dry and semi-dry fermented sausages

Fermented sausages have been around for hundreds of years and their distinctive flavor and appearance still appeal to people around the world. Their inherent tangy flavor is due to the lactic acid that is produced during fermentation. Semi-dry sausages are usually not cooked; however, they are fairly shelf stable because of the acidity produced during fermentation and the smoke compounds that are present, if they are smoked. They are sometimes cold smoked. They generally take just one to two weeks to produce. Examples of semi-dry sausages are summer sausages, Lebanon bologna, and cervalats. One of the most well-known dry sausages is salami. Dry sausages require quite a bit of care and attention because of the length of time that they are aged. Their manufacture requires the most pristine production processes as well as attention to their environment while they age.

## *Ingredients*

Fermented sausages are typically made from beef or pork, water (60 to 70 percent of the weight of the meat), salt, curing agents such as nitrate and nitrite, and sugars such as dextrose and sucrose. Often, a starter is added to the mixture (especially in semi-dry sausage) in order to increase the amount of friendly bacteria present that will carry out the fermentation process in the meat. It is imperative to use pork that is labeled certified pork (see page 236 for definition) to be certain that it is trichinosis-free. The meat should be free from a lot of connective tissue because it will not break down, since the sausages are not cooked before they are eaten. It is also important to maintain a proper moisture ratio in the sausage because excess water promotes an environment where bacteria can grow that might cause spoilage. The salt acts to help break down the proteins and add flavor, and has anti-microbial properties, but if there is too much added, it will slow fermentation. The sugar acts as food for the organisms required for fermentation.

## Production

During production of fermented sausage, it is vital to inhibit or eliminate the growth of bacteria that can cause spoilage. Some ingredients that have antimicrobial properties are salt, curing agents, garlic, cloves, cinnamon, and, to a lesser extent, crushed red pepper, sage, and oregano. When mixing the meat with the salt and curing agents, it is key to mix the meat very well to get even distribution of the salt and curing agents. The meat should be cured for 2 to 3 days before adding the remaining seasonings and grinding the meat (see Fig 6-5a).

It is essential to keep the meat extremely cold, if not nearly frozen. The meat should be between 28°F and 30°F / –2°C and –1°C and the fat should be between 5°F and 10°F / –15°C and –23°C. After grinding, the only step left is to stuff and smoke the sausage if desired.

However, the sausages must be stuffed properly (see Fig 6-5b). Understuffing the sausages will produce air pockets and overstuffing the sausages may cause ruptures.

While they age, keep the sausages in an environment that is climate-controlled. It is crucial to maintain a proper humidity level. As the sausages dry, the water evaporates from the surface of the sausage and moisture is then drawn from the inside of the sausage to maintain an equilibrium of moisture content in the cells (see Fig 6-5c).

If the humidity is too low, the surface of the sausage dries out faster than the moisture can be drawn from within the sausage and the casing effectively forms a hard shell through which no moisture can escape (called case hardening). If the humidity is too high, the moisture will not evaporate from the surface of the sausage. The humidity should be decreased as the sausage ages in order to maintain a constant rate of evaporation. As a general guideline, the sausage should not lose more than 1 percent of its weight per day. The sausages will begin to firm up as they dry because the lactic acid is denaturing the proteins.

## Finished sausage

The fermentation during the drying process produces lactic and acetic acid, which lower the pH level to between 4.6 and 5.2 for semi-dry sausages and to a pH level between 5.0 and 5.3 for dry sausages. Semi-dry sausages may lose 15 percent of their original weight as they age and dry sausage could lose up to 30 percent. The combined factors of reduced moisture content and lower pH extend the shelf life of these products by creating a hostile environment for bacteria to grow. The finished product should be brightly colored and have a slight yeast flavor and a smooth, slightly chewy texture (see Fig 6-5d).

Occasionally, dry sausages will accumulate a white mold (mycelium) on the surface of the sausages but this is not harmful. The finished sausages can be sliced thinly and simply served with cheeses, cornichons, and slices of baguette.

**FIG 6-5A** *Meat for fermented sausages must be cured for two to three days before grinding.*

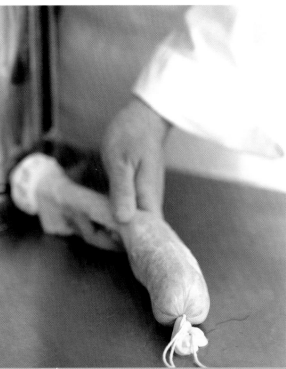

**FIG 6-5B** *Once ground, stuff the meat into the prepared casing, taking care not to over- or understuff.*

**FIG 6-5C** *As the sausage dries, moisture evaporates from its surface and is pulled out from its interior, which tightens the casing and firms up the texture.*

**FIG 6-5D** *Once fully dried, the finished sausage should be brightly colored with a smooth, slightly chewy texture.*

# Emulsion sausages

**Emulsion** sausages such as frankfurters and mortadella are made from a basic mixture referred to as **5-4-3 forcemeat,** which reflects the ratio of ingredients: 5 parts trimmed raw meat to 4 parts fat (pork jowl fat) to 3 parts water (in the form of **ice**) by weight. Many emulsion-style sausages are poached before smoking. Once finished, the sausages should be properly packaged, wrapped, and refrigerated. If your production needs demand it, you can freeze uncooked emulsion-style sausages very successfully.

1. **Cure the meat and then grind through the fine die.** Meats should be trimmed of any gristle, sinew, or connective tissue. Add the cure mix, tossing to coat the meat evenly. The cured meat is ground through the fine plate of the meat grinder and must be kept very cold while grinding the fat (see Fig 6-6a). The meat and the fat should be kept separate at this point.

2. **Grind the chilled fatback through the fine grinder die.** The fat (jowl fat is typical) may be partially frozen after it is cubed. Grind it through a fine grinder plate and keep the ground fat well chilled until needed.

3. **Chop together the ground meat and crushed ice and process until the temperature drops to below 30°F / –1°C.** Place the meat in the bowl of a high-speed chopper or processor. If the chopper or processor is not powerful enough, a proper emulsion will not form. Add the ice on top of the meat and start to process the mixture (see Fig 6-6b). Process until the temperature first drops below 30°F / –1°C and then begins to climb up.

4. **Add the ground fat to the meat when the temperature reaches 40°F / 4°C (see Fig 6-6c).** Check the temperature frequently to be sure that the mixture is within the desired temperature range. The fat is added just at this point to form a good emulsion with the lean meat. The mechanical mixing action, as well as the friction created by the coarse ice and the effect of the salt, produces a light, almost spongy texture.

5. **Add the nonfat dry milk (and any remaining seasonings) when the temperature reaches between 45°F / 7°C and 50°F / 10°C.** Continue to process the forcemeat until it reaches 58°F / 14°C. This process requires the sausage to reach a higher temperature than other sausages and forcemeats so that the fat will liquefy enough to blend very evenly with the lean meat. The texture of an emulsion sausage must be very even (see Fig 6-6d). To ensure the best results, scrape down the bowl as the sausage is mixed.

   Make a **test** and evaluate the forcemeat before garnishing, shaping, and finishing the sausage (see Fig 6-7). This important step takes some time to do properly, but it can save you time and money. To make a test, wrap a 1-oz / 28-g portion of the forcemeat in plastic wrap and poach it to the appropriate internal temperature (145°F / 63°C for fish, 150°F / 66°C for pork, beef, veal, lamb, and game, and 165°F / 74°C for any item including poultry and poultry liver). Cool the forcemeat to the correct service temperature before you taste it. You will be checking for flavor, seasoning, and consistency.

**FIG 6-6A** *Working over ice, grind the chilled meat and fatback separately though the fine die of a meat grinder.*

**FIG 6-6B** *Combine the meat and ice and blend continuously until the mixture drops below 30° F/ −1° C.*

**FIG 6-6C** *Once the meat and ice mixture has risen up to 40° F/ 4° C after continuous mixing, add the ground fatback and continue mixing.*

**FIG 6-6D** *The finished emulsion sausage will have a homogenous and almost spongy texture.*

# Garnishing

Some sausage recipes may call for a **garnish.** Usually, the garnish item is diced and added to the forcemeat after it has been tested and adjusted. Cheeses, vegetables, cured or smoked meats, nuts, and dried fruits are all examples of garnishes that can be added to sausages. Add the garnish by folding it into the base mixture in the electric mixer, if desired, or working by hand over an ice bath.

# Sausage shaping

Sausage meat may be used either in **bulk (loose) form,** made into patties, or stuffed into natural or synthetic **casings** and then formed into links, loops, spirals, or other special shapes.

## Loose or bulk sausages

To shape bulk sausage into a roll, place about 1 lb / 454 g sausage on a square of plastic wrap. Roll it up, and twist the ends to form a solid log. Once rolled, the sausage can be sliced into patties. Bulk sausage can also be shaped into patties and wrapped in caul fat if desired.

## Sausages in casings

Various types of casings, both natural and synthetic, are available today. **Natural casings** are made from the intestines and stomach of sheep, hogs, and cattle (see Fig 6-8). **Synthetic casings** are made from a variety of food-grade materials, some edible and some not (see Fig 6-9). They may be colored, lined with herbs, or netted. The advantage to synthetic casing for commercial use is that a standard amount is required to fill each one and therefore makes the sausage stuffing process more uniform and efficient.

    **Beef casings** are made from various parts of the intestines: **middle, round,** and **bung.** The diameter of each type of casing varies. Individual links are typically made from lamb, **sheep,** or **hog casings.** Larger sausages are made using beef middles or bungs. (See Table 6.2 on following page for casing charts.)

table 6.2 Casing Chart

**Sheep Casings**

| ITEMS | SIZE | LENGTH | CAPACITY | COMMENTS/USES |
|---|---|---|---|---|
| *Sheep casing* | Inch measure 0.7 in / 18 mm and less | 100 yd / 91 m per hank | 38 to 41 lb / 17.23 to 18.59 kg | Cocktail franks |
| *Sheep casing* | Inch 0.95 in / 24 to 26 mm (4 ft per lb) | 100 yd / 91 m per hank | 60 to 64 lb / 27.21 to 29.04 kg | Pork sausage, frankfurters, andouille |
| *Sheep casing* | Inch measure 1.1 in / 28 mm and up | 100 yd / 91 m per hank | 65 to 70 lb / 29.48 to 31.75 kg | |

**Hog Casings**

| ITEMS | SIZE | LENGTH | CAPACITY | COMMENTS/USES |
|---|---|---|---|---|
| *Hog casing (small intestine)* | 1.26 to 1.38 in / 32 to 35 mm (2 ft per lb) | 100 yd / 91 m per hank | 105 to 115 lbs / 47.63 to 52.16 kg | Country-style and pork sausage, large frankfurters, pepperoni |
| *Hog middles (middle of intestine)* | 4 in / 10 cm | 13 ft / 3.3 m (27 ft / 6.9 m per set) | | |
| *Hog bung (end)* | 2 in / 5 cm and up | 4 ft / 1.2 m long | | |
| *Sewed hog bungs* | 4 in / 10 cm wide | 36 in / 91 cm long | 8½ to 9½ lb / 3.86 to 4.31 kg | Salami, liverwurst, casings |

**Beef Casings**

| ITEMS | SIZE | LENGTH | CAPACITY | COMMENTS/USES |
|---|---|---|---|---|
| *Beef round (tight curl)* | 1.69 to 1.81 in / 43 to 46 mm | 100 ft / 33.52 m per set | 75 to 80 lb (15 ft per lb) | Ring liver, ring bologna, sausage kielbasa, blood and Mettwurst Holsteiner |
| *Beef middle (large intestine)* | 2.36 to 2.56 in / 60 to 65 mm | 57 ft / 17.37 m per set | 70 to 80 lb (9 ft per lb) | Lyoner–style sausages and other types of bologna, dry and semi–dry cervelats, dry and cooked salami, kishka (stuffed derma), and veal sausage |
| *Beef bung* | 4.72 in / 120 mm | 23 to 27 in / 58 to 69 cm | 17 to 20 lb / 7.71 to 9.07 kg | Capicolla, large bologna cap, lebanon and cooked salami |

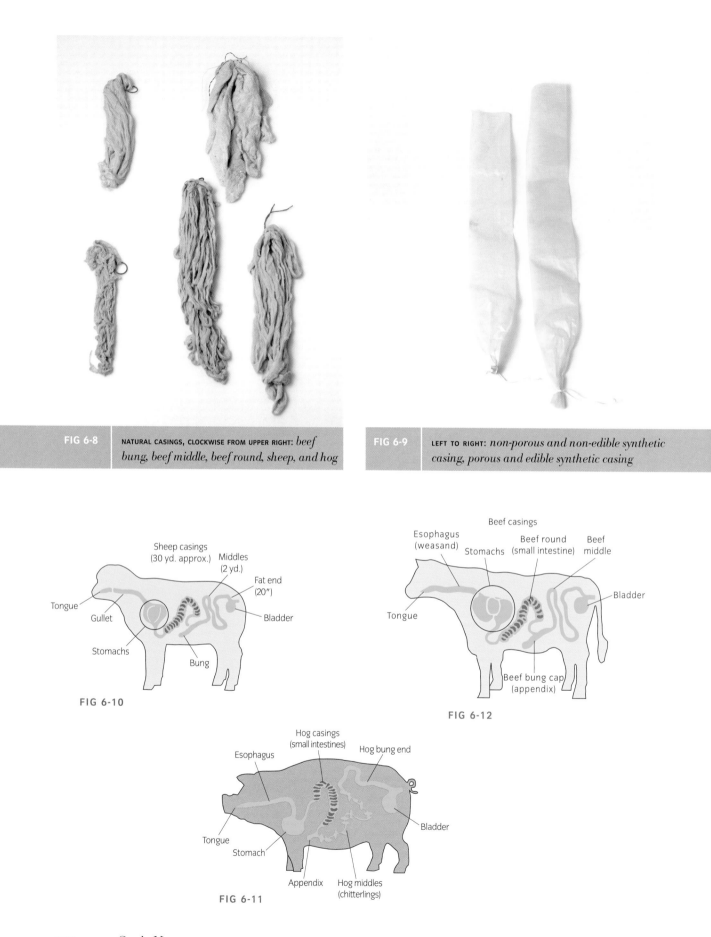

**FIG 6-8** NATURAL CASINGS, CLOCKWISE FROM UPPER RIGHT: *beef bung, beef middle, beef round, sheep, and hog*

**FIG 6-9** LEFT TO RIGHT: *non-porous and non-edible synthetic casing, porous and edible synthetic casing*

**FIG 6-10**

Sheep casings (30 yd. approx.)
Middles (2 yd.)
Fat end (20″)
Tongue
Gullet
Bladder
Stomachs
Bung

**FIG 6-12**

Beef casings
Esophagus (weasand)
Beef round (small intestine)
Beef middle
Stomachs
Tongue
Bladder
Beef bung cap (appendix)

**FIG 6-11**

Hog casings (small intestines)
Hog bung end
Esophagus
Tongue
Bladder
Stomach
Appendix
Hog middles (chitterlings)

## Preparing natural casings

1. Rewind the casings and store covered in salt (see Fig 6-13a). Lay out the casings and remove any knots. Form into bundles of the required length. If you will be holding the casings for a few days, store them covered with salt (see Fig 6-13b).

2. Before using the casings, rinse them thoroughly in tepid water, forcing the water through the casing to flush out the salt (see Fig 6-13c). Repeat this step as often as necessary to remove all traces of salt and any other impurities.

3. Cut the casing into lengths if necessary (consult specific recipes) and tie a bubble knot in one end of the casing (see Figs 6-13d and 6-14).

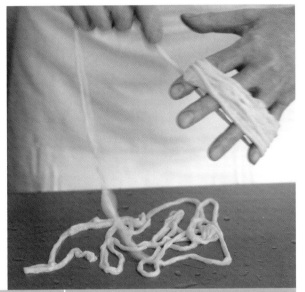

**FIG 6-13A** *Natural casings should be rewound from their original groups to make smaller bundles that are easier to handle.*

**FIG 6-13B** *If not being used immediately, rewound casings should be packed in salt and refrigerated until needed.*

**FIG 6-13C** *To prepare the casings for use, flush them through with cold water to remove all of the residual salt and impurities.*

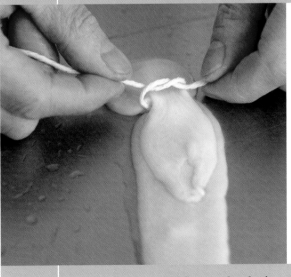

**FIG 6-13D** *Seal the cleaned casings by using butcher's twine to tie a bubble knot on one end.*

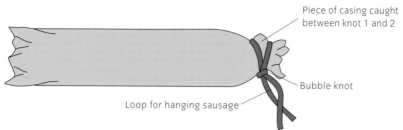

Piece of casing caught between knot 1 and 2

Bubble knot

Loop for hanging sausage

**FIG 6-14** *To properly tie a bubble knot, secure the casing at one end with a simple knot, then fold the overhanging casing back over the knot and secure it in place with another knot.*

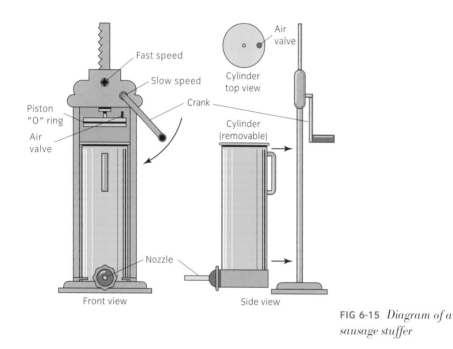

Fast speed

Slow speed

Air valve

Cylinder top view

Crank

Piston "O" ring

Air valve

Cylinder (removable)

Nozzle

Front view

Side view

**FIG 6-15** *Diagram of a sausage stuffer*

## Stuffing the casing

The following method describes the procedure for filling sausage casings using a sausage-stuffing machine.

1.  **Assemble and fill the sausage stuffer properly (see Fig 6-15).** Keep the **nozzle** of your stuffer as well as the work table lubricated with a bit of water as you work to prevent the casing from sticking and tearing. Be sure that all parts of the sausage stuffer that will come in contact with the forcemeat are clean and chilled. Fill the stuffer with the sausage meat, tamping it down well to remove any air pockets.

2.  **Press the sausage into the prepared casing.** Gather the open end of the casing over the noz- zle of the sausage stuffer. Press the sausage into the casing (if you are using a hand stuffer or piping the sausage into the casing, slide the open end over the nozzle of the hand stuffer or over the tip of the pastry bag). Support the casing as the forcemeat is expressed through the nozzle and into the casing (see Fig 6-16a).

3.  **Twist or tie the sausage into the appropriate shape.** If the sausage is to be made into links, use either of the following methods: Press the casing into links at the desired intervals and

then twist the link in alternating directions for each link, or tie the casing with twine at the desired intervals (see Fig 6-16b).

Larger sausages should be secured with a second **bubble knot,** to allow the sausage to expand as it cooks. After the sausage has been formed into links, loops, or other shapes, pierce the casing with a **teasing needle,** sausage maker's knife, or similar tool to allow the **air bubbles** to escape (see Fig 6-16c).

FIG 6-16A | *Having fitted the casing onto the end of the feeder tube, begin stuffing by slowly drawing the casing off of the feeder tube as the forcemeat is extruded out.*

FIG 6-16B | *Once the casings have been completely filled and tied off, section off the links by rolling segments and securing them with butcher's twine.*

FIG 6-16C | *Inspect the links for any air bubbles trapped inside the casing and remove them with a teasing needle.*

FIG 6-16D | *The size of a casing will vary depending on what animal it comes from; pictured clockwise from top, mortadella stuffed in beef bung, kielbasa stuffed in beef middle, smoked turkey and apple breakfast sausage stuffed in sheep casing, and chorizo stuffed in hog casing.*

# Breakfast Sausage

YIELD: *11 lb / 4.99 kg bulk; 88 links (2 oz / 57 g each)*

10 lb / 4.54 kg boneless pork butt, cubed (70% lean, 30% fat)

SEASONINGS

1¾ oz / 50 g salt

¾ oz / 21 g ground white pepper

⅓ oz / 9 g poultry seasoning

16 fl oz / 480 mL ice-cold water

42 ft / 12.80 m sheep casings, rinsed (optional)

1. Toss the pork butt with the combined seasonings. Chill well, until nearly frozen.

2. Grind through the medium plate (¼ in / 6 mm) of a meat grinder into a mixing bowl over an ice bath.

3. Mix on low speed with mixer's paddle attachment for 1 minute, gradually adding water.

4. Mix on medium speed for 15 to 20 seconds, or until the sausage mixture is sticky to the touch.

5. Make a test. Adjust seasoning and consistency before shaping into patties, cylinders, or filling casings and shaping into individual links 5 in / 13 cm long (see Fig. 6-17).

6. Pan fry, bake, grill, or broil the sausage to an internal temperature of 150°F / 66°C, or refrigerate for up to 3 days.

*Variation*   *Smoked Breakfast Sausage: Add ⅓ oz / 9 g tinted curing mix to the seasoning mixture. Stuff into sausage casings; pinch and twist into links 5 in / 13 cm long. Refrigerate uncovered overnight to dry and cold smoke for 1 hour. Prepare for service as directed above.*

**FIG 6-17**   *Portion the prepared sausage into patties for later cooking and serving.*

# Green Chile Sausage

YIELD: *11 lb 8 oz/ 5.22 kg bulk; 46 links or patties (4 oz/ 113 g each)*

10 lb / 4.54 kg boneless pork butt, cubed (70% lean, 30% fat)

SEASONINGS

3½ oz / 99 g salt

1½ oz / 43 g chili powder

5 tsp / 10 g cumin

5 tsp / 12 g sweet Spanish paprika

5 tsp / 10 g chopped oregano

5 tsp / 10 g chopped basil

1½ tsp / 3 g onion powder

6 garlic cloves, minced

5 tsp / 25 mL Tabasco sauce

12 oz / 340 g poblano chiles, roasted, seeded, peeled, and cut into ⅛-in / 3-mm dice (about 7)

3 jalapeños, seeded and minced

12 fl oz / 360 mL ice-cold water

21 ft / 6.41 m hog casings, rinsed

1. Toss the pork butt with the combined seasonings. Chill well, until nearly frozen.

2. Grind through the fine plate (⅛ in / 3 mm) of a meat grinder into a mixing bowl over an ice bath.

3. Mix on low speed for 1 minute, gradually adding poblanos, jalapeños, and ice water. Mix on medium speed for 15 to 20 seconds, or until the sausage mixture is sticky to the touch. Make a test. Adjust seasoning and consistency before filling the prepared casings and shaping into links 4 in / 10 cm long.

4. Pan fry, bake, grill, or broil the sausage to an internal temperature of 150°F / 66°C, or cover and refrigerate for up to 3 days.

*Variation*   *Smoked Green Chile Sausage: Add ½ oz / 7 g tinted curing mix (TCM) to the seasonings. Cold smoke at 80°F / 27°C for 2 hours, then cut into separate links.*

# Mexican Chorizo

YIELD: *11 lb / 4.99 kg bulk; 88 links (2 oz / 57 g each)*

10 lb / 4.54 kg boneless pork butt, cubed (70% lean, 30% fat)

SEASONINGS

3¼ oz / 92 g salt

3 oz / 85 g ground dried chiles

1 oz / 28 g Spanish paprika

1¾ oz / 50 g minced garlic, sautéed and cooled

5 tsp / 12 g ground cinnamon

5 tsp / 10 g chopped oregano

5 tsp / 10 g chopped thyme

5 tsp / 10 g ground cumin

5 tsp / 11 g black pepper

2½ tsp / 5 g ground cloves

2½ tsp / 5 g ground ginger

2½ tsp / 5 g nutmeg

2½ tsp / 5 g coriander

2½ tsp / 5 g bay leaf

6 fl oz / 180 mL red wine vinegar

42 ft / 12.80 m sheep casings, rinsed (optional)

1. Toss the pork butt with the combined seasonings. Chill well, until nearly frozen.

2. Grind through the medium plate (¼ in / 6 mm) of a meat grinder into a mixing bowl over an ice bath.

3. Mix on low speed for 1 minute, gradually adding red wine vinegar a little at a time.

4. Mix on medium speed for 15 to 20 seconds, or until the sausage mixture is sticky to the touch.

5. Make a test. Adjust seasoning and consistency before shaping into patties, or filling casings and shaping into individual links 5 in / 13 cm long.

6. Pan fry, bake, grill, or broil to an internal temperature of 150°F / 65°C, or cover and refrigerate for up to 3 days.

*Presentation idea*  Fill fried tortilla cups with the sautéed chorizo and garnish with minced onion and tomato, sour cream, and cilantro pluches.

# Venison Sausage

YIELD: *11 lb / 4.99 kg; 85 links (2 oz / 57 g each)*

5 lb / 2.25 kg boneless venison shoulder, cubed

2.5 lb / 1.13 kg boneless pork butt, cubed

2.5 lb / 1.13 kg fatback, cubed

SEASONINGS

3¾ oz / 106 g salt

1½ oz / 43 g dextrose

4½ oz / 128 g onion powder

2 tsp / 4 g ground black pepper

2½ tsp / 4 g crushed juniper berries

½ tsp / 0.75 g garlic powder

2½ tbsp / 5 g minced sage

14⅔ fl oz / 440 mL Venison Stock (page 592), cold

40 ft / 12 m sheep casings, rinsed

1. Toss the venison, pork butt, and fatback with the combined seasonings. Chill well, until nearly frozen.

2. Grind through the fine plate (⅛ in / 3 mm) of a meat grinder into a mixing bowl over an ice bath.

3. Mix on low speed for 1 minute, gradually adding cold venison stock a little at a time. Mix on medium speed for 15 to 20 seconds, or until the sausage mixture is sticky to the touch. Make a test. Adjust seasoning and consistency before filling prepared casings and shaping into links 5 in / 13 cm long.

4. Pan fry, bake, grill, or broil the sausage to an internal temperature of 150°F / 66°C, or cover and refrigerate for up to 3 days.

*Variation*   *Smoked Venison Sausage: Add ⅓ oz / 9 g tinted curing mix (TCM) to the seasoning mixture. Stuff into sausage casings and shape into links 5 in / 13 cm long. Twist them and cut into individual links. Refrigerate uncovered overnight to dry and cold smoke for 1 hour. Prepare for service as directed above.*

*Chef's note*   *Venison sausage makes excellent use of less tender cuts and trim from the shoulder or leg. These sausages can be used to add another dimension to a main course featuring prime cuts such as loin or chops.*

# Sweet Italian Sausage

YIELD: *11 lb / 4.99 kg bulk; 44 links (4 oz / 113 g each)*

| | |
|---|---|
| 10 lb / 4.54 kg boneless pork butt, cubed (70% lean, 30% fat) | 1 oz / 28 g whole fennel seeds |
| | ¼ oz / 7 g sweet Spanish paprika |
| SEASONINGS | 16 fl oz / 480 mL ice-cold water |
| 3½ oz / 99 g salt | |
| 1 oz / 28 g dextrose | 23 ft / 7.01 m hog casings, rinsed |
| 1 oz / 28 g coarse ground black pepper | |

1. Toss the pork butt with the combined seasonings. Chill well, until nearly frozen.

2. Grind through the coarse plate (⅜ in / 9 mm) of a meat grinder into a mixing bowl over an ice bath.

3. Mix on low speed for 1 minute, gradually adding water.

4. Mix on medium speed for 15 to 20 seconds, or until the sausage mixture is sticky to the touch. Make a test. Adjust seasoning and consistency before shaping.

5. Stuff into prepared casings and twist into links 5 in / 13 cm. Cut into individual links.

6. Pan fry, bake, grill, or broil the sausage to an internal temperature of 150°F / 66°C, or wrap and refrigerate for up to 3 days.

*Variations*   *Hot Italian Sausage: Replace the fennel seeds and sweet paprika with 4 oz / 113 g of the Hot Italian Spice Blend (page 591).*

*Italian Sausage with Cheese: Grind 2 lb / 907 g cubed provolone cheese, 1 lb / 454 g cubed Parmesan cheese, and 2 oz / 57 g chopped parsley along with the pork in step 2. This recipe makes approximately 50 links weighing 4½ oz /128 g each. Or cut the casings into 15-in / 38-cm lengths and coil into a spiral as shown on page 261. Secure the spiral with a skewer 6 in / 15 cm long and bake or broil before serving.*

*Low-Fat Italian Sausage: Trim all the exterior fat from the pork butt. Grind 2 lb / 907 g of well-cooked rice pilaf along with the pork in step 2. May be seasoned as desired with sweet or hot spice blends.*

*Smoked Italian Sausage: Add ⅓ ounce / 9 ml tinted curing mixture (TCM) to the cubed pork, before grinding. Cold smoke the sausages at 80°F / 27°C for 2 hours. Since the sausages are cold smoked, they must be fully cooked before service as directed above.*

# Greek Sausage (Loukanika)

YIELD: *12 lb / 5.44 kg bulk; 64 patties (3 oz / 85 g each)*

| | |
|---|---|
| 10 lb / 4.54 kg fatty lamb shoulder, cubed | 1 tbsp / 3 g chopped oregano |
| SEASONINGS | 1½ tsp / 1.50 g chopped thyme |
| 3½ oz / 99 g salt | 1 lb 4 oz / 567 g minced onion, sautéed and cooled |
| 4 oz / 113 g minced orange peel | |
| 1 tbsp / 6 g ground black pepper | 1½ tsp / 4.50 g minced garlic, sautéed and cooled |
| 1 tsp / 2 g ground bay leaves | |
| 1 tsp / 2 g ground allspice | 10 fl oz / 300 mL ice-cold water |
| 1 tsp / 2 g crushed red pepper | 2 lb 8 oz / 1.13 kg caul fat (optional) |
| 1 tsp / 2 g cayenne | 48 flat-leaf parsley pluches (optional) |
| 3 tbsp / 9 g chopped flat-leaf parsley | |

1. Toss the lamb with the combined seasonings; chill well, until nearly frozen. Progressively grind from the coarse (⅜ in / 9 mm) through the fine plate (⅛ in / 3 mm) of a meat grinder into a mixing bowl over an ice bath.

2. Mix on low speed for 1 minute, gradually adding water. Mix on medium speed for 15 to 20 seconds, or until the sausage mixture is sticky to the touch. Make a test. Adjust seasoning and consistency before shaping.

3. Portion sausage meat into patties weighing approximately 3 oz / 85 g. If desired, wrap each patty in a piece of caul fat, placing pluches of parsley below the caul fat and folding edges over sausage.

4. Pan fry, bake, grill, or broil the sausage to an internal temperature of 150°F / 65°C, or wrap and refrigerate for up to 3 days.

*Chef's note*  *Traditionally made with lamb and scented with orange peel, this makes a wonderful grilled or roasted sausage. Pork can be substituted for the lamb, if desired.*

# German Bratwurst

YIELD: *11 lb / 4.99 kg bulk; 44 links (4 oz / 113 g each)*

10 lb / 4.54 kg boneless pork butt, cubed
(70% lean, 30% fat)

SEASONINGS

3 oz / 85 g salt

½ oz / 14 g rubbed sage

¾ oz / 21 g ground white pepper

½ tsp / 1 g ground celery seed

½ tsp / 1 g ground mace

16 fl oz / 480 mL ice-cold water

22 ft / 6.71 m hog casings, rinsed and tied at
one end

1. Toss the pork with the combined seasonings. Chill well, until nearly frozen.

2. Grind the pork through the fine plate (⅛ in / 3 mm) of a meat grinder into a chilled mixing bowl.

3. Mix on low speed for 1 minute, gradually adding water. Mix on medium speed for 15 to 20 seconds, or until the sausage mixture is sticky to the touch. Make a test. Adjust seasoning and consistency before shaping.

4. Stuff into prepared casings and twist into links 5 in / 13 cm long.

5. Poach the sausages in simmering water (165°F / 74°C) to an internal temperature of 150°F / 66°C (15 to 18 minutes), then shock in an ice-water bath to an internal temperature of 60°F / 16°C.

6. Sauté, grill, broil, or bake the sausage just until hot, or wrap and refrigerate for up to 7 days.

*Chef's note*   *Smaller bratwurst may be made using sheep casings and twisting the sausages into links 4 in / 10 cm long.*

*Variation*   *Smoked Bratwurst: Add ½ oz / 14 g tinted curing mix (TCM) to the seasonings. Do not separate the sausages into links until after cold smoking at 80°F / 27°C for 2 hours. Cook the sausage as directed above before serving.*

# Merguez

YIELD: *10 lb / 4.54 kg bulk; 27 links (6 oz / 170 g each)*

7 lb / 3.18 kg lean lamb trim, cubed

SEASONINGS

1½ cups / 360 mL red wine

2 tsp / 5½ g tinted curing mix (TCM)

3½ oz / 99 g salt

2 tbsp / 24 g sugar

2 lb / 907 g beef fat from the plate, cubed

1 lb / 454 g red peppers, roasted, skinned and seeded

1 tbsp / 4.50 g crushed chili peppers

2 oz / 57 g Harissa (page 533)

1½ tsp / 3 g Quatre Épices (page 588)

1½ oz / 42 g minced garlic

38 ft / 11.58 m sheep casings, rinsed

1. Combine lamb trim, red wine, TCM, salt, and sugar and marinate for at least 1 hour.

2. Add remaining ingredients except for the sheep casings and mix thoroughly. Chill well, until nearly frozen.

3. Grind through a medium (¼ in / 6 mm) plate.

4. Mix on low speed for 1 minute and then on medium speed for 15 to 20 seconds, or until the mixture is sticky.

5. Make a test. Adjust seasoning and consistency before shaping.

6. Stuff into prepared sheep casings, and twist into links 15 in / 38 cm long. Cut into individual links. Make a spiral with each link and secure with a skewer 6 in / 15 cm long.

7. Pan fry, bake, grill, or broil the sausage to an internal temperature of 150°F / 66°C, or wrap and refrigerate for up to 7 days.

# Szechwan-Style Sausage

YIELD: *11 lb / 4.99 kg bulk; 44 links (4 oz / 113 g each)*

15⅛ lb / 6.86 kg boneless pork butt, cubed (70% lean, 30% fat)

SEASONINGS

2¾ oz / 78 g salt

2¾ tbsp / 13 g Prague Powder II

5½ oz / 156 g sugar

2¾ oz / 78 g chili powder

1½ tsp / 3 g ground white pepper

½ oz / 14 g Chinese Five-Spice Powder (page 587)

4½ tsp / 9 g Szechwan peppercorn powder

5½ fl oz / 165 mL soy sauce

3½ fl oz / 105 mL white liquor or vodka

32 ft / 9.50 m hog casings, rinsed and tied at one end

1. Toss the pork butt with the combined seasonings, soy sauce, and liquor. Chill well, until nearly frozen.

2. Grind through the medium plate (¼ in / 6 mm) of a meat grinder into a mixing bowl over an ice bath.

3. Mix on low speed for 1 minute, then mix on medium speed for 15 to 20 seconds, or until the sausage mixture is sticky to the touch. Make a test. Adjust seasoning and consistency before shaping.

4. Stuff into prepared casings and twist into links 8 in / 20 cm long.

5. Dry for 3 days.

6. Poke small holes in the casing. Steam to an internal temperature of 150°F / 66°C, about 15 minutes. Sauté, grill, broil, or bake sausage just until hot, or wrap and refrigerate up to 7 days.

# Kassler Liverwurst

**YIELD:** *16 sausages (1 lb / 454 g each)*

5 lb / 2.27 kg boneless pork butt, cubed

4 lb / 1.81 kg pork liver

3 lb / 1.36 kg jowl fat, cubed, or skinless pork bellies

SEASONINGS

4 oz / 113 g salt

½ tsp / 2.5 g tinted curing mix (TCM)

2 tsp / 5½ g ground white pepper

2 tsp / 4 g Pâté Spice (page 590)

4 oz / 113 g onions, minced

12 oz / 340 g potato starch

8 fl oz / 240 mL dry white wine

12 whole eggs

1 lb / 454 g small-dice boiled ham

4½ oz / 128 g pistachio nuts, blanched, peeled, and halved

16 pieces beef middle casings, rinsed, cut in 12-in / 30-cm lengths and tied at one end

1. Combine pork, liver, and jowl fat with seasonings.

2. Progressively grind from the coarse (⅜ in / 9 mm) through the fine plate (⅛ in / 3 mm) of a meat grinder into a mixing bowl over an ice bath.

3. Blend the meat mixture with the onions and potato starch in a mixer on low speed, about 1 minute.

4. Add the wine and eggs and mix on low speed for 1 minute, or until relatively homogenous. Mix on medium speed for 15 to 20 seconds, or until the sausage mixture is sticky to the touch. Make a test. Adjust seasoning and consistency before garnishing and shaping.

5. Fold the ham and pistachio nuts into the forcemeat by hand over an ice bath.

6. Stuff into prepared casings and tie ends with a bubble knot.

7. Poach at 165°F / 74°C to an internal temperature of 155°F / 68°C, then shock and blot dry.

8. Cold smoke at 80°F / 27°C until desired color, for 2 to 4 hours.

9. Poach, sauté, grill, or bake the sausage just until hot, or wrap and refrigerate up to 1 week.

# Smoked Pheasant Sausage

YIELD: *11 lb / 4.99 kg bulk; 85 links (2 oz / 57 g each)*

7 lb / 3.18 kg pheasants

3 lb / 1.36 kg fatback, cubed

SEASONINGS

3 oz / 85 g salt

1 tbsp / 8.25 g tinted curing mix (TCM)

1 oz / 28 g sugar

½ oz / 14 g ground white pepper

½ oz / 14 g poultry seasoning

1 tbsp / 6 g onion powder

12 fl oz / 360 mL ice-cold water or stock

44 ft / 13.41 m sheep casings, rinsed

1. Remove the meat from the breast and legs and cut into cubes. (You should have 7 lb / 3.18 kg of meat.) Toss pheasant with the fatback and the combined seasonings. Chill well, until nearly frozen.

2. Grind through the medium plate (¼ in / 6 mm) of a meat grinder into a mixing bowl over an ice bath.

3. Mix on low speed for 1 minute, gradually adding water. Mix on medium speed for 15 to 20 seconds, or until the mixture is sticky to the touch. Make a test. Adjust seasoning and consistency before shaping.

4. Stuff into prepared casings and twist into links 5 in / 13 cm long.

5. Hang uncovered overnight in refrigerator to air-dry and form a pellicle.

6. Cold smoke at 80°F / 26°C for 1 to 2 hours.

7. Poach, sauté, bake, or grill to an internal temperature of 165°F / 73°C, or wrap and refrigerate for up to 3 days.

*Variation*   *Pheasant Sausage with Wild Rice: Reduce the amount of fatback to 2 lb 8 oz / 1.13 kg. Add 8 oz / 227 g cooked wild rice to the meat after it has been ground, before the second mixing in step 3.*

# Spicy Lamb Sausage

YIELD: *10 lb/4.54 kg bulk*

7 lb / 3.18 kg lamb shoulder, cut into 1-in / 25-mm cubes

2 lb / 907 g jowl fat cut into 1-in / 25-mm cubes

1 lb / 454 g pancetta, cut into ½-in / 1-cm cubes

1 oz / 28 g minced garlic

4 oz / 113 g minced shallots

2 oz / 57 g salt

1 tsp / 2 g ground black pepper

1 tsp / 2 g crushed red pepper flakes

1½ tsp / 3 g pimenton

2 tsp / 4 g ground coriander

1 tsp / 2.6 g tinted curing mix (TCM)

1 oz / 28 g honey

2 tbsp / 6 g coarsely minced thyme leaves

¼ tbsp / 12 g Italian chopped parsley

2 tsp / 3 g coarsely chopped rosemary

6 fl oz / 180 mL chicken stock, ice cold

24 ft / 7.32 m hog casings, flushed and rinsed

1. Combine the lamb meat, jowl fat, and pancetta; mix with the garlic, shallots, salt, peppers, spices, TCM, honey, and herbs. Chill well, until nearly frozen.

2. Progressively grind from the coarse (⅜ in / 9 mm) through the medium plate (¼ in / 6 mm) of a meat grinder into a mixing bowl over an ice bath.

3. Mix the forcemeat with a paddle attachment on low speed for one minute, gradually adding the stock. Mix on medium speed for 15 to 20 seconds until the mixture is sticky to the touch.

4. Prepare a poach test and adjust seasonings as necessary. Stuff into prepared casings and twist into links 5 in / 13 cm long.

5. Refrigerate overnight uncovered on a wire rack on a sheet pan to air-dry and form a pellicle.

6. Cold smoke for 2 hours at 80°F / 27°C.

7. The sausage may be poached, grilled, or sautéed to an internal temperature of 150°F / 66°C.

# Cajun Boudin

*YIELD: 8 to 10 lb / 3.63 to 4.54 kg*

| CAJUN SPICE MIX | BOUDIN |
|---|---|
| 5 oz / 142 g kosher salt | 1 pork butt, 6 to 6½ lb / 2.72 to 2.95 kg |
| 2 tsp / 4 g cayenne | 24 fl oz / 720 mL medium-grain sushi rice |
| 2 tsp / 4 g black pepper | 32 fl oz / 960 mL water |
| 1 tsp / 2 g white pepper | 8 green onions, coarsely chopped |
| 2 oz / 57 g paprika | 1 oz / 28 g parsley, coarsely chopped |
| 1 tbsp / 6 g onion powder | |
| 1 tbsp / 6 g garlic powder | |

1. Make the spice mix and reserve.

2. Cut the pork butt into three pieces and cover with cold water in a stock pot. Add ¼ cup / 35 g spice mix and simmer until the meat is fork tender, about 1½ hours. Remove the meat and cool to room temperature. Strain the broth, cool to room temperature, and reserve.

3. Meanwhile, rinse the rice in a fine mesh strainer under cold water until the water runs clear. Place the rice in a thick-bottomed pan or rice cooker and add the 32 fl oz / 960 mL water. Bring to a simmer over low heat, cover, and place in a 350°F / 177°C oven for 15 to 20 minutes or until the rice is cooked. Hold at room temperature until ready to use.

4. Remove some (not all) of the excess fat from the pork butt. Grind the meat through a ¼-in / 6-mm die. Place in a large mixing bowl. Add the cooked rice to the meat with 2 to 3 tbsp / 18 to 27 g Cajun spice mix, green onions, and parsley. Mix well and add 16 to 24 fl oz / 480 to 720 mL reserved broth. Check seasonings.

5. Fill sheep casings loosely and chill. Alternatively, roll into balls 1 in / 3 cm in diameter and chill.

6. The sausage links can be steamed to 145°F / 63°C to be reheated. The boudin balls should be deep fried in oil heated to 350°F / 177°C until golden brown. Drain on absorbent paper towels.

# Fresh Kielbasa

YIELD: *10 lb / 4.54 kg*

10 lb / 4.53 kg pork butt, 70/30, cut into ½- to 1-in / 1- to 3-cm cubes

3 tbsp / 30 g salt

2½ tsp / 6 g freshly ground black pepper

1 tsp / 2 g garlic powder

½ tbsp / 3 g freshly ground allspice

½ tbsp / 6 g celery salt

¾ oz / 21 g mustard seed, crushed

1 lb / 454 g ice

7.5 ft / 2.29 m beef round casing

1. Toss the pork with the combined seasonings. Chill well, until nearly frozen.

2. Grind the pork through a medium plate (¼ in / 6 mm). Add the ice and mix until sticky.

3. Cut the beef round casings into 16-in / 41-cm lengths and tie a bubble knot at the end of each one. Stuff the casings and prick all of the air bubbles before tying a bubble knot in each sausage to seal it.

4. The sausage may be poached, grilled, or sautéed to an internal temperature of 150° F / 66° C.

# Andouille Sausage

YIELD: *11 lb / 4.99 kg bulk; 25 links (8 oz / 227 g each)*

8.59 lb / 3.89 kg boneless pork butt, cubed (70% lean, 30% fat)

SEASONINGS

3 oz / 85 g salt

⅓ oz / 9 g tinted curing mix (TCM)

⅔ oz / 19 g dextrose

3 tbsp 1½ tsp / 17.50 g cayenne

1½ tsp / 3 g ground mace

1½ tsp / 3 g ground allspice

1½ tsp / 3 g ground marjoram

1 tsp / 2 g ground thyme

⅓ tsp / 0.66 g ground cloves

1 lb 11½ oz / 780 g coarsely chopped onions

1¾ oz / 50 g minced garlic

5½ oz / 156 g nonfat dry milk

44 ft / 13.42 m sheep casings, rinsed

1. Toss the pork butt with the combined seasonings, onion, and garlic. Chill well, until nearly frozen.

2. Progressively grind from the coarse (⅜ in / 9 mm) through the fine plate (⅛ in / 3 mm) of a meat grinder into a mixing bowl over an ice bath.

3. Add dry milk.

4. Mix on low speed for 1 minute or until the sausage mixture is sticky to the touch. Make a test. Adjust seasoning and consistency before shaping.

5. Stuff into prepared casings and tie into links 10 in / 25 cm long. Do not cut. Hang overnight in refrigerator to air-dry and form a pellicle.

6. Cold smoke at 80°F / 26°C for 12 to 14 hours. Allow the sausages to dry in a cool, dry area or curing room for an additional 12 to 24 hours.

7. Poach, sauté, grill, or bake the sausage just to an internal temperature of 155°F / 68°C, or wrap and refrigerate for up to 2 weeks.

# Summer Sausage

YIELD: *11 lb / 4.99 kg bulk; 10 links (1 lb 2 oz / 511 g each)*

| | |
|---|---|
| 5 lb 8 oz / 2.50 kg boneless beef shoulder clod, cubed (70% lean, 30% fat) | 2 oz / 57 g dextrose |
| | 4 tsp / 9 g ground black pepper |
| 4 lb 12 oz / 2.14 kg boneless pork butt, cubed (70% lean, 30% fat) | 4½ tsp / 9 g ground coriander |
| | 5 tsp / 9 g ground mustard |
| SEASONINGS | 1½ tsp / 3 g garlic powder |
| 3 oz / 85 g salt | |
| 4¾ oz / 135 g Fermento | 10 pieces beef middle casings, rinsed, cut in |
| 2¾ tsp / 7.3 g tinted curing mix (TCM) | 10-in / 25-cm lengths and tied at one end |

1. Grind the beef through the medium plate (¼ in / 6 mm) of a meat grinder. Chill if necessary.

2. Toss the beef and pork with the combined seasonings and mix thoroughly. Transfer to a container, cover with plastic wrap, and refrigerate at 38°F / 3°C to 40°F / 4°C for 2 to 3 days to cure.

3. Progressively grind meat from the coarse (⅜ in / 9 mm) through the fine plate (⅛ in / 3 mm) of a meat grinder into a mixing bowl over an ice bath. Mix on low speed for 1 minute. Mix on medium speed for 15 to 20 seconds, or until the sausage mixture is sticky to the touch. Make a test. Adjust seasoning and consistency before shaping.

4. Stuff into casings, tying with bubble knot. Refrigerate uncovered overnight to air-dry and form a pellicle.

5. Cold smoke at 80°F / 26°C for 12 to 14 hours. Hot smoke at 160°F / 71°C to an internal temperature of 155°F / 68°C. Dry 1 to 2 hours in a smoker.

6. Slice and serve the sausage immediately, or wrap and refrigerate for up to 2 weeks.

*Presentation idea* *Summer sausage can be sliced and used to top stuffing or served inside potatoes.*

# Landjäger

YIELD: *11 lb / 4.99 kg bulk; 37 links (4¾ oz / 135 g each)*

10¾ lb / 4.88 kg beef

7 lb 3 oz / 3.26 kg certified pork butt, trimmed (see Chef's Notes)

SEASONINGS

6½ oz / 184 g salt

4¼ oz / 120 g Fermento

.72 oz / 20 g Prague Powder II

1 tbsp / 6 g ground caraway seeds

1½ oz / 43 g dextrose

1 oz / 28 g ground black pepper

2 tsp / 10 mL garlic powder

7 fl oz / 210 mL ice-cold water

57 ft 6 in / 17.5 m hog casings, rinsed and tied at one end

1. Toss the beef and certified pork with the combined seasonings. Chill well, until nearly frozen.

2. Grind through the fine plate (⅛ in / 3 mm) of a meat grinder into a mixing bowl over an ice bath.

3. Mix on low speed for 1 minute, gradually adding water, until the sausage mixture is sticky to the touch. Make a test. Adjust seasoning and consistency before shaping.

4. Stuff into prepared hog casings and twist into links 6 in / 15 cm long. Cut at every other twist to separate into pairs of links.

5. Press in landjäger press (see Chef's Notes).

6. Place on a plastic sheet pan, cover with another plastic sheet pan, press with 2 cutting boards, and refrigerate for 2 to 4 days.

7. Cold smoke at 80°F / 26°C for 12 to 24 hours, then dry until desired firmness, 3 to 4 days.

*Chef's notes* This is a dry-type sausage and is not cooked, so the pork used must be certified to prevent trichinosis. Certified pork may be purchased, or you can certify it yourself by freezing the pork at the appropriate temperature for a prescribed period (see page 236).

A landjäger press is used to shape the sausage. The press is typically made of a hard wood and is approximately 18 to 20 in / 45 to 50 cm long. There is a rectangular well in the center of the mold, about 1 in / 3 cm wide and ¾ in / 2 cm deep. Once the sausage is stuffed into the casing, the links are laid into the mold and then covered with plastic wrap (see Fig 6-22). Weight the sausages by setting 2 wooden cutting boards on top of the press. This creates the typical rectangular shape of landjäger sausages.

FIG 6-22  *After shaping the sausages in a landjäger mold, line them up on a sheet tray, packing them tightly next to each other to preserve their shape.*

# Smoked Turkey and Dried Apple Sausage

YIELD: *13 lb / 5.90 kg*

10 lb / 4.54 kg whole turkey, trimmed and cut into 1-in / 3-cm cubes

3 lb / 1.36 kg jowl fat, cut into 1-in / 3-cm cubes

4 oz / 113 g salt

1 tbsp / 8 g tinted curing mix (TCM)

½ oz / 14 g sugar

½ oz / 14 g ground black pepper

2 oz / 57 g coarsely chopped thyme

2 oz / 57 g coarsely chopped sage

3 tbsp / 12 g Bell's poultry seasoning

2 oz / 60 g minced garlic

6 oz / 170 g minced shallots

2 fl oz / 60 mL vegetable oil

8 oz / 227 g dried apples, chopped

24 fl oz / 720 mL chicken stock

45 ft / 13.72 m sheep casings

1. Combine the turkey meat and fatback; mix with the salt, TCM, sugar, pepper, thyme, sage, and poultry seasoning.

2. Sweat the garlic and shallots in a small sauté pan over low heat in oil until tender, about 4 to 5 minutes. Drain off excess fat and cool completely in the refrigerator. When cool, add to the meat. Chill well, until almost frozen.

3. Grind the meat through a medium die (¼ in / 6 mm) of a meat grinder and reserve. Remove half of the ground meat and put through a fine die of a meat grinder (⅛ in / 3 mm) or pulse in a robot coupe until desired consistency is reached. Combine both meats together and place in a mixing bowl over ice.

4. Simmer the apples in the stock in a small saucepot over low heat until the apples become tender, about 8 to 10 minutes. Drain well, reserving the stock; dry, and cool. Cut the cooled apples into a rough small dice and add to the forcemeat. Chill 12 fl oz / 360 mL of the stock until cold.

5. Mix the forcemeat with a paddle attachment on low speed for 1 minute, gradually adding the chilled reserved stock. Mix on medium speed for 15 to 20 seconds until the mixture is sticky to the touch.

6. Prepare a poach test and adjust the seasoning as necessary.

7. Stuff into prepared casings and twist into links 4 in / 10 cm long.

8. Refrigerate overnight uncovered on a wire-racked sheet pan to air-dry and form a pellicle.

9. Cold smoke for 2 hours at 80°F / 27°C.

10. Poach, grill, or sauté the sausage to an internal temperature of 165°F / 74°C.

# Smoked Duck Sausage

YIELD: *5 lb / 2.26 kg*

3 lb 8 oz / 1.58 kg duck meat, cut into 1-in / 3-cm cubes, chilled

1 lb 8 oz / 680 g jowl fat, cut into 1-in / 3-cm cubes, chilled

1½ oz / 43 g salt

¼ tsp / 0.50 g ground black pepper

½ tsp / 1.3 g tinted curing mix (TCM)

½ oz / 14 g honey

1½ oz / 43 g thyme, finely chopped

2 tsp / 3 g coarsely chopped rosemary

4 tsp / 3 g coarsely chopped sage

2 oz / 57 g minced garlic

4 oz / 113 g minced shallots

2 oz / 57 g rendered duck fat

12 ft / 3.66 m hog casings, flushed and rinsed

1. Combine the duck meat and jowl fat; mix with the salt, pepper, TCM, honey, and herbs.

2. Sweat the garlic and shallots in a small sauté pan over low heat in the duck fat until tender, about 2 to 3 minutes. Drain off excess fat and refrigerate until completely cooled.

3. When cool, add garlic and shallots to the meat. Chill well, until nearly frozen.

4. Grind the meat through a medium plate (¼ in / 6 mm) of a meat grinder and place in a mixing bowl over ice.

5. Add the chicken stock and mix the forcemeat with a paddle attachment on low speed for 15 to 20 seconds until the mixture is sticky to the touch.

6. Prepare poach test and adjust seasonings as necessary.

7. Stuff into prepared casings and twist into links 5 in / 13 cm long.

8. Refrigerate overnight uncovered on a wire-racked sheet pan to air-dry and form a pellicle.

9. Cold smoke at 80°F / 27°C for 2 hours.

10. The sausage may be poached, grilled, or sautéed to an internal temperature of 165°F / 74°C.

# Cajun Andouille Sausage

YIELD: *12 lb / 5.44 kg*

| CAJUN SPICE MIX | SAUSAGE |
|---|---|
| ½ cup / 24 g kosher salt | 10 lb / 4.54 kg pork butt |
| 1 tsp / 2 g cayenne | ¼ oz / 7 g tinted curing mix (TCM) |
| 1 tsp / 2 g ground black pepper | ½ oz / 14 g sugar |
| ½ tsp / 1 g ground white pepper | 3 oz / 85 g nonfat dry milk |
| ¼ cup / 28 g paprika | 4 oz / 113 g Cajun spice mix |
| 1½ tsp / 3 g onion powder | ½ tsp / 1 g cayenne |
| 1½ tsp / 3 g garlic powder | 16 fl oz / 480 mL water |
| | |
| | 16 ft / 4.88 m hog casings, rinsed |

1. Prepare the Cajun spice mix by combining all of the spices. Reserve until needed.

2. Trim and cut the pork butt into 1-in / 3-cm cubes. Combine with the TCM, sugar, milk powder, Cajun spice mix, cayenne, and water. Mix well. Chill well, until nearly frozen.

3. Grind the meat through a medium die (¼ in / 6 mm) and then through a fine die (⅛ in / 3 mm). Mix the meat together until it is tacky.

4. Make a test of the forcemeat to assess flavor and texture. After the poaching test, the sausage should be homogenous and some moisture should come out when it is squeezed. Adjust seasoning as necessary.

5. Stuff into the prepared casings and twist into links 5 to 6 in / 13 to 15 cm long.

6. Hang the sausages overnight in a place with low humidity and good airflow to air-dry and form a pellicle.

7. Cold smoke at 40 to 70°F / 4 to 21°C for 4 to 5 hours and then refrigerate until needed. Cook as desired, or wrap and refrigerate for 1 week or freeze for up to 6 months.

# Colombian Chorizo

YIELD: *10 lb 8 oz / 4.76 kg*

5 lb / 2.27 kg pork butt, cut into 1-in / 3-cm cubes

2 lb / 907 g beef shoulder or plate, trimmed and cut into 1-in / 3-cm cubes with no visible fat

2 lb / 907 g fatback, skinned

3¼ oz / 92 g salt

5½ oz / 156 g nonfat dry milk

½ oz / 14 g dextrose

2 tsp / 5.3 g tinted curing mix (TCM)

¼ oz / 7 g ground white pepper

¾ oz / 21 g ground cumin

1 oz / 28 g Spanish paprika

6 oz / 170 g green onions, cut into ¼-in / 6-mm dice

5 fl oz / 150 mL ice-cold water

21 ft / 3.2 m hog casings

1. Chill the equipment and mix the pork and the beef with all of the seasonings, except for the scallions. Chill well, until nearly frozen.

2. Grind meat through a coarse die (⅜ in / 9 mm).

3. Freeze the fatback. Grind fatback through a medium die (¼ in / 6 mm).

4. Place ground meats and fat back in the mixer, and add green onions and water. Mix on low speed for 1 minute and on second speed for 10 to 20 seconds, or until tacky.

5. Prepare taste test; adjust seasoning if needed.

6. Stuff into prepared hog casings, measure, and pinch into 5-in / 13-cm lengths. Tie with thin string. Do not cut.

7. Hang the sausages in the refrigerator overnight, uncovered, to air-dry and form a pellicle.

8. Cold smoke for 12 to 14 hours, or until the sausages are smoked to taste. Dry an additional 12 hours if necessary. Dry the sausage for an additional 1 to 3 days, if desired, to concentrate the flavor by further removing moisture.

*Chef's note*   This can be made as fresh sausage if TCM is omitted.

# Frankfurter

YIELD: *11 lb / 4.99 kg bulk; 70 links (2½ oz / 71 g each)*

4 lb 6 oz / 1.98 kg lean boneless beef shoulder clod, cubed

3 lb 8 oz / 1.59 kg jowl fat, cubed, partially frozen

2 lb 10 oz / 1.20 kg crushed ice

CURE MIX

2¾ oz / 78 g salt

1¾ tsp / 4.8 g tinted curing mix (TCM)

1 oz / 28 g dextrose

SPICE BLEND

½ oz / 14 g onion powder

¼ oz / 7 g ground white pepper

¼ oz / 7 g ground coriander

¼ oz / 7 g ground nutmeg

½ tsp / 1 g garlic powder

6¾ oz / 189 g nonfat dry milk

44 ft / 13.42 m sheep casings, rinsed

1. Toss the beef with the cure mix; chill well, until nearly frozen. Progressively grind from the coarse plate (⅜ in / 9 mm) through the fine plate (⅛ in / 3 mm) of a meat grinder into a mixing bowl over an ice bath. Place in freezer until semi-frozen (just beginning to freeze but not solid).

2. Freeze the jowl fat. Progressively grind from the coarse plate (⅜ in / 9 mm) through the fine plate (⅛ in / 3 mm) of a meat grinder into a mixing bowl over an ice bath; reserve.

3. Transfer the ground beef to a chilled chopper bowl. Add the ice and the spice blend on top of the ground beef. Process the ingredients in a high-powered processor or chopper until the mixture drops to a temperature of 30°F / –1°C. Continue running the machine until the mixture's temperature rises to 40°F / 4 °C.

4. Add the jowl fat and process until the mixture reaches 45°F / 7°C. Add the nonfat dry milk and continue processing until the mixture reaches 58°F / 14 °C. Make a test. Adjust seasoning and consistency before shaping.

5. Stuff into prepared casings, twist, and tie into 6-in / 15-cm links. Hang uncovered overnight in refrigerator to air-dry and form a pellicle.

6. Hot smoke at 160°F / 71°C until desired color is achieved, approximately 45 minutes. Poach in water at 165°F / 73°C to an internal temperature of 155°F / 68°C, about 10 to 20 minutes, then shock in ice water to an internal temperature of 60°F / 16°C. Blot dry.

7. Sauté, grill, broil, or bake the sausage just until hot, or wrap and refrigerate for up to 7 days.

*Variation*   *Reduced-Fat Frankfurter: For lower-fat frankfurters, increase the amount of meat by 2 lb / 907 g and decrease the amount of fat by 2 lb / 907 g. If desired, other combinations of pork, veal, or beef may be used.*

# Bologna

YIELD: *11 lb / 4.99 kg bulk; 14 links*

4 lb 6 oz / 1.98 kg boneless beef shoulder clod, cubed

3 lb 8 oz / 1.59 kg jowl fat, cubed, partially frozen

2 lb 10 oz / 1.20 kg crushed ice

CURE MIX

2¾ oz / 78 g salt

1¾ tsp / 4.8 g tinted curing mix (TCM)

1 oz / 28 g dextrose

SPICE BLEND

1⅓ oz / 38 g onion powder

½ oz / 14 g ground white pepper

1¾ tsp / 3.5 g ground caraway seeds

1¾ tsp / 3.5 g ground nutmeg

6¾ oz / 191 g nonfat dry milk

1 piece beef bung, or 8 pieces beef middle casings, cut into 6-in / 15-cm lengths, tied at one end with a bubble knot

1. Toss the beef with the cure mix. Chill well, until nearly frozen. Progressively grind from the coarse plate (⅜ in / 9 mm) through the fine plate (⅛ in / 3 mm) of a meat grinder into a mixing bowl over an ice bath. Place in freezer until semi-frozen (just beginning to freeze but not solid).

2. Progressively grind the jowl fat from the coarse plate (⅜ in / 9 mm) through the fine plate (⅛ in / 3 mm) of a meat grinder into a mixing bowl over an ice bath; reserve. Transfer the ground beef to a chilled high-speed chopper or processor bowl. Add the ice and the spice blend on top of the ground beef. Process the ingredients until the mixture drops to a temperature of 30°F / –1°C. Continue running the machine until the mixture's temperature rises to 40°F / 4°C.

3. Add the jowl fat and process until the mixture reaches 45°F / 7°C. Add the nonfat dry milk and continue processing until the mixture reaches 58°F / 14°C. Make a test. Adjust seasoning and consistency before shaping.

4. Stuff into prepared casings and tie each end with a bubble knot. Hang uncovered in refrigerator overnight to air-dry and form a pellicle.

5. Hot smoke at 160°F / 71°C until desired color is achieved, approximately 1 to 2 hours. Poach in water at 165°F / 74°C to an internal temperature of 155°F / 68°C (10 to 30 minutes for beef round, 1 to 3 hours for beef bung), then shock in ice water to an internal temperature of 60°F / 16°C. Blot dry.

6. The bologna is ready to slice and serve now, or wrap and refrigerate for up to 2 weeks.

*Variation*  Ham Bologna: Add 3 lb 8 oz / 1.59 kg cured pork, cut into ¾- to 1-in / 2- to 3-cm cubes, to the mixture. This variation will produce 10 sausages of 14 in / 35 cm each using beef casing (casings should be precut into pieces 16 in / 40 cm long and tied) or 1 sausage weighing 14 lb 8 oz / 6.6 kg if using beef bung.

# Kielbasa Krakowska

YIELD: *10 lb / 4.54 kg*

10 lb / 4.54 kg fresh ham, boneless, cut into ½-in / 1-cm dice and chilled until nearly frozen

2 lb / 907 g pork butt, cut into ½- to 1-in / 1- to 3-cm dice and chilled until nearly frozen

2 lb / 907 g pork fatback, cut into ½- to 1-in / 1- to 3-cm dice and chilled until nearly frozen

16 fl oz / 480 mL ice-cold water

2¼ oz / 64 g salt

2 tsp / 2 g Insta-cure #1

2 tbsp / 12 g dextrose powder

3½ tbsp / 23 g garlic powder

1¼ tsp / 3 g ground white pepper

1 tsp / 2 g coriander

2 tbsp / 11 g ground mustard

½ tsp / 1 g marjoram, chopped coarsely

7.5 ft / 2.28 m beef middle casings

1. Grind half of the fresh ham through the coarse die of a meat grinder (⅜ in / 9 mm). Reserve the remaining ham for garnish.

2. Progressively grind the pork butt from the coarse die (⅜ in / 9 mm) through the fine plate (⅛ in / 3 mm) of a meat grinder into a mixing bowl over an ice bath.

3. Progressively grind the fatback from the coarse die (⅜ in / 9 mm) through the fine die (⅛ in / 3 mm) of a meat grinder into a mixing bowl over an ice bath.

4. Place meats and fatback in mixing bowl and add all of the remaining ingredients except for the casings.

5. Mix on low speed for 1 minute and on second speed for 10 to 20 seconds, making sure all spices are mixed evenly.

6. Stuff into the prepared casings and twist into links 24 in / 61 cm long.

7. Hang the sausages uncovered in the refrigerator overnight to air-dry and form a pellicle.

8. Hot smoke at 130°F / 54°C for about 1 hour.

9. Apply a heavy smoke and increase smoke temperature to 160 to 165°F / 71 to 74°C.

10. Keep sausages in smoker until they reach an internal temperature of 152°F / 67°C, 2 to 3 hours, depending on the smoker.

11. When sausage is cooked, place in cold water to shock to internal temperature of 60°F / 16°C.

12. Refrigerate overnight.

*Chef's note* *Krakowska is made from fresh hams. Hams are boned and the lean meat is kept separate.*

# French Garlic Sausage

YIELD: *11 lb / 4.99 kg bulk; 7 links*

5 lb 4 oz / 2.38 kg boneless pork butt, diced into ¼- to ½-in / 6-mm to 1-cm cubes

2 lb 4 oz / 1.02 kg lean beef shoulder clod, diced into ¼- to ½-in / 6-mm to 1-cm cubes

1 lb 12 oz / 794 g jowl fat, diced into ¼- to ½-in / 6-mm to 1-cm cubes and partially frozen

1 lb 5 oz / 595 g crushed ice

CURE MIX

1½ oz / 43 g salt

⅓ oz / 10 g tinted curing mix (TCM)

1 oz / 28 g dextrose

SPICE BLEND

2 tbsp / 16 g chopped garlic

½ oz / 14 g ground white pepper

¼ oz / 7 g dry mustard

3½ oz / 99 g nonfat dry milk

8.36 ft / 2.55 m beef middle casings, rinsed, cut into 14-in / 36-cm lengths and tied at one end

1. Toss the pork with half the cure mix. Chill well and reserve for garnish.

2. Toss the beef with the remaining cure mix and the spice blend. Chill well until nearly frozen. Progressively grind from the coarse plate (⅜ in / 9 mm) through the fine plate (⅛ in / 3 mm) of a meat grinder into a mixing bowl over an ice bath. Place in freezer until semi-frozen (just beginning to freeze but not solid).

3. Progressively grind the jowl fat from the coarse plate (⅜ in / 9 mm) through the fine plate (⅛ in / 3 mm) of a meat grinder into a mixing bowl over an ice bath; reserve.

4. Transfer the ground beef to a chilled high-speed chopper or processor bowl. Add the ice to the ground beef. Process the ingredients until the mixture drops to a temperature of 30°F / –1°C. Continue running the machine until the mixture's temperature rises to 40°F / 4°C.

5. Add jowl fat and process until the mixture reaches 45°F / 7°C. Add the nonfat dry milk and continue processing until the mixture reaches 58°F / 14°C. Make a test. Adjust seasoning and consistency before shaping.

6. Fold the pork garnish into the sausage in a mixer or by hand over an ice bath. Stuff into prepared casings and tie each end with a bubble knot. Hang uncovered in the refrigerator overnight to air-dry and form a pellicle.

7. Poach in water at 165°F / 74°C to an internal temperature of 150°F / 66°C, then shock in ice water to an internal temperature of 60°F / 16°C. Blot dry. Slice and serve the sausage immediately, or wrap and refrigerate for up to 7 days.

*Chef's note* *For more smoke color, cold smoke at 80°F / 27°C for up to 12 hours, then finish cooking by poaching, as described in step 7 above.*

*Variation* *Duck Sausage: Substitute duck meat for all meats; instead of beef casings, substitute hog casings, cut into 5-in / 13-cm lengths; follow the same method as above.*

# Fine Swiss Bratwurst

YIELD: *11 lb / 4.99 kg bulk; 88 links (2 oz / 57 g each)*

3 lb 5½ oz / 1.52 kg boneless veal top or bottom round, cut into cubes and partially frozen

3 lb 5½ oz / 1.52 kg jowl fat, cut into cubes and partially frozen

3 lb / 1.36 kg crushed ice

CURE MIX

3¼ oz / 92 g salt

¾ oz / 21 g dextrose

SPICE BLEND

3½ tsp / 9 g ground white pepper

5 tsp / 9 g dry mustard

1½ tsp / 3 g ground mace

1 tsp / 2 g ground ginger

6¾ oz / 191 g nonfat dry milk

44 ft / 13.42 m sheep casings, rinsed

1. Toss the veal with the cure mix. Chill well, until nearly frozen. Progressively grind from the coarse plate (⅜ in / 9 mm) through the fine plate (⅛ in / 3 mm) of a meat grinder into a mixing bowl over an ice bath. Progressively grind the jowl fat from the coarse plate (⅜ in / 9 mm) through the fine plate (⅛ in / 3 mm) of a meat grinder into a mixing bowl over an ice bath; reserve separately. Place in freezer until semi-frozen (just beginning to freeze but not solid).

2. Transfer the ground veal to a chilled high-speed chopper or processor bowl. Add the crushed ice and the spice blend on top of the ground veal.

3. Run the machine and process the ingredients until the mixture reaches a temperature of 30°F / −1°C. Continue running the machine until the mixture's temperature rises to 40°F / 4°C.

4. Add the fat and process until the mixture reaches 45°F / 7°C. Add the nonfat dry milk and continue processing until the mixture reaches 58°F / 14°C. Make a test. Adjust seasoning and consistency before shaping.

5. Stuff into prepared casings, twist, and tie into links 5 in / 13 cm long.

6. Poach in water at 165°F / 73°C to an internal temperature of 150°F / 66°C, about 10 to 20 minutes, then shock in ice water to an internal temperature of 60°F / 16°C. Blot dry.

7. Sauté, grill, broil, or bake the sausage just until hot, or wrap and refrigerate for up to 7 days.

*Variations* Chipolata: *Prepare as directed above, stuffing the sausage into sheep casings and shaping into links 3 in / 8 cm long.*

Smoked Bratwurst: *Add ⅓ oz / 10.27 g tinted curing mix (TCM) to the cure mix. Stuff into casings and shape into links 5 in / 13 cm long. Twist and cut into individual links. Refrigerate uncovered overnight and cold smoke for 1 hour.*

Weisswurst: *Omit the ginger and mustard. Add finely chopped lemon zest as needed.*

# Mortadella

YIELD: *11 lb / 4.99 kg bulk; 11 links (1 lb / 454 g each)*

3 lb 14 oz / 1.75 kg boneless pork butt, cut into cubes and partially frozen

3 lb 2 oz / 1.41 kg jowl fat, cut into cubes and partially frozen

2 lb 5 oz / 1.05 kg crushed ice

CURE MIX

2½ oz / 71 g salt

½ oz / 14 g dextrose

1½ oz / 43 g tinted curing mix (TCM)

2¾ fl oz / 82.5 mL dry white wine

SPICE BLEND

4 tsp / 11 g ground white pepper

1 tbsp / 5.50 g ground mace

2¼ tsp / 5.50 g sweet Spanish paprika

2½ tsp / 5.50 g ground nutmeg

2¾ tsp / 5.50 g ground coriander

¾ tsp / 1.50 g ground cloves

¾ tsp / 1.50 g ground bay leaves

⅜ tsp / 0.75 g garlic powder

6 oz / 170 g nonfat dry milk

GARNISH

13 oz / 369 g pork fat, diced, blanched, cooled

5½ oz / 156 g pistachios, blanched and peeled

11 pieces beef middles, rinsed, cut in 10-in / 25-cm lengths and tied at one end

1. Toss the pork with the cure mix. Chill well, until nearly frozen. Progressively grind from the coarse plate (⅜ in / 9 mm) through the fine plate (⅛ in / 3 mm) of a meat grinder into a mixing bowl over an ice bath. Place in freezer until semi-frozen (just beginning to freeze but not solid).

2. Progressively grind the jowl fat from the coarse plate (⅜ in / 9 mm) through the fine plate (⅛ in / 3 mm) of a meat grinder into a mixing bowl over an ice bath; reserve.

3. Transfer the ground pork to a chilled chopper bowl. Add the crushed ice and spice blend on top of the ground pork. Run the machine and process the ingredients until the mixture reaches a temperature of 30°F / −1°C. Continue running the machine until the mixture's temperature rises to 40°F / 4°C.

4. Add the fat and process until the mixture reaches 45°F / 7°C. Add the nonfat dry milk and continue processing until the mixture reaches 58°F / 14°C. Make a test. Adjust seasoning and consistency before shaping.

5. Working over an ice bath, stir in the garnish ingredients. Stuff into prepared casings and tie with a bubble knot.

6. Hang uncovered in the refrigerator overnight to air-dry and form a pellicle.

7. Poach at 165°F / 74°C to an internal temperature of 150°F / 65°C, 2½ to 3 hours, then shock in ice water to an internal temperature of 60°F / 16°C. Blot dry.

8. Refrigerate uncovered overnight on absorbent paper towel–lined trays to form a pellicle.

9. If desired, cold smoke at 80°F / 26°C for 1 to 2 hours. Slice and serve the sausage immediately, or wrap and refrigerate for up to 3 weeks.

See photo on page 295.

*Presentation idea* *For a nontraditional garnish, add 13 oz / 369 g pork fat, cut into ¼-in / 6-mm dice, blanched and cooled, and 1¼ oz / 35 g whole black peppercorns, soaked in hot water and drained.*

# Chicken and Vegetable Sausage

YIELD: *11 lb / 4.99 kg bulk; 88 links (2 oz / 57 g each)*

4 lb 13 oz / 2.19 kg chicken thigh meat, diced

1 lb 6 oz / 624 g jowl fat, diced

2 lb 1 oz / 936 g crushed ice

CURE MIX

2¼ oz / 64 g salt

¾ oz / 21 g dextrose

GARNISH

5½ oz / 156 g small-dice carrots

5½ oz / 156 g small-dice celery

11 oz / 312 g small-dice onions

¾ fl oz / 22 mL vegetable oil

1 lb 6 oz / 624 g small-dice mushrooms

5½ fl oz / 165 mL dry white wine

1½ tbsp / 5 g chopped flat-leaf parsley

SPICE BLEND

½ oz / 14 g ground white pepper

2½ tsp / 5 g poultry seasoning

¾ tsp / 1½ g powdered thyme

5½ oz / 156 g nonfat dry milk

34.38 ft / 10.48 m sheep casings, rinsed and tied at one end

1. Toss the chicken with the cure mix. Progressively grind from the coarse plate (⅜ in / 9 mm) through the fine plate (⅛ in / 3 mm) of a meat grinder into a mixing bowl over an ice bath. Progressively grind the jowl fat from the coarse plate (⅜ in / 9 mm) through the fine plate (⅛ in / 3 mm) of a meat grinder into a mixing bowl over an ice bath and refrigerate separately. Place in freezer until semi-frozen (just beginning to freeze but not solid).

2. Sauté the carrots, celery, and onions in oil, until cooked; add the mushrooms. Sauté until mushrooms release water, then add wine and reduce until almost dry. Chill.

3. Transfer the ground chicken to a chilled high-speed chopper or processor bowl. Add the crushed ice and the spice blend on top of the ground chicken. Run the machine and process the ingredients until the mixture reaches a temperature of 30°F / –1°C. Continue running the machine until the mixture's temperature rises to 40°F / 4°C.

4. Add the fat and process until the mixture reaches 45°F / 7°C. Add the nonfat dry milk and continue processing until the mixture reaches 58°F / 14°C. Transfer to a bowl. Stir in the garnish, working over an ice bath. Make a test. Adjust seasoning and consistency before shaping.

5. Stuff into prepared casings and tie off into links 5 in / 13 mm long. Poach in water at 170°F / 77°C to an internal temperature of 165°F / 74°C, then shock in ice water to an internal temperature of 60°F / 16°C and blot dry.

6. Sauté, grill, or broil the sausage just until hot, or wrap and refrigerate for up to 3 days.

# Braunschweiger

YIELD: *11 lb / 4.99 bulk; 11 sausages (1 lb / 454 g each)*

4 lb 9 oz / 2.08 kg pork liver, cubed

1 lb 13 oz / 822 g boneless pork butt, cubed

2 lb 12 oz / 1.25 kg slab bacon, cubed

1 lb ½ oz / 468 g crushed ice

CURE MIX

3¼ oz / 92 g salt

1¾ tsp / 15 g tinted curing mix (TCM)

1 oz / 28 g dextrose

SPICE BLEND

½ oz / 14 g onion powder

1 tbsp / 6 g ground white pepper

½ tsp / 1 g ground allspice

½ tsp / 1 g ground cloves

½ tsp / 0.50 g rubbed sage

½ tsp / 1 g ground marjoram

½ tsp / 1 g ground nutmeg

½ tsp / 1 g ground ginger

7⅓ oz / 208 g nonfat dry milk

11 ft / 3.36 m beef middles, rinsed, cut into 10-in / 25-cm lengths and tied at one end

1. Toss the liver and pork butt with the cure mix. Chill well, until nearly frozen. Progressively grind from the coarse plate (⅜ in / 9 mm) through the fine plate (⅛ in / 3 mm) of a meat grinder into a mixing bowl over an ice bath. Place in freezer until semi-frozen (just beginning to freeze but not solid).

2. Grind the ground bacon through the fine plate (⅛ in / 3 mm); reserve separately.

3. Transfer the ground liver and pork to a chilled high-speed chopper or processor bowl. Add the crushed ice and the spice blend on top of the ground pork. Process the ingredients until the mixture drops to a temperature of 30°F / –1°C. Continue running the machine until the mixture's temperature rises to 40°F / 4°C.

4. Add the ground bacon and process until the mixture reaches 45°F / 7°C. Add the nonfat dry milk and continue processing until the mixture reaches 58°F / 14°C. Make a test. Adjust seasoning and consistency before shaping.

5. Stuff into prepared casings and tie closed with a bubble knot. Hang uncovered overnight in the refrigerator to air-dry and form a pellicle.

6. Hot smoke at 160°F / 71°C until desired color is achieved, 1½ to 2 hours.

7. Poach in water at 165°F / 74°C to an internal temperature of 150°F / 66°C, then shock in ice water to an internal temperature of 60°F / 16°C. Blot dry. Slice and serve immediately, or wrap and refrigerate for up to 2 weeks.

# Blood Sausage with Apples

YIELD: *11 lb / 4.99 kg bulk; 44 links (4 oz / 113 g each)*

2¾ oz / 78 g fresh white bread crumbs

22 fl oz / 660 mL heavy cream

88 fl oz / 2.64 L beef blood

1¼ oz / 35 g salt

1 tsp / 2 g Quatre Épices (page 588)

1 oz / 28 g brown sugar

3 lb 10¾ oz / 1.66 kg fatback, small diced

2 lb 12 oz / 1.25 kg fine-dice onions

2 lb 4 oz / 1.02 kg cored and peeled apples, sautéed and puréed

44 ft / 13.38 m hog casings, cut into 24-in / 61-cm lengths and tied at one end

1. Soak the bread crumbs in the heavy cream to make a panada. Knead gently to moisten evenly.

2. Mix the blood with the salt, quatre épices, and brown sugar.

3. Render 14 oz / 397 g fatback in a heavy sautoir.

4. Add the onions and sweat until translucent but not brown.

5. Stir in the rest of the diced fatback, the apples, panada, and seasoned blood.

6. Gently heat, stirring until mixture reaches about 100°F / 38°C. Remove from heat.

7. Tie a knot at one end of the hog casings. Fill the casings with the help of a funnel, making sure all the components are distributed evenly. Take care not to overstuff to prevent them from bursting when cooking.

8. Poach the sausages in 165°F / 74°C water and cook for 20 minutes, then prick with a teasing needle. If brown liquid comes out, they are done; if blood comes out, let cook a few more minutes and check again.

9. When cooked, shock sausages in ice water for 5 minutes, drain them, dry them with absorbent paper towels, lay them on a pan, and brush them with melted lard or duck fat. Refrigerate to finish cooling.

*Chef's note*   *Unlike other sausages, the blood sausage mixture is loose enough to pour through a funnel into the prepared casings.*

*Presentation idea*   *To serve, cut the sausages into lengths, prick them all over with a fork, and sauté or grill them. Traditional accompaniments are mashed or home-fried potatoes, fried apple rings, and sauerkraut.*

# Seafood Sausage

**YIELD:** *11 lb / 4.99 kg bulk; 88 links (2 oz / 57 g each)*

MOUSSELINE

3 lb 5½ oz / 1.52 kg sole fillet, diced

3 lb 5½ oz / 1.52 kg sea scallops, muscle tabs removed

½ oz / 14 g salt

4 tbsp / 27 g Old Bay seasoning

3½ oz / 99 g fresh white bread crumbs

44 fl oz / 1.32 L heavy cream, cold

11 egg whites

GARNISH

1 lb 2 oz / 510 g shrimp, peeled and deveined, cut into ¼-in / 6-mm dice

1 lb 2 oz / 510 g crab- or lobster meat, diced (from three 1¼-lb / 567-g blanched lobsters)

1 lb 2 oz / 510 g salmon meat, cut into ¼-in / 6-mm dice

1 lb 2 oz / 510 g bay scallops, muscle tabs removed

2 tbsp / 7 g chopped fresh parsley

39.6 ft / 12.08 m sheep casings, rinsed, or 20 ft / hog casings, rinsed

1. Combine the sole, scallops, salt, and Old Bay seasoning. Grind through the fine plate (⅛ in / 3 mm) of a meat grinder. Chill in freezer 15 minutes.

2. Soak bread crumbs in half of the heavy cream to make a panada.

3. Pureé the seafood in food processor as smooth as possible. Add the egg whites and panada. Pulse in the remaining cream. Make a test. Adjust seasoning and consistency before shaping.

4. Fold in the garnish ingredients until evenly distributed; cover and refrigerate.

5. Stuff into prepared casings and twist and tie into 5-in / 3-cm links.

6. Poach in water at 165°F / 74°C to an internal temperature of 145°F / 63°C. Shock in ice water to an internal temperature of 60°F / 16°C. Blot dry.

7. To serve, remove the strings and either sauté the sausage in clarified butter until golden brown, or reheat in a 350°F / 177°C oven for 10 to 12 minutes. Serve immediately, or wrap and refrigerate for up to 3 days.

*Chef's note*  *The sausages can be twisted into links 3 in / 8 cm long for an appetizer-sized sausage. The sausage is shown here with fingerling potatoes.*

# Duck and Foie Gras Sausage

YIELD: *8 lb / 3.63 kg*

2 lb / 907 g duck meat from a whole duck

1 lb 8 oz / 680 g chicken leg meat

4 oz / 113 g minced shallots

2 oz / 57 g butter

1½ lb / 680 g foie gras, B grade; only remove large vein

2 tsp / 5.3 g tinted curing mix (TCM)

2 fl oz / 60 mL brandy

2 oz / 57 g salt

3½ to 4 cups / 840 mL to 960 mL heavy cream

2 oz / 57 g salt

½ tsp / 1 g ground white pepper

2 oz / 57 g truffles, coarsely chopped

2 bunches chives, minced

2 bunches chervil, coarsely chopped

30 ft / 9.14 m sheep casings, rinsed

1. Cube the duck and chicken into ½-in / 1-cm cubes. Chill or partially freeze. Grind the meat through a medium plate (¼ in / 6 mm) of a meat grinder. Combine the shallots and butter. Sweat in a small pan over low heat until tender, 6 to 8 minutes. Drain off excess butter and cool under refrigeration. Dice the foie gras into rough ⅓-in / 8-mm cubes.

2. Combine the ground duck, chicken, foie gras, shallots, TCM, brandy, and salt. Place in chilled robot coupe, pulse for 5 seconds, and scrape down sides with a rubber spatula. Repeat this step 3 or 4 more times or until the mixture becomes partially smooth.

3. Add the cream in four additions, repeating step 3 after each addition until a smooth, homogenous mixture is formed. Pass through a tamis.

4. Season the forcemeat with salt and pepper; add the truffles and herbs.

5. Prepare a poach test to check flavor and consistency.

6. Stuff into the sheep casings and twist into links 2 in / 5 cm long. Pierce with a teasing needle.

7. Poach the sausages in 165°F / 74°C water until an internal temperature of 165°F / 74°C is reached; drain and cool in an ice bath. The sausage may be finished by poaching, sautéing, or grilling.

# Garlic Sausage

YIELD: *7 lb / 3.18 kg (4 sausages; 10 in / 25 cm each)*

5 lb / 2.27 kg pork butt, fresh, cut into
½- to 1-in / 1- to 3-cm cubes, partially frozen

1 lb / 454 g jowl fat, cut into ½- to 1-in /
1- to 3-cm cubes, partially frozen

10 oz / 284 g ice-cold water

1½ oz / 43 g salt

½ oz / 14 g sugar

4½ tsp / 9 g coarse-ground black pepper

¾ oz / 21 g garlic, mashed to a paste

Pinch cayenne

1 tsp / 2 g garlic powder

⅛ oz / 3 g tinted curing mix (TCM)

8 ft 9 in / 2.66 m beef round casing, cut into
15-in / 38-cm lengths, tied at one end

1. Grind pork and fat separately through a coarse plate of a meat grinder (⅜ in / 9 mm).

2. Mix meat and fat in mixer with the paddle attachment on low speed. Add water and seasoning and mix until the ingredients are combined, about 1 minute.

3. Place the mixer on second and mix for 30 to 40 seconds, or until emulsified.

4. Make a test and adjust seasoning as needed.

5. Stuff into casings, leaving enough extra string to tie both bubble knots together, and leaving enough string so they can be hung.

6. Hang the sausages uncovered overnight in the refrigerator to air-dry and form a pellicle.

7. Cold smoke sausages in a 70°F / 21°C cold-smoke box for about 6 hours, or until the sausages achieve a rosy, mahogany color from the smoke. (They will not shrink too much because they were cold smoked.)

8. Place sausage in 170°F / 77°C water, reduce heat to low, and poach slowly to an internal temperature of 155°F / 68°C, about 25 minutes. Refrigerate until needed.

9. These sausages are intended to be served cold or only slightly room temperature, as with lukewarm potato salad.

# Kielbasa (Polish-Style Sausage)

YIELD: *6 lb 8 oz / 2.95 kg*

5 lb / 2.26 kg pork butt, fresh, cut into ½- to 1-in / 1 to 3-cm cubes and chilled

1 lb 8 oz / 680 g fatback, cut into ½- to 1-in / 1- to 3-cm cubes and chilled

6 fl oz / 180 mL ice-cold water

1½ oz / 43 g salt

½ oz / 14 g sugar

4¾ tsp / 9.50 g coarse-ground black pepper

¾ oz / 21 g garlic, mashed to a paste

⅛ oz / 3.5 g tinted curing mix (TCM)

4 ft 10½ in / 1.49 m beef round casing, cut into 16-in / 41-cm lengths

1. Grind the pork through the coarse die (⅜ in / 9 mm) of a meat grinder.

2. Grind the fatback through the fine die (⅛ in / 3 mm) of a meat grinder.

3. Place meat and fatback in the mixer, add water and seasonings, and mix on low speed until just combined.

4. Place mixer on second speed and mix for 30 to 40 seconds until the mixture is emulsified and slightly sticky to the touch.

5. Make a test and adjust seasoning as needed.

6. Tie the end of each length of casing into a bubble knot. Stuff the sausage into the casings, using a bubble knot to seal each sausage. Tie both ends together, leaving enough string so that they may be hung.

7. Hang the sausages uncovered in the refrigerator to air-dry and form a pellicle. Hang the sausages in an area with adequate airflow and low humidity.

8. The next day, cold smoke the sausages at 40 to 70°F / 4 to 21°C for 6 hours.

9. Place the sausages in 170°F / 77°C water, reduce heat, and poach slowly to an internal temperate of 155°F / 68°C, about 25 minutes. Refrigerate until needed.

10. These sausages are intended to be served cold or slightly warm, as with lukewarm potato salad.

# Southwest Dry Sausage

YIELD: *11 lb / 4.99 kg*

6 lb / 2.72 kg diced beef, partially frozen

4 lb 2 oz / 1.87 kg diced certified pork, partially frozen (see page 236)

2¾ tsp / 6 g garlic powder

4½ fl oz / 135 mL cold water

3¾ tsp / 8 g chili powder

1¾ tsp / 4 g onion powder

1¾ tsp / 3.50 g ground cumin

7¼ tsp / 16 g coarse ground black pepper

1 tsp / 5 mL Tabasco

½ oz / 14 g Prague Powder #2

7½ oz / 212 g dextrose

3¾ oz / 106 g salt

2¾ oz / 78 g Fermento

20 ft / 6.1 m hog casings, rinsed

1. Progressively grind the beef and pork from the coarse plate (⅜ in / 9 mm) through the fine plate (⅛ in / 3 mm) of a meat grinder into a mixing bowl over an ice bath.

2. Add all remaining ingredients to the ground meats; mix on low speed for 1 minute and then on second speed for 10 to 20 seconds, or until meat feels sticky to the touch. Make a test. Adjust seasoning and consistency before shaping.

3. Place sausage meat into stuffer and tamp down to remove any air pockets.

4. Stuff into prepared hog casings and tie into links 9 in / 23 cm long, using bubble knots to secure the links.

5. Arrange on drying sticks and cure for 4 days. (See Chapter 5, page 192, for the USDA regulations for dry-curing sausages.)

6. Cold smoke at 80°F / 27°C for 24 to 36 hours to the desired color. Allow the sausage to continue to dry until desired firmness.

# Dried Chorizo

YIELD: *10 lb / 4.54 kg*

| | |
|---|---|
| 10 lb / 4.54 g pork butt, cut into cubes and chilled | 2 tsp / 4 g black pepper |
| 2½ oz / 71 g salt | 2 tsp / 4 g Insta-cure #2 |
| 8 fl oz / 240 mL white vinegar | 3 tbsp / 61 g corn syrup solids |
| 1 oz / 28 g Spanish paprika | 12 fl oz / 360 mL Fermento |
| 3 tbsp / 18 g cayenne | 8 fl oz / 240 mL ice-cold water |
| 3 tbsp / 32 g granulated garlic powder | 20 ft / 6.096 m hog casings, 13½ to 15 in / 35 to 38 mm |
| 3 tbsp / 9 g dried oregano | |

1. Chorizo can be made using any combination of lean meats or 100% pork butt. Grind all chilled meats (32 to 34°F / 0 to 2°C) through a coarse plate of a meat grinder (⅜ in / 9 mm).

2. Add all ingredients except casings to meat and mix well by hand. Transfer meat to a container and press air out. Cover with a tight-fitting lid and refrigerate at 34 to 36°F / 1 to 3°C overnight to cure.

3. Before stuffing, re-grind meat through a medium or coarse die.

4. Stuff into the prepared casings and twist into links 5 to 6 in / 13 to 15 cm long.

5. Place sausage on smoke sticks, spaced properly, 3 to 4 inches apart, and allow to ripen 3 days at 70 to 75°F / 21 to 24°C, with a humidity of 70 to 80%. After that, space the sausage 3 to 4 in / 8 to 10 cm apart and dry for 15 days at 50 to 55°F / 10 to 13°C, with a humidity of 60 to 70%. The sausage should be crumbly and have about a 10% moisture loss.

6. Sausage may be placed in containers that are then filled with lard. This is an especially popular method of storage in Cuba.

See photo on page 295.

# Cotechino

YIELD: *6 lb 8 oz / 2.95 kg*

| | |
|---|---|
| 8 oz / 227 g pork skin, cut into ¼- by ¾-in / 6-mm to 2-cm strips | 1¼ oz / 35 g salt |
| 1 vanilla bean | 1½ tsp / 3 g ground black pepper |
| 6 fl oz / 180 mL white wine | 1 lb 8 oz / 680 g pork jowl fat, cut into 2-in / 5-cm cubes, partially frozen |
| 5 garlic cloves, minced | 4 oz / 113 g Prague Powder #2 |
| ¼ tsp / 0.50 g ground allspice | 1½ tsp / 3.5 g whole black peppercorns |
| 8 bay leaves | |
| 4 lb 8 oz / 2.04 kg pork butt, lean | 4 ft 10½ in / 1.49 m beef middle casings, cut into 16-in / 41-cm lengths |

1. Boil the skins with the vanilla bean in enough water to cover them until the skins are tender, about 1½ hours. Strain the skins and remove the vanilla bean.

2. While hot, toss the skins with white wine, garlic, allspice, and bay leaves and allow the mixture to cool to room temperature.

3. Grind the pork skins through a medium die of a meat grinder (¼ in / 6 mm).

4. Season the pork butt with salt and ground pepper and grind through the coarse die of a meat grinder (⅜ in / 9 mm).

5. Grind jowl fat through a medium die of a meat grinder (¼ in / 6 mm).

6. Combine pork butt, pork skin, jowl fat, whole peppercorns, and Prague Powder #2. Mix well.

7. Stuff mixture into casings and finish with bubble knots on either side of the sausage. Weigh sausages. Hang dry until the outside is dry, not tacky, and the sausages have lost about 10% of their weight, 4 to 6 weeks.

8. Poach at 165°F / 74°C over low heat until the sausage registers an internal temperature of 165°F / 74°C and is firm, about 1 hour.

# California Spicy Sopressata

YIELD: *Approx. 6 lb / 2.72 kg (20 sausages; 8 in / 20 cm each)*

| | |
|---|---|
| 8 oz / 227 g pork fatback | 1 tsp / 2 g cayenne |
| 5 lb 8 oz / 2.5 kg pork butt, 75/25, cut into ½- to 1-in / 1- to 3-cm cubes | 1 tsp / 2 g Insta-cure #2 |
| 2 oz / 57 g salt | 1 tbsp / 6 g red pepper flakes, crushed med fine |
| 2 tsp / 4 g coarsely ground black pepper | 4 fl oz / 120 mL ice-cold grappa |
| 1 tsp / 2 g garlic powder | 2 tsp / 4 g anise seed, crushed |
| 1½ oz / 43 g corn syrup | |
| 1 tbsp / 6 g hot paprika | 4 ft 6 in / 1.37 m bung casing |

1. Cut the fatback into ¼-in / 6-mm dice and freeze until it is 30 to 32°F / –1 to 0°C. Grind through a medium die (¼ in / 6 mm) of a meat grinder and refrigerate until needed.

2. Mix the cubed meat with the salt, black pepper, garlic powder, corn syrup, paprika, cayenne, and insta-cure until thoroughly combined. Place in the freezer until the internal temperature of the meat reaches 30 to 32°F / –1 to 0°C. Alternately, the meat can be frozen overnight and then thawed at room temperature for 30 minutes.

3. Grind the meat with large die (⅜ in / 9 mm), passing through 2 times, then grind half of the mixture through a medium die (¼ in / 6 mm). Remember to chill thoroughly between passes.

4. Combine the ground meat, ground fatback, red pepper flakes, grappa, and anise seed and mix until tacky.

5. Make a test of the forcemeat to assess flavor and texture. After poaching the test, the sausage should be homogenous and some moisture should come out when it is squeezed. Adjust seasoning as necessary.

6. Stuff into the prepared casings and twist into 8-in / 20-cm lengths. Weigh sausages. Hang for 4 days in a 50°F / 10°C, low-humidity, drafty area. The sausage should lose 30 to 40% of its weight during this time.

7. Place in the refrigerator until firmness similar to a pepperoni is achieved, about 4 weeks. The water activity level should be within the safety zone.

   See photo on page 295.

*Variation*  Spicy Duck Cappicola: Use duck legs and thighs in place of the pork.

# Sonoma Peppered Salami

YIELD: *Approx. 10 lb / 4.54 kg, 8 sausages; 18 in / 46 cm long*

| | |
|---|---|
| 10 lb / 4.54 kg pork butt, 70/30, cut into ½-in / 1-cm cubes | 1 tbsp / 6 g red pepper flakes, crushed med fine |
| 3¾ oz / 106 g salt | 2 tsp / 4 g granulated or powdered garlic |
| 2 tsp / 4 g Insta-cure #2 | 4 oz / 113 g light corn syrup |
| 3 oz / 85 g Fermento | ½ oz / 14 g hot Spanish paprika (pimenton) |
| ½ tsp / 1 g sodium erythorbate | 1 tbsp / 6 g anise seed, crushed |
| 4 fl oz / 120 mL ice-cold grappa | 7 ft 6 in / 2.28 m beef middle casings |
| 2 oz / 57 g coarse-ground black pepper | |

1. Combine the pork with the salt, Insta-cure #2, and Fermento and mix well. Place in a plastic container and press the air out. Cover with plastic wrap and a tight-fitting lid and refrigerate 7 days to cure.

2. Grind the cured pork with coarse die (⅜ in / 9 mm), passing 2 times. Then put half of the mixture through the medium die (¼ in / 6 mm). Remember to chill mixture thoroughly between passes.

3. Combine sodium erythorbate with the iced grappa and mix until sodium erythorbate is completely dissolved.

4. Combine the ground pork with the black pepper, red pepper, garlic, corn syrup, and paprika and anise and mix until thoroughly combined. Add the sodium erythorbate dissolved in the iced grappa at the last moment.

5. Make a test poach and adjust seasoning as necessary.

6. Stuff the sausage into the prepared casings and twist and tie into 18-in / 46-cm lengths. Hang for 5 days in 60°F / 16°C environment with 70 to 80% humidity with plenty of air movement to air-dry and form a pellicle.

7. Hang in refrigerator for additional 3 to 4 weeks or until it forms a white mycelium finish.

*Chef's note*   *For regular Genoa-style salami, omit the pimenton and red pepper flakes.*

CLOCKWISE FROM UPPER RIGHT: *Dried Chorizo (page 291), Mortadella (page 282), Spicy Duck Cappicola (page 293), Sonoma Peppered Salami, provolone cheese, California Spicy Sopressata (page 293), served with cornichons, Dijon mustard, and baguette*

# 7

# Terrines, pâtés, galantines, and roulades

The French are famous for their contributions to the world of terrines, pâtés, and other forcemeat specialties. From the rustic appeal of a peasant-style pâté grand-mère to a luxurious foie gras and truffle pâté, these dishes are part of the worldwide tradition of classic cold dishes.

In this chapter, we will look at the methods for preparing four basic forcemeat styles (straight, country, gratin, and mousseline) and the shaping methods to produce items from forcemeats (terrines, pâtés en croûte, galantines, and roulades), as well as a special commodity featured in the cold kitchen (foie gras). In addition, we give several examples of nontraditional "terrines" made without forcemeats.

# Forcemeats

One of the basic components of charcuterie and garde manger items is a preparation known as a **forcemeat.** A forcemeat is a lean meat and fat **emulsion** that is established when the ingredients are processed together by grinding, sieving, or puréeing. Depending on the grinding and emulsifying methods and the intended use, the forcemeat may have a smooth consistency or may be heavily textured and coarse. The result must not be just a mixture but an emulsion, so that it will hold together properly when sliced. Forcemeats should have a rich and pleasant taste and feel in the mouth.

Forcemeats may be used for quenelles, sausages, pâtés, terrines, roulades, and galantines, as well as to prepare stuffings for other items (a salmon forcemeat may be used to fill a paupiette of sole, for example). Each forcemeat style will have a particular texture. The four basic forcemeat styles are:

- **Straight** forcemeats combine pork and pork fat with a dominant meat in equal parts, through a process of **progressive grinding** and emulsification. The meats and fat are cut into cubes, seasoned, cured, rested, ground, and processed.
- **Country-style** forcemeats are rather coarse in texture. They are traditionally made from pork and pork fat, often with a percentage of liver and other garnish ingredients.
- In **gratin** forcemeats, some portion of the dominant meat is sautéed and cooled before it is ground. The term *gratin* means "browned."
- **Mousseline,** a very light forcemeat, is based on tender, lean white meats such as veal, poultry, fish, or shellfish. The inclusion of cream and eggs gives mousselines their characteristic light texture and consistency.

## Main ingredients

Forcemeats, like sausages, are made from raw products, with the exception of the gratin forcemeat. Some classic choices for forcemeats include pork; fish such as pike, trout, or salmon; seafood such as shrimp and scallops; game meats such as venison, boar, or rabbit; poultry and game birds; and poultry, game, veal, or pork livers. When selecting cuts of red and white meat, opt for well-exercised cuts, since they have a richer flavor than very tender cuts, such as the tenderloin or loin. However, meats to be used as garnishes can easily be the more delicate portions: tenderloin of lamb, rabbit, or pork, or poultry breasts, for example. Often, recipes for shrimp or scallop mousseline call for a quantity of pike to ensure a good primary **bind.**

An adequate amount of **fat** is also important. Fatback is considered to have a neutral flavor and can be paired with most meats. Mousselines made from delicate white meats, fish, or shellfish generally call for heavy cream.

To prepare the meat and fatback for a forcemeat, it should first be trimmed of any gristle, sinew, or skin. The meat is then cut into dice, so it can drop easily through the feed tube of a grinder or be quickly processed to a paste in a food processor.

FIG 7-1A | *When shaped into quenelles and poached, forcemeats can be used as a garnish.*

FIG 7-1B | *Prepared forcemeats can be used to fill tortellini and other filled pastas.*

FIG 7-1C | *Forcemeats can be shaped into a roulade and poached for service.*

FIG 7-1D | *When portioned into a terrine, forcemeats can be cooked and served as large slices.*

# Salt and seasonings

**Salt** plays a vital role in producing good force-meats. The salt acts to draw out the proteins in the meat (these proteins are the primary source of the forcemeat's "bind"), and it also adds its own unique flavor. Classic recipes often call for ground spices such as *quatre épices*, which is a combination of pepper, nutmeg, cinnamon, and cloves. **Seasoning** or marinating meat prior to grinding will further enhance its flavor.

Herbs, aromatic vegetables such as onions or mushrooms, wines, cognacs, grain-based spirits, or vinegars may also be added. In some cases, a reduction of garlic or shallots, herbs, wines, glace de viande or volaille, and other flavoring ingredients may be made. This reduction should be thoroughly chilled before adding it to the meats.

It is always important to follow basic formulas carefully as you are learning to make forcemeats, and to properly test and taste forcemeats each time you make them.

# Secondary binders

The proteins in meats and fish are the basic source of the forcemeat's structure, texture, and bind. In some special cases, however, you may need to add a **secondary binder,** which is generally required for country-style and gratin forcemeats. There are three basic types of secondary binders: eggs, nonfat dry milk powder, and panadas (see Fig 7-2). **Panadas** are made from starchy (farinaceous) items—well-cooked, puréed rice or potatoes, bread soaked in milk, or pâte à choux, which is a dough made from flour, water, butter, and eggs.

# Garnish ingredients

**Garnishes** give the chef an opportunity to add color, flavor, and texture to a basic formula. Some traditional garnishes include the poultry breast, pork, beef, veal, or lamb tenderloin portions, nuts (especially pistachios and pine nuts), mushrooms, truffles, and diced foie gras. The quantity of garnish added to a forcemeat can range from a few chopped nuts scattered throughout a pâté to a terrine in which there is a predominant garnish bound together with a small amount of forcemeat or aspic.

You can add garnishes to a forcemeat in two ways. They can be simply folded into the forcemeat; in that case they are known as **internal** or **random garnishes** (see Fig 7-3a).

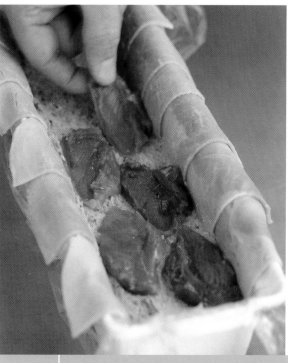

The second means of introducing the garnish is to place it in the forcemeat as you are filling the mold or laying it out for a roulade or galantine. These garnishes are known as **inlays,** though you may also hear them called **centered garnishes** (see Fig 7-3b).

Care should be taken to shape and place the garnish so that each slice will have a uniform, consistent appearance, whether the slice comes from the end or center of the pâté.

If you are preparing forcemeat items for display or competition, you may want to dust garnish items very lightly with a bit of powdered gelatin or albumen (dried and powdered egg whites) or a combination of these two items, to glue them into place. This will improve the adherence of the forcemeat to the garnish, making it less likely that they will separate when the item is cut into slices.

## *Making forcemeats*

### Chill ingredients, chill equipment

Maintaining both the ingredients and equipment is imperative when preparing forcemeat. This helps keep the forcemeat below 40°F / 4°C, which keeps the food out of the danger zone, reducing the risk of food-borne illness. Temperature control is also the key to achieving the best results. When forcemeats are kept well chilled throughout processing, mixing, and cooking, they require less fat, yet still have a smooth texture and an appealing mouth feel. The flavor of the forcemeat itself is generally better, as well.

### Grinding

The most common piece of equipment for grinding the meats for straight, country, and gratin force-meats is a meat grinder. Review all the cautions and instructions found on page 239 in chapter 6.

Some forcemeat formulas will call for some or all of the meats and fat to be ground using a method called **progressive grinding** (see page 240). Review the recipe to determine if you will need one or more grinding plates. Grind the meat directly into a well-chilled mixing bowl set over ice.

Mousseline forcemeats are typically made from start to finish in a food processor, although some chefs prefer to grind the meat or fish before placing it in the bowl of the food processor. If you make a significant quantity of forcemeats using a food processor, it is a good idea to dedicate one very sharp blade to that purpose only.

### Mixing and processing

Once ground, the forcemeat is mixed in order to blend any seasonings, panadas, or other ingredients thoroughly and evenly. More importantly, an adequate mixing period is crucial to the development of the correct texture.

**Mixing** can be done by beating the forcemeat with a rubber spatula or wooden spoon over an ice bath, in a mixer, or in a food processor. Care should be taken not to overmix, especially when you use a machine. Be careful not to overload the bowl. Depending on the amount of product, one to three minutes at the lowest speed should be sufficient. The forcemeat's color and texture will change slightly when it is properly mixed.

Mixing in a food processor is very fast and provides a smoother texture. Most food processors handle relatively small batches. It is critical to keep an eye on the forcemeat as it processes. Your forcemeat can go from properly processed to overworked in a matter of seconds. This can cause pockets or bubbles to form in the item you are preparing, a distraction on a plated item presented to a guest and grounds for losing points in competition work.

## Testing a forcemeat

Forcemeats are poached directly in a liquid (as for galantines, roulades, or quenelles) or in a water bath (terrines), or baked in a crust (pâté en croûte). You can only be sure of the quality of the force-meat after it is cooked, and the method below for **testing** a forcemeat will give you an opportunity to evaluate the quality, seasoning, and texture.

The test portion itself will not taste or feel exactly the same as the finished product, since it is a general practice to allow the forcemeat items to rest two or three days before they are served. However, with experience, you can train your palate to recognize the evidence of quality or to detect a flaw in a forcemeat. This is the same **taste memory,** built up through experience and practice, that permits a cellar master to foretell with some accuracy the qualities a wine will have when it is mature, even when the wine is actually far too young to drink.

If the texture is poor, evaluate just what kind of problem you have. Rubbery forcemeat can be improved by adding more fat and cream. Loose forcemeat, on the other hand, may be improved by adding egg whites or a bit of panada. However, take into account whether or not the item will be pressed or coated with aspic before you make a dramatic change.

# Straight forcemeat

This basic forcemeat is used to prepare pâtés, terrines, and galantines. It is generally made by grinding the meat and fat through a medium plate, then further processing it in a mixer or food processor (see Fig 7-4a).

Process the ground meat with any additional ingredients (see Fig 7-4b). An egg may be added to the forcemeat to give a better bind. A quantity of heavy cream may also be included in some recipes to give the forcemeat a smooth texture and a richer flavor, if desired.

Once the forcemeat is tested and any adjustments to seasoning or consistency have been made, you may add garnish ingredients. This may be done in the mixer or by hand, working over an ice bath to keep the forcemeat properly chilled.

Straight forcemeats may be used to fill a pâté en croûte, or to prepare terrines and galantines. (For more information on preparing a pâté en croûte, terrines, and galantines, see pages 308 to 318.)

| FIG 7-4A | *Straight forcemeats begin with a combination of ground meat and any desired seasonings.* |

| FIG 7-4B | *Once thoroughly mixed, the meat and seasonings should be homogenously dispersed and the forcemeat should be slightly tacky.* |

## Country-style forcemeat

**Country-style forcemeats** are less refined in texture and heartier in flavor than others and are traditionally made from pork and pork liver.

The texture of this forcemeat is achieved by grinding the pork through a coarse die, then reserving most of this coarse grind. If desired, a portion of the ground meat may be ground again through a medium die before the forcemeat is blended with its panada and processed as for a straight forcemeat (see Fig 7-5a).

The coarsely ground meat as well as the processed forcemeat is then combined. Because at least part of the forcemeat is left as a coarse grind, a panada is almost always included to help the finished product hold together after cooking.

## Gratin forcemeat

A **gratin forcemeat** is similar to a straight forcemeat, with the exception of the way in which the main meat is handled. The meat is very quickly seared—just enough to enhance the flavor and color, but not enough to cook it through. The meat is changed enough by the searing that a panada is required to help produce the desired texture.

The first step is to sear the meat. Get the pan or grill very hot, sear the meat on all sides as quickly as possible, and just as quickly cool it down (see Fig 7-6a).

The best way to accomplish this is to work in small batches and to avoid crowding the meat in the pan. Remove it to a sheet pan, and cool it quickly in the refrigerator or freezer. An optional step is to prepare an aromatic reduction to flavor the forcemeat.

FIG 7-5A  *Country-style forcemeats are characterized by the inclusion of two different grinds of meat, often with the addition of a panada.*

FIG 7-5B  *The prepared forcemeat will have a sticky texture and retain a somewhat coarse texture from the different grinds of meat.*

| FIG 7-6A | *Gratin forcemeat gets its flavor from searing the main meat before processing.* | FIG 7-6B | *Prepared gratin forcemeat, like straight forcemeat, will have a homogenous texture and be slightly tacky.* |

Follow the same procedure for grinding as for a straight forcemeat, and process it with a panada and any additional ingredients as suggested or required by the recipe (see Fig 7-6b). Be sure to test the forcemeat properly before continuing to add the garnish ingredients.

Gratin forcemeats can be used in the same general applications as straight forcemeats.

## Mousseline forcemeat

Although individual recipes will differ, the formula shown below for **mousseline forcemeat** works as an excellent starting point. The amount of cream indicated will produce a good texture for terrines and other forcemeat items that will be sliced. If the mousseline will be used to prepare a timbale or other similar applications, the quantity of cream can be increased by nearly double the amount indicated below:

Meat or fish—1 lb / 454 g
Salt—1 tsp / 3 g
Egg (or egg white)—1 large
Cream—8 fl oz / 240 mL

When preparing a mousseline forcemeat, you may simply dice the main ingredients and proceed to grind them in the food processor, or you may wish to grind the main ingredient through a coarse or medium plate before processing it with an egg white. When using shellfish, it is important to keep in mind that some types of shellfish, such as lobster and wet pack sea scallops, retain more moisture than others and therefore require less cream than the standard ratio indicates.

Process the meat and salt just long enough to develop a paste with an even texture. Add the egg white, followed by the cream (see Fig 7-7a).

In order to blend the mousseline properly, it is important to scrape down the bowl. Continue processing only until the forcemeat is smooth and homogenous, generally around thirty seconds.

Optional: For a very light mousseline, you may prefer to work the cream in by hand. This is more time-consuming and exacting than using a food processor, but the results are worth the extra effort. Both the base mixture and the cream must be very cold in order to add the cream in higher proportions than those suggested in the basic formula above. Work over an ice bath for the best results.

Fine forcemeats may be passed through a drum sieve (tamis) to be sure that a very delicate texture is achieved (see Fig 7-7b). Be sure that the forcemeat is very cold as you work, and work in small batches to prevent the forcemeat from heating up as you work.

Mousseline forcemeats are often featured as appetizers, fillings, or stuffings, or to coat or wrap poached fish or poultry suprêmes. Another interesting way to use this forcemeat is to layer mousselines with different colors to create a special effect in a terrine.

FIG 7-7A    *Finish mousselines with cream to give them a silky texture and mouth feel.*

FIG 7-7B    *Once mixed, mousselines may be passed through a drum sieve or tamis to ensure a very fine texture.*

FIG 7-8 EACH TYPE OF FORCEMEAT RESULTS IN A DIFFERENT TEXTURE ONCE COOKED.
LEFT TO RIGHT, TOP TO BOTTOM: *straight forcemeat, country-style force-*
*meat, gratin forcemeat, mousseline forcemeat*

# Terrines

**Terrines,** the shortened name of a dish known classically as **pâté en terrine,** are traditionally understood to be forcemeat mixtures baked in an earthenware **mold** with a tight-fitting lid. This preparation gets its name from its association with the material used to make the mold, once exclusively earthenware of unglazed clay, or terra cotta. Today, terrine molds are produced from materials such as stainless steel, aluminum, ceramic, enameled cast iron, ovenproof plastic, or glazed earthenware. These materials are more durable and more sanitary than the unglazed earthenware once favored by charcutières. Terrine molds also come in any number of shapes, including triangle, half-circle, and trapezoidal (see Fig 7-9). These materials and shapes offer the garde manger chef an effective way to impress the guest.

Traditionally, terrines were served directly from the mold. Now it is more common to present terrines in slices. This improves the chef's ability to control both the presentation and the portioning of the dish. This is clearly in the best interest of both the guest and the chef. In some special cases, however, terrines are still served in their molds. A terrine of foie gras, for instance, may be presented in a small decorative mold, accompanied by toasted brioche. Guests use a special service spoon or knife to serve themselves.

Today, some non-traditional terrines are also made by binding items such as roasted meats or poultry, roasted or grilled vegetables, poached salmon, or seared lamb loins with a little **aspic,** making them similar to a head cheese. One example from among the recipes in this chapter is Seared Lamb, Artichoke, and Mushroom Terrine (page 332). Terrines made from layered vegetables can be bound with a custard or cheese. Roasted Vegetable Terrine with Fresh Goat Cheese (page 338) and Mozzarella, Prosciutto, and Roasted Tomato Terrine (page 340) are two examples.

FIG 7-9 TERRINE MOLDS, CLOCKWISE FROM TOP: *pâté en croûte mold, trapezoidal terrine mold, triangular terrine mold, half cylinder terrine mold, two-pound enameled cast-iron terrine mold, three-pound enameled cast-iron terrine mold*

# *Making forcemeat terrines*

1.  **Prepare the terrine mold by lining it.** Terrine molds were traditionally lined with fatback, then filled with a forcemeat and any garnish called for by the recipe. This **liner**, also referred to as a **chemise** or jacket, is still used today, but fatback may be replaced today with proscuitto, bacon, caul fat, crêpes, leeks, spinach, or even seaweed. A liner is not always required, and may be replaced with plastic wrap; this makes it easy to remove the terrine neatly from the mold.

2.  **Fill the prepared mold with forcemeat and any garnish required.** Use a spatula to work the forcemeat into all corners and remove any air pockets (see Fig 7-10a). Then the liner is folded over the forcemeat to completely encase it, and a lid or foil covers the terrine. Firmly tap the assembled terrine on the countertop to further eliminate air pockets.

3.  **Cook the terrine gently in a water bath (bain-marie).** Terrines must be properly cooked at a carefully regulated temperature. A water bath can insulate the terrine from temperature extremes. Set the filled, covered terrine mold in a baking pan on a clean side towel or several layers of paper towels, if desired. Add enough simmering water to come about two-thirds to three-quarters of the way up the mold's sides (see Fig 7-10b). Monitor the water bath's temperature; it should be at a constant 170°F / 77°C. An oven temperature of approximately 300°F / 149°C should keep the water bath's temperature where it belongs, but if necessary, adjust the oven temperature.

4.  **Cook to the correct internal temperature.** Check for doneness by measuring the terrine's internal temperature with an instant-read thermometer. Remember to allow for **carryover cooking** when deciding whether the terrine is ready. The amount of carryover cooking will vary, depending upon the material used to make the mold, the forcemeat, and the overall shape and size of the mold.

5.  **Cool, press, and store the terrine until ready to serve.** Remove the fully cooked terrine from the water bath and allow it to rest at room temperature until the internal temperature drops to 90°F / 32°C. Set a **press plate** on the terrine. You can create a press plate by cutting Styrofoam, Plexiglas, or wood to the inside dimensions of the mold. Wrap the press plate in plastic wrap or foil to lengthen its useful life. Place a 2-lb / 907-g mold on top of the press plate (see Fig 7-10c). Set this assembly in a hotel pan and refrigerate the terrine for at least two to three days to mellow and mature the flavor. If desired, coat the terrine with melted aspic (see Fig 7-10d). Techniques and ratios for aspic gelée can be found on page 22.

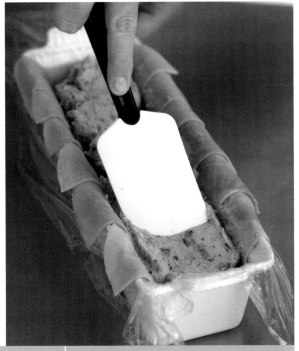

FIG 7-10A | *After lining a terrine mold with plastic wrap and a desired liner, in this case ham, fill it with prepared forcemeat, smoothing over the top.*

FIG 7-10B | *Bake the terrine in a water bath to regulate its temperature while in the oven.*

FIG 7-10C | *Once it has cooled after baking, press the terrine with a press plate and weights overnight under refrigeration.*

FIG 7-10D | *If desired, a terrine can be coated with melted aspic once completely cooled.*

*Terrines, pâtés, galantines, and roulades* 311

FIG 7-11A | *When preparing an aspic-bound terrine, use only enough aspic as is appropriate to bind the main ingredients without overpowering them.*

FIG 7-11B | *Working over ice, assemble the terrine in layers of aspic-bound fillings and lay-in garnishes, allowing each layer of aspic to set slightly before applying the garnish.*

FIG 7-11C | *Once the terrine is completely assembled and wrapped, apply a press plate and weight to it until it is completely set.*

FIG 7-11D | *Unmold the finished terrine by inverting it on a cutting board, anchoring the plastic wrap that hangs over the edge, and pulling the mold away from the terrine.*

## Aspic-bound terrines

To produce high-quality aspic-bound terrines, you should, of course, season and prepare the main ingredients with care; they are the foundation of the terrine. The aspic, though an important part of the dish, should be added only as needed to bind the major flavoring ingredients properly (see Fig 7-11a).

Still, it is important to take the time to select a rich, full-flavored base liquid. Clear stocks, broths, consommés, juices, or wines can be used singly or in combination to prepare an aspic of slicing strength.

An alternative to an aspic is a reduced stock, glace de viande, or essence. The action of cooking the stock down drives off the water but leaves the gelatinous proteins in place.

The aspic can be prepared in advance and refrigerated. To use it, warm the aspic over a hot water bath just enough to melt it. It should be incorporated while still warm, so that it will blend properly with the ingredients. The ingredients should not be too cold or else the aspic will set up upon contact with them.

# Pâté en croûte

## Making pâté en croûte

Today, **pâtés en croûte** are often made in rectangular molds. The advantage of these molds is that they have regular dimensions and straight sides. This encourages even baking and helps reduce the chances of undercooking the dough. Another reason to choose a rectangular mold is the ability to make uniform slices. However, an oval pâté en croûte may be a more dramatic presentation if it is being served whole on a buffet or being displayed uncut, as a retail item for sale.

1. **Line the pâté mold with dough.** First, roll out sheets of dough to a thickness of approximately ⅛ to ¼ in / 3 to 6 mm. It is important to roll the dough evenly and to handle it gently to avoid tearing or stretching the dough as you line the mold.

    Now, mark the dough by pressing all sides of the mold very lightly into the dough. This will produce the appropriate pattern for the interior of the mold. To line a straight-edged terrine mold, allow an overhang of ½ in / 1 cm on one side piece as well as enough to fold over the mold's opening, plus ½ in / 1 cm to secure it into the sides. Allow an overhang of about 1 to 1½ in / 3 to 4 cm for oval or round molds.

    The excess dough in the corners should be cut out before the dough is transferred to the mold. Reserve the excess dough to make the reinforcements for the vent holes you will cut in the top of the pâté, as well as any decorations you may wish to apply.

    Set the dough in the mold so that the overhang on one side of the mold is enough to completely cover the top of the mold and extend down into the mold on the opposite side at least ½ in / 1 cm. The overhang on the other side will be about ½ in /1 cm. Use eggwash to "glue" the pastry together in the corners and pinch the **seams** (see Fig 7-12a).

    If you wish, a second liner may be added at this time. Fatback is commonly used, but prosciutto and other thinly sliced cooked meats can be used to create a special effect.

At this point, the mold should be filled with the forcemeat and any inlay garnish (see Fig 7-12b).

Fold the liner and then the excess dough over the top of the forcemeat. Pinch the edges of the overlapping dough slightly so that when the dough is overlapped, it has the same thickness as the other three sides.

A top crust, or **cap**, is the traditional way to finish enclosing the forcemeat in pastry. Straight-sided pâtés can be prepared without a separate cap piece as follows: Remove the **pins** of the mold, place the bottom of the mold on the top of the pâté, reinsert the pins, and invert the entire assembly. This will give a smooth, neat top piece, without any extra layers of dough. It also allows the weight of the pâté and mold to hold the seams along the edges of the mold, preventing them from blowing out as the pâté bakes.

Oval pâtés or other shapes should have a separate cap piece. Cut a piece of dough large enough to completely cover the mold. Trim away any excess and tuck the edges down into the mold.

2. Bake the pâté, adding the chimney and any additional dough garnishes as desired. The top crust of the pâté should be vented by cutting a hole in the top to permit steam to escape during baking. If the vent is not cut, the pressure will cause the dough to burst. Be sure that the cut extends completely through every layer of dough and liner. Reinforce the vent's opening by gluing a ring of dough around the hole into place with some egg wash (see Fig 7-12c).

Insert a cylinder of rolled aluminum foil, known as a chimney, to keep the hole from closing as the pâté bakes.

Any decorations made from dough scraps can be added now. You can complete these tasks before baking the pâté. Egg wash should be brushed over the entire surface for color and sheen, as well as to secure the reinforcing ring of dough and any decorations to the top crust.

An alternate method is to cover the pâté with foil and partially bake at 450°F / 232°C for 15 minutes, or until the dough has a dry and light brown appearance. Remove the foil, and use round cutters to make one or two holes in the top piece and brush with egg wash.

Secure any additional decorative pieces to the cap piece, gluing them in place with egg wash. Finally, egg wash the entire top of the pâté. Return the uncovered pâté to the oven and finish baking at 350°F / 177°C to the appropriate internal temperature.

3. Cool the pâté en croûte and finish with aspic. Let the pâté cool to 90° to 100°F / 32° to 38°C. Insert a funnel into the foil chimney and ladle in melted warm aspic (see Fig 7-12d).

Refrigerate the pâté at least twenty-four hours and up to three days before slicing and serving the pâté. Once a pâté en croûte is shaped, baked, and finished with aspic, it may be held for approximately five to seven days.

FIG 7-12A | *Using sections of dough that have been cut to the size of each side, line the mold with the dough, sealing the seams where the sections of dough meet.*

FIG 7-12B | *After lining the dough, in this case with fatback, evenly spread a prepared forcemeat into the mold.*

FIG 7-12C | *After enclosing the forcemeat by overlapping the overhanging sections of dough, cut a small hole in the top of the dough and adhere a chimney ring to the top of the cut-*

FIG 7-12D | *Once baked and cooled, seal the pâté en croûte by pouring or funneling melted aspic through the chimney.*

*Terrines, pâtés, galantines, and roulades*    315

# Galantines and roulades

**Galantines,** as we know them, have been popular since the time of the French Revolution (1789–99). The chef from the house of Marquis de Brancas, an M. Prévost, began producing the savory cold dish, made from boned poultry, sewn back into the bird's **skin,** poached in a rich stock, and preserved in the natural jelly. The origin of the dish appears relatively straightforward. The origins of the word, however, are less obvious.

According to *Larousse Gastronomique,* the term derives primarily from an old French word for chicken: *géline* or *galine.* According to this source, the association with chicken is so specific, in fact, that all by itself, *galantine* presumes chicken, unless it is specified otherwise in the title. Other experts have promoted the idea that galantine more likely comes from the word *gelatin,* with the current spelling gradually superseding other forms of the word, such as *galentyne, galyntyne, galandyne,* and *galendine.*

Two additional terms, **ballotine** and **dodine,** are occasionally used in the same way as galantine. Ballotines may be served hot or cold. Dodines, also normally made from poultry, especially duck and goose, are quite similar to galantines except that they are roasted rather than poached, and they are always served hot.

**Roulades** differ from galantines in that they are rolled in cheesecloth or plastic wrap, not in the natural skin "casing" featured in galantines. Another distinction between the two items is that, while galantines are firmly associated with poultry, roulades have no such identity. Instead, roulades are made from a wide range of base products, including foie gras or mousseline forcemeats made of fish or poultry.

## *Making galantines and roulades*

1. **Carefully remove the skin and bone the bird for a galantine.** The first step in preparing a galantine is to carefully remove the skin from the bird. Make an incision along the backbone, and carefully pull and cut away the skin from the meat (see Fig 7-13a). Keep the skin in a single piece and trim it to an even rectangle.

    You may wish to save the breast portion or tenderloin to use as a garnish. These choice parts can be seared or cured, if desired. They may be placed as a center garnish or flattened to form the exterior of the galantine.

2. **Fill and roll the galantine or roulade.** Lay out plastic wrap and/or cheesecloth, which should be several inches larger than the skin's dimensions. If you are using cheesecloth, remember to rinse it well and wring it dry, until it is damp but not dripping wet.

    Lay out the skin on the cheesecloth or plastic wrap and fill it with the forcemeat and any garnish (see Fig 7-13b).

    The chicken breast may be pounded and laid on the skin with the forcemeat in the middle, or the forcemeat can be spread on the skin and the chicken breast can be used as a garnish. Roll the galantine or roulade carefully around the forcemeat. The skin should just overlap itself by about ½ in / 1 cm, forming a seam. A roulade can be rolled like a jelly roll to create a spiral effect, or as you would for a galantine to keep a centered garnish in place. Secure the galantine or roulade by crimping each end and smoothing the forcemeat away from the ends. You may need a pair of extra hands to maintain a compact shape while you tie the ends (see Fig 7-13c).

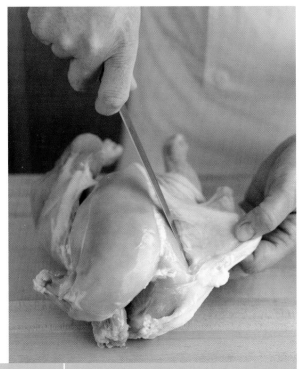

FIG 7-13A | *Remove the skin from the chicken, reserving it as one whole piece.*

FIG 7-13B | *Layer a garnish, in this case whole chicken breasts, and prepared forcemeat over the reserved skin.*

FIG 7-13C | *After rolling the galantine, secure it by tying off both ends with butcher's twine and securing the middle with two bands of cheesecloth.*

FIG 7-13D | *Finish the galantine by poaching it in chicken stock.*

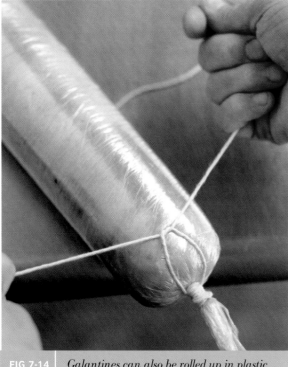

FIG 7-14 | *Galantines can also be rolled up in plastic wrap, but they still need to be tightly secured.*

FIG 7-15 | *A galantine can be roasted on a rack, wrapped in aluminum foil, then seared to provide additional color.*

3. **Prepare the galantine or roulade by poaching or roasting.** Galantines and roulades are commonly poached. Lower the galantine or roulade into a simmering pot of stock (water is fine if the roulade has been wrapped in plastic wrap rather than cheesecloth) (see Figs 7-13d and 7-14).

To keep the galantine submerged, weight it with small plates. This helps to cook the galantine evenly. A roasted galantine is placed on a bed of mirepoix or a rack and cooked, uncovered, to the appropriate internal temperature. Another method for roasting a galantine is employed by wrapping the galantine in foil and roasting it in the oven until it is cooked, unwrapping it, and then searing the skin to create a mahogany color on the outside (see Fig 7-15). This method allows the filling to set during cooking so that the cylindrical shape of the galantine is maintained.

Once properly cooked (check the internal temperature for accurate results), galantines should be completely cooled. They may be cooled directly in the cooking liquid; roulades are generally removed from the poaching liquid and cooled. Galantines and roulades should be rewrapped to produce an even, appealing texture.

# Foie gras

**Foie gras** is one of the world's great luxury items. The earliest records of foie gras go back to 2500 B.C.E. The tombs dedicated to Ti, an Egyptian counselor to the Pharaoh, show scenes of Egyptians hand-feeding figs to geese.

The first published recipe for **pâté de foie gras** appeared in *Le Cuisinier Gascon,* a cookbook published in 1747. Jean-Pierre Clause developed another classic preparation in Strasbourg. He took a foie gras and truffles, wrapped them in a pastry case, and baked the dish. Escoffier included a version of this same dish, Pâté Strasbourgeois, in *Le Guide Culinaire.*

Today, foie gras is produced from both **geese** and **ducks.** Fresh foie gras is finally available to chefs in the United States. Izzy Yanay, an Israeli who moved to the United States in 1981, is currently producing **domestic foie gras** from the **moulard** duck, a hybrid breed resulting from cross-breeding Muscovy (or Barbary) and Pekin ducks.

# Working with foie gras

## Grades

Foie gras may receive an **A, B, or C grade,** based on the size, appearance, and texture of the liver (see Fig 7-16).

To receive a grade of A, the liver must weigh at least 1 lb 8 oz /680 g. It should be round and firm, with no blemishes. These livers are used for terrines and pâtés.

B-grade foie gras weighs between 1 lb / 454 g and 1 lb 3 oz / 539 g. It should have a good texture but are not necessarily as round in shape as foie gras graded A. This is a good choice for roasting or sautéing.

Foie gras that weighs less than 1 lb / 454 g, is slightly flattened, and has some visual imperfections will receive a grade of C. These livers may have some soft spots. They are used primarily for mousses.

## Upon arrival

1. **Inspect the foie gras.** This is an expensive product, whatever grade you buy. So take the time to be certain that you are getting the quality you are paying for. First, look to be certain that the packaging is still intact. Any rips or punctures may have damaged the foie gras. Weigh the foie gras yourself, and inspect it carefully for any unexpected imperfections.

2. **Prepare the foie gras for refrigerated storage.** Set the foie gras on a bed of crushed ice in a perforated hotel pan, set inside a standard hotel pan. Pack more ice around the liver and keep this assembly in the refrigerator until you are ready to prepare the foie gras.

3. **Temper the foie gras before cleaning.** Soak the foie gras in salted water and/or milk at room temperature for at least two hours. This will **temper** the foie gras, making it easier to manipulate as you remove the veins. Inspect the surface and remove visible bruises or blemishes or traces of green bile with a sharp paring knife.

| FIG 7-16 | **GRADES OF FOIE GRAS, FROM LEFT TO RIGHT:** *A, B, C* |

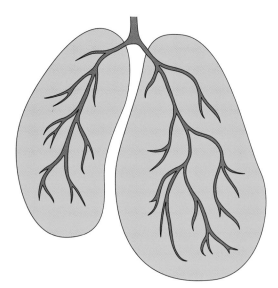

**FIG 7-17** *Vein network of foie gras*

4. **Separate the foie gras into lobes and remove the veins.** Holding the liver in both hands, gently pull the two lobes apart at their natural seam. Cut about one-third of the way into the lobe. Using a combination of pulling and loosening, expose the vein network (see Fig 7-17).

Starting from the top of the lobe, where the veins are thickest, pull out the veins, using tweezers, the tip of a knife, and/or your fingertips. Try to remove as much of the vein network in one piece as possible. Once the small vessels break, they are very hard to grip. Work carefully, but quickly, to avoid overhandling the foie gras. You want to keep the lobes as intact as possible.

This procedure takes practice, but once mastered it should take only a few minutes to complete. If you are not ready to proceed with a recipe, be sure to store the cleaned foie gras, well wrapped in plastic, at approximately 34°F / 1°C. It is important to keep the foie gras as cold as possible, both to keep it safe and wholesome and to keep it firm enough to slice or dice neatly.

## Marinating foie gras

Foie gras terrines, pâtés, and roulades typically call for **marinated** foie gras. Place the cleaned foie gras in a suitable container and add seasonings as indicated by the recipe. Sauternes, port, cognac, and Armagnac are among the classic marinade ingredients. You may also wish to incorporate additional flavorings, such as quatres épices, cinnamon, or allspice, to give the dish finished a special flavor. Turn the foie gras to coat it evenly with the marinade, and let it rest, covered, refrigerated for at least 12 and up to 24 hours.

Pâtés, roulades, and terrines of foie gras are still made according to time-honored methods (recipes for these items appear on pages 329, 341, 342, and 436). Today they may be presented to the guest still in their ceramic crock, cut into slices or shaped into quenelles. A classic presentation, made famous by Fernand Point, features foie gras baked in brioche (see page 435 for recipe). Foie gras mousse is another popular item, and has been used with great effect to make special canapés and appetizers (see page 341 for mousse recipe).

# Pâté Grand-Mère

YIELD: *1 terrine [3 lb / 1.36 kg 18 to 20 servings (2½ oz / 71 g each)]*

1 lb 4 oz / 567 g chicken livers, sinew removed

1 lb 1 oz / 482 g pork butt, cubed

1 tsp / 2.75 g tinted curing mixture (TCM)

1 tbsp / 15 mL vegetable oil, as needed

1 fl oz / 30 mL brandy

SEASONINGS

1½ oz / 43 g salt

1 tsp / 2 g coarse-ground black pepper (plus more as needed for liner)

¼ tsp / 0.50 g ground bay leaf

½ tsp / 1 g ground thyme

1 oz / 28 g shallots, minced

1 tbsp / 3 g chopped flat-leaf parsley

2½ oz / 71 g crustless white bread, cut into small dice

5 fl oz / 150 mL milk, warm

2 eggs

3 fl oz / 90 mL heavy cream

¼ tsp / 0.50 g ground white pepper

Pinch freshly ground nutmeg

8 slices fatback (¹⁄₁₆ in / 1.50 mm thick), or as needed for liner

6 to 8 fl oz / 180 to 240 mL Aspic Gelée, melted (page 58) (optional)

1. Sear the livers briefly in hot oil; remove them from the pan, and chill. Sauté the shallots in the same pan; deglaze with the brandy and add to the livers. Mix in seasoning. Chill thoroughly.

2. Progressively grind the pork butt, the liver and shallot mixture, and parsley from the coarse plate (⅜ in / 9mm) to the fine plate (⅛ in / 3 mm) of a meat grinder into a bowl set over an ice bath.

3. Combine the bread and milk; let soak to form a panada. Add the eggs, heavy cream, pepper, and nutmeg. Mix with the ground meats on medium speed until homogenous, about 1 minute. Test the forcemeat and adjust seasoning if necessary before proceeding.

4. Line a terrine mold with plastic wrap and then the fatback slices, leaving an overhang. Sprinkle the fatback with more ground pepper, pack the forcemeat into the mold, and fold over the liners. Refrigerate overnight to cure. Cover the terrine and bake in a 170°F / 77°C water bath in a 300°F / 150°C oven to an internal temperature of 165°F / 74°C, about 60 to 75 minutes.

5. Remove the terrine from the water bath and allow it to cool to an internal temperature of 90°F / 32°C to 100°F / 38°C. Apply a press plate and a 2-lb / 907-g weight and press overnight. Alternately, pour off the juices from the terrine, add enough aspic to coat and cover the terrine, and refrigerate for 2 days. The terrine is now ready to slice and serve, or wrap and refrigerate for up to 10 days.

# Pâte de Campagne

YIELD: *1 terrine (3 lb / 1.36 kg; 18 to 20 servings)*

1 lb 8 oz / 680 g pork butt, trimmed of excess fat

8 oz / 227 g chicken liver or foie gras; ½-in / 1-cm dice

4 oz / 113 g pork fatback, skin off, cut into ½-in / 1-cm cubes

¾ oz / 21 g salt

¼ tsp / 0.50 g coarsely ground black pepper

2 oz / 57 g shallots, minced

3 garlic cloves, minced

½ tsp / 1.3 g tinted curing mix (TCM)

4 juniper berries, finely crushed

2 tsp / 2 g fresh thyme, chopped

2 tbsp / 6.5 g Italian parsley, chopped

⅛ tsp / 0.25 g pâté spice

2 tsp / 4 g dried cèpes, ground into powder

PANADA

2 oz / 57 mL heavy cream

1 egg

1½ oz / 42.5 g fresh white bread crumbs

½ oz / 15 mL calvados

GARNISH

1 oz / 28 g black truffles cut into ³⁄₁₆-in / 5-mm dice

3 oz / 85 g pork fatback, cut into ³⁄₁₆-in / 5-mm dice and blanched

1 tsp / 2 g green peppercorns

1½ oz / 43 g pistachios, blanched, peeled

1 lb / 454 g smoked ham, thinly sliced

1. Cut 8 oz / 227 g trimmed pork butt into ³⁄₁₆-in / 5-mm dice and reserve for garnish. Dice the remaining pound of pork and toss together with the seasonings. Progressively grind the mixture along with the chicken liver or foie gras and fatback from a ¼-in / 6-mm die to a ⅛-in / 3-mm die. Combine the panada ingredients in a bowl and whisk together until smooth. Add to the ground meat mixture along with the diced pork butt.

2. Prepare a poach test and adjust seasoning as necessary.

3. Combine the truffles, blanched fatback, peppercorns, and pistachios and add to the forcemeat.

4. Line desired mold with plastic wrap followed by the thin slices of ham, leaving an overhang on both. Pack the forcemeat into the terrine and fold over the ham and plastic wrap.

5. Bake the terrine in a 170°F / 77°C water bath in a 300° F / 149° C degree oven until a finished internal temperature of 165°F / 74°C (if using chicken) or 145°F / 63°C (if using foie gras) is reached. (This does not take into consideration carry over cooking.)

6. Weigh the terrine with a 1-lb / 454-g weight and refrigerate at least 24 hours. Cut into slices approximately ¼ in / 6 mm thick.

*Chef's note*    *2 lb / 907 g fatback that is pounded to flatten the bottom, frozen, and sliced thin can be substituted for the ham.*

# Chicken Liver Pâté

YIELD: *1 terrine (3 lb / 1.36 kg; 18 to 20 servings)*

2 lb 4 oz / 1.02 kg chicken livers, cleaned, sinew removed

24 fl oz / 720 mL milk, or as needed for soaking

¾ oz / 21 g salt

¼ tsp / 0.66 g tinted curing mix (TCM)

12 oz / 340 g fresh fatback, cut into medium dice

2½ oz / 71 g minced shallots

3 garlic cloves, minced

2 tsp / 4 g ground white pepper

¾ tsp / 1.5 g ground allspice

¾ tsp / 1.5 g dry mustard

2 oz / 55 g fresh white bread crumbs

1½ fl oz / 45 mL sherry

4½ oz / 128 g bread flour

1 tbsp / 9 g powdered gelatin

5 eggs

9 fl oz / 270 mL heavy cream

1. Soak the chicken livers in the milk with 2¼ tsp / 7 g salt and the TCM for 12 to 24 hours. When ready to use, drain well and pat dry with paper towels.

2. Purée all ingredients except the cream in a blender to a smooth, loose paste.

3. Pass through a wire-mesh strainer into a stainless-steel bowl.

4. Stir in the cream.

5. Refrigerate the mixture for 2 hours.

6. Pour into a terrine mold lined with plastic wrap, cover, and poach in a 170°F / 77°C water bath in a 300°F / 149°C oven to an internal temperature of 165°F / 74°C, about 45 minutes to 1 hour.

7. Remove from the oven and let cool at room temperature for 30 minutes.

8. Press with a 1-lb / 454-g weight and refrigerate overnight before unmolding and slicing.

*Variation*   *Smoked Chicken Liver Pâté: Cut 12 oz / 340 g livers into medium dice and pan-smoke (see page 200) for a flavorful contrasting garnish. For even more flavor, the terrine can also be lined with sliced ham.*

# Duck and Smoked Ham Terrine

YIELD: *1 terrine (3 lb / 1.36 kg; 18 to 20 servings)*

1 lb 3 oz / 539 g duck leg and thigh meat, skinned and boned

9¾ oz / 276 g fatback

GARNISH

1¼ oz / 35 g butter

1¼ skinless duck breasts, cut into ½-in / 1-cm dice

15 oz / 425 g smoked ham, cut into ½-in / 1-cm dice

1 oz / 28 g minced shallots

1¼ tsp / 4 g minced garlic

2½ fl oz / 75 mL port wine

1¼ tbsp / 8 g all-purpose flour

¼ tsp / 0.50 g tinted curing mix (TCM)

½ oz / 14 g salt

1 egg

4¾ fl oz / 143 mL heavy cream

1¼ tsp / 2.50 g coarse-ground black pepper

¾ tsp / 1.50 g poultry seasoning

1. Cut the leg and thigh meat and the fatback into ½-in / 1-cm dice. Reserve.

2. Prepare the garnish: Melt the butter in a sauté pan. Brown the duck breast and ham; remove and chill. Sweat the shallots and garlic. Add the port wine and reduce to a thick syrup; chill well.

3. Combine the leg meat mixture with the flour, TCM, and salt; toss to coat evenly. Progressively grind from the coarse (⅜ in / 9 mm) through the fine plate (⅛ in / 3 mm) of a meat grinder into a mixing bowl over an ice bath.

4. Transfer the ground meats to a chilled mixing bowl. Add the egg and heavy cream. Mix on medium speed for 1 minute, until homogenous. Add the black pepper and poultry seasoning; mix to incorporate.

5. Test the forcemeat and adjust seasoning if necessary before proceeding.

6. Fold the garnish mixture into the forcemeat by hand over an ice bath.

7. Line a terrine mold with plastic wrap, leaving an overhang. Pack the forcemeat into the mold, and fold over the liner. Cover the terrine and bake in a 170°F / 77°C water bath in a 300°F / 150°C oven to an internal temperature of 165°F / 74°C, about 60 to 75 minutes.

8. Remove the terrine from the water bath and allow it to cool to an internal temperature of 90°F / 32°C to 100°F / 38°C. Apply a press plate and a 2-lb / 907-g weight and press overnight. Alternately, pour off the juices from the terrine, add enough aspic to coat and cover the terrine, and refrigerate for 2 days. The terrine is now ready to slice and serve, or wrap and refrigerate for up to 5 days.

# Venison Terrine

**YIELD:** *1 terrine [(3 lb; 18 to 20 servings (2½ oz / 71 g each)]*

2 lb / 907 g venison shoulder or leg meat

1 lb / 454 g fatback

SEASONINGS

2 fl oz / 60 mL red wine

½ tsp / 1 g ground cloves

1 tsp /6 g crushed black peppercorns

1 oz / 2¾ g tinted curing mix (TCM)

1 oz / 28 g minced onions, sautéed and cooled

1½ tbsp / 15 g salt

2 tsp / 4 g ground black pepper

1 oz / 28 g dried cèpes or morels, ground to powder

3 eggs

6 fl oz / 180 mL heavy cream

1 tbsp / 3 g chopped tarragon

1 tbsp / 3 g chopped flat-leaf parsley

GARNISH

2 oz / 57 g golden raisins, plumped in 4 fl oz / 120 mL brandy

4 oz /113 g mushrooms, diced, sautéed, and cooled

8 thin slices ham ( 1¹⁄₁₆ in  / 1.50 mm), or as needed for liner

1.  Dice venison and fatback into 1-in / 2-cm cubes. Marinate them with the seasonings and refrigerate overnight.

2.  Prepare a straight forcemeat by grinding the marinated venison and fatback into a chilled mixing bowl. Mix in the eggs, heavy cream, tarragon, and parsley on medium speed until homogenous, about 1 minute. Fold the raisins and mushrooms into the forcemeat.

3.  Line a terrine mold with plastic wrap, then with the ham, leaving an overhang. Pack the forcemeat into the terrine mold and fold over the ham and plastic. Cover the terrine.

4.  Bake forcemeat in a 170°F / 77°C water bath in a 300°F / 149°C oven to an internal temperature of 150°F / 66°C, about 60 to 70 minutes.

5.  Remove the terrine from the water bath and allow it to cool to an internal temperature of 90°F / 32°C to 100°F / 38°C. Apply a press plate and a 2-lb / 907-g weight. Refrigerate and press overnight. The terrine is now ready to slice and serve, or wrap and refrigerate for up to 10 days.

# Duck Terrine with Pistachios and Dried Cherries

YIELD: *1 terrine (3 lb / 1.36 kg; 18 to 20 servings)*

1 lb 12 oz / 794 g duck meat, trimmed and cubed (from 4- to 5-pound bird)

8 oz / 227 g fatback

SEASONINGS

1 tbsp / 9 g salt

2 tbsp / 6 g chopped sage

1 tsp / 5 mL white pepper

1 tbsp / 3 g chopped flat-leaf parsley

¼ tsp / 0.66 g tinted curing mix (TCM)

GARNISH

4 oz / 113 g ham, cut into small dice

3 oz / 85 g roasted and peeled pistachios

2½ oz / 71 g dried cherries

8 thin slices ham (¹⁄₁₆ in / 1.5 mm), or as needed for liner

1. Combine 1 lb / 454 g of the duck meat, the fatback, and the seasonings, and grind through the medium plate (¼ in / 6 mm) and then the fine plate (⅛ in / 3 mm) of a meat grinder.

2. Sear the remaining duck meat and the diced ham; let cool.

3. Test the forcemeat and adjust seasoning before adding garnish.

4. Fold in the seared duck, ham, pistachios, and cherries, working over an ice bath.

5. Line a terrine mold with plastic wrap and ham slices, leaving an overhang, then pack with the forcemeat. Fold the liners over the terrine and cover the mold. Bake in a 170°F / 77°C water bath in a 300°F / 149°C oven to an internal temperature of 165°F / 74°C, about 50 to 60 minutes.

6. Let the terrine rest for 1 hour. Weight it with a 2-lb / 907-g press plate and refrigerate overnight or up to 3 days. Slice and serve immediately, or wrap and refrigerate for up to 7 days.

# Lobster Terrine with Summer Vegetables

YIELD: *1 terrine (3 lb / 1.36 kg; 18 to 20 servings)*

6 oz / 170 g diced scallops

6 oz / 170 g diced shrimp

SEASONINGS

1¼ fl oz / 22.50 mL Pernod

1½ tsp / 7.50 mL lemon juice

1½ tsp / 5 g salt

¾ tsp / 2 g ground white pepper

¾ tsp / 2.25 g grated lemon zest

pinch cayenne pepper

1½ egg whites

7½ fl oz / 225 mL heavy cream, chilled

GARNISH

15 oz / 425 g assorted vegetables, cut into

¼-in / 6-mm dice, cooked, cooled, and drained (see Chef's note)

15 oz / 425 g lobster meat, poached and cut into medium dice

1. Make a mousseline forcemeat by grinding the scallops, shrimp, and seasonings in the bowl of a food processor. Process to a relatively smooth paste. Add the egg whites. With the machine running, add the heavy cream and process just to incorporate. Pass the forcemeat through a drum sieve if desired.

2. Test the forcemeat and adjust seasoning if necessary before proceeding.

3. Fold in the garnish by hand, working over an ice bath.

4. Oil a terrine mold and line it with plastic wrap, leaving an overhang. Pack the forcemeat into the lined mold, making sure to remove any air pockets. Fold the liner over the forcemeat to completely encase the terrine, and cover.

5. Bake the terrine in a 170°F / 77°C water bath in a 300°F / 149°C oven to an internal temperature of 145°F / 63°C, 60 to 75 minutes.

6. Remove the terrine from the water bath and allow it to cool to 90°F / 32°C. Apply a press plate and 2-lb / 907-g weight to the terrine and press overnight.

7. Let the terrine rest at least overnight and up to 3 days, refrigerated and weighted with a 2-lb /907-g press plate if desired. Slice and serve immediately, or wrap and refrigerate for up to 7 days.

*Presentation idea*  Serve with Basic Mayonnaise (page 36) flavored with chopped basil, and tomato concassé garnish.

*Chef's note*  For vegetable garnish, choose from broccoli, carrots, zucchini, squash, and shiitake or other mushrooms.

# Chicken and Crayfish Terrine

YIELD: *1 terrine (3 lb / 1.36 kg; 18 to 20 servings)*

MOUSSELINE

1 lb 8 oz / 680 g ground chicken breast

3 egg whites

1 tbsp / 10 g salt

¾ tsp / 1.50 g ground black pepper

9 fl oz / 270 mL Shellfish Essence, chilled (recipe follows)

3 fl oz / 90 mL heavy cream, chilled

GARNISH

12 oz / 340 g cooked crayfish tails, shelled and deveined

1½ chipotles in adobo sauce, minced

9 shiitake mushrooms, cut into medium dice, sautéed, and chilled

3 tbsp / 9 g chopped cilantro

1½ tbsp / 4.50 g chopped dill

1. Make a mousseline forcemeat: Process the ground chicken, egg whites, salt, and pepper. Add the shellfish essence and heavy cream with the machine running, and process just to incorporate. Pass the forcemeat through a drum sieve if desired.

2. Test the forcemeat and adjust seasoning if necessary before proceeding.

3. Fold in the crayfish tails, chipotles, mushrooms, cilantro, and dill, working over an ice bath.

4. Oil a terrine mold and line it with plastic wrap, leaving an overhang. Pack the forcemeat into the lined mold, making sure to remove any air pockets. Fold the liner over the forcemeat to completely encase the terrine; cover.

5. Bake the terrine in a 170°F / 77°C water bath in a 300°F / 149°C oven to an internal temperature of 165°F / 74°C, about 60 to 75 minutes.

6. Remove the terrine from the water bath and allow it to cool to 90°F / 32°C. Apply a press plate and 2-lb / 907-g weight to the terrine and press overnight.

7. Let the terrine rest, refrigerated, at least overnight and up to 3 days, weighted with a 2-lb / 907-g press plate if desired. The terrine is now ready to slice and serve, or wrap and refrigerate for up to 7 days.

*Chef's note*  The Shellfish Essence can be prepared using the shells reserved from this recipe or from other uses. Be sure to freeze the shells if they cannot be used within 12 hours.

# Shellfish Essence

YIELD: *9 fl oz / 270 mL*

1 lb 8 oz / 680 g crayfish, shrimp, or lobster shells

1½ tbsp / 22.50 mL vegetable oil

3 shallots, minced

3 garlic cloves, minced

18 fl oz / 540 mL heavy cream

4½ bay leaves

1 tbsp / 6 g poultry seasoning

1½ tbsp / 9 g chili powder

1½ fl oz / 45 mL Glace de Volaille or Viande (page 594)

1. Sauté the shells in the vegetable oil until bright red. Add the shallots and garlic; sauté until aromatic.

2. Add the heavy cream, bay leaves, poultry seasoning, and chili powder; reduce to half of original volume. Add the glace and squeeze through cheesecloth (final volume should be 9 fl oz / 270 mL); chill to below 40°F / 4°C.

# Sweetbread and Foie Gras Terrine

**YIELD:** *1 terrine (2 lb 12 oz/ 1.25 kg; 16 to 18 servings)*

| | |
|---|---|
| 1 lb / 454 g veal sweetbreads | 8 fl oz / 240 mL heavy cream |
| 8 fl oz / 240 mL milk | 2 tbsp / 20 g salt |
| 64 fl oz / 1.44 L Court Bouillon (page 594) | ½ tsp / 1 g ground white pepper |
| 12 oz / 340 g foie gras, B-grade | 1 tbsp / 3 g chopped chervil |
| ½ oz / 14 g albumen powder or powdered gelatin (optional) | 1 tbsp / 3 g chopped chives |
| | 8 thin slices cooked smoked tongue (¹⁄₁₆ in / 1.5 mm), or as needed for liner |
| MOUSSELINE | |
| 1 lb / 454 g lean veal | |
| 1 egg white | |

1. Soak sweetbreads overnight in the milk. Drain and poach in the court bouillon at 170°F / 77°C until just done and still pink inside. Cool and remove membranes. Break the sweetbreads into pieces approximately 1 in / 2 cm square.

2. Cut foie gras into cubes 1 in / 2 cm square. Dust with the albumen powder (if using).

3. Make a mousseline-style forcemeat by processing the veal, egg white, cream, salt, and pepper until smooth.

4. Test the forcemeat and adjust if necessary before proceeding.

5. Fold the sweetbreads, foie gras, and herbs into the forcemeat.

6. Line a terrine mold with plastic wrap and the sliced tongue, leaving an overhang.

7. Fill the mold with the forcemeat and smooth with a palette knife. Fold over the tongue and plastic wrap. Bake in a 170°F / 77°C water bath in a 300°F / 149°C oven until an internal temperature of 138°F / 58°C is reached, about 60 to 70 minutes.

8. Remove the terrine from the water bath and allow it to cool to an internal temperature of 90°F / 32°C to 100°F / 38°C. Press with approximately 6-lb / 2.72-kg weight. Let the terrine rest, refrigerated, overnight. Slice and serve immediately, or wrap and refrigerate for up to 3 days.

# Mediterranean Seafood Terrine

YIELD: *1 terrine (3 lb / 1.36 kg; 18 to 20 servings)*

MOUSSELINE

4 oz / 113 g shrimp, peeled, deveined, and diced

10 oz / 283 g scallops, diced

2 tsp / 6 g salt

½ tsp / 1 g ground white pepper

2 egg whites

5 fl oz / 150 mL heavy cream, infused with saffron and chilled (see Chef's Note)

GARNISH

8 oz / 227 g shrimp (16/20 count), split and cut into eighths

8 oz / 227 g sea scallops, quartered

1 tbsp / 3 g chopped parsley

2 tsp / 2 g chopped basil

1. Prepare a mousseline-style forcemeat by processing the shrimp, scallops, salt, pepper, egg whites, and saffron-infused cream until smooth.

2. Test the forcemeat and adjust if necessary before proceeding.

3. Fold the garnish ingredients into the forcemeat, working over an ice bath.

4. Line a terrine mold with plastic wrap, leaving an overhang, and fill it with the forcemeat. Fold over the plastic and cover the terrine.

5. Bake the terrine in a 170°F / 77°C water bath in a 300°F / 149°C oven to an internal temperature of 140°F / 60°C, about 20 to 25 minutes.

6. Remove the terrine from the water bath and allow it to cool to an internal temperature of 90°F / 32°C to 100°F / 38°C. Let the terrine rest, refrigerated, overnight. Slice and serve immediately, or wrap and refrigerate for up to 3 days.

*Presentation idea*  This terrine can be served with Red Pepper Coulis (page 55).

*Chef's note*  To make saffron-infused cream, heat 5 fl oz / 150 mL heavy cream to 160°F / 71°C. Add a pinch of crushed saffron and allow the saffron to steep in the cream away from the heat until it turns a brilliant yellow-gold color. Chill the cream well before using in the mousseline.

# Carolina Barbecue Terrine with Apricot Barbecue Sauce

YIELD: *1 terrine (3 lb / 1.36 kg; 18 to 20 servings)*

| | |
|---|---|
| 1 pork butt | 1 tbsp / 12 g sugar |
| DRY RUB | 1 tbsp / 6 g crushed red pepper |
| 1 oz / 28 g sweet Spanish paprika | 1 tsp / 3 g salt |
| 2 tbsp / 20 g salt | ½ tsp / 1 g finely ground black pepper |
| 1 oz / 28 g sugar | |
| 1 oz / 28 g dark brown sugar | 1 lb / 454 g collard greens, cleaned, blanched, and rough chopped |
| 2 tbsp / 12 g ground cumin | |
| 2 tbsp / 13 g chili powder | 4 fl oz / 120 mL Chicken or Turkey Stock (page 592) |
| 1 tbsp / 6 g finely ground black pepper | |
| 1 tbsp / 6 g cayenne | 4 fl oz / 120 mL Glace de Volaille, warmed (page 594) |
| SPICED VINEGAR | 2 pork tenderloins, brined overnight in Basic Meat Brine, and hot smoked (see page 220) |
| 2 fl oz / 60 mL cider vinegar | |

1. Trim pork butt of excess fat, leaving approximately ¼ in / 6 mm fat cover. Score fat in criss-cross pattern.

2. Combine the dry rub ingredients and rub into the butt. Refrigerate overnight.

3. Combine the ingredients for the spiced vinegar in a saucepan. Heat and allow to steep for 30 minutes.

4. Smoke-roast the pork butt at 225°F / 107°C for 4 to 6 hours to an internal temperature of 150°F / 66°C until tender, basting with the spiced vinegar. Remove from the oven and allow to rest until cool enough to handle.

5. Pull the meat from the bones, discarding any fat and gristle. Shred the meat into small pieces and combine with the collards, stock, and glace.

6. Oil a terrine mold and line with plastic wrap, leaving an overhang. Pack half of the meat into the mold. Place the fully cooked pork tenderloins in the center as garnishes. Fill to the top of the mold with the remaining meat. Fold over liner.

7. Let the terrine rest, refrigerated, for 2 to 3 days, weighted with a 4-lb / 1.81-kg press plate if desired. Slice and serve immediately, or wrap and refrigerate for up to 7 days.

# Seared Lamb, Artichoke, and Mushroom Terrine

YIELD: *1 terrine (3 lb / 1.36 kg; 18 to 20 servings)*

1½ whole lamb loin, bone-in

SPICES

2¼ tsp / 4.50 g curry powder

2¼ tsp / 5.25 g celery seed

2¼ tbsp / 11.25 g whole coriander seeds

1½ tbsp / 9 g ground za'atar (see Chef's Notes)

1½ tbsp / 10 g fennel seed

3 tbsp / 30 g salt

3 tbsp / 18 g cumin seed

1½ tsp / 2 g anise seed

1½ tbsp / 22.50 mL olive oil

4½ oz / 128 g cèpes, quartered

Salt, as needed

Ground white pepper, as needed

ASPIC

1½ oz / 42 g tomato paste

12 oz / 340 g Mirepoix (page 586)

24 fl oz / 720 mL Chicken Stock (page 592)

1 oz / 28 g powdered gelatin

4½ artichoke bottoms, cooked and quartered

3 tbsp / 9 g chopped tarragon

3 tbsp / 9 g chopped parsley

1. Bone the loin, reserving the loins and tenderloins separately. Reserve the bones to prepare a stock.

2. Cut lamb loins lengthwise into two pieces, making 4 loin strips plus 2 tenderloin pieces.

3. Toast the spices; grind and rub over lamb. Marinate for 4 hours.

4. Sear the lamb to medium rare in a very hot sauté pan in olive oil. Cool and reserve.

5. Sauté the cèpes in hot oil, season with salt and pepper, and cook through. Cool and reserve.

6. Brown the lamb bones in the oven. Add the tomato paste and mirepoix; brown. Transfer bones and mirepoix to saucepan; add the chicken stock. Bring to a simmer and reduce by one third.

7. Strain through cheesecloth and cool. When cool, add the gelatin; bloom and heat to clear. Heat the aspic to 120°F / 49°C.

8. Oil a terrine mold and line it with plastic wrap, leaving an overhang. Mix the lamb, artichokes, cèpes, tarragon, and parsley. Mix in all but 6 fl oz / 180 mL of the aspic thoroughly and pack into the terrine mold. Pour the remaining aspic on top, spreading it over the entire length of the terrine. Use more stock if necessary.

9. Fold over liner and weight with a 2-lb / 907-g press plate. Refrigerate at least 24 hours before slicing and serving, or wrap and refrigerate for up to 10 days.

*Presentation idea*   *Serve this terrine with Hummus (page 52) and pita triangles.*

*Chef's note*   *One average bone-in lamb loin will yield approximately 1 lb / 454 g loin and tenderloin meat.*

*Za'atar is a Middle Eastern spice blend made of ground sumac and thyme. It can be purchased or made as needed.*

# Mushroom Terrine

YIELD: *1 terrine (3 lb / 1.36 kg; 18 to 20 servings)*

2 lb 4 oz / 1.02 kg assorted mushrooms, sliced

3 shallots, minced, sautéed, and cooled

4½ garlic cloves, minced, sautéed, and cooled

1½ fl oz / 45 mL vegetable oil

6 fl oz / 180 mL Madeira

3 fl oz / 90 mL brandy

3 tbsp / 9 g minced tarragon

3 tbsp / 9 g minced chives

3 tbsp / 9 g minced flat-leaf parsley

1½ fl oz / 45 mL Glace de Volaille (page 594), melted

1 tbsp / 9 g salt

¾ tsp / 1.50 g ground white pepper

1 lb 2 oz / 510 g chicken breast, raw, diced

1½ eggs

12 fl oz / 360 mL heavy cream

1. Sauté the mushrooms, shallots, and garlic in the vegetable oil.

2. Add the Madeira and brandy and reduce until ¾ fl oz / 23 mL liquid remains. Transfer to a bowl and add the tarragon, chives, parsley, glace, and half the salt and pepper. Chill.

3. Make a mousseline-style forcemeat by processing the chicken, the remaining salt and pepper, eggs, and cream until smooth.

4. Test the forcemeat and adjust seasoning if necessary before proceeding.

5. Fold in the mushroom and herb mixture, working over an ice bath.

6. Oil a terrine mold and line it with plastic wrap, leaving an overhang. Pack the forcemeat into the lined mold, making sure to remove any air pockets. Fold the liner over the forcemeat to completely encase the terrine, and cover.

7. Poach the terrine in a 170°F / 77°C water bath in a 300°F / 149°C oven until an internal temperature of 150°F / 66°C is reached, about 45 to 60 minutes.

8. Remove the terrine from the water bath and allow it to cool to an internal temperature of 90 to 100°F / 32 to 38°C. Weight with a 2-lb / 907-g weight and refrigerate overnight. Slice and serve immediately, or refrigerate for up to 3 days.

*Chef's note*  Scallops or salmon fillet can be substituted for the chicken.

# Terrine of Roasted Pheasant

**YIELD:** *1 terrine (2 lb 8 oz / 1.13 kg; 14 to 16 servings)*

| | |
|---|---|
| 1 pheasant, about 3 pounds | 4 fl oz / 120 mL Madeira |
| 64 fl oz / 1.44 L Basic Poultry Brine, chilled (page 217) | ½ oz / 14 g whole black peppercorns |
| ASPIC | 4 oz / 113 g baby braising greens, blanched and rough chopped |
| 32 fl oz / 960 mL Chicken Stock (page 592) | 2 tbsp / 6 g chopped flat-leaf parsley |
| ½ bunch parsley stems | 2 tsp / 6 g salt |
| 4 thyme sprigs | ½ tsp / 1 g coarse-ground black pepper |
| 2 tsp / 3 g crushed juniper berries | 1 tsp / 2 g Old Bay seasoning |

1. Cover the pheasant with the brine and weight with a plate to be sure it is completely submerged. Cure overnight. Remove the pheasant and rinse thoroughly.

2. Roast the pheasant to an internal temperature of 165°F / 74°C, about 35 to 45 minutes. Remove the pheasant from the oven and allow to cool.

3. Pull the meat from the bones. Reserve the bones and discard the skin. Shred the meat coarsely, cover, and refrigerate until ready to assemble the terrine.

4. Place the bones in a large pot and cover with the chicken stock. Bring to a slow, even simmer. Add the parsley stems, thyme, juniper, Madeira, and peppercorns; continue to simmer until the stock has a good flavor, at least 2 hours.

5. Strain the stock through a fine-mesh strainer, return it to the stove, and reduce it to 1 cup. Keep warm.

6. Line a terrine mold with plastic wrap, leaving an overhang. Combine the pheasant with the aspic, braising greens, chopped parsley, salt, pepper, and Old Bay. Pack into the mold. Fold over the liner.

7. Let the terrine rest, refrigerated, for at least 24 hours and up to 2 days. Slice and serve immediately, or wrap and refrigerate for up to 7 days.

*Chef's note* *Do not use red beet greens or red Swiss chard; they will discolor the terrine. A julienne of vegetables can also be added.*

# Poached Chicken Terrine

YIELD: *1 terrine (3 lb / 1.36 kg: 18 to 20 servings)*

3 lb / 1.36 kg chicken breast

1½ gal / 5.76 L Chicken Stock (page 592)

1½ standard Sachet d'Épices (page 587)

1½ tsp / 4.50 g salt

¾ tsp / 1.75 g ground white pepper

1½ oz / 43 g gelatin powder

12 oz / 340 g zucchini

12 oz / 340 g yellow squash

1 lb 14 oz / 851 g spinach, cleaned, seasoned, and blanched

1½ oz / 43 g minced Fines Herbes (page 590)

12 oz / 340 g carrots, cut into small dice and fully cooked

1. Skin the chicken and simmer in the chicken stock with the sachet d'épices until chicken is tender.

2. Shred the chicken meat into thick strips (about ¼ by 3 in / 6 mm by 7.5 cm).

3. Degrease and strain the stock; return to heat and reduce to approximately 36 fl oz / 1.08 L. Season with the salt and pepper. Cool. Sprinkle gelatin on top of stock. Let bloom 10 minutes. Melt over double boiler until clear.

4. Remove the seeds from the zucchini and yellow squash. Cut into small dice and blanch.

5. Lay the spinach leaves out on a piece of plastic wrap 8 by 12 in / 20 by 30 cm so that each leaf slightly overlaps the previous one. Cover with another piece of plastic wrap and roll over with a rolling pin to flatten.

6. Lay the spinach in the plastic wrap in the mold. Remove the top piece of plastic and paint the spinach leaves with a small amount of reduced stock. Sprinkle a thin layer of Fines Herbes over the painted spinach. Gently line a terrine mold with the spinach, leaving an overhang.

7. Mix the chicken and vegetables and any remaining Fines Herbes. Place this mixture in the mold. Pour in the stock. Fold over the liner.

8. Cover the terrine with plastic wrap and refrigerate overnight. Slice and serve immediately, or wrap and refrigerate for up to 7 days.

*Presentation idea*  Serve two thin slices of the terrine with 2 oz / 57 g Papaya and Black Bean Salsa (page 44) or Mango-Lime Salsa (page 43) or with Mustard-Walnut Vinaigrette (page 31)

*Chef's note*  The vegetables should be blanched separately to ensure even coloring and to prevent color transfer.

# Poached Salmon and Lemon Terrine

**YIELD:** *1 terrine (3 lb / 1.36 kg; 18 to 20 servings)*

2 lb / 907 g salmon fillet

64 fl oz / 1.92 L Court Bouillon (page 594), or as needed

24 fl oz / 720 mL Aspic Gelée (page 58), made with Fish Stock

Salt, as needed

GARNISH

3 egg whites, poached, cut into small dice

4 lemons, sectioned and seeded

½ oz / 14 g lemon zest, blanched and chopped fine

6 oz / 170 g roasted red pepper, peeled, seeded, and cut into small dice

2 tbsp / 6 g rough-chopped flat-leaf parsley

1 tbsp / 3 g rough-chopped tarragon

1 oz / 28 g fine-dice shallots

½ tsp / 1 g white pepper

1. Cut the salmon fillet into 5 strips the length of the terrine mold and about ¾ in / 1.75 cm square. Poach in the court bouillon until barely cooked, about 10 minutes. Drain and chill well.

2. Season the gelée with salt. Line a terrine with plastic wrap, leaving an overhang, then brush the sides and bottom with a thin layer of the gelée.

3. Working over an ice bath, fit the salmon and the combined garnish ingredients into the mold, covering each layer with fish aspic gelée. Make sure garnish is evenly distributed from end to end.

4. Fold over the plastic wrap, cover, and refrigerate at least 24 hours, weighted with a 2-lb / 907-g press plate if desired. Slice and serve immediately, or wrap and refrigerate for up to 4 days.

# Roasted Vegetable Terrine with Goat Cheese

**YIELD:** *1 terrine (3 lb / 1.36 kg; 18 to 20 servings)*

2 lb / 907 g zucchini (about 3)

2 lb / 907 g yellow squash (about 3)

1 lb 4 oz / 567 g eggplant (about 1 large)

2 lb / 907 g tomatoes (about 4)

2 portobello mushrooms

MARINADE

1 fl oz / 30 mL olive oil

1 tbsp / 15 g Dijon mustard

1 tbsp / 3 g chopped flat-leaf parsley

1 tbsp / 3 g chopped chives

2 garlic cloves, minced, sautéed, and cooled

2 tsp / 2 g chopped rosemary

2 tsp / 10 g anchovy paste (about 4 fillets)

½ oz / 14 g honey

2 tsp / 6 g salt

½ tsp / 1 g ground white pepper

8 oz / 227 g fresh goat cheese

1 egg

1. Cut all vegetables lengthwise into slices ⅛ in / 3 mm thick.

2. Combine the marinade ingredients and add to the vegetables.

3. Line sheet pans with oiled parchment and lay out the vegetables in a single layer.

4. Dry in 200°F / 93°C oven for 1 hour, or until dry but not brittle. Remove from oven and cool.

5. Mix the goat cheese with the egg to make the custard.

6. Line a terrine mold with plastic wrap, leaving an overhang, and assemble the terrine by alternating layers of vegetables and the cheese mixture until the terrine is filled. Fold over the liner.

7. Cover the terrine and bake in a 170°F / 77°C water bath in a 300°F / 150°C oven to an internal temperature of 145°F / 63°C, about 60 minutes.

8. Remove the terrine from the water bath and allow it to cool slightly.

9. Refrigerate the terrine at least overnight and up to 3 days, weighted with a 2-lb / 907-g press plate if desired. Slice and serve immediately, or wrap and refrigerate for up to 7 days.

*Chef's note* *Using a piping bag for the goat cheese custard makes it easier to distribute the custard evenly within the terrine. Vegetables can be marinated and grilled instead of dried.*

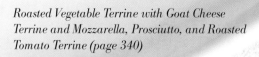

*Roasted Vegetable Terrine with Goat Cheese
Terrine and Mozzarella, Prosciutto, and Roasted
Tomato Terrine (page 340)*

# Mozzarella, Prosciutto, and Roasted Tomato Terrine

YIELD: *1 terrine (3 lb / 1.36 kg; 18 to 20 servings)*

| | |
|---|---|
| 9½ oz / 269 g Spinach Pasta (page 604) | 2½ tsp / 7.50 g salt |
| 14½ oz / 411 g Mozzarella Cheese (page 384) | 2½ tsp / 5 g ground black pepper |
| 3 lb 9½ oz / 1.63 kg ripe tomatoes | 9½ oz / 269 g thin slices prosciutto (⅟₁₆ in / 1.5 mm) |
| 6 tbsp / 15 g basil chiffonade | |
| 2½ fl oz / 75 mL olive oil | |

1. Prepare the spinach pasta as directed on page 604. Roll the pasta into thin sheets and trim as necessary to match the dimensions of the terrine mold. Cook the sheets until tender in simmering salted water. Drain, refresh in cold water, and drain again. Reserve.

2. Prepare the mozzarella as directed on page 384 through step 4. Roll and stretch the mozzarella into thin sheets (⅛ in / 3 mm thick) and trim as necessary to match the dimensions of your terrine mold. Or, if using purchased mozzarella, cut into thin slices to layer into terrine.

3. Cut tomatoes into slices ¼ in / 6 mm thick and season with basil, olive oil, salt, and pepper.

4. Lay tomatoes on a roasting rack and dry in a 200°F / 93°C oven for 2 to 3 hours. Cool and reserve.

5. Line the terrine mold with plastic wrap, leaving an overhang.

6. Assemble the terrine by layering pasta sheets, prosciutto, mozzarella, and roasted tomatoes, creating layers that cover the entire surface of the mold. Repeat process until ingredients are used up and mold is filled, finishing with a layer of pasta. Fold plastic wrap over and smooth over the top.

7. Cover with a lid and place in a water bath in a 250°F / 121°C oven for 30 minutes.

8. Cover with a 2-lb / 907-g press plate and refrigerate overnight. Slice and serve immediately, or refrigerate up to 3 days.

9. For service, cut into slices ³⁄₁₆ in / 9 mm thick with plastic wrap still on. Remove plastic wrap after slices have been plated.

*Presentation idea* This terrine may be served with a vinaigrette such as a tomato or balsamic, and a green salad. Grissini (page 602) or French bread slices topped with Tapenade (page 53) are also good accompaniments.

# Foie Gras Mousse Terrine

YIELD: *1 terrine (2 lb / 907 g; 10 to 12 servings)*

| | |
|---|---|
| 1 lb 8 oz / 680 g foie gras grade A, cleaned and veins removed | 2 oz / 57 g minced shallots |
| 2 tsp / 6 g salt | 1 garlic clove, minced |
| ½ tsp / 1 g ground white pepper | 4 oz / 113 g butter |
| 2 fl oz / 60 mL Sauternes | 6 fl oz / 180 mL heavy cream, whipped to medium peaks |

1. Marinate the foie gras in the salt, pepper, and wine overnight.

2. Drain foie gras and cut into chunks 1 in / 2 cm square.

3. Sauté the shallots and garlic in the butter until soft; do not brown.

4. Add the foie gras and cook over high heat, stirring continuously, until foie gras is cooked through, 4 to 5 minutes.

5. Cool mixture to 90°F / 32°C and purée in a food processor. Pass this mixture through a drum sieve into a 64-fl oz / 1.92-L bowl set over an ice bath.

6. Stir mixture continuously until it begins to thicken. Fold the whipped cream into the mixture, and adjust seasoning.

7. Line a terrine mold with plastic wrap, leaving an overhang. Fill with the foie gras mousse and smooth the top. Wrap and refrigerate at least overnight or up to 3 days before serving.

*Presentation idea* Foie gras mousse is best enjoyed on simple toasted croutons, but it can be used to embellish other hors d'oeuvre, such as prunes soaked in Armagnac and then filled with this mousse.

# Foie Gras Terrine

YIELD: *1 terrine (2 lb / 907 g; 10 to 12 servings (2½ oz / 71 g each)*

| | |
|---|---|
| 2 lb 12 oz / 1.25 kg foie gras, grade A | 1 tbsp / 12 g sugar |
| 2 tbsp / 18 g salt | ¼ tsp / 0.66 g tinted curing mix (TCM) |
| 2 tsp / 4 g ground white pepper | 16 fl oz / 480 mL white port or Sauternes |

1. Clean the livers, remove all veins, and dry well (see Fig 7-20a). Combine 1 tbsp / 9 g salt, 1 tsp / 2 g of the pepper, the sugar, TCM, and port. Add the livers to the mixture and refrigerate overnight.

2. Line a terrine mold with plastic wrap.

3. Remove the marinated foie gras from the refrigerator, place it on a cutting board, and slice into large pieces that will fit snugly into the mold. Place them in the mold so that the smooth sides of the foie gras pieces form the exterior of the terrine (see Fig 7-20b); season as needed with the remaining salt and pepper. Fill the mold up to the inner lip and press the pieces down tightly to remove any air pockets. Cover the terrine mold.

4. Bake the terrine in a hot water bath, maintaining it at a constant 160°F / 71°C, for 45 to 50 minutes. The oven temperature may need to be adjusted to keep the water at a constant temperature. If it gets too hot, add cold water immediately to lower the temperature. Foie gras has the best texture and flavor when cooked to an internal temperature of 118°F / 48°C. (Be sure to check with your local and state health authorities, however.)

5. Remove the terrine from the water bath and allow it to rest for 2 hours at room temperature, then pour off the fat (see Fig 7-20c). Cover the terrine with a press plate and top with a 1- to 2-lb / 454- to 907-g weight. Refrigerate for at least 24 hours and up to 48 hours to mellow and mature.

6. Remove the plastic wrap and carefully remove the congealed fat. Then tightly rewrap the terrine in fresh wrap. Slice and serve immediately (see Fig 7-20d) or refrigerate for up to 3 days.

*Presentation ideas*  Foie gras terrines may be sliced for plated presentations or served directly in the terrine.
Take the time to select the most appropriate accompaniments. You may want to consult with your sommelier or make suggestions yourself to the dining room staff so that they can help guests choose the most appropriate wine or other beverage to enjoy with the terrine.
When you are ready to serve the terrine, remove the weight and carefully pull off the press plate. To neaten up the appearance, smooth out the top with a small knife and clean the edges of the terrine with a towel. Or you may wish to score the top in a cross-hatched pattern if it is to be served directly in the terrine.

*Chef's notes*  To determine the amount of foie gras needed to fill any size terrine mold, simply measure the volume of water the terrine can hold. The number of fl oz / mL in volume will correlate to the number of oz / g in weight of foie gras necessary to fill the mold.
For easier service, slice the terrine with the plastic wrap on. Remove the plastic after the slices have been plated. A warm beveled knife works best. Save any fat removed in step 5 to use to sauté vegetables or potatoes.

*Variation*  Foie Gras Roulade: Prepare the foie gras as directed for the terrine. Arrange the marinated foie gras on a large sheet of plastic wrap; wrap tightly around the foie gras to form a roulade. If desired, insert whole truffles into the foie gras lobes before rolling the roulade. Poach in a 160°F / 71°C water bath to an internal temperature of 118°F / 48°C. Remove from the water, cool, and rewrap.Refrigerate for at least 24 hours before slicing. This roulade may also be baked in brioche (see page 435) and served as an appetizer.

*Working carefully, remove the vein network from the interior of each lobe of foie gras.*

*Pack the foie gras into a plastic-wrap-lined terrine mold to form it to the mold's shape.*

*After allowing the baked terrine to rest, pour off the excess fat and reserve it for other uses.*

*The finished terrine will be evenly colored and hold its shape once sliced.*

# Grilled Portobello Mushroom Terrine with Roasted Peppers, Olives, and Coach Farm Goat Cheese

YIELD: *1 terrine (2 lb / 907 g; 14 servings)*

### GRILLED PORTOBELLOS

5⅓ fl oz / 158 mL pure olive oil

2 tbsp / 18 g finely minced garlic

3 tbsp / 9 g coarsely minced thyme

2 tbsp / 9 g coarsely minced rosemary

Salt, as needed

Black pepper, as needed

6 lb / 2.72 kg portobello mushrooms

4 oz / 120 mL chicken stock, hot

### ROASTED GARLIC

16 large garlic cloves, peeled

1 tbsp / 15 mL pure olive oil

1 tsp / 3 g salt

### ARTICHOKES

3 artichokes

2 fl oz / 60 mL lemon juice

24 fl oz / 720 mL water

1 tsp / 3 g salt

### OVEN-DRIED TOMATOES

1 lb 4 oz / 567 g plum tomatoes

1 tsp / 1 g thyme leaves

1 tsp / 1 g minced oregano

1 tsp / 1 g chopped basil

Salt, as needed

Sugar, as needed

1 tbsp / 15 mL extra-virgin olive oil

### ROASTED PEPPERS

1 lb / 454 g red peppers

1 lb / 454 g yellow peppers

### BALSAMIC VINAIGRETTE

3 fl oz / 90 mL balsamic vinegar

3 fl oz / 90 mL water

4 tsp / 20 mL powdered gelatin

1 garlic clove, minced

2 shallots, minced

Tabasco sauce, as needed

Salt, as needed

Coarsely ground black pepper, as needed

1½ tsp / 11 g honey

1½ tbsp / 4.5 g coarsely chopped marjoram

2 tbsp / 6 g coarsely chopped thyme

6 fl oz / 180 mL extra-virgin olive oil

3 fl oz / 90 mL Wesson oil

### SAUCE AND GARNISH

8 fl oz / 240 mL balsamic vinegar

5 oz / 142 g Coach Farm goat cheese

24 Kalamata olives

24 picholine olives

24 Niçoise olives

24 caper berries, cut in half

¾ oz / 21 g chervil sprigs

6 fl oz / 180 mL Tomato Oil (page 548)

1. For the mushrooms: Whisk together the oil, garlic, herbs, salt, and pepper. Remove the stems and gills from the mushrooms and combine with the oil mixture.

2. Place mushrooms cap side down on a medium high grill until brown grill marks are achieved, 3 to 4 minutes. Turn over and grill on the gill side until browned grill marks are achieved, 2 to 3 minutes. Remove and place in a hotel pan along with the hot stock and cover with foil. At this point the mushrooms should be only halfway cooked.

3. Bake at 350°F / 177° C until the mushrooms are tender, approximately 10 minutes. Refrigerate until needed.

4. For the garlic: Toss the garlic cloves with a small amount of olive oil, season with salt, and place on a square of aluminum foil 12 by 12 in / 30 by 30 cm. Fold the corners together to make a pouch.

5. Bake at 300°F / 149°C until tender, approximately 30 minutes. Remove the garlic in whole pieces and refrigerate until needed.

6. For the artichokes: Combine the lemon, water, and salt. Trim the artichokes down to the hearts and cook in the acidulated water until tender.

7. Cool the artichokes over an ice bath in their own liquid and reserve.

8. For the tomatoes: Remove the cores from the tomatoes, cut in half lengthwise, and place on a half racked sheet pan, cut side up.

9. Sprinkle the herbs and seasonings on the tomatoes and drizzle with olive oil.

10. Bake in a 225°F / 107°C oven until more than halfway dried, 1 to 2 hours. Refrigerate until needed.

11. For the peppers: Grill the peppers over medium heat to lightly blister the skins. Place in a bowl and cover with plastic for ten minutes.

12. Peel, seed, and cut the peppers into strips 1½ in / 3 cm wide. Set aside until needed.

13. For the vinaigrette: Combine the balsamic vinegar and water and bring to room temperature. Sprinkle with the gelatin and allow the gelatin to bloom for 5 minutes. Heat over a double boiler until the gelatin is dissolved completely, about 5 minutes.

14. Combine mixture with the garlic, shallots, Tabasco, salt, pepper, honey, and herbs.

15. Whisk in the oils. Adjust seasoning.

16. Line a triangular terrine mold 2 in by 2 in by 12 in / 5 cm by 5 cm by 30 cm with plastic wrap, leaving an overhang. Lightly brush two thirds of the portobellos with the vinaigrette and use them to line the sides of the terrine, lightly overlapping.

17. On the bottom of the terrine, lay the garlic cloves and lightly brush with enough vinaigrette to coat them.

18. Lay the artichokes in the bottom of the mold and brush with enough vinaigrette to lightly coat them.

19. Lay the tomato halves in the bottom of the mold and brush with enough vinaigrette to lightly coat them.

20. Lay the roasted peppers down and brush with enough vinaigrette to lightly coat them.

21. Lay the remaining mushrooms on top and brush with the vinaigrette. Cover tightly with the excess plastic wrap. Place a plastic press plate on top and weight with a 1-lb / 454-g weight. Refrigerate overnight.

22. Unmold onto a half sheet pan and refrigerate for service.

23. For the sauce and garnish: Place the balsamic vinegar in a small sauce pot and reduce over medium heat until syrupy, about 15 minutes.

24. Stir the goat cheese until smooth.

25. Cut a slice from the terrine ¾ in / 2 cm thick and place in the middle of an appetizer plate 8 in / 20 cm in diameter, positioned so the top of the terrine faces 12 o'clock.

26. Using two demitasse spoons, form three quenelles of goat cheese and place them around the plate.

27. Lay 2 olives and 2 caper berries around the plate.

28. Lay 3 sprigs of chervil around the plate.

29. Sprinkle a small amount of tomato oil and a small amount of reduced balsamic vinegar on the plate. Serve immediately.

# Country-Style Terrine

YIELD: *1 terrine (3 lb / 1.36 kg; 18 to 20 servings)*

10 oz / 284 g pork butt, cut into ½- to 1-in / 1- to 3-cm cubes

1 lb / 454 g veal shoulder, cut into ½- to 1-in / 1- to 3-cm cubes

8 oz / 227 g fatback, cut into ½- to 1-in / 1- to 3-cm cubes

½ oz / 14 g butter

2 shallots, thinly sliced

2 garlic cloves, minced

4 fl oz / 120 mL sherry

1½ tbsp / 9 g pâté spice

2 tbsp / 20 g salt

1 tsp / 2 g black pepper

⅛ tsp / 0.25 g tinted curing mixture (TCM)

EMULSION

1 large egg

4 fl oz / 120 mL heavy cream

1 tbsp / 9 g salt

1½ oz / 14 g fresh white bread crumbs

GARNISH

6 oz / 170 g smoked ham

6 oz / 170 g fatback, diced

3 oz / 85 g raisins, quartered, plumped in white wine

4 oz / 113 g almonds, toasted, coarsely chopped

3 tbsp / 27 g coarsely chopped flat-leaf parsley

2 tbsp / 1 g chives, cut into ¼- to ½-in / 6-mm to 1-cm lengths

1. Cut the fat and sinew off of the pork butt and veal. Clean any skin and glands off of the fatback. Refrigerate until needed.

2. Heat a small sauté pan over medium low heat and melt the butter in it. Sweat the shallots and garlic in the butter until they are a light golden brown, 2 to 3 minutes. Deglaze with 1 fl oz / 30 mL sherry and allow the mixture to cool to room temperature. Add the cooled, sweated shallots and garlic to the veal and pork.

3. Add pâté spice, salt, pepper, and TCM.

4. Grind once with largest die (⅜ in / 9 mm) and hold cold over ice. Grind half of mixture a second time with the medium die (¼ in / 6 mm). Mix together the two batches of ground meat.

5. Add the emulsion ingredients to the forcemeat over an ice bath.

6. Mix well and fold in garnish.

7. Poach a test sample and adjust seasoning, if necessary.

8. Lightly grease a terrine mold and then line it with plastic wrap, leaving an overhang.

9. Pipe in one third of the mixture and spread in an even layer. Pipe another third of the mixture into the mold and spread in an even layer. Repeat with the remaining mixture. Cover the terrine with the plastic overhang and cover.

10. Bake the terrine in a 160 to 170°F / 71 to 77°C water bath at 350°F / 177°C until the terrine reaches an internal temperature of 155°F / 68°C.

11. Cool the terrine to room temperature, place a press plate on top, and weight with a 2-lb / 907-g weight. Refrigerate overnight.

12. Unwrap the terrine and rewrap it in plastic wrap. To serve, cut the terrine into slices ¼ in / 6 mm thick and then in half across the diagonal, if desired.

# Terrine of Scallops, Truffles, and Salmon

YIELD: *1 terrine (2 lb / 907 g; 14 servings)*

12 oz / 340 g salmon fillet, frozen

6 green asparagus stalks, peeled

1 carrot, peeled

1 lb 14 oz / 851 g bay scallops, cleaned

2 egg whites

7 fl oz / 210 mL heavy cream

1 tbsp / 15 mL lemon juice

2 tbsp / 20 g kosher salt

¼ tsp / 0.50 g ground white pepper

Pinch cayenne

2 to 4 oz / 57 to 113 g black winter truffles, finely chopped

2 oz / 57 g chives, finely chopped

½ tsp / 2 g agar powder

½ tsp / 2 g powdered gelatin

4 to 6 nori sheets

1. Cut the frozen salmon into bâtonnet. Wrap the strips in plastic wrap and keep frozen until needed.

2. Cut the asparagus and carrot into bâtonnet, blanch, and shock in an ice bath. Dry the vegetables and refrigerate until needed.

3. In a food processor with a chilled bowl and blade, purée the scallops to a fine purée. Pass the purée through a drum sieve and place it in a stainless-steel bowl over an ice bath.

4. Add the egg whites and combine thoroughly. Add the cream, lemon juice, salt, white pepper, cayenne pepper, truffles, and chives and combine thoroughly. Refrigerate until needed.

5. Mix the agar powder and powdered gelatin together until combined thoroughly.

6. Brush the nori sheets with water and separate the nori into two stacks of three sheets each. Place the stacks next to each other to form one long strip.

7. Place the salmon strips, asparagus strips, and carrot strips in rows lengthwise along the nori sheets. Sprinkle with some of the powdered agar-gelatin mixture and roll tightly. The roll should be 1 in / 3 cm in diameter.

8. Fill the terrine mold with water and then discard the water. Line the terrine mold with plastic wrap, leaving an overhang.

9. Pipe one third of the scallop mousseline into the terrine. Sprinkle some of the agar-gelatin mixture onto the scallop mixture and place the nori cylinder in the center. Sprinkle the remaining agar-gelatin mixture over the cylinder and pipe the rest of the mousseline on top of the cylinder.

10. Smooth the top of the mousseline using a palette knife and wrap the overhanging plastic wrap over the top of the mousseline.

11. Place the terrine mold in a full-size hotel pan 4 in / 10 cm deep and fill the pan halfway with 160°F / 77°C water. Place the pan in a 300°F / 149°C oven and poach until the terrine reaches an internal temperature of 145°F / 63 °C, 40 to 50 minutes.

12. Remove the terrine from the water bath and refrigerate for 2 hours.

13. To serve, cut into slices ½ in / 1 cm thick.

# Salmon Pâté en Croûte

YIELD: *1 terrine (2 lb 8 oz / 1.13 kg; 14 to 16 servings)*

1 lb / 454 g shrimp (16/20 count), peeled, deveined, and cut into medium dice

12 oz / 340 g salmon, diced

1 oz / 28 g salt

¼ oz / 7 g ground black pepper

2 egg whites

18 fl oz / 540 mL heavy cream

2 tbsp / 16 g Old Bay seasoning

8 drops Tabasco sauce

6 oz / 170 g crayfish tails, cleaned

2 tbsp / 6 g snipped chives

3 tbsp / 9 g chopped basil

1 truffle, cut into small dice (optional)

1 lb 8 oz / 680 g Saffron Pâte Dough (page 599)

3 pieces salmon fillet, cut into strips 1 in / 3 cm wide and length of mold

2 fl oz / 60 mL egg wash (1 whole egg beaten with 1 tbsp milk)

6 to 8 fl oz / 180 to 240 mL Aspic Gelée, melted, or as needed to coat terrine (page 58)

1. Grind 12 oz / 340 g shrimp, the diced salmon, salt, and pepper through the medium die (¼ in / 6 mm) of a meat grinder.

2. Make a mousseline-style forcemeat by processing the ground seafood, egg whites, cream, Old Bay seasoning, and Tabasco sauce until smooth. Test the forcemeat and adjust seasoning if necessary before proceeding.

3. Fold the remaining shrimp, the crayfish, chives, basil, and truffle into the forcemeat, working over an ice bath.

4. Roll out the pâte dough and line a hinged mold, leaving an overhang.

5. Pack half the forcemeat into the lined mold. Place the salmon strips down the center; cover with remaining forcemeat.

6. Fold the dough over the forcemeat, cutting away any excess. Add a cap piece (see Chef's Note). Cut and reinforce vent holes; brush the surface with egg wash.

7. Bake at 450°F / 232°C for 15 to 20 minutes; reduce the heat to 350°F / 177°C and finish baking to an internal temperature of 145°F / 63°C, about 50 minutes.

8. Remove the pâté from the oven and allow it to cool to 90 to 100°F / 32 to 38°C. Ladle the aspic through a funnel into the pâté. Refrigerate for at least 24 hours. Slice and serve immediately, or wrap and refrigerate for up to 3 days.

*Presentation idea*  Serve with Red Pepper Coulis (page 55).

*Chef's note*  *Instead of making a separate cap piece, you may invert the pâté before cutting vent holes, as described on page 314.*

# Turkey Pâté en Croûte

YIELD: *2½ lb / 1.13 kg; 14 to 16 servings (2½ oz / 71 g each)*

12 oz / 340 g turkey leg and thigh meat, cleaned and cubed

6 oz / 170 g pork butt, cubed

6 oz / 170 g fatback, cubed

¼ tsp / 0.75 g tinted curing mix (TCM)

2 tsp / 6 g salt

2 shallots, minced

2 garlic cloves, minced

1 tbsp / 15 mL vegetable oil

3 fl oz / 90 mL brandy

6 juniper berries, crushed

1 oz / 28 g Dijon mustard

1 tbsp / 3 g chopped sage

1 tbsp / 3 g chopped thyme

Pinch ground nutmeg

½ tsp / 1 g ground black pepper

1 fl oz / 30 mL Glace de Viande or Volaille, melted (page 594)

1 egg

GARNISH

1 oz / 28 g dried cherries, plumped in Triple Sec

1 oz / 28 g dried apricots, quartered, plumped in Triple Sec

1 lb 8 oz / 680 g Sweet Potato Pâte Dough (page 600)

8 slices thin-sliced ham (¹⁄₁₆ in / 1.5 mm), or as needed for liner

3 pieces turkey breast, cut into strips 1 inch wide and length of mold

2 fl oz / 60 mL egg wash (1 whole egg beaten with 1 tbsp / 15 mL milk)

6 to 8 fl oz / 180 to 240 mL Aspic Gelée, melted (page 58)

1. Combine the leg and thigh meat, pork butt, fatback, TCM, and salt and grind through the fine die (⅛ in / 3 mm) of a meat grinder.

2. Sweat the shallots and garlic in the oil; deglaze with the brandy. Cool.

3. Combine the ground meats, shallot mixture, juniper berries, mustard, sage, thyme, nutmeg, pepper, and glace; marinate 1 hour.

4. Transfer the ground meats to a food processor with a chilled bowl and blade and add the egg. Process for 1 minute, or until smooth.

5. Test the forcemeat and adjust seasoning if necessary before proceeding.

6. Drain the garnish ingredients and fold into the forcemeat, working over an ice bath.

7. Roll out the dough and line a hinged mold. Line the dough with the sliced ham, leaving an overhang.

8. Pack half the forcemeat into the lined mold. Lay in the turkey breast; cover with remaining forcemeat.

9. Fold the ham and the dough over the forcemeat, cutting away any excess. Add a cap piece (see Chef's Note). Cut and reinforce vent holes; brush the surface with egg wash.

10. Bake at 450°F / 232°C for 15 to 20 minutes; reduce the heat to 350°F / 177°C and finish baking to an internal temperature of 165°F / 74°C, about 50 minutes.

11. Remove the pâté from the oven and allow it to cool to 90 to 100°F / 32 to 38°C. Ladle the aspic through a funnel into the pâté. Refrigerate the pâté for at least 24 hours. Slice and serve immediately, or wrap and refrigerate for up to 5 days.

*Chef's note*   *Instead of making a separate cap piece, you may invert the pâté before cutting the vent holes, as described on page 314.*

# Rabbit Pie in Parmesan-Prosciutto Crust

YIELD: *1 tart (10 in / 25 cm in diameter; 16 servings)*

1 lb / 454 g lean rabbit meat (from a 3-lb / 1.36-kg rabbit)

8 oz / 227 g fatback

2 oz / 57 g minced shallots

1 garlic clove, minced

1 oz / 28 g butter

½ tsp / 1.30 g tinted curing mix (TCM)

2 tsp / 6 g salt

1 fl oz / 30 mL sherry

1 egg

4 fl oz / 120 mL heavy cream

1 tbsp / 3 g chopped flat-leaf parsley

1 tsp / 2 g poultry seasoning

½ tsp / 1 g ground white pepper

1 recipe Parmesan Prosciutto Crust (recipe follows)

1. Cut the rabbit meat and fatback into medium dice.

2. Sweat the shallots and garlic in the butter until soft. Cool.

3. Combine the shallots and garlic with the rabbit meat, fatback, TCM, salt, and sherry; marinate 6 hours.

4. Grind through the medium die (¼ in / 6 mm) of a meat grinder. Chill if necessary before grinding through the fine plate (⅛ in / 3 mm).

5. Transfer the ground meat to a chilled mixing bowl. Add the egg and cream and mix on medium speed for 1 minute, until homogenous. Add the parsley, poultry seasoning, and pepper. Mix well.

6. Test the forcemeat and adjust seasoning if necessary before proceeding.

7. Place the crust in a 10-in / 25-cm tart pan and the forcemeat in the crust. Bake at 300°F / 149°C to an internal temperature of 165°F / 74°C, approximately 40 minutes. Chill 24 hours. Slice and serve immediately, or wrap and refrigerate for up to 5 days.

*Presentation idea* Serve the pie garnished with quartered Seckel pears that have been poached in sweet wine.

# Parmesan-Prosciutto Crust

YIELD: *Crust for 1 tart 10 in / 25 cm in diameter*

4 oz / 113 g fresh white bread crumbs

½ oz / 14 g flour

2 tsp / 4 g coarse-ground black pepper

1 tsp / 1 g dried oregano

1 tsp / 1 g dried basil

1 tsp / 1 g dried thyme

2 oz / 57 g butter, melted

2 egg yolks

1 oz / 28 g grated Parmesan

2 oz / 57 g fine-dice prosciutto

1. Combine bread crumbs, flour, pepper, oregano, basil, and thyme. Add the butter and egg yolks; mix well with kitchen fork. Mix in Parmesan cheese and prosciutto.

2. Press into a buttered tart pan 10 in / 25 cm in diameter. Bake at 350°F / 177°C until slightly brown, about 10 minutes. Cool. Fill and bake as directed.

# Pheasant Galantine

YIELD: *14 by 2-in /35 by 5-cm galantine; 10 to 12 servings (2½ oz/ 71 g each)*

| | |
|---|---|
| 1 pheasant (about 3 lb / 1.36 kg) | 2 tsp / 2 g chopped sage |
| 1 fl oz / 30 mL vegetable oil | 2 tsp / 2 g chopped flat-leaf parsley |
| 8 oz / 227 g Mirepoix (page 586) | 2 tsp / 2 g chopped thyme |
| 8 fl oz / 240 mL Madeira | 3 juniper berries, crushed |
| 96 fl oz / 2.88 L Chicken Stock (page 592) | 1 egg |
| 10 whole black peppercorns | GARNISH |
| 3 bay leaves, crushed | ¾ oz / 21 g dried currants, plumped in Madeira |
| 4 oz / 113 g pork butt, trimmed of visible fat, diced | ¾ oz / 21 g dried cherries, plumped in Madeira |
| 4 oz / 113 g fatback, diced | ¾ oz / 21 g dried apricots, quartered, plumped in Madeira |
| ¼ tsp / 1.25 g tinted curing mix (TCM) | |
| 2 tsp / 6 g salt | 1 tsp / 2 g whole pink peppercorns |
| 2 tsp / 2 g chopped rosemary | |

1. Debone the pheasant and remove the skin, keeping it intact. Dice the meat. Chop the carcass. Reserve the skin.

2. Brown the carcass in the oil; add the mirepoix and brown. Add the Madeira, 16 fl oz / 480 mL chicken stock, the peppercorns, and the bay leaves. Simmer for 3 hours. Strain, return to heat, and reduce to 2 fl oz / 60 mL. Chill.

3. Combine the pheasant meat, pork, and fatback. Add the reduced pheasant stock, TCM, salt, rosemary, sage, parsley, thyme, and juniper. Mix well and marinate overnight, refrigerated.

4. Grind the meat through the medium die (¼ in / 6 mm) of a meat grinder. Chill if necessary before grinding through the fine die (⅛ in / 3 mm).

5. Transfer the ground meats to a chilled food processor bowl. Process on medium speed for 1 minute, until homogenous. Add the egg and process until smooth.

6. Test the forcemeat and adjust seasoning if necessary before proceeding.

7. Drain the plumped fruit. Stir the garnish ingredients into the forcemeat, working over an ice bath.

8. Place damp cheesecloth on a work surface and lay the pheasant skin on top. Spread the forcemeat over the skin in an even layer. Use the cheesecloth to help roll the galantine. Carefully lap the skin over itself at the seam. Tie.

9. Heat the remaining chicken stock in a pot to 170°F / 77°C. Place the galantine in the chicken stock and poach to an internal temperature of 165°F /74°C, about 45 to 50 minutes. Remove the pot from the heat and place over an ice bath. Let the galantine cool in the chicken stock. Refrigerate overnight. Rewrap the galantine and refrigerate at least 12 hours. Slice and serve immediately, or cover and refrigerate for up to 5 days.

*Presentation idea*  Serve with a Cranberry Relish (page 529), Apricot-Cherry Chutney (page 527), or Dried Apricot Relish (page 529).

*Chef's note*  Replace the garnish ingredients with equal parts dried cherries and whole pistachios.

# Roasted Asian Duck Galantine

YIELD: *1 galantine (2 lb / 907 g; 10 to 12 servings)*

1 duck (4 to 5 lb / 1.81 to 2.27 kg)

16 fl oz / 480 mL Poultry Brine (page 217)

MARINADE

3 garlic cloves, minced

2 shallots, minced, sautéed, and cooled

2 tsp / 6 g minced ginger

1 tbsp / 15 mL vegetable oil

6 oz / 170 g lean pork butt, cubed

6 oz / 170 g fatback, cubed

1 tbsp / 15 mL oyster sauce

1 tbsp / 15 mL soy sauce

2 tsp / 10 mL sesame oil

1 tbsp / 3 g minced thyme

1 tbsp / 3 g minced cilantro

1 jalapeño, stemmed, seeded, and chopped fine

½ tsp / 1 g Chinese Five-Spice Powder (page 587)

1 tbsp / 21 g honey

¼ tsp / 0.66 g tinted curing mix (TCM)

6 shiitake mushrooms, stems removed, cut into fine dice

4 oz / 113 g carrots, finely diced and fully cooked

3 green onions, minced

2 tsp / 9.50 g powdered gelatin

1. Remove the skin from the duck in one piece, starting from the back. Debone the duck; reserve legs for forcemeat and breast for garnish. Square off the ends of the breasts and add the pieces of trim to the forcemeat.

2. Cover the duck breasts with the brine; refrigerate for 4 hours.

3. Lay the skin out on a sheet pan lined with plastic wrap and freeze. When the skin has frozen, remove all the excess fat using a chef's knife in a scraping motion.

4. Sweat the garlic, shallots, and ginger in the vegetable oil and cool. Combine this mixture with the duck leg and thigh meat, trim from breasts, pork, fatback, oyster sauce, soy sauce, sesame oil, thyme, cilantro, jalapeño, five-spice powder, honey, and TCM; marinate for 1 hour.

5. Grind the meat through the medium die (¼ in / 6 mm) of a meat grinder. Chill if necessary before grinding through the fine die (⅛ in / 3 mm).

6. Transfer the ground meats to a chilled mixing bowl. Mix on medium speed for 1 minute, until homogenous.

7. Test the forcemeat and adjust seasoning if necessary before proceeding.

8. Toss the mushrooms, carrots, and green onions with the gelatin. Fold the vegetables into the forcemeat, working over an ice bath.

9. Place the duck skin on a large piece of plastic wrap. Pipe the forcemeat onto the skin and smooth with a pallet knife. Place the breasts in the middle and roll into a galantine. Wrap galantine into foil forming a roulade.

10. Place the galantine on a sheet pan and roast in a 300°F / 149°C oven to an internal temperature of 165°F / 74°C, about 50 to 60 minutes.

# Pork Tenderloin Roulade

YIELD: *1 roulade (3 lb / 1.36 kg; 18 to 20 servings)*

1 pork tenderloin (about 1 lb 12 oz / 794 g)

BRINE

20 fl oz / 600 mL Basic Meat Brine (page 220)

3 star anise pods

2½ oz / 71 g ginger, roughly chopped

2½ tsp / 3 g Szechwan peppercorns

MOUSSELINE

1 lb 3 oz / 539 g ground chicken breast

2½ tsp / 8 g salt

2½ oz / 71 g egg whites

9½ fl oz / 285 mL heavy cream

2½ tsp / 7.50 g minced garlic

2½ tsp / 7.50 g minced ginger

1¼ tsp / 6 mL dark soy sauce

1¼ tsp / 6 mL sherry

3½ green onions, minced

¾ tsp / 1.50 g ground black pepper

1¼ fl oz / 38 mL Glace de Volaille or Viande (page 594), warm

1. Trim the pork tenderloin; you should have 10 to 12 oz / 284 to 340 g after trimming.

2. Cover the pork with the brine ingredients; use small plates or plastic wrap to keep it completely submerged. Refrigerate for 12 hours. Rinse tenderloin and dry well.

3. Prepare the chicken mousseline: Place the ground chicken and salt in the bowl of a food processor. Process to a relatively smooth paste. Add the egg whites. With the machine running, add the heavy cream and process just to incorporate. Pass the forcemeat through a drum sieve and fold in the remaining ingredients.

4. Test the forcemeat and adjust the seasoning if necessary before proceeding.

5. Spread half of the mousseline on a sheet of plastic wrap. (Dust the tenderloins with albumen/gelatin powder, if desired; see Chef's Note below.) Place the tenderloin in the middle and spread the other half of the mousseline evenly over the tenderloin. Roll tightly into a cylinder and secure ends with twine. Poach in a 170°F / 77°C water bath in a 300°F / 149°C oven to an internal temperature of 165°F / 74°C, about 50 to 60 minutes.

6. Remove the roulade from the water bath and allow it to cool. Rewrap the roulade tightly to properly bind the tenderloin and forcemeat together.

7. Refrigerate at least 24 hours and up to 2 days. Slice and serve immediately, or wrap and refrigerate for up to 7 days.

*Chef's note* *Make a mixture that is comprised of 50% powdered albumen and 50% powdered gelatin. Dust the tenderloins with this mixture in order to trap the moisture that is released by the tenderloins as they cook so that the forcemeat doesn't absorb extra moisture.*

# Chicken Galantine

YIELD: *1 galantine (4 lb / 1.8 kg; 28 to 30 servings)*

PANADA

2 eggs

1½ fl oz / 45 mL brandy

1 tsp / 2 g Pâté Spice (page 590)

3 oz / 85 g flour

1 tbsp / 10 g salt

¼ tsp / 0.50 g ground white pepper

8 fl oz / 240 mL heavy cream, heated

1 chicken (about 3 lb / 1.36 kg), boned, wing tips removed, skin removed intact

1 lb / 454 g pork butt, cut into 1-in / 3-mm cubes and chilled

6 fl oz / 180 mL Madeira

4 oz / 113 g fresh ham or cooked tongue, cut into ¼-in / 6-mm cubes

3 tbsp / 16 g black truffles, chopped

4 oz / 113 g pistachios, shelled, blanched

Chicken Stock (page 592), as needed

1. Prepare the panada: mix the eggs with all the panada ingredients except the cream.

2. Temper the egg mixture with the hot cream. Add the cream to the egg mixture and cook over low heat until thickened.

3. Weigh the leg and thigh meat from the chicken. Add an equal amount of pork butt, or enough for approximately 2 lb / 907 g meat. Grind the chicken leg and thigh meat and pork twice, using the fine die (⅛ in / 3 mm) of a meat grinder.

4. Keep the breast of the chicken in large pieces as you bone out the bird. Butterfly or slice the breast meat.

5. Pound the chicken breast to a thickness of ⅛ in / 3 mm, place on a sheet pan lined with plastic wrap, cover with plastic wrap, and refrigerate.

6. Cut the chicken tenderloin into ½- to ¾-in / 1- to 2-cm cubes. Season as needed. Combine the meat and the Madeira and refrigerate for at least 3 hours.

7. Drain the chicken breast, reserving the Madeira. Add the Madeira and panada to the ground meat mixture. Blend well.

8. Fold in the ham, truffles, and pistachios. Mix well.

9. Lay out the reserved skin on plastic wrap and lay the pounded chicken breast on top. Add the forcemeat and roll the galantine securely.

10. Poach the galantine at 170°F / 77°C in enough chicken stock to cover, to an internal temperature of 165°F / 74°C, about 60 to 70 minutes.

11. Transfer the galantine and the poaching liquid to a storage container. Let cool at room temperature. Remove the galantine from the stock and wrap it in new cheesecloth to firm its texture; chill at least 12 hours. Unwrap and slice the galantine to serve.

*Chef's note* Classically, galantines are wrapped in cheesecloth and poached in fortified chicken stock.

# 8

# Cheese

Wines, sausages, dried foods, and cheeses are all fruits of preservation practices known to ancient humankind, then refined, recorded, and evolved over time. We know that cheeses were enjoyed by the ancient Sumerians, whose writings about many aspects of daily life are believed to date from 3000 B.C.E. Early records of cheese have been found on earthenware vessels from Egyptian tombs dating as far back as 2300 B.C.E. The Romans were the first to mass-produce cheese to be carried on long journeys and used by their armies as a convenient form of concentrated nutrition. They carried their formulas into conquered lands as their empire expanded, marrying them with indigenous cheeses in Europe.

uring the period of European history known as the Dark Ages, the traditions of cheese making were preserved and refined by religious houses and monasteries, as were the traditions of wine and spirit making. Some of these religious orders are still creating handmade cheeses using the same original formulas and methods. Until the early to mid-1800s, cheese production continued on an individual home or cottage level, by families who were fortunate enough to own sheep, goats, and cows. As farms grew in size and were able to supply communities with agricultural products, so the cheese business grew as well, although the cheese-making process continued to be both painstaking and time-consuming.

This chapter explores the basic cheese-making process and artisan dairies in order to provide a better understanding of the special characteristics of the cheeses and why some special cheeses are so highly prized. Also discussed are the basic cheese categories—fresh, rind-ripened, semi-soft, blue cheeses, *pasta filata,* hard, and very hard—and the basic principles used to select cheeses for a cheese course offered on the menu, a cheese platter or tray for a buffet, or a cheese cart for the dining room.

Fresh cheeses can be produced with relatively little in the way of special equipment. These cheeses are served very fresh and can easily become a signature piece in an appetizer, salad, sandwich, entrée, or dessert item. Mozzarella, mascarpone, ricotta, and cultured dairy items such as crème fraîche and yogurt are among the recipes and techniques included in this chapter.

# Cheese making
## *What is cheese?*

**Cheese** is defined as a food product made from the pressed curd of milk. Like wine, cheese is thought of as a living food because of the "friendly" living **bacteria** that are continually changing it. You may hear cheeses referred to as **"natural"** to distinguish them from highly **processed cheeses** that are not expected to ripen.

It is believed that sheep's and goat's milk were first used to make cheese, as these were probably the first domesticated animals appropriate for milking. Today, cow's milk is the base for many cheeses, followed by goat's milk, then sheep's milk. The milk of water buffalo, yak, camel, and llama are also used to create the special cheeses of the societies where these animals were domesticated.

## *Cheese production*

The techniques used today to produce cheese have changed little since the times of the Romans and the medieval monasteries, but scientific discoveries have led to better control of the natural processes involved in cheese making: acidification and coagulation of the milk, salting, cutting and draining the curds, shaping the cheese, and finally, ripening.

In the nineteenth century, scientists were able to identify the many bacteria present in the milk, the air, and the caves used for ripening. Bacteria that would interfere with the process could be eliminated, and the individual strains that contribute to the desirable character of individual cheeses could be cultivated and standardized. By the turn of the century, **"pure cultures"** were made available and allowed for more uniform results from cheese maker to cheese maker when producing cheese within a single variety.

## Artisan cheeses and dairies in the United States

In 1851, the first real cheese factory in America was established in Rome, New York, by Jesse Williams. It was obvious that the market for cheese was ready, because within the next fifteen years there would be five hundred more of these operations established in New York alone. Around the same period of time, Wisconsin, California, Ohio, and Vermont were also beginning to establish themselves as states with producers of high-quality cheeses. These cheese makers were trying to make cheeses that emulated those of their homelands and ended up creating fine versions of Limburger and Cheddar as well as a new American cheese, Colby. By 1900, cheese makers in California were producing soft-ripened, soft, and washed-rind cheeses as well as the American-invented Monterey Jack cheese. Their efforts created a market for cheese that just kept expanding. In 1990 alone, over eight billion pounds of cheese and cheese-related products were produced in the United States.

Increasing renown is being accorded to today's high-quality, handcrafted cheeses. Since the early 1990s, the number of artisan dairies in the US has grown from a handful to more than 200 and it could keep growing. These artisan cheeses are being produced all over the country, on the same small scale and with the same high standards of years ago. Familiar varieties as well as brand new cheeses are becoming available on the local level, making a better opportunity for the garde manger to feature excellent and unusual cheeses all the time.

There are many high-quality small dairies throughout the country producing some of the best cheese available today and it is well worth the effort to seek them out. There has been a boom of these small dairies in the last two decades, which has been largely attributed to a decline in milk prices in the late 1980s and mid-1990s. A number of dairy farmers turned to cheese making as a way to still make a profit from their milk, and ended up creating handmade products that rival many European imports in quality and flavor. Although the number of artisan dairies is increasing, cheese making is a very expensive, laborious undertaking. A label that says **artisanal** or handmade implies just that; that it is handmade with little or no mechanization. If the label reads "farmstead," the cheese makers use the milk from the animals on their farm.

Farmers also turned to other animals to provide milk to make cheese. Goat- and sheep's-milk cheeses have gained widespread popularity and are regularly featured on cheese courses and in local gourmet cheese shops. One of the most popular trends in today's American dairy is using old-world recipes but giving them a new, modern twist. Some dairies, such as Coach Farm, are also mixing different milks together to produce new and exciting cheeses.

Buying cheese from an artisan dairy allows the retail store or restaurant the opportunity to get to know the source of the cheese. They can ask the farmer directly about the conditions in which the cheese was produced and any questions about its flavor and texture. The widespread use of the Internet has made marketing and selling cheese a reality for a small operation with no room for a sales department. It may be possible one day for the artisan dairy to produce cheese to exacting specifications from a particular chef, but that day is probably a little ways off.

# The cheese-making process

For the most part, the only changes in cheese making since the early days have been in understanding how we can control the complicated interaction of various biological agents and processes, all integral to cheese making. The basic stages in the modern production process are:

- **Milk** and its **pretreatment**, including **homogenizing**, **pasteurizing**, or **heating**
- **Acidification** of milk, to change the pH level
- **Coagulating** (curdling) the milk to create curds
- **Separating** the **curds** and **whey**
- **Salting** the curds
- **Shaping**, cutting, or molding the curds into their appropriate shapes
- **Ripening**

Considering how few ingredients are needed to make cheese, there is astonishing variety in the types of cheeses that can be produced. Hundreds of distinct cheeses can be made by introducing only slight modifications: Choosing sheep's milk instead of cow's; using a different starter culture; draining the cheese a little more or less; cutting the curds very fine or leaving them whole or in slabs; rubbing the cheese with salt at a different point in the process; or shaping it into a disk, wheel, or round will produce different cheeses, with unique textures, flavors, and aromas.

Different steps applied during the ripening process can play a critical role as well: The rind may be washed with brine or coated with wax, additional molds or cultures can be introduced directly to the cheese or applied to the surface, and so forth.

## *Milk*

The type of milk the cheese maker chooses is critical to the development and final outcome of the cheese. Not only are there different milks (cow, sheep, goat, yak, llama, buffalo, mare, and others) with different fat contents, there are also various ways to collect, blend, and treat milk. One famous cheese, Morbier, is traditionally made by layering the richer milk collected in the evening with the leaner milk of the next day's first milking.

In large-scale cheese production, milk is routinely handled as follows: it is tested for quality, pasteurized, and homogenized, and the milk's fat content is standardized. Although cheeses aged more than sixty days may be made from raw milk, the majority of cheese in this country is produced from pasteurized milk.

Pasteurization is the process by which a liquid, in this case milk, is heated to a particular temperature and held there for a specific period of time to destroy the naturally occurring bacteria in the milk. This landmark discovery in food safety came at a price for cheese makers. The down side is that the process destroys not only pathogens but also the "friendly" bacteria, which are not only safe but also play an important role in producing cheeses. However, there are several dairies in the US that are producing wonderful pasteurized-milk cheeses because the risks involved are lower than those associated with raw milk cheeses.

The importance of food safety outranks the changes to the flavor and quality of the cheese, however, and cheese makers have worked to compensate for the loss of naturally present bacteria and changes in flavor.

## Acidification of milk

The serious business of cheese making gets under way when the milk is acidified, or soured. The milk is heated to a specific temperature and a starter is added that contains either an acid or an organism that produces lactic acid.

To produce many of the soft fresh cheeses featured in this chapter, lemon juice, vinegar, or citric or tartaric acid—the acid starters—can be used. Mozzarella and provolone (known as pasta filata) as well as most ripened cheeses are produced by souring the milk with a culture composed of a lactic acid-producing organism—the enzyme starters. Acid development is critical in order to control the growth of undesirable organisms and the rate of coagulation.

The starter is added at a ratio that will produce the appropriate level of acid. If there is too much acid, the curd may take several days to release the whey. If there is too little, a seemingly dry cheese may begin to leak whey several weeks after it has been shaped and pressed.

## Coagulating (curdling) the milk

**Acid starters** will change the milk rapidly, souring the milk as well as forming curds. The effect of any acid on a protein is to tighten it. This is the basic action in curdling milk. **Enzyme starters,** including **rennet,** result in a sweeter curd. The action of the so-called friendly bacteria (either in the milk or in the starter) produces lactic acid, resulting in a sweeter-tasting curd, since less overall acid is required.

Rennet was originally obtained from the fourth stomach of young ruminant animals such as cows, sheep, and goats. It can also be derived from certain plants. Today both animal- and plant–based forms are available, as well as a genetically engineered substitute called **chymosin.** The rennet that gives the cheese the desired flavor is the one that the cheese maker will use.

## Separating the curds and whey

When the milk coagulates, it generally forms a soft mass curd that must be broken up to allow the noncoagulated portion of the milk, known as the whey, to drain off (see Fig 8-1).

If the curd is cut only a little, you can create soft, creamy cheeses. When the curd is cut quite small, more of the whey will drain away, and the cheese will have a drier texture. For some very dry cheeses, the curds and whey are even cooked to further shrink the curds and allow even more moisture to escape.

**FIG 8-1**  *A cheesecloth-lined colander set over a bowl is one system that will separate the curds and whey during cheese production.*

## Salting

Salt may be added at various points in the cheese-making process but it is usually done after draining the whey from the curd. It may be stirred into the milk along with the starter or shortly after the starter is added. Coarse salt may be spread over the surface of the curd, or the cut and drained curd may be submerged in or rubbed with salt brine.

Salt is important to cheese making in a number of ways. In addition to adding its own flavor, salt affects the cheese's flavor because of its role in controlling fermentation. The quantity of carbon dioxide and alcohol produced as a by-product of this bacterial activity gives each cheese its unique flavor. Salt limits spoilage by creating an inhospitable environment for the organisms that cause spoilage. It also affects the finished texture of the cheese, acting to dry the cheese. The drier the cheese, the longer its useful life. Very dry grating cheeses, such as Pecorino Romano, are so salty they can be used as a substitute for some of the salt added in a dish.

## Shaping

There are a number of methods for draining and shaping cheeses, each specified both by tradition and by the role that those methods play in producing the desired flavor and texture in the finished cheese. After the curds are drained of the freed whey, some are placed in cheesecloth bags, baskets, or molds, and set on racks or hung and allowed to drain and dry for the prescribed time. For fresh and soft cheeses, draining and shaping is accomplished simultaneously. Some cheeses—notably Cheddars—are shaped into thick slabs and then stacked, so that the weight of the cheese itself presses out the whey.

## Ripening

The last stage of cheese making is ripening, also known as **aging** or **curing.** This is where the "magic" of flavor development takes place. The ripening process may take anywhere from thirty days to several years, depending upon the cheese being made. During that time, the cheese undergoes changes that will affect its flavor, body, texture, and occasionally its color. What began as rubbery fresh cheese curd is transformed into smooth and mellow ripened cheese.

Originally cheeses were aged in caves, where conditions were perfect for the magic of ripening to take place. Today, most cheeses are aged in temperature- and humidity-controlled environments that simulate caves.

Cheeses may be ripened in leaves, ashes, wax rinds, or no rind at all. Some are rubbed or washed, and some are simply left to cure naturally. In some cases, holes are made in the cheeses to allow gases produced by bacteria to escape; in others, the gases are confined to form a variety of holes ranging in size from tiny to the size of a quarter, as in some Swiss or Swiss-style cheeses. Special additional bacteria cultures or molds are introduced in many cheeses by injecting, spraying, or washing them. Once these steps are done, the rest of the work is left to nature.

# Cheese classifications

With so many cheeses available today, there are several categories by which they can be referenced. Milk type, country of origin, region, handling, aging, and texture are some of the various classification strategies that have been used. Although most experts agree that none of these classifications are completely adequate, so far no one has been able to come up with one that really covers all the variables. Even when two experts agree on which method to use, they do not necessarily agree on which cheeses fall into which categories.

For the sake of discussion, this section presents several broad groups of cheese that have been loosely categorized according to texture.

## Soft fresh cheeses

**Soft fresh cheeses** are those cheeses that are unripened and generally have a fresh, clean, creamy flavor. These cheeses are typically the most perishable and are sometimes held in brines. Examples of soft fresh cheeses are cottage cheese, pot cheese, queso blanco, and cream cheese (see Fig 8-2).

Ricotta cheese, made from recooking whey, actually began in Italy as a by-product of the cheese-making industry. (The name literally means "recook.") When whey is heated, the proteins fuse

FIG 8-2 FRESH CHEESES. CLOCKWISE FROM TOP LEFT: *cheese curd, soft ash goat cheese, queso fresco, feta, farmer's cheese, Boursin, ricotta, cottage cheese, mascarpone*

together and create a new curd that, when drained, becomes a snowy white ricotta high in moisture and naturally low in fat. It is commonly used in Italian cooking as a filling for pastas or as a base for cheesecakes. Today, some ricottas are made with added part-skim or whole milk for a richer flavor.

Mascarpone is a fresh cheese made by curdling heavy cream with citric acid. The process releases excess moisture and yields a rich, creamy cheese that is mildly acidic and adapts to both sweet and savory preparations. One of the most famous uses of mascarpone is in the dessert tiramisù, in which the rich cheese is layered with sponge cake or ladyfingers that have been dipped in espresso and Marsala wine. Savory mascarpone dishes such as dips and spreads may also include herbs and spices.

In the United States, fresh goat's milk cheeses have become very popular of late and are being produced in many parts of the country. They can be found in a variety of shapes and may be coated in herbs or edible ash.

*table 8.1*  ## Soft Cheeses

| Variety | Description | Common Culinary Uses |
|---|---|---|
| *Chèvre* | Goat's milk; white block, pyramid, button, wheel, or log; mild to tangy flavor (depending on age), may be flavored with herbs or peppercorns; soft to crumbly texture (depending on age); also known as goat cheese; Montrachet is a popular variety | Spread; filling; in salad |
| *Cottage cheese* | Whole or skim cow's milk; packaged in containers; white curds; mild flavor; soft, moist texture | With fruit; in dip |
| *Cream cheese* | Whole cow's milk, plus cream; white block; mild, slightly tangy flavor; soft, creamy texture; also known as Neufchâtel in many parts of the United States (with a lower fat content), though Neufchâtel is a different cheese in France and Switzerland | Spread; cooking ingredient; in cheesecake; in dip |
| *Feta* | Sheep's, goat's, or cow's milk; white block; tangy, salty flavor; soft, crumbly texture | In salad; filling for Spanakopita |
| *Fromage blanc* | Whole or skim cow's milk; white; mild, tangy flavor; soft, slightly crumbly texture | Cooking ingredient |
| *Mascarpone* | Cow's cream; formless, packaged in containers; pale yellow; buttery, sweet, rich flavor; soft, smooth texture | With fruit; in tiramisù; to enrich dishes |
| *Mozzarella* | Whole or skim cow's or buffalo's milk; irregular sphere; white, greenish-yellow tint; mild flavor; tender to slightly elastic texture (depending on age); may be smoked | Pizza, pasta; with tomatoes and basil in a Caprese salad |
| *Ricotta* | Whole, skim, or low-fat cow's milk; soft, white curds; mild flavor; moist to slightly dry, grainy texture | Cooking ingredient; desserts; filling for cannoli; makes excellent cheesecake |
| *Farmer's cheese* | Cow's milk; white, curdless; firm enough to cut; mild flavor; grainy texture; spoonable | With fresh fruit and vegetables; dips, desserts, pasta |
| *Boursin* | Whole cow's milk and cream; white rounds; flavored or herbed cream cheese spread; smooth texture | Spread |
| *Queso fresco* | Cow's milk; off-white to white rounds; mild, salty flavor; texture similar to ricotta or farmer's cheese—crumbly, slightly grainy | Topping or filling for many Mexican dishes |

# Soft ripened cheeses

**Soft ripened cheeses** are those that have typically been sprayed or dusted with a mold and allowed to ripen. The two most popular varieties are probably Brie and Camembert. Neither name is protected by law, so both have been counterfeited in many places with vast differences in quality. Soft ripened cheeses are available in varying degrees of richness. For example, single-, double-, and triple-cream cheeses have 50, 60, and 70 percent **butterfat,** respectively (see Fig 8-3).

Soft ripened cheeses should be eaten only when properly ripened. An underripe cheese is firm and chalky; an overripe cheese will run when cut. A cheese ready for eating will "bulge" when cut and barely hold its shape. Soft ripened cheeses will ripen only until they are cut into. After that they will begin to dry and deteriorate. To check for ripeness before cutting, press firmly but gently in the middle of the cheese. It should have some feel of softness to the center. An **overripe** cheese can be identified by an ammonia odor.

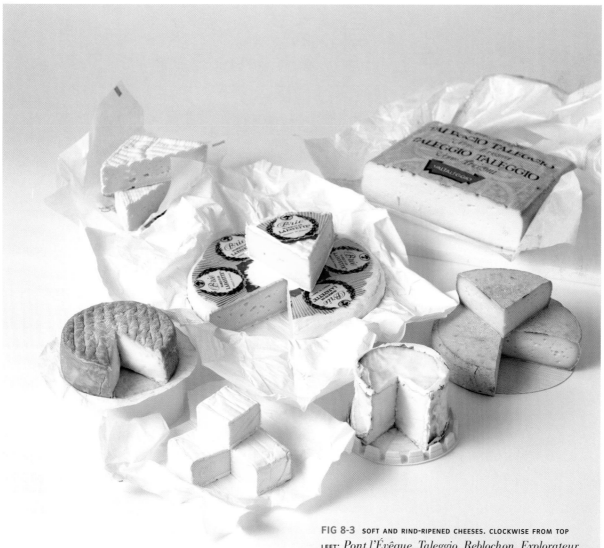

FIG 8-3 SOFT AND RIND-RIPENED CHEESES. CLOCKWISE FROM TOP LEFT: *Pont l'Évêque, Taleggio, Reblochon, Explorateur, Hudson Valley Camembert, Epoisses, Brie*

Soft ripened cheeses can be served at room temperature as a dessert cheese or as an appetizer. For those who are not purists, these cheeses can also be served warm by baking them in a crust of flaky dough or toasted almonds. It still remains a matter of taste as to whether soft ripened cheeses should be eaten with the rind. Even the "experts" don't agree on that age-old discussion, so it should be left up to the individual.

## Rind-ripened cheeses

Washed-rind cheeses are periodically washed with brine, beer, cider, wine, brandy, or oils during the ripening period. This remoistening encourages bacterial growth, sometimes known as a **smear,** which allows the cheese to be ripened from the outside in. Popular examples of this type of cheese include Limburger and its famous American counterpart Liederkranz, both of which are intensely pungent, as well as Muenster, Saint Paulin, and Port-Salut.

*table 8.2*  Soft Ripened and Washed-Rind Cheeses

| Variety | Description | Common Culinary Uses |
| --- | --- | --- |
| **SOFT RIPENED** | | |
| Brie | Pasteurized whole or skim cow's and goat's milk, sometimes cream; light yellow wheels; buttery, pungent flavor; soft, smooth, creamy texture with edible rind | Sandwiches, salads; table cheese |
| Camembert | Raw or pasteurized whole cow's and goat's milk; light yellow disk; mild, mushroom-like flavor; soft, creamy texture, with edible rind | Sandwiches; table cheese |
| Explorateur | Whole cow's milk and cream; pale yellow barrels, disks, or wheels; rich, mild flavor; soft, creamy, smooth texture | Table cheese; excellent with Champagne |
| **WASHED RIND** | | |
| Limburger | Whole or low-fat cow's milk; light yellow block, brown exterior; very strong flavor and aroma, salty; soft, smooth, waxy texture | Table cheese, with fruit and vegetables |
| Pont l'évêque | Whole cow's milk; light yellow square; piquant, strong aroma and flavor; soft, supple texture with small holes and edible golden-yellow crust | Dessert, crêpes, salads; table cheese |
| Taleggio | Raw cow's milk; light yellow square; tart, salty, buttery, and powerful flavor (depending on age); has some small holes | Salads; cooking ingredient; table cheese |
| Epoisses | Cow's milk; blonde, almost straw-colored disks; rich, huge flavor; pleasantly smelly, barnyard-like aroma; smooth texture | Table cheese; dish accompaniment |
| Reblochon | Cow's milk; ivory disk; sweet, powerful, nutty flavor; creamy, velvety texture | Table cheese, with fruit or bread |

## Semi-soft cheeses

**Semi-soft cheeses** include a wide variety ranging from mild and buttery to very pungent and aromatic (see Fig 8-4). They are allowed to ripen in several ways. **Dry-rind cheeses** are those that are allowed to form a natural rind during ripening. Gouda and Edam are semi-soft cheeses that are sealed in wax prior to the aging process. These cheeses, which get their names from two towns in Holland, have been made for eight hundred years. Gouda is made from whole milk and tends to be softer and richer than Edam, which is made from part-skim milk and is firmer in texture. These cheeses may be either flavored or smoked, and are available in mild and aged varieties.

FIG 8-4 SEMISOFT CHEESES. CLOCKWISE FROM BOTTOM LEFT: *Monterey Jack, Muenster, caciotta, caraway Havarti, Fontina, Morbier*

*table 8.3*

## Semi-soft Cheeses

| Variety | Description | Common Culinary Uses |
|---|---|---|
| *Fontina* | Whole cow's or sheep's milk; medium yellow wheel; mild, grassy, fruity, and nutty flavor | Table cheese; in sandwiches; in cooking; in fondues; great melting cheese |
| *Havarti* | Cream-enriched cow's milk; white to light yellow blocks or wheels; very mild, buttery flavor, often flavored with herbs, spices, or peppers; creamy texture, with small holes | Great on sandwiches |
| *Morbier* | Whole cow's milk; light yellow wheel with edible ash layer and a brown crust; fruity and nutty flavor, with hay-like aroma; creamy, smooth texture | Table cheese |
| *Monterey Jack* | Whole, pasteurized cow's milk; light yellow wheel or block; mild flavor (may be flavored with jalapeños) | Table cheese; great for melting |
| *Muenster* | Whole cow's milk; light yellow wheel or block; rind may be orange; mild to pungent flavor (depending on age and country of origin); smooth, waxy texture with small holes. French muenster is made with raw milk, has a washed rind, and has an aroma similar to Epoisses. | Great for melting |
| *Port-salut* | Whole or low-fat cow's milk; yellow block; orange rind; buttery, mellow to sharp flavor; smooth texture with tiny holes | Table cheese paired with raw onions and beer; great for melting |
| *Caciotta* | Whole cow's milk; thick, yellowish wax; aged for 2 months; mellow and savory flavor (available flavored with chiles or herbs); semi-soft texture with some curd holes | Table cheese; great for melting |

# *Blue-veined cheeses*

Blue or **blue-veined cheeses** are thought to have been among some of the first cheeses produced. Although there is no specific research to prove the theory, it is believed that the mold was first introduced to cheese from moldy bread that had come in contact with the cheese.

In the modern production of blue cheeses, needles are used to form holes and introduce the mold to the cheese as well as to allow the gases to escape and oxygen to enter to support mold growth within the cheese. This process is why when you cut a wedge or cross section of factory-made blue cheese, you will notice the bluing tends to follow those puncture lines vertically with little even horizontal growth. The cheese is then salted or brined and allowed to ripen in caves or under "cavelike conditions." Some of the most famous blue cheeses are the French Roquefort, Italian Gorgonzola, English Stilton, Danish blue, and American Maytag blue (see Fig 8-5).

**Roquefort** is made strictly from raw sheep's milk and has been made since ancient times in the Rouergue area of southern France. It is made by introducing the mold while the cheese is still curds and before it has been molded or shaped. The mold *Penicillium roqueforti* is taken from moldy bread and grated into a powder before it is mixed in with the curds. The Roquefort Association, Inc., ensures that quality standards and name integrity are protected. Today the cheeses are still ripened in the caves of Cambalou for three months to develop their unique character. They may be eaten after the initial ripening but are more typically stored for an additional three to twelve months as the market allows.

One of the things that makes Roquefort unique is the fact that the mold is not grown in a laboratory, as are molds for many other blue cheeses. Instead, Roquefort mold is developed naturally from rye bread. Roquefort should therefore be highlighted for what it is, and when used in dips or dressings should be clearly identified on the menu.

Gorgonzola is another special blue cheese. Unlike Roquefort, Gorgonzola is made from cow's milk, and its mold is from a completely different strain, which is now commercially produced. Gorgonzola is made with evening milk and the following day's morning milk. There are two varieties available: sweet or "dolce," which is aged three months, and "naturale" or mountain, which is aged further and has a fuller, more robust flavor.

FIG 8-5 BLUE CHEESES. CLOCKWISE FROM TOP LEFT: *Roquefort, Gorgonzola, Spanish blue, Pont Reyes, Stilton (center)*

table 8.4

## Blue Cheeses

| Variety | Description | Common Culinary Uses |
|---|---|---|
| *Danish blue* | Whole cow's milk; white blocks or drums, no rind; strong, sharp, salty flavor; firm, crumbly texture | Dressings, salads; slices, spreads |
| *Gorgonzola* | Whole cow's and/or goat's milk; medium yellow wheel with blue or green marbling; tangy, piquant flavor; semi-soft, creamy texture; crumbles well | Table cheese with fruit; salad, pizza; cooking ingredient; slices, spreads |
| *Roquefort* | Raw sheep's milk; ivory cylinder with blue-green marbling; deep, full, spicy flavor; semi-soft texture, crumbly | Table cheese; salads |
| *Stilton* | Whole cow's milk; tall cylinder, ivory-colored paste with blue-green marbling; full, rich, cheesy flavor; spicy aroma; firm yet crumbly texture | Table cheese; salads |
| *Spanish blue (valde-on, cabrales, picon)* | Cow's, sheep's, or goat's milk; straw-colored cylinder with veins of purplish-blue color; salty, sharp and tangy flavor; moist, crumbly texture; common variety is Cabrales | Table cheese; salads |
| *Pont reyes* | Cow's milk; bone-colored cylinder with little blue veining; full-flavored with hints of lemongrass and sea salt; creamy texture | Table cheese; dressings, salads |
| *Maytag blue* | Whole cow's milk; medium yellow cylinder, with blue marbling; spicy, peppery, earthy flavor; hard, creamy, crumbly texture | Table cheese; dressings, salads |

# Hard cheeses

A variety of **hard cheeses** are produced throughout the world. Cheddars and Swiss-style cheeses are among the most well known (see Fig 8-6).

Originating in England, Cheddar has become one of the most popular hard cheeses in the United States. The Pilgrims brought Cheddar formulas to the United States, and by 1790, it was produced in such quantities that it was exported back to England. Cheddar derives its name from the process used in its manufacture. The **cheddaring** process involves turning and stacking the slabs of young cheese to extract more whey and give the cheese its characteristic texture. The yellow color of some Cheddars is achieved through the addition of annatto seed paste and has nothing to do with the flavor.

Once the cheddaring process is complete, the cheeses are wrapped in cheesecloth that has been dipped in wax and allowed to ripen. Cheddars are categorized by age. Current Cheddar is aged for thirty days, mild for one to three months, medium for three to six months, sharp for six to nine months, and extra-sharp for nine months to five years.

Many cheeses that originated in the United States are produced using the cheddaring method. American cheese is said to have gotten its name after the American Revolution when the proud producers of Cheddar in the United States did not want their cheeses to be mistaken for anything that might have originated in England, and aptly labeled them "American cheese."

Colby is another truly American cheese that was invented in the town of Colby, Wisconsin, in 1874. When Colby slabs are cut in half, they are popularly known as "longhorns."

The family of cheeses generically referred to as Swiss are also hard cheeses. These cheeses are sometimes characterized by holes, called **eyes,** which range in size from tiny to the size of a quarter. Swiss cheeses are often mellow in flavor and have excellent melting properties. Some of the more well-known varieties of Swiss cheese include Gruyère and Emmentaler. Beaufort is a French cheese made in the French Alps since Roman times that is similar to Swiss Gruyère. It is known as the Prince of Gruyères or King of the Mountain and has AOC status as well. Jarlsberg is another famous cheese that is Swiss-style; it comes from Norway.

FIG 8-6 HARD CHEESES. CLOCKWISE FROM TOP LEFT: *Emmentaler, aged provolone, Gruyère, manchego, aged Gouda, aged Cheddar, aged pecorino antico mugella, ricotta salata*

table 8.5

## Hard Cheeses

| Variety | Description | Common Culinary Uses |
|---|---|---|
| *Cantal* | Whole cow's milk; light yellow cylinder; mild, buttery flavor; crumbly, firm texture | Salads, sandwiches, with fruit |
| *Cheddar* | Whole cow's milk; light to medium yellow wheels or rectangles; mild to sharp (depending on age) flavor; sweet grassy aroma; buttery, rich texture | Table cheese; with beer, sandwiches; cooking ingredient; great melting cheese |
| *Emmentaler* | Raw or pasteurized, part-skim cow's milk; light yellow wheel; full-flavored, nutty, fruity aroma; smooth, shiny texture with large holes; commonly called Swiss cheese | Great melting cheese; in fondues, sandwiches |
| *Gouda* | Whole cow's milk; wheel (usually coated with red wax), ranges from golden to amber (depending on age); mild, creamy, slightly nutty flavor; smooth texture, may have tiny holes; may be smoked | Table cheese; great for melting; aged Gouda can be grated |
| *Jarlsberg* | Part-skim cow's milk; light yellow wheel; sharp, nutty flavor; smooth texture with large holes | Great melting cheese; very popular in the United States |
| *Manchego* | Whole sheep's milk; white to yellowish wheels with brownish-gray rinds; slightly briny, nutty flavor; smooth slightly oily texture; may have tiny holes | Table cheese; in salads; can be grated |
| *Provolone* | Whole cow's milk; shaped like a pear, sausage, or round balls; pale yellow with yellow to golden-brown rind; sharp flavor; elastic, oily texture; may be smoked | Table cheese with olives, bread, raw vegetables, or salami; in sandwiches; for melting |
| *Ricotta salata* | Whole sheep's milk; pure white cylinder; mild, nutty flavor; smooth but crumbly texture | Pasta, salads; with salami, fruit, and vegetables |
| *Gruyère* | Whole raw cow's milk; flat beige wheels with brown rind; fruity and nutty flavor; smooth, creamy texture that becomes drier and slightly grainy when fully aged | Fondue; gratins, soups, sandwiches; cooking ingredient |

# Very hard cheeses

In Italy, these cheeses are known as the **granas,** or grainy cheeses, because of their granular texture. The most popular of these cheeses are Parmesan and Romano, which are now produced in the United States and South America but are different from their predecessors. **Very hard cheeses** are most often grated or shaved, but they are also traditionally eaten in chunks broken off with a special knife (see Fig 8-7).

True Parmigiano-Reggiano is often referred to as the "king of cheeses." It is believed that the formula for this cheese has not changed in more than seven hundred years, and its origins date back even further. This legendary cheese is made slowly and carefully following strict guidelines that require it to be aged a minimum of fourteen months, although most are aged for twenty-four months. Stravecchio, or extra aged, is ripened for as much as three years. The flavor of Parmigiano-Reggiano is complex and unique.

Romano cheeses—named for the city of Rome—come in several different varieties. Pecorino Romano, which is made with sheep's milk, is probably the best known. Caprino Romano is a very sharp goat's milk version, and vacchino Romano is a mild version made from cow's milk.

FIG 8-7 GRATING CHEESES: *Asiago, Parmigiano-Reggiano, grana Padano, ancho chile caciotta, Pecorino Romano, Spanish goat cheese, sapsago, dry Monterey Jack (center)*

table 8.6

## Very Hard Cheeses

| Variety | Description | Common Culinary Uses |
|---|---|---|
| *Asiago* | Whole or part-skim cow's milk; light yellow to tan or gold wheels with gray rind; mild to sharp flavor (depending on age) | Salads, pasta; with fruit and bread |
| *Parmigiano-Reggiano* | Part-skim cow's milk; large drums, straw interior with golden rind; sharp, nutty, salty flavor; very hard, dry, crumbly texture | Table cheese; grated over pasta or risotto; in salads; rind is used in vegetable stocks |
| *Dry Monterey Jack* | Whole or part-skim cow's milk; pale yellow with a rich, sharp, slightly nutty flavor; also known as Aged Monterey Jack | Table cheese; grated over pasta, in salads |
| *Pecorino Romano* | Whole sheep's milk; tall cylinders, white with thin, black rind; very sharp, salty, peppery flavor; dry, crumbly texture | Table cheese; grated over pasta or risotto, in salads |
| *Sapsago* | Skim cow's milk; light green flattened cone; piquant, sharp, sage- and lettuce-like flavor; very hard, granular texture; also known as Glarner Schabzieger | Grated on noodles, salads, or soups; mixed with butter or yogurt in dips |
| *Grana padano* | Cow's milk; drums, golden colored; mild flavor; very hard texture | Grating; a less-expensive alternative to Parmigiano-Reggiano |

# Pasta filata cheeses

**Pasta filata cheeses** are a group of cheeses that are related by the process used in their manufacture, rather than by their textures. In fact, the textures of pasta filata cheeses run the gamut from soft to hard, depending upon how they are aged, if at all.

Pasta filata literally means "spun curds" or "spun paste." During manufacture, the curds are dipped into hot water and then stretched or spun until the proper consistency and texture is achieved. They are then kneaded and molded into the desired shapes.

The most common cheese of this category is mozzarella. In 1990, over 1.5 billion pounds of mozzarella were produced in America alone. Today there are two types of mozzarella available: the traditional fresh style, which is available in a variety of shapes and sizes, and the newer American invention of low-moisture mozzarella, which has a longer shelf life than the fresh style. Both whole-milk and part-skim varieties are available. A recipe for making Mozzarella Cheese is on page 384 (see Figure 8-12).

Provolone is another popular pasta filata cheese that is similarly handled but is made with a different culture. Once the curd is stretched and kneaded, it is rubbed with brine and tied into shape. It is then hung and left to dry in sizes ranging from 250 g to 200 lb. Provolone is often smoked and/or aged for additional character and firmer texture.

# Cheese service
## Selecting the cheese

A variety of approaches may be taken when developing a cheese board. Cheeses should be selected based on color, shape, texture, richness, and intensity. A modest selection might simply include cheeses of the best quality selected from the soft, blue, and hard categories. More extensive selections continue to build their offerings by expanding selections within categories and developing a special selection to feature local or regional favorites.

**Cheese plates, boards, or carts** often contain a variety of cheeses, but sometimes it is interesting to compose a board that features only one type of milk, sometimes referred to as a **flight of cheeses,** in the same way that a flight of Chardonnays or Pinot Noirs might be offered. A sheep's milk cheese board, for instance, gives the guest a chance to taste and compare a variety of cheeses made from the same main ingredient. This is an opportunity that many people have never had, but would probably be interested in trying.

## Presenting the cheese

Cheeses should be allowed to come to room temperature before they are served. This process, known as **aromatization,** brings out the fullest flavor of the cheese, so that all its nuances can be enjoyed.

### Styles of presentation

Cheeses may be served as a **course** in and of themselves, often preceding or in place of dessert. In à la carte service, some restaurants present their customers with a cheese cart from which they may sample a variety of cheeses. The customer chooses which cheeses he or she would like to try, and their server then prepares a plate tableside, consisting of the desired cheeses, bread or crackers, and occasionally some fruit (see Fig 8-8).

On a **buffet,** cheese boards are eye-catching items that have always been popular. The board itself can be as simple as a piece of wood, reserved strictly for cheese board service, which has been decoratively lined with clean, nontoxic leaves. More common, however, are service platters, mirrors, or marble.

## Partners and accompaniments for cheese

Three types of foods have a natural affinity for cheese: wine, beer, and fortified wines; varieties of bread and crackers; and fruit. Bread is probably the original **accompaniment** to cheese; the combination provided portable sustenance for the traveler and a convenient meal for others.

Wine, particularly tannic wine, offers a perfect contrast to the richness of cheese. The wine's acidity cuts through the cheese's butterfat. Beer, on the other hand, works well to contrast the salt component of cheese, making it an ideal accompaniment.

The sweet juiciness of many fruits also pairs well with the earthy richness of cheese. Classic examples include apples with Cheddar and pears with blue cheese.

FIG 8-8    *Cheese service styles can vary to include different types of cheese, bread or crackers, or fruit*

# Caring for cheeses: storage and handling

Because cheese is a **living food** with active biological attributes, it is critical to maintain the highest standards in sanitation during handling. Cheese can be a potentially hazardous food if handled improperly.

When handling cheese that is not going to be cooked, it is important to either use utensils or wear food-service gloves to prevent the **contamination** of the cheese with bacteria from your hands (as well as preventing unsightly fingerprints on the cheese). All food contact areas should be cleaned and sanitized properly with hot soapy water and sanitizing solution to prevent cross-contamination. All cheese-cutting equipment should be similarly sanitized.

If cheeses become unnaturally moldy, they may be trimmed by cutting ½ to 1 in / 1 to 2 cm past the mold. Care should be taken not to transfer the mold to the good portion.

Cheeses should never be allowed to sit out at room temperature for extended periods of time beyond that required to aromatize the cheeses. The exception to this rule, of course, is the time that they spend maturing when they are being made. Always keep cheeses and cheese preparations covered and refrigerated properly. Cheese should not be wrapped in plastic for storing. Waxed paper and aluminum foil are preferable as they allow the cheese to breathe while not drying out. Wrapping cheese in plastic effectively "kills" it by not allowing the bacteria access to air. Most cheese purchased commercially will, unfortunately, be wrapped in plastic. When storing cheese, do not freeze it either, as that will certainly destroy its texture.

# Making cheese in the kitchen

Cheese making, especially for the fresh cheeses in the accompanying recipes, is a practical and reasonable way to expand the handcrafted specialty items you can offer your guests. The raw ingredients can be obtained easily, and most of the necessary equipment is already part of a standard kitchen setup. Because cheese making involves acid, the equipment should be made of or lined with **nonreactive materials,** such as stainless steel, enamel, or food-grade plastic. All equipment should be thoroughly sterilized before use.

- Whole milk, heavy cream, and half-and-half are used to prepare the fresh cheeses here. You can often substitute (in whole or in part) lower-fat milk for whole milk or heavy cream for half-and-half, or substitute milk from sheep or goats, if it is available in your area. The milk should be pasteurized and homogenized to help produce consistent results.
- Fresh cheeses are most often curdled with an acid. Our recipes use cider vinegar, citric acid, tartaric acid, and lemon juice. Each acid has a particular effect on the finished cheese, and you may wish to experiment with different starters to find one that gives you the flavor you want.
- The curd for mozzarella is prepared with a rennet or other enzymatic starter. The curd can be purchased and used to prepare fresh mozzarella.
- Two of the recipes in this section call for **direct-set cultures.** These cultures start curdling the milk almost instantly, without requiring an extended incubation period.

# Mascarpone

YIELD: *32 fl oz / 960 mL*

64 fl oz / 1.92 L heavy cream

½ tsp / 2.5 mL tartaric acid

1. Heat the cream to 180°F / 80°C, stirring often to prevent scorching. Remove from the heat. Add the tartaric acid, and let the cream coagulate into a curd.

2. Pour the curd into a strainer lined with a coffee filter or damp cheesecloth, if desired (see Fig 8-9a) and refrigerate for 24 hours to drain. Serve immediately, or transfer to a storage container, cover, and refrigerate for up to 1 week.

*Chef's note*  *This is a delicious, rich cheese with a very high fat content. It can be used as a base for sauces by sweetening or adding fruit purées, or it can be served as is to accompany fresh or poached fruits.*

| FIG 8-9A | *Once the cream is curdled, pour it into a colander lined with dampened cheesecloth.* | FIG 8-9B | *Finished mascarpone is somewhat thick with a smooth, creamy consistency.* |

# Whole-Milk Ricotta Cheese

YIELD: *2 lb / 907 g*

| | |
|---|---|
| 4 tsp / 20 mL citric acid | 4 gal / 15.36 L whole milk |
| 8 fl oz / 240 mL water | 8 tsp / 24 g salt |

1. Dissolve the citric acid in the water.

2. Heat the milk, citric acid solution, and salt to 185°F / 85°C, stirring often to prevent scorching. Skim away the scum as it rises to the surface (see Fig 8-10a).

3. When the milk reaches 185°F / 85°C, turn off the heat and allow the milk to set for 10 minutes.

4. Pour the curd into a damp cheesecloth-lined colander or a cheesecloth or muslin bag set over a bowl and refrigerate for at least 1 hour and up to 3 hours to drain.

5. Serve immediately or transfer to a storage container, cover, and refrigerate for up to 1 week.

*Chef's notes*   *Although ricotta cheese is traditionally made by recooking the whey, it can also be made by substituting milk for some or all of the whey. This version calls for whole milk. If you prefer a lower-fat cheese, use skim milk for all or part of the whole milk.*
*If desired, substitute 2 fl oz / 60 mL diluted liquid citric acid for the 4 tsp of citric acid. If a creamier product is desired, add 8 oz / 240 mL heavy cream to the curd.*

| FIG 8-10A | *Remove and discard the scum that forms on the surface of the milk as it is heating up.* |

| FIG 8-10B | *Once the whey has been drained from the curds, the finished cheese will have a moist, granular texture.* |

# Lemon Cheese

YIELD: *2 lb / 907 g*

| | |
|---|---|
| 64 fl oz / 1.92 L milk | 1¼ tsp / 3.75 g salt |
| 2⅔ cups / 640 mL heavy cream | ¾ tsp / 2.25 g grated lemon zest |
| 6¾ fl oz / 202 mL lemon juice, strained and chilled | |

1. Heat the milk and cream over simmering water to exactly 100°F / 38°C (not higher).

2. Remove from the heat and add the lemon juice. Stir very gently and briefly until the milk and cream mixture starts to curdle or thicken.

3. Rest at room temperature for 3 to 4 hours.

4. Pour the curd into a cheesecloth-lined colander or a cheesecloth or muslin bag set over a bowl and refrigerate for 8 to 12 hours to drain.

5. Transfer the cheese to a bowl and work in the salt and lemon zest with wooden spoons. Be careful not to overwork the cheese.

6. Press into a mold, top with a weight, and refrigerate overnight. Unmold and serve immediately, or wrap and refrigerate for up to 4 days.

*Chef's note*  *This cheese has a pronounced lemon flavor. The texture is a bit dryer and coarser than mascarpone, the result of using a slightly lower-fat dairy product, as well as the additional draining and pressing this cheese undergoes.*

*Variations*  *Peppered Lemon Cheese: Add 4 tsp / 8 g coarse-ground black pepper with the lemon zest in step 5.*
*Dried Fruit and Hazelnut Cheese: Replace the lemon zest with 1¾ oz / 50 g toasted chopped hazelnuts, 2 oz / 57 g each toasted hazelnuts, and 1¾ oz / 50 g dried cherries.*

# Queso Blanco

YIELD: *2 lb / 907 g*

64 fl oz / 1.92 L whole milk

1 fl oz / 30 mL cider vinegar

2 tbsp / 20 g kosher salt

1. Heat the milk to 185°F / 85°C, stirring often to prevent scorching.

2. Add the vinegar and salt gradually, stirring constantly. Remove from the heat when the milk has solidified into a curd.

3. Drain the curd, refrigerated, for at least 1 hour and up to 3 hours in a cheesecloth-lined colander or a cheesecloth or muslin bag set over a bowl.

4. Serve immediately or transfer to a storage container. Cover and refrigerate for up to 1 week.

*Chef's note* *Queso blanco is a white, slightly salty fresh cheese featured in Mexican and other Latin American cuisines. Its texture is somewhat firm and crumbly, similar to that of farmer's cheese. It is used as a quesadilla filling on page 463.*

# Fromage Blanc

YIELD: *48 fl oz / 1.44 L*

64 fl oz / 1.92 L whole milk

1 packet direct-set Fromage Blanc Starter Culture

1. Warm the milk to 72°F / 22°C.

2. Stir in the starter culture.

3. Cover and allow to set (incubate) for 24 hours, or until a solid white curd forms.

4. Drain the curd, refrigerated, at least 3 hours and up to 6 hours in a cheesecloth-lined colander or a cheesecloth or muslin bag set over a bowl.

5. Serve immediately or transfer to a storage container, cover, and refrigerate for up to 1 week.

*Chef's notes* *Fromage blanc (French for "white cheese") has the texture of cream cheese without the calories. It can be used to make dips and spreads for sandwiches and hors d'oeuvre. Fresh herbs, spices, and dried and fresh fruits and vegetables can be added to this cheese to give it additional flavor and texture.*
*A shorter draining gives a spreadable consistency; longer draining yields a cream cheese–like consistency.*

# Herbed Yogurt Cheese

YIELD: *32 fl oz / 960 mL*

| | |
|---|---|
| 64 fl oz / 1.92 L plain yogurt | 2 tsp / 2 g chopped thyme |
| 1 tbsp / 9 g salt | 2 small chiles, split |
| 2½ tsp / 5 g coarse-ground black pepper | 2 bay leaves |
| 1 tbsp / 3 g chopped oregano | 16 fl oz / 480 mL extra-virgin olive oil |

1. Mix the yogurt, salt, and pepper and let drain, refrigerated, 3 days in a cheesecloth-lined colander or a cheesecloth or muslin bag set over a bowl.

2. Divide the cheese into 2-oz / 57-g portions and place on parchment-lined trays. Allow to drain and dry, refrigerated, overnight (see Fig 8-11).

3. Combine the remaining ingredients for a marinade. Add the cheese and marinate 24 hours before serving. The cheese can be covered and refrigerated in the marinade up to 4 weeks.

*Chef's note*  Yogurt cheese can be made from low-fat or nonfat yogurt with good results. It can be used as a dip or a spread.

**FIG 8-11** | *Once allowed to refrigerate overnight, the cheese will develop a tacky skin and plastic consistency.*

# Marinated Sheep's Cheese with Herbes de Provence

YIELD: *12 servings (4 oz / 113 g each)*

| | |
|---|---|
| 3 lb / 1.36 kg fresh sheep's cheese | 12 grape leaves, rinsed |
| 2½ oz / 71 g Herbes de Provence (page 591) | 12 fl oz / 360 mL extra-virgin olive oil |
| 1¾ tsp / 5.25 g salt | 24 slices peasant-style bread |
| 1 tsp / 2 g ground black pepper | |

1. Divide the cheese logs into 5 equal portions.

2. Mix together the herbs, salt, and pepper and press gently into cheese, shaping the cheese portions into even disks about 3 in / 7.50 cm in diameter.

3. Wrap the disks in grape leaves and place in a container. Pour the oil over the wrapped cheeses, cover, and refrigerate overnight. Serve immediately or cover and refrigerate up to 3 days.

*Variations*  *Grilled Marinated Sheep's Cheese with Country Bread: Brush slices of country-style bread with olive oil. Grill the bread and the drained wrapped cheese over hot coals until marked on both sides. The cheese should be soft and runny. Serve the cheese on a bed of greens, if desired, with the toasted bread, or arrange it on a platter for buffet-style service.*

*Marinated Goat Cheese: Substitute buttons or logs of fresh goat cheese for the sheep's cheese.*


# Crème Fraîche

YIELD: *24 to 32 fl oz / 720 to 960 mL*

| | |
|---|---|
| 32 fl oz / 960 mL half-and-half | 1 packet direct-set Crème Fraîche Starter Culture |

1. Warm the half-and-half to 72°F / 22°C.

2. Stir in the starter culture.

3. Cover and allow to set (incubate) for 24 hours, until a very thick curd forms.

4. Serve immediately or transfer to a storage container, cover, and refrigerate up to 1 week.

*Chef's note*  *Crème fraîche is made by fermenting heavy cream that has a butterfat content as high as 60 percent with a lactic acid and the appropriate bacterial cultures. The flavor of newly prepared crème fraîche is sweet, and it has a loose, almost pourable texture. As it ages, the flavor becomes more pronounced and tart, and it thickens to the point at which it can nearly hold a spoon upright. It is important to the garde manger as a base or spread for canapés, in salad dressings, and served with fresh fruit.*

*Variation*  *Lime-Flavored Crème Fraîche: Add fresh lime juice to taste.*

# Mozzarella Cheese

YIELD: *2 lb / 907 g*

5½ oz / 156 g salt

1 gal / 3.84 L water

2 lb / 907 g cheese curd, cut into ½-in / 1-cm cubes

1. Add the salt to the water and bring to 160°F / 71°C. Remove the pot from the heat.

2. Place the cheese curd in a colander and lower the colander into the hot water. The curds must be completely submerged.

3. Work the curd with wooden spoons, stretching it until it becomes a smooth but stringy mass (see Fig 8-12a). Maintain the water temperature at a constant 155°F / 68°C during this process, rewarming the pot as needed.

4. Remove the cheese from the water and continue stretching until the curd is smooth.

5. Shape the cheese into 4-oz / 113-g balls and allow the cheese to cool slowly in the liquid in which it was melted (see Fig 8-12b). Store wrapped in plastic wrap or in brine. Cover and refrigerate up to 5 days.

*Variations*  *Marinated Bocconcini: Prepare the mozzarella as directed through step 4. On plastic wrap, form a long tube, about 1 in / 3 cm in diameter, and roll up (see Fig 8-13a). Tie at 1-in / 2.5-cm intervals to form balls (see Fig 8-13b). Refrigerate at least 8 hours. Cut into individual balls and remove the plastic wrap. Combine 1½ fl oz / 45 mL olive oil, 1 tbsp / 15 mL sherry vinegar, 1 tbsp / 3 g basil chiffonade, and ½ tsp / 1 g red pepper flakes. Marinate cheese overnight. This recipe makes about 60 pieces. If desired, accompany the marinated bocconcini with roasted peppers.*

FIG 8-12A  *Gently stretch the mozzarella curds until they have melted and formed a smooth, stringy mass.*

FIG 8-12B  *Once kneaded until smooth, portion the cheese into balls and store them in the same water in which the curds were melted.*

*Mozzarella Roulade with Prosciutto: Prepare the mozzarella through step 4. Working on a plastic tray or plastic wrap, stretch the curd into a rectangle (see Fig 8-14a). It should be about ¼ in / 6 mm thick and 12 in by 14 in / 30 cm by 36 cm. While the cheese is still warm, lay 10 paper-thin slices of prosciutto and 20 basil leaves over the mozzarella in an even layer. Roll into a roulade with plastic wrap and secure the ends tightly with string (see Fig 8-14b). Return to the hot water for 2 to 3 minutes to lock in the garnish. Remove from the water and retie the ends to secure. Chill the roulade overnight in a water bath before slicing. The wrapped roulade can be refrigerated up to 7 days. This recipe makes about thirty 1-oz / 28-g servings.*

**FIG 8-13A** | *Shape the prepared mozzarella into a log and wrap it in plastic wrap.*

**FIG 8-13B** | *Portion the log into small balls, securing each one with butcher's twine.*

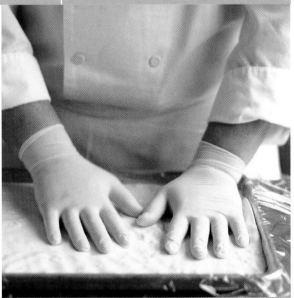

**FIG 8-14A** | *Stretch the prepared mozzarella into a plastic-wrap-lined tray, working it evenly into all corners.*

**FIG 8-14B** | *After laying the desired garnish over the cheese, tightly roll up the roulade and secure the ends with string.*

# Hudson Valley Camembert Crisps

*YIELD:* *12 servings (2 oz / 57 g each)*

6 sheep's milk Camembert (4 oz / 113 g each)

12 phyllo dough sheets

6 oz / 170 g butter, melted (as needed for preparing phyllo and sautéing)

4 fl oz / 120 mL egg wash (2 whole eggs beaten with 1 tbsp / 15 mL milk)

Vegetable oil for pan frying, as needed

1. Cut the Camembert squares from corner to corner, forming equal triangles.

2. Layer three sheets of phyllo, brushing each layer with the melted butter. Repeat with remaining sheets for a total of four stacks.

3. Cut each layered phyllo stack lengthwise into three equal strips. Wrap 1 strip around a triangle of cheese. Secure the seam by brushing with a bit of egg wash. Repeat procedure until all cheese is wrapped in phyllo. Continue to step 4 or cover tightly so phyllo doesn't dry out, and refrigerate up to 24 hours before preparing further.

4. Pan fry the wrapped Camembert over high heat in the oil until well browned on both sides and quite crisp. Drain briefly on absorbent paper towels and serve hot or at room temperature.

*Presentation idea*   *This can be served warm with a fruit chutney, peasant-style bread, air-dried venison, and a tossed salad.*

# Blue Cheese Tart

YIELD: *12 tarts (4 in / 10 cm in diameter)*

2 lb 8 oz / 1.13 kg Pâte Dough (page 598)

1 lb 3 oz / 539 g cream cheese

1 lb 3 oz / 539 g blue cheese

5 large eggs

7½ fl oz / 225 mL sour cream

9½ fl oz / 285 mL heavy cream

2½ tbsp / 7.50 g minced chives

2½ tbsp / 7.50 g minced flat-leaf parsley

5 tsp / 5 g minced thyme

2½ tsp / 7.50 g minced shallots, sautéed and cooled

1¼ tsp / 3.75 g salt

½ tsp / 1 g ground white pepper

1. Roll out the dough and use it to line 12 tart pans 4 in / 10 cm in diameter. Blind bake at 350°F / 177°C for 15 to 20 minutes. Let cool while making filling.

2. Cream the cheeses in mixer until smooth. Add the eggs gradually, scraping the sides often. Add the sour cream, heavy cream, herbs, and seasonings.

3. Pour into prepared crusts and bake at 300°F / 150°C until knife comes out clean when inserted in the center of the tarts, about 20 minutes.

4. Let the tarts rest at least 10 to 15 minutes before slicing. They may be served warm or at room temperature.

*Chef's note* For canapé, pour the custard into 120 prepared barquette pans and bake as directed above. Garnish with chopped toasted walnuts or pistachios.

# Savory Roquefort Cheesecake

YIELD: *1 cake (9 in / 23 cm in diameter; 24 servings)*

CRUST

2 oz / 57 g dry bread crumbs

1 oz / 28 g butter

2¼ oz / 64 g chopped walnuts, toasted

12 oz / 340 g Roquefort

1¼ lb / 567 g cream cheese

½ oz / 14 g all-purpose flour

3 shallots, minced, sautéed, and cooled

4 eggs

2 fl oz / 60 mL heavy cream

2 tbsp / 6 g chopped dill

1. Brown the bread crumbs in the butter; add the toasted walnuts. Cool.

2. Press into a springform pan 9 in / 23 cm in diameter as for a graham cracker crust.

3. Line pan with a paper collar about 3 in / 7.5 cm high.

4. In a food processor, blend the cheeses until smooth.

5. Add the flour, shallots, eggs, and cream.

6. Blend in the dill and pour into the prepared pan.

7. Bake in a 160°F / 71°C water bath in a 300°F / 149°C oven until set, 30 to 40 minutes.

8. Cool to room temperature, then cover and refrigerate overnight. Cut into 24 equal slices. Bring to room temperature before serving.

*Presentation idea*  This recipe makes an excellent element on any buffet or reception offering. Serve a wedge of it as an intermezzo salad on a bed of dressed greens, with a cheese course, or as an accompaniment to a wine tasting.

# Pear and Blue Cheese Tart

**YIELD:** *12 tarts (5 in / 13 cm in diameter)*

½ recipe Pâte Sucrée (page 599)

3¾ oz / 106 g almonds, slivered, toasted

6 Bosc or Anjou pears, poached in white wine, halved, peeled, and cored

8 oz / 227 g Maytag or Pont Reyes blue cheese

8 fl oz / 240 mL heavy cream

4¾ oz / 135 g sugar

2 eggs

1. On a floured work surface, working in batches, roll out the pastry dough ⅛ to ¼ in / 3 to 6 mm thick. Cut out 12 circles 6 in / 15 cm in diameter. Line 12 individual tart pans 5 in / 13 cm in diameter with the dough. Trim any excess dough from the edges. Chill for 30 minutes to an hour.

2. Preheat an oven to 400°F / 204°C. Lay a small square of aluminum foil inside each tart pan and fill it with dried beans to weight the dough during baking. Blind bake the tarts 15 minutes, then turn down the oven to 350°F / 177°C and bake 5 more minutes. If the edges of the tart start to brown too quickly during the baking process, line the edges with aluminum foil. Once the crusts are finished baking, remove the foil and beans, prick the bottoms with a fork, and set them aside to cool, leaving them in their molds.

3. Divide the almonds evenly and sprinkle into the bottom of each crust.

4. Place one pear half on your work surface at a time. Working with your knife at a diagonal, slice each half crosswise into ¼-in / 6-mm slices. Arrange the slices of one pear half evenly over the almonds.

5. Place the cheese in a food processor and mix until smooth. Add the cream, sugar, and eggs. Mix for about 30 seconds, or until the mixture is smooth. Scrape the bowl down periodically while mixing.

6. Divide the mixture evenly over the pears in the crust, scraping the bowl out with a rubber spatula. Spread the mixture gently with a rubber spatula to make sure it covers everything fairly evenly.

7. Bake the tarts in a 350°F / 177°C oven for 35 minutes, or until set.

8. Allow the tarts to cool slightly before removing them from the molds. Slice the tarts and serve them warm.

*Chef's note*  *The tarts can be sliced in half for a lunch-size serving or into 6 to 8 pieces for hors d'oeuvre.*

# 9

*objectives*

- Compare and contrast appetizers and hors d'oeuvre

- Identify composed hors d'oeuvre including canapés, profiteroles, tartlets, and barquettes

- Discuss the role of appetizers in à la carte, buffet, and tasting menu situations

- Explain how to select and prepare appetizers

- Recognize the principles of presenting appetizers

- Understand the preparation of cold savory mousses, sorbets, and espumas

- Classify types of caviar and its role in garde manger

# Appetizers and hors d'oeuvre

The distinctions between appetizers and hors d'oeuvre have more to do with how and when they are served than the actual foods being served. Typically served as preludes to a meal, hors d'oeuvre are some of the most intriguing and demanding items produced by the garde manger. Appetizers are served as the first course of a meal. For every rule you read about what types of foods should or shouldn't constitute an appetizer, you will find at least one good exception.

**W**hat most appetizers have in common is the careful attention to portioning and proper technical execution and plating. Typically, appetizers are small servings of very flavorful items, meant just to take enough edge off the appetite to permit thorough enjoyment of an entrée. The usual practice of "building" a menu from one course to the next calls for some logical connection between the appetizer and all of the courses that follow.

The term **hors d'oeuvre,** which translates from French as "outside the work," is universally recognized; we have not developed an exact equivalent in English capable of conveying as much information as this short French phrase. Hors d'oeuvre also have a place on a menu, where they may be featured as antipasti or hors d'oeuvre variées. You may be familiar with the "chef's tasting" or amuse-gueule, a small portion of something exotic, unusual, or otherwise special that is served when the guests are seated.

Even though hors d'oeuvre are small bite-sized items, today it is increasingly common for clients to request an entire menu made up of hors d'oeuvre to serve at a reception or cocktail party. These **"standing meals"** can be quite extensive, running the gamut from small servings of cold soups, meats, fish, cheeses, vegetable dishes, and pastas, to desserts and confections. In a break with the traditional notion that hors d'oeuvre should be small enough to eat in one bite and never require a knife and fork, some items at these special receptions may be plated. For these events to run smoothly, it is important to have adequate service staff on hand to continually relieve guests of used plates and cups or picks and napkins.

The items you choose to serve as hors d'oeuvre may be very simple, requiring little if any preparation on the part of the garde manger beyond slicing and presenting. Nuts, plain or marinated olives, and hard-cooked eggs are all traditional offerings. Dips and spreads are often served with crudité (raw or chilled lightly blanched vegetables), crackers, or chips. Sausages, pâtés, terrines, and cheeses are also served as reception or buffet items, as are thinly sliced or hand-carved smoked fish and meats. One "simple" but elegant food, caviar, is also featured on its own as an elegant hors d'oeuvre.

There are a few precepts to remember in general hors d'oeuvre preparation and presentation:

- When selecting hors d'oeuvre, keep in mind the nature of the event, as well as the menu to follow.
- Ice carvings and ice beds are sometimes used to keep seafood and caviar very cold, as well as for their dramatic appeal. Be certain that the ice can drain properly and that the food that is served follows all sanitary guidelines.
- Hors d'oeuvre served on platters or passed on trays butler-style should be thoughtfully presented, so that the last person to take an hors d'oeuvre is not rummaging among jumbled garnishes.
- Today, chefs have many imaginative ways to present hors d'oeuvre. Some top-name chefs have companies making plates and platters designed by them specifically for their appetizers and hors d'oeuvre. Choose something eye-catching that will show off the design of the hors d'oeuvre.

# Composed hors d'oeuvre

**Composed hors d'oeuvre** are built from two or more components. When planning elaborate hors d'oeuvre, you may want to envision an appetizer or an entrée that would be reduced to a bite or two. Many of these components can be prepared in advance, but often the final assembly and garnish has to be done at nearly the last minute. When planning to include composed hors d'oeuvre in an event, it is important to take into account the timing for the hors d'oeuvre and the size of the event. These special items—including tartlets, barquettes, canapés, profiteroles, and spoons—can add greatly to the variety of offerings as well as provide an interesting combination of flavors. Cured and smoked foods, pâtés, foie gras, salads, and vegetables are all appropriate as elements in any composed hors d'oeuvre. One versatile item, **mousse,** can be featured as a spread, piped into molds or edible containers, rolled into a roulade and sliced, or shaped into quenelles.

## Barquettes and tartlets

Pâté dough (page 598) can be used to line a pâté en croûte as well as to create small edible containers, known as **barquettes** or **tartlets.** They may be filled with a cold mousse or other savory fillings. The dough should be rolled out in a thin sheet by hand or using a pasta machine. Cut out the dough to fit the mold (see Fig 9-1a). Set the dough in the mold, and top with a second mold to press it into shape (see Figs 9-1b and 9-1c). Set this assembly upside down on a sheet pan. Bake until golden brown, unmold, and store in an airtight container until needed (see Fig 9-1d).

These shells can be filled and garnished as for canapés, though it is generally not necessary to add a separate spread. Select the filling carefully. Very moist fillings can quickly make the pastry shell soggy. These hors d'oeuvre are best when assembled as close as possible to service time. Other **pastry or bread wrappers** can be used to prepare hors d'oeuvre. Some classics from cuisines around the world include bouchées, empanadas, beurrecks and tiropettes, dim sum, and spring rolls.

## Canapés

**Canapés** are small open-faced sandwiches (see Sandwiches, page 146). The "base" for a canapé is a small piece of bread, cut to shape and toasted. A spread of some sort—usually a plain or flavored butter, spreadable cheese, or mayonnaise—is applied to the bread to act as a moisture barrier.

The filling or topping is added next. It should be cut neatly, so that nothing hangs over the edge of the canapé. A **garnish** gives a fresh and appealing look to the canapé, but take the time to select something attractive and appropriate for the flavor profile of the canapé.

## Profiteroles

**Profiteroles** are small, round, hollow puffs made from pâte à choux. They can be made in varying sizes depending on the application and can be filled with sweet or savory filling. They are very often baked, sliced in half, filled, and garnished as desired. Alternately, a hole can be made in the bottom of the puff while they are still warm and then a smooth filling such as a mousse can be piped in. Pâté a choux is extremely versatile and is not terribly difficult to make. The dough can be flavored in a variety of ways and filled however is desired. The pâte à choux can also be baked and frozen, making it a very valuable product for the kitchen.

**FIG 9-1A**   *Cut out the barquettes with a paring knife using the mold as a guide and leaving space around the edge.*

**FIG 9-1B**   *Sandwich the cut dough between two molds, taking care not to squeeze the dough more than is necessary to shape it in the molds. Pressing too hard will make the dough thinner in some places, which will cause it to bake unevenly.*

**FIG 9-1C**   *Use a paring knife to trim off the excess overhanging dough from the edge of each mold.*

**FIG 9-1D**   *Bake the barquettes upside down and sandwiched between two molds.*

## *Spoons*

Hors d'oeuvre spoons have evolved somewhat in recent years but the basic principle remains the same. They are used as a base for an hors d'oeuvre, similar to a canapé base, so that you can layer a variety of items that have different flavors, colors, and textures. One of the biggest advantages to using the spoon as a base is that you can add a liquid element to the hors d'oeuvre, in the form of a sauce or gelée, which you cannot easily do with a canapé or tartlet because they will get soggy. Spoons also offer the functionality of having the utensil built into the presentation so that the guests don't have to use their fingers and extra serving pieces do not need to be set.

# Appetizers on the "à la carte menu"

When creating appetizers for the menu, it is important to provide enough appropriate options that work with the main course offerings. In an "à la carte situation," the garde manger may have relatively little control over what a guest might choose. Furthermore, there is no guarantee that the guests will order an appetizer just as a first course. This has led to some interesting and challenging new approaches to featuring appetizers on the menu. **Grazing menus** or **degustation menus** are produced by selecting a series of appetizer-size portioned items served in a logical sequence.

Guests today may look for appetizers that can be shared, or that can be ordered in a larger size to enjoy as a main course. In some restaurants, waitstaff may suggest an appetizer for the table to share and enjoy while their entrées are being prepared, both as a way to expose guests to something new or unusual as well as to "sell up the menu."

# Appetizer tasting menus

Over the past few years, the American restaurant scene has seen the advent of restaurants that feature entire menus made up of little appetizers or **tapas.** The menus from the newer tapas restaurants allow the diner to taste a wide variety of dishes because the plates are only a few bites each. In typical tasting menus, the chef decides on the appetizer that will help build a menu that has complementary flavors through the entrée and dessert. A disadvantage for this type of tasting menu is the limited amount that the customer gets to choose from, while tapas restaurants offer the patrons their choice of little dishes. This freedom of choice along with the lively, welcoming atmosphere makes these restaurants a popular destination for people to unwind from the stress of the day.

Classically, tapas were small pieces of bread that were used to cover glasses of sherry ("tapa" means lid). Tapas in Spain evolved as bar and restaurant owners began to feature their regional products alongside their sherries and wine. Tapas were given free to all patrons and each bar had its own specialties. Going from bar to bar to sample different tapas became one of the main social activities before dinner in order to get together with friends and discuss everything from politics to sports. Seasonality is very important in Spanish tapas, and bars tend to feature simple items that use the regional ingredients that are in season at the time. Typical regional dishes can range from items like anchovies, Spanish olives such as Manzanilla and Arbequira, chorizo sausage, Serrano ham, manchego cheese, and peppers to dishes such as fried calamari, Shrimp with Garlic (page 509), tortilla de papas, and Chicken Chilendron (page 505). Chefs have a chance to showcase their favorite ingredients and flavors in a variety of preparations.

However, Spain doesn't have the market cornered for these small dishes. Most cuisines worldwide have a well-established form of preparing and presenting appetizers and hors d'oeuvre. The *zakuski* table served before banquets in Russia features smoked and pickled fish, blinis with caviar, and a host of special salads. "Little dishes" known as *meze* are popular throughout the Mediterranean regions and feature olives, nuts, dips, spreads, and highly seasoned items such as grilled kebabs of meat or fish. In the Scandinavian countries, a **smorgasbord** showcases the special dishes, hot and cold, of that region, including herring, cheeses, and pickled foods.

# Appetizers for a banquet

Banquet menus frequently call for one or more appetizers. In this case, the chef does have the ability to **"build" a menu,** progressing from one flavor and texture experience to the next, so in this instance, thoughtful consideration of how each element of the menu will relate to what precedes and follows is the key to success. Taking a cue from the principles used by sommeliers to build from one wine to another, going from the more understated to the more robust, is a common practice for the meal to progress from **subtle** to more **assertive flavors**.

It is important to consider the entire experience when designing appetizers in a banquet menu. They should be served in sensible portions, perhaps smaller than you might offer on an à la carte menu, so that guests can sample a few appetizers and still enjoy their main course and dessert.

# Selecting and preparing appetizers

Classic hors d'oeuvre can usually be served as appetizers if you increase the portion size slightly and take into consideration the plating of the appetizer. The new appetizer may require a sauce or a different garnish than the smaller hors d'oeuvre. Perfectly fresh clams and oysters, for example, shucked as close to service time as possible and served with sauces designed to enhance their naturally briny savor, or a classic shrimp "cocktail," served with a cocktail sauce, salsa, or other pungent sauce, are perennial favorites in any appetizer category.

Smoked fish, meats, or poultry; sausages, pâtés, terrines, and galantines; air-dried hams and beef sliced paper thin—all of these items can be used to create appetizer plates, on their own with a few accompaniments or garnishes or as a sampler plate. Refer to Chapters Five, Six, and Seven for specific recipes and presentation ideas.

Salads are also served as appetizers. Several salads in Chapter Three can fit this category quite well. You may prefer to change the portion size, substitute a different sauce or garnish to give your menu items a special look, vary it from season to season, or showcase a range of flavors and textures from other cuisines.

Warm and hot appetizers may include small servings of pastas, such as ravioli or tortellini, served on their own or in a sauce or broth. Puff pastry shells can be cut into vols au vent or made into turnovers and filled with savory ragoûts or foie gras. Broiled or grilled fish, shellfish, or poultry may be featured. Crêpes, blinis, and other similar dishes are popular presentations in many different cuisines. Global influences can be seen on menus across the country. Asian and Pacific Rim spices and infusions are very popular, as are Mediterranean dishes. Empanadas share space in the garde manger's repertoire with kefta (spicy kebabs made from ground lamb). Vegetables are more important than ever as appetizers. Sometimes they are presented very simply; for example, steamed artichokes may be served with a dipping sauce such as a flavored mayonnaise or vinaigrette, chilled asparagus may be served drizzled with a flavored oil, or a plate of grilled vegetables may be accompanied by a vinaigrette sauce.

Another popular concept when selecting an appetizer is cooking an item more than one way on a plate. For example, the duck confit from the leg can be served with a potato crisp that is cooked in the garlicky fat alongside slices of smoked duck breast. This principle is also considered by some chefs as a great way to utilize the whole duck while being creative with the presentation. Of course this could apply to a multitude of items such as salmon, shellfish, and poultry.

# Principles for presenting appetizers

The recipes in this chapter include such traditional favorites as carpaccio, melon and prosciutto, and foie gras in brioche. Keep in mind some of the following basic principles as you select, prepare, and plate appetizers:

- Serve all appetizers at the **proper temperature.** Remember to chill or warm plates as required by the preparation. Serving different components of an appetizer at different temperatures also creates a more interesting appetizer.
- Season all appetizer items with meticulous care. Appetizers are meant to stimulate the appetite, so **seasoning** is of the utmost importance because you shouldn't overwhelm the palate when there are more courses to come. When creating your appetizer you should consider things like umami and glutamates found naturally in your ingredients and make sure that you have several sources of flavor to ensure that your dish has plenty of interest.
- Slice, shape, and **portion** appetizers properly. There should be just enough of any given item to make the appetizer interesting and appealing from start to finish, but not so much on the plate that the guest is overwhelmed.
- **Neatness** always counts, but especially with appetizers. Your guests will most likely judge their entire meal based on the impression the appetizer gives.
- When offering **shared appetizers,** consider how they will look when they come to the table. It may create a more visually appealing presentation if the chef splits a shared plate in the kitchen, rather than expecting the guests to divide it up themselves.
- Color, shape, and "white space" play a role in the overall **composition** of your plate. Take the time to choose the right size and shape serving pieces and to provide the guest with all the items necessary for the appetizer, including cups for dipping sauces, special utensils, and if necessary, finger bowls.
- Consider the garnish for the appetizer carefully and be sure that it adds something to the plate, whether it is a complementary or contrasting flavor or texture.

# Cold savory mousses

The French word *mousse* literally means "foam" or "froth." For the garde manger, it indicates a cold item prepared by combining three basic elements: a **base,** a **binder,** and an **aerator.** Mousses are often featured as hors d'oeuvres, piped decoratively on a canapé base or into a barquette or tartlet mold. They can be used to fill a cucumber cup or endive leaf, shaped in a special mold as a single serving perhaps topped with a layer of crystal-clear aspic gelée, or as loaves or roulades ready to be sliced and served.

A cold mousse as the term is understood today is one that is not cooked after being assembled. It is never served hot, since subjecting the gelatin or fat binder in the mousse to heat would melt the mousse and deflate it. A "hot mousse" indicates a small serving of a mousseline forcemeat that has been molded in a fashion similar to a cold mousse before being cooked and served hot.

## The base

Mousse prepared by the garde manger is produced from savory items such as cooked or smoked meats and fish, cheeses, or prepared vegetables. This base is then puréed until very smooth (see Fig 9-2a).

In some cases it may be necessary to add a liquid or moist product such as velouté, béchamel, unwhipped cream, or mayonnaise to adjust the consistency. The intent is to have the base at a consistency similar to that of pastry cream before adding the binder, if it is required, and the aerator. For the best possible texture, sieve the puréed base. This removes any last bits of sinew or fiber and gives a very delicate finished product.

## The binder

Gelatin, either powdered or in sheets, is added in a proportion similar to that called for when preparing an aspic gelée. Soften the gelatin in a cool liquid (known as "blooming"). Warm it to 90°F / 32°C to 110°F / 43°C to dissolve the granules or melt the sheets. Stir the dissolved gelatin into the base. It is important to blend the gelatin evenly throughout the entire base (see Fig 9-2b).

In some cases, the base product has enough body and bind to hold the mousse together without an additional binder. Cheese is a good example of one of these base products.

The key is to have the proper balance of binder and base so that the mousse will keep a distinct shape when chilled without melting or sagging but also without being rubbery because there is too much binder. The amount of binder in a product should be adjusted depending on the final use of the product. For example, if a mousse must be sliced and lined up on a buffet platter that will be sitting out for any length of time, it will need more binder (gelatin) than would a single serving of mousse that is taken directly from the refrigerator immediately before it is served.

## The aerator

Beaten egg whites and/or whipped cream give the mousse its frothy texture. Beat the whites or cream to soft peaks for the best results. If the aerator is overbeaten, it could begin to collapse or give the mousse a grainy appearance and texture.

Fold the aerator into the base carefully (see Fig 9-2c). It is a good idea to add about one-third of the total amount of aerator first to make it easier to fold in the remaining two thirds. This technique keeps the maximum volume in the finished mousse.

FIG 9-2A  *Prepare the mousse base by puréeing it and passing it through a drum sieve, repeating as necessary to acquire a perfectly smooth consistency.*

FIG 9-2B  *Working over ice to keep the ingredients cold, incorporate the melted binder solution into the puréed base.*

FIG 9-2C  *Continuing to work over ice, gently fold the aerator into the base mixture, ensuring that the aerator is not deflated during mixing.*

FIG 9-2D  *The finished mousse must be immediately piped or portioned as desired before the binder has a chance to set.*

## Basic formula for a mousse

Although each base ingredient may call for an adjustment in the amount of binder and aerator, this basic formula is a good checkpoint. It can and should be altered depending on the type of mousse being made and the intended use of the final product.

*Basic Formula for a Mousse*

| | |
|---|---|
| Base | 2 lb / 907 g |
| Binder* | 1 oz / 28 g gelatin (*if required by recipe) |
| Liquid** | 8 fl oz / 240 mL (**to bloom gelatin) |
| Aerator | 16 fl oz / 480 mL |

Once the mousse is prepared, it should be shaped in the desired way. Transfer immediately to a pastry bag and pipe out without delay into the desired "container" or apply it as a topping or filling for tea sandwiches and canapés (see Fig 9-2d).

A mousse can also be rolled in the same way as a roulade (pages 316–318), carefully secured, and chilled before slicing. Terrine molds may be used to shape a mousse into a loaf (page 309); be sure to oil the mold and line it with plastic wrap to make it easy to remove the mousse once it is properly chilled.

# Savory waters, jellies, and sorbets

One of the staples of the garde manger kitchen has been flavored waters that can either be used as broths for meats, poultry, fish, and vegetable entrees, frozen as sorbets and granitas, or thickened with a variety of agents to make jellies. When making sorbets, granités, or jellies from savory waters, it is important to check the seasonings because they often need to be increased when the waters are used for cold applications.

Jellies are a fantastic product that can add a luscious texture contrast to most dishes. They retain their shape on the plate but also melt in the mouth, depending on the amount of gelatin that is used. The typical range for gelatin in jellies is 1 percent to 3 percent of the total weight, but can be increased depending on the firmness required for the product. Do not add too much gelatin or the jelly could get rubbery. The most well known of the savory jellies is aspic, but the flavors of jellies have expanded beyond meats to include a myriad of flavors. Jellies can be made by adding gelatin to almost any base, such as wine, liquor, and fruit and vegetable juices. Choose your base carefully because acids and salt weaken gelatin, and some fruits, like pineapple and papaya, have enzymes that break down gelatin.

Savory sorbets and granités have been used for some time to tease the palate as an intermezzo or to add a contrasting frozen element to an entrée or appetizer. Savory sorbets with a high amount of natural sugars, like tomato sorbet, are smoother, while vegetable juices and purees with lower sugars will develop larger ice crystals and are more like a granité. Herbs or acids are often added to savory sorbets to brighten the flavor.

## *Alternative thickeners*

Gelatin is probably the most widely available and widely utilized thickener in professional kitchens. However, other thickeners have become more prevalent as the scope of the foods made by the garde manger has expanded. Some examples are:

### Agar

Agar (also agar agar) is a carbohydrate-based gelling agent manufactured from seaweed. It takes a lesser concentration of agar than gelatin to fully set a product, and agar has a crumbly texture in comparison with the texture of gelatin. To use it, soak it in cold water and bring it to a boil, mix it with the base, and then strain the mixture before cooling to set it. The defining difference between agar and gelatin is that agar melts at a much higher temperature, so it won't melt in the mouth but it can be served hot.

### Carageenan

This red algae-based thickener has been used by many countries from China to Ireland for many years. This is a popular stabilizer that is used by large manufacturers for ice cream and other products. Its texture can range from delicate to fairly flexible or elastic.

### Alginate

This is also a carbohydrate-based gelling agent that is made from brown seaweed. It only gels in the presence of calcium, which makes it an ideal candidate for thickening milk and cream and for spherical preparations that are gelled in calcium solutions (see below).

# Savory foams and encapsulations

One of the exciting developments in recent years in professional kitchens has been cold and hot savory foams and encapsulations. They are a continuation of the ideas that were used for developing savory water, jellies, and sorbets. Cold and hot foams use methods such as agitation and nitrous oxide canisters to create foam out of vegetables and fruit purees, fish, foie gras, and even cheese. These foams can be savory or sweet and give foods like asparagus and cauliflower a different texture that will contrast beautifully with almost any foods with which they are served. The bases for these preparations have to be carefully constructed, taking into account their acidity level and their seasoning. The bases may require more seasoning because the bubbles extend the flavor over a larger surface area.

Vegetable and fruit purées are especially appropriate for foams because the carbohydrates in their cell walls prevent the bubbles from disintegrating too quickly. You can shake the purées until air bubbles are incorporated and then scoop off the foam and add it to food. You can also force bubbles into the purée with the incorporation of nitrous oxide through a whipped-cream canister and pipe out the foam for its desired application. It is possible to extend the life of the foam by adding an emulsifier such as soy lecithin to the base. The bases for foams are often also thickened with a substance such as gelatin or alginate in order to stabilize them. There are also powders that you can add to bases with a high acid content so that you can still thicken them with gelatin before making a foam out of them.

These foams are typically used in high-end restaurants to test the boundaries of the dining experience and expand the palates of their customers. Chefs have taken the cold foam one step further by making the bases hot (about 80°F / 27°C) before placing them in the canisters and creating foams out of them. These foams can be bruléed and add a surprising touch to any dish. Following the development of foams were airs that are much lighter than foams and that require the addition of soy lecithin to make them retain their air. These airs are similar to the froth on a cappuccino while the cold and hot foams are much denser.

Encapsulations take the concept of the foam to the next level. The bases are thickened with alginate, possibly injected with nitrous oxide, and then piped or dripped into calcium solutions. Once the film forms around the soft mixture in the center, the spheres are removed and washed. The more concentrated the calcium solution, the thicker the pellicle or film becomes. This makes spherical items such as small orbs of fruit purée that look like caviar or a tea sphere that can surround a lemon center. The spheres can be served warm or cold, depending on how they are prepared.

# Caviar

**Caviar,** a delicacy made from the **roe** of a sturgeon, was described by Aristotle in the fourth century B.C.E. During the Roman Empire, trumpets heralded the arrival of caviar to the table, presented with garlands of flowers.

Today caviar remains among the most expensive and exclusive of all preserved foods, partly because of overfishing and pollution and partly because caviar is both labor-intensive to produce, and extremely perishable. Caviar will probably never again be given away with glasses of beer "to encourage libation" as it once was in this country.

## From roe to caviar

The **roe sac** must be harvested from the sturgeon while it is still alive (if the fish is dead, the membranes surrounding the individual eggs will deteriorate and rupture). The roe sacs are carefully rubbed over a sieve; the **eggs** (or **berries**) are caught in a container, washed in fresh water, drained, and then graded.

The master grader looks for consistency of grain, size, color, fragrance, flavor, gleam, firmness, and vulnerability of the roe skin. The bigger and lighter in color the eggs, the more rare and expensive the finished caviar.

Eggs of the highest quality are prepared by a method called *malossol* or "little salt," indicating that salt is added at a rate of less than 5 percent of the eggs' weight. Lesser-quality caviar will be processed with greater amounts of salt. Salt both preserves the caviar and gives it its texture and flavor. However, even though caviar is a salted food, it remains quite perishable, and must be carefully refrigerated throughout processing and storage.

## Types of caviar

In France, only the processed roe of sturgeon can be called caviar; France still strictly enforces this rule. In the United States, however, the law has been interpreted more leniently, and as long as the type of fish is identified on the label, various kinds of fish roe may be sold as caviar (see Fig 9-3).

## True caviar

The major sturgeon species used to produce true caviar today are **beluga, osetra,** and **sevruga. Sterlet,** which is nearly extinct, was the source of the fabled "**golden caviar** of the Czars." One of the reasons caviar is so expensive is directly related to the age and size a sturgeon must reach before developing the valuable roe.

The individual eggs, or berries, are graded for color, with 000 indicating the lightest-colored and better-quality caviar and 0 denoting the darkest. Color alone, however, does not indicate quality. The eggs are also sized. Beluga caviar has the largest eggs, graded large or coarse; osetra eggs are slightly smaller than beluga; sevruga is the smallest of all.

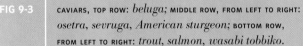

**FIG 9-3** CAVIARS, TOP ROW: *beluga;* MIDDLE ROW, FROM LEFT TO RIGHT: *osetra, sevruga, American sturgeon;* BOTTOM ROW, FROM LEFT TO RIGHT: *trout, salmon, wasabi tobbiko.*

- Beluga caviar ranges in color from light steel gray to dark gray. The beluga sturgeon takes as long as twenty years to achieve maturity, when it may weigh up to two thousand pounds. This long growth cycle means that beluga caviar is the most expensive and least readily available. It is typically sold in blue jars or tins.

- Osetra caviar is a brownish color with a golden tinge and can be distinguished from other caviar by the strong nutty flavor. This sturgeon reaches a size of ten feet and five hundred pounds and grows to maturity in twelve to fourteen years. It is usually sold in yellow jars or tins.

- Sevruga caviar berries are dark brown, the smallest of the true caviars, with a strong flavor. Sevruga can grow to seven feet and about 150 pounds in eight to ten years. Sevruga caviar is less expensive than beluga and osetra. It is normally sold in red jars or tins.

- **Pressed caviar** (known in Russian as *pajusnay*) is made from mature, broken, or overripe eggs. The salted eggs are put into a linen sack and pressed (using a grape press) until all of the fatty liquid is released. The result is a marmalade-like substance, doted on by the Russians, who spread it on black bread and enjoy it with chilled vodka. The flavor of pressed caviar is more intense than other caviars, and the eating experience is quite different. Pressed caviar is also used to prepare special dishes and cold sauces.

## Caviar from farm-raised sturgeon

The demand for caviar has given rise to a market for farm-raised sturgeon caviar. Sacramento River sturgeon is one of the few sturgeons that are currently being farmed to market size. The rate at which the fish matures is making the farm-raised caviar much more affordable because the caviar can be harvested after five years rather than twelve to fourteen years. Two advantages of farm-raised sturgeon caviar are its availability and the size and quality of the caviar eggs. The caviar from farm-raised sturgeon is typically graded at 00 and is similar in size to the osetra caviar. The flavor of the caviar is very approachable and mild and the texture is comparable to that of osetra caviar.

Although there still has been no progress in techniques to harvest the roe without killing or sterilizing the fish in the process, the market is there for the flesh of the fish and the fillets have a variety of uses. They can be cooked in any number of ways and are especially delicious when they are smoked. The flavor of the fish is slightly milder than that of wild cod but it is also very adaptable to a number of preparations.

### Other types of caviar

Other fish roes or non-sturgeon caviars can be processed in the same manner as sturgeon. The United States and other countries also produce caviar from the roe of salmon, paddlefish, whitefish, lumpfish, and cod. These caviars are available pasteurized or fresh. Each type is different in size, texture, and taste.

Salmon caviar is either golden or pink in color. The eggs are large, flavorful, and attractive.

Whitefish from the Great Lakes and Canada produces a roe with a natural golden color, crunchy texture, and a mild fresh taste.

The processed roe of cod and carp are quite small and are often salted, pressed, and sold as *tarama*. The gray mullet is also the source of the Mediterranean delicacy known as *poutargue* or *boutargue* in France and *botarga* in Italy. In Greece, **tarama** caviar is made from the roe of the gray mullet. To further confuse the issue, in the United States, tarama, which is imported, is made not from mullet but from the roe of tuna.

The roe of crab, flying fish (*tobikko*), cod (*tarako*), and sea urchin (*uni*) are also processed in a similar fashion and are staples of sushi bars in Japan. They are sometimes flavored with wasabi or other ingredients to produce special flavors and colors.

Lumpfish roe, though widely available and inexpensive, is not a good substitute for true caviar. Because lumpfish roe has an unappetizing off-gray color, it is typically dyed red, gold, or black using vegetable-based dyes or cuttlefish ink.

## Buying and storing caviar

Fresh sturgeon caviar should be plump and moist, with each individual egg shiny, smooth, separate, and intact. When you taste caviar, the eggs should release a savory flavor, faintly nutty with a hint of the sea. It should be surrounded by its own thick natural oils, but never appear to be swimming in oil.

Caviar should always be properly stored at 28°F / −2°C to 32°F / 0°C. True caviar can be refrigerated, unopened, for 4 weeks, and opened for 2 to 3 days. Pressed caviar will keep unopened at 40°F / 4°C for 10 days to 2 weeks; once opened it should be eaten within 5 days. One of the primary reasons caviar goes bad after opening is cross contamination. Be sure to use a clean spoon each time you dip some caviar from its container.

Pasteurized "caviars" and those processed with greater amounts of salt will keep in the refrigerator unopened for several weeks or even months, but once opened, they too should be consumed within 2 to 3 days.

Caviar can be purchased in jars weighing from 1 to 2½ oz / 28 to 71 g. Larger quantities are generally packed in tins, and are available in various weights from 4 oz to 2 lb 3 oz / 113 to 992 g).

# Serving caviar

The best caviar needs no special accompaniments. It is often served in special iced containers, with mother-of-pearl, bone, horn, or glass spoons to avoid any flavor change that might occur if metal spoons are used. Toast points, brioche, or blinis are often served as a base for a caviar canapé, perhaps with a few dollops of crème fraîche (see Fig 9-4).

This precious item is also used as a garnish for other hors d'oeuvre and appetizers. Lesser-quality caviar may be appropriate for garnishing some items. Remember that caviar should never be added to foods as they are cooking.

FIG 9-4  *Formal caviar service*

# Beef Carpaccio

YIELD: *10 servings*

1 lb 8 oz / 680 g beef sirloin or tenderloin, trimmed of all fat

1 fl oz / 30 mL pure olive oil

1 tbsp / 3 g chopped rosemary

1 tbsp / 3 g chopped sage

1 tbsp / 3 g chopped thyme

1 tbsp / 15 mL balsamic vinegar

2 tsp / 6 g kosher salt

1 tbsp / 14 g mignonette pepper

GARNISH

10 oz / 284 g mixed greens, washed and dried

5 fl oz / 150 mL Lemon Vinaigrette (page 30)

2 fl oz / 60 mL extra-virgin olive oil

3 oz / 85 g Parmesan, shaved into curls

2 tbsp / 6 g chopped flat-leaf parsley

2 oz / 57 g capers, rinsed, dried, and fried in hot oil (optional)

1. If desired, tie the beef to give it a uniform shape. Heat the oil over high heat and sear the beef on all sides. Remove it from the heat and cool.

2. Combine the herbs, vinegar, salt, and pepper and coat the beef evenly with this mixture. Wrap tightly in plastic wrap and freeze just until solid to be able to slice thinly.

3. Appetizer Assembly: For each serving, cut 6 or 7 very thin slices of beef by hand or with an electric slicer. Arrange on a chilled plate. Toss 1 oz / 28 g greens with 1 tbsp / 15 mL vinaigrette and arrange on the plate. Drizzle the meat with a few drops of extra-virgin olive oil and add a few Parmesan curls, parsley, and capers.

# Salsa Cruda di Tonno

YIELD: *10 servings*

1 lb 9 oz / 709 g tuna fillet, very cold

SALSA CRUDA

8 fl oz / 240 mL extra-virgin olive oil

5 oz / 142 g picholine olives, pitted and finely chopped

4 oz / 113 g celery hearts (stalks and leaves reserved separately), thinly sliced

2 oz / 57 g red onion, cut into brunoise

2 oz / 57 g jalapeño, cut into brunoise

1 oz / 28 g salted capers, soaked twice for 20 minutes each time

1 oz / 28 g flat-leaf parsley leaves, cut into chiffonade

1 tsp / 3 g garlic, minced to a paste

1 oz / 28 g lemon zest, blanched, cut into brunoise

Sea salt, as needed

Freshly ground black pepper, as needed

SALAD

4 oz / 113 g frisée, white leaves only

4 oz / 113 g arugula, picked and clean

4 oz / 113 g radish, cut into julienne

4 oz / 113 g fennel fronds

½ oz / 14 g celery leaves

3½ fl oz / 105 mL Lemon-Parsley Vinaigrette (page 30)

10 oz / 284 g Croutons, brunoise (page 613)

1. Slice the tuna very thin and flatten it between layers of plastic wrap, using a mallet, to the dimensions of your appetizer plate. Cover and keep chilled until ready to assemble the appetizer.

2. Combine olive oil, olives, celery, onion, jalapeño, capers, parsley, garlic and lemon zest. Taste and adjust seasoning with salt and pepper. Cover and refrigerate for at least 24 hours.

3. Toss together the frisée, arugula, radish, and fennel fronds. Reserve until ready to assemble the appetizer.

4. For each serving, lay 2 oz / 57 g sliced tuna on a chilled plate and mound about 1 oz / 28 g salsa cruda in the center of the tuna. Toss about 1 oz / 28 g mixed greens and radishes with 2 tsp / 10 mL lemon-parsley vinaigrette and mound on the plate. Scatter croutons over the plate and serve.

# Escabèche of Tuna

YIELD: *10 servings*

| | |
|---|---|
| 30 oz / 851 g tuna steak | ½ oz / 14 g small-dice red onion |
| Salt, as needed | ½ serrano chile, minced |
| Ground black pepper, as needed | 1 green onion, thinly sliced on the bias |
| 2 fl oz / 60 mL olive oil | ½ tsp / 1.50 g minced garlic |
| 3 tbsp / 45 mL lime juice | 1 tsp / 1 g chopped cilantro |
| 3 oz / 85 g small-dice tomato concassé (see page 607) | |

1. Cut the tuna into 1-in / 3-cm cubes or 3-oz / 85-g steaks. Season with salt and pepper, rub with 1 fl oz / 30 mL of the oil, and sear in a hot, well-seasoned pan. (It should be cooked "black and blue"—colored on the exterior but still extremely rare.)

2. Remove the tuna and chill thoroughly.

3. To make the marinade, mix the remaining olive oil with the lime juice, tomato, onion, chile, green onion, garlic, and cilantro.

4. Pour the marinade over the tuna and turn or gently toss to coat evenly. Cover and refrigerate at least 12 hours or overnight before serving.

*Presentation idea*  This dish can be served with a small salad as an appetizer, used to fill cucumber cups as an hors d'oeuvre, or served as part of an antipasti offering.

# Fennel and Chorizo Strudel

YIELD: *10 servings*

| | |
|---|---|
| 5 oz / 142 g butter, melted | 1 egg |
| 2 shallots, minced | 7 oz / 198 g dry bread crumbs |
| 4 oz / 113 g chorizo, sliced thin, skin off | 1 tsp / 3 g salt |
| 10 to 12 oz / 284 to 340 g fennel bulb, diced | ¼ tsp / 0.50 g ground black pepper |
| 1½ tbsp / 4.50 g tarragon leaves, minced | 6 phyllo dough sheets, thawed |
| ½ tbsp / 1.50 g minced chives | |

1. Heat about 1 oz / 28 g of the butter in a sauté pan over medium heat. Add the shallots and sauté them until they are translucent. Add the chorizo and allow some of the fat to render. Add the fennel and gently cook it until tender. It may be necessary to reduce the heat slightly so that the mixture does not burn. Allow the mixture to cool to room temperature.

2. Process the mixture to a coarse paste in a food processor.

3. Add the tarragon leaves, chives, egg, and enough bread crumbs (about 1¾ oz / 50 g) to lightly bind the mixture. Adjust seasoning as needed with salt and pepper.

4. Brush each sheet of phyllo dough with melted butter and sprinkle it evenly with about 1 to 1½ tsp / 2 to 3 g bread crumbs. Top this with another sheet of phyllo dough and repeat the process.

5. When three sheets are stacked, place half of the chorizo-fennel mixture down the left side of the dough and roll the sheets over the chorizo-fennel mixture.

6. Brush the top with butter.

7. Repeat with the remaining dough and filling.

8. Chill the strudel for about 30 minutes and score the top on the diagonal to divide each strudel into 10 sections.

9. Bake the strudels at 400°F / 204°C until they are browned, 10 to 15 minutes.

10. Slice and serve immediately.

# Seafood Strudel with Lobster-Infused Oil

YIELD: *10 servings*

### SEAFOOD STRUDEL

1 lb / 454 g shrimp, 16/20 count, peeled and deveined

1 egg

10 fl oz / 300 mL heavy cream

1 oz / 28 g butter

2 bunches green onions, sliced on a bias

6 oz / 170 g Chinese sausage, minced

6 oz / 170 g lobster meat, cooked and cut into medium dice

6 oz / 170 g sea scallops, dry packed, cut into quarters

6 oz / 170 g crayfish, tail meat, cooked

1 oz / 28 g Pommery mustard

1 oz / 28 g Dijon mustard

8 phyllo dough sheets, thawed

4 oz / 113 g butter, melted

4 oz / 113 g panko bread crumbs

### PLATE COMPONENTS

2½ cups / 600 mL micro greens

8 fl oz / 240 mL Lobster Oil (page 597)

10 cups / 2.4 L Marinated Tomato Salad (page 108)

1. Place cleaned shrimp in food processor and blend into a smooth, sticky paste, about 2 minutes.

2. Add the egg and pulse to incorporate, about 1 to 2 minutes.

3. Slowly add the heavy cream in a steady stream, stopping to scrape down the sides.

4. Heat the butter over medium low heat in a small sauté pan. Cook the green onions in the butter until soft, about 2 to 3 minutes. Fold the green onions into the sausage and lobster meat. Refrigerate the mixture until completely cooled.

5. Fold the scallops, crayfish tails, lobster mixture, and the mustards into the shrimp mixture. Adjust seasoning, cover, and refrigerate until needed.

6. Lay 1 sheet phyllo dough on a cutting board with the shorter side facing you. Brush it lightly with the melted butter. Sprinkle some of the breadcrumbs on top of each layer of phyllo after brushing with butter. Place another sheet of phyllo directly on top of the buttered sheet and brush it lightly with butter. Repeat two more times to make one stack with four layers. Repeat this procedure with the remaining phyllo layers in a separate stack.

7. Divide the seafood mixture between the phyllo stacks, placing the mixture along the edge closest to you. Roll the phyllo over the filling to encase it and fold the sides in toward the middle, if desired (see Fig 9-7a). Continue rolling the phyllo until you reach the end of the dough. Repeat with the remaining dough.

8. Brush both rolls with butter and score the dough halfway through the sheets on the bias at ¼- to ½-in / 6-mm to 1-cm intervals (see Fig 9-7b).

9. Bake on parchment paper at 400°F / 204°C until golden brown, 15 to 20 minutes.

10. Allow the strudel to cool for 5 minutes, then slice the strudel where the score marks are.

11. Appetizer Assembly: Place 2 oz / 57 g greens in the center of the plate and place 1 cup tomato salad slightly to the side of the greens. Lean two slices of strudel against the salad and drizzle 1 tbsp / 15 mL oil around the plate.

*After layering the phyllo with butter, roll the filling up inside it.*

*Once the strudel has been rolled up, score the dough halfway through the phyllo sheets on the bias.*

# Herbed Goat Cheese in Phyllo Dough

YIELD: *10 servings*

4½ oz / 128 g goat cheese

1½ tbsp / 4.50 g chopped basil

1½ tbsp / 3 g chopped chervil

1½ tbsp / 4.50 g chopped tarragon

1½ tbsp / 4.50 g chopped chives

6 fl oz / 180 mL heavy cream

½ tsp / 1.50 g salt

½ tsp / 1 g ground black pepper

9 phyllo dough sheets, thawed (14 by 18 in / 36 by 46 cm)

6 oz / 170 g clarified butter, melted

1. Combine the goat cheese, basil, chervil, tarragon, chives and heavy cream. Adjust seasoning with salt and pepper. Cover and refrigerate until needed.

2. Brush a sheet of phyllo dough with melted butter. Lay another sheet of dough on top of it and brush it with butter. Repeat this process once more so that there are three layers of phyllo dough stacked on top of each other. Cut the dough lengthwise into strips 2 in / 5 cm wide.

3. Place 1 oz / 14 g filling at the base of each strip and fold into triangles (See Spanakopita recipe, page 476). Brush the triangles with additional melted butter and place on a sheet pan.

4. Repeat with the remaining phyllo dough and filling until all of it is used.

5. Bake the triangles at 400°F / 204°C until they are browned, 10 to 12 minutes.

6. Serve immediately.

# Empanada Gallega de Cerdo (Pork Pepper Pie)

YIELD: *10 servings*

FILLING

1 lb / 454 g pork loin

2 fl oz / 60 mL olive oil

2 Spanish onions, cut into small dice

2 green peppers, cut into small dice

2 garlic cloves, minced

2 tsp / 12 g tomato paste

4 oz / 113 g Serrano ham

1 tsp / 2 g sweet Spanish paprika

Salt, as needed

DOUGH

2 lb / 907 g all-purpose flour

1 fl oz / 30 mL white wine

1 fl oz / 30 mL olive oil

1 oz / 28 g clarified butter

Pinch salt

1 oz / 28 g sugar

12 fl oz / 360 mL water

Egg yolk

1. To prepare the filling: Cut the pork loin in strips and sauté them in the olive oil until browned; remove.

2. Sweat the onion and peppers in the same oil and cook until they start to caramelize. Add the garlic and cook for 2 minutes.

3. Mix in the tomato paste, add the ham, and season with the paprika and salt.

4. To prepare the dough: Sift the flour and make a well in the center. Add the white wine, olive oil, clarified butter, salt, sugar, and the lukewarm water.

5. Mix all the ingredients and knead until making a flexible dough.

6. Wrap and refrigerate for about 30 minutes.

7. Divide the dough in two pieces.

8. Roll out each piece of dough to 12 in / 30 cm in diameter and ⅛ in / 3 mm thick, and lay in a pie plate 10 in / 25 cm in diameter. Add the filling and cover with the other piece of dough, sealing the edges with your fingers.

9. Brush the top with egg yolk and bake in a 350°F / 177°C oven until browned, about 30 minutes.

*Chef's note*   *The dough and filling can be prepared as tapas by making them into individual empanadas. Use the same shaping technique as described in the Pork Piccadillo Empanadas (page 464). It may be necessary to seal the edges of the empanada by crimping them with the tines of a fork. Brush the empanadas with egg wash and bake in a 350°F / 177°C oven until golden brown.*

# Grilled Vegetable Appetizer with Balsamic Vinaigrette

YIELD: *10 servings*

| | |
|---|---|
| 4 fl oz / 120 mL olive oil | 1 lb 8 oz / 680 g red peppers (about 3), cut into eighths |
| ½ bunch thyme, leaves only | 12 oz / 340 g yellow peppers (about 2), cut into eighths |
| Salt, as needed | |
| Ground black pepper, as needed | 1 lb / 454 g portobello mushrooms, stem removed |
| 1 lb / 454 g eggplant, sliced into rounds ½ in / 1 cm thick | |
| | 5 plum tomatoes, cored and halved |
| 1 lb / 454 g zucchini, sliced on the bias ½ in / 1 cm thick | 10 green onions, trimmed |
| | 15 fl oz / 450 mL Balsamic Vinaigrette (page 28) |
| 1 lb / 454 g yellow squash, sliced on the bias ½ in / 1 cm thick | |

1. Combine the olive oil with the thyme, salt, and pepper. Brush the vegetables with this mixture. Grill the eggplant until very soft and cooked through. Grill or broil the remaining vegetables to mark on all sides; they should be tender and very hot. Slice the portobellos as necessary to make 10 servings.

2. Appetizer Assembly: For each serving, arrange 2 to 3 slices each of eggplant, zucchini, and yellow squash on each plate. Add 2 strips of red pepper and 1 of the yellow pepper, a grilled tomato half, and a green onion. Drizzle with vinaigrette and serve warm or at room temperature.

*Chef's note* *Use a variety of tomatoes if available for extra color in this dish. If preferred, the tomatoes may be lightly broiled just until hot. They should still retain their shape.*

# Marinated Tomatoes with Mozzarella

YIELD: *10 servings*

2 lb 8 oz / 1.13 kg Marinated Tomatoes (page 108)

2 lb / 907 g Mozzarella Cheese (page 384)

1 red tomato

1 yellow tomato

3 tbsp / 9 g basil chiffonade

1. Prepare the tomato salad and reserve until ready to assemble appetizer.

2. Cut the mozzarella into slices ¼ in / 6 mm thick and reserve.

3. Cut the tomatoes into slices ¼ in / 6 mm thick, and halve or quarter the slices. Reserve.

4. Appetizer Assembly: For each serving, mound 4 oz / 113 g tomato salad on a chilled plate. Arrange 3 oz / 85 g sliced mozzarella and several slices of red and yellow tomatoes around the tomato salad. Scatter a little basil chiffonade over the appetizer. Serve chilled or at room temperature.

*Chef's note* *For buffet presentation, mound the tomato salad on a chilled platter, and arrange sliced tomatoes and mozzarella around the salad. You may wish to add a small bed of mixed green salad, lightly dressed with a Basic Red Wine or Balsamic Vinaigrette (page 28), for individual servings.*

# Prosciutto and Summer Melon Salad

YIELD: *10 servings*

1 lb 4 oz / 567 g prosciutto di Parma

1 lb 14 oz / 851 g sliced or diced mixed melons (cantaloupe, honeydew, casaba, etc.)

1 fl oz / 30 mL aged balsamic vinegar (optional)

Cracked black pepper, as needed

20 Grissini (page 602)

1. Slice prosciutto as thin as possible, laying it out on butcher's paper for easy handling. This should be done as close to service time as possible.

2. Appetizer Assembly: For each serving, arrange the melon on the plate, and add the prosciutto (drape it over melon slices or arrange it next to diced melon).

3. If desired, drizzle a few drops of excellent aged balsamic vinegar on the melon just before serving. Scatter a little pepper on the plate and serve with two grissini.

*Chef's note*  *This simple appetizer can be prepared as a plattered item for buffet service. Or individual cubes or spears of melon may be wrapped with a bit of prosciutto and skewered for service as an hors d'oeuvre.*
*If you have a prosciutto slicing stand in the dining room, this appetizer can be prepared with the prosciutto sliced to order in front of the guest, as long as the melon mise en place has been properly assembled by the kitchen staff.*

# Smoked Breast of Duck Niçoise Style

YIELD: *10 servings*

1 lb 4 oz / 567 g Smoked Duck Breast (page 218)

8 oz / 227 g haricots verts

1 lb 9 oz / 709 g Mediterranean Potato Salad (page 112)

5 tomatoes, blanched, peeled, seeded, and cut into strips

2 fl oz / 60 mL Basic Red Wine Vinaigrette (page 28)

2½ fl oz / 75 mL Tapenade (page 53)

1. Slice the duck breast thin and reserve until ready to assemble the appetizer.

2. Blanch the haricots verts and refresh.

3. Appetizer Assembly: For each serving, arrange 2½ oz / 71 g potato salad on the plate. Fan 2 oz / 57 g sliced duck on the plate. Toss ¾ oz / 21 g haricots verts and several strips of tomato in the vinaigrette and arrange on the plate. Garnish with 1½ tsp / 7.50 mL tapenade.

# Duck Confit with Frisée and Roasted Shallot Vinaigrette

YIELD: *10 servings*

10 pieces Duck Confit, legs only (page 230)

5 Idaho potatoes, peeled and sliced into 1½- by ⅛-in / 3¾-cm by 3-mm disks

32 fl oz / 960 mL duck fat, for frying

Salt, as needed

Coarse-ground black pepper, as needed

2 lb / 907 g frisée lettuce, washed and dried

15 fl oz / 450 mL Roasted Shallot Vinaigrette (page 32)

1. Scrape off excess fat from duck legs, reserving fat for frying potatoes. Roast duck legs in a 450°F / 230°C oven until warm and crisp, approximately 15 minutes. Keep warm.

2. Fry the potatoes in duck fat heated to 350°F / 175°C until browned and crisp, about 8 minutes. Drain on absorbent paper, season with salt and pepper, and keep warm.

3. Appetizer Assembly: For each serving, toss 3 oz / 85 g frisée in 1½ fl oz /45 mL vinaigrette and mound on a chilled plate. Top with a duck leg, 2 oz / 57 g fried potatoes, and a few roasted shallots from the dressing. Serve at once.

*Chef's note*  Serve this as an appetizer, composed salad, or light meal.

# Smoked Duck Tart

YIELD: *1 tart (10 in / 25 cm in diameter; 12 servings)*

| | |
|---|---|
| 8 oz / 227 g Pâté Dough (page 598) | 2 tbsp / 30 mL brandy |
| 1 Smoked Duck (page 218) | 4 fl oz / 120 mL heavy cream, whipped |
| ¼ oz / 7 g powdered or sheet gelatin | 36 Candied Pecan halves (page 512) |

1. Roll out the dough to a thickness of about ³⁄₁₆ in / 5 mm. Line a tart pan with a removable bottom with the dough, trimming the edges. Blind-bake at 350°F / 175°C until golden brown and fully baked, about 8 minutes. Reserve until the mousse is prepared.

2. Remove the bones and skin from the duck. Trim the breast portions and slice very thin for garnish; reserve. Dice the leg and thigh meat, removing all sinew and gristle.

3. Make a mousse as described on pages 339–402: Grind leg, thigh, and any additional useable trim through the medium plate (¼ in / 6 mm) of a meat grinder. Purée the ground duck to a fine paste. Bloom the gelatin in the brandy, warm to dissolve the gelatin, and fold into the duck mixture. Fold in the cream.

4. Fill the prepared tart shell with mousse and top with thin-sliced duck breast arranged symmetrically in a spiral pattern covering the surface of the tart. Garnish the rim of the tart with candied pecans (see Fig 9-9). Refrigerate at least 4 hours before slicing and serving.

5. Appetizer Assembly: Slice the tart into 12 servings and serve on chilled plates.

*Chef's note* There are a variety of tart pan shapes available and this recipe can be adapted to fit into most tart pans, such as the rectangle shown here.

FIG 9-9    *Garnish the sides of the assembled tart with candied pecan halves.*

# Tofu with Red Curry Paste, Peas, Green Onions, and Cilantro

YIELD: *10 servings*

Grapeseed oil, as needed

1 lb / 454 g tofu, drained, cut into 1-in / 3-cm cubes

1 fl oz / 30 mL lime juice

3½ oz / 99 g small dice onion

¾ oz / 21 g minced garlic

8 fl oz / 240 mL coconut milk

2 oz / 57 g red curry paste

¼ oz / 6 g ground turmeric

Salt, as needed

Ground black pepper, as needed

7 oz / 198 g peas, blanched

6 oz / 170 g grape tomatoes, cut in half

⅓ bunch cilantro, chopped

½ bunch green onions, minced

1 lb 2 oz / 510 g brown rice, cooked

10 oz / 284 g baby greens

6 oz / 170 g black sesame seeds

1. Heat a small amount of the oil in a medium nonstick sauté pan. Add tofu and cook until moisture is evaporated and the tofu is a light golden brown. Remove tofu from pan and sprinkle with lime juice.

2. Heat more oil in the pan, add the onions, and cook until translucent. Add the garlic and cook for an additional 2 minutes.

3. Add the coconut milk, curry paste, and turmeric. Season with salt and pepper. Reduce heat and simmer until the sauce has slightly thickened.

4. Add the peas, tomatoes, and tofu to the mixture and simmer just to combine. Adjust seasoning if necessary. Toss the mixture with the cilantro and green onions.

5. Place a molded 2½ fl oz / 75 mL cylinder of rice in the center of each of 10 small bowls. Divide the tofu mixture between the bowls in front of rice. Rest 1 oz / 28 g greens against rice. Sprinkle black sesame seeds on top of rice.

# Shrimp and Avocado Quesadillas

YIELD: *10 servings*

2 lb / 907 g Smoked Shrimp (21/25 count) (page 207)

8 oz / 227 g tomatillos, charred, husks removed (about 9)

2 avocados, pitted, peeled, and diced

1 onion, diced and sautéed until golden

¼ bunch cilantro, chopped

1 tbsp / 6 g toasted cumin seeds

Salt, as needed

Ground black pepper, as needed

20 flour tortillas (4 in / 10 cm in diameter)

8 oz / 227 g Monterey Jack cheese, shredded

1 fl oz / 30 mL olive oil

2 bunches watercress, washed and dried

10 fl oz / 300 mL Orange Vinaigrette (page 34)

1. Peel and devein the shrimp; reserve.

2. Chop the tomatillos fine. Combine with the diced avocado and onion and work with a wooden spoon or a fork to form a coarse paste. Stir in the cilantro and cumin and season with salt and pepper. Spread this mixture on a tortilla, top with ¾ oz / 21 g cheese, and close with a second tortilla. Continue until 10 quesadillas are filled. This may be done up to 1 hour in advance.

3. Appetizer Assembly: When ready to serve, lightly oil both sides of the quesadillas, and cook over low heat in a well-seasoned or nonstick pan until golden brown on both sides. Place each quesadilla on a plate; top with 4 shrimp. Dress ¾ oz / 21 g watercress with 2 tsp / 10 mL vinaigrette and arrange on the plate. Drizzle the perimeter of the plate with another 2 tsp / 10 mL vinaigrette.

# Crabmeat Rolls with Infused Pepper Oils, Fried Ginger, and Tamari-Glazed Mushrooms

YIELD: *10 servings*

1 lb 8 oz / 680 g lump crabmeat

4 oz / 113 g carrots, cut into fine julienne

1 oz / 28 g red pepper, cut into brunoise

1 oz / 28 g yellow pepper, cut into brunoise

1 oz / 28 g green pepper, cut into brunoise

½ oz / 14 g minced chives

1 tbsp / 6 g black sesame seeds

1½ fl oz / 45 mL rice wine vinegar

Salt, as needed

Ground white pepper, as needed

10 rice paper wrappers (8 in / 20 cm in diameter)

10 oz / 284 g Tamari-Glazed Mushrooms (see Chef's Note)

2 fl oz / 60 mL Red Pepper Oil (page 547)

2 fl oz / 60 mL Green Pepper Oil (page 547)

2 fl oz / 60 mL Yellow Pepper Oil (page 547)

2 pieces ginger (2 in / 5 cm long), peeled, sliced thin, and fried for garnish

1. Clean the crabmeat, removing any shell or cartilage. Combine with the carrots, peppers, chives, sesame seeds, and rice wine vinegar. Season with salt and pepper.

2. Moisten the rice paper wrappers and fill each one with about 3 oz / 85 g crabmeat mixture. Roll the wrapper to completely encase the filling; it should be about 1 in / 3 cm in diameter. Cover with a lightly dampened cloth and refrigerate until ready to serve.

3. Appetizer Assembly: For each serving, cut 1 crab roll on the bias and arrange on a chilled plate. Add 1 oz / 28 g tamari-glazed mushrooms, 1 tsp / 5 mL each of the pepper-flavored oils, and a few pieces of fried ginger.

*Chef's note* *To make tamari-glazed mushrooms, sauté 1 lb / 454 g of sliced shiitake mushrooms in 1 fl oz / 30 mL olive oil until very hot. Add 1 oz / 28 g tamari to deglaze the pan, and adjust seasoning as needed with sugar, dark sesame oil, salt, and pepper.*

# Shrimp Cakes with Rémoulade Sauce

YIELD: *10 servings*

½ oz / 14 g unsalted butter,

1 oz / 28 g peeled, finely diced celery stalk

1 oz / 28 g finely sliced green onions

1 oz / 28 g panko bread crumbs

2 dashes Tabasco

1 oz / 28 g eggs, well beaten

1 fl oz / 30 mL Basic Mayonnaise (page 36)

½ oz / 14 g chives, finely snipped

1 lb / 454 g shrimp, cleaned, deveined, ¼-in / 6-mm dice

¼ tsp / 75 g salt

Pinch ground black pepper

6 oz /170 g fresh white bread crumbs

Clarified butter, as needed

10 fl oz / 300 mL Remoulade Sauce (page 38)

1. Melt the butter in a sauté pan over medium heat. Sweat the celery in the butter until slightly translucent. Add the green onions and continue cooking over medium heat until soft. This will happen quickly.

2. Transfer the mixture into a bowl and allow to cool to room temperature.

3. Add the panko crumbs, Tabasco, eggs, mayonnaise, chives, and shrimp; season with salt and pepper.

4. Add approximately 1½ oz / 43 g bread crumbs to the shrimp mixture. If the mixture is too wet, add more bread crumbs until the mixture is only slightly moist.

5. Dividing the mixture into 2-oz / 57-g servings, shape into small cakes 2 in / 5 cm in diameter. Dip both sides of each shrimp cake in the remaining bread crumbs.

6. Heat the clarified butter in a sauté pan over medium high heat and cook the cakes until the shrimp is fully cooked and the cakes are golden brown, 4 to 5 minutes on each side.

7. Arrange the cakes on individual plates or on a platter and serve the Rémoulade Sauce on the side.

# Seared Sea Scallops with Artichokes and Peperonato

YIELD: *10 appetizers*

2 lb / 907 g sea scallops

2 lb / 907 g Peperonato (recipe follows)

Hearts of Artichoke Salad (page 104)

Salt, as needed

Ground black pepper, as needed

5 oz / 142 g olive oil

5 oz / 142 g Red or Yellow Pepper Oil (page 547)

1. Remove and discard the muscle tab from the scallops.

2. For each serving, heat 3 oz / 85 g peperonato and 2 pieces baby artichoke or 4 pieces artichoke bottoms. Adjust seasoning with salt and pepper. Keep warm.

3. Heat 1 oz / 28 g olive oil in a sauté pan over medium high heat. Add 3 oz / 85 g scallops and sear on both sides until golden brown but still translucent in the center, 1 to 2 minutes per side.

4. Mound the peperonato on a heated plate and arrange the artichoke and scallops on the plate. Drizzle with red or yellow pepper oil and serve immediately.

# Peperonato

YIELD: *10 servings*

2 fl oz / 57 g extra-virgin olive oil

5 oz / 142 g onions, thinly sliced

½ oz / 14 g garlic cloves, thinly sliced

½ tsp / 0.50 g dry oregano (Italian)

½ tsp / 1 g red pepper flakes

1 lb / 454 g red peppers, cut into julienne

1 lb / 454 g yellow peppers, cut into julienne

1 lb / 454 g green peppers, cut into julienne

½ oz / 14 g flat-leaf parsley, chopped

1 tbsp / 3 g thyme leaves

Salt, as needed

Ground black pepper, as needed

1. Heat the olive oil in a sauté pan over medium heat. Add the onions and sauté, stirring occasionally, until tender and translucent with no color, about 8 minutes. Add the garlic, oregano, and red pepper flakes; sauté until aromatic, about 1 minute. Add the peppers and continue to cook, stirring from time to time, until the peppers are soft and tender, 5 to 6 minutes more.

2. Add the parsley and thyme. Taste and adjust seasoning with salt and pepper. Simmer over low heat until flavorful, stirring as necessary to avoid browning the mixture, about 15 minutes.

3. Serve immediately or cool, cover, and refrigerate up to 5 days.

# Shrimp Mousse with Dill Gelée

YIELD: *10 servings*

32 fl oz / 960 mL Court Bouillon (page 594)

½ bunch dill, separated into leaves and stems

1 lb / 454 g shrimp (still in the shell)

¼ oz / 7 g powdered or sheet gelatin

1 fl oz / 30 mL cool water

4 egg whites, whipped to soft peaks

8 fl oz / 240 mL heavy cream, whipped to soft peaks

Salt, as needed

Ground white pepper, as needed

Lemon juice, as needed

Pinch cayenne

GARNISH

½ oz / 14 g caviar

2 seedless cucumber, sliced thin

2 fl oz / 60 mL Lemon Vinaigrette (page 30)

1. To cook the shrimp and prepare the aspic: Bring the court bouillon and dill stems to a simmer. Add the shrimp and poach just until cooked through, about 5 minutes. Remove the shrimp. Strain the court bouillon and reserve 7 fl oz / 210 mL; keep warm (90°F / 32°C). Bloom the gelatin in the water and add the mixture to 4 fl oz / 120 mL warm court bouillon. Stir until the gelatin is completely dissolved. Reserve.

2. To prepare the mousse: Shell and devein the shrimp. Split 5 shrimp in half lengthwise. Dice the remaining shrimp and purée with 3 fl oz / 90 mL court bouillon mixture to form a smooth paste. Transfer to a mixing bowl and fold in the egg whites and cream. Season with salt, pepper, lemon juice, and cayenne.

3. Pipe the mousse into 2-in / 5-cm PVC pipe molds (or other molds as desired). Top each mousse with a shrimp half and ½ oz / 14 g aspic. Refrigerate at least 3 hours before unmolding. Serve garnished with caviar, dill, and cucumbers dressed in vinaigrette.

# Lobster and Truffle Salad

YIELD: *10 servings*

| | |
|---|---|
| 5 whole lobsters (1 lb / 454 g each) | Salt, as needed |
| 8 oz / 227 g haricots verts | Ground white pepper, as needed |
| 5 bunches mâche | 4 fl oz / 120 mL extra-virgin olive oil |
| **VINAIGRETTE** | **GARNISH** |
| 9 fl oz / 270 mL orange juice | 1 tomato, peeled, seeded, and cut into diamond shapes |
| 2 fl oz / 60 mL Champagne vinegar | ½ oz / 14 g chervil pluches |
| 1½ oz / 43 g minced Fines Herbes (page 590) | 1 oz / 28 g truffles |

1. Cook the lobsters in simmering salted water until fully cooked, 9 to 10 minutes. Remove and refrigerate until cold. When cold, remove the tail and claw meat. Slice each tail in half to make 10 equal servings; cover and refrigerate until ready to assemble the appetizer.

2. Blanch the haricots verts in boiling salted water until bright green; refresh, drain, and refrigerate until ready to assemble the appetizer.

3. Rinse the mâche carefully and divide each bunch in half. Dry thoroughly and refrigerate until ready to assemble the appetizer.

4. To prepare the vinaigrette, combine the orange juice, vinegar, fines herbes, salt, and pepper. Gradually add the oil, whisking constantly. Adjust seasoning and reserve.

5. Appetizer Assembly: For each serving, slice 1 lobster tail half into medallions. Dress ¾ oz / 21 g haricots verts and ½ bunch mâche with the vinaigrette and arrange on chilled plates. Add the lobster tail medallions and a claw piece. Garnish with tomato diamonds and a chervil pluche. Shave a few pieces of truffle over the salad and serve immediately.

# Foie Gras in Brioche

YIELD: *10 servings*

2 lb 8 oz / 1.13 kg Brioche Dough (page 604)

½ recipe Foie Gras Roulade (page 342), well chilled

20 fl oz / 600 mL Port Wine Gelée (page 58)

20 red grapes, seeded and sliced very thin

1. Roll or press the brioche dough into a rectangle as long as a Pullman loaf pan and twice its width.

2. Unwrap the foie gras roulade and center it on the dough. Roll the dough around the roulade, pressing the dough to seal the seams. Set in a well-greased Pullman loaf pan, seam side down. Place the lid on the Pullman pan. Allow the brioche dough to rise for 30 minutes. Bake at 350°F / 177°C until the brioche is thoroughly baked, about 40 minutes. Let cool before unmolding and cutting into 10 equal slices.

3. Appetizer Assembly: Pool 2 fl oz / 60 mL of gelée on each plate, decorate with sliced grapes, and refrigerate until firm. At service, top with a slice of foie gras in brioche.

*Presentation idea* A slice of the foie gras in brioche served with a green salad and some Cranberry Relish (see page 529) makes for a great light lunch.

# Foie Gras Roulade with Roasted Beet Salad and Smoked Duck Breast

YIELD: *10 servings*

1 lb / 454 g Foie Gras Roulade or Terrine (page 342)

15 oz / 425 g Smoked Duck Breast (page 218)

20 oz / 567 g Roasted Beet Salad (page 102), made with gold and red beets

20 Parsnip Crisps (page 541)

1¼ oz / 35 g baby beet greens

5 fl oz / 150 mL Beet Vinaigrette (page 33)

1. Slice the foie gras roulade into 10 servings, each weighing about 1½ oz / 43 g. If done in advance, cover and refrigerate the slices until ready to assemble the appetizer.

2. Slice the duck breasts thin; you will serve 4 slices per appetizer.

3. Appetizer Assembly: For each serving, place 1 slice of foie gras on the plate and serve with 2 oz / 57 g beet salad, 4 slices of duck breast, 2 parsnip chips, and ⅛ oz / 3 g baby beet greens; drizzle the plate with 1 tbsp / 15 mL of vinaigrette.

*Chef's note*   This photo shows both red and golden beet salads made using the same recipe. Fresh figs can also be used to garnish this dish.

# Tomato Dome Stuffed with Tofu with Mozzarella and Basil Oil

YIELD: *10 servings*

2 lb 13 oz / 1.28 kg yellow vine-ripe tomatoes (about 10 medium)

14 oz / 397 g fresh buffalo mozzarella, cut into small dice

14 oz / 397 g medium-firm tofu, cut into small dice

6 oz / 170 g basil leaves

1½ oz / 43 g shiso leaves

¾ oz / 21 g finely chopped shallots

12 fl oz / 360 mL freshly squeezed grapefruit juice

12 fl oz / 360 mL extra-virgin olive oil

12 fl oz / 360 mL grapeseed oil

12 oz / 340 g baby amaranth salad

Salt, as needed

Pepper, as needed

1. Remove the core from the tomatoes. Blanch tomatoes in boiling water until the skin just begins to peel off, 20 to 30 seconds. Shock in an ice bath and remove the skin from the tomatoes, being careful not to damage the flesh. Slice off enough of the stem end to make interior accessible in order to remove the seeds and pulp from the tomato. Hollow out the tomato to form a tomato cup.

2. In a small bowl combine mozzarella and tofu. Tear 18 basil leaves into 6 to 8 pieces each. Tear 9 shiso leaves into 10 to 12 pieces each. Combine the leaves, shallots, grapefruit juice, and 3 fl oz / 60 mL olive oil with the mozzarella mixture. Adjust seasoning with salt and pepper.

3. Stuff the tomatoes with just enough mozzarella mixture to be flush with the tomato where it is sliced. Do not overstuff. The stuffed tomatoes can be assembled ahead, covered, and refrigerated, but they are best assembled just before service.

4. Blanch the remaining basil in 32 fl oz / 960 mL boiling water until the basil starts changing color and the green deepens in color, 1 to 2 minutes. Shock in an ice bath and squeeze out excess water. Puree with the grapeseed oil and 6 fl oz / 120 mL olive oil. Season with salt and pepper to produce basil oil. Strain through a chinois. Place in a squeeze bottle and hold until service.

5. Appetizer Assembly: In a deep, medium-sized chilled bowl, place tomato with the open end down. Drizzle 1 tbsp / 15 mL basil oil around the tomato. Drizzle some of the remaining olive oil on top of the tomato. Season with cracked black pepper and garnish with leftover shiso leaves. Toss the amaranth leaves with a little oil and top the dome with some of the amaranth leaves for garnish. Serve immediately.

# Cucumber Granité

YIELD: *32 fl oz / 960 mL*

1 lb 8 oz / 680 g cucumbers (about 3), peeled, seeded, and roughly chopped

1½ fl oz / 45 mL white wine vinegar

½ oz / 14 g granulated sugar

¾ oz / 21 g egg white, lightly beaten

1. Purée the cucumber in a blender until very smooth.

2. Combine the cucumber purée with the vinegar, sugar, and egg white and stir until combined.

3. Pour the mixture into a hotel pan, cover with plastic wrap, and freeze for at least 3 hours, stirring every 25 minutes. To serve, scrape a kitchen spoon over the surface and shape into quenelles or balls. Serve immediately.

# Celery Granité

YIELD: *32 fl oz / 960 mL*

1 bunch celery (about 2 lb / 907 g)

1½ fl oz / 45 mL white wine vinegar

½ oz / 14 g granulated sugar

¾ oz / 21 g pasteurized egg white, lightly beaten

1. Trim the celery, cut into dice, and juice or purée in a blender until liquid. Strain through a fine sieve to remove fibers.

2. Combine the celery with the vinegar, sugar, and egg white and stir until combined.

3. Pour the mixture into a hotel pan, cover with plastic wrap, and freeze for at least 3 hours, stirring every 25 minutes. To serve, scrape a kitchen spoon over the surface and shape into quenelles or balls. Serve immediately.

# Lime Granité

YIELD: *32 fl oz / 960 mL*

32 fl oz / 960 mL water

1 lb / 454 g sugar

1 oz / 28 g lime zest, minced fine

4 fl oz / 120 mL lime juice

Combine all ingredients in a hotel pan. Cover with plastic wrap and freeze until firm, about 3 hours, stirring every 25 minutes. To serve, scrape a kitchen spoon over the surface and shape into quenelles or balls. Serve immediately.

# Tomato-Basil Sorbet

YIELD: *32 fl oz / 960 mL*

2 oz / 57 g sugar

2 fl oz / 60 mL water

6 ripe tomatoes

4 fl oz / 120 mL lemon juice

¾ tsp / 2.25 g salt

¾ oz / 21 g tomato paste

2 oz / 57 g chopped basil

1. Bring the sugar and water to a boil in a small saucepan. Remove from the heat and cool to room temperature.

2. Blanch the tomatoes in boiling water until the skin just begin to peel off, about 15 to 20 seconds, and shock them in an ice bath. Peel and seed the tomatoes.

3. Puree the tomatoes until smooth in a food processor. Combine the puree with the simple syrup, lemon juice, salt, tomato paste, and basil.

4. Process the mixture in an ice-cream maker according the manufacturer's instructions, and freeze until needed.

*Tomato-Basil Sorbet*

# Profiteroles

YIELD: *60 pieces*

| | |
|---|---|
| 12 fl oz / 360 mL water | 6¾ oz / 191 g all-purpose flour, sifted |
| 6 oz / 170 g butter | 6 eggs |
| Salt, as needed | |

1. Combine the water, butter, and salt and bring to a boil.

2. Add the sifted flour all at once and stir in well; cook over medium heat just until mass comes away from the pot.

3. Transfer to a mixer and mix on medium speed for about 1 minute. Add the eggs one at a time, mixing well after each addition, to achieve a stiff but pliable texture.

4. Transfer the dough to a pastry bag with a No. 5 plain tip and pipe out in the desired shape onto parchment-lined sheet pans (see Fig 9-16a). For profiteroles, pipe balls 1 in / 2.50 cm in diameter; other shapes such as éclairs may also be prepared.

5. Bake at 400°F / 204°C until golden brown, then reduce oven temperature to 325°F / 163°C to cook through, 12 to 15 minutes (see Fig 9-16b).

6. When ready to fill, slice off the tops with a sharp knife. Add filling of choice, and replace the top.

**FIG 9-16A** *Prepared pâte à choux will be stiff yet pliable, with a pale yellow color.*

**FIG 9-16B** *Once baked, profiteroles take on an even golden brown coloration and develop a hollow center.*

# Gougères (Gruyère Cheese Puffs)

YIELD: *60 pieces*

| | |
|---|---|
| 12 fl oz / 360 mL water | 1½ oz / 43 g egg whites |
| 6 oz / 170 g butter | 6 eggs |
| Salt, as needed | 4½ oz / 128 g grated Gruyère |
| 6¾ oz / 191 g all-purpose flour, sifted | 1½ tbsp / 8 g grated Parmesan |

1. Combine the water, butter, and salt and bring to a boil.

2. Add the sifted flour all at once and stir in well; cook over medium heat. stirring constantly, just until mass comes away from the sides of the pot.

3. Transfer to a mixer and mix on medium speed for about 1 minute. Add the egg white and eggs one at a time, mixing well after each addition, to achieve a stiff but pliable texture.

4. Add the grated Gruyère and Parmesan and continue mixing for 1 minute.

5. Transfer the dough to a pastry bag with a No. 5 plain tip and pipe out in the desired shape onto parchment-lined sheet pans.

6. Bake at 400°F / 204°C until golden brown, then turn down to 325°F / 163°C to cook through, 12 to 15 minutes. Serve warm or store in airtight container, as for crackers.

*Chef's note*  *These puffs make a great snack item or casual reception food with cocktails. They are best when served warm from the oven, but they can be cooled, held in airtight containers, and served at room temperature if necessary.*

# Palmiers with Prosciutto

YIELD: *40 to 45 pieces*

8 oz / 227 g Blitz Puff Pastry sheets
(page 601)

2 oz / 57 g tomato paste

12 prosciutto slices

¾ oz / 21 g finely grated Parmesan

1. Lay out the puff pastry sheets and brush each with a small amount of tomato paste.

2. Lay thin slices of prosciutto over the puff pastry and dust with cheese. Roll long sides in toward center. Cut into slices ¼ in / 6 mm thick and arrange on parchment-lined sheet pans. Cover with a second sheet of parchment and bake at 400°F / 205°C until golden brown, about 10 minutes.

*Chef's notes* *Parchment paper on top and bottom will help the pieces stay flat. The paper can be removed for the last few minutes to allow for browning.*
*These can be made up in batches and frozen, then baked as needed and served warm.*

# Cheese Sticks (Paillettes)

YIELD: *30 pieces*

1 egg yolk

1 tbsp / 15 mL whole milk

1 Blitz Puff Pastry sheet (page 601)

1½ oz / 43 g grated Parmesan

Sweet Spanish paprika, as needed

1. Whisk together the egg yolk and milk to make an egg wash. Brush the puff pastry sheet with the egg wash.

2. Sprinkle the cheese and paprika evenly over the puff pastry sheets.

3. Cut pastry into strips ¼ in / 6 mm wide, the length of the sheet.

4. Bake on parchment-lined sheet pans at 400°F / 205°C until golden brown, about 10 minutes.

*Chef's note* *Cajun Spice Blend (page 589), cayenne, poppy seeds, or sesame seeds may be used as alternate garnishes.*

*Presentation idea* *Cheese sticks are a quick and simple way to add a signature look and flavor to a reception table, dining table, or bar. The sticks may be twisted, curled, or shaped as desired before baking. Fanciful shapes presented in tall glasses or jars serve as eye-catching edible decorations.*

CLOCKWISE FROM UPPER LEFT: *Cheese Sticks, Palmiers with Prosciutto, Gougères (page 443)*

# Southwest Chicken Salad in Profiteroles

YIELD: *30 pieces*

2 chicken legs, cooked and cut into small dice

1 tomato cut into concassé

1 lime, segments only, cut into small dice

½ oz / 14 g small-dice roasted pepper

1 tsp / 2 g minced jalapeño

1 oz / 28 g minced shallots

1 garlic clove, minced

2 tbsp / 6 g chopped cilantro

2 tsp / 2 g chopped marjoram

2 tsp / 2 g minced chives

Salt, as needed

Ground black pepper, as needed

30 Profiteroles (page 442)

1. Combine the chicken, tomato, lime, peppers, shallots, garlic, and herbs. Season with salt and pepper. Cover and refrigerate 2 hours to marinate.

2. Split the puffs and fill with the chicken salad.

# Yorkshire Pudding with Duck Ragoût

YIELD: *30 pieces*

DUCK RAGOÛT

1 lb 8 oz / 680 g duck legs

1¾ oz / 50 g minced shallots

1 oz / 28 g minced garlic

1 oz / 28 g tomato paste

½ oz / 14 g all-purpose flour

24 fl oz / 720 mL chicken stock

SACHET D' ÉPICES

1 oz / 28 g dried cèpes

1 rosemary sprig

2 thyme sprig

1 sage sprig

1 bay leaf

3 tbsp / 9 g finely chopped flat-leaf parsley leaves

1 tbsp / 9 g minced garlic

6 juniper berries, crushed

2 black peppercorns, crushed

1 fl oz / 30 mL rendered duck fat

1 fl oz / 30 mL olive oil

4 oz / 113 g shiitakes, cut into slices ⅛ in / 3 mm thick

1¾ oz / 50 g minced shallots

5⅓ fl oz / 160 mL red wine

4 fl oz / 120 mL Tomato Concassé (see page 607)

1 tbsp / 3 g coarsely chopped Italian parsley

½ tsp / ½ g coarsely chopped tarragon

1 oz / 28 g butter

Salt, as needed

Ground black pepper, as needed

YORKSHIRE PUDDING

1¼ oz / 35 g all-purpose flour

1 tsp / 3 g salt

10 fl oz / 300 mL whole milk

¾ fl oz / 22.5 mL water

3 eggs, beaten

2 fl oz / 60 mL rendered duck fat

2 oz / 57 g grated Parmesan

1. For the duck ragoût: Trim excess fat from the duck legs.

2. Lightly sauté the shallots and garlic in the olive oil in a small sauté pan over low heat until tender, about 3 to 4 minutes. Add the tomato paste and cook until it reaches a light mahogany brown, about 1 minute. Add the flour and cook until it has a pale color and slightly toasted aroma, about 2 to 3 minutes. Add the chicken stock and the sachet and simmer over medium low heat to make brown sauce, about 40 to 45 minutes.

3. Sear the duck legs in the olive oil in a sauté pan over medium heat. Add the brown sauce and bring the mixture to a simmer. Skim the fat off the top of the sauce and braise legs in a 325°F / 163°C oven until meat can be pulled from the bones, about 1½ hours.

4. Strain the sauce through a chinoise and reserve it separately. Coarsely shred the duck meat while still warm.

5. Sauté the sliced shiitakes in 1 tbsp / 15 mL of the reserved duck fat in a small sauté pan over medium heat until tender, and reserve.

6. At service, sweat shallots in the remaining rendered duck fat in a saucepan over medium heat until tender, about 3 to 4 minutes. Add red wine and reduce to a sec, about 4 to 5 minutes. Add the reserved brown sauce and finish with concassé and fresh herbs. Carefully fold in the duck and mushrooms and monte au beurre. Season with salt and pepper.

7. Hold warm in a bain-marie until service.

8. For the Yorkshire pudding: Sift together the flour and salt; make a well in the center, add the milk and water, and mix just until smooth. Add eggs and mix until smooth.

9. Brush 30 mini muffin tins with duck fat and preheat in a 450°F / 232°C oven. Fill each cup a little more than half full with batter (about 1 tbsp / 15 mL batter) and bake until browned and puffed, 12 to 18 minutes.

10. Garnish with ½ oz / 14 g ragoût and a pinch of Parmesan.

# Duck Confit and White Bean Hash Cake with Cippolini Onion Marmalade

YIELD: *30 pieces*

DUCK CONFIT

1 lb 8 oz / 680 g duck legs

2½ oz / 71 g salt

1 oz / 28 g garlic, coarsely chopped

4 crushed black peppercorns

½ oz / 15 mL coarsely chopped thyme

48 fl oz / 1.44 L rendered duck fat, melted and cooled slightly

DUCK CONFIT AND WHITE BEAN HASH CAKE

2 oz / 57 g bacon, finely chopped

1 fl oz / 30 mL rendered duck fat

2 oz / 57 g minced onions

½ oz / 14 g minced garlic

8 fl oz / 240 mL risotto rice

2⅔ fl oz / 80 mL white wine

32 fl oz / 960 mL chicken stock

2 tbsp / 7 g chopped flat-leaf parsley

1 tsp / 3 g chopped thyme

2 tbsp / 6 g minced chives

2 tsp / 2 g chopped rosemary

1 cup / 720 mL white beans, cooked, roughly chopped

4 oz / 113 g duck confit, shredded finely

2 eggs, lightly beaten

1 cup / 240 mL fresh bread crumbs

Salt, as needed

Ground black pepper, as needed

6 oz / 170 g all-purpose flour

4 eggs, whisked together

4 oz / 113 g panko bread crumbs

12 fl oz / 360 mL vegetable oil, for pan-frying

Cippolini Onion Marmalade (recipe follows)

1. Trim duck legs and arrange in a single layer in a hotel pan. Combine the seasonings and sprinkle over the duck legs Top with a press plate and a 2-lb / 907-g weight. Cover and refrigerate overnight to cure.

2. Rinse the seasonings from the legs; pat dry. Cover the legs in the duck fat. Simmer the legs gently in a small pot until the duck meat is completely tender, about 2 hours.

3. Remove the meat. Shred most of the confit small for the hash cake and reserve 30 large pieces for the garnish.

4. Render the bacon in the duck fat over low heat in a small pan until the bacon just starts to brown. Add the onions and garlic and continue to sweat over low heat until tender, approximately 6 to 8 minutes. Add the rice and sauté for one minute; deglaze with the wine and reduce by half. Add the stock in four additions and simmer gently until the rice is tender and very dry, 20 to 25 minutes.

5. Cool the rice to room temperature and add the herbs, beans, confit, eggs, fresh bread crumbs, and seasonings until just combined.

6. Form into balls weighing 1¼ oz / 35 g; flatten balls into discs 1 to 1¼ in / 2.5 to 3 cm in diameter. Cover and refrigerate until thoroughly cold.

7. Coat the cakes using the flour, eggs, and panko in the standard breading procedure (see page 612). Heat oil to 350°F / 177°C and pan fry cakes until golden brown, 2 to 3 minutes per side.

8. Rewarm the reserved duck confit pieces and place on top of the cakes along with ¼ oz / 7 g onion marmalade.

# Cippolini Onion Marmalade

YIELD: *16 fl oz / 480 mL*

1 lb 8 oz / 680 g cippolini onions, peeled

3 oz / 85 g butter

4 tsp / 20 g honey

2 fl oz / 30 mL sherry vinegar

4 tsp / 12 g chopped thyme

Salt, as needed

Ground black pepper, as needed

Combine the onions and butter in a sauté pan and cook over low heat until golden brown; add the honey and vinegar. Cover with a lid and bake in a 325°F / 163° C oven until tender, 15 to 20 minutes. Season with thyme, salt, and pepper and cut into rough medium dice.

# Duck Rillettes in Profiteroles

YIELD: *30 pieces*

4 oz / 113 g Duck Rillettes (page 232)

1 fl oz / 30 mL duck fat, melted

1 oz / 28 g Dijon mustard

30 Profiteroles (page 442), split

1 oz / 28 g green peppercorns, crushed
(1 per profiterole)

Salt, as needed

Ground black pepper, as needed

1. In a mixing bowl on low speed, work rillettes until softened.

2. Fold the duck fat and mustard gently but thoroughly into the rillettes. Adjust seasoning with salt and pepper, if needed.

3. Pipe the rillette mixture into the profiteroles. Garnish each with a green peppercorn. Replace the top.

# Smoked Salmon Mousse Barquettes

YIELD: *30 pieces*

5 oz / 142 g Smoked Salmon (pages 208–209), diced

6 fl oz / 180 mL Fish Velouté (page 595)

1 fl oz / 30 mL Aspic Gelée (page 58), softened

4 fl oz / 120 mL heavy cream

¼ tsp / 1.25 mL Tabasco sauce

2 tsp / 6 g kosher salt

Ground black pepper, as needed

30 barquettes made from Pâte Dough (pages 395, 598), prebaked

2 oz / 57 g salmon roe

30 dill sprigs

1. Make the mousse by puréeing the smoked salmon and velouté in a food processor until very smooth. Add the warm aspic gelée while the processor is running. Transfer to a bowl once fully incorporated.

2. Whip the cream to soft peaks and fold gently but thoroughly into the salmon mixture. Season with Tabasco, salt, and pepper.

3. Barquette Assembly: Pipe approximately ½ oz / 14 g salmon mousse into each barquette, garnish with a little salmon roe and a dill sprig, and chill until firm. The barquettes are now ready to serve, or can be covered and refrigerated up to 1 hour.


# Creamed Wild Mushroom Tartlets

YIELD: *30 pieces*

1 lb / 454 g assorted wild mushrooms (shiitake, porcini, oyster, etc.), cut into small dice

2 shallots, minced

2 oz / 57 g butter

1 tbsp / 15 mL brandy

1 tbsp / 15 mL sherry

2 fl oz / 60 mL heavy cream

GARNISH

2 oz / 57 g finely grated dry Jack cheese

1 oz / 28 g chopped flat-leaf parsley

2 tsp / 4 g ground black pepper

30 tartlet shells made from Pâte Dough (page 395, 598), baked blind

1. Sauté the mushrooms and shallots in the butter; add the brandy, sherry, and cream to finish the duxelles.

2. Combine the garnish ingredients and reserve.

3. Tartlet Assembly: Fill each tartlet shell with a tablespoon of duxelles and top with a sprinkle of the garnish mixture. Serve warm.

# Steak Tartare Canapé

YIELD: *30 pieces*

1 lb / 454 g beef tenderloin

1 oz / 28 g pasteurized egg yolks

1 oz / 28 g minced onions

¾ oz / 21 g chopped capers

Salt, as needed

Ground black pepper, as needed

Worcestershire sauce, as needed

30 rye bread canapé bases, toasted

5 oz / 142 g Anchovy Butter (page 596), softened

2 oz / 57 g hard-cooked egg, chopped, or as needed

2 oz / 57 g minced onion, or as needed

2 oz / 57 g minced parsley, or as needed

1. Chop the tenderloin fine. At service time, combine the beef, egg yolks, onions, and capers to prepare the tartare. Add salt, pepper, and Worcestershire as needed.

2. Canapé Assembly: Spread the canapé base with 1 tsp / 5 mL anchovy butter and ½ oz / 14 g tartare mixture, and top with chopped eggs, onions, and parsley.

# Salt Cod Canapé with Piperada

YIELD: *30 pieces*

1 lb 4 oz / 567 g salt cod fillets (about 3 fillets)

6½ fl oz / 195 mL olive oil

8 oz / 227 g onions, cut into julienne

1 tsp / 4 g sugar

Salt, as needed

Ground black pepper, as needed

2 oz / 57 g red pepper, cut into small dice

2 oz / 57 g green pepper, cut into small dice

30 baguettes, cut into slices ¼ in / 6 mm thick

1. Soak the salt cod in cold water for 24 hours, changing the water several times. Remove from the water and pat dry. Remove the blood line. Shred the fish and set aside.

2. Heat 1½ fl oz / 45 mL olive oil in a large sauté pan over medium heat. Add the onions and sweat, stirring often until softened but not browned, approximately 15 minutes.

3. Increase the heat to medium-high and add the cod and sugar. Sauté until heated through and well combined, approximately 3 to 4 minutes. Season as needed with salt and pepper.

4. To make the piperada, heat 1 tbsp / 15 mL olive oil in a small sauté pan over medium-high heat. Add the peppers and cook, stirring often, until softened, about 5 minutes. Remove from heat and set aside.

5. Brush the slices of bread with remaining olive oil and toast lightly in a 350°F / 177°C oven.

6. Top each bread slice with ½ oz / 14 g cod mixture. Garnish with the piperada and serve warm.

# Sun-Dried Tomato and Goat Cheese Tartlets

YIELD: *30 pieces*

| | |
|---|---|
| 1 lb / 454 g Blitz Puff Pastry (see page 601) | 3 eggs |
| 1 tbsp / 9 g minced garlic cloves | 1 tbsp / 7 g all-purpose flour |
| 1 tsp / 2 g ground white pepper | 4 oz / 113 g fresh goat cheese, crumbled |
| 3 tbsp / 9 g chopped basil | 1 oz / 28 g green onions, minced |
| 6 fl oz / 180 mL whole milk | 3½ oz / 99 g sun-dried tomatoes, minced |
| 2 fl oz / 60 mL dry sherry | |

1. Roll the puff pastry dough to ⅛ in / 3 mm thick.

2. Cut 30 rounds from the puff pastry using a 2-in / 5-cm cm round cutter and press gently into tart molds 1¾ in / 4.50 cm in diameter. Dock the dough with a fork.

3. Cover the dough in the molds with a small piece of foil and fill with uncooked dried beans or pastry weights. Bake in a 425°F / 220°C oven for 5 minutes. Allow to cool completely and remove the foil and beans or weights.

4. Combine the garlic, pepper, basil, milk, and sherry in a food processor. Add the eggs and flour and process until just blended.

5. Toss together the goat cheese, green onion, and sun-dried tomatoes.

6. Place 2½ tsp / 12.50 mL of the goat cheese mixture into each tartlet.

7. Fill each tartlet two-thirds full with the egg mixture.

8. Bake in a 350°F / 177°C oven until set, about 15 minutes.

*Prosciutto and Melon Canapé*

# Prosciutto and Melon Canapé

YIELD: *30 pieces*

8 very thin slices prosciutto (about 5 oz / 142 g)

30 white bread canapé bases, toasted

5 oz / 142 g Mascarpone Cheese Spread (see Chef's Note)

90 petit-pois size honeydew melon balls

90 petit-pois size canteloupe melon balls

30 mint leaves, cut into fine chiffonade

1. Cut prosciutto to fit canapé bases.

2. Canapé Assembly: Spread the canapé bases with some of the mascarpone spread and top with a piece of prosciutto. Pipe a small mound of mascarpone spread in the center of each canapé, and top with melon balls and mint.

*Chef's note*  To prepare Mascarpone Cheese Spread, add Tabasco, Dijon mustard, salt, and pepper as needed to 5 oz / 142 g mascarpone (page 377). Mix well.

# Barbecued Shrimp and Bacon

YIELD: *30 pieces*

30 small bamboo skewers

30 shrimp (16/20 count), peeled and deveined

15 strips Basic Bacon (page 222), partially cooked and cut in half

8 fl oz / 240 mL Barbecue Sauce (page 156)

1. Preheat the broiler. Soak bamboo skewers in water for 30 minutes.

2. Wrap each shrimp with a bacon strip. Thread each shrimp on a bamboo skewer.

3. Place the skewers on a wire rack set into a foil-lined metal tray.

4. Broil the shrimp 1 to 2 minutes on the first side. Turn and broil on the second side until the bacon is crispy and the shrimp are just cooked through, 1 to 2 minutes. Remove from the broiler and baste with the barbecue sauce.

*Chef's note*  Soak the skewers in water before using to prevent them from catching fire when the shrimp are cooking.

*Variation*  Serrano-Wrapped Shrimp: Replace the bacon with thin slices of Serrano ham. Baste lightly with oil before grilling or broiling as directed above.

# Blue Cheese Mousse

YIELD: *2 lb / 907 g*

| | |
|---|---|
| 1 lb 4 oz / 567 g blue cheese | ½ tsp / 1 g ground black pepper |
| 12 oz / 340 g cream cheese | 4 fl oz / 120 mL heavy cream, whipped to soft peaks |
| 1 tbsp / 10 g kosher salt | |

1. Purée the blue and cream cheeses until very smooth. Season with salt and pepper.

2. Fold the whipped cream into the mousse until well blended. There should be no lumps.

3. The mousse is now ready to use to prepare canapés or as a filling or dip.

*Variation*   Goat Cheese Mousse: Substitute fresh goat cheese for the blue cheese.

*Presentation idea*   The mousse can be piped into tartlets and garnished with paper-thin slices of baby golden and candy-striped beets, about ½ in / 1 cm in diameter.

# Smoked Trout Mousse

YIELD: *24 fl oz / 720 mL*

| | |
|---|---|
| 1 lb / 454 g boneless Hot Smoked Trout fillets (page 215) | ¼ tsp / 1.25 mL Tabasco sauce |
| 8 fl oz / 240 mL Aspic Gelée (page 58) made from Fish Stock, warmed | 1 tbsp / 15 mL dry white wine |
| | ½ oz / 14 g horseradish (prepared) |
| 4 fl oz / 120 mL Basic Mayonnaise (page 36) | 1 tsp / 5 mL lemon juice |
| 1 tsp / 5 mL Worcestershire sauce | 6 fl oz / 180 mL heavy cream, whipped to soft peaks |

1. Place trout, aspic, mayonnaise, Worcestershire sauce, Tabasco, wine, horseradish, and lemon juice in a food processor and process until very fine.

2. Fold in the whipped cream.

3. The mousse is now ready to use to prepare canapés, for profiteroles, or for other applications.

Blue Cheese Mousse

# Beef Negimaki

YIELD: *30 pieces*

| | |
|---|---|
| 1 lb 12 oz / 794 g beef strip loin | ¼ oz / 7 g garlic, minced to a paste |
| 6 fl oz / 180 mL water | 6 oz / 170 g green onions, green tops only, left whole |
| 5 fl oz / 150 mL soy sauce | |
| 3 oz / 85 g honey | 1¼ tsp / 3.75 g cornstarch |
| 1 oz / 28 g ginger, peeled and grated | ¾ oz / 21 g sesame seeds |
| 1 tbsp / 15 mL dark sesame oil | ¼ oz / 7 g chives, chopped |

1. Remove the silverskin and fat from the beef, leaving only the muscle. Wrap well and freeze just until very firm, but not frozen solid, about 3 hours.

2. Combine the water, soy sauce, honey, ginger, sesame oil, and garlic in a saucepan. Simmer over low heat until flavorful, about 5 minutes. Strain the marinade, cool, and refrigerate until needed.

3. Using an electric slicer, slice the semi-frozen beef into thin slices, about 1 oz / 28 g each. Lay them out overlapping in groups of 8 on a parchment-lined sheet pan.

4. Divide the the green onions evenly among the sliced beef and arrange lengthwise on the beef slices. Roll the beef tightly around the green onions. Transfer the rolls to a hotel pan and pour three-fourths of the marinade over the beef. Cover and refrigerate at least 4 and up to 12 hours to marinate.

5. To prepare the glaze, make a cornstarch slurry by stirring 1 tbsp / 15 mL cool water into the cornstarch. Bring the remaining marinade to a simmer in a saucepan. Add the cornstarch slurry to the simmering marinade while stirring or whisking constantly. When the mixture has a coating consistency, remove it from the heat.

6. Squeeze the beef rolls to remove the excess marinade and arrange seam side down on a greased sheet pan.

7. Broil the rolls under high heat until the beef is browned and cooked through, about 5 minutes. Remove them from the broiler or salamander, brush lightly with the glaze, and sprinkle with sesame seeds and chives.

8. Use skewers or picks to secure the rolls and mark into servings. Cut into bite-size pieces and serve immediately.

# Lamb Brochettes with Mint Pesto

YIELD: *30 pieces*

| | |
|---|---|
| 2 lb 8 oz / 1.13 kg leg of lamb, boned and trimmed of connective tissue | 2 tbsp / 6 g chopped mint |
| 1 fl oz / 30 mL lemon juice | 30 bamboo skewers |
| 3 garlic cloves, crushed | 8 oz / 227 g pancetta or bacon, thinly sliced (about 15 slices) |
| 1 tsp / 3 g salt | 16 fl oz / 480 mL Mint Pesto Sauce (page 49) |
| ½ tsp / 1 g ground black pepper | |
| 2 oz / 57 g extra-virgin olive oil | |

1. Cut the lamb into ¾-in / 2-cm cubes. Combine the lemon juice, garlic, salt, and pepper, whisk until blended, and add the oil and mint.

2. Toss the lamb in the mixture to coat well, then cover and refrigerate, tossing occasionally, for a minimum of 4 hours.

3. If using bamboo skewers, soak them in water for at least 30 minutes to prevent burning.

4. Thread 2 pieces of lamb and ½ slice of pancetta on each skewer and arrange on a sheet pan.

5. Roast in a 450°F / 232°C oven until the lamb is nicely browned outside yet still pink and juicy inside, 8 to 12 minutes.

6. Serve with mint pesto sauce for dipping.

*Chef's note*   *If using bacon, blanch in a large saucepan of slowly simmering water for 5 minutes. The bacon will become opaque and firm. Drain and pat dry before using.*

# Beef Saté

YIELD: *30 pieces*

| | |
|---|---|
| 1 lb 14 oz / 851 g tenderloin tips or sirloin tips | 2 tbsp / 6 g chopped cilantro |
| 4 tsp / 12 g minced garlic | 2 fl oz / 60 mL soy sauce |
| 2 tsp / 6 g minced ginger | 1 fl oz / 30 mL sesame oil |
| 1 small chile, crushed | 1 tbsp / 3 g minced lemongrass (optional) |
| 2 tsp / 4 g curry powder | 30 bamboo skewers, 6 in / 15 cm long |
| | 8 fl oz / 240 mL Peanut Sauce (page 51) |

1. Slice the meat lengthwise into portions about 1 oz / 28 g each.

2. Combine the garlic, ginger, chile, curry, cilantro, soy sauce, sesame oil, and lemongrass. Add the meat to the mixture and turn to coat. Cover and refrigerate for 1 hour and up to 2 hours.

3. Soak the skewers in water for 30 minutes.

4. Remove the meat from the marinade, scraping off any excess. Weave each slice of meat onto a skewer.

5. Sear on a hot griddle, or broil until medium rare, about 1 minute per side.

6. Serve with warm peanut dipping sauce.

*Chef's note*  Lamb may be substituted for the beef.

# Pinchon Moruno (Moorish-Style Shish Kebobs)

YIELD: *30 pieces*

| | |
|---|---|
| 6 fl oz / 180 mL extra-virgin olive oil | ½ oz / 14 g lemon zest |
| 1½ tsp / 3 g fresh ground cumin | 2 fresh bay leaves, chopped |
| 12 garlic cloves, thinly sliced | 2 lb 8 oz / 1.13 kg pork loin, cut into ¾-in / 2-cm cubes |
| 4 tsp / 16 g pimenton | |
| ¼ tsp / 0.50 g cayenne | 30 wooden skewers, 6 in / 15 cm long, soaked for two hours |
| Black pepper, as needed | |
| 3 tbsp / 9 g thyme, coarsely chopped | Salt, as needed |
| | 2 fl oz / 60 mL lemon juice |

1. Combine the olive oil, cumin, garlic, pimenton, cayenne, pepper, thyme, lemon zest, and bay leaves and pour over the pork cubes. Cover and refrigerate 24 hours to marinate.

2. Skewer the pork, season with salt, and grill. After grilling, sprinkle with lemon juice and season with salt.

# Small Seared Lobster and Vegetable Quesadillas

YIELD: *10 servings (2 quesadillas per serving)*

3 lb 8 oz / 1.59 kg lobster (2 lobsters)

½ tsp / 1 g cumin, toasted and ground

¼ tsp / 0.50 g chili powder

Pinch cayenne

Olive oil, as needed, for sautéing

4 oz / 113 g onion, cut into ¼-in / 6-mm dice

1½ tsp / 4.5 g chopped garlic

7 oz / 198 g poblano chiles, roasted and cut into ¼-in / 6-mm dice

3 oz / 85 g red bell pepper, roasted and cut into ¼-in / 6-mm dice

Pinch salt

3 oz / 85 g queso blanco, grated

8 flour tortillas (8 in / 20 cm in diameter)

Olive oil, as needed

1. Cook the lobsters in simmering salted water for 6 minutes. De-shell and coat the meat with the cumin, chili powder, and cayenne.

2. Heat olive oil in a sauté pan over high heat and pan-sear the lobster. Cut the lobster into ¼-in / 6-mm dice.

3. Heat the olive oil over moderate heat and sauté the onion and chopped garlic.

4. Mix the onion and peppers together and adjust seasoning with salt.

5. Mix the lobster with the vegetable mixture and the queso blanco.

6. Using a 2½-in / 6-cm ring mold, cut 20 rounds from the tortillas.

7. Heat some olive oil in a sauté pan and lightly sauté both sides of the tortilla rounds over medium high heat.

8. Place ½ oz / 14 g of filling on each of 10 of the tortilla rounds and top with the remaining rounds.

9. Arrange the assembled quesadillas on a parchment-lined half sheet pan. Place a half sheet of parchment paper on top of the quesadillas. Weigh down the quesadillas with a half sheet pan to flatten them.

10. Bake in a 400°F / 205°C oven until the cheese has melted, 8 to 10 minutes, or brown the quesadillas in a cast-iron pan. Serve immediately.

*Chef's note* Smoked chicken works well as a substitution for the lobster.
This will make 30 hors d'oeuvre using 1-in / 3-cm tortilla rounds and 1 tsp / 4 g filling.

# Pork Piccadillo Empanadas

YIELD: *30 pieces*

PORK FILLING

2 tsp / 10 mL olive or vegetable oil

12 oz / 340 g pork butt, coarse grind

½ oz / 14 g jalapeño, minced

2 tsp / 4 g chili powder

1 tsp / 2 g ground cumin

1 tsp / 2 g ground cinnamon

¼ tsp / 0.50 g ground allspice

2 oz / 57 g golden raisins, plumped in warm water

1¾ oz / 50 g blanched almonds, toasted and chopped

1½ fl oz / 45 mL lime juice

Salt, as needed

Ground black pepper, as needed

1 fl oz / 30 mL sour cream

EMPANADA DOUGH

6¾ oz / 191 g all-purpose flour

4 oz / 113 g masa harina

3½ tsp / 10.50 g baking powder

1 tsp / 3 g salt

4 oz / 113 g lard, melted and cooled

6 fl oz / 180 mL water, or as needed

2 eggs

8 fl oz / 240 mL Salsa Verde, Salsa Fresco, or Chipotle Pico de Gallo (pages 43, 44, 46)

1. Heat the oil in a sauté pan over medium heat. Add the pork and sauté, breaking up the meat, until it is no longer pink, about 10 minutes. Stir in the jalapeño, chili powder, cumin, cinnamon, and allspice. Continue to sauté until most of the liquid evaporates, 5 to 6 minutes more. Transfer to a bowl and fold in the raisins and almonds. Season with lime juice, salt, and pepper. Fold in the sour cream, adding just enough to gently bind the filling. Cool the filling, cover, and refrigerate until ready to assemble the empanadas, up to 2 days.

2. To prepare the dough, blend the flour, masa harina, baking powder, and salt in a mixing bowl. Add the lard and mix by hand or on low speed until evenly moistened. Blend 4 fl oz / 120 mL water and 1 egg and add the mixture gradually to the dough, stirring or blending with a dough hook as you work. Knead the dough until it is pliable, about 3 minutes.

3. Whisk together the remaining egg and 2 fl oz / 60 mL water to make an egg wash.

4. To assemble the empanadas, roll out the dough to a thickness of 1/16 in / 1.5 mm and cut into circles 3 in / 8 cm in diameter to make at least 30 circles. If necessary, gently knead the dough scraps together and roll the dough out again to obtain 30 circles. Place ½ oz / 14 g filling on each circle. Brush the edges with egg wash, fold in half, and seal the seams. Transfer to parchment-lined sheet pans, cover, and refrigerate until ready to fry the empanadas. (They may be refrigerated up to 24 hours, or frozen for up to 3 weeks.)

5. Heat the oil in a deep fryer (or to a depth of 2 in / 5 cm in a rondeau) to 350°F / 177°C. Add the empanadas to the hot oil and fry, turning if necessary to brown both sides evenly, until golden brown and crisp, 4 to 5 minutes. Drain on absorbent paper towels and blot briefly. Serve while very hot with the salsa or pico de gallo.

# Fried Wontons

YIELD: *30 pieces*

| | |
|---|---|
| 8 oz / 227 g pork, ground (from shoulder) | 1½ tsp / 7 mL oyster sauce |
| 4 oz / 113 g savoy cabbage, shredded very fine | 1½ tsp / 7 mL soy sauce |
| 2½ oz / 71 g red bell pepper, minced very fine | 1½ tsp / 1.50 g coarsely chopped cilantro |
| 2½ oz / 71 g shiitake mushroom, minced very fine | 1½ tsp / 7 mL dark sesame oil |
| | ½ tsp / 1.50 g salt, or as needed |
| 1 oz / 28 g green onions, sliced (about ½ bunch) | ½ tsp / 1 g ground black pepper, or as needed |
| 1½ tsp / 4.50 g ginger, minced very fine or grated | 1 egg |
| | 1 fl oz / 30 mL water |
| 1½ tsp / 4.50 g garlic, minced to a paste | 30 wonton wrappers |

1. Sauté the pork in a wok or skillet over high heat until the pork is cooked through, about 6 minutes. Drain the pork in a colander to remove excess fat.

2. Return the pan to high heat and add the cabbage, bell pepper, and shiitake mushrooms. Sauté, stirring the vegetables as necessary, until they are almost tender, about 10 minutes. Add the green onions, ginger, and garlic and cook until aromatic, 2 to 3 minutes. Add the pork to the vegetable mixture.

3. Remove the pork and cabbage mixture from heat and stir in oyster sauce, soy sauce, cilantro, sesame oil, salt, and black pepper. Allow the mixture to rest for 20 minutes to blend the flavors.

4. Whisk together the egg and water to make egg wash.

5. To fill the wontons, place approximately 1 tbsp / 15 mL filling in a wrapper and brush the edges with egg wash (see Fig 9-24a). Pull the wrapper over the top of the filling and seal the edges (see Fig 9-24b). Pull the tips back toward each other and pinch together (see Fig 9-24c).

6. Heat oil to 350°F / 177°C and fry the wontons, turning as necessary, until evenly brown and crispy, 3 to 4 minutes (see Fig 9-24d).

*Chef's note* If preparing this filling mixture in advance, cool it rapidly, cover, and refrigerate. Make a sample wonton and check seasoning. Make any necessary adjustments before filling the wrappers.

*Presentation idea* Serve 3 of the wontons with 1 fl oz / 30 mL Asian-Style Dipping Sauce (page 50).

**FIG 9-24A** *Place a small amount of filling in the center of a wonton wrapper.*

**FIG 9-24B** *After egg-washing each side of the wrapper, seal it by bringing diagonal corners together to form a triangle whose sides are just shy of lining up.*

**FIG 9-24C** *Pull the tips of the longest side of the triangle back and together, forming them into a ring, and seal them with a little water if necessary.*

**FIG 9-24D** *Fry the wontons until evenly brown and crispy.*

# Chinese Skewered Bites

YIELD: *30 servings (½ oz / 14 g each)*

32 fl oz / 960 mL dry red wine

14 oz / 397 g green onions, minced

8 fl oz / 240 mL light soy sauce

6 fl oz / 180 mL plum sauce

4 fl oz / 120 mL dark sesame oil

2 oz / 57 g sesame seeds, toasted

½ oz / 14 g garlic, finely minced

1 tsp / 1 g dried thyme leaves

1 lb / 454 g pork loin, cut into bite-size pieces

30 bamboo skewers, 2 in / 5 cm long, soaked in water

1. Combine the red wine, green onions, soy sauce, plum sauce, sesame oil, sesame seeds, garlic, and thyme in a small saucepan and boil for 5 minutes. Allow the mixture to cool to room temperature.

2. Pour the red wine marinade over the pork and refrigerate, covered, for at least 1 hour.

3. Place the marinated pork on the skewers.

4. Simmer the marinade for 10 minutes, until thick.

5. While the marinade is simmering, broil or grill the meat for 5 to 7 minutes, or until done.

6. Strain the marinade and use it for a dipping sauce.

*Variation*  Substitute beef or chicken for the pork.

# Steamed Wontons with Shrimp

**YIELD:** *30 pieces*

14½ oz / 411 g shrimp, peeled and deveined

4 tsp / 20 mL sesame oil

2¾ tsp / 11 g sugar

1¼ tsp / 3.75 g very finely minced ginger

1¼ tsp / 3.75 g very finely minced garlic

1¼ tsp / 1 g minced parsley

Salt, as needed

Ground black pepper, as needed

4¾ oz / 135 g brown rice, completely cooked

30 wonton wrappers

¾ oz / 21 g green onions, sliced thin on the bias

½ oz / 14 g sesame seeds, toasted

1. Make the filling in a food processor by puréeing the shrimp, sesame oil, sugar, ginger, garlic, parsley, salt, and pepper into a coarse paste, pulsing the machine on and off in short blasts. Transfer the shrimp mixture to a bowl. Purée the rice in the food processor very briefly, just enough to break up grains. Fold the rice into the shrimp mixture until evenly blended, making sure to scrape the bowl while folding. (If made in advance, cover, label, and refrigerate for up to 24 hours. Make a sample wonton and check seasoning. Make any necessary adjustments before filling the wrappers.)

2. To assemble the wontons, brush the edges of each wrapper with water. Transfer shrimp and rice filling to pastry bag with no tip. Fill each wrapper with 1 tsp / 4 g filling. Fold the wonton in half to make a triangle. Press to seal the edges securely. Bring the two corners along the base of the triangle in toward each other, overlap them, and press to seal securely. Transfer to a parchment-lined sheet pan and refrigerate until ready for service. The wontons can be covered and refrigerated up to 24 hours or frozen for up to 3 weeks.

3. For each serving, arrange 3 to 4 wontons in a small bamboo steamer and steam over boiling water until the wrappers are tender and translucent and the filling is completely cooked, 10 to 12 minutes. Transfer the steamer to a plate, and garnish with sliced green onions and sesame seeds. Serve with a container of Asian-style Dipping Sauce (page 50) (1½ fl oz / 45 mL per serving) in the center of the basket with chopsticks.

# Shrimp Tempura

YIELD: *30 pieces*

2 lb / 907 g shrimp (16/20 count), peeled and deveined

16 fl oz / 480 mL vegetable oil

8 fl oz / 240 mL peanut oil

8 fl oz / 240 mL sesame oil

TEMPURA BATTER

3 eggs, beaten

16 fl oz / 480 mL water

8 oz / 227 g ice, crushed

13 oz / 369 g all-purpose flour, plus more for dredging

Cornstarch, as needed

15 fl oz / 450 mL Asian-style Dipping Sauce (page 50)

1. If desired, make two incisions on the stomach side of each shrimp so that it stays straight. Refrigerate until service.

2. Combine the vegetable, peanut, and sesame oils in a deep pot or fryer. Heat the oil to 350°F / 177°C.

3. To make the batter, combine the eggs, water, and ice. Add the flour and mix gently. Do not overmix.

4. To prepare the shrimp for frying, press the shrimp quite firmly on a board with cornstarch so as to break most of the muscles and stop the shrimp from curling up as it cooks. Try to keep the shrimp straight and always make sure that your shrimp or vegetables are lightly dusted in cornstarch before dipping in the batter.

5. Lightly dredge the shrimp in flour. Pick up the shrimp by their tails and dip the bodies only in the batter to lightly coat. Immediately deep-fry the shrimp until crispy and white or light golden brown.

6. Blot the tempura on absorbent paper towels or drain on a rack and serve immediately with the dipping sauce.

*Variation*   *Vegetable Tempura: 2 lb 12 oz / 1.25 kg assorted vegetables (e.g. broccoli, zucchini, mushrooms) may be substituted for the shrimp. The vegetables will need to be blotted dry before seasoning and frying.*

*Chef's notes*   *The reason for adding the ice is to keep the gluten from forming in the flour, therefore flour with very little gluten is ideal. Cake flour may also be used.*

*To devein shrimp for tempura, peel all but the tail and remove the vein from the back of the shrimp with a skewer or point of a paring knife so that the shrimp remains round-bodied.*

# Mussels Stuffed with Vegetables

YIELD: *30 pieces*

| | |
|---|---|
| 30 mussels, cleaned (about 1 lb 5 oz / 595 g) | 1 oz / 28 g flour |
| 2 fl oz / 60 mL white wine | 8 fl oz / 240 mL milk |
| 1 oz / 28 g butter | 1 egg yolk |
| 2 oz / 57 g onion, minced | Salt, as needed |
| 1 garlic clove, minced | Pepper, as needed |
| 2 oz / 57 g carrots, brunoise | 5 oz / 142 g bread crumbs |
| 1 oz / 28 g leek, white part only, minced (a section about 2 in / 5 cm in length) | 1½ fl oz / 45 mL olive oil |

1. Clean the mussels and remove the beards. Combine the mussels and white wine in a large pot over high heat and bring to a boil. Cover and steam the mussels until all have just opened, 3 to 5 minutes.

2. Remove the meat from the shells and chop. Reserve the steaming liquid. Separate the shells and discard half of them. Rinse and dry the remaining shells and set aside.

3. Heat the butter in a saucepot over medium heat. Add the onions, garlic, carrot, and leek and sweat for 3 minutes. Add the flour and cook, stirring constantly, until the flour begins to turn a golden brown.

4. Whisk in the milk and 2 fl oz / 60 mL reserved steaming liquid. Simmer the mixture, stirring occasionally, for 12 to 15 minutes or until the sauce has thickened.

5. Temper the egg yolk into the thickened sauce. Add the mussel meat. Stir for 1 minute, until the meat is heated through. Adjust seasoning with salt and pepper.

6. Fill each of the shells with ½ oz / 14 g filling and refrigerate until cool.

7. Combine the bread crumbs with the olive oil and sprinkle evenly over the filled shells.

8. Broil until golden brown and heated through, about 2 minutes.

9. Serve hot as individual passed hors d'oeuvre or 3 each for an appetizer serving.

# Risotto Croquettes with Fontina

YIELD: *30 pieces*

1 oz / 28 g fine-dice onions

2 oz / 57 g butter

1 lb / 454 g arborio rice

8 fl oz / 240 mL white wine

48 fl oz / 1.44 L Chicken Stock (page 592), hot

4 oz / 113 g Parmesan

Salt, as needed

15 oz / 425 g Fontina, cut into 30 cubes
(¼ in / 6 mm square)

4½ oz / 128 g flour

2 eggs, beaten with 2 tbsp water or milk

3½ oz / 99 g bread crumbs

8 oz / 227 g plum tomatoes, cut into 30
slices and roasted

Olive oil, as needed

Herbs (thyme, basil, marjoram), as needed

1. Sauté the onions in the butter. Add the rice and coat with butter; cook until parched.

2. Add the white wine; simmer until absorbed, then add the stock in 3 additions.

3. Cook over low heat, stirring frequently, until rice is cooked through, about 18 minutes. Add Parmesan.

4. Transfer the risotto to a sheet pan and spread in an even layer. Allow rice to cool completely. Season with salt if necessary.

5. Form the chilled risotto into small balls wrapped around a cube of Fontina.

6. Coat the balls using flour, eggs, and bread crumbs in the standard breading procedure (see page 612).

7. Deep-fry croquettes at 350°F / 175°C until golden brown, 4 to 5 minutes.

8. Garnish each with an oven-roasted tomato slice, olive oil, and fresh herbs.

*Chef's note*   *This recipe works best when the risotto is prepared a day in advance. Other fillings can be used in place of Fontina, such as cooked sausage, seafood, vegetables, or Toasted Almonds (page 513).*

# Risotto and Pancetta Cakes with Sun-Dried Tomato Pesto

YIELD: *30 pieces*

| | |
|---|---|
| 8 oz / 227 g pancetta, thinly sliced | Ground pepper, as needed |
| 1 oz / 28 g butter | 14 oz / 397 g panko bread crumbs |
| 1 oz / 28 g onion, minced | 3 eggs |
| 7 oz / 198 g arborio rice | 4 fl oz / 120 mL milk |
| 28 fl oz / 840 mL chicken stock, hot | 8 oz / 227 g all-purpose flour, or as needed |
| 2 tbsp / 6 g minced parsley | 8 fl oz / 240 mL vegetable oil for frying, or as needed |
| 2 tbsp / 30 mL dry white wine | |
| 4 oz / 113 g grated Parmesan | 12 oz / 340 g Sun-dried Tomato Pesto (page 49) |
| Salt, as needed | |

1. Bake the pancetta slices in a single layer on sheet pans in a 350°F / 175°C oven until crisp, 10 to 12 minutes. Let cool, roughly chop, and set aside.

2. Heat the butter in a saucepot over medium high heat. Add the onions and sweat until softened and translucent, about 6 to 8 minutes. Increase the heat to high and add the rice. Cook, stirring constantly, for 1 minute.

3. Add one-third of the stock to the rice and cook, stirring every 3 to 5 minutes, until the rice has absorbed the stock. Repeat using half of the remaining stock. Add the remaining stock and stir the risotto until the rice is tender and most of the liquid has been absorbed.

4. Remove from the heat and stir in the parsley, wine, pancetta, and 2 oz / 57 g Parmesan. Adjust seasoning with salt and pepper.

5. Evenly spread the risotto onto a quarter sheet pan lined with lightly oiled parchment paper. Cover and refrigerate until firm and cool.

6. Cut the chilled risotto into 30 pieces, about 1½ in / 4 cm square.

7. For the breading, combine the bread crumbs and remaining 2 oz / 57 g Parmesan. Whisk together the eggs and milk. Dip a risotto cake into the flour and tap off excess. Dip in the egg mixture and then in the breadcrumb mixture, turning to coat thoroughly each time. Repeat with remaining cakes.

8. Heat the oil in a large skillet over medium-high heat to 350°F / 175°C. Pan-fry the risotto cakes until golden brown and crisp, about 1 to 2 minutes on each side.

9. Serve hot, garnished with dollop of Sun-dried Tomato Pesto.

*Chef's note* For appetizer-size pieces, cut the chilled risotto into 10 equal pieces, about 1¾ in by 3½ in / 4 by 9 cm.

# Warm Phyllo Triangles Filled with Camembert and Dried Apple and Fig Marmalade

YIELD: *30 each*

| | |
|---|---|
| 4 oz / 113 g shallots, minced | 24 fl oz / 720 mL apple cider |
| 1 oz / 28 g butter | 2 fl oz / 60 mL sherry vinegar |
| 8 oz / 227 g dried apples, cut into ½-in / 1-cm dice | ⅔ bunch thyme leaves, coarsely chopped |
| 4 fl oz / 120 mL dried black figs, cut into ½-in / 1-cm dice | 1 lb / 454 g Hollow Farms Camembert |
| | 1 lb / 454 g phyllo dough sheets (30 sheets) |
| | 8 oz / 227 g clarified butter, melted |

1. Sweat the shallots in the butter over medium-low heat in a 1-quart saucepot until tender, about 3 to 4 minutes. Drain off the excess fat. Add the apples, figs, cider, and vinegar. Cook until the liquid is completely absorbed and the apples and figs are tender and cooked through, about 5 to 10 minutes. Remove from the pan and cool.

2. Stir the thyme leaves into the marmalade.

3. Cut the Camembert into 30 pieces by cutting each piece into thirds lengthwise and then cutting those pieces into ¼- to ½-in / 6-mm to 1-cm slices. You should be able to get 18 to 20 pieces out of each one.

4. Lay 1 sheet of phyllo dough on a cutting board with the shorter side facing you. Brush it lightly with the melted butter. Place another sheet of phyllo directly on top of the buttered sheet and brush it lightly with butter. Repeat with a third sheet.

5. Cut the phyllo dough lengthwise into 3 even strips. Place a piece of cheese on the bottom right corner of each phyllo strip and top with 1 tablespoons of marmalade.

6. Fold the bottom right corner of a strip diagonally to the left side of the strip to create a triangle of dough encasing the filling (see Fig 9-25a). Fold the bottom left point of the dough up along the left side of the dough to seal the filling.

7. Fold the bottom left corner of the dough diagonally to the right side of the dough to form a triangle. Fold the bottom right point up along the right edge of the dough. Repeat until the end of the strip is reached and you have a triangle of layered phyllo dough with the filling wrapped inside (see Fig 9-25b). Repeat with each strip.

8. Repeat the layering, filling, and folding procedure with the remaining phyllo sheets, cheese, and marmalade.

9. Place the phyllo triangles on a parchment-lined sheet pan and brush each one with melted clarified butter.

10. Bake in a 400°F / 204°C oven until golden brown, 15 to 20 minutes. Serve immediately.

| FIG 9-25A | *Fold the bottom right corner of the strip diagonally over to create a triangle of dough that encases the cheese and filling.* | FIG 9-25B | *Continue folding the triangle diagonally over itself to the opposite side of the dough strip to completely encase the filling.* |

# Mini Stilton Popovers

YIELD: *36 mini popovers*

| | |
|---|---|
| 4 large eggs | 1 tsp / 3 g salt |
| 16 fl oz / 480 mL whole milk | ¼ tsp / 0.50 g pepper |
| 2 oz / 57 g butter | 6 oz / 170 g Stilton, crumbled |
| 8¼ oz / 234 g all-purpose flour | 4 oz / 113 g walnuts, toasted and chopped |

1. Combine all ingredients, cover, and refrigerate for 30 minutes.

2. Grease 36 mini muffin cups (2 in / 5 cm in diameter by 1 in / 3 cm deep). Fill the tins half to three-quarters full with the mixture, or about 1½ to 2 tbsp / 22.5 to 30 mL per muffin cup.

3. Bake in a 425°F / 218°C oven until the popovers are golden brown and a toothpick inserted into the center comes out clean, 12 minutes.

# Spanakopita

YIELD: *30 pieces*

| | |
|---|---|
| 1¼ oz / 35 g butter | 7½ oz / 205 g feta cheese, crumbled |
| 2½ oz / 70 g minced shallots | 2½ oz / 71 g mozzarella cheese, grated |
| 2½ tbsp / 23 g minced garlic | 1¼ tsp / 3.75 g salt |
| 15 oz / 425 g spinach, cleaned and stems removed | Pinch ground black pepper |
| | 15 phyllo sheets |
| 1¼ tsp / 2.50 g nutmeg | 10 oz / 284 g butter, melted |
| 1¼ tbsp / 3.75 g chopped dill | |

1. Melt the butter in a sauté pan over moderate heat until it starts to bubble. Add the shallots and garlic to the butter and sweat until translucent.

2. Add the spinach, nutmeg, and dill and sauté gently until the spinach is wilted, 1 to 2 minutes. Transfer the spinach mixture to a stainless-steel bowl and allow it to cool to room temperature. Add the cheeses and season with salt and pepper. Keep the filling refrigerated until needed.

3. Lay one sheet of phyllo dough on a cutting board. Brush it lightly with melted butter. Place another sheet of phyllo dough directly on the buttered sheet and brush it lightly with butter. Repeat with a third sheet of phyllo.

4. Cut the phyllo dough lengthwise into 6 even strips. Place 1 oz / 28 g spinach filling on the bottom right corner of each strip. Fold the bottom right corner of a strip diagonally to the left side of the strip to create a triangle of dough encasing the filling. Fold the bottom left point of the dough up along the left side of the dough to make a triangle and seal in the filling.

5. Fold the bottom left corner of the dough diagonally to the right side of the dough to form a triangle. Fold the bottom right point up along the right edge of the dough. Repeat until the end of the strip is reached and you have a triangle of layered phyllo dough with the filling wrapped inside. Repeat with each strip.

6. Place the phyllo triangles on a parchment-lined sheet pan and brush each with melted butter.

7. Bake in a 400°F / 205°C oven until golden brown, 15 to 20 minutes. Serve immediately.

# Stuffed Grape Leaves

YIELD: *30 pieces*

| | |
|---|---|
| 1 onion, cut in small dice | 1 oz / 28 g grated ginger |
| 1 tsp / 2 g minced garlic | 2 oz / 57 g fresh currants |
| 2 fl oz / 60 mL olive oil | ⅛ tsp / 0.25 g cinnamon |
| 4 oz / 113 g green onions, sliced on the bias into ⅛-in / 3-mm slices | 72 fl oz / 2.16 L vegetable stock |
| 4 oz / 113 g parsley, coarsely chopped | 8 oz / 227 g long-grain rice |
| 2 oz / 57 g dill, coarsely chopped | 2 eggs |
| 2 tsp / 2 g coarsely chopped mint | Salt, as needed |
| 1½ fl oz / 45 mL lemon juice | Pepper, as needed |
| 1½ tsp / 3 g turmeric | 36 jarred grape leaves, rinsed |
| ½ tsp / 0.50 g oregano | 2 fl oz / 60 mL olive oil |
| 1 tbsp / 6 g cumin | 2 tsp / 2 g coarsely chopped mint |
| 1 tsp / 2 g coriander | 1 tsp / 1 g coarsely chopped oregano |
| 1 tsp / 2 g fennel seed | 1 fl oz / 30 mL lemon juice |
| 2 oz / 57 g pine nuts | 1 tbsp / 9 g lemon zest |

1. Sauté onions and garlic in olive oil over medium heat in a sauté pan until golden brown, about 2 minutes.

2. Add the green onions, parsley, dill, and mint and sauté briefly until the green onions wilt, 1 to 2 minutes. Cool the mixture to room temperature.

3. Mix the lemon juice, turmeric, oregano, cumin, coriander, fennel seed, pine nuts, ginger, currants and cinnamon with onion and garlic mixture.

4. Bring 20 fl oz / 600 mL stock to a boil and stir in the rice. Bring the mixture to a simmer, cover it, and place the pan in a 350°F / 177°C oven. Cook until the rice grains are fluffy and fully cooked, 18 to 20 minutes. Spread the rice out on a sheet pan to cool to room temperature. Combine the rice with the onion-spice mixture and season. Add the eggs and stir until fully combined.

5. Soak the grape leaves in water and place 1½ tsp / 7 g filling toward the bottom edge of one of the leaves. Roll the bottom of the grape leaf over the filling to encase it and fold the sides in toward the middle. Continue rolling the grape leaf until you reach the end. Repeat with the remaining leaves and filling. The rolls should be 2 in / 5 cm long and ½ in / 1 cm thick.

6. Pack the rolls tightly in a 2-in / 5-cm-deep perforated full hotel pan and cover with aluminum foil. Place the remaining vegetable stock in a 4-in / 10-cm-deep full hotel pan. Place the perforated pan inside the deeper hotel pan. Steam the leaves for 1 to 2 hours, or until cooked through.

7. Combine the olive oil, mint, oregano, lemon juice, and lemon zest. After the leaves have cooled for a few minutes, brush grape leaves with olive oil mixture. Serve immediately.

# Wrapped Shrimp with Asian Barbecue Sauce

YIELD: *30 pieces*

1 lb / 454 g pineapple, cleaned and trimmed

1 lb / 454 g shrimp, medium, peeled and deveined

Salt, as needed

Pepper, as needed

15 strips bacon, par-baked and halved

30 bamboo skewers (6 in / 15 cm long)

1 tbsp / 15 mL olive oil or vegetable oil

2¼ oz / 64 g onions, diced

1½ oz / 43 g celery, diced

1 garlic clove, chopped

1 fl oz / 30 mL rice vinegar

4 oz / 113 g ketchup

4 oz / 113 g chili sauce

1 fl oz / 30 mL soy sauce

2¼ oz / 68 mL plum sauce

2 tsp / 10 mL Worcestershire sauce

2⅓ oz / 66 g green onions, thinly sliced

3 oz / 85 g toasted coconut

1. Cut thirty ½-in / 1-cm chunks of pineapple and finely chop the rest.

2. Season the shrimp with salt and pepper. Place a chunk of pineapple on each shrimp and wrap with a piece of bacon.

3. Place a skewer through the bacon, pineapple, and shrimp and reserve. (Do not hold for too long as the pineapple will denature the shrimp.)

4. Heat the oil in a large skillet over medium heat and sweat the onions, celery, and garlic until softened but not brown, about 3 to 4 minutes.

5. Add the reserved pineapple, vinegar, ketchup, chili sauce, soy sauce, plum sauce, and Worcestershire sauce to the onion mixture. Bring to a simmer and cook for 15 minutes or until sauce is glossy and thickened. Adjust the consistency with water if necessary and season with salt and pepper. Keep the sauce warm.

6. To cook the shrimp, spoon or brush a small amount of sauce (about 1 tsp / 5 mL) over each skewer and place in a 400°F / 204°C oven until the meat just turns white, about 10 minutes.

7. Remove from oven and arrange on serving platters. Garnish with the green onions and coconut. Serve immediately with the remaining sauce on the side for dipping.

*Potato Crêpes with Crème Fraîche and Caviar*

# Potato Crêpes with Crème Fraîche and Caviar

YIELD: *30 pieces*

| | |
|---|---|
| 12 oz / 340 g puréed cooked potatoes | Pinch grated nutmeg |
| 1 oz / 28 g flour | Vegetable oil, as needed |
| 2 eggs | 4 fl oz / 120 mL Crème Fraîche (page 382) |
| 3 egg whites | 1 oz / 28 g caviar |
| 2 fl oz / 60 mL heavy cream, or as needed | Dill sprigs, as needed |
| Salt, as needed | 6 oz / 170 g smoked salmon slices (optional) |
| Ground white pepper, as needed | |

1. Combine the potatoes and flour in a mixer. Add the eggs one at a time, then the whites. Adjust consistency with cream to that of a pancake batter; season with salt, pepper, and nutmeg.

2. Hors d'oeuvre Assembly: Coat a nonstick griddle or sauté pan lightly with oil. Pour batter as for pancakes into silver-dollar-size servings. Cook until golden brown; turn and finish on the second side, about 2 minutes total cooking time.

3. Serve the crêpes warm with small dollops of crème fraîche and caviar, a small dill sprig, and a smoked salmon slice, if desired.

*Chef's note*  *For dill crêpes, chop some of the dill. Warm the heavy cream and add the chopped dill. Cool before preparing the crêpe batter.*

# Tuna with Capers and Olive Oil

YIELD: *30 each*

| | |
|---|---|
| 1 lb 8 oz / 680 g tuna loin, center-cut | Black pepper, as needed, freshly ground |
| 1¼ fl oz / 37.5 mL lemon juice | 2 tbsp / 12 g coarsely chopped chives |
| ¾ oz / 21 g shallots, minced | 4 tsp / 4 g coarsely chopped dill |
| 3 oz / 85 g capers | Sea salt, as needed |
| 5⅓ fl oz / 160 mL extra-virgin olive oil | 30 French baguette crostini (¼ in / 6 mm thick) |

1. Remove the connective tissue from the tuna loin and cut into very small but rough brunoise.

2. Combine the lemon juice, shallots, capers, oil, pepper, and herbs in a blender and puree until smooth, or approximately one minute.

3. At service time, combine the tuna with the vinaigrette, season with salt as needed, and place on baguette.

# Bluepoint Oysters with Beluga Caviar

YIELD: *30 pieces*

MIGNONETTE SAUCE

1¼ oz / 35 g minced shallots

2 oz / 60 mL chopped chives

2⅔ fl oz / 80 mL Champagne vinegar

1½ oz / 45 mL cracked black pepper

30 oysters

1 oz / 28 g beluga caviar

1. Combine the shallots, chives, vinegar, and pepper and reserve.

2. Shuck the oysters, loosen muscle from bottom shell, then remove oyster with top shell.

3. Hors d'oeuvre Assembly: Place the shells on a bed of crushed ice. Place an oyster inside each shell. Top each with mignonette sauce and a dollop of caviar.

*Presentation idea*  *Place the muscle and liquor in an Asian soup spoon. Top each spoon with mignonette sauce and a dollop of caviar. If desired, arrange spoons on a bed of ice.*

# Pickled Shrimp

YIELD: *30 pieces*

4 fl oz / 120 mL white vinegar

8 fl oz / 240 mL water

1½ tsp / 4.5 g salt

1 garlic clove, crushed

1½ tsp / 6 g mustard seed

1½ tsp / 4 g celery seed

½ tsp / 1 g ground cumin

1 clove

6 allspice berries

½ oz / 14 g light brown sugar

1½ jalapeños, minced

2 bay leaves

30 shrimp (21/25 count), peeled, deveined, and cooked

1. Combine vinegar, water, salt, garlic, mustard seed, celery seed, cumin, clove, allspice, brown sugar, jalapeños, and bay leaves. Bring mixture to a boil. Cool thoroughly.

2. Pour the cold pickling mixture over the shrimp and marinate overnight.

*Bluepoint Oysters with Beluga Caviar*

# Grapes Rolled in Blue de Bresse

YIELD: *30 pieces*

2½ oz / 71 g Blue de Bresse (or other blue cheese)

2½ oz / 71 g cream cheese

30 seedless green grapes

2½ oz / 71 g pistachios, shelled

1. Combine the blue cheese and the cream cheese in a mixer with a paddle and mix well; there should be very few lumps. Cover and refrigerate for 1 hour.

2. Wrap a small amount of cheese around each grape by rolling in the palms of your hands. Store on a parchment-lined sheet pan. Cover and refrigerate at least 1 hour and up to overnight.

3. Pulse the pistachios in a food processor; force through a drum sieve.

4. Roll the grapes in the nut powder and shape with the palms of your hands. This can be done up to 1 hour before service. Do not refrigerate the grapes once they have been rolled in the nut powder.

*Presentation idea* The grapes can be arranged on a platter in the shape of a natural bunch of grapes.

# Scallop Seviche in Cucumber Cups

YIELD: *30 pieces*

6 oz / 170 g sea scallops, cut into brunoise

1 tomato, peeled and seeded, cut into brunoise

1 tsp / 1 g minced chives

1 tbsp / 3 g chopped cilantro

½ jalapeño, minced

¼ green pepper, cut into brunoise

1 tbsp / 15 mL olive oil

5 drops Tabasco sauce

1 to 2 fl oz / 15 to 30 mL lime juice

1 tsp / 3 g kosher salt

Ground black pepper, as needed

3 cucumbers, cut into ½-in / 1-cm slices (30 slices total)

Sour cream, as needed (optional)

2 tsp / 2 g cilantro leaves (optional)

1. To make the seviche, combine the scallops, tomatoes, herbs, peppers, olive oil, and Tabasco. Add enough lime juice to cover the scallops. Season with salt and pepper.

2. Cover and refrigerate at least 8 hous, stirring occasionally.

3. Trim the cucumber slices with a round cutter to remove the peel. Use a small Parisienne scoop to scoop a pocket out of the middle of the cucumber slices. Do not cut all the way through the slice.

4. Fill the cucumber cups with the seviche. Garnish each seviche cup with a small dot of sour cream and a cilantro leaf if desired. Serve immediately.

*Scallop Seviche in Cucumber Cups*

# Sushi

YIELD: *30 Pieces*

| | |
|---|---|
| 5 sheets nori | 2 oz / 57 g cucumber, julienned |
| Hand Vinegar (page 491), as needed | 3 oz / 85 g crabmeat, picked over and shell removed |
| 1 lb 14 oz / 851 g Sushi Rice (page 491), cooled (about 5 cups / 1.2 L) | Rice vinegar, as needed |
| 2 oz / 57 g avocado, julienned | |

1. Cover a bamboo mat with plastic wrap. Place the bamboo mat on a cutting board and lay one sheet of nori on top. Lightly moisten hands with the hand vinegar.

2. Evenly spread 4 oz / 113 g rice (or enough to create a 2-grain-thick layer of rice) over three-quarters of the sheet closest to you, leaving a ½-in / 1-cm band along the long side of the nori sheet exposed (see Fig 9-30a).

3. Place ½ oz / 14 g each avocado, cucumber, and crabmeat on the rice across the long edge of the nori sheet (see Fig 9-30b). Roll up carefully, brush the exposed strip of nori with rice vinegar, and press to seal (see Fig 9-30c).

4. Cut each roll into 6 even pieces and serve immediately (see Fig 9-30d). Repeat with remaining ingredients.

*Variations*    *Cucumber Roll: Follow the recipe as above but sprinkle 1 tsp / 3 g unhulled sesame seeds over the rice layer and replace the filling ingredients with 1 oz / 28 g peeled, seeded, and julienned cucumber per roll.*

*Avocado Roll: Follow the recipe as stated above but sprinkle 1 tsp / 3 g unhulled sesame seeds over the rice layer and replace the filling ingredients with 1 oz / 28 g julienned avocado per roll.*

FIG 9-30A  *Evenly spread the rice over three-quarters of the side of the nori sheet closest to you.*

FIG 9-30B  *Lay the garnish ingredients across the long end of the nori sheet.*

FIG 9-30C  *Carefully roll up the nori sheet, enclosing the garnishes inside and using the bamboo mat to preserve the round shape.*

FIG 9-30D  *Once rolled and sealed, cut the roll into six pieces and serve immediately.*

# Sushi Maki—Maguro (Tuna) Roll

YIELD: *30 pieces*

5 sheets nori

Hand Vinegar (page 491), as needed

1 lb 4 oz / 567 g Sushi Rice (page 491), cooled (about 5 cups / 1.2 L)

¾ fl oz / 21 mL Wasabi Paste (page 534)

5 oz / 142 g yellowfin tuna, sushi grade, cut into thin strips

1. Cover a bamboo mat with plastic wrap. Place the bamboo mat on a cutting board and lay one sheet of nori on top. Lightly moisten hands with the hand vinegar.

2. Evenly spread 4 oz / 113 g rice (or enough to create a 2-grain thick layer of rice) over three-quarters of the sheet closest to you, leaving a ½-in / 1-cm band along the long side of the nori sheet exposed.

3. Place 1 oz / 28 g tuna down the center of the rice. Roll up carefully, brush the exposed strip of nori with rice vinegar, and press to seal. Repeat with remaining ingredients.

4. Cut each roll into 6 even pieces and serve immediately.

*Chef's note*  The plate may be garnished with wasabi paste, pickled ginger, julienned daikon, and julienned carrots. Wrapping the mat with plastic film is a common practice that makes clean-up a bit easier. Also the plastic helps when you are preparing inside-out rolls.

# Inari

YIELD: *30 pieces*

30 inari tofu pouches (canned)

3 lb oz / 1.36 kg Sushi Rice (page 491) cooled

Wasabi Paste (page 534), as needed

Sesame seeds, black and white, as needed

1. Stuff the pouches with sushi rice.

2. Place a small amount of wasabi on the rice and garnish with sesame seeds.

*Chef's note*  The pouches may also be garnished with a small amount of enoki mushrooms or sprouts.

SUSHI, CLOCKWISE FROM UPPER RIGHT: *Sushi Maki, Inari, Sushi (page 486), Nigiri (page 490), Sea Urchin (page 490), Pickled Ginger (page 539)*

# Nigiri

YIELD: *30 pieces*

| | |
|---|---|
| 30 shrimp, 31/35 count | Wasabi Paste (page 534), as needed |
| Hand Vinegar (page 491), as needed | 30 nori strips, 3½ by ¼ in / 9 cm by 6 mm (optional) |
| 1 lb 8 oz / 680 g Sushi Rice (page 491) (about 3 cups / 720 ml), cooled | |

1. Skewer the shrimp along the length of shell and poach for 3 minutes or until the shrimp is cooked through.

2. Shock the shrimp in ice water and peel them. Trim the tail to create a sharp V and cut the underside of the shrimp to butterfly them. Reserve until needed.

3. Dip your fingers into the hand vinegar and rub your palms together. Shape about ¾ oz / 21 g sushi rice into a roughly rectangular form or finger shape about 1½ by ¾ in / 4 cm by 2 cm square.

4. Place a small amount of wasabi on the rice and place a shrimp on top. If desired, wrap the nigiri with a band of nori. Serve immediately.

*Chef's note*  *There are a number of different items that can be used to top the rice such as tuna, salmon, omelet, or vegetables.*

# Uni (Sea Urchin) Roll

YIELD: *24 pieces*

| | |
|---|---|
| 6 sheets nori | 24 shiso leaves |
| 1 cup / 240 mL Hand Vinegar (see page 491) | 12 oz / 340 g sea urchin |
| 1 lb 8 oz / 680 g Sushi Rice (page 491) (about 3 cups / 720 mL), cooled | 2 tbsp / 6 g minced chives |

1. Cut each sheet of nori into 4 rectangles.

2. Dip your fingers into the hand vinegar and rub your palms together. Pick up about ¾ to 1 oz / 21 to 28 g sushi rice and shape into a roughly rectangular form (or "finger") about 1½ by ¾ in / 4 by 2 cm.

3. Wrap the mold of rice in the nori sheet, leaving a short "wall" above the rice to hold the sea urchin. Encircle the roll with your hands for about 20 seconds in order to bind the ends of the nori sheet together. Place a shiso leaf inside the cavity, allowing its top to stick up over the edge of the nori. Fill the cavity with ½ oz / 14 g sea urchin and garnish with ½ tsp / 0.50 g chives.

# Sushi Rice

YIELD: *3 lb / 1.36 kg*

| | |
|---|---|
| 1 piece kombu (dried kelp) 4½ in / 11.50 cm square | 2 oz / 57 g sugar |
| | 1 tbsp / 9 g salt |
| 4 fl oz / 120 mL Japanese unseasoned rice vinegar | 1 lb 12 oz / 794 g short-grain rice |
| | 34 fl oz / 1.02 L water |

1. Wipe kombu with a damp cloth to remove any sand. Do not remove the flavorful white powder.

2. Combine vinegar, sugar, salt, and kombu in a small saucepan. Heat over low heat, stirring to dissolve sugar and salt. Do not let mixture boil. Cool to room temperature.

3. Place the rice in a large bowl; fill with cool water. Gently stir the rice and drain. Repeat this process about 5 times or until water remains semi-clear. Cover the rice with water and soak for 1 hour. Drain well.

4. Bring the rice to a boil over high heat and then reduce to a simmer. Cover the pan and cook for 12 to 15 minutes. Do not uncover the pan or stir the rice while cooking. Turn off the heat and allow the rice to rest for 5 minutes.

5. Turn cooked rice out onto a parchment-lined sheet pan. Vent the rice with a bamboo paddle or 2 chopsticks. Fan with a small tray until steam ceases.

6. Divide the rice between two 2-in / 5-cm full hotel pans and drizzle with the vinegar mixture. Using a wooden rice paddle, "cut" and fold rice with horizontal strokes as the rice is fanned. Continue to process until mixture has cooled and takes on a shiny appearance.

7. Put rice into 1 hotel pan and cover with plastic wrap. Refrigerate until needed.

# Hand Vinegar (Tteuz)

YIELD: *8 fl oz / 240 mL*

8 fl oz / 240 mL cold water

1 tbsp / 15 mL Japanese unseasoned rice vinegar

Combine ingredients and reserve until needed. This mixture is used to prevent the rice from sticking to your hands. The hands are dipped in the water, then slapped together, an effective—and theatrical—way to remove the excess water. The tip of the knife is also dipped in this water and then the handle is tapped so the bead of liquid runs down the blade. This is done before slicing sushi into servings.

*Chef's note*  Lemon juice may be substituted for the rice vinegar.

# Crab Cakes

YIELD: *30 pieces*

| | |
|---|---|
| 10 oz / 284 g blue crabmeat | 4 tsp / 4 g minced chives |
| 2½ shallots, minced | ¼ tsp / 1 mL Tabasco |
| 2 tsp / 10 mL vegetable oil, or as needed | 1 oz / 28 g cracker crumbs, finely crumbled |
| 1½ fl oz / 45 mL mayonnaise | Salt, as needed |
| 1 egg | Black pepper, as needed |
| ½ oz / 14 g whole-grain mustard | 30 Pullman bread slices, cut into rounds |
| 2 tsp / 2 g coarsely chopped parsley | 1¼ in / 3 cm in diameter |

1. Pick through the crabmeat to remove all shells.

2. Sweat the shallots in the vegetable oil in a small sauté pan over low heat until translucent, about 5 to 6 minutes. Cool to room temperature and add to the picked crabmeat.

3. Combine the mayonnaise, egg, mustard, parsley, chives, and Tabasco. Fold the mayonnaise mixture into the crabmeat without shredding it. Fold in the cracker crumbs and adjust seasoning with salt and pepper.

4. Portion into cakes weighing ½ oz / 14 g, about 1¼ in / 3 cm in diameter (the weight is more important than the exact diameter).

5. Sauté in vegetable oil in a large sauté pan over medium-low heat until golden brown on both sides, about 1 to 1½ minutes per side.

6. Toast the bread under the salamander on both sides, about 20 seconds, and reserve separately.

7. Place the crabcakes on the bread rounds and garnish as desired. Serve immediately.

*Presentation idea* Spoon a teaspoon of Red Onion Confit on top of the crabcake.

# Croquetas

YIELD: *30 pieces (about 1½ oz / 43 g each)*

32 fl oz / 960 mL whole milk

4 oz / 113 g yellow onions, finely chopped

5 cloves

1 bay leaves

8 oz / 227 g Serrano ham, finely chopped

2 oz / 57 g butter

14 oz / 397 g all-purpose flour

3 eggs

1 lb / 454 g fresh bread crumbs

1 gal / 3.84 L pure olive oil

Salt, as needed

1. Simmer the milk with the onion and spices until the flavor has developed, about 20 minutes.

2. Strain the milk; add the Serrano ham and simmer for 2 minutes or until the milk is infused with the flavor of the ham. Do not strain out the ham.

3. Prepare a pale roux with the butter and 6 oz / 170 g flour.

4. Thicken the milk with the roux and simmer until the sauce is very thick and the flour taste has cooked out, about 30 minutes.

5. Line a half sheet pan with plastic and spread the béchamel uniformly; refrigerate until firm, or overnight.

6. Set up a breading station with the eggs, bread crumbs, and remaining flour. Form the béchamel into balls 1¼ in / 3 cm in diameter. Bread using the standard breading procedure and refrigerate for 20 to 30 minutes.

7. Heat olive oil to 350°F / 177°C and fry croquetas until golden brown, about 3 minutes. Drain on absorbent paper towels and lightly season with salt. Serve immediately.

# Mango Curry Shrimp Salad in Wonton Cups

YIELD: *30 pieces*

MANGO CHUTNEY

2 green onions, coarsely chopped

1 oz / 28 g dried currants

½ tbsp / 7 mL sherry vinegar

1 tsp / 3 g peeled and grated ginger

12 oz / 340 g mango, peeled, seeded, and cut into ¼-in / 6-mm dice

SHRIMP SALAD

15 wonton wrappers, cut into rounds 2 in / 5 cm in diameter

1 tbsp / 15 mL vegetable oil

2 fl oz / 60 mL mayonnaise

1 tbsp / 3 g coarsely chopped cilantro

1¼ fl oz / 37.5 mL lime juice

½ tsp / 2.5 mL Thai green curry paste

12 oz / 340 g shrimp, 16/20 count, peeled, cooked, and cut into ¼- to ½-in / 6-mm to 1-cm dice

30 cilantro pluches

1. For the mango chutney: Combine all of the ingredients and mix until thoroughly blended. Cover and refrigerate for at least 1 hour and up to 6 hours, tossing occasionally.

2. For the shrimp cups: Preheat the oven to 325°F /163°C. Place the wonton rounds on a cutting board and brush lightly with oil.

3. Press each wonton into mini muffin cups 2 in / 5 cm in diameter by 1 in / 3 cm deep, oiled side down.

4. Bake until wonton cups are golden brown, about 10 minutes. Cool in pans.

5. Remove the cups from tins and store in an airtight container at room temperature until needed.

6. Whisk mayonnaise, chopped cilantro, lime juice, 1½ tbsp / 23 mL chutney, and curry paste in a medium bowl until fully blended.

7. Stir in the diced shrimp and season the salad as needed with salt and pepper.

8. Fill the wonton cups three-quarters full with the shrimp salad, garnish with additional chutney as needed, and serve.

# Dim Sum with Chili Sauce

YIELD: *30 pieces*

1½ fl oz / 45 mL vegetable oil

8 to 10 garlic cloves, crushed

1 lb 8 oz / 680 g ground pork

1 lb 8 oz / 680 g bok choy, shredded

2¼ fl oz / 67 mL light soy sauce

1½ tsp / 7 mL sesame oil

30 spring roll wrappers, 10-in / 30-cm square, thawed if frozen

Oil, for deep-frying, such as peanut oil or ultrafry, as needed

4 fl oz / 120 mL Chili Sauce (recipe follows)

1. Preheat a wok over medium-high heat. Add the oil and heat until it shimmers and there is a slight haze coming off it. Add the garlic and stir fry for 30 seconds or until the garlic is light golden but not browned. Add the pork and stir fry until lightly colored, 2 to 3 minutes.

2. Add the bok choy, soy sauce, and sesame oil to the wok and stir fry until the water starts to come out of the cabbage and it becomes limp, 2 to 3 minutes. The cabbage should still be green and should not start to turn yellow. Remove from the heat and refrigerate mixture to 40°F / 4°C.

3. Working with 6 to 8 at a time, spread out the spring roll wrappers on a work surface and spoon 2 tbsp / 28 g pork mixture along 1 edge of each wrapper. Roll the edge over the filing and fold in the sides. Roll up completely to make a sausage/egg roll shape, brushing the edges with a little water to seal. Set the dim sum rolls aside for 10 minutes to seal firmly. Repeat with remaining wrappers and filling.

4. Heat the oil for deep-frying in a wok until almost smoking, then reduce the heat slightly to medium and deep-fry the rolls, in batches if necessary, until golden brown, 3 to 4 minutes. Remove the rolls from the oil with a slotted spoon and drain on absorbent paper towels. Serve immediately with the chili sauce.

# Chili Sauce

YIELD: *4 fl oz / 120 mL*

2 oz / 57 g sugar

2 fl oz / 30 mL rice vinegar

1 fl oz / 30 mL water

2 Thai red bird chiles, finely chopped

1. Heat the sugar, vinegar, and water in a small saucepan over medium low heat, stirring until the sugar dissolves.

2. Bring the mixture to a boil and boil rapidly until a light syrup forms, about 5 to 8 minutes.

3. Remove from the heat and stir in the chopped red chiles. Allow the sauce to cool to room temperature before serving. Do not strain.

# Japanese Cucumber with Sea Urchin Mousse and Beluga Caviar

YIELD: *32 servings*

2 to 4 Japanese cucumbers, about ½ in / 1 cm in diameter and 8 to 10 in / 20 to 30 cm in length

10 to 12 oz / 284 to 340 g sea urchin roe

8 fl oz / 240 mL heavy cream

4 tsp / 20 mL powdered gelatin

5⅓ fl oz / 160 mL fish or vegetable velouté

Salt, as needed

White pepper, as needed

4 tsp / 20 mL Beluga caviar

1. Peel cucumbers and cut into rounds 1 in / 3 cm thick, making 16 total. Poach rounds in salted water for 20 seconds and shock in ice bath. Drain.

2. Scoop seeds out with a Parisienne scoop, making sure not to go further than halfway through the round. Let cups drain upside down until they will be used.

3. Pass sea urchin roe through a tamis to get a smooth paste; keep cool.

4. Whip heavy cream until soft peaks form, and refrigerate until needed.

5. Bloom gelatin in the cooled velouté; once gelatin is bloomed, reheat velouté in bain-marie in a water bath to dissolve the gelatin, stirring constantly, about 2 to 3 minutes. Allow the mixture to cool to room temperature.

6. When cooled, combine gelatin-velouté mixture with the sea urchin and fold in whipped cream. Adjust seasoning with salt and pepper.

7. Place mixture in piping bag with desired tip and pipe mixture into cucumber cups, decorate with caviar, and serve.

# Shot Glass with Tomato Gelée and Crayfish

YIELD: *32 servings*

4 lb / 1.81 kg vine-ripe tomatoes

12 to 16 crayfish

96 fl oz / 2.88 L court bouillon

1/2 oz / 14 g gelatin (ratio for gelatin is 1 oz of gelatin to 1 pint of liquid)

3 tbsp / 9 g chopped tarragon

4 fl oz / 120 mL sherry

Salt, as needed

White pepper, as needed

1. Cut tomatoes in half, place in mixing bowl, and squeeze by hand to work juices from tomatoes until they are the consistency of crushed tomatoes.

2. Place tomato mixture in china cap lined with cheesecloth and place a 3- to 4-lb / 1.36- to 1.81-kg weight on top of mixture to press the tomato juice out; leave to drain overnight; discard pulp.

3. Poach crayfish in court bouillon until opaque and bright red in color, 3 to 4 minutes. Cool completely in the refrigerator.

4. When cooled, peel the tails and reserve the head for decoration (optional).

5. After tomato water has drained overnight, add gelatin to bloom.

6. Warm up tomato water in bain-marie over a water bath to dissolve gelatin. Allow the mixture to cool to 65°F / 18°C.

7. Add chopped tarragon, sherry wine, and salt and pepper to tomato water mixture.

8. Pour 2 fl oz / 60 mL mixture into 2½-oz / 71-g shot glasses and place one crayfish tail in each glass; place in cooler and allow tomato gelatin to set, about 30 minutes to 1 hour.

9. Decorate with reserved crayfish head, if desired, and serve.

*Presentation idea* *Depending on the size of the shot glass, the crayfish head may or may not be used. A small dollop of crème fraîche and a wild dill sprig may be substituted as a garnish.*

# Spoon of Quail Eggs on Lobster Medallion with Champagne Emulsion

YIELD: *30 servings*

### COURT BOUILLON

1¼ yellow onion, cut into ½-in / 1-cm dice

1¼ celery stalk, cut into ½-in / 1-cm dice

1¼ leek, white parts only, cut into ½-in / 1-cm dice

1¼ carrot, cut into ½-in / 1-cm dice

20 to 25 parsley stems

2½ oranges, cut in half and juiced

5 bay leaves

2½ tsp / 5 g peppercorns

2 gal 64 fl oz / 9.6 L water

2½ lobsters, 1 lb 8 oz / 680 g each

### POACHING LIQUID FOR QUAIL EGGS

1¼ fl oz / 38 mL Champagne vinegar

¾ tsp / 2.25 g salt

1 gal 32 fl oz / 4.80 L water

15 quail eggs

### CHAMPAGNE EMULSION

6 fl oz / 180 mL Champagne vinegar

2½ shallots, minced

2½ tsp / 13 g mustard

2½ tbsp / 53 g honey

14 fl oz / 420 mL grapeseed oil

10 fl oz / 300 mL olive oil

2½ red peppers, cut into fine brunoise

2½ yellow peppers, cut into fine brunoise

2½ green peppers, cut into fine brunoise

30 chervil leaves for garnish

1. Prepare court bouillon by bringing all of the ingredients except the lobsters to a simmer for 15 minutes.

2. Reduce the heat and poach the lobsters just until the meat is opaque, 8 to 10 minutes. Remove the tail after 8 minutes. Refrigerate until cold.

3. Meanwhile prepare poaching liquid for quail eggs by bringing the ingredients to poaching temperature (160° to 185°F / 71° to 85°C). Poach eggs 2 to 3 minutes, and shock them in an ice bath.

4. Pat poached eggs dry and chill. When eggs are cold, peel and cut them in half.

5. Combine the Champagne vinegar, shallots, mustard, and honey; whisk together. Whisk in the oils and reserve at room temperature. Combine with peppers and toss to mix evenly.

6. Remove shell from lobster and cut tail into medallions ¼ in / 6 mm thick.

7. Place medallion in a 1-oz / 30-ml serving spoon and nappé with ½ tsp / 2.5 mL Champagne emulsion. Top with a quail egg half, and garnish with ½ tsp / 2.5 mL bell pepper confetti from the Champagne Emulsion and one chervil leaf.

# Spoon with Kumamoto Oysters, Apple Mint Gelée, and Wasabi Tobikko

YIELD: *30 servings*

| | |
|---|---|
| 1 lb 8 oz / 680 g Granny Smith apples | 9 to 12 mint leaves, finely minced |
| ⅜ tsp / 2 mL ascorbic acid, or as needed | Salt, as needed |
| 3 oz / 85 g gelatin | White pepper, as needed |
| 30 fresh Kumamoto oysters (or any other small fresh oyster) | 6 to 9 red radishes |
| 3 fl oz / 90 mL lemon juice | ¾ oz / 21 g wasabi tobikko |

1. Cut Granny Smith apples in quarters and place in juicer; add ascorbic acid to juice to prevent oxidation. This should yield approximately 16 fl oz / 480 mL apple juice.

2. Sprinkle gelatin and allow to bloom; meanwhile, shuck the oysters.

3. Warm up gelatin mixture in bain-marie over a water bath to dissolve gelatin, and then refrigerate until temperature is below 65°F / 18°C.

4. Add lemon juice, mint, and seasonings

5. Refrigerate the gelatin mixture until set; meanwhile, cut radishes into fine julienne.

6. When mixture is set, place oysters on individual spoons, top with apple gelée and radishes, and decorate with wasabi tobikko.

# Barquettes with Foie Gras Mousse and Rhubarb Compote

**YIELD:** *24 servings*

### RHUBARB COMPOTE

1 to 2 rhubarb stalks

2 oz / 57 g butter

4 oz / 113 g honey

8 fl oz / 240 mL port

4 fl oz / 120 mL grenadine

1 sachet of 5 to 6 peppercorn, 1 bay leaf, 2 cloves, and 1 cinnamon stick

### FOIE GRAS MOUSSE

1 lb / 454 g foie gras lobe, B grade, deveined

64 fl oz / 1.92 L duck fat, melted

1 sachet of 1 tsp / 2 g peppercorns, 3 to 4 thyme leaves, 2 bay leaves, 2 garlic cloves, and 1 star anise

4 fl oz / 120 mL heavy cream

2 fl oz / 60 mL chicken or vegetable velouté

2 tbsp / 18 g gelatin

½ oz / 14 g cognac

Salt, as needed

White pepper, as needed

24 barquettes, 1½ in / 4 cm long

1. Wash and peel rhubarb and cut pieces 2 in / 5 cm in length.

2. Sweat rhubarb in butter in a 64-fl oz / 1.92-L saucepot over medium low heat until the rhubarb is translucent, about 4 minutes.

3. Add honey, port, grenadine, and sachet.

4. Cook until rhubarb is fork-tender and liquid has reached a syrupy consistency, about 10 to 12 minutes.

5. Place foie gras lobe in melted duck fat and add sachet. Bring fat to 160°F / 71°C and poach until meat reaches 120°F / 749°C, about 35 minutes. Remove from heat and allow foie gras to cool in fat to room temperature.

6. Pass foie gras through a tamis to get a smooth paste; refrigerate until needed.

7. Whip heavy cream until soft peaks form, and refrigerate until needed.

8. Bloom gelatin in the cooled velouté; once gelatin is bloomed, reheat velouté in bain-marie in a water bath to dissolve the gelatin, stirring constantly, 2 to 3 minutes. Allow the mixture to cool to room temperature.

9. When cooled, combine gelatin-velouté mixture with the foie gras paste and fold in whipped cream, cognac, salt and pepper.

10. Place mixture in piping bag fitted with #1 star tip (or other desired tip) and fill barquettes with approximately ½ oz / 14 g foie gras mousse. Dot mousse with rhubarb compote to garnish.

11. Chill until firm; refrigerate up to 1 hour.

# Parmesan Crisps with Truffled Goat Cheese

YIELD: *30 servings*

24 fl oz / 720 mL Parmigiano-Reggiano from moist piece of cheese

3 oz / 85 g black truffles

½ oz / 14 g flat-leaf parsley, finely minced

1 lb 8 oz / 680 g goat cheese, softened

12 to 18 fl oz / 360 to 540 mL heavy cream

Salt, as needed

White pepper, as needed

1. Grate the Parmigiano-Reggiano and reserve until needed.

2. Place 2-in / 5-cm round ring cutters on a sheet pan lined with a Silpat.

3. Add about ¾ oz / 21 g grated cheese to each mold, or just enough to cover the bottom. Repeat with remaining cheese and molds.

4. Bake at 325°F / 163°C until golden brown, 8 to 10 minutes.

5. Remove from the oven and immediately mold crisps into small 2 fl oz / 60 mL cup shapes. You may need to perform this on the open oven door to allow for the heat to keep crisps pliable. Allow to cool to room temperature and set.

6. Cut the truffles into a fine brunoise. Reserve ¾ oz / 21 g truffles for garnish. Squeeze the parsley in cheesecloth to remove the chlorophyll.

7. Combine soft goat cheese and heavy cream; mix until creamy and of a soft consistency.

8. Add chopped truffles and parsley, and fold in lightly. Season with salt and pepper.

9. Place mixture in piping bag with desired tip and fill Parmigiano-Reggiano crisps with approximately ½ oz / 14 g filling. Garnish with chopped truffles.

# Pollo Al Chilindron—Chicken with Peppers (Navarra)

YIELD: *30 servings*

3 lb 6 oz / 1.53 kg boneless, skinless chicken thighs

Salt, as needed

6 fl oz / 180 mL olive oil

2¾ fl oz / 80 mL brandy

1 lb 8 oz / 680 g Spanish onion, minced

3 green pepper, small diced

3 red pepper, small diced

3 oz / 85 g Serrano ham, small diced

12 garlic cloves

12 tomatoes, concassé (see page 607), cut into small dice

1 tbsp / 7 g pimenton

12 fl oz / 360 mL chicken stock

1 tbsp / 3 g parsley, chopped

1. Cut the chicken into 1-in / 3-cm cubes. Season the chicken with salt.

2. Sauté the chicken in the olive oil until the outside is just cooked; add the brandy and flambé it. Remove the chicken and reserve until needed.

3. Add the onions, peppers, and ham to the same pan. Cook until browned, then add the garlic and cook for 2 more minutes.

4. Stir in the tomatoes and pimenton; add the chicken stock and the reserved chicken.

5. Stew for about 15 minutes at low heat. Add the parsley and adjust seasoning if needed.

# Tortilla d'España

YIELD: *2 omelets (8 in / 20 cm; 16 servings each)*

1 lb / 454 g eggplant, peeled, cut into slices ⅓ in / 8 mm thick

Salt, as needed

6 oz / 170 g Spanish onions, cut into ⅓-in / 8-mm dice

3 fl oz / 90 mL extra-virgin olive oil

4 oz / 113 g red pepper, roasted, peeled, cut into ⅓-in / 8-mm dice

6 oz / 170 g zucchini, cut into ⅓-in / 8-mm dice

6 oz / 170 g tomato concassé (see page 607)

8 oz / 227 g Serrano ham, julienned

10 eggs, beaten

Ground black pepper, as needed

1. Spread the eggplant over some absorbent paper towels and sprinkle lightly with salt. Let sit for 30 minutes or until you see moisture loss on the paper towels and then pat dry.

2. Sauté the onions in the olive oil in a large sauté pan over medium-low heat until tender, about 7 to 8 minutes. Add the eggplant, red pepper, and zucchini and cook until tender, about 8 to 10 minutes; add the tomato and cook until sauce has thickened, about 5 to 7 minutes; add the ham and warm through, about 1 minute. Adjust seasoning.

3. In an 8-in / 20-cm nonstick omelet pan, heat some of the reserved extra-virgin olive oil over medium low and add half of the eggplant mixture in an even layer. Gently ladle in half of the eggs, making sure they are spread evenly on top. Cook until the bottom is lightly caramelized, and three-fourths of the egg body is stiff, about 5 to 6 minutes. Flip it over in the pan and finish cooking, about 2 to 3 minutes. Repeat with remaining ingredients.

4. Slide the omelet out of the pan and cut each omelet into 16 wedges for hors d'oeuvre.

# Mejillones al Estilo de Laredo/Mussels with Olives (Cantabria)

YIELD: *32 servings*

| | |
|---|---|
| 64 mussels | 2 garlic cloves, minced |
| 8 oz / 227 g dry white wine | 2 fl oz / 60 g olive oil |
| 2 Spanish onions, sliced | 12 tomatoes, concasséd and cut into small dice |
| 2 bay leaves | |
| Salt, as needed | 4 oz / 113 g black olives, pitted and chopped |
| 4 shallots, minced | 8 anchovy fillets, chopped |

1. Scrub the mussels under running water, removing the beards.

2. In a pot combine the wine, onions, bay leaves, and salt; bring to a boil.

3. Add the mussels to the liquid; cover and steam until they open.

4. Remove the mussels from the shell and hold on the side. Reserve the cooking liquid and half the shells.

5. Sauté the shallots and garlic in the olive oil until translucent.

6. Add the tomatoes, the olives, and the anchovy fillets.

7. Add the mussel liquid and reduce by half.

8. Return the mussels to the sauce and adjust seasoning.

9. Serve inside the shells. Place one mussel inside each shell and spoon ½ to 1 tsp / 2.5 to 5 mL of the sauce over the mussel.

# Gambas al Ajillo (Shrimp with Garlic)

YIELD: *30 servings (2 shrimp each)*

15 fl oz / 450 mL extra-virgin olive oil

Red pepper flakes, as needed

30 garlic cloves, sliced very thin

2 lb 8 oz / 1.13 kg shrimp (31/35 count), peeled and deveined (60 shrimp)

Salt, as needed

30 fl oz / 900 mL white wine or lemon juice

16 fl oz / 480 mL roughly chopped flat-leaf parsley

1. In a sauté pan, heat the olive oil over medium-high heat.

2. Add the pepper flakes, garlic, and shrimp. Adjust seasoning with salt.

3. Add the white wine and reduce by three-fourths, shaking the pan to emulsify the sauce.

4. Finish the sauce with chopped parsley.

TAPAS, CLOCKWISE FROM UPPER RIGHT: *Mussels with Olives (Mejillones al Estilo de Laredo) (page 507), Pork Pepper Pie (Empanada Gallega de Cerdo) (page 417), Manchego Cheese with Olive Oil, Chicken with Peppers (Pollo al Chilindron) (page 505), Shrimp with Garlic (Gambas al Ajillo), Potato Omelet (Tortilla d'España) (page 506), Chorizo Sausage and Serrano Ham (center)*

# Spiced Mixed Nuts

YIELD: *1 lb / 454 g*

| | |
|---|---|
| 1½ oz / 43 g butter | ½ tsp / 1 g chili powder |
| 1 tbsp / 15 mL Worcestershire sauce | ¼ tsp / 0.50 g ground cumin |
| 1 lb / 454 g unsalted raw whole mixed nuts | ⅛ tsp / 0.25 g cayenne |
| ½ tsp / 1 g celery seed | ½ tsp / 1.50 g salt |
| ½ tsp / 1 g garlic powder | |

1. Melt the butter over medium heat. Add the Worcestershire and bring to a simmer. Add the nuts and toss well to coat evenly.

2. Sprinkle the combined spices and salt over the nuts and toss well to coat evenly.

3. Place the nuts on a nonstick or well-greased sheet pan and bake in a 375°F / 191°C oven, stirring occasionally, for 10 to 12 minutes, or until evenly browned. Let cool completely before serving.

4. Store at room temperature in an airtight container for up to 2 weeks.

*Chef's note* If saltier nuts are desired, sprinkle with kosher salt while still warm.

# Chili-Roasted Peanuts with Dried Cherries

YIELD: *1 lb / 454 g*

| | |
|---|---|
| 1 oz / 28 g unsalted butter | 1 tbsp / 10 g salt |
| 1 lb / 454 g raw peanuts | ½ tsp / 1 g dried oregano |
| 1 tbsp / 6 g mild chili powder | ½ tsp / 1 g cayenne |
| 2 tsp / 4 g ground cumin | 8 oz / 227 g dried cherries (or raisins) |
| 2 tsp / 4 g ground white pepper | |

1. Melt the butter in a small saucepan.

2. Add the raw peanuts and toss to coat evenly with the melted butter.

3. Mix together the chli powder, cumin, white pepper, salt, oregano, and cayenne; reserve.

4. Spread peanuts in a single layer on a large sheet pan and lightly toast in a 300 to 325°F / 149 to 163°C oven for about 10 minutes, shaking pan occasionally.

5. Transfer the peanuts into a large bowl and coat with the dry ingredients. Mix in cherries until uniformly blended.

6. Cool completely, then cover and store at room temperature up to 2 weeks.

*Chili-Roasted Peanuts with Dried Cherries*

# Candied Pecans

YIELD: *1 lb / 454 g*

| | |
|---|---|
| 1 lb / 454 g whole pecans | 2 tsp / 4 g ground ginger |
| 2 egg whites beaten with 2 tbsp water | 2 tsp / 4 g ground cardamom |
| 4½ oz / 128 g superfine sugar | 1½ tsp / 3 g ground allspice |
| 2 tsp / 6 g salt | 1 tsp / 2 g ground coriander |
| 1 tbsp / 6 g ground cinnamon | ⅛ tsp / ¼ g cayenne |

1. Preheat the oven to 250°F / 121°C.

2. Stir the nuts into the beaten egg white mixture until completely coated. Drain well in a colander.

3. Combine the sugar, salt, and spices and toss the nuts in this mixture until evenly coated.

4. Turn onto a sheet pan and spread in a single layer. Bake for about 10 minutes, then lower the oven temperature to 225°F /107°C and bake, stirring occasionally, for another 10 minutes, or until the nuts are dark golden brown.

5. Let cool completely before serving.

6. Store in an airtight container for up to 2 weeks.

*Chef's note*  *These nuts are used to garnish the Smoked Duck Tart (page 423).*

# Spicy Curried Cashews

**YIELD:** *1 lb / 454 g*

| | |
|---|---|
| 1 lb / 454 g whole raw cashews | ¼ tsp / 0.50 g garlic powder |
| 1 oz / 28 g unsalted butter, melted | ¼ tsp / 0.50 g onion powder |
| ½ tsp / 1.50 g salt | ⅛ tsp / 0.25 g cayenne |
| 1 tbsp / 6 g curry powder | |

1. Preheat the oven to 350°F / 175°C.

2. Toss the cashews and melted butter together until evenly coated.

3. Combine the salt and spices; reserve.

4. Place the cashews on a sheet pan and bake until golden brown.

5. Remove the cashews from the oven and toss with the combined spices while still warm. Allow to cool before serving.

6. Store in an airtight container for up to 10 days.


# Toasted Almonds

**YIELD:** *1 lb / 454 g*

| | |
|---|---|
| 1 lb / 454 g almonds, whole | Salt, as needed |
| 1 fl oz / 30 mL pure olive oil | 2 tsp / 10 mL pimenton |

1. Bake the almonds in a 300°F / 149°C oven until crispy and dried out, about 8 to 10 minutes. Add the remaining ingredients and toss to coat evenly. Let cool before serving.

2. Cover and store up to 2 weeks.

# 10

*objectives*

- Identify condiments such as mustard, ketchup, chutney, relish, and compote

- Understand the process of making flavored oils and vinegars

- Explain the role of pickles

- Describe the process of making chips and crisps

# Condiments, crackers, and pickles

Condiments, crackers, and pickles are those little extras that can elevate a dish from the ordinary to the sublime. Although most of these foods are available commercially, they are not difficult to produce, and are always more interesting when made by hand because you can customize the flavor profile of the condiment and come up with inventive ways to feature seasonal ingredients.

# Condiments

**Condiments** are assertive sauce-like creations, typically served on the side and added at the diner's discretion (see Fig 10-1). However, condiments can also be found as spreads or dips, adding a little extra flavor to sandwiches, dressings, and salads.

FIG 10-1 CONDIMENT VARIETIES, CLOCKWISE FROM TOP: *Red Onion Confiture (page 531), Beer Mustard with Caraway Seeds (page 529), Rhubarb Compote (pages 503, 532), Pickles (page 537), Tomato Ketchup (page 525), Papaya Chutney (page 528)*

# Mustard

Plain and flavored **mustards** have a wonderful aroma and a complex flavor that pairs beautifully with meats, cheeses, and poultry; mustard can even be served as a dip. It is frequently added to vinaigrettes and other dressings to act as an emulsifier or used to glaze meats as they roast. Special mustards from around the world have their own unique qualities: some are very hot, while others are mild; some are very smooth, and others are grainy. American-style mustard is made from white mustard seeds and gets its distinctive yellow color from turmeric. European mustards are made from brown mustard seeds and can be grainy or smooth.

# Ketchup

Lancelot Sturgeon, a British author, wrote that **ketchup** was invented by the French in the seventeenth century. However, early French cookbooks claim that the British formulated the condiment. Still others trace its origins to East Asia. Early English recipes for ketchup called for such ingredients as kidney beans, mushrooms, anchovies, liver, and walnuts. Now predominantly tomato-based, the product, which is also sometimes called "catsup" or even "catchup," is defined by its slightly sweet, vinegary flavor and thick consistency. Ketchup can be used as a dipping sauce or as extra flavor on sandwiches or eggs.

# Chutney

**Chutneys** are sweet-and-sour condiments, often fruit-based (though vegetable-based versions exist as well) and generally highly spiced, and are favored in Indian cuisines. Chutneys may be cooked, similar to a pickle or relish, or they may be raw, making them similar to other cold raw sauces such as salsa.

Mango chutney is probably most familiar worldwide, but tomatoes, eggplant, melons, apples, and pineapples are also commonly used to prepare chutneys. The use of chutneys has expanded beyond a spoonful or two on top of an entrée. They are very popular as accompaniments for cheese courses, spreads on sandwiches, and as dips. Chutneys offer an easy way to add intriguing spices and flavor to any dish.

# Relish

A **relish** may be as simple as a mound of sliced cucumbers or radishes, or as complex as a curried onion relish, cooked in a pickle or brine, highly seasoned and garnished with dried fruits. Relishes are served cold to act as a foil to hot or spicy foods, or to liven up dishes that need some extra kick.

# Compote

**Compotes** are often made by cooking fruits in syrup. For the garde manger, savory compotes can be used to accompany galantines or pâtés in much the same way that a chutney is used.

# Flavored oils and vinegars

Good-quality oils and vinegars can be infused with spices, **aromatics,** herbs, and fruits or vegetables to create products with many applications. They work well as condiments, added in a drizzle or as droplets to lend a bit of intense flavor and color to a plated dish. They also are excellent to use as a dressing for vegetables, pastas, grains, or fruits. And, of course, they are well suited to use as part of vinaigrettes and other dressings for a special effect.

To infuse oils and vinegars, use one of the following methods:

## *Method 1: a warm infusion*

Heat the oil or vinegar very gently over low heat with flavoring ingredients such as citrus zest or spices, just until the aroma is apparent. Let the oil or vinegar steep off of the heat with the flavoring ingredients until cool, then pour into storage bottles or containers. You may opt to strain the vinegar or oil for a clearer final product, or leave the flavoring ingredients in for a more intense flavor. It is recommended to use damp cheesecloth when straining flavored vinegars.

FIG 10-2A  *Flavoring agents, such as the basil used here, can also be puréed along with oil and vinegar, then strained away to produce infused oil and vinegar.*

FIG 10-2B  *Oils and vinegars can be infused or steeped with any number of flavors, such as shallots and tarragon (left) or lemon and thyme (right).*

## Method 2: steeping

Place the herbs or other aromatics in a glass or plastic bottle. Heat the oil or vinegar briefly, just until warm. Pour the warm oil or vinegar over the aromatics, and let the vinegar rest until the desired flavor is achieved. You may wish to add fresh aromatics after the oil or vinegar has steeped for several days to give an even more intense flavor.

## Method 3: purées

**Purée** raw, blanched, or fully cooked vegetables, herbs, or fruits and bring the purée to a simmer, reducing if necessary to concentrate the flavors. Add the oil or vinegar and transfer to a storage container. You may leave the oil or vinegar as is, and use it as you would a purée. Or you may strain it to remove the fiber and pulp (see Fig 10-2a).

## Method 4: cold infusion

Combine room-temperature oil or vinegars with ground spices and transfer to a storage container (see Fig 10-2b). Let the mixture settle until the vinegar or oil is clear and the spices have settled in the bottom of the container. Carefully decant the vinegar or oil once the desired flavor is reached.

Note: When you introduce fresh or raw ingredients to an oil or vinegar, you run the risk of food-borne illness if the finished products are not carefully stored. Although commercially prepared versions of flavored oils and vinegars are shelf-stable, you should keep yours refrigerated, especially if you have used raw garlic or shallots. Use them within a few days to be sure that they will have the best flavor and color.

# Pickles

**Pickles** encompass any food that has been brined. They can be made from a variety of ingredients such as vegetables, fruit, or eggs. The **brine** often contains **vinegar,** though a **salt brine** can also be used to make special pickles. Pickles may be extremely tart, such as cornichons, or sweet, like the Sweet Pickle Chips on page 534.

Pickles are used as a traditional condiment in India and Southeast Asia, but these pickles are different from typical European pickles because they use oil as the pickling agent instead of vinegar. Chopped fruits, vegetables, or aromatics are added to oil and spices, then left to marinate for up to three weeks, after which they become similar in texture to a relish. Each region has a distinct blend of spices and features seasonal, local fruits, vegetables, and aromatics in its pickles. It is very easy to produce these pickles and they can add an international flair to many dishes.

# Chips and crisps

Crackers and other breads may be eaten alone or as a support item that adds flavor and a textural counterpoint. They are served to accompany dips and spreads, or with a salad or appetizer to add a bit of crunch to the plate.

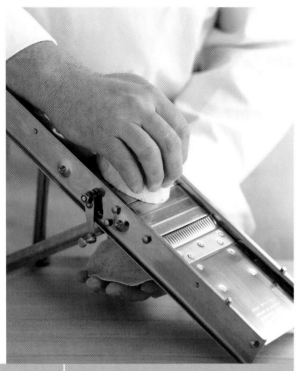

*Thinly slice the desired fruits or vegetables on a mandoline or slicer.*

*Frying the slices in oil produces chips.*

*The slices can be baked in an oven to produce a crisp.*

*Store prepared chips and crisps in even layers, separating each layer with parchment paper.*

# Fried and baked chips

We are all familiar with potato chips, which are made by slicing potatoes very thin and frying them in oil until crisp. Other vegetables can also be made into chips: sweet potatoes, beets, and artichokes are all excellent choices (see Figs 10-3a and 10-3b).

**Baked chips** or crisps are also wonderful additions to salads and composed appetizers, or on their own as "snack food." Pears, apples, bananas, and other fruits can be sliced thin and then baked until they are dry and crisp (see Fig 10-3c). If they are sliced a little thicker and baked at a lower temperature, they take on an appealing chewy texture.

# Crackers

**Crackers** can be produced in a number of ways. **Icebox-style crackers** are made in much the same way as cookies. A savory dough is prepared, rolled into a log, chilled, then sliced and baked. Cheese and nuts are often used to season and flavor these crackers. Cracker dough can also be rolled out by hand or using a pasta machine for a thin, uniform cracker. These crackers can have garnish ingredients folded into the dough, or you can brush the dough with a little egg wash and sprinkle sesame seeds, poppy seeds, coarse sea salt, spice blends, or any number of other toppings. Be sure that the toppings will not burn when the crackers are baked.

Still other crackers are made from a **batter** that is baked. These delicate crackers can be shaped before baking by spreading them on a greased sheet pan or silicone baking pad. They can be shaped when they are still warm from the oven by draping them over rolling pins or pressing them into cups or other molds.

# Heywood's Mustard

YIELD: *32 fl oz / 960 mL*

4½ oz / 128 g dry mustard

1 oz / 28 g sugar

2 tsp / 6 g salt

12 oz / 340 g eggs

16 fl oz / 480 mL malt vinegar

¼ tsp / 1.25 mL Tabasco sauce

3 oz / 85 g honey

1. Combine the mustard, sugar, and salt.

2. Add the eggs and mix until smooth.

3. Whisk in the vinegar, Tabasco, and honey. Cover and refrigerate for 1 to 2 hours.

4. Beat in a double boiler over hot water until thick and creamy. Cover and refrigerate until cold.

5. Transfer to a clean storage container. Cover and refrigerate for up to 2 weeks.


# Southwestern Spicy Green Chile Mustard

YIELD: *32 fl oz / 960 mL*

3 oz / 85 g dry mustard

6 fl oz / 180 mL dark Mexican beer

6 fl oz / 180 mL sherry wine vinegar

12 egg yolks

1 tbsp / 15 mL soy sauce

6 oz / 170 g green chiles, diced

1 jalapeño, minced

¾ oz / 21 g cumin seeds, toasted whole

2 tbsp / 6 g dry Mexican oregano

3 oz / 85 g honey

1½ tbsp / 13.5 g salt

1. Combine the mustard, beer, vinegar, egg yolks, and soy sauce in a stainless-steel bowl.

2. Cover and refrigerate for 1 hour.

3. Beat in a double boiler over hot water until thick and creamy.

4. Add the green chiles, jalapeño, cumin, oregano, honey, and salt. Mix well.

5. Transfer to a clean storage container. Cover and refrigerate for up to 2 weeks.

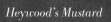
*Heywood's Mustard*

# Dried Cranberry Mustard

YIELD: *32 fl oz / 960 mL*

| | |
|---|---|
| 3 oz / 85 g dry mustard | ½ tsp / 2.5 g salt |
| 6 eggs | 1 tbsp / 15 mL Worcestershire sauce |
| 8 fl oz / 240 mL cranberry juice | 2 oz / 57 g packed brown sugar |
| 3 fl oz / 90 mL white vinegar | 2½ oz / 71 g chopped dried cranberries |

1. Combine mustard, eggs, cranberry juice, vinegar, salt, Worcestershire sauce, and brown sugar in a stainless-steel bowl.

2. Cook over boiling water, stirring constantly until thick and smooth.

3. Add cranberries and mix well. Cover and refrigerate for at least 48 hours before using.

4. Cover and refrigerate for up to 2 weeks.


# Beer Mustard with Caraway Seeds

YIELD: *32 fl oz / 960 mL*

| | |
|---|---|
| 12 fl oz / 360 mL dark beer | 1 tsp / 5 mL Worcestershire sauce |
| 6 eggs | 2 oz / 57 g packed brown sugar |
| 4½ oz / 128 g dry mustard | 2 fl oz / 60 mL white vinegar |
| 2 tsp / 6 g salt | ½ oz / 14 g caraway seeds, toasted |

1. Combine beer, eggs, mustard, salt, Worcestershire sauce, brown sugar, and vinegar and mix well.

2. Let mixture rest at room temperature for 1 hour.

3. Cook in a double boiler over boiling water until thick and smooth.

4. Add the caraway seeds and mix well.

5. Transfer to a clean storage container. Cover and refrigerate for up to 2 weeks.

# Swedish Mustard Sauce

YIELD: *32 fl oz / 960 mL*

| | |
|---|---|
| 5⅓ fl oz / 160 g prepared mustard | 1 tsp / 3 g salt |
| 2¼ oz / 64 g minced fresh horseradish | 2 tsp / 10 mL Worcestershire sauce |
| 16 fl oz / 480 mL Basic Mayonnaise (page 36) | 8 fl oz / 240 mL heavy cream, whipped |

1. Purée mustard, horseradish, mayonnaise, salt, and Worcestershire sauce.

2. Fold in the cream; cover and refrigerate until cold.

3. Transfer to a clean storage container. Cover and refrigerate for up to 12 hours.


# Tomato Ketchup

YIELD: *32 fl oz / 960 mL*

| | |
|---|---|
| 3½ oz / 99 g sugar | 2 roasted red peppers, chopped |
| 3 oz / 85 g minced onion | 8 fl oz / 240 mL red wine vinegar |
| 1 tbsp / 9 g minced garlic | 4 fl oz / 120 mL balsamic vinegar |
| 96 fl oz / 2.88 L crushed tomatoes | Cayenne, as needed |

1. Cook the sugar over moderate heat until it turns an amber color.

2. Add the onion and garlic.

3. Add the tomatoes and roasted peppers; cook 5 to 10 minutes over moderate heat.

4. Add the vinegars and reduce until thickened, about 20 minutes.

5. Season with cayenne as needed (the flavor should be mild).

6. Strain through a fine sieve.

7. Transfer to a clean storage container. Cover and refrigerate for up to 2 weeks.

# Yellow Pepper Ketchup

YIELD: *32 fl oz / 960 mL*

2 lb / 907 g yellow peppers, seeded and coarsely chopped (about 8)

3 oz / 85 g jalapeños, seeded and chopped (about 4)

12 oz / 340 g onions, coarsely chopped (about 2)

2 tbsp / 18 g chopped garlic

Vegetable oil, as needed

6 fl oz / 180 mL red wine vinegar

5¼ oz / 149 g sugar

Salt, as needed

Ground white pepper, as needed

1. Sauté the peppers, jalapeños, onions, and garlic in oil until tender but not browned, about 12 minutes.

2. Add the vinegar and sugar; simmer 30 to 45 minutes.

3. Purée until smooth.

4. Adjust seasoning with salt and pepper.

5. Cool and transfer to a clean storage container. Cover and refrigerate for up to 2 weeks.


# Spicy Mango Chutney

YIELD: *32 fl oz / 960 mL*

3 mangoes, peeled and chopped

3½ oz / 99 g raisins

1 jalapeño, minced

4 garlic cloves, minced

1 tbsp / 9 g minced ginger

7¾ oz / 220 g packed dark brown sugar

8 fl oz / 240 mL white wine vinegar

½ tsp / 1.50 g salt

1 tsp / 2 g turmeric

1. Combine the mangoes, raisins, jalapeño, garlic, ginger, and sugar. Cover and refrigerate for 24 hours.

2. Add the vinegar; bring to a boil and simmer 15 minutes.

3. Add the salt; simmer 10 minutes.

4. Add the turmeric; simmer 5 minutes.

5. Cool and transfer to a clean storage container. Cover and refrigerate for up to 2 weeks.

# Apricot-Cherry Chutney

YIELD: *32 fl oz / 960 mL*

| | |
|---|---|
| 4 oz / 113 g onion, sliced thin | 2 fl oz / 60 mL lemon juice |
| 2 tbsp / 18 g minced ginger | ½ tsp / 1 g ground coriander |
| 1 tbsp / 15 mL peanut oil | ¼ tsp / 0.50 g ground cardamom |
| 4 fl oz / 120 mL cider vinegar | ½ tsp / 1 g curry powder |
| 3 oz / 85 g honey | ¼ tsp / 0.50 g red pepper flakes |
| 8 fl oz / 240 mL orange juice | 8 oz / 227 g dried apricots, halved |
| 16 fl oz / 480 mL water | 8 oz / 227 g dried cherries |

1. Sauté the onion and ginger in the peanut oil until limp, but not browned.

2. Add the remaining ingredients and simmer for 20 minutes. Add more water if the chutney is too thick.

3. Cool and transfer to a clean storage container. Cover and refrigerate for up to 2 weeks.

# Beet Chutney

YIELD: *32 fl oz / 960 mL*

| | |
|---|---|
| 6 beets | 1 fl oz / 30 mL red wine vinegar |
| Water, as needed | 1 tbsp / 15 mL lime juice |
| 1 tsp / 3 g kosher salt | ¼ tsp / 0.50 g cayenne |
| 1 tbsp / 9 g finely chopped ginger | 1 tsp / 6 g finely chopped jalapeño |
| 2 fl oz / 60 mL vegetable oil | 1 tbsp / 3 g finely chopped cilantro |
| 2 tsp / 6 g salt | |

1. Preheat the oven to 375°F / 191°C.

2. Wash the beets well. Leave 1 in / 3 cm stem attached to the beets. Put the beets in a 2-in / 5-cm hotel pan, in a single layer, and add water just to cover the bottom of the pan. Season with kosher salt. Cover the pan with aluminum foil and roast the beets until fork-tender, about 1 hour depending on size. Shake the pan every 20 minutes so the beets do not stick or burn.

3. When the beets are done but still warm, remove the skin. Cut the beets into small dice and combine with remaining ingredients. (Note: If preferred, add the peppers and cilantro on the day of service.) This chutney should be very spicy.

4. Cool and transfer to a clean storage container. Cover and refrigerate for up to 2 weeks.

# Apple Chutney

YIELD: *3 lb / 1.36 kg*

6 oz / 170 g light brown sugar

5 oz / 142 g onion, fine dice

4 oz / 113 g golden raisins

2 oz / 57 g walnuts, toasted and chopped

2 oz / 57 g cider vinegar

1 fl oz / 30 mL lemon juice

½ oz / 14 g ginger, grated

½ oz / 14 g chile, chopped

2 tsp / 6 g lemon zest, minced or finely grated

1 tsp / 3 g garlic, minced to a paste

½ tsp / 1 g ground mace

½ tsp / 1 g ground cloves

2 lb 4 oz / 1.02 kg Granny Smith apples, peeled, cored, cut into medium dice

1. Combine brown sugar, onion, raisins, walnuts, cider vinegar, lemon juice, ginger, chile, zest, garlic, mace, and cloves in a saucepot and simmer, covered, over low heat for 10 minutes.

2. Add the apples and simmer until the apples are very tender and the juices are reduced and slightly thickened, 10 to 15 minutes. Cool, then cover and refrigerate until service.

# Papaya Chutney

YIELD: *32 fl oz / 960 mL*

4 fl oz / 120 mL vegetable oil

5 oz / 142 g onion, peeled, small dice

8 oz / 227 g red pepper, small dice

6 oz / 170 g green pepper, small dice

4 garlic cloves, minced

2 tsp / 4 g ground allspice

2 tsp / 4 g curry powder

2 tsp / 4 g ground cumin

1 lb / 454 g papaya, ripe, peeled, seeded, small dice

4 fl oz / 120 mL white vinegar

8 fl oz / 240 mL pineapple juice

1½ oz / 43 g molasses

2 fl oz / 60 mL lemon juice

1 tsp / 3 g salt

½ tsp / 1 g ground black pepper

1. In a large sauté pan, heat the vegetable oil over medium heat until hot but not smoking. Add the onions and sauté 5 to 7 minutes, stirring frequently, until onions have become lightly caramelized.

2. Add the red and green peppers and cook an additional 2 minutes, or until the peppers just begin to soften, stirring frequently. Add the garlic and spices and cook an additional 2 minutes, stirring constantly. The mixture will be quite dry at this point.

3. Add the papaya, vinegar, pineapple juice, and molasses, stir well, and allow to come to a boil. Reduce the heat to low and cook until the mixture coats the back of a spoon.

4. Add the lemon juice, salt, and pepper as needed. Cool, then cover and refrigerate.

# Cranberry Relish

YIELD: *32 fl oz / 960 mL*

| | |
|---|---|
| 12 oz / 340 g cranberries | 3 oz / 85 mL sugar |
| 3 fl oz / 90 mL orange juice | 2 oranges, zest and suprêmes |
| 3 fl oz / 90 mL triple sec (optional) | |

1. Combine cranberries, orange juice, triple sec, sugar, and orange zest in a saucepot and stir to combine.

2. Cover and let simmer 15 to 20 minutes, stirring occasionally.

3. Cook until all the berries have burst and liquid starts to thicken. Remove from heat and add the orange segments. Adjust sweetness with sugar.

4. Transfer to a clean storage container. Cover and refrigerate for up to 2 weeks.

# Dried Apricot Relish

YIELD: *32 fl oz / 960 mL*

| | |
|---|---|
| 1 lb / 454 g medium-dice dried apricots | 6 oz / 170 g honey |
| ½ tsp / 1.50 g minced garlic | 2 tbsp / 30 mL soy sauce |
| 2 drops Tabasco sauce | 16 fl oz / 480 mL ginger ale |
| 3 tbsp / 45 mL lemon juice | 4 oz / 113 g sliced almonds, toasted |
| ¼ oz / 7 g lemon zest | |

1. Combine apricots, garlic, Tabasco, lemon juice and zest, honey, soy sauce, and ginger ale in a saucepot; simmer for 20 minutes. Cool.

2. Stir in the almonds.

3. Cool and transfer to a clean storage container. Cover and refrigerate for up to 2 weeks.

*Curried Onion Relish*

# Curried Onion Relish

YIELD: *32 fl oz / 960 mL*

| | |
|---|---|
| 2 lb / 907 g onions, cut into ¼-in / 6-mm dice | 1 tsp / 3 g salt |
| 2 garlic cloves, minced | ¾ oz / 21 g pickling spice, tied into a sachet |
| 16 fl oz / 480 mL white vinegar | 2 tbsp / 12 g curry powder |
| 14 oz / 396 g sugar | |

1. Combine all ingredients; mix well.

2. Simmer, covered, in a small nonreactive saucepan until tender and mostly dry. Stir often, being careful not to scorch. Refrigerate until cold.

3. Transfer to a clean storage container. Cover and refrigerate for up to 2 weeks.

# Red Onion Confiture

YIELD: *32 fl oz / 960 mL*

| | |
|---|---|
| 1 fl oz / 30 mL vegetable oil | 6 fl oz / 180 mL red wine |
| 1 lb 8 oz / 680 g red onion, thinly sliced | Salt, as needed |
| 6 oz / 170 g honey (see Chef's Note) | Ground white pepper, as needed |
| 4 fl oz / 120 mL red wine vinegar | |

1. Heat the oil in a sauté pan over high heat. Sweat the onions.

2. Stir in the honey; cook the mixture until the onions are lightly caramelized.

3. Add the vinegar and wine; reduce until the liquid is almost completely cooked away.

4. Adjust seasoning with salt and pepper.

5. Cool and transfer to a clean storage container. Cover and refrigerate for up to 2 weeks.

*Chef's note* *Grenadine can be substituted for the honey for sweetness; it will enhance the color as well.*

# Rhubarb Compote

YIELD: *32 fl oz / 960 mL*

| | |
|---|---|
| 2 lb / 907 g rhubarb, trimmed and diced | 2 oz / 57 g dried currants (Zante) |
| 8 oz / 227 g sugar | ½ oz / 14 g finely minced garlic |
| 8 fl oz / 240 mL water | ¾ oz / 21 g finely minced ginger |
| 8 fl oz / 240 mL red wine vinegar | ½ oz / 14 g finely grated lemon zest |

1. Combine the rhubarb, sugar, water, vinegar, currants, garlic, ginger, and lemon zest. Bring to a boil, then reduce the heat and simmer until the compote thickens and has a good flavor, about 20 minutes. Skim the surface as necessary while simmering.

2. Transfer the compote to a clean container and cool completely before storing. The compote may be covered and refrigerated for up to 3 weeks.

# Roasted Red Pepper Compote

YIELD: *32 fl oz / 960 mL*

| | |
|---|---|
| 4 red peppers | Salt, as needed |
| 8 oz / 227 g red onion, minced | Ground black pepper, as needed |
| 3 fl oz / 90 mL pure olive oil | 2 fl oz / 60 mL aged balsamic vinegar |
| 3 oz / 85 g capers, finely chopped | ½ oz / 14 g dill, coarsely chopped |

1. Roast the peppers over a grill.

2. Place the peppers in a stainless steel bowl and cover with plastic wrap. Peel and seed the peppers and cut into ⅛-in / 3-mm dice.

3. Sweat the onions in the oil over low heat until tender, 6 to 8 minutes. Cool and add to the peppers.

4. Combine the peppers and onions with the remaining ingredients. Allow the mixture to sit for 20 minutes.

# Quince Compote

YIELD: *24 fl oz / 720 mL*

| | |
|---|---|
| 1 oz / 28 g whole butter | 8 fl oz / 240 mL white wine |
| 3 oz / 85 g shallots, minced | 16 fl oz / 480 mL apple cider |
| 1 lb 2 oz / 510 g quince, peeled, ¼-in / 6-mm dice | 2 oz / 57 g sugar |

1. Heat the butter until melted. Add the shallots and sauté over low heat until tender; add the quince and sauté for 2 minutes or until the outside starts to soften.

2. Add the remaining ingredients and cook over low heat until a thick consistency is achieved and the fruit is tender, about 20 minutes. Cool and transfer to a clean container. Cover and refrigerate.

*Variation*   *An equal amount of Granny Smith apples or Bartlett pears may be substituted for the quince.*


# Harissa

YIELD: *16 fl oz / 480 mL*

| | |
|---|---|
| 10 jalapeños, roasted, peeled, and seeded | ¾ oz / 21 g hot Hungarian paprika |
| 3 to 4 red peppers, roasted, peeled, and seeded | 1½ tsp / 3 g cayenne |
| 1 tbsp / 6 g whole cumin seeds, toasted and ground | 6 fl oz / 180 mL olive oil |
| 1 tbsp / 9 g garlic paste | 1½ fl oz / 45 mL lemon juice |
| | Salt, as needed |

1. Combine the jalapeños, peppers, cumin, garlic paste, paprika, and cayenne in a blender. Grind to a paste-like consistency.

2. Remove the paste to a bowl. Slowly whisk in the oil to create a smooth sauce. Add the lemon juice and salt as needed.

3. Transfer to a clean storage container. Cover and refrigerate for up to 2 weeks.

*Chef's note*   *This intense sauce can be used as a condiment or to flavor dips and spreads.*

# Wasabi Paste

YIELD: *2 fl oz*

⅔ oz / 19 g wasabi powder
Cool tap water, as needed

1. Place the wasabi powder in a small bowl. Add water as needed , stirring until a smooth paste is achieved. Spread the mixture across the bottom of the bowl; wrap tightly with plastic wrap.

2. Reserve for 10 minutes until the flavor is developed.

*Chef's notes*  *When mixing the wasabi powder with water, stand back, as the fumes that rise will burn your eyes. Warm water yields a more pungent paste.*
*Mix to a play-dough consistency for shaping as a garnish, or to the consistency of toothpaste for spreading.*

# Sweet Pickle Chips

YIELD: *2 lb / 907 g*

2 lb / 905 g cucumbers
8 oz / 227 g onions
12 fl oz / 360 mL cider vinegar
1½ tsp / 4.50 g salt
½ tsp / 1 g mustard seeds
14 oz / 397 g sugar

32 fl oz / 960 mL water
10 fl oz / 300 mL white vinegar
1 tbsp / 6 g celery seed
1½ tsp / 3 g whole allspice, crushed
1 tsp / 2 g turmeric

1. Wash the cucumbers and slice ¼ in / 6 mm thick. Slice the onions ¼ in / 6 mm thick.

2. Combine the cucumber and onions with cider vinegar, salt, mustard seeds, 1 tbsp / 15 g of the sugar, and the water in a saucepot.

3. Simmer for 10 minutes and drain. Discard liquid.

4. Bring the white vinegar, celery seed, allspice, turmeric, and remaining sugar to a boil.

5. Pour the vinegar mixture over the cucumbers and onions and refrigerate for 3 to 4 days before serving. Cover and refrigerate for up to 1 week.

# Half-Sour Pickles

YIELD: *3 lb / 1.36 kg*

4 lb / 1.81 kg pickling cucumbers, cut into spears

BRINE

½ oz / 14 g dill sprigs

3 garlic cloves, smashed

2 bay leaves

64 fl oz / 1.92 L water

6 oz / 170 g salt

8 fl oz / 240 mL white vinegar

1. Place the dill, garlic, and bay leaves in a noncorrosive container. Pack the spears on top.

2. Bring the water, salt, and vinegar to a boil, pour over cucumbers, and allow to cool.

3. Cover and refrigerate at least 3 days and up to 4 weeks.

*Chef's note*  *The pickles will change in texture from half-raw/half-cured to a fully cured pickle the longer they sit in the refrigerator.*


# Pickled Vegetables

YIELD: *2 lb / 907 g*

10 fl oz / 300 mL water

2¾ fl oz / 82 mL malt vinegar

¾ oz / 21 g salt

2¼ oz / 64 g sugar

1¼ fl oz / 28 g pickling spices

2 lb / 907 g assorted vegetables: baby golden, red, or Chioggia beets; pearl onions; okra; baby carrots; broccoli, trimmed and cut into small pieces

2 tsp / 6 g minced garlic

1 dill sprig

1. Bring the water, vinegar, salt, sugar, and pickling spices to a boil to make a brine.

2. Pack vegetables, garlic, and dill sprig in a noncorrosive container. Pour the brine over the vegetables. Let cool, then cover and refrigerate.

3. Allow to marinate for at least 24 hours before serving. Holding ability will depend on choice of vegetables.

# Pickled Grapes or Cherries

YIELD: *32 fl oz / 960 mL*

1 lb 12 oz / 794 g sugar

22 fl oz / 660 mL white wine vinegar

1½ cinnamon sticks

½ tsp / 1.50 g salt

2½ lb / 1.13 kg seedless grapes or sweet cherries (grapes removed from stems; cherries pitted)

1. Combine the sugar, vinegar, cinnamon sticks, and salt in a saucepot. Simmer for 5 minutes.

2. Pour mixture over the grapes or cherries, allow to cool, then cover and and refrigerate.

3. Serve immediately or cover and refrigerate overnight.


# Pickled Red Onions

YIELD: *32 fl oz / 960 mL*

12 fl oz / 360 g red wine vinegar

3 oz / 85 g sugar

6 fl oz / 180 mL water

1½ tsp / 4.50 g salt

½ tsp / 1 g cracked black pepper

1 lb 2 oz / 510 g red onions, sliced in thin rings

1. Combine the vinegar, sugar, water, salt, and pepper in a small non-reactive saucepan and bring to a boil. Remove from the heat, but keep hot.

2. Bring a large pot of water to a boil. Add enough salt to flavor the water. Add the red onions and boil for 1 minute, or until tender. Drain immediately.

3. Pour the hot vinegar mixture over the blanched onions. Cool the onions in the vinegar solution to room temperature, then refrigerate for 6 to 8 hours or overnight.

4. Transfer to a clean storage container. Cover and refrigerate for up to 2 weeks.

# Dill Pickles (Fresh-Pack Dill Pickles)

YIELD: *50 lb / 22.68 kg*

40 to 50 lb / 18.14 to 22.68 kg Kirby pickling cucumbers

2 lb 6 oz / 1.07 kg salt

6 gal / 23.04 L water

1 gal 16 fl oz / 4.32 L white vinegar

6¾ qt / 5.04 L water

6 oz / 170 g sugar

8 oz / 227 g mixed pickling spices

4 whole heads garlic

3 bunches dill (or 3½ oz / 99 g dill seed)

21 pepper pods, small

1. Wash cucumbers thoroughly; rinse and drain. Cover with brine made of 1 lb 9 oz / 709 g salt and 6 gal / 23.04 L cool water and allow to stand overnight.

2. Mix vinegar, 6¾ qt / 6.48 L water, remaining salt (13 oz / 369 g), sugar, and mixed pickling spices (tied in two cloth bags) and heat to a boil. Keep hot.

3. Pack half the cucumbers to within ½ in / 1 cm of the top of a 5-gal / 19.20-L tub, cover with hot pickling liquid, and top with one sachet. Fill a second tub with remaining cucumbers, picking liquid, and sachet.

4. Place lids on tubs and seal tightly.

5. Let stand for three weeks, remove sachets, and hold for use.


# Pickles

YIELD: *64 fl oz / 1.92 L*

2 lb 4 oz / 1.02 kg seedless cucumbers, sliced ⅛ in / 3 mm thick

2 white onions, thinly sliced

2 tbsp / 20 g salt

5¼ oz / 149 g sugar

8 fl oz / 237 mL white wine vinegar

1. Combine the cucumbers, onions, and salt. Cover and refrigerate for 3 hours, stirring often.

2. In a small saucepot, dissolve the sugar in the vinegar over medium heat. Allow mixture to cool.

3. Drain the cucumbers and onions and rinse.

4. Combine the vinegar mixture with the cucumbers and onions. Refrigerate until cold before serving.

*Acar Jawa (Javanese Pickled Vegetables)*

# Acar Jawa (Javanese Pickled Vegetables)

YIELD: *32 fl oz / 960 mL*

| | |
|---|---|
| 2 tsp / 10 mL minced dried shrimp (soak in hot water until soft, then mince and measure) | 6½ oz / 184 g carrots, roll cut into ¾-in / 2-cm pieces |
| 5 oz / 142 g red jalapeños, seeded and minced | 2½ oz / 71 g broccoli florets, cut into ¾-in / 2-cm pieces |
| 4 oz / 113 g shallots, minced | 6 oz / 170 g seedless cucumber, cut in half lengthwise and thinly sliced |
| ½ oz / 7 g garlic, minced | 4 fl oz / 120 mL vegetable oil |
| 4 oz / 113 g cauliflower florets, cut into ¾-in / 2-cm pieces | 8 oz / 227 g granulated sugar |
| 4½ oz / 128 g yellow squash, roll cut into ¾-in / 2-cm pieces | 8 fl oz / 240 mL white wine vinegar |
| | 4 fl oz / 120 mL coconut milk |
| 3¾ oz / 106 g green beans, cleaned, cut in half (if desired) | 1 tsp / 3 g salt, or as needed |

1. Using a mortar and pestle, pound together the dried shrimp, jalapeño chilies, shallots, and garlic.

2. Blanch each of the vegetables separately in the order given until crisp and tender, 2 to 5 minutes depending on the vegetable. Once cooked, shock each vegetable in an ice water bath. Once cooled, transfer each vegetable to a mixing bowl and reserve.

3. Heat the vegetable oil in a small skillet over medium heat. Add the chili paste and cook until fragrant, 6 to 8 minutes. Add the sugar, vinegar, coconut milk, and salt and simmer for 4 to 5 minutes.

4. Pour the sauce over the cooked vegetables and let them marinate for 30 minutes to 1 hour before serving. Serve at room temperature.

# Pickled Ginger

YIELD: *1 lb / 454 g*

| | |
|---|---|
| 1 lb / 454 g ginger, peeled, sliced very thin | 16 fl oz / 480 mL unseasoned rice vinegar |
| 2 tbsp / 20 g salt | 8 shiso leaf, chiffonade (optional) |
| 5¼ oz / 149 g sugar | |

1. Place ginger slices in a bowl with 1 tsp / 3 g of the salt for 10 minutes. Rinse in hot water; drain well.

2. Place sugar, vinegar, shiso and remaining salt in a small nonreactive pan and bring to a boil. Pour vinegar mixture over ginger and cool. Cover and refrigerate overnight before serving.

# Sweet and Sour Onions

YIELD: *16 oz / 170 g*

20 oz / 567 g pearl onions

1 tbsp / 15 mL olive oil

1 fl oz / 30 mL tomato paste, dissolved in 16 fl oz / 480 mL water

5¼ oz / 149 g golden raisins

5⅓ fl oz / 160 mL red wine vinegar

4 oz / 113 g sugar

2 rosemary sprigs (2 in / 5 cm long)

1 tsp / 3 g salt

½ tsp / 1 g ground black pepper

1. In a 32-fl oz / 960-mL saucepan, blanch onions in boiling water 3 minutes, then drain and rinse under cold water. Peel onions.

2. Heat the oil in a 9-in / 23-cm sauté pan over medium heat until hot but not smoking.

3. Add onions and cook until browned, about 4 minutes.

4. Add remaining ingredients, stirring until sugar is dissolved, then simmer, stirring occasionally, until onions are tender and most liquid is evaporated, 40 to 45 minutes.

5. Cool onions completely and discard rosemary sprig.

6. Cool mixture until it reaches room temperature, about 2 hours, then refrigerate.

7. Bring to room temperature before service.

8. Serve with bruschetta.

# Assorted Vegetable Chips

YIELD: *30 servings*

| | |
|---|---|
| 8 oz / 227 g taro root | 8 oz / 227 g beets |
| 8 oz / 227 g sweet potatoes | 8 oz / 227 g plantains |
| 8 oz / 227 g parsnips | Vegetable oil, as needed for frying |
| 8 oz / 227 g carrots | Salt, as needed |
| 8 oz / 227 g baking potatoes (such as Idaho or russet) | |

1. Peel all vegetables. Slice all of them very thin (1/16 in / 1.50 mm). Hold taro and potato slices separately in cold water; all other vegetables may be held dry. Keep the vegetables separate since they all require different cooking times.

2. Heat a fryer with clean oil to 275°F / 135°C. Fry each vegetable separately until crisp, drain on absorbent paper towels, and season with salt.

3. Serve immediately or store in an airtight container, as you would crackers, for later service. Serve within 24 hours for best quality.

*Variations*  *Artichoke Chips: Remove choke and some of the stem. Slice trimmed artichokes very thin (1/16 in / 1.50 mm) on a slicer and fry in 350°F / 177°C oil until crisp. Drain on absorbent paper towels and salt as needed.*

*Fennel Chips: Remove stem ends from fennel bulbs, trim root end, and halve or quarter (depending upon the size of the fennel bulb). Slice very thin (1/16 in / 1.50 mm) using a knife, electric slicer, or mandoline. Fry in 350°F / 177°C vegetable oil in a deep fryer or over medium heat until crisp. Drain on absorbent paper towels and salt as needed.*

*Garlic Chips: Use large garlic (elephant garlic) and slice peeled cloves very thin (1/16 in / 1.50 mm) using a knife or a garlic slicer. Fry in olive oil over moderate heat until lightly browned. Reserve the flavored oil for other use, if desired. Drain on absorbent paper towels.*

*Apple or Pear Chips: Remove the core from rinsed apples or pears, slice thin (1/16 in / 1.50 mm), and bake on a silicone baking pad or a lightly oiled sheet pan in a 375°F / 190°C oven until crisp, 20 to 30 minutes. Drain on absorbent paper towels.*

# Pepper Jack and Oregano Crackers

YIELD: *100 crackers*

8¼ oz / 234 g all-purpose flour

8 oz / 227 g shredded pepper Jack cheese

2 tsp / 2 g dried oregano, or 1 tbsp / 3 g fresh oregano

½ tsp / 1.50 g salt

½ tsp / 1 g ground black pepper

4 fl oz / 120 mL vegetable oil

4 to 5 fl oz / 120 to 150 mL water

SPICE MIXTURE

¼ tsp / 0.50 g cayenne

1 tsp / 4 g sugar

1 tsp / 3 g kosher salt

1. Combine the flour, cheese, oregano, salt, and pepper in a food processor or by hand. Add the oil and mix just to a coarse meal consistency. Add the water gradually until the dough forms a cohesive ball that pulls away from the sides of the bowl.

2. Divide the dough equally into pieces, wrap, and refrigerate. Combine the spice mixture ingredients; reserve.

3. Roll the dough through a pasta machine to ⅛ in / 3 mm thickness (see Fig 10-7a).

4. Cut the dough using a pizza cutter, knife, or shaped cutters into the desired cracker shapes and place on a doubled sheet pan. Sprinkle with the spice mixture (see Fig 10-7b).

5. Bake at 325°F / 165°C until lightly golden; turn and bake until medium golden brown, 15 to 20 minutes.

*Chef's note*  Chill the dough if it becomes soft during rolling or cutting.

FIG 10-7A  *Roll the chilled dough through a pasta machine to achieve the desired thickness.*

FIG 10-7B  *Sprinkle the cut-out dough with the spice mixture before baking the crackers.*

# Sesame Crackers

YIELD: *2 lb / 907 g*

4¾ oz / 135 g durum flour

4½ oz / 128 g all-purpose flour

¼ tsp / 0.75 g salt

1 tsp / 3 g baking powder

1½ fl oz / 45 mL extra-virgin olive oil

8 fl oz / 240 mL water

3 large egg whites

5 oz / 142 g sesame seeds

3 tbsp / 30 g kosher salt

1. Preheat oven to 350°F / 177°C.

2. Combine the flour, salt, and baking powder in the bowl of an electric mixer and mix on medium speed until the ingredients are fully combined.

3. Add the oil to the dry ingredients and mix until incorporated, about 1 to 2 minutes. Add the water and mix until a pliable ball forms, about 3 to 5 minutes.

4. Allow the dough to rest for one hour, covered, at room temperature.

5. Working with about one quarter of the dough at a time, roll out the dough on a pasta machine to 1⁄16 in / 1.50 mm. Be sure to dust the machine with flour periodically so that the dough doesn't stick.

6. Cut the dough into 2-in / 5-cm rounds or other desired shape. The dough can also be baked in sheets and then broken into crackers.

7. Brush the dough with the egg white, then sprinkle the rounds with the sesame seeds and salt.

8. Bake the crackers in the preheated oven until light golden brown, about 5 minutes.

9. Store the crackers between layers of absorbent paper towels in an airtight container for up to 3 days.

# Cheddar and Walnut Icebox Crackers

YIELD: *About 100 small crackers*

| | |
|---|---|
| 4 oz / 113 g butter | 1 tsp / 3 g salt |
| 8 oz / 227 g aged Cheddar cheese, grated | 2 oz / 57 g finely chopped walnuts |
| 6 oz / 170 g all-purpose flour | |

1. Cream the butter; add cheese and mix well.

2. Add the flour and salt and mix well. Blend in the nuts.

3. Roll out into 3 logs, about 1½ in / 4 cm in diameter. Chill at least 1 hour.

4. Cut into slices ⅛ in / 3 mm thick and place on a parchment-lined sheet pan. Bake at 350°F / 175°C for 8 to 10 minutes until crisp (see photo). Cool on a wire rack. Store in an airtight container. Serve within 3 days.

*Variation*  *Blue Cheese and Pecan Crackers: Substitute an equal amount of blue cheese for the Cheddar and pecans for the walnuts.*


# Potato Crisps

YIELD: *100 crisps*

2 lb / 908 g russet potatoes
4 oz / 113 g egg whites
Milk, as needed

1. Bake the potatoes until done, about 1 hour.

2. Scoop out the pulp and pass through a food mill. Cool.

3. Mix in the egg whites; add milk and mix to the consistency of crêpe batter.

4. Lay out a thin layer of the mixture on a silicone baking pad or nonstick sheet pan and bake in a convection oven at 300°F / 150°C for 3 to 4 minutes. Score into crackers of the size and shape desired; finish baking until golden, 2 to 3 minutes. Cool on a wire rack and store in an airtight container. Serve within 3 days.

*Variations*  *Parsnip Crisps: Replace potatoes with parsnips.*

*Celeriac Crisps: Replace potatoes with peeled celeriac (celery root).*

*Cheddar and Walnut Icebox Crackers*

# Basil Oil (Basic Herb Oil)

YIELD: *16 fl oz / 480 mL*

3 oz / 85 g basil leaves

1 oz / 28 g flat-leaf parsley leaves

16 fl oz / 480 mL pure olive oil

1. Blanch the basil and parsley leaves in salted water for 20 seconds. Shock and drain on absorbent paper towels.

2. Combine the blanched herbs with half the oil in a blender and purée very fine. Add this purée to the remaining oil. Strain the oil through cheesecloth, if desired.

3. Transfer to a storage container or squirt bottle. Keep chilled. Use within 3 to 4 days.

*Chef's note*   *This recipe will work well with most green herbs, such as chives, tarragon, chervil, or parsley.*

*Variation*   *Chive Oil: Replace the basil leaves with chives. Blanching is not necessary.*


# Cinnamon Oil (Basic Spice Oil)

YIELD: *16 fl oz / 480 mL*

19 fl oz / 570 mL sunflower oil

12 cinnamon sticks, crushed

1 nutmeg, quartered

1. Heat the oil in a small saucepot with the cinnamon and nutmeg until approximately 150°F / 65°C. Remove from heat and allow to cool.

2. Strain the oil into a bottle or other clean container. Allow to cool, and recap.

3. Store in a cool, dark area. Use within 3 to 4 days.

*Variation*   *Curry Oil: Replace the cinnamon and nutmeg with 2 oz / 57 g Curry Powder (page 589).*

# Orange Oil (Basic Citrus Oil)

YIELD: *16 fl oz / 480 mL*

12 fl oz / 360 mL pure olive oil

12 fl oz / 360 mL extra-virgin olive oil

3 oranges, zest only, cut into 1 by 3-in / 3 by 8-cm strips

1. Combine both oils and heat to 140°F / 60°C. Do not leave oil unattended—it warms very quickly.

2. Add the orange zest. Transfer to a storage container and refrigerate to infuse overnight.

3. The next day, taste the oil and strain if the flavor is good. If stronger flavor is desired, allow to infuse longer.

4. Cover and refrigerate. Use within 3 to 4 days.

# Red Pepper Oil

YIELD: *16 fl oz / 480 mL*

8 red peppers

2 oz / 57 g prepared mustard

20 fl oz / 600 mL extra-virgin olive oil

Salt, as needed

1. Wash the peppers, remove the stems and seeds, and rough-cut into small dice.

2. Purée the peppers very fine in a blender. Place this purée juice in a stainless-steel saucepan and reduce to one-fourth the original volume. Strain through a chinois and cool.

3. When the pepper purée is cool, add the mustard. Add the olive oil. Season with salt.

4. Transfer to a clean storage container or squirt bottle and refrigerate. Use within 2 to 3 days.

*Chef's note*   *Yellow or green peppers can be substituted with excellent results. For a spicy variation, use chiles and omit the mustard.*

# Tarragon Oil

YIELD: *12 fl oz / 360 mL*

1 oz / 28 g spinach leaves, blanched

1 bunch tarragon

8 fl oz / 240 mL vegetable oil

1. Blanch the spinach leaves for 30 seconds to set the color. Shock the leaves, drain them, and squeeze out the excess moisture.

2. In a blender, combine all of the ingredients.

3. Blend for 2 minutes on high speed.

4. Place the puréed oil into a medium saucepan over medium heat. Bring to a simmer, then remove from the heat and cool for 5 minutes.

5. Strain the oil through a coffee filter and cool to room temperature. Cover and refrigerate.

# Tomato Oil

YIELD: *12 fl oz / 360 mL*

2 garlic cloves, minced

1 oz / 28 g onions, minced

1 oz / 28 g carrot, finely chopped

1½ fl oz / 45 mL olive oil

8 oz / 227 g canned plum tomatoes, seeded, drained

3 tbsp / 9 g basil, chiffonade

8 fl oz / 240 mL extra-virgin olive oil

Salt, as needed

1. Sweat the garlic, onions, and carrots in the olive oil in a small sauté pan over low heat until tender and without color.

2. Add the tomatoes and gently simmer for 10 minutes or until the flavor is intensified. Cool the mixture for 10 minutes. Add the basil and purée in a food processor for 30 seconds.

3. Place tomato purée back into a saucepot and add the oil. Bring to a simmer and cook very slowly until the flavor is infused into the oil, about 30 minutes. Strain through a chinois.

4. Season and transfer to a squeeze bottle. Refrigerate until service. Use within 4 to 5 days.

# Raspberry and Thyme Vinegar (Basic Flavored Vinegar)

YIELD: *16 fl oz / 480 mL*

16 fl oz / 480 mL red wine vinegar

8 to 10 thyme sprigs

4 fl oz / 120 mL raspberries (about 25 )

1. Heat the vinegar until slightly warm, about 120°F / 50°C.

2. Place the thyme sprigs and raspberries in a glass jar or other storage container.

3. Pour the vinegar over the herbs and berries.

4. Allow to cool, and recap.

5. Refrigerate and use within 5 to 6 days.

*Chef's note*  Champagne wine vinegar can be substituted for the red wine vinegar.


# Rosemary-Garlic Vinegar

YIELD: *16 fl oz / 480 mL*

16 fl oz / 480 mL white wine vinegar

4 garlic cloves

6 to 8 rosemary sprigs

1 opal basil sprig (optional)

1 tbsp / 6 g whole black peppercorns

1. Heat the vinegar until slightly warm, about 120°F / 50°C.

2. Thread the garlic on a skewer. Place it in a glass or plastic bottle with the rosemary, basil (if desired), and peppercorns.

3. Pour the vinegar over the herbs and garlic.

4. Allow to cool, and recap.

5. Refrigerate and use within 5 to 6 days.

# 11

# Buffet presentation

Buffets are one of the garde manger's most exciting professional challenges. They demand a unique blend of culinary and management skills. The practical aspects of a buffet make them advantageous to virtually any type of operation. The creative challenges and opportunities they open up to the garde manger make them a meaningful way to advance and develop a career.

The work of the garde manger as banquet chef can be divided into four distinct phases. In the first phase, the concept or theme is identified so that planning can begin. In the second phase, the menu, price, and theme are worked out together, culminating in a production plan that makes good culinary and business sense from the menu to the plans for food presentation and service. In the third stage, the chef prepares plans for the layout and setup of the buffet lines, tables, and platters that are intended to make the buffet attractive and welcoming for the guests as well as efficient and practical for the service staff to replenish. The final stage, the actual production and display of the food, flows directly from the planning and preparation in the preceding stages.

Flexible enough to incorporate new trends—both the foods that you serve and the style of service you offer—buffets are an important aspect of many foodservice operations, no matter what their size or menu. All facets of the foodservice industry have found effective uses for buffets, from fast food outlets through supermarkets and delis to family or multi-unit restaurants and fine-dining establishments as well as corporate and institutional dining.

# Concepts and themes

A buffet may center on a particular meal period, special occasion, holiday, or ethnic presentation. The event's theme is typically the starting point for developing a plan for the buffet itself. Another fundamental decision is a **menu** that is developed around a theme.

The season, weather, and the guests' comfort and expectations hold together the theme. They have a direct impact upon the specific dishes selected for the buffet as well as the ways they are presented. When a buffet is part of a special event or celebration, the food should set the mood and enhance the occasion without overshadowing the occasion itself.

When the **concept** or **theme** is maintained throughout the buffet presentation, guests can easily recognize it as the concept or theme. At each stage of buffet work, from the development of the menu through replenishing the platters during the event, the theme or concept guides you to the best choice for the particular situation.

Buffets are integral to many special events. The event could be a personal or family occasion, such as a wedding, birthday, anniversary, christening, or bar mitzvah. It may have a seasonal or holiday celebration, such as New Year's Eve, Mother's Day, or Thanksgiving. Cities, states, countries, and continents all can be used as inspiration to develop regional and ethnic menus for a buffet that will highlight a variety of flavors. Buffets can be part of a fundraiser or a gala, or part of an opening reception for a new business, product, or exhibit at a gallery. Buffets are a part of many meetings, conferences, conventions, and similar corporate events. Buffets that are planned around a special event such as a fundraiser, gala, or wedding are generally planned with the client and must be tailored to their needs and budget.

A featured-concept buffet is designed to attract guests to the restaurant. Examples include Sunday brunches, pasta, or seafood buffets as well as "quick service" breakfast or lunch menus. The chef chooses foods for these buffets that have wide appeal and that work to improve the operation's bottom line. One popular example of a "featured-concept" buffet is the ubiquitous breakfast buffet. Operations that regularly present breakfast bars include hotels, motels, resorts, casinos, and restaurants. A smaller version of a breakfast buffet might include muffins, croissant and Danish, fresh fruit, bagels, toast and jam, coffee, orange juice, and milk and cereal. This type of breakfast buffet, when featured at a hotel or motel, may be included in the price of the hotel stay in order to give the customer a "value-added" experience.

A menu from a more extensive breakfast buffet might include several action stations such as a carving station for hams, roasts, and lox, an omelet station that creates omelets to order, or a crêpe station making filled crêpes. These stations would be in operation where a person is alongside an extensive buffet that would include many breakfast items such as scrambled eggs, bacon, waffles, hash browns, quiche, and the above-mentioned muffins, bagels, toast, and fruit.

# Menu development for buffets

Menu development is a process aimed at crafting a menu that satisfies the guest or client as well as makes a profit for the operator. It is the responsibility of the banquet chef to consider all aspects of the banquet, including the overall theme, the price range, and the guest's expectations.

First, review the concept or theme and establish the appropriate menu selections for the buffet. The number of options within those categories and the exact dishes to be prepared from one area in which the chef can make adjustments. When you begin to select a potential menu, highlight any special requests, seasonal or holiday items, and the like. These items will require special consideration as you refine the list. Another point to consider is that, although the food may all be presented at the same time, most guests expect to see options for the soup course, main course, side dishes, salads, and dessert on a dinner buffet menu.

Some menu items may be drawn from previous events. The advantage in working with familiar recipes and presentations is that you already know what they cost to produce and serve. Other menus may be made up of items that are new to your repertoire of buffet recipes. The advantage in offering new items is the ability to reflect popular trends, customize a menu for a special event, or introduce a new concept or theme.

After addressing the special needs and items that the guest may want, continue to develop the menu by listing other items that might work within the theme that you've established. Assign them to menu categories and work toward establishing a list that appropriately covers all the courses your menu should include.

# The menu

Because they can maintain a focus on the guest, banquet chefs have the enviable ability to create a unique dining experience. The menu selections and their presentation convey an integrated message to the guest. Buffet-style service offers guests variety, the freedom to choose from different categories, and the option of unlimited portions.

In most operations, buffets also serve as a creative and profitable outlet for a wide range of foods if **priced** properly. Whenever you can sell more of the food you bought, you lower overall food costs for the entire business. Banquets are a good way to attract new **market segments** or keep your current **clientele** coming back regularly. They also allow you to showcase new additions to the menu.

Throughout the menu-development and -planning process, the banquet chef needs to keep abreast of current **trends** and the **competition** to be sure that the menu is one that meets customers' expectations as well as showcases the skills and abilities of the facilities and the staff.

The food is generally the focal point for the guest. Food supplies the majority of the drama, excitement, and interaction, and it falls to the garde manger to produce food that is flavorful and attractive. The successful banquet chef generates and executes menus that please guests whether they are looking for global flair or traditional elegance.

# Price range

Establish the price range for any buffet at the outset of planning. There are a variety of factors to consider, including the competition's price for a comparable buffet and your guest's expectations or special requests, as well as any special conditions or limitations on the menu or the service.

The price range determines, to some extent, the number of options that can be offered as well as the specific ingredients or dishes you choose. **Food cost** can be difficult to estimate if you cannot predict the exact number of guests. But, even if you can, there is no certainty that guests will eat the foods you prepared in the amounts you estimated.

Food cost is an important piece of information. Use standard costing procedures to arrive at a cost per piece or portion. (For more information about food costing, see *Culinary Math, 3rd Edition* by Hill and Blocker, Wiley.) This step identifies costly ingredients or those that may have a limited shelf life. This does not mean that these items must be dropped from the menu, though you may wish to revise the portion size, presentation, or preparation method to help control costs.

In addition to the cost of the food for a buffet, the banquet chef considers other items as well. The cost to produce a specific item can be calculated (**labor cost**) and used as part of the overall evaluation of any item. High labor costs on one item may be offset by low costs for others. However, any item that has markedly higher labor costs than the other items on the menu should be reviewed to determine where those costs could be cut or if the item is appropriate for a buffet.

You may be able to use different **purchasing strategies** to reduce labor and/or service costs. Pre-cut or pre-portioned items that meet your quality standards may be one way to reduce labor, for instance. **Organizing** the workload differently, such as grouping mise en place in such a way that it is more efficiently done, may reduce costs as well.

Foods must be at the height of quality when presented, but many buffet foods may be prepared well in advance and then held. These foods, along with foods that are prepared just before they are served, must also maintain their quality while they are on the buffet line.

Review each proposed item to determine how well it will hold before and during the meal period. Consider how the food will taste and look, the safety of the guests, and any restrictions imposed by the pace of service, budget, equipment, and the skills of the buffet attendants.

Some foods lend themselves readily to banquet service, like carved or sliced meats, salads, some pasta dishes, and canapés. Foods that must be prepared and served immediately may require special handling during preparation or presentation; this can increase the cost of serving the food. Whenever possible, weed out items that require special handling, not only to make service more efficient but also to reduce the cost of service items like chafing dishes, heat lamps, and portable cooking devices.

Although not all dishes are equally suitable for buffets, there are often techniques and strategies you can employ to execute a dish that is particularly important to the guest or the theme. These strategies may affect both labor cost and food cost. One such strategy is to present these foods at an **action station,** especially foods such as pasta or omelets that are made or finished to order. Another is **pre-plating** (for more about pre-plating and its role in buffets, see page 566.).

Well-planned menus leave no detail to chance. They take advantage of every opportunity to meet and exceed customers' expectations, in terms not only of the food, but also of its presentation and display. Equally important in all these considerations is the development of a menu that is profitable for the operation. Your goal is to create a balance between cost control and the guests' freedom of choice.

# Meeting and exceeding expectations

As you develop the menu items for a specific event, make a list of those items that guests expect—or a **development list**. If it is a special occasion, this may include dishes specifically requested by the client. If the buffet has a regional theme, appropriate dishes to represent the region should be featured. For a dinner brunch, the guests in your area may expect a certain number of courses to be represented.

**Authenticity** is the key to the success of an ethnic or regional buffet. Customs, methods, and foods should be studied carefully. Researching the items for your menu may mean reading about a special cuisine or it may mean reviewing notes from previous banquets. Learning about the menus and prices for other buffets in your area is another important research tactic.

It is safest to have more items on your development list than you intend to actually serve. As you go through the process of evaluating each item, some will be dropped and others may be modified. Keep in mind that, from the guests' point of view, two of the main advantages of buffets are the **variety of choices** and the **amount of food offered.**

A careful review process for every menu item identifies areas you can improve, modify, or adapt to meet all of your objectives: great food, great service, a great experience, and, when the day is done, a profit.

The successful banquet chef uses specific strategies to deliver uncompromising high quality in all areas to the guest, coupled with a wide range of strategies to control costs.

Before making a final menu selection for dishes to feature at an interactive station, consider the specific skills necessary to successfully staff the station, as well as the needs of the attendant during service, especially space and equipment availability.

# Action stations

If your buffet plans include action or demonstration stations, select foods for those stations carefully. They should add something more than simply another menu item. Guests enjoy these stations because they see them as a custom experience; foods are made, sliced, or presented to their order as they watch. Highlight the special talents of your staff as they make crêpes and fill them or carve a steamship round of beef. They are also a good way to introduce interaction between the guests and the staff. For example, a cheese display staffed with a knowledgeable attendant is effective not only as far as serving the guests is concerned, but it also increases the chances that the guest will return.

These stations add to the overall cost of the buffet because you have to have one person dedicated to this station and this person must have the skills to execute the preparation on the station. Also, there may be special equipment needed to produce the item, such as an induction burner or extra refrigeration. However, the items on an action station almost always draw a higher price from the client and can be a cost-effective way to cook food that otherwise may have been sold for less.

**Action stations** can now be adapted to encompass nearly any food item on a menu. New developments in equipment such as the induction burner have expanded the possibilities for the items that you can feature on an action station. With the new items that may be featured, the skill level required to work on an action station can be high. Action stations can even have more than one person working on a single item. For instance, in order to create an appetizer of potato blinis with smoked salmon and caviar, one person may be sautéing the blinis while the second person is slicing the salmon and plating the appetizer. Some resorts and casinos have up to 20 people working on action stations in a single buffet. These higher-end items are usually reserved for events where the cost can be passed on to the client.

Action stations are expanding beyond the buffet as well. Action stations can be featured at an event that features passed hors d'oeuvre; the chef could make the hors d'oeuvre at an action station in the dining room for the service staff to pass to the guests. This eliminates guests having to wait in line for food and still gives them an attractive presentation that they are sure to enjoy. Restaurants that have open kitchens feature a sort of action station. The chefs are making food for customers in full view and must keep the same level of quality and cleanliness as a station in a buffet. Some restaurants that have chefs making tapas to order for bar customers have action stations.

Some examples of action stations are listed below.

# Raw bar

A **raw bar** setup is a sure way to impress your guests. They are very popular and will make any event look and feel more extravagant (see Fig 11-1).

Oysters, clams, mussels, shrimp, and crab are the seafood typically used for service at a raw bar. When serving raw seafood, it is important to be aware of the associated hazards. All raw shellfish must come with a tag stating the point of origin, the date of harvest, and the wholesale grower and seller. These stipulations, set by the National Shellfish Sanitation Program, guarantee that shellfish may be traced in the case of a disease outbreak. The warning on the tag reads: RETAILERS INFORM YOUR CUSTOMERS.

Thoroughly cooking foods of an animal origin such as shellfish reduces the risk of food-borne illness. Individuals with certain health conditions such as liver disease, chronic alcohol abuse, diabetes, cancer, or stomach, blood, or immune disorders, may be at higher risk if these foods are consumed raw or undercooked. Consult your physician or public health official for further information.

With this risk in mind, it is important to use only the freshest and highest-quality shellfish for raw bar service.

## Oysters

Throughout the world, oysters are commonly eaten raw. Four species of oyster that are typically cultivated for consumption include: the **Atlantic oyster** (Crassostrea *virginica,* also known as the Eastern or American oyster), the **Pacific oyster** (Crassostrea *gigas,* also known as the Japanese Oyster), the **European flat oyster** (Ostrea *edulis*), and finally, the **Kumamoto oyster** (Crassostrea *sikamea*). Each species of oyster has one of two distinct **flavor profiles,** which is a result of the water in which they were cultivated. Warm-water oysters are mild, with a buttery flavor and a creamy texture. Cold-water varieties, on the other hand, are characteristically briny, with a metallic flavor and a firm, crisp texture. When served raw, the delicate and subtle flavor differences between each oyster variety becomes apparent.

## Checking oysters for freshness

Oysters do not open and close as readily as clams and mussels do, making it difficult to determine **freshness** from their outside appearance. Good indicators of freshness are shellfish that do not open easily, meat that is moist and plump, and a fresh smell.

When preparing oysters for service in a raw bar, it is important to **shuck** the shellfish carefully. This will prevent damage of the oyster's flesh, and ensure that the bottom shell remains intact.

**FIG 11-1** *A raw bar adds an impressive touch to buffet seafood service.*

# Clams

Clams served raw on the half shell, while popular in select regions throughout the world, are much less common than raw oysters. Only varieties of **hard-shell clams** (Mercenaria *mercenaria*) are served raw, with **Littlenecks** and **Topnecks** being the most popular varieties, as they are the smallest and most tender. **Cherrystones** are medium-sized clams that are slightly tougher than Littlenecks and Topnecks; nevertheless, they are commonly served raw.

## Checking clams for freshness

**Fresh** clams should have a tightly closed shell, moist plump flesh, and a sweet smell. **Shucking** for service on the half shell, as with oysters, must be done carefully to prevent damaging the clam's flesh.

## Steamed mussels

The remaining seafood popularly served on a raw bar—mussels, shrimp, and crab—are not actually served raw; rather, they are steamed. The majority of the mussels purchased today are cultivated; therefore, they are free of barnacles. Typically, a **cultivated mussel** has a better meat-to-shell ratio than do **wild mussels.** Cultivated mussels are more uniform in size, cleaner, and less frequently have broken shells.

## Checking mussels for freshness

**Fresh** mussels, like clams, will have a tightly closed shell, moist plump flesh, and a sweet smell. Mussels must be cleaned before steaming: remove and discard any mussels with cracked or broken shells, and debeard as close to service as possible.

## A basic method for steaming mussels

Flavor the **steaming** liquid with shallots, white wine, cracked black pepper, and garlic. Bring the mixture to a boil, add the mussels, cover, and steam until just open. Steam mussels as close to service as is feasible.

## Shrimp

The varieties of shrimp are too numerous to mention; however, for culinary purposes shrimp are available as **small, large,** or **jumbo,** and are sold in a variety of forms: **PUD** (peeled un-deveined), **PND** (peeled and deveined), and **IQF** (individually quick-frozen). Head-on shrimp may also be purchased to provide a dramatic display, although, unless purchased very fresh, they are generally of lesser quality.

## Checking shrimp for freshness

**Fresh** shrimp will be free of any ammonia odor, slimy feel, or residue, and will be sweet-smelling.

## A basic method for poaching or steaming shrimp

Prepare a court bouillon or other flavorful liquid and simmer for a short time to develop the flavors. Place the shrimp in the liquid, and **poach** just until firm and opaque, being careful not to overcook them. Drain the shrimp and allow them to cool at room temperature before refrigerating. Shrimp should be fully defrosted before they are cooked and the pan should not be overcrowded. To preserve flavor, shrimp that will be served cold should be peeled after cooking.

## Crabs

Steamed crabs, available in many varieties, are a pleasant addition to any raw bar. **Claws** are generally the only part of the crab that is served; however, the **legs** of some varieties such as king crab are eaten as well. Crab claws are most often purchased cooked, either in or out of the shell. The most common crabs served on a raw bar include King, Snow, Jonah, Dungeness, and Stone Crabs.

The Red King Crab is of higher quality than most of the other varieties. For this reason, the Red King Crab is a popular choice for raw bar use. Claws and legs of the crab are served. The Snow Crab and the Jonah Crab, of lesser quality than the King Crab, are also known as "Cocktail Claws." A rather expensive crab from the Gulf Coast Region and Florida is the Stone Crab. The Stone Crab, though purchased cooked, must be cracked prior to service.

## Raw bar safety

In order to ensure the safety of a raw bar, purchase depurated oysters, clams, and mussels. **Depuration** is a system that purges the shellfish of **impurities** and sand. The process occurs when the shellfish are placed in tanks and fresh water is pumped throughout.

To further decrease the risks associated with raw bar, it is advisable to purchase **cultivated** oysters, clams, and mussels. Cultivated shellfish are raised in a controlled environment, and therefore are generally cleaner and safer.

## Service instructions for the raw bar

Prior to service all shellfish should be scrubbed, and held on ice between 35 and 40°F / 2 to 4°C for only two to three days. Shellfish should be served with accompaniments, on a tray filled with ice, and replenished as consumed. When the raw bar is presented as an action station, the chef has two ways to present the shellfish. The chef can either shuck the shellfish and create plates to order for the customers or the chef can shuck the shellfish and place the different varieties on a platter or ice bed where the guests can help themselves. The latter presentation is more efficient and still allows the guest the opportunity to interact with the chef and ask questions about the shellfish that is being served.

Popular accompaniments to a raw bar include but are not limited to: lemons, cocktail sauce, hot sauce such as Tabasco, vinegars like malt vinegar, salsas, seaweed salad, and mignonette sauce in the Bluepoint Oysters with Beluga Caviar (page 482).

Some equipment that is essential for a safe, functional, and attractive raw bar includes ice, knives for shucking, gloves (although there is a NY State glove law, the metal gloves used at the raw bar offer protection while shucking), and self-draining displays that are available in a variety of shapes and materials.

# Omelet station

The omelet station is perhaps the most well-known of the action stations. In addition to requiring a certain skill level, this station also demands speed and competence of the person who is operating the station. During a weekend breakfast or brunch, there is usually a near-constant line of customers waiting for a delicious, custom-made breakfast.

Having your mise en place in order is crucial to being able to run an omelet station efficiently. In addition to cracked, whipped eggs, the chef may need cheese, diced ham, chopped scallions, crumbled sausage, chopped onions, chopped peppers, or any number of ingredients that the chef decides to feature that day. The mise en place for cooking the omelet is just as important. This may

**FIG 11-2** *An omelet station adds an interactive element to a breakfast bar.*

include a bain-marie of oil or clarified butter for greasing the pans, omelet pans (usually ones that are reserved especially for the station and are kept in near pristine condition), paper towels, rubber spatulas, ladles, gloves, towels, warm plates, and a portable or induction burner. Be sure to have plenty of backup mise en place prepared so that someone can help you replenish your station at a moment's notice.

Safety considerations also need to be addressed to ensure that all of the items on the omelet station remain out of the danger zone at all times. This may entail purchasing a special mobile station or extra refrigeration in order to contain all of the various sizes of hotel pans that hold the chef's mise en place.

# Pasta station

Pasta stations are also very familiar and popular action stations. They allow the chef to feature any number of combinations of sauces, types of pastas, and main ingredients like poultry, beef, pork, cured meats, or shellfish. The chef can prepare dishes like pasta with puttanesca sauce because the chef can prepare the sauce à la minute by sautéing the aromatics and adding the remaining ingredients along with shrimp or chicken, as desired.

As with the raw bar, the chef can prepare single orders of pasta for individual guests or the chef can prepare a few portions and place them in a bowl at the front of the station for the guests to serve themselves.

Mise en place is very important for this station as well. The pasta should be cooked al dente before service so that it can be finished à la minute with the sauce and main item. Consider each item and the tools required to cook it when choosing the equipment necessary for the station. If the main item is raw, it is imperative to have sufficient refrigeration to store the item properly. It is important to have enough mise en place prepared so that you can replenish the station as needed.

# Mise en place and production for buffets

Menu selection and development leads to the next phase of planning. At this point, information about the number or count to be prepared and **portioning** is finalized. The chef analyzes the menu to determine the best scheduling for mise en place and production work. By maintaining a direct concentration on the important aspects of the buffet—the theme, the anticipated number of guests, customer expectations, and the pace of service—it is possible to improve quality and efficiency.

Chefs use a variety of means to arrive at the number of portions or pieces to make for each menu item. You cannot simply make enough for every guest to have a specific number of each item; guests may ignore one item altogether but devour another. The problem is magnified if there is no firm guest count, as there might be at a luncheon or dinner buffet. Chefs rely upon information from previous buffets to make an educated guess; throughout the course of each buffet, they have another opportunity to collect more information. Keeping track of not only actual **production** but also actual **consumption** is an important activity during the buffet itself. It is also important to improving the quality and profitability of future buffets.

Portions for buffets are typically smaller than for à la carte service. Smaller portions are an advantage to the guest facing a full buffet. They can take small portions of many items, or take as much of a single item as they wish. At the same time that this approach increases freedom of choice for the guest, it also reduces the amount of food that is wasted. Large portions that are only partially consumed are of no use to the guest or to the chef. It becomes a more difficult task to get accurate information about customer preferences to use in the future.

The banquet chef organizes food production to maximize the quality of the food, lower the overall labor cost, and cut down on food loss. Writing a logical, simple, but detailed plan is vital to good organization. In some operations, this plan is known as a **buffet production order.** These instructions set out the flow of food throughout preparation and service. Assign a specific individual (or individuals) to be responsible for the food, making sure that safe food-handling practices are observed, that foods are properly prepared and portioned, and that exact counts are taken and recorded.

Tasks can be organized to prevent a last-minute scramble. Some foods can be prepared, either up to the point of service or to some intermediate point, well in advance, as long as adequate and appropriate storage space is available.

## Arranging foods

An interesting and challenging aspect of cooking for a buffet is that you must make large quantities of food and then portion it into many small pieces. Excellent **cutting skills** and **precise work** are mandatory. The banquet chef's knives and cutters must be perfectly sharp. Clean cuts, straight edges, and precise angles do more to naturally enhance the foods you serve than any garnish, and show off a food's color, texture, and shape.

Arranging the food for service is the banquet chef's responsibility as well as his or her opportunity to improve the quality of the guest's experience. Food is necessarily handled as it is transferred to platters and other service pieces. From a food safety standpoint, it is critical to avoid contaminating the food as you work. Gloves, tongs, spatulas, and other tools keep you from touching the food with your bare hands and prevent cross contamination. They also cut down on the number of smudges or fingerprints that might mar the food or the platter. Cleanliness and order are critical to a successful food presentation, regardless of the overall design (for more about buffet design and enhancing food presentation, see pages 563 and 567). These two aspects of presentation assure the guest that foods have been properly and professionally handled.

As you place items on a platter, pay attention to the spacing between pieces and between other lines. It should be as regular as possible. Individual pieces of items like canapés or crab cakes should be regularly shaped and evenly sized.

## Slicing and sequencing

**Slicing** and **sequencing** foods that have tapered shapes, such as turkey breasts, or which have an internal garnish, such as a terrine, make it possible to create strong lines from foods that are not perfectly regular in shape and size.

Set up a complete station mise en place to be sure that you have all the tools you need to slice and hold the food—knives, a steel, a holding tray, and plastic wrap or dampened toweling to keep foods from discoloring or toughening as you work.

You may choose to include an element on your platter or tray known as a **grosse pièce,** which is simply a large piece of the sliced item you are displaying. If your platter calls for a grosse pièce, determine which portion of the item to keep whole and how large the piece should be before you start to slice. Working from the opposite end, make even slices. As each piece is carved, transfer it to a work tray and keep it in numerical sequence. Work in a logical and consistent order to avoid mistakes in sequencing later when you arrange the slices on the platter. Keep the same side of each slice facing up, especially if the item you are slicing has an internal garnish. This prevents you from reversing the slices as you arrange them. Transfer the slices from the holding tray back to the platter so that the last piece that was sliced is the closest to the grosse pièce.

# Buffet design

Once the theme for an event is determined and you have made your best estimate of the anticipated head count, you can diagram the layout for tables, buffet lines, and stations. In addition, you can choose the serving pieces and centerpieces for the buffet. As you work through the various tasks involved in preparing the buffet's design, evaluate your decisions to see if they help to reinforce the theme, improve service, and control costs.

## Number and placement of lines and stations

One of the ways that buffets differ from à la carte service is that the food is on display as it is being served to the guest. In an à la carte setting, the chef has control over how foods are arranged on the plate. During a buffet, the chef's challenge is to create an attractive, thematic, logical, and functional display of food. This stage of buffet planning may send you right back into an earlier stage, such as menu development, in order to overcome a specific problem of service or presentation. Even a long-established buffet can often be improved by a careful analysis of its design.

The number of guests you anticipate directly affects how many lines or stations you need for a given buffet, and it also changes how crowded the room may be once it is full of guests. Practical considerations must always be kept in mind. Buffet lines should be placed so that there is an adequate amount of room to walk around them.

The buffet should make it easy for guests to access the food, as well as for attendants to serve guests or replenish the line. Keeping it as close as possible to the kitchen means that waiters can deliver food more quickly, so that it tastes and looks fresher.

Buffet lines should not block entrances, emergency exits, or other doors used by either the servers or the guests. If electricity is required, it makes sense to try to locate lines and stations close to the electrical source.

In some cases, there may be a specific style of seating to which your buffet design must adapt. For instance, at a wedding buffet, a dance floor may take up some of the floor space. At a lecture, there may be theater- or classroom-style seating to contend with.

When there are tables where the guests can sit as they eat or there is a dance floor or presentation area, they take up floor space. However, the presence of tables can be turned to an advantage, since **utensils,** glassware, and napkins, as well as some condiments or other items, can be removed from the buffet line to the tables.

If the guests are expected to serve themselves from a buffet and then sit down to eat, try to place lines and stations so that they can get from the buffet line to their table in the fewest possible steps.

Account for elements in the room, such as pillars or columns, to avoid placing a line or station too close to these immovable objects.

All of these possibilities should be evaluated to determine the best combination of numbers of lines and stations, as well as their placement in the room.

# Lines

A buffet **line** permits the guest to select from a variety of dishes. The more lines you have, the more quickly all the guests are served. Depending upon the overall configuration of the room, it may be possible to establish two or more zones to reduce time guests spend standing in line.

# Stations

Smaller stations, sometimes referred to as **satellite** or **action stations,** break up the traditional "line" for a more contemporary service style. With stations, you can showcase special items or cooking demonstrations, encourage interaction between the guests and the attendants, and make traffic flow more smoothly through the room.

One of the drawbacks of traditional buffets is that they result in long lines that tend to build up during the initial stages of buffet service. In some settings, traditional single- or double-sided buffet lines are reconfigured as a number of smaller stations. These stations may be self-service, attended, or interactive. Stations make it easier for the guests to hone in on the dishes they find most appealing—without a long wait.

Setting up and staffing several stations puts additional demands on the kitchen and service staff. For some buffets, especially a featured concept buffet that offers speedy service, stations are kept to a minimum or not used at all.

# Table configuration and setup

The **configuration** and setup of the tables for a buffet plays an important role in how the guest perceives the event. They can improve access to food, make replenishing unobtrusive and efficient, control the flow of traffic by speeding or slowing it, and maintain the appearance of a bountiful, varied display throughout the meal.

You can adapt a configuration to **control consumption,** which may be a concern in an unlimited, all-you-can-eat setting with an extended service period, by using a one-sided display and limiting the number of satellite stations. It is even possible to eliminate a traditional line in favor of more demonstration or action stations. This configuration encourages a more leisurely pace of service. Certain configurations lend themselves to large displays and centerpieces. Others accommodate many dishes and stations in a relatively small amount of floor space.

The size and shape of the tables and their configuration add to the mood of the meal. The simplest layout is a long, **straight line,** arranged to serve foods from one or both sides of the table. A **serpentine line,** made by combining a series of horseshoe tables, is a more fluid, contemporary look with the ability to hold more food than a straight line.

You can also create other configurations by combining round, square, rectangular, and serpentine tabletop shapes. The ability to create a number of different configurations in the dining room permits you to adapt the buffet table and the amount of access guests have (from one side, two sides, or all around) as in the case of large rounds, squares, and T- and L-shaped arrangements.

Rectangles, squares, H-, T- V-, or L-shapes, and zigzags are made by combining rectangular and/or square tables. These configurations are conducive to multiple lines and zones. They can be single sided or double sided. If there are multiple zones, each zone must be completely set up with food and service items. Round, half-round, and serpentine table shapes joined together create circles or oval shapes, alone or in combination with squares and rectangles. Less common single-table shapes are sometimes available, including octagons, triangles, and ovals.

Tables can be joined together in such a way that they are left open in the center as well as at one end. If the configuration is a single-sided display, the open center of a circle, square, or U-shape can be used to hold very large or tall display pieces. If possible, arrange the tables so that access to the center of the configuration is positioned as close as possible to the kitchen or other food holding area to make replenishing easy and unobtrusive.

## Linens

We can thank the Roman Empire for the tablecloth. At Roman feasts, tablecloths reached from the table to the floor and served as napkins, while the napkins the guests brought with them were reserved for "doggy bags." Today, **linens,** including tablecloths, napkins, and skirting, are made in a wide range of colors, materials, textures, and weights. Prints, stripes, bold or subtle colors, and geometric shapes are a great way to spice up the look and feel of a buffet. Use dramatic and innovative draping techniques for special effects with skirting. Try out various napkin folds to add color, height, and texture to a tabletop. Or, use a popular tactic seen in Japanese banquet halls: strip the table bare to let gleaming wood show.

## China, flatware, glassware

The china and flatware settings also are important to the look and feel of the buffet. Plates are located on the line for guests to serve themselves or to hold plated presentations from carving or demonstration stations. The location of flatware and glassware may be either preset on tables or located on the line itself, generally at the end of the line.

When tabletops are preset, you can introduce special elements, including centerpieces, candles, and place cards. Plain white china works with almost any style of food or service, but for a more custom look, you can often find china with an unusual shape, color, or pattern that works with the food and the overall theme.

## Service pieces

Match the size of the serving piece to the number of pieces or servings. Leave enough room between pieces or lines to permit the foods to be easily arranged in the kitchen and served in the dining room.

Platters, **steam tables, chafing dishes**, and bowls are the most common service pieces used in buffet service.

Use steam tables and chafing dishes to keep foods hot. They are usually best for soft, spoonable, or pourable items like soups or vegetable dishes. Standard-size chafing dishes have inserts in a wide range of sizes. This allows the chef to choose the best size for the pace of service, the quality of the food, and the size of the staff. Platters of many shapes and sizes can be used to present both hot and cold food, but will not, unless specifically adapted to that purpose, keep them hot or cold for very long. Oval, round, square, and rectangular platters are widely available, some with handles to make service and replenishing easier.

The color, texture, and shape of your serving pieces can bolster the theme. Instead of bowls or platters, for instance, you might use copper cookware, slabs of stone or marble, or glass. Specially made presentation pieces add interest and functionality to the buffet line. Hollowed vegetables and other natural "containers" promote a feeling that the buffet is fresh and natural.

Whether the buffet is formal or informal, you may be able to introduce whimsy or fun by using items we do not normally think of as serving pieces to display foods. Children's beach toys, toy boats, paper or lacquered boxes and trays, sporting paraphernalia, or fashion accessories can join ranks with your steam tables and platters for a unique display. However, it is imperative that the foods do not come into contact with surfaces that could contaminate the food, and it is a good practice to line any of these items before placing food on them.

## Serving tools

Spoons, ladles, tongs, spatulas, and other serving pieces not only make it possible for the food to get from the service piece onto the guest's plate, they also have a direct impact on how the food looks and how certain foods are portioned.

Generally speaking, kitchen tools are not the best choice for buffet service. Not only do they look inappropriate in the dining room, they are often too large. As you consider a serving piece's use, try to anticipate how big a portion the tool can lift or hold as well as how easily the food will release from the serving tool onto the plate. Long-handled ladles can be awkward. Foods may stick and build up on serving pieces. Assign a specific tool for each menu item during menu development to be sure these tools are on hand for the buffet.

## Planning for waste

Some foods generate waste—shrimp shells, skewers, or strawberry stems, for instance. Guests may take a clean plate to try new items, leaving a dirty plate behind. The ability to clear away this waste makes the difference between cleanliness and chaos.

You may need or want to include **waste receptacles** as part of the buffet line's design. This may mean positioning containers and either labeling them or "seeding" them with a skewer or shell to make their purpose clear to guests. Attentive service can also regulate the amount of waste. Removing debris from the line throughout service should be a high priority for anyone involved with staffing the buffet.

## Pre-plating

Foods that are difficult to present and serve as individual portions from larger platters or chafing dishes may be pre-plated. For the guest, **pre-plating** adds elegance and ease to a self-service line or station. For the chef, it means better control over portioning and far less waste.

As a further advantage to pre-plating, the chef can use this strategy to create a focal point or a permanent display. For instance, if slices of cake are pre-plated and arranged around a whole fully decorated cake, the cake becomes part of the display, and won't be cut into.

On the other hand, pre-plating does increase labor and service costs. It takes more skill and time to make up a large number of uniformly presented plates. Those plates, too, take up more valuable space on the line than a platter. Finally, the wait staff will need to work harder at replenishing such a display.

## *Garnishes*

To be most successful and to create the best and most integrated theme, consider the type of garnish you might add to a dish. This may mean garnishing individual portions or plates as well as larger platters or trays containing multiple portions.

When foods are purchased and prepared with quality in mind, they develop the best possible flavor, texture, and colors. A garnish cannot make up for poor or marginal quality.

**Garnishes** can be used to add visual, textural, or flavor appeal to a dish or a platter. Rather than a last-minute decision based upon whatever is closest at hand, garnish selection as part of overall menu development and review is a sensible part of planning. You will be better equipped not only when it is time to order, but also during scheduling and food production.

Garnishes are often applied to individual plates or portions. These garnishes are selected using the same criteria as you would to select an individual item to be part of an overall menu. The garnish should make sense in terms of the rest of the dish. Some common garnishes include fresh herbs; these make the most sense if they either echo or complement the other flavors and herbs already in the dish. They make sense because they function as an aromatic or flavoring as well as a visual element.

When the only purpose for a garnish is to add a shape or a color, find a better option. Sprigs of parsley or watercress added to a platter simply for a bit of green color are **non-functional garnishes.** But, if the watercress is actually a bed for a marinated salad or other item, and the flavor and texture of the watercress becomes a significant element in the dish, it is a **functional garnish.**

The selection of a garnish for individual items may be governed by tradition, but it is often the development of an original garnish that creates the impression of a "new" item, something that is modern, trendy, and fashionable.

# Enhancing food presentation

The banquet chef or garde manger can take advantage of many opportunities to enhance the foods' presentation and, at the same time, enhance the guests' experience. Food presentation is the banquet chef's chance to emphasis the theme and showcase the talents of the garde manger staff.

## *Practical considerations in food presentation: function and meaning*

A good **design** serves a function. The **function** of a buffet is to serve the guest. Therefore, a properly devised buffet design places foods logically. Guests should be able to tell what they are eating. They should be able to reach the food easily, and to find all the appropriate service tools, including plates and silverware, positioned where they are easy to see and easy to reach. If there is a chance that a food might cause an allergic reaction, guests should be warned, either through placards or a printed menu or by positioning knowledgeable wait staff on the line. The design and layout should account for keeping foods properly heated or chilled and safe from cross contamination. These elements of the overall design must be accounted for first.

Guests typically expect that a buffet will provide a wide array of choices as well as the option to take as much as they like of any offering. The design of a buffet should support this expectation. At this stage of banquet planning, menu items have already been scrutinized for their costs, appropriateness to the theme, and customer acceptance. The banquet chef next begins to apply design principles and elements. The result is a composition that is echoed throughout every part of the buffet, from a single, tiny garnish on an individual canapé to ice carvings and display buffets.

# The role of design

When we like the way many elements are combined together in a single display, we use a variety of words to describe the effect: simple, elegant, balanced, integrated, unified, organic, or even synergistic. The banquet chef's task is to exploit the full sensory potential of every dish to create a presentation that is practical, functional, and appealing to all the senses. Planning a design that enhances food presentation is an important way to highlight the work of the garde manger and to benefit from the special skills that go into planning and producing a unified, thematic, and successful buffet.

## Judgments about what is fashionable or beautiful are subjective

They change over time, sometimes quite rapidly. However, the basic principles behind good design and presentation remain constant, even if the specific expressions of those principles keep evolving into new styles and trends.

### One of the primary purposes of food presentation is to be functional and practical

Enhanced food presentations integrate all aspects of the buffet, including the theme, the menu, the style of service, and your clients' expectations. The goal is never to simply meet those expectations and standards, but to exceed them. A well thought-out and executed plan is a distinct advantage in any successful buffet. It is important to remember and always think of these techniques as enhancements to the food's appeal; the real importance and focus of the food should always lie, ultimately, in its flavor and texture.

### Balance, as it relates to the work of the banquet chef, is achieved by combining the physical aspects of food in the context of specific design principles

Food supplies the important visual elements: colors, textures, and shapes. Additionally, the foods you serve also supply two important, but non-visual, elements: aroma and flavor. The design principles at the chef's disposal include **symmetrical** or **asymmetrical** compositions, contrasting or complementary arrangements, and the use of lines to create patterns or indicate motion. In creating a balanced presentation, be sure to also take into consideration the accessibility of each item to be placed on the platter. Place larger items in the rear and lower items in front. Items such as sauce boats should be kept in an area that does not disturb the design, but allows the guest easy access (see Fig 11-4).

**FIG 11-4** *A balanced spread should be arranged to make its components visually appealing while also ensuring that each item is accessible to the guest.*

A certain amount of regularity and repetition is comfortable and appealing, but too much of anything becomes monotonous, whether it is an ingredient, a **color,** a **shape,** a **flavor,** or a **texture.** Introducing **contrasting** elements adds energy and motion to an arrangement. However, when every element seems to stand on its own, the effect can be chaotic.

Throughout menu development and buffet design, record information about each menu item. Include not only estimates of amounts to prepare and portioning information, but also colors, textures, and other important characteristics. You can use this information as you plan the layout for individual platters or other displays.

## A food's natural color is one important tool in platter presentation

The color of a food can be used as an element in design (see Fig 11-5). We associate with colors in very specific ways. Greens give the impression of freshness and vitality. Browns, golds, and maroons are warming, comforting, and rich. Orange and red are intense, powerful colors. Colors that harmonize are those that touch each other on the color wheel (for example, green, blue, and violet are complementary colors, while blue and orange are contrasting). Clashing colors are rarely a problem. A more common concern is the overuse of one color on a single display.

**FIG 11-5** *Food's natural color should be taken into consideration and balanced when preparing a spread, as was done with the oranges, greens, and browns of this display.*

### Texture is important to the way food looks, as well as the way it feels in our mouths

The surface of a food will have a tendency to either reflect light or absorb it, making some foods glossy and others matte. Some foods have highly textured exteriors while others are very smooth. The way the food feels when you bite into it is another aspect of texture that the chef needs to include in a plan. Too much of the same texture is monotonous.

Cooking technique is vital to great presentation, because no matter how artful the display, the way the food tastes is the most important element. In addition to assuring that foods are flavorful and at the right temperature, the process of cooking gives the chef a chance to enhance the food in other significant ways. "Visual flavor" is an important concept to the garde manger chef when creating a cold food display. Unlike hot foods, with their abundant aromas to entice the guest, the aromas of cold foods are less apparent, making it necessary for guests to "see" the flavors. Some techniques deepen or darken the food's exterior; grilling, roasting, and smoking are a few examples. With these cooking methods it is also relevant for the guests to be able to see the seasonings used on the food, i.e., specks of seasonings and herbs or the shine of oil from a dressing. Other techniques introduce new elements, such as coatings or wrappers; pan frying and deep-frying are two such techniques. For an interesting selection throughout the menu, introduce a number of different techniques for a variety of flavors, colors, and textures.

### The shape and height of the food is an important part of buffet presentation

Food has three dimensions. Cubes, cylinders, spheres, and pyramids are just some of the shapes food can assume. Alternating or repeating shapes in a design is one way to add visual interest to food arrangements (see Fig 11-6). You can alter the natural shape of a food by cutting or slicing it. To give height to foods that are naturally flat, you can roll or fold them, arrange them in piles or pyramids, or use serving pieces such as pedestals, columns, or baskets to raise foods.

### A focal point serves an important function on a platter

It introduces a large shape into a field of smaller shapes. It adds height. It can make the arrangement logical and sensible to the guest; one common focal point is a grosse pièce (literally "big piece"). The guest can instantly identify the food on the platter. Sometimes, in place of a grosse pièce, there may be one or more significant garnish elements. The garnish elements are things that can possibly identify what is contained in the food, such as an herb or citrus zest or other ingredient. They can also be ingredients or items that suggest a style or region where the food originated. Such a garnish functions in the same way as a grosse pièce; they too are most effective, and attractive, when they offer some information about the food instead of simply adding a spot of color.

### Strong, clean lines arrange the food neatly and logically

Lines can be straight, curved, or angled. When two lines meet, they create a shape. When you repeat a line, you create a pattern. The more evenly spaced the lines, the more obvious the pattern. The wider the spaces, the more obvious they are as discrete lines. In order to have a line, you need a starting and ending point; the focal point in an arrangement is that reference point. Lines can move from or toward this point and thereby introduce a sense of flow or motion into the arrangement.

### The platter's layout can be symmetrical or asymmetrical

The position of the **focal point** on a platter or plate determines how the food is arranged. A focal point positioned off-center means that one side of the arrangement appears to have more weight than the other. The lines extending away from the focal point are of different lengths. When the

**FIG 11-6** *Utilizing a variety of shapes and heights, such as those in this antipasto spread, will create a visually dynamic buffet presentation.*

focal point is positioned in the center, it gives the impression that both sides of the arrangement are in equilibrium. The lines radiating from the focal point are the same length. Asymmetrical arrangements tend to look natural while symmetrical arrangements look formal.

## Arrangement of items on a line

Since a buffet line contains more than one offering or dish, give some thought to the sequence and arrangement of those dishes. Arrange dishes on the buffet line so that they are easy to see, easy to reach, and easy to serve.

What follows is a collection of general guidelines you can use to determine the best display sequence. Not every one will be useful for every type of buffet, though each of them has a practical purpose. Some of the most popular and creative solutions used in buffets today were arrived at only by creatively disregarding a widely accepted rule.

- Place plates where they are easy to see at the start of a line and at each independent station where they are easy to reach. They should also be easy for the wait staff to monitor and replenish. Utensils and napkins are best at the end of the line, so guests won't have to juggle them as they make their selections.
- Keep foods that might drip or spill closest to the guests.
- Use pedestals and similar devices to lift some platters higher. This is especially effective when you need to save space or when you would like to control the service of expensive items.
- Keep hot foods near one another; likewise, group chilled foods in their own area.
- Place sauces and condiments directly with the foods they accompany so that guests understand how to use them. Each one should have its own underliner and a serving tool if required.

## Replenishing

Exchanging full serving pieces for empty ones is an important part of service for any buffet. Obviously, no empty platter or chafing dish should be left sitting on the line for any appreciable amount of time. Each operation may have a different standard concerning exactly when to pull a platter and replace it with a fresh one. It depends somewhat upon the item being served and the size of the serving piece itself. However, the decision should be made ahead of time, then clearly communicated to the entire staff. The kitchen should be prepared to supply full platters promptly. The dining room staff should remove platters and chafing dishes as appropriate and immediately replace those items to avoid disrupting service (see Fig 11-7).

Large mirrors or silver platters provide a dramatic backdrop for the food displays that are the hallmark of a buffet. They demand considerable space on the buffet and considerable time to set up and dismantle, however. They are also a challenge to replenish. Moving big pieces around during service invariably inconveniences the guest and slows service. It can be awkward or dangerous to attempt moving marble slabs or big mirrors with guests in proximity to the buffet table.

If the buffet is meant to accommodate quests over a long period—for instance, throughout a two-hour reception—it can be difficult to keep the display attractive. As the guests help themselves from the display, the arrangement begins to look messy and, eventually, skimpy.

The modern buffet often features a more contemporary approach to food display in order to make the buffet as attractive, fresh, and appealing as possible, as well as to make it easier to replenish the buffet.

**FIG 11-7** *As a serving dish becomes depleted, it should be removed by service staff and replaced with one that is full.*

Instead of using one large piece, the garde manger is more likely to arrange foods on smaller serving pieces, then arrange these individual serving pieces into a larger overall composition (see Fig 11-8). Use that arrangement to reinforce or to enhance the concept or theme, as well as the arrangement of each platter.

Another distinct advantage of more frequent replenishment of smaller platters or chafing dishes is that it permits you to adapt quickly to the guests' behavior. During planning for food production, you estimate how many platters containing a certain number of items to prepare. If your prediction is off, you can more easily adapt to prevent shortages or to cut losses on items that are not in significant demand. This information can help you keep the customer satisfied and control costs by limiting wasted food.

**FIG 11-8** *Plating buffet foods on smaller platters adds visual interest to a spread and eases the task of replenishing serving dishes as they empty.*

Smaller serving pieces generally eliminate the temptation to combine fresh items with those that have already been on display. Uneaten portions should be counted and recorded on the appropriate form and then dealt with according to safe food-handling policy.

There should be a clear-cut policy on how to handle foods that are returned unused to the kitchen. Foods still safe for use in other applications should be carefully processed to keep them safe and wholesome.

## *Centerpieces and displays*

Any truly successful garnish or focal point adds excitement and interest to a presentation. But they can do more than simply that. They also improve the quality of the entire experience. They reinforce or magnify the buffet's theme or concept. They provide important visual elements that help the guest decipher the function or meaning of any presentation.

When you turn your attention to the presentation of the entire line or even the entire room, you can see that **centerpieces** and **displays** can and should serve the same functions as focal points or garnishes. They too should fit in with the featured concept or theme. It isn't enough that they match the other elements of the design, however. Just as you should develop a garnish to have a purpose and a meaning, you can also develop a similar plan for the buffet's centerpieces and displays.

These important design elements may be composed of edible or non-edible materials. Some traditional examples include ice, salt, or tallow sculptures, floral arrangements, or displays of fruits, vegetables, breads, or even wines.

Take care of practical considerations as you incorporate these elements into your overall design. Tall centerpieces and very large displays need to be carefully located. They should not block the guests' view or make it difficult to reach the food. Position any display pieces that might drip or shed well away from the food. Stabilize tall or top-heavy pieces during the buffet setup to be certain they do not wobble or fall over.

# Ice carving

Ice is a challenging medium for the sculptor and makes special demands. Unlike marble, stone, or clay, ice carvings eventually melt. The costs of acquiring and storing the ice, the skills needed to carve it into an attractive three-dimensional sculpture or display piece, transporting it, and setting it up are significant. Yet, ice carvings remain a powerful tool for setting the tone at any event. The fleeting life span of an **ice carving,** coupled with its high demands in terms of skill and artistry, sends out a vivid message to guests, offering them entertainment, excitement, and a good dose of the highly desirable "wow" factor.

The recent resurgence of this historic art form at catered events, buffets, banquets, weddings, and high-end sporting events brings it out of the eighteenth century and into the twenty-first. It has truly become an industry in itself. Although some carvers traditionally had a foodservice background and might have learned ice carving as an additional skill, professionals are now deciding to specialize in this field as a career. Exposure for the field is growing in scope and national competitions are getting increased funding and attendance.

# Ice sculptures

There are two sources of **ice blocks** available in the industry today. One is natural ice, which comes from frozen lakes, and the other is commercial ice, which is produced in ice houses and is more widely used in the industry. Typical manufactured blocks of ice weigh 300 pounds and measure approximately 10 inches by 20 inches by 40 inches. Some blocks may vary in size depending on the region of the country where they are produced. The ice should be free of rough edges, clean, clear, and free from impurities and bubbles, and should not have a cloudy core, sometimes referred to as feathered ice. To prevent feathered ice, the water is constantly circulated while it is being frozen.

Typically, as the ice block freezes from the bottom up, the impurities are pushed to the top and then scraped off after the ice is frozen solid. The result is a clear block of ice. Ice houses are equipped to freeze ice so that it has no core, but it is difficult for an individual operator to freeze ice without some feathered ice in the finished piece.

One of the central features of ice is its unique optical property. It refracts the light that is transmitted through the ice at different speeds and directions. This gives allure and uniqueness to ice which, unlike any other sculpture material, helps to make ice sculptures "come alive." The surface of an ice carving can be very smooth for a glass-like effect, or the surface can be scored to give it texture and a three-dimensional quality.

Large and small ice carvings are used for both display and individual service. In addition to the standard ice carving, a somewhat recent technique entails the carver sculpting mirror images into the ice and packing it with snow, which creates a white-on-clear display that looks almost like a holograph. Less-demanding displays are made from a split block of ice that sandwiches a logo. The snow-filled ice-carving technique described above is also quite popular when making logos. Numerals and letters are relatively easy to carve into the face of the ice as a bas-relief. Simple bowls or cups of ice can be made using molds and then set on the table filled with individual appetizers, such as shrimp cocktail. By the use of channels or depressions, ice carvings can be used to dispense drinks. Some ice carvings are intended to hold food, but they must be maintained carefully to ensure that the food being served meets sanitary guidelines at all times. Others can be finished with fresh flowers, fruits, vegetables, and other decorations to complement a theme.

The quality of molds for both large and small ice display pieces has improved and the costs have dropped, making them more affordable for smaller operations. The molds make it easier for the chef to create a display piece that is profitable and requires less time and effort than carving larger blocks of ice. However, the ice can cloud, the molds have size limitations, and some clients still prefer something original, made just for them.

# Ice carving tools

The chef need not be a world-class artist, but the proper tools certainly make it easier to look like one. Ice carving tools have come a long way in recent years, especially with the new technology made accessible through electronic tools (see Fig 11-9). There is computer-aided design (CAD) equipment available that can replicate nearly all of a previously made sculpture and the carver needs only to add the detail. On a smaller scale, there are many power tools that can help speed the production of the sculpture. Chainsaws are the most common electric tool used in ice carving today. They can draw straight and curved lines, are a quick way to cut away large pieces of excess ice, and can gouge and sand as well. Augers are tools designed to bore into the ice. Disk sanders, dremels,

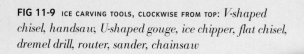

**FIG 11-9** ICE CARVING TOOLS, CLOCKWISE FROM TOP: *V-shaped chisel, handsaw, U-shaped gouge, ice chipper, flat chisel, dremel drill, router, sander, chainsaw*

routers, and drill bits are all used for shaping the ice. Disk sanders are used to round off the ice, and dremels and routers work in the same way that chisels do but they are much faster. Drill bits are used to provide detail in the sculpture. Irons can be used to smooth the ice as can sheets of metal that are at an ambient temperature. These two tools can also be used to warm the edges of two pieces of ice so that you can join them together. Gum remover or freeze spray is also handy to have when you need to join two pieces of ice together. Just be sure to use it carefully or ice fissures may form.

The more modern electric tools are not preferred by all. Hand tools are often more expensive, but some feel that they are more true to the art of ice sculpting. Some hand tools used for ice carving include handsaws, ice tongs, chippers, and a variety of chisels. Handsaws are available in a variety of tooth sizes and lengths. The larger teeth are used for rough cuts and the smaller teeth are used for finer cuts. The chisels can be straight, rounded or U-shaped (also called a gouge), or V-shaped, and are used for shaving and shaping the ice. These shapes produce corresponding grooves and shapes in the ice. There are single- and multi-pronged ice chippers that can be used to remove chunks of ice, shave ice, make holes, and score the ice. Ice tongs are pincers used to lift, seize, hold, or handle the ice.

Keep the ice and your tools as clean as possible to avoid contaminating the ice, especially if the ice carving will hold food to be served to the guests. Be sure that tools are stored dry with a little oil wiped on them so that they don't rust, and that they are kept sharp.

## The method for ice carving

The thermal sensitivity of ice must be well understood by the ice carver because the molecular structure of ice is changed by temperature. This means that the ice will have different structure and will react to light and touch differently. Experienced ice carvers know that the ice block has to be at the right temperature. The ice can't be too cold or it will fracture; on the other hand, if it is too warm it will break off in cubes or splinter. One of the causes of ice's sensitivity to temperature, touch, light, and other variables is that the solid structure of ice crystals is held together by weak hydrogen bonds. The strength of these bonds is primarily dependent on the thickness and temperature of the ice. The ice carver is allowed to sheer or glide the tools through the ice, without destroying the continuity of the crystal bonds.

Ice carving can be explained in any number of steps but here it is organized into five sections. Becoming proficient at ice carving takes many years of practice and lots of training. It is not difficult to learn, but it is difficult to master. Most professional ice sculptors carve the ice in the freezer to maintain an ideal carving temperature; however, this is not feasible for all operations and sometimes it has to be done in a walk-in or on a loading dock. When this is necessary, it is imperative to temper the block of ice before you start carving. Tempering is the process of allowing the ice to come up to temperature slowly so that it is consistent with the air temperature surrounding it. If there is a drastic temperature change, the ice could crack or pop, similar to what an ice cube does in warm soda. The ice block should be placed in the walk-in refrigerator for a minimum of 4 hours and preferably overnight. The blocks should be covered to prevent sublimation. Sublimation is when the ice passes from a solid to a gaseous state without melting, which causes the ice to dehydrate. Care should be taken when storing both ice blocks and the finished ice sculptures.

# The five steps for carving ice

1. **First, you need a design.** The finished sculpture can only be as good as the carver's preparatory drawing. You can sketch from life or find appropriate images in magazines or books, or from the Internet. Examine the design and try to break it down into one or more of the following basic shapes: cube, cone, cylinder, or sphere. Leave a base for the carved portion of the sculpture to sit on. The base is normally the full size of the end of the block and about 5 inches tall, but you may prefer to have an oversized base that raises small carvings up higher for better show. Professional ice sculptors always carve a pattern into the base such as brick or rock so that there is no wasted space on the ice sculpture.

   As ice carvings melt, their shape stays the same, since melting happens evenly for all parts of the sculpture. At room temperature, on average, the ice melts at the rate of half an inch per hour. The location and temperature of the place where the ice sculpture will be displayed should be taken into consideration when designing the piece. If your panther ice carving is resting on four legs, be sure those legs start out big enough to last throughout the service without giving way under the weight of the panther's body.

   Transfer the sketch to graph paper and then use a predetermined scale to enlarge the design. Enlarging the original design can also be done using an overhead or opaque projector. Trace this design onto chart paper or a similar material and cut the design out using a sharp blade. Alternately, the paper can be applied to the ice block and cut out using a chain saw or chipper.

2. **Select the tools that you will need to create the sculpture.** Be sure to take into consideration all safety precautions when selecting your tools, clothing, and protective wear. Transfer the design to the ice block by spraying the block with water and immediately affixing the paper template directly to the ice. It is important that the ice block be below freezing when applying paper templates, whether you are working with it inside or outside of a freezer. Smooth the paper so that there are no bubbles and make sure that the template is square to the edge of the block (see Fig 11-10a).

3. **Etch the pattern into the ice and then remove the excess ice around the template to create an outline for the sculpture (see Fig 11-10b).** This can be done with saws and possibly chisels but be careful to follow the lines set forth on the template. The colder the ice is when you carve it, the easier carving is. The ideal temperature range for carving is between 26 and 28°F; the warmer the air where you are working, the more quickly you must work to compensate for faster melting.

4. **Carve the ice sculpture into 3-D.** This can be done using saws, power tools, chisels, and chippers (see Fig 11-10c). It is important to take your time and step back every once in a while to look at the sculpture. If the design is larger than one piece of ice, extra pieces can be carved out of ice and attached using the following technique: Carve a 4-inch-deep notch into the base piece of ice. Carve a peg that corresponds to the size of the notch into the piece that will be joined to the base sculpture. Place the peg in the notch and pack the seam with snow. Hold the two pieces together until they freeze, then remove the excess snow. When designing the sculpture, take into account the size of the extra pieces, their weight, and the location where they will be pegged in place. The seams should come at a natural place in the sculpture and the place where the extra piece is affixed should be able to bear the weight of the extra pieces.

5. **Carve the details into the sculpture to show texture (see Fig 11-10d).** Extreme care should be taken when making these details and they should be made as close to life as possible to make the sculpture recognizable. These details include feathers, eyes, fingers, patterns, etc. This can be done with chisels, dremels, routers, dies, or chippers. Scoring the ice creates contrast and texture in the sculpture. Wash and clean the ice to remove any chips before finishing the detail work.

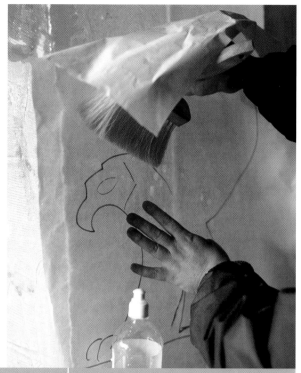

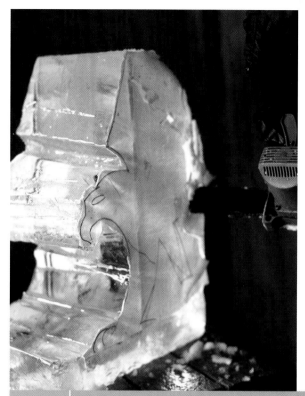

FIG 11-10A *Apply the template to the block of ice by wetting the ice, smoothing the template over it, and removing any air bubbles with a soft-bristled brush.*

FIG 11-10B *Taking care to follow the template, remove the excess ice from around the outline to create an outline for the sculpture.*

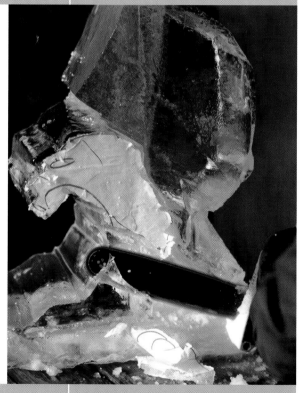

FIG 11-10C *Once outlined, add 3-D elements to the sculpture to give it the desired shape and form.*

FIG 11-10D *Details are carved into the sculpture to give it texture and a sense of realism.*

## Displaying ice carvings

Large ice carvings must be set up carefully. Usually, allowing the ice carving to rest at room temperature for at least an hour before the event is enough time to make the carving glisten. Display them on very sturdy and level tables or stands. To capture the melting water that runs off the carving, set the carving directly in a pan fitted with a valve or drain that connects to a hose. The water is siphoned away from the carving and into a collection bucket or tub. Alternatively, set the sculpture on wooden blocks in a pan large and deep enough to hold water. Drape the pan set-up with cloths or camouflage it with flowers, ferns, or other display items.

Be sure that any lights used in or near the display are properly installed. Spotlights should be located far enough away and the bulbs should be of low enough wattage so that their heat does not melt the ice carving. Lights can be placed directly beneath or behind the carving for a dramatic look, but great care must be taken to be certain that water will not drip on the lights or wiring. Check that any wiring, cords, or drainage items are discreetly positioned and cannot trip unwary guests or servers. Fog machines or dry ice can also create dramatic effects when used around an ice sculpture.

## Grafting or repairing the sculpture

Use great care when transporting ice carvings; they break as easily as glass. If a carving does break, you can "weld" pieces back onto the carving to replace or repair the damage. Use the same technique that you would to attach appendages to carvings that are bigger than a single block (wings, tusks, or tails, for instance). When creating the replacement piece, carve a peg at the end of the piece. Notch an indentation in the carving at the appropriate location that matches the size of the peg, insert the piece, pack it with wet snow or slush, and freeze for one or two days. Scrape away any excess snow before displaying the sculpture. If an ice carving has a small break, you can usually repair it by sprinkling both surfaces of the break with slush, then holding the pieces together until they fuse again.

**FIG 11-11A** *Once the site of grafting or repairing has been aligned, prepare some slush to pack the seam with.*

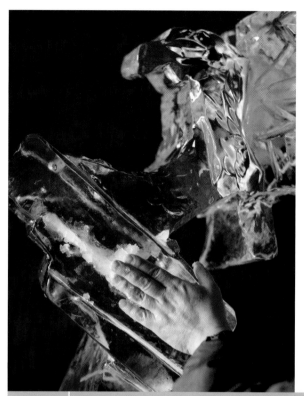

**FIG 11-11B** *Pack the seam copiously with slush, taking care to fill the seam itself as well as the area surrounding it.*

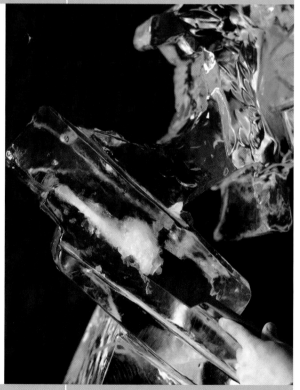

**FIG 11-11C** *Once allowed to freeze momentarily, the excess slush is removed from the surface of the seam.*

**FIG 11-11D** *The sealed seam should have a smooth surface and exhibit very subtle markings at the point of contact.*

12

# Mirepoix

YIELD: *1 lb / 454 g*

8 oz / 227 g onions, peeled and chopped

4 oz / 113 g celery, trimmed and chopped

4 oz / 113 g carrots, trimmed and chopped

Cut the vegetables into an appropriate size based on the cooking time of the dish.

*Variation*   *White Mirepoix: For 1 lb / 454 g: Reduce the onions to 4 oz / 113 g. Replace the carrots with 4 oz / 113 g each chopped leeks (white parts only) and parsnips. If desired, add 2 to 3 oz / 57 to 85 g mushroom trimmings.*

# Standard Bouquet Garni

YIELD: *1 bouquet, enough to flavor 1 gal / 3.84 L stock*

4 oz / 113 g whole celery stalk, trimmed

1 bay leaf

3 to 4 fresh parsley stems

2 to 3 leek leaves

1 fresh thyme sprig

1.  Halve the celery stalk crosswise. Sandwich the herbs between the celery pieces and fold the leek leaves around the herbs and celery.

2.  Tie the bundle securely with butcher's twine, leaving a long tail of string to tie the bouquet to the stockpot handle.

*Chef's note*   *Savory, sage, or other fresh herbs may be used in addition to or in place of the ingredients called for above, depending on the recipe or desired result.*

# Standard Sachet d'Épices

YIELD: *1 sachet, enough to flavor 1 gal / 3.84 L of stock*

3 or 4 fresh parsley stems

½ tsp / 1.50 g fresh thyme leaves

1 bay leaf

½ tsp / 1 g peppercorns, cracked

1 garlic clove, crushed (optional)

Place all ingredients on a piece of cheesecloth approximately 4 in / 10 cm square. Gather up the edges and tie with butcher's twine, leaving a long tail of twine to tie to the stockpot handle.

*Chef's note*   *Cloves, dill, tarragon stems, juniper berries, star anise, allspice, and other herbs and spices may be included, depending on the recipe or desired result.*

# Chinese Five-Spice Powder

YIELD: *about 4 oz / 113 g*

2 oz / 57 g star anise

3 tbsp / 16 g cloves

3 tbsp / 10 g Szechwan pepper

¾ oz / 21 g fennel seeds

¾ oz / 21 g cinnamon (or cassia)

Grind the spices in a spice mill or with a mortar and pestle. Store any unused spice powder in an airtight container in a cool, dry place. Keeps well for several weeks.

# Barbecue Spice Mix

YIELD: *about 4 oz / 113 g*

1 oz / 28 g hot Hungarian paprika

2 tbsp / 13 g chili powder

2 tbsp / 18 g salt

4 tsp / 8 g ground cumin

4 tsp / 16 g sugar

1 tbsp / 3 g dried thyme

2 tsp / 4 g dry mustard

2 tsp / 4 g ground black pepper

2 tsp / 2 g dried oregano

2 tsp / 4 g curry powder

1 tsp / 2 g cayenne

Combine all ingredients thoroughly. Store any unused spice blend in an airtight container in a cool, dry place.

# Quatre Épices

YIELD: *about 4 oz / 113 g*

2 oz / 57 g black peppercorns

3 tbsp / 20 g ground nutmeg

2 tbsp / 14 g ground cinnamon

2 tbsp / 11 g cloves

Grind together the spices in a spice mill or with a mortar and pestle. Store any unused spice blend in an airtight container in a cool, dry place.

*Chef's note* Add 2 tbsp / 14 g ground ginger, if desired.

# Cajun Spice Blend

YIELD: *about 4 oz / 113 g*

1½ oz / 42 g hot Hungarian paprika

1 tbsp / 10 g kosher salt

2 tbsp / 13 g onion powder

2 tbsp / 13 g garlic powder

2 tbsp / 11 g cayenne

1 tbsp / 6 g ground white pepper

1 tbsp / 6 g ground black pepper

1 tbsp / 3 g dried thyme

1 tbsp / 3 g dried oregano

Combine all ingredients thoroughly. Store any unused spice blend in an airtight container in a cool, dry place.

# Curry Powder

YIELD: *about 4 oz / 113 g*

4½ tbsp / 27 g cumin seeds

4½ tbsp / 22 g coriander seeds

1 tbsp / 12 g whole mustard seeds

12 dried red chiles, or as needed

3 tbsp / 21 g ground cinnamon

3 tbsp / 21 g ground turmeric

3 tbsp / 21 g ground ginger

1. Combine all the seeds and chiles. Roast them in a 350°F / 177°C oven for 5 minutes. Remove and cool slightly. Split the chiles and remove and discard the seeds.

2. Grind the whole seeds, ground spices, and chiles in a spice mill or with a mortar and pestle until evenly blended. Store any unused powder in an airtight container in a cool, dry place.

*Chef's note*  Add hot Hungarian paprika, cloves, or fresh curry leaves to the blend.

# Fines Herbes

YIELD: *2 oz / 57 g*

½ oz / 14 g chervil leaves

½ oz / 14 g chives

½ oz / 14 g parsley leaves

½ oz / 14 g tarragon leaves

Wash all herbs. Combine all the herbs and chop or mince to the desired fineness. Use immediately.

# Pâté Spice

YIELD: *4 oz / 113 g*

½ oz / 14 g white peppercorns

1 oz / 28 g coriander seeds

½ oz / 14 g dried thyme

½ oz / 14 g dried basil

1 oz / 28 g whole cloves

½ oz / 14 g grated nutmeg

20 bay leaves

¼ oz / 7 g mace

⅓ oz / 9 g dried cèpes (optional)

Combine all ingredients and grind them using a mortar and pestle or a blender. Store any unused spice blend in an airtight container in a cool, dry place.

# Hot Italian Sausage Blend

YIELD: *about 4 oz/ 113 g*

3 tbsp / 20 g fennel seeds

2 tbsp / 12 g ground coriander

1 tbsp / 12 g sugar

2 tbsp / 14 g sweet Spanish paprika

2 tbsp / 14 g hot Hungarian paprika

1½ tsp / 3 g cayenne

4 tbsp / 19 g crushed red pepper

1 tbsp / 6 g coarse-ground black pepper

Combine all ingredients. Store any unused spice blend in an airtight container in a cool, dry place.

# Herbes de Provence

YIELD: *about 4 oz/ 113 g*

1¼ oz / 35 g dried thyme

1¼ oz / 35 g dried marjoram

1¼ oz / 35 g dried savory

2½ tbsp / 7.50 g dried rosemary

2½ tsp / 2.50 g dried sage

2½ tsp / 2.50 g dried mint

2½ tsp / 2.50 g fennel seeds

2½ tsp / 2.50 g dried lavender flowers

Combine all ingredients. Store any unused spice blend in an airtight container in a cool, dry place. The herbs may be crushed fine with a mortar and pestle before use if desired.

*Chef's note*  *Crushed bay leaves are sometimes included in this blend. As with other spice blends in this chapter, amounts of herbs may be adjusted according to personal taste.*

# Brown Veal Stock

YIELD: *1 gal /3.84 L*

8 lb / 3.63 kg veal bones, including knuckles and trim

1½ gal / 5.76 L cold water

1 lb / 454 g Mirepoix (page 586)

6 oz / 170 g tomato paste

1 Standard Sachet d'Épices (page 587)

1. Rinse the bones and dry them well. Preheat an oiled roasting pan in a 450°F / 232°C oven. Brown the bones in the roasting pan in the oven.

2. Combine the bones and water in a stockpot. Bring the stock to a boil over low heat. Simmer for about 6 hours, skimming the surface as necessary.

3. Brown the mirepoix and tomato paste; add to the stock in the last hour of simmering. Deglaze the drippings in the roasting pan with water and add to the stock. Add the sachet d'épices.

4. Simmer an additional hour. Strain the stock. Cool and refrigerate.

*Variation*  *Venison Stock: Replace the veal bones with an equal weight of venison bones and lean trim. Include fennel seeds and/or juniper berries in standard sachet d'épices, if desired.*

# Chicken Stock

YIELD: *1 gal/ 3.84 L*

8 lb / 3.63 kg chicken bones, cut into 3-in / 8-cm lengths

1½ gal / 5.76 L cold water

1 lb / 454 g Mirepoix (page 586)

1 Standard Sachet d'Épices (page 587)

1. Rinse the bones in cool water. Combine the bones and water in a stockpot.

2. Bring the stock to a boil over low heat. Skim the surface, as necessary. Simmer 4 to 5 hours.

3. Add the mirepoix and sachet d'épices in the last hour of simmering. Strain the stock. Cool and referigerate.

*Variations*  *White Duck Stock: Substitute equal amounts of duck bones for the chicken bones.*

*Turkey Stock: Substitute equal amounts of turkey bones for the chicken bones.*

*White Beef Stock: Substitute equal amounts of beef bones for the chicken bones. Increase the simmering time in step 2 to 6 to 7 hours.*

# Shellfish Stock

YIELD: *1 gal / 3.84 L*

10 lb / 4.54 kg shellfish shells (lobster, shrimp, or crab)

2 fl oz / 60 mL vegetable oil

1 lb / 454 g Mirepoix (page 587)

3 to 4 oz / 85 to 113 g tomato paste

1 gal 32 fl oz / 4.8 L cold water

1 Standard Sachet d'Épices (page 587)

8 fl oz / 240 mL white wine

1. Sauté the shellfish shells in the oil until deep red. Add the mirepoix and continue to sauté another 10 to 15 minutes. Add the tomato paste and sauté briefly.

2. Add the water, sachet, and wine and simmer 30 minutes. Strain the stock. Cool and refrigerate.

*Variation*   Fish Stock: Substitute an equal amount of bones and trim from lean white-fleshed fish for the shellfish shells. In step 1, sauté in oil over low heat until the bones become white. Use White Mirepoix. Omit the tomato paste.


# Vegetable Stock

YIELD: *1 gal / 3.84 L*

2 fl oz / 60 mL vegetable oil

4 oz / 113 g onions, sliced

4 oz / 113 g leeks, green and white parts, chopped

2 oz / 57 g celery, chopped

2 oz / 57 g green cabbage, chopped

2 oz / 57 g carrots, chopped

2 oz / 57 g turnips, chopped

2 oz / 57 g tomatoes, chopped

3 garlic cloves, crushed

1 gal 16 fl oz / 4.32 L cold water

1 Standard Sachet d'Épices (page 587), with:

    1 tsp / 2 g fennel seeds (place in sachet)

    3 whole cloves (place in sachet)

1. Heat the oil. Add the vegetables and garlic and sweat for about 5 minutes.

2. Add the water and sachet d'épices and simmer for 30 to 40 minutes. Strain the stock. Cool and refrigerate.

# Glace de Viande

YIELD: *4 to 8 oz / 113 to 227 g (see Chef's Note)*

32 fl oz / 960 mL Brown Veal Stock (page 592)

1. Place the stock in a heavy-gauge pot over moderate heat. Bring to a simmer and reduce until volume is halved, then transfer to a smaller pot.

2. Continue to reduce, transferring to successively smaller pots, until very thick and syrupy.

*Chef's note*  The yield will vary depending on cooking time and desired consistency.

*Variation*  Glace de Volaille: Substitute Chicken Stock (page 592) for the brown veal stock.

# Court Bouillon

YIELD: *1 gal / 3.84 L*

80 fl oz / 2.4 L cold water

80 fl oz / 2.4 L white wine

2 tsp / 6 g salt (optional)

12 oz / 340 g carrots, sliced

1 lb / 454 g onions, sliced

Pinch dried thyme leaves

3 bay leaves

1 bunch fresh parsley stems

½ oz / 14 g black peppercorns

1. Combine water, wine, salt (if using), carrots, onions, thyme leaves, bay leaves, and parsley stems.

2. Simmer for 50 minutes.

3. Add the peppercorns and simmer for an additional 10 minutes. Strain the court bouillon before using.

*Variation*  Vinegar Court Bouillon: Double the amount of water. Replace all the white wine with 8 fl oz / 240 mL vinegar. This court bouillon is considered standard in many kitchens.

# Chicken Consommé

YIELD: *1 gal / 3.84 L*

CLARIFICATION

1 lb / 454 g Mirepoix (page 586)

3 lb / 1.36 kg lean chicken, ground

10 egg whites, beaten

12 oz / 340 g tomato concassé

1 gal 32 fl oz / 4.8 L Chicken Stock
(page 592), cold

1 Standard Sachet d'Épices (page 587), plus:

    1 clove (place in sachet)

    2 allspice berries (place in sachet)

1 tsp / 3 g kosher salt

½ tsp / 1 g ground white pepper

1. Mix the ingredients for the clarification and blend with the stock. Mix well.

2. Bring the mixture to a slow simmer, stirring frequently, until raft forms.

3. Add the sachet d'épices and simmer for 45 minutes, or until the appropriate flavor and clarity are achieved. Baste raft occasionally.

4. Strain the consommé; adjust seasoning with salt and white pepper.

# Velouté

YIELD: *64 fl oz / 1.92 L*

80 fl oz / 2.4 L Chicken Stock (page 592)

4 to 8 oz / 113 to 227 g white or blonde roux, as needed

½ tsp / 1.50 g salt

¼ tsp / 0.50 g ground black pepper

1. Bring the stock to a boil.

2. Whip the roux into the stock; work out all the lumps.

3. Simmer for 30 to 40 minutes, skimming the surface as necessary.

4. Season with salt and pepper as needed and then strain the sauce.

*Variations*   *Fish Velouté: Use Fish Stock (page 593) instead of chicken stock.*

   *Shellfish Velouté: Use Shellfish Stock (page 593) instead of chicken stock.*

   *Vegetable Velouté: Use Vegetable Stock (page 593) instead of chicken stock.*

# Pimiento Butter

YIELD: *1 lb / 454 g*

12 oz / 340 g butter, softened

3½ oz / 99 g pimientos, minced

¼ tsp / 0.75 g minced garlic

1 tbsp / 15 mL lemon juice

Salt, as needed

Pepper, as needed

1. Purée all ingredients and mix well.

2. Wrap tightly and refrigerate until needed.

3. Soften if needed for spreading.


# Anchovy Butter

YIELD: *1 lb / 454 g*

1 lb / 454 g butter, softened

1 to 1½ fl oz / 30 to 45 mL lemon juice

1 to 2 oz / 28 to 57 g anchovy paste

Salt, as needed

Ground black pepper, as needed

1 tbsp / 9 g chopped drained capers

1. Combine all ingredients and mix well.

2. Wrap tightly and refrigerate until needed.

3. Soften if needed for spreading.


# Horseradish Butter

YIELD: *1 lb 4 oz / 567 g*

3 oz / 85 g prepared horseradish

1 lb / 454 g butter, softened

1 tbsp / 15 g prepared mustard

2 tsp / 10 mL Worcestershire sauce

1 tbsp / 12 g sugar

1 tsp / 5 mL lemon juice

1. Squeeze excess liquid out of the horseradish.

2. Combine all ingredients and mix well.

3. Wrap tightly and refrigerate until needed.

4. Soften if needed for spreading.

# Lobster-Infused Oil

YIELD: *8 fl oz / 240 mL*

1 lb / 454 g lobster shells

4½ oz / 128 g tomato paste

2 fl oz / 60 mL white wine

¼ oz / 7 g hot Hungarian paprika

8 fl oz / 240 mL extra-virgin olive oil

1. Roast the shells in a 400°F / 204°C oven until crisp and brittle, about 15 minutes.

2. Place the shells and tomato paste in a saucepot over medium heat and cook, stirring frequently, until the tomato paste has a rusty color, about 4 to 5 minutes.

3. Stir in the white wine and paprika and reduce until there is no liquid left, about 2 to 3 minutes.

4. Add the oil and heat the mixture to 190°F / 88°C. Remove the pan from the heat and allow the mixture to steep for 20 minutes. Strain the oil through a cheesecloth-lined strainer, pressing the solids to release as much oil as possible.

5. Transfer to a clean storage container or squirt bottle and refrigerate.

# Mayonnaise Collée

YIELD: *24 fl oz / 720 mL*

16 fl oz / 480 mL Basic Mayonnaise (page 36)

8 fl oz / 240 mL Aspic Gelée (page 58), firm gel strength, warmed to 110°F / 43°C

2 tsp / 6 g kosher salt

1¼ oz / 35 g ground white pepper

Tabasco sauce, as needed

Combine mayonnaise with aspic, strain, and add seasonings.

# Pâte Dough

YIELD: *1 lb 8 oz / 680 g*

| | |
|---|---|
| 1 lb / 454 g bread flour | 4 oz / 113 g butter or lard, cold, cut into cubes |
| 2 tsp / 6 g baking powder | 1 egg |
| ½ oz / 14 g salt | 2 tsp / 10 mL cider vinegar |
| 1 tsp / 4 g sugar | 8 fl oz / 240 mL whole milk |

1. Combine the dry ingredients and mix well.

2. With two knives or a pastry cutter, cut the butter into the dry ingredients. Work the dough until it becomes crumbly (see Fig 12-1a ).

3. Mix the wet ingredients into the dough until fully incorporated. Knead the dough until smooth and not sticky (see Fig 12-1b).

4. Shape the dough into a disc 10 in / 25 cm in diameter. Wrap and refrigerate for at least 1 hour or overnight.

FIG 12-1A · *Cut the fat into the dry ingredients until it resembles a granular texture slightly larger than cornmeal.*

FIG 12-1B · *Once the dough has been kneaded to a smooth consistency, shape it into a block to be wrapped and stored.*

# Tomato Cilantro Pâte Dough

YIELD: *1 lb 8 oz / 680 g*

| | |
|---|---|
| 1 lb 8 oz / 680 g Pâte Dough (page 598) | 1½ oz / 43 g tomato paste |
| 2 tsp / 4 g ground coriander | 2 tbsp / 5 g chopped cilantro |
| 2 tsp / 4 g ground cumin | |

Prepare the pâte dough according to the basic recipe, adding the coriander and cumin in step 1, and the tomato paste and cilantro in step 2.


# Saffron Pâte Dough

YIELD: *1 lb 8 oz / 680 g*

| | |
|---|---|
| Large pinch saffron | 2 tbsp / 6 g chopped dill (optional) |
| 5 fl oz / 150 mL warm water | 2 tbsp / 6 g chopped chives (optional) |
| 1 lb 8 oz / 680 g Pâte Dough (page 598) | |

Infuse the saffron in the water. Replace 5 fl oz / 150 mL milk with the saffron water in the basic pâte dough recipe. Add the chopped herbs in step 2.


# Pâte Sucrée

YIELD: *5 lb / 2.27 kg*

| | |
|---|---|
| 8 oz / 227 g butter | 3 eggs |
| 13 oz / 369 g sugar | 3 egg yolks |
| ¼ tsp / .75 g salt | 2 lb 6 oz / 1.077 kg pastry flour |
| ¼ tsp / 1¼ mL vanilla extract | |

1. Cream together the butter, sugar, salt, and vanilla on medium speed using a paddle attachment, scraping down the bowl periodically, until smooth and light in color. Be careful not to overcream the mixture. Add the eggs and yolks gradually, scraping down the bowl and blending until smooth after each addition. Add the flour all at once and mix on low speed until just blended.

2. Turn the dough out onto a lightly floured work surface. Scale the dough as desired. Wrap tightly and refrigerate for at least 1 hour before rolling. The dough can be held under refrigeration or frozen.

# Sweet Potato Pâte Dough

YIELD: *1 lb 8 oz / 680 g*

| | |
|---|---|
| 1 lb 8 oz / 680 g Pâte Dough (page 598) | ½ tsp / 1 g ground mace |
| ½ tsp / 1 g ground cinnamon | 5 oz / 142 g sweet potato, baked, boiled, |
| ½ tsp / 1 g ground cardamom | or steamed, and puréed |

Prepare the pâte dough according to the basic recipe, adding the ground spices in step 1 and the sweet potato in step 2. You may need to reduce the amount of milk called for in the original pâte dough recipe.

*Chef's note*  *To make decorative display pieces with the pâte dough, roll the dough into thin sheets using a pasta machine. Pâte dough can be cut to give the effect of fish netting. Score the dough with a lattice cutter. Gently pull apart the dough, lay it on crumbled foil, and paint with egg wash. The crumbled foil gives additional height and texture to the pâte dough netting. Bake at 325°F / 163°C until dried and cooked through, 8 to 10 minutes.*

# Blitz Puff Pastry

*Makes 2 lb 8 oz / 1.13 kg*

8 oz / 227 g cake flour

8 oz / 227 g bread flour

1 lb / 454 g butter, cubed and chilled

9 fl oz / 270 mL ice-cold water

¼ oz / 7.50 g salt

1. Combine the cake and bread flours in the bowl of a stand mixer. Add the butter and toss with your fingertips until the butter is coated with flour. Combine the water and salt; add all at once. Mix on low speed with the dough hook until the dough forms a shaggy mass.

2. Tightly cover the mixture with plastic wrap and refrigerate until the butter is firm but not brittle, about 20 minutes.

3. Place the shaggy mass on a lightly floured work surface and roll out into a rectangle ½ in / 1.25 cm thick and approximately 12 in by 30 in / 30.5 cm by 76 cm (see Fig 12-2a).

4. Administer a book fold, roll out the dough to the same dimensions, and administer a second book fold. Tightly wrap the dough in plastic wrap and refrigerate 30 minutes.

5. Repeat this process two more times for a total of 4 book folds, refrigerating and turning the dough 90° each time before rolling. After completing the final fold, wrap the dough in plastic wrap and refrigerate until firm, at least 1 hour (see Fig 12-2b). (The dough can be refrigerated or frozen until use.)

*Chef's note*   *More folds will yield finer and more even layers with less height. Fewer folds yield a lighter product, with irregular layers and more height.*

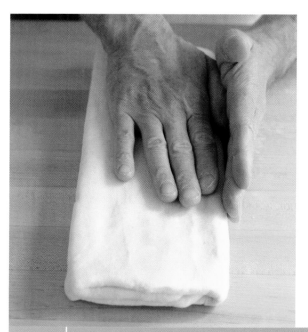

FIG 12-2A   *Blitz puff pastry should have large, visible chunks of butter dispersed throughout the dough before being folded.*

FIG 12-2B   *Once all of the folds have been made, the dough should have a smooth, even appearance.*

# Focaccia

*YIELD: 3 lb / 1.36 kg*

Cornmeal, as needed

18 fl oz / 540 mL water

½ oz / 14 g compressed yeast

2 fl oz / 60 mL extra-virgin olive oil

1 lb 12 oz / 794 g hard wheat flour

½ oz / 14 g salt

GARNISH OPTIONS

Crumbled goat cheese, as needed

Olives, pitted and sliced, as needed

Pine nuts, as needed

Sun-dried tomatoes, as needed

Chopped herbs such as basil and oregano, as needed

1. Line baking sheets with parchment. Scatter with cornmeal.

2. Combine the water, yeast, and oil until yeast is dissolved. Add the flour and salt. Mix the dough until smooth and elastic. Cover the bowl and allow the dough to ferment for 75 minutes. Punch down and scale the dough at 10 oz / 284 g per foccacia. Round off dough. Set dough on prepared sheet pan and proof at room temperature 1 hour.

3. Press the balls of dough flat and stretch slightly. Brush with olive oil and add any optional garnish items desired. Pan-proof an additional 30 minutes.

4. Bake in a 425°F / 218°C oven for approximately 30 minutes.

*Variation* Grissini: Prepare the dough through step 2. Punch down and scale at 1½ oz / 43 g. Round off the dough. Set on a sheet pan and proof at room temperature 1 hour. Roll the balls into long, thin sticks. Brush with olive oil or egg wash and top with desired seasoning: kosher salt, sesame seeds, or fresh herbs. Pan-proof an additional 15 minutes. Bake in 425°F / 218°C oven for 10 to 12 minutes.

*Chef's note* Focaccia may be lightly brushed with garlic and olive oil and served on its own, used as the base of an hors d'oeuvre or sandwich (see pages 163 and 170), or dressed with various additions.

# Pasta Dough

YIELD: *1 lb 8 oz / 680 g*

| | |
|---|---|
| 1 lb / 454 g all-purpose or bread flour | 2 tsp / 6 g salt |
| 4 to 6 eggs | 2 fl oz / 60 mL water, or as needed |

1. Combine all ingredients in a large bowl and knead the mixture until it is smooth and elastic. Add more water if necessary.

2. Cover the dough and allow to rest, refrigerated, for 1 hour before rolling and shaping.

*Variations*  Spinach Pasta: Add 6 oz / 170 g puréed raw spinach. Add additional flour if necessary.

Malfatti Pasta: Run the basic pasta dough through a pasta machine to create thin sheets. Cut the pasta into rectangles 1½ by 2½ in / 3.75 by 6.25 cm.

# Brioche Dough

YIELD: *3 lb / 1.36 kg dough*

| | |
|---|---|
| 1 lb 8 oz / 680 g bread flour | 2 oz / 57 g sugar |
| ⅜ oz / 10 g instant dry yeast | 1 tbsp / 10 g salt |
| 8 oz / 227 g eggs, at 40°F / 4°C (about 4 large eggs) | 12 oz / 340 g butter, cut into cubes, softened but still pliable (60 to 65°F / 16 to 19°C) |
| 4 fl oz / 120 mL whole milk | |

1. Combine the flour and yeast in the bowl of a 5-qt / 4.8-L mixer. Add the eggs, milk, sugar, and salt; mix with a dough hook on low speed until evenly blended, scraping down the bowl as needed, 4 minutes.

2. Gradually add the butter with the mixer running on low speed, scraping down the bowl as necessary, 2 minutes. After the butter has been fully incorporated, increase to medium speed and mix until the dough begins to pull away from the sides of the bowl and is quite elastic, 15 minutes.

3. Remove the dough from the bowl, shape into a brick, wrap well, and refrigerate at least 12 hours before using. Brioche dough can be frozen for up to 2 months.

# Whole Wheat Pita Bread

YIELD: *12 pitas*

| | |
|---|---|
| 2¼ tsp / 8 g active dry yeast (⅓ oz) | 1 lb / 454 g whole wheat flour |
| 20 fl oz / 600 mL warm water (100°F / 38°C) | 1 tbsp / 9 g salt |
| 1 lb / 454 g bread flour | ¾ fl oz / 22.5 mL olive oil |

1. Combine the yeast with the warm water and mix well.

2. Add the remaining dry ingredients and mix the dough on low speed until it is quite elastic, 3 to 4 minutes.

3. Place the dough in a large bowl. Brush it with olive oil, cover, and allow it to double in size at room temperature, approximately 1 to 2 hours. Punch the dough down.

4. Scale the dough to pitas 4 oz / 113 g each and line them three by five on an oiled sheet pan. Cover with plastic wrap. Allow the scaled pita breads to double in size before rolling.

5. Dust the workspace with flour. Roll the pita dough out to a disc about 7 in / 18 cm in diameter.

6. Rest, covered, at room temperature until the dough is well relaxed, 15 minutes.

7. Load the pitas directly onto the deck of a 500°F / 260°C oven, or onto a baking stone or a preheated sheet pan, and bake until puffed but not browned, 3 to 4 minutes. Stack the pitas 5 high and wrap each stack in a cloth. Cool before serving.

# Simple Syrup

YIELD: *32 fl oz / 960 mL*

32 fl oz / 960 mL water

8 oz / 227 g sugar

4½ fl oz / 135 mL lemon juice

9 fl oz / 270 mL orange juice

1. Bring the water and sugar to a boil; stir until sugar dissolves; cool.

2. Flavor with lemon and orange juice. Cover and refrigerate until needed.

# Roasting Garlic and Shallots

*The flavor of garlic and shallots becomes rich, sweet, and smoky after roasting. Roasted garlic can be found as a component of marinades, glazes, and vinaigrettes, as well as a spread for grilled breads and focaccia.*

1. Place the unpeeled head of garlic (or shallot bulbs) in a small pan. Some chefs like to place it on a bed of salt, which holds the heat, roasting the garlic quickly and producing a drier texture in the finished product.

2. Roast at a moderate temperature until the garlic or shallots are quite soft. Any juices that run from the garlic or shallots should be browned. The aroma should be sweet and pleasing, with no hints of harshness or sulfur.

FIG 12-4    *Properly roasted garlic will develop a soft texture and take on a light golden brown color and sweet aroma.*

# Tomato Concassé

*Make only enough tomato concassé to last through a single service period. Once peeled and chopped, tomatoes begin to lose some of their flavor and texture.*

1. Cut away the tomatoes' core ends and score skin away using a paring knife.

2. Bring a pot of water to a rolling boil. Drop the tomatoes into the water. After 10 to 35 seconds (depending upon the tomatoes' age and ripeness), remove them with a slotted spoon, skimmer, or spider. Immediately plunge them into very cold or ice water. Pull away the skin.

3. Halve each tomato crosswise at its widest point and gently squeeze out the seeds. (Plum tomatoes are more easily seeded by cutting lengthwise.)

4. Cut the flesh into dice or julienne, as desired.

*Chef's note*  One of the primary reasons for skinning and de-seeding the tomato is to avoid a bitter end product, which can be the result if the seeds and skin are used.

# Oven-Roasted Tomatoes

*Makes 10 servings*

| | |
|---|---|
| 4 lb 8 oz / 2.04 kg tomatoes | 2 tsp / 2 g chopped oregano |
| 3 fl oz / 90 mL extra-virgin olive oil | 1 tsp / 1 g chopped thyme |
| ½ oz / 14 g minced garlic | Salt, as needed |
| ½ oz / 14 g minced shallots | Ground black pepper, as needed |
| 2 tsp / 2 g chopped basil | |

1. Remove the cores from the tomatoes and cut into the desired shape (halved, quartered, wedged, or sliced). Arrange in a single layer in a shallow pan.

2. Combine the oil, garlic, shallots, basil, oregano, and thyme. Season with salt and pepper. Drizzle this mixture over the tomatoes and turn carefully to coat them.

3. Arrange the tomatoes on racks set in sheet pans. Roast in a 275°F / 135°C oven until tomatoes are dried and lightly browned, 1 to 1½ hours.

4. Serve immediately or cool, cover, and refrigerate.

# Roasting Peppers

*To roast and peel small quantities, roast the peppers over a flame:*

1. Hold the pepper over the flame of a gas burner with tongs or a kitchen fork, or place the pepper on a grill. Turn the pepper and roast it until the surface is evenly charred.

2. Place in a plastic or paper bag or under an inverted bowl to steam the skin loose.

3. When the pepper is cool enough to handle, remove the charred skin, using a paring knife if necessary.

*For larger quantities, oven-roast the peppers:*

1. Halve the peppers and remove stems and seeds. Place cut side down on an oiled sheet pan.

2. Place in a 475°F / 246°C oven or under a broiler. Roast or broil until evenly charred.

3. Remove from the oven or broiler and cover immediately, using an inverted sheet pan, aluminum foil, or plastic wrap (see Fig 12-5a). This will steam the peppers, making the skin easier to remove.

4. Peel, using a paring knife if necessary (see Fig 12-5b).

FIG 12-5A | *As soon as they have finished roasting, cover the peppers and allow them to steam, making the skin easier to remove.*

FIG 12-5B | *Peel the roasted peppers and use as desired.*

# Preparing Artichokes

*Artichokes can be cut in a number of ways, depending on the desired final presentation.*

To prepare whole artichokes:

1. First, cut away the stem. The amount of stem removed is determined by how the artichoke is to be served, as well as by how tender or tough the stem is. Cutting the stem away even with the bottom of the artichoke makes a flat surface, allowing the artichoke to sit flat on the plate.

2. Peel the stem with a paring knife.

3. Cut off the top of the artichoke.

4. Snip the barbs from each leaf with kitchen scissors.

5. Rub the cut surfaces with lemon juice to prevent browning, or hold the trimmed artichoke in acidulated water (a mixture of lemon juice and water).

6. The artichoke can be simmered or steamed at this point, if desired, or the center of the artichoke, the choke, may be removed prior to cooking. To remove the choke, spread the leaves of the cooked or raw artichoke open. The choke can now be scooped out using a spoon.

To prepare artichoke bottoms:

1. Pull away the leaves from around the stem and trim the stem as desired. Make a cut through the artichoke at its widest point, just above the artichoke bottom, to remove the tips of the leaves.

2. Use a paring knife to trim the tough outer leaves away from the artichoke bottom.

3. Scoop out the center of the artichoke bottom, known as the choke. Hold trimmed artichoke bottoms in acidulated water to prevent browning.

To prepare artichoke halves or quarters:

1. Pull away the leaves from around the stem and trim just the woody end of the stem. The stem may also be removed, if desired.

2. Peel the stem with a paring knife.

3. Cut the top third of the artichoke off. Remove the tough outer leaves from the artichoke.

4. Cut the artichokes into halves or quarters. Hold in acidulated water until needed to prevent oxidation.

# Roasting Corn

*To roast corn, dampen the husk and place in a hot (475 to 500° F/ 245 to 260° C) oven or over hot coals. Roast or grill for approximately 15 to 20 minutes. The husks should become a deep brown. The corn should be tender (to check for doneness, pull back some of the husk and pierce a kernel). When the corn is cool enough to handle, pull away the corn and the silk. Cut the corn away from the cob with a sharp paring knife.*

# Preparing Leeks

*A leek grows in layers, trapping grit and sand between each layer, and one of the biggest concerns when working with leeks is removing every trace of dirt. Careful rinsing and cleaning is essential.*

1. To clean leeks, rinse off all the surface dirt, paying special attention to the roots, where dirt clings. Lay the leek on the cutting board, and using a chef's knife, trim away only the heavy, dark green portion of the leaves. By cutting on an angle, you can avoid losing the tender light green portion of the leek. Reserve the dark green portion of the leek to make bouquet garni or for other uses.

2. Trim away most of the root end, being careful not to cut away too much of the white part. Cut the leek lengthwise into halves, thirds, or quarters, depending on the final use of the leek. Gently pull apart the layers and rinse the leek thoroughly under running water to remove any remaining grit or sand.

3. Cut the leek into the desired shape. Leeks may be left in halves or quarters with the stem end still intact for braising. Or they may be cut into slices, chiffonade, julienne, dice, or paysanne-style cuts.

# Plumping Dried Fruits and Vegetables

1. Check the dried ingredient and remove any obvious debris or seriously blemished or moldy specimens.

2. Place the ingredient in a bowl or other container and add enough boiling or very hot liquid (water, wine, fruit juices, or broth can all be used) to cover.

3. Let the dried ingredient steep in the hot water for several minutes, until softened and plumped.

4. Pour off the liquid, reserving it if desired for use in another preparation. If necessary, the liquid can be strained through a coffee filter or cheesecloth to remove any debris.

# Toasting Nuts, Seeds, and Spices

*Toasting nuts, seeds, and spices improves their flavor, as long as they are not allowed to scorch.*
*To toast small quantities, use a dry skillet (cast iron is an excellent choice, but other materials will also work well).*

1. Heat the skillet over direct heat and add the nuts, seeds, or spices.

2. Toss or stir frequently, stopping just as a good color and aroma are achieved.

3. Pour the nuts, seeds, or spices out into a cool sheet pan and spread into a thin layer to stop any further browning.

Large quantities can be toasted in a moderate oven.

1. Spread out the nuts, seeds, or spices on a dry sheet pan and toast just until a pleasant aroma is apparent. The oils in nuts, seeds, and spices can scorch quickly, so be sure to check frequently.

2. Stir them often to encourage even browning.

3. Be sure to transfer nuts and spices toasted in the oven to a cool sheet pan immediately, so they don't become scorched from residual heat in the pan.

*Toasting dried chiles: Dried chiles may be toasted in the same manner, in a dry skillet or in the oven. They may also be passed repeatedly through a flame until toasted and softened. The pulp and seeds are then scraped from the skin, or the whole chile may be used, according to individual recipes.*

# Rendering Fats

*Occasionally the fat from ducks, geese, or pork may be required for such dishes as confit or rillettes.*

1. Cube or coarsely grind the fat, if necessary.

2. Place the fat in a sauteuse. Add about ½ in / 1 cm water to the uncooked fats if there are no drippings present.

3. Cook over low heat until the water evaporates and the fat is released. (This is the actual clarifying process.)

4. Remove the cracklings, if any, with a slotted spoon (they may be reserved for garnish).

5. Cool the rendered fat, cover, and refrigerate for up to several weeks.

# Parmesan Crisp

To prepare a parmesan crisp, shred Parmesan cheese. Preheat an oven to 350°F / 175°C and line a sheet pan with parchment paper. If desired, trace a circle or other shape on the paper. Allow room on the tracing to permit some spread (about ½ in / 1 cm). Scatter the cheese in an even layer (enough to cover the paper, but not too thick, or the cheese will not crisp). Bake the cheese for 10 minutes, or until cheese is melted and bubbly and looks like lace. Remove the sheet pan from the oven and allow the cheese to cool for a few minutes. The warm cheese crisp can be rolled or draped inside bowls or over dowels or cups to create containers or fans, as desired. Cheese crisps will keep for several days, stored in a parchment-lined airtight container.

# Bread Crumbs

*Bread crumbs may be "dry" or "fresh." Fresh bread crumbs (mie de pain) are prepared by grating or processing a finely textured bread, such as 1- or 2-day-old hard rolls. Dry bread crumbs can be prepared from slightly stale bread that has been additionally dried or toasted in a warm oven.*

# Standard Breading Procedure

*For the best possible results, breading needs a little time to firm up before it is pan fried. If you bread an item and then immediately put it into hot oil, there is a good chance that the breading will fall away. Not only will this have a negative impact on the dish's finished texture, it will also make the cooking oil break down quickly, and subsequent batches cooked in the same oil will blacken without cooking properly.*

1. Dry the main item well, then hold it in one hand (left hand if you are right-handed, and right hand if you are left-handed) and dip it in flour. Shake off any excess flour, and transfer the food to a container of egg wash.

2. Switch hands, pick up the food, and turn it if necessary to coat it on all sides. Transfer it to a container of bread crumbs. Use your dry hand (the first hand) to pack bread crumbs evenly around the food. Shake off any excess, then transfer the food to a holding tray.

3. Refrigerate at least 1 hour before continuing with pan frying.

4. Discard any unused flour, egg wash, and bread crumbs.

# Croutons

YIELD: *1 lb / 454 g*

| | |
|---|---|
| 1 lb / 454 g white bread | 1 tsp / 3 g salt, or as needed |
| 4 oz / 113 g butter, melted or olive oil, as needed | ½ tsp / 1 g pepper (optional), or as needed |

1. Remove the crust from the bread if desired. Slice and cube the bread into desired size (from small cubes to garnish soups served in cups to large slices to garnish salads). If the bread is very fresh, let the bread cubes dry out in the oven for 5 minutes before continuing.

2. Toss the bread, butter or oil, and seasonings together on a sheet pan or in a hotel pan.

3. Bake at 450°F / 232°C until lightly golden, 8 to 10 minutes.

*Chef's note* *Croutons can be prepared in advance and stored in an airtight container for several days. For smaller batches, the croutons can be cooked on top of the stove in a skillet or sauté pan. Deep-fat frying is not recommended for croutons. While it is a quicker cooking method, they absorb too much oil and become greasy.*

*Variations* *Garlic-Flavored Croutons: Add 2 tsp / 6 g very finely minced garlic (garlic paste) to the oil or butter before tossing with the bread cubes.*
*Cheese Croutons: After the bread cubes have been tossed with the butter, toss generously with grated Parmesan, Romano, or other hard grating cheese as needed.*
*Herb-Flavored Croutons: Add chopped fresh or dried herbs (such as oregano or rosemary) as needed to the bread cubes along with the butter.*

# Robialo Cheese Croutons

YIELD: *20 croutons (2 per serving)*

| | |
|---|---|
| ½ baguette, 20 in / 50 cm in length | 2 tbsp / 30 mL extra-virgin olive oil |
| 8 oz / 227 g Robialo cheese or Tallegio cheese | Salt, as needed |
| | Ground black pepper, as needed |

1. Cut the baguettes on the bias into slices ¼ in / 6 mm thick (about 20 slices).

2. Cut the cheese into 20 slices.

3. Lightly brush olive oil on each bread slice. Bake at 450°F / 232°C until lightly crisp, about 4 minutes. Remove from the oven.

4. Flip each crouton over. Put one slice cheese on each crouton and season with salt and pepper. Return to oven until cheese is melted, about 30 seconds. Serve 2 croutons with each serving of salad.

# Cooked Lobster

To remove the meat from the shell, pull away the tail. Split the shell on the underside with kitchen shears and pull out the tail meat in one piece. To remove the meat from the claw, crack the claw in half with the spine of a knife. Pull out the meat carefully, in order to keep the meat intact. Cut the knuckles from end to end and remove nuggets of meat.

# Cleaning a Soft-Shell Crab

1. Bend back the apron and twist to remove it and the intestinal vein at the same time (see Fig 12-6a).

2. Peel back the pointed shell and scrape away the gill filament on each side (see Fig 12-6b).

3. Cut off the head and carefully squeeze out the green bubble behind the eyes (see Fig 12-6c).

FIG 12-6A *Remove the tail flap (or apron) with a slight twisting motion, which will draw out the intestinal vein at the same time.*

FIG 12-6B *Peel back the pointed shell and remove the gill filament on each side of the crab.*

FIG 12-6C *Cut the eyes and mouth away from head just behind the eyes, and squeeze gently to force out the green bubble, which has an unpleasant flavor.*

FIG 12-6D *The cleaned crab with the tail flap, head, and gill filaments removed.*

# Glossary

**Acid:** A substance having a sour or sharp flavor. A substance's degree of acidity is measured on the pH scale; acids have a pH of less than 7. Most foods are somewhat acidic. Foods generally referred to as "acids" include citrus juice, vinegar, and wine. See also Alkali.

**Action station:** A part of a buffet where the chef prepares food to order for the guest. Some typical examples of action stations are omelet stations, pasta stations, and raw bars.

**Aerobic bacteria:** Bacteria that require the presence of oxygen to function.

**Aïoli (Fr.):** Garlic mayonnaise, often based on olive oils (Italian, *allioli;* Spanish, *aliolio*).

**Air drying:** Exposing meats and sausages to proper temperature and humidity conditions to change both flavor and texture for consumption or further processing. Times and temperatures will vary depending upon the type of meat or sausage.

**Albumen:** The white of an egg; also the major protein in egg whites (also spelled *albumin*); used in dry form in some cold food preparations.

**Alkali:** A substance that tests at higher than 7 on the pH scale. Alkalis are sometimes described as having a slightly soapy flavor. Olives and baking soda are some of the few alkaline foods. See also *Acid.*

**Allumette (Fr.):** Vegetables, potatoes, or other items cut into pieces the size and shape of matchsticks; ⅛ by ⅛ in by 1 to 2 in / 3 by 3 mm by 3 to 5 cm is the standard measure for the cut.

**Anaerobic bacteria:** Bacteria that do not require the presence of oxygen to function.

**Andouille:** A spicy pork sausage that is French in origin, but is now more often associated with Cajun cooking. There are hundreds of varieties of this regional specialty.

**Antipasto (It.):** Italian for "before the pasta." Typically a platter of cold hors d'oeuvre that includes meats, olives, cheese, and vegetables.

**AP/As-purchased weight:** The weight of an item before trimming or other preparation (as opposed to edible portion weight, or EP).

**Appareil (Fr.):** A prepared mixture of ingredients used alone or as an ingredient in another base preparation, such as duchesse potatoes or duxelle.

**Appetizer:** One or more of the initial courses in a meal. These may be hot or cold, plated or served as finger food. They should stimulate the appetite and should go well with the remaining meal.

**Aromatics:** Plant ingredients, such as herbs and spices, used to enhance the flavor and fragrance of food.

**Arrowroot:** A powdered starch made from cassava, a tropical root. Used primarily as a thickener. Remains clear when cooked.

**Aspic:** A clear jelly made from clarified stock (or occasionally from fruit or vegetable juices) thickened with gelatin. Used to coat foods, or cubed and used as a garnish.

# B

**Bacteria:** Microscopic organisms. Some have beneficial properties; others can cause food-borne illnesses when contaminated foods are ingested.

**Bain-marie (Fr.):** A water bath used to cook foods gently by surrounding the cooking vessel with simmering water. Also, a set of nesting pots with single, long handles used as a double boiler. Also, a round steam-table insert.

**Barbecue:** A variation of a roasting method involving grilling or slow smoke-roasting food over a wood or charcoal fire. Usually some sort of rub, marinade, or sauce is brushed on the item during cooking.

**Bard:** To cover an item with thin slices or sheets or strips of fat, such as bacon or fatback, to baste it during roasting. The fat is usually tied on with butcher's twine.

**Barquette (Fr.):** A boat-shaped tart or tartlet, which may have a sweet or savory filling.

**Baste:** To moisten food during cooking with pan drippings, sauce, or other liquid. Basting prevents food from drying out, improves color, and adds flavor.

**Baton/Batonnet (Fr.):** Literally, "stick" or "small stick." Items cut into pieces somewhat larger than allumette or julienne; ¼ by ¼ in by 2 to 2½ in / 6 by 6 mm by 5 to 6 cm is the standard measure for this cut.

**Béchamel:** A white sauce made of milk thickened with white or pale roux and flavored with onion. It is one of the grand sauces.

**Binder:** An ingredient or appareil used to thicken a sauce or hold together a mixture of ingredients.

**Blanch:** To cook an item briefly in boiling water or hot fat before finishing or storing it. This sets the color and, if applicable, can make the skin easier to remove.

**Blood sausage:** Also called black pudding or blood pudding, a sausage where the main ingredient is liquid blood.

**Bloom:** To soften gelatin in lukewarm liquid before use. Also, to allow casing on smoked sausage to darken at room temperature after smoking.

**Boil:** A cooking method in which items are immersed in liquid at or above the boiling point of water (212°F / 100°C).

**Botulism:** A food-borne illness caused by toxins produced by the anaerobic bacterium *Clostridium botulinum*.

**Bouchée (Fr.):** A small puff pastry shell that may be filled with meats, cheese, seafood, or even fruit. Served as an hors d'oeuvre or as a garnish on a larger entrée.

**Boucher (Fr.):** Butcher.

**Bouillon (Fr.):** Broth.

**Bouquet garni (Fr.):** A small bundle of herbs tied with string, used to flavor stocks, braises, and other preparations. Usually contains bay leaf, parsley, thyme, and possibly other aromatics, such as leek and celery stalk.

**Braise:** A cooking method in which the main item, usually a tough cut of meat, is seared in fat, then simmered in a specific quantity of stock or another liquid in a covered vessel, slowly tenderizing it by breaking down collagen.

**Brine:** A solution of salt, water, and seasonings used to flavor and preserve foods.

**Brisket:** A cut of beef from the lower forequarter, best suited for long-cooking preparations like braising. Corned beef is cured beef brisket.

**Broil:** A cooking method in which items are cooked by a radiant heat source placed above the food.

**Brunoise (Fr.):** Small dice; ⅛ in / 3 mm square is the standard measure for this cut. For a brunoise cut, items are first cut in julienne, then cut crosswise. For a fine brunoise, 1⁄16 in / 1.5 mm square; cut items first into fine julienne.

**Bubble knot:** Also called a triple knot. Used to tie beef round, middle, and bung casings. A piece of casing is caught between the two first knots, and a third knot is used to lock the previous knots in place. A length of string is often left at the end for hanging.

**Buffet:** Historically a traditional Swedish mode of dining where people serve themselves from a table or sideboard. Buffet foods commonly include cold meat and cheese platters, pickled fish, salads, sandwiches, and desserts but have expanded to include action stations (see page 553).

**Bulk sausage:** Sausage that is not contained in a casing. Sausages commonly found in bulk include breakfast sausage and Italian sausages meant to be used in pizzas or other dishes. Generally only fresh sausage is packaged in bulk.

**(Beef) Bung cap:** Beef appendix, typically used for larger sausages such as bologna and mortadella. Generally 2 to 2 ½ ft / 61 to 76 cm long with a diameter of about 4 to 6 in / 10 to 15 cm, a beef bung can hold from 10 to 20 lb / 4.54 to 9.07 kg of sausage.

**Butcher:** A chef or purveyor responsible for butchering meats, poultry, and, occasionally, fish. In the brigade system, the butcher may also be responsible for breading meat and fish items and other mise en place operations involving meat.

**Butterfly:** To cut an item (usually meat or seafood) and open out the edges like a book or the wings of a butterfly, to promote attractive appearance and even cooking. Butterflied cuts of meat can be stuffed, rolled, and tied as well.

# C

**Canapé (Fr.):** An hors d'oeuvre consisting of a small piece of bread or toast, often cut in a decorative shape, garnished with a savory spread or topping.

**Caramelization:** The process of browning sugar in the presence of heat. The temperature range in which sugar begins to caramelizes is approximately 320° to 360°F / 160° to 182°C.

**Carry-over cooking:** Heat retained in cooked foods that allows them to continue cooking even after removal from the cooking medium; especially important to roasted foods. The internal temperature rises as the meat rests, a function of cooling as the meat or item seeks equilibrium of temperature.

**Casing:** A synthetic or natural membrane (usually pig, beef, or sheep intestines) used to enclose sausage forcemeat.

**Cassoulet (Fr.):** A stew of beans baked with pork or other meats, duck or goose confit, and seasonings.

**Caul fat:** A fatty membrane from a pig or sheep that lines the stomach and resembles fine netting; used to bard roasts and pâtés and to encase sausage forcemeat.

**Cellulose:** A complex carbohydrate; the main structural component of plant cells.

**Charcuterie (Fr.):** The preparation of pork and other meat items, such as hams, terrines, sausages, pâtés, and other forcemeats that are usually preserved in some manner, such as smoking, brining, and curing.

**Chaud-froid (Fr.):** Literally, "hot-cold." A sauce that is prepared hot but served cold as part of a buffet display, usually as a decorative coating for meats, poultry, or seafood; classically made from béchamel, cream, or aspic.

**Cheesecloth:** A light, fine-mesh gauze cloth used for straining liquids and making sachets and in many other kitchen operations including cheese making.

**Chiffonade:** Leafy vegetables or herbs cut into fine shreds; often used as a garnish.

**Chile:** The fruit of certain types of capsicum peppers (not related to black pepper), used fresh or dry as a seasoning. Chiles come in many types (for example, jalapeño, serrano, poblano) and varying degrees of spiciness and heat, measured in Scoville units.

**Chili powder:** Dried, ground, or crushed chiles, often including other ground spices and herbs.

**Chipolata:** A small, spicy sausage usually made from pork or veal and stuffed into a sheep casing.

**Chitterlings:** Hog middle intestines.

**Chop:** To cut into pieces of roughly the same size. Also, a small cut of meat including part of the rib.

**Choucroute (Fr.):** Sauerkraut; preserved cabbage with a sour flavor. Choucroute garni is sauerkraut garnished with various meats such as cured meats and sausages.

**Clarification:** The process of removing solid impurities from a liquid (such as butter or stock). Also, a mixture of ground meat, egg whites, mirepoix, tomato purée, herbs, and spices used to clarify stock for consommé.

**Clarified butter:** Butter from which the milk solids and water have been removed, leaving pure butterfat. Has a higher smoking point than whole butter but less butter flavor. Also known as ghee.

**Coagulation:** The curdling or clumping of protein, usually due to the application of heat or acid.

**Coarse chop:** To cut into pieces of roughly the same size; used for items such as mirepoix, where appearance is not important.

**Cold smoking:** A procedure used to give smoked flavor to products without cooking them.

**Collagen:** A fibrous protein found in the connective tissue of animals, which is used to make sausage casings as well as glue and gelatin. Breaks down into gelatin when cooked in a moist environment for an extended period of time.

**Collagen casing:** Casings made from collagen that is usually obtained from animal hides. Collagen casings are easy to use and store and have the advantage of being uniform and consistent.

**Compote (Fr.):** A dish of fruit—fresh or dried—cooked in syrup flavored with spices or liqueur.

**Compound butter:** Whole butter combined with herbs or other seasonings and usually used to sauce grilled or broiled items, vegetables or pastas, or as a spread for sandwiches and canapés.

**Concassé/concasser (Fr.):** To pound or chop coarsely. Usually refers to tomatoes that have been peeled, seeded, and coarsely chopped.

**Condiment:** An aromatic mixture, such as pickles, chutney, and some sauces and relishes, that accompanies food (usually kept on the table throughout service).

**Confit (Fr.):** Preserved meat (usually goose, duck, or pork) cooked and preserved in its own fat.

**Confiture (Fr.):** Referring to jam or preserves.

**Corned beef:** Beef brisket preserved with salt and spices. The term "corned" refers to the chunks of salt spread over the brisket during the corning process.

**Cornichon (Fr.):** A small, sour, pickled cucumber.

**Cornstarch:** A fine, white powder milled from dried corn; used primarily as a thickener for sauces and occasionally as an ingredient in batters. Viscous when hot, gelatinous when cold.

**Coulis:** A thick purée, usually of vegetables or fruit. (Traditionally meat, fish, or shellfish purée; meat jus; or certain thick soups.)

**Country style:** A forcemeat that is coarse in texture, usually made from pork, pork fat, liver, and various garnishes.

**Court bouillon (Fr.):** Literally, "short broth." An aromatic vegetable broth that usually includes an acidic ingredient, such as wine or vinegar; most commonly used for poaching fish.

**Crème fraîche (Fr.):** Heavy cream cultured to give it a thick consistency and a slightly tangy flavor; used in hot preparations, as it is less likely to curdle when heated than sour cream or yogurt.

**Cross contamination:** The transference of disease-causing elements from one source to another through physical contact.

**Croustade (Fr.):** A small baked or fried edible container for meat, chicken, or other mixtures, usually pastry, but may be made from potatoes or pasta.

**Crouton (Fr.):** A bread or pastry garnish, usually toasted or sautéed until crisp.

**Crudité (Fr.):** Usually raw vegetables but sometimes fruit, served as an appetizer or hors d'oeuvre. Some vegetables may be blanched to improve taste and appearance.

**Cuisson (Fr.):** Poaching liquid—stock, fumet, court bouillon, or other liquid—that may be reduced and used as a base for the poached item's sauce.

**Cure:** To preserve a food by salting. Also, the ingredients used to cure an item.

**Curing salt:** A mixture of 94 percent table salt (sodium chloride) and 6 percent sodium nitrite used to preserve meats. Also known as *tinted curing mixture,* or *TCM.* Curing salt is distinguished by its pink color.

**Curry:** A mixture of spices used primarily in Indian cuisine; may include turmeric, coriander, cumin, cayenne or other chiles, cardamom, cinnamon, clove, fennel, fenugreek, ginger, and garlic. Also, a dish seasoned with curry.

# D

**Deglaze/Déglacer (Fr.):** To use a liquid, such as wine, water, or stock, to dissolve food particles and/or caramelized drippings left in a pan after roasting or sautéing.

**Degrease/Dégraisser (Fr.):** To skim the fat off the surface of a liquid, such as a stock or sauce, or to pour off excess fat from a sauté pan before deglazing.

**Demi-glace (Fr.):** Literally, "half-glaze." A mixture of equal proportions of brown stock and brown sauce that has been reduced by half. One of the grand sauces.

**Dice:** To cut ingredients into small cubes (⅛ in / 3 mm for small or fine; ¼ in / 6 mm for medium; ¾ in / 2 cm for large are standard measures for these cuts).

**Drawn:** A whole fish that has been scaled and gutted but still has its head, fins, and tail.

**Dressed:** Prepared for cooking or service; a dressed fish is gutted and scaled, and its head, tail, and fins are removed (same as pan-dressed). Dressed poultry is plucked, drawn, singed, trimmed, and trussed. Also, coated with dressing, as in a salad.

**Drum sieve:** A sieve consisting of a screen stretched across a shallow cylinder of wood or aluminum. Also known as a *tamis.*

**Dry cure:** A combination of salts and spices used usually before smoking to process meats and forcemeats.

**Dumpling:** Any of a number of small soft dough or batter items that are steamed, poached, or simmered (possibly on top of a stew); may be filled or plain.

**Duxelles (Fr.):** An appareil of finely chopped mushrooms and shallots sautéed gently in butter.

# E

**Egg wash:** A mixture of beaten eggs (whole eggs, yolks, or whites) and a liquid, usually milk or water, used to coat baked goods before or during baking to give them a sheen or to enhance browning.

**Emincer (Fr.):** To cut an item, usually meat, into very thin slices.

**Emulsion:** A mixture of two or more liquids, one of which is a fat or oil and the other of which is water-based, so that tiny globules of one are suspended in the other. This may involve the use of stabilizers, such as egg or mustard. Emulsions may be temporary, permanent, or semipermanent.

**En croûte (Fr.):** Encased in a bread or pastry crust.

**Encapsulation:** A preparation in which a base that sometimes includes alginate is dropped into a calcium solution where it forms a pellicle or film. The center of the sphere-shaped capsule remains soft.

**EP/Edible portion:** The weight of an item after trimming and preparation (as opposed to the purchased weight, or AP).

# F

**Facultative bacteria:** Bacteria that can survive both with and without oxygen.

**Farce (Fr.):** Forcemeat or stuffing (*farci* means "stuffed").

**Fat:** One of the basic nutrients used by the body to provide energy. Fats also provide flavor in food and give a feeling of fullness.

**Fatback:** Pork fat from the back of the pig, used primarily for barding.

**Fermentation:** The breakdown of carbohydrates into carbon dioxide gas and alcohol, usually through the action of yeast on sugar.

**Fermento:** A commonly used brand of dairy-based fermentation product for semi-dry fermented sausages, used to lower pH and give a tangy flavor.

**Fillet/Filet (Fr.):** A boneless cut of meat, fish, or poultry.

**Fine mesh strainer:** A conical sieve made from fine metal mesh screen, used for straining and puréeing foods.

**Fines herbes (Fr.):** A mixture of fresh herbs, usually equal parts by volume of parsley, chervil, tarragon, and chives.

**Foie gras (Fr.):** The fattened liver of a force-fed duck or goose.

**Food-borne illness:** An illness in humans caused by the consumption of an adulterated food product. In order for a food-borne illness outbreak to be considered official, it must involve two or more people who have eaten the same food and it must be confirmed by health officials.

**Food mill:** A type of strainer with a crank-operated, curved blade; used to purée soft foods.

**Food processor:** A machine with interchangeable blades and disks and a removable bowl and lid separate from the motor housing. It can be used for a variety of tasks, including chopping, grinding, puréeing, emulsifying, kneading, slicing, shredding, and cutting julienne.

**Forcemeat:** A mixture of chopped or ground meat or seafood and other ingredients used for pâté, sausages, and other preparations.

**Fumet (Fr.):** A type of stock in which the main flavoring ingredient is smothered with wine and aromatics; fish fumet is the most common type.

# G

**Galantine (Fr.):** Boned meat (usually poultry) that is stuffed into its own skin, rolled, poached, and served cold, usually in aspic.

**Garde manger (Fr.):** Cold kitchen chef or station; the position responsible for cold food preparations, including salads, cold appetizers, and pâtés.

**Garnish:** An edible decoration or accompaniment to a dish.

**Gelatin:** A protein-based substance found in animal bones and connective tissue. When dissolved in hot liquid and then cooled, it can be used as a thickener or stabilizer.

**Gelatinization:** A phase in the process of thickening a liquid with starch in which starch molecules swell to form a network that traps water molecules.

**Gherkin:** A small pickled cucumber.

**Giblets:** Organs and other trim from poultry, including the liver, heart, gizzard, and neck.

**Glace (Fr.):** Reduced stock; ice cream; icing.

**Glaze:** To give an item a shiny surface by brushing it with sauce, aspic, icing, or another appareil. For meat, to coat with sauce and then brown in an oven or salamander.

**Gratiné (Fr.):** Browned in an oven or under a salamander (*au gratin, gratin de*). Gratin can also refer to a forcemeat in which some portion of the dominant meat is seared and cooled before grinding.

**Gravlax:** Raw salmon cured with salt, sugar, and fresh dill. A regional dish of Scandinavian origin.

**Grill:** A technique in which foods are cooked by a radiant heat source placed below the food. Also, the piece of equipment on which grilling is done. Grills may be fueled by gas, electricity, charcoal, or wood.

**Grill pan:** An iron skillet with ridges that is used on the stove top to simulate grilling.

**Grinder:** A machine used to grind meat, ranging from small hand-operated models to large capacity motor-driven models. Meat or other foods are fed through a hopper into the grinder where the worm or auger pushes them into a blade. The blade cuts and forces the item through different-size grinder plates. Care should be taken to keep the machine as clean as possible to lessen the chances of cross contamination.

**Grinder plates:** Used to determine the texture of the ground meat, plates come in varying sizes, from as small as ⅛ in / 3 mm for fine-textured ground meat, to as large as ⅜ in / 9 mm, used mostly to create garnishes for emulsion sausages.

**Griswold:** Brand name for a pot, similar to a rondeau, made of cast iron; may have a single short handle rather than the usual loop handles.

**Grosse pièce (Fr.):** Literally, "large piece." The main part of a pâté or terrine that is left unsliced and serves as a focal point for a platter or other display.

**Gumbo:** A Creole soup-stew thickened with filé or okra.

# H

**Haricot (Fr.):** Bean. *Haricots verts* are thin green beans.

**Head cheese:** A jellied meat product typically made from diced boiled pork head meat held together by the natural gelatin contained in the reduced stock left over from boiling the head. Garnished with pickles, pimientos, and parsley and flavored with vinegar.

**Hock:** The lowest part of an animal's leg; could be considered the ankle. The most familiar example is ham hock.

**Hog casings:** Casings are made from the small and middle hog intestine. Used for countless sausages, hog casings range in diameter from 1¼ to 1⅓ in / 32 to 35 mm (used for bratwurst and Italian sausage) to 1½ to 1⅔ in / 38 to 42 mm (used for Polish sausage and pepperoni). The type of hog casing used will depend on the intended application.

**Hors d'oeuvre (Fr.):** Literally, "outside the work."

**Hot smoking:** A technique used when a fully cooked smoked item is desired. Both cured and uncured items can be hot smoked. Smoking temperature and time will depend on the product.

**Hygiene:** Conditions and practices followed to maintain health, including sanitation and personal cleanliness.

# I

**Infusion:** Steeping an aromatic or other item in liquid to extract its flavor. Also, the liquid resulting from this process.

**Instant-read thermometer:** A thermometer used to measure the internal temperature of foods. The stem is inserted in the food, producing an instant temperature readout.

# J

**Julienne (Fr.):** Vegetables, potatoes, or other items cut into thin strips; ⅛ by ⅛ in by 1 to 2 in / 3 by 3 mm by 3 to 5 cm is the standard measure for this cut. Fine julienne is 1⁄16 by 1⁄16 in by 1 to 2 in / 1.5 by 1.5 mm by 3 to 5 cm.

**Jus (Fr.):** Juice. *Jus de viande* is meat juice. Meat served *au jus* is served with its own juice.

**Jus lié (Fr.):** Meat juice thickened lightly with arrowroot or cornstarch.

## K

**Kosher:** Prepared in accordance with Jewish dietary laws.

**Kosher salt:** Pure, refined rock salt often preferred for pickling because it does not contain magnesium carbonate and thus it does not cloud brine solutions. Also used to kosher items. Also known as *coarse salt* or *pickling salt*.

## L

**Lard:** Rendered pork fat used for pastry and frying. Also the process of inserting strips of fat or seasonings into meat before roasting or braising to add flavor and succulence.

**Lardon (Fr.):** A strip of pork fat, used for larding; may be seasoned. Also can mean a small strip of cooked bacon commonly used as a garnish.

**Liaison (Fr.):** A mixture of egg yolks and cream used to thicken and enrich sauces. Also, loosely applied to any appareil used as a thickener.

**Links:** Segments of sausage created when a filled casing is twisted or tied off at intervals.

**Liquid smoke:** Distilled and bottled smoke that can be used in place of actual smoking to provide a smoked flavor.

**Looped sausage:** Also known as *ring-tied sausages*; kielbasa is an example of these longer sausages. Also refers to sausage made in beef round casings.

## M

**Maillard reaction:** A complex browning reaction that results in the distinctive flavor and color of foods that do not contain much sugar, including roasted meats. The reaction, which involves carbohydrates and amino acids, is named after the French scientist who first discovered it. There are low-temperature and high-temperature Maillard reactions; high temperature starts at 310°F / 154°C.

**Mandoline (Fr.):** A slicing device of stainless steel with carbon-steel blades. The blades may be adjusted to cut items into various cuts and thicknesses.

**Marbling:** The intramuscular fat found in meat that makes it tender and juicy when cooked.

**Marinade (Fr.):** An appareil used before cooking to flavor and moisten foods; may be liquid or dry. Liquid marinades are usually based on an acidic ingredient, such as wine or vinegar; dry marinades are usually salt- or spice-based.

**Mayonnaise:** A cold emulsion sauce made of oil, egg yolks, vinegar, mustard, and seasonings.

**Medallion (Fr.):** A small, round scallop-shaped cut of meat.

**Mesophilic:** A term used to describe bacteria that thrive within the middle-range temperatures—between 60° and 100°F / 16° and 43°C.

**Microgreens:** Seedlings of various herbs, greens, and vegetables that are typically used in salads or as a garnish.

**Mie de pain (Fr.):** The soft part of bread (not the crust) used to make fresh white bread crumbs.

**Mince:** To chop into very small pieces.

**Mirepoix (Fr.):** A combination of chopped aromatic vegetables—usually two parts onion, one part carrot, and one part celery—used to flavor stocks, soups, braises, and stews.

**Mise en place (Fr.):** Literally, "put in place." The preparation and assembly of ingredients, pans, utensils, and plates or serving pieces needed for a particular dish or service period.

**Molasses:** The dark brown, sweet syrup that is a by-product of sugar cane refining.

**Mousse (Fr.):** A dish made with beaten egg whites and/or whipped cream folded into a flavored base appareil; may be sweet or savory, and should be foamy or frothy. Can be made with cooked items, bound with gelatin, and served cold.

**Mousseline (Fr.):** A very light forcemeat based on white meats or seafood lightened with cream and eggs.

# N

**Napper/Nappé (Fr.):** To coat with sauce. Also, thickened.

**New potato:** A small, waxy potato that is usually prepared by boiling or steaming and is often eaten with its skin. Refers to "new" harvest; not always small but with very thin skin.

# O

**Offal:** Variety meats including head meat, tail, and feet as well as organs such as brains, heart, kidneys, lights (or lungs), sweetbreads, tripe, and tongue.

**Oignon piqué (Fr.):** Literally, "pricked onion." A whole, peeled onion to which a bay leaf is attached, using a whole clove as a tack; used to flavor béchamel sauce and some soups.

**Organ meat:** Meat from an organ, rather than the muscle tissue of an animal.

# P

**Panada (It.):** An appareil based on starch (such as flour or crumbs), moistened with a liquid; used as a binder.

**Parchment:** Heat-resistant paper used to line baking pans, cook items en papillote, construct pastry cones, and cover items during shallow poaching.

**Parcook:** To partially cook an item before storing or finishing by another method; may be the same as blanching.

**Pâte (Fr.):** Pastry or noodle dough.

**Pâté (Fr.):** A rich forcemeat of meat, game, poultry, seafood, and/or vegetables, baked in pastry or in a mold or dish.

**Pâte à choux (Fr.):** Cream-puff paste, made by boiling a mixture of water, butter, and flour, then beating in whole eggs. (Also known as *choux paste*.)

**Pâte brisée (Fr.):** Short (rich) pastry for pie crusts.

**Pâté de campagne:** Country-style pâté, with a coarse texture.

**Pâté en croûte:** Pâté baked in a pastry crust.

**Paysanne/fermier cut:** A knife cut in which ingredients are cut into flat, square pieces; ½ by ½ by ⅛ in / 1 by 1 by 3 cm is the standard measure for this cut.

**Pellicle:** A sticky "skin" that forms on the outside of produce, salmon, sausage, or meats through air drying and helps smoke particles adhere to the food, resulting in better, more evenly smoked product.

**Pesto (It.):** A thick, puréed mixture of an herb, traditionally basil, and oil used as a sauce for pasta and other foods and as a garnish for soup. Pesto may also contain grated cheese, nuts or seeds, and other seasonings.

**pH scale:** A scale with values from 0 to 14 representing degree of acidity. A measurement of 7 is neutral, 0 is most acidic, and 14 is most alkaline. Chemically, pH measures the concentration/activity of the element hydrogen.

**Phyllo dough:** Flour-and-water dough rolled into very thin sheets; layered with butter and/or crumbs to make pastries. Also known as *filo*.

**Pickling spice:** A mixture of herbs and spices used to season pickles; often includes dill seed, coriander seed, cinnamon stick, peppercorns, and bay leaves.

**Pilaf:** A technique for cooking grains in which the grain is sautéed briefly in butter, then simmered in stock or water with various seasonings. Also known as *pilau, pilaw, pullao, and pilav*.

**Pincé (Fr.):** To caramelize an item by sautéing; usually refers to a tomato product.

**Poach:** A method in which items are cooked gently in liquid at 160° to 180°F / 71° to 80°C.

**Proscuitto:** A dry-cured ham. True proscuitto comes from Parma, Italy, although variations can be found throughout the world.

**Purée (Fr.):** To process food by mashing, straining, or chopping very fine in order to make it into a smooth paste. Also, a product made using this technique.

# Q

**Quenelle (Fr.):** A light, poached dumpling based on a forcemeat (usually chicken, veal, seafood, or game) bound with eggs and typically shaped into an oval.

## R

**Ramekin:** A small, ovenproof dish, usually ceramic. Also, in French, *ramequin*.

**Reduce:** To decrease the volume of a liquid by simmering or boiling; used to provide a thicker consistency and/or concentrated flavors and color.

**Reduction:** The product that results when a liquid is reduced.

**Refresh:** To plunge an item into, or run under, cold water after blanching to prevent further cooking. Also referred to as *shocking*.

**Render:** To melt fat and clarify the drippings for use in sautéing or pan frying.

**Rennet:** An enzyme used in cheese-making to turn milk into cheese; usually taken from the stomach lining of a calf or reproduced chemically in a laboratory.

**Roast:** A dry-heat cooking method in which items are cooked in an oven or on a spit over a fire.

**Roe:** Fish or shellfish eggs.

**Roulade (Fr.):** A slice of meat or fish rolled around a stuffing. Also, filled and rolled sponge cake.

## S

**Sachet d'épices (Fr.):** Literally, "bag of spices." Aromatic ingredients encased in cheesecloth that are used to flavor stocks and other liquids. A standard sachet contains parsley stems, cracked peppercorns, dried thyme, bay leaf, and sometimes garlic.

**Salé (Fr.):** Salted or pickled.

**Salt cod:** Cod that has been salted and dried to preserve it. Also referred to as *baccalà* or *bacalao*.

**Saltpeter:** Potassium nitrate. Formerly used to preserve meat. It is a component of curing salt; it gives certain cured meats their characteristic pink color. Not used commercially since 1975 because its residual amounts are not consistent.

**Sanitation:** The practice of preparation and distribution of food in a clean environment by healthy food workers.

**Sanitize:** To kill pathogenic organisms by chemicals and/or moist heat.

**Sauté:** A cooking method in which naturally tender items are cooked quickly in a small amount of fat in a pan on the range top.

**Sauteuse (Fr.):** A shallow skillet with sloping sides and a single, long handle; used for sautéing. Often referred to as a *sauté pan*.

**Savory:** Not sweet. Also, the name of a course served after dessert and before port in traditional British meals. Also, a family of herbs (including summer and winter varieties).

**Scald:** To heat a liquid, usually milk or cream, to just below the boiling point. May also refer to blanching fruits and vegetables.

**Score:** To cut the surface of an item at regular intervals to allow it to cook or cure evenly.

**Sea salt:** Salt produced by evaporating sea water. Available refined or unrefined, crystallized or ground. Also, *sel gris*, French for "gray salt."

**Sear:** To brown the surface of food in fat over high heat before finishing by another method (for example, braising) to add flavor and color.

**Shallow poach:** A method in which items are cooked gently in a shallow covered pan of simmering liquid. The liquid can then be reduced and used as the basis of a sauce.

**Sieve:** A container made of a perforated material, such as wire mesh, used to drain, rice, or purée foods. Also known as a *tamis*.

**Silverskin:** The tough, connective tissue that surrounds certain muscles.

**Simmer:** To maintain the temperature of a liquid just below boiling. Also, a cooking method in which items are cooked in simmering liquid.

**Slurry:** Starch (flour, cornstarch, or arrowroot) dispersed in cold liquid to prevent it from forming lumps when added to hot liquid as a thickener.

**Smearing:** A fault in sausages; if sausage is processed at too high a temperature, fat will soften and become smeared throughout the sausage. Smeared fat has a tendency to leak out of the sausage and leave it dry.

**Smoke roasting:** Roasting over wood or chips in a oven to add a smoky flavor. A method for roasting foods in which items are placed on a rack in a pan containing wood chips that smolder and emit smoke when the pan is placed on the range top or in the oven.

**Smoking:** Any of several methods for preserving and flavoring foods by exposing them to smoke. Methods include cold smoking (in which smoked items are not fully cooked), hot smoking (in which the items are cooked), and smoke roasting.

**Smoking point:** The temperature at which a fat begins to smoke when heated.

**Smörgasbord:** A classic Swedish manner of dining, where guests serve themselves from a table laden with food; one of the earliest forms of buffets.

**Sodium:** An alkaline metal element necessary in small quantities for human nutrition; one of the components of most salts used in cooking.

**Sodium nitrate:** Used in curing meat products that are not going to be heated by cooking, smoking, or canning.

**Sodium nitrite:** Used in curing meat products that are going to be heated by either cooking, smoking, or canning.

**Stabilizer:** An ingredient (usually a protein or plant product) that is added to an emulsion to prevent it from separating (for example, egg yolk, cream, or mustard). Also, an ingredient, such as gelatin, that is used in various desserts to prevent them from separating (for example, Bavarian creams).

**Standard breading procedure:** The procedure in which items are dredged in flour, dipped in beaten egg, then coated with crumbs before being pan fried or deep fried.

**Stock:** A flavorful liquid prepared by simmering bones and/or vegetables in water with aromatics until their flavor is extracted. It is used as a base for soups, sauces, and other preparations.

**Straight forcemeat:** A forcemeat combining pork and pork fat with another meat made by grinding the mixture together.

**Sweetbreads:** The thymus glands of young animals, usually calves but possibly lambs. Usually sold in pairs of lobes.

# T

**Table salt:** Refined, granulated rock salt. May be fortified with iodine and treated with magnesium carbonate to prevent clumping.

**Tapas:** Small hors d'oeuvre that are thought to have originated in Spain. The varieties of tapas are numerous and are meant to give just a taste of the dish.

**Tart:** A shallow pie without a top crust; may be sweet or savory.

**Tartlet:** A small, single-serving tart.

**TCM/tinted curing mix:** See Curing Salt.

**Temper:** To heat gently and gradually. May refer to the process of incorporating hot liquid into a liaison to gradually raise its temperature. May also refer to the proper method for working with chocolate.

**Tenderloin:** A cut of tender expensive meat from the loin or hind quarter, usually beef or pork

**Terrine (Fr.):** A loaf of forcemeat, similar to a pâté but cooked in a covered mold in a bain-marie. Also, the mold used to cook such items, usually a loaf shape made of ceramic.

**Thermophilic:** Heat-loving; describes bacteria that thrive within the temperature range of 110° to 171°F / 43° to 77°C.

**Timbale (Fr.):** A small, pail-shaped mold used to shape rice, custards, mousselines, and other items. Also, a preparation made in such a mold.

**Tomalley:** Lobster liver, which is olive green in color and turns red when cooked or heated.

**Total utilization:** The principle advocating the use of as much of a product as possible in order to reduce waste and increase profits.

***Trichinella spiralis:*** A spiral-shaped parasitic worm that invades the intestines and muscle tissue; transmitted primarily through infected pork that has not been cooked sufficiently.

**Trichinosis:** The disease transmitted by *Trichinella spiralis*.

**Tripe:** The edible stomach lining of a cow or other ruminant. Honeycomb tripe, the most popular, comes from the second stomach and has a honeycomb-like texture.

**Truss:** To tie up meat or poultry with string before cooking it in order to give it a compact shape for more even cooking and better appearance.

# V

**Variety meat:** Meat from a part of an animal other than the muscle; for example, organs.

**Velouté (Fr.):** A sauce of white stock (chicken, veal, or seafood) thickened with blond or pale roux; one of the grand sauces. Also, a cream soup made with a velouté sauce base and flavorings (sometimes puréed) that is usually finished with a liaison.

**Venison:** Originally meat from large game animals; now specifically refers to deer meat.

**Vertical chopping machine (VCM):** A machine similar to a blender that has rotating blades used to grind, whip, emulsify, or blend foods.

**Vinaigrette (Fr.):** A cold sauce of oil and vinegar, usually with flavorings; it is a temporary emulsion sauce. The standard proportion is three parts oil to one part vinegar.

# W

**Whip:** To beat an item, such as cream or egg whites, to incorporate air. Also, a special tool. A whisk for whipping made of looped wire attached to a handle.

**White mirepoix:** Mirepoix that does not include carrots and may include parsnips and chopped mushrooms or mushroom trimmings; used for pale or white sauces and stocks.

**White stock:** A light-colored stock made with bones and/or vegetables that have not been browned.

# Y

**Yeast:** Microscopic fungus whose metabolic processes are responsible for fermentation; used for leavening bread and in making cheese, beer, and wine.

**Yogurt:** Milk cultured with bacteria to give it a slightly thick consistency and sour flavor.

# Z

**Zest:** The thin, brightly colored outer part of citrus rind. It contains volatile oils, making it ideal for use as a flavoring.

# Bibliography and Recommended Reading

Amendola, Joseph. *Ice Carving Made Easy.* 1st rev. ed. Chicago: National Restaurant Association, 1969.

Andrés, José, with Richard Wolffe. *Tapas: A Taste of Spain in America.* New York: Clarkson Potter, c2005.

Aylward, Larry. "The Absolute Wurst." *Meat Marketing and Technology,* February 1996.

Batterberry, Ariane. "High Livers." *Food Arts,* July–August 1993, pp. 58–60.

Beard, James. *American Cookery.* Boston: Little Brown, 1972.

Beard, James. *Beard on Bread.* New York: Knopf, 1973.

Black, Maggie. *The Medieval Cookbook.* New York: Thames and Hudson, 1996.

Blomquist, Torsten, and Werner Voëli. *A Gastronomic Tour of the Scandinavian Arctic.* Stockholm: Timbro, 1987.

Braudel, Ferdinand. *The Structures of Everyday Life: The Limits of the Possible.* Berkley, Calif.: 1992.

Brown, Dale. *The Cooking of Scandinavia.* New York: Time Life Books, 1968.

Cerveny, John G. "Effects of Changes in the Production and Marketing of Cured Meats on the Risk of Botulism." *Food Technology,* May 1980, pp. 240–53.

Cetre, F. O. *Practical Larder Work.* London: Sir Isaac Pitman and Sons, 1954.

Church, Ruth Ellen. *Mary Meade's Sausage Cook Book.* Chicago: Rand McNally, 1967.

Clayton, Bernard. *The Breads of France.* Indianapolis: Bobbs-Merrill, 1978.

Costner, Susan. *Great Sandwiches.* New York: Crown Publishers, 1990.

Coxe, Antony Himmisley. *The Great Book of Sausages.* Woodstock, N.Y.: Overlook Press, 1992.

Culinary Institute of America. *The New Professional Chef 5th and 6th eds.* Linda Glick Conway, ed. New York: John Wiley & Sons, Inc., 1991.

———. *Techniques of Healthy Cooking.* New York: John Wiley & Sons, Inc., 1993.

Dahl, J. O. *Kitchen Management: Construction, Planning, Administration.* New York: Harper and Brothers, 1928.

De Gouy, Louis Pullig. *Sandwich Manual for Professionals.* Stamford, Conn: The Dahls, 1939.

Desaulniers, Marcel. *Burger Meisters.* New York: Simon and Schuster, 1993.

Diggs, Lawrence, J. *Vinegar.* San Francisco: Quiet Storm Trading Co., 1989.

Dornenburg, Andrew, and Karen Page. "Tall Food Tales." *National Culinary Review,* January 1997, pp. 12–15.

Ehlert, Friedrich W., Edouard Longue, Michael Raffael, and Frank Wesel. *Pâtés and Terrines.* New York: Hearst Books, 1984.

Escoffier, Auguste. *The Complete Guide to the Art of Modern Cookery.* London: Heinemann, 1986.

———. *The Escoffier Cookbook: A Guide to the Fine Art of Cookery.* American ed. New York: Crown, 1976. (Translation of *Le Guide Culinairé,* 4th ed.)

Flower, Barbara, and Elisabeth Rosenbaum, eds. *The Roman Cookery Book by Apicius.* London: Harrap, 1961.

"The Foie Gras Story." *Wine Spectator,* November 1993, pp. 71–72.

Freeland-Graves, Jeanne Himich, and Gladys C. Peckham. *Foundations of Food Preparation.* 6th ed. New York: Prentice Hall, 1996.

Garlough, Robert. *Ice Sculpting the Modern Way.* New York: Thomson/Delmar Learning, 2004.

Gerard, C. "Let Them Eat Foie Gras." *Art Culinaire* 26 (Fall 1992).

Giascosa, Ilaria Gozzini. *A Taste of Ancient Rome.* London: University of Chicago Press, 1992.

Gingrass, David. "Hand-Crafted Salamis: An Experienced Sausagemaker Shares His Method." *Fine Cooking,* February–March 1995, pp. 56–59.

Guy, Christian. *An Illustrated History of French Cuisine.* New York: Bramhall House, 1962.

Halvorsen, Francine. *Catering Like a Pro.* Hoboken, N.J.: John Wiley & Sons, 2004.

Harlow, Jay. *The Art of the Sandwich.* San Francisco: Chronicle Books, 1990.

Hazan, Giuliano, and Marcella Hazan. *The Classic Pasta Cookbook.* London, New York: Dorling Kindersley, 1993.

Hodgson, W. C. *The Herring and Its Fishery.* London: Routledge and Kegan Paul, 1957.

Holmes, Jerry. *Ice Sculpting Techniques.* Nebraska: J.D. Technical Design; Texas: CHIPS Books, 1999.

Igoe, Robert S. *Dictionary of Food Ingredients.* New York: John Wiley & Sons, Inc., 1989.

Iowa State University. *Dry and Semi-Dry Sausage Short Course.* April 8–10, 2003.

Janericco, Terrence. *The Book of Great Hors d'oeuvre.* New York: John Wiley & Sons, Inc., 1990.

Jensen, Albert C. *The Cod.* New York: Thomas Y. Crowell Company, 1972.

Jordan, Michele Anna. *The Good Cook's Book of Oil and Vinegar.* Reading, Mass: Perseus Press, 1992.

Joyce, Jennifer. *Small Bites.* New York: DK Pub., 2005.

Kaufman, William. *The Hot Dog Cookbook.* Garden City, N.Y.: Doubleday, 1966.

Killeen, Johanne, and George Germon. *Cucina Simpatica: Robust Trattoria Cooking.* New York: Harper, 1991.

Klein, Maggie Blyth. *The Feast of the Olive.* San Francisco: Chronicle Books, 1994.

Lang, Jenifer Harvey, ed. *Larousse Gastronomique.* New York: Crown Publishers, 1984.

Lawrie, R. A. *Meat Science.* New York: Pergamon Press, 1991.

Leader, Daniel, Judith Blahnik, and Patricia Wells. *Bread Alone: Bold Fresh Loaves from Your Own Hands.* New York: William Morrow & Company, 1993.

Leto, M. T., and W. K. H. Bode. *The Larder Chef.* London: Heinemann, 1969.

Martin, Richard. "Foie Gras: Richly Diverse." *Nation's Restaurant News,* February 8, 1993, pp. 27, 33.

Martini, Anna. *Pasta and Pizza.* New York: St. Martin's Press, 1977.

McCalman, Max, David Gibbons. *Cheese: A Connoisseur's Guide to the World's Best.* New York: Clarkson Potter, 2005.

McGee, Harold. *The Curious Cook: More Kitchen Science and Lore.* San Francisco: North Point Press, 1990.

———. *On Food and Cooking, 2nd ed.* New York: Collier Books, 1988.

McHenry, ed. *The New Encyclopedia Britannica.* Chicago: Encyclopedia Britannica, 1992.

McNeill, F. Marian. *The Scots Kitchen: Its Traditions and Lore with Old-Time Recipes.* London: Blackie and Son, 1971.

Mengelatte, Pierre, Walter Bickel, and Albin Abelanet. *Buffets and Receptions.* English language ed. Surrey, England: Couldson, Virtue 1988.

Metz, Ferdinand E., and the United States Culinary Olympic Team. "The 1984 Culinary Olympics Cookbook: U.S. Team Recipes from the Sixteenth International Culinary Competition (International Kochkunst Ausstellung), Frankfurt, West Germany." Des Plaines, Ill.: *Restaurants & Institutions,* Cahners Pub., 1985.

Metz, Ferdinand E., L. Timothy Ryan. "Taste of Gold, the 1988 U.S. Culinary Team Cookbook: The Road to the World Championship." Des Plaines, Ill.: *Restaurants & Institutions,* Cahners Pub., 1989.

Meyer, Danny, and Michael Romano. *The Union Square Cafe Cookbook.* New York: Harper, 1994.

Midgley John. *The Goodness of Vinegars.* New York: Random House, 1994.

Murray, Joan. "Is Free-Range Better?" *Washingtonian,* October 1994.

Nicolas, Jean F. *Elegant and Easy: Decorative Ideas for Food Presentations.* Boston: CBI Publishing Company, 1983.

Nish, Wayne. "Understanding Foie Gras." *Fine Cooking Magazine,* December 1994–January 1995.

"Nitrate, Nitrite, and Nitroso Compounds in Foods." *Food Technology,* April 1997, pp. 127–36.

"Non Meat Ingredients." *Meat Industry,* 1986.

O'Neill, Molly. "Can Foie Gras Help the Heart?" *New York Times,* November 17, 1991.

Pearson, A. M., and F. W. Tauber. *Processed Meats.* New York: John Wiley & Sons, Inc., 1984.

Pellaprat, Henri-Paul, and John Fuller, eds. *Modern French Culinary Art: The Pellaprat of the 20th Century.* London: Virtue, 1978.

Perdue, Charles L., ed. *Pig's Foot Jelly and Persimmon Beer: Foodways from the Virginia Writers' Project.* Santa Fe: Ancient City Press, 1992.

Peterson, Sarah T. *Acquired Taste: The French Origins of Modern Cooking.* Ithaca, N.Y.: Cornell University Press, 1994.

Phalon, Richard. "Diversifying into Pâté de Foie Gras." *Forbes,* November 21, 1994.

Price, James F., and Bernard S. Schweigert, eds. *The Science of Meat and Meat Products.* Westport, Conn.: Food & Nutrition Press, 1987.

Regenstein, Joe M., and Carrie E. Regenstein. *Introduction to Fish Technology.* New York: John Wiley & Sons, Inc., 1991.

Revel, Jean François. *Culture and Cuisine.* New York: Doubleday, 1982.

Rey, Alain. *Dictionnairie Historique de la Langue Française.* Paris: Dictionnaires le Robert, 1995.

Romans, John. *The Meat We Eat.* Danville, Ill.: Insterstate Printers & Publishers, 1985.

Root, Waverly, and Richard de Rochemont. *Eating in America: A History.* New York: Ecco Press, 1981.

Rosengarten, David. "Bringing Home the Game." *Wine Spectator,* November 30, 1993, pp. 67–70.

Schmidt, Arno. *Chefs' Book of Formulas, Yields, and Sizes.* New York: John Wiley & Sons, Inc., 1990.

Shaw, Timothy. *The World of Escoffier.* New York: St. Martin's Press, 1995.

Silverton, Nancy with Teri Gelber. *Nancy Silverton's Sandwich Book.* New York: A.A. Knopf, 2002.

Sonnenschmidt, Frederic H., and Jean Nicolas. "The Professional Chef's Art of Garde Manger." *Institutions/Volume Feeding,* 1973.

———. *The Professional Chef's Art of Garde Manger.* 4th ed. New York: John Wiley & Sons, Inc., 1988.

Soyer, Alexis. *The Pantropheon: Or a History of Food and Its Preparation in Ancient Times.* New York: Paddington Press, 1977.

Strayer, Joseph R., ed. *Dictionary of the Middle Ages,* vol. 13. New York: Charles Scribner's Sons, 1983.

Tapper, Richard. *Tapas.* Boston: Periplus; North Clarendon, Vt.: Distributed by Tuttle Pub., c2001.

Time-Life Books, eds. "Terrines, Pâtés & Galantines." *The Good Cook: Techniques and Recipes.* Alexandria, Va.: Time-Life Books, 1982.

Tobias, Doris. "Gascon Commissary: Game and Foie Gras from the Wilds of Jersey City." *Wine and Spirits,* October 1993, pp. 43–45.

Toussaint-Samat, Maguelonne. *A History of Food.* Cambridge, Mass.: Blackwell Reference, 1992.

Uvezian. Sonia. *The Complete International Sandwich Book.* New York: Stein and Day, 1982.

Veale, Wency. *Step by Step Garnishing.* London: Quintet Publishing, 1989.

Verroust, Jacques Winker, Michel Pastoureau, and Raymond Buren. *Le Cochon.* Paris: Sang de la Terre, 1987.

Vongerichten, Jean-Georges. *Simple Cooking.* New York: Prentice Hall Press, 1990.

Weir, Joanne. *From Tapas to Meze.* New York: Crown, c1994.

Werlin, Laura. *The All American Cheese and Wine Book.* New York: Stewart, Tabori & Chang, 2003.

Werlin, Laura. *The New American Cheese.* New York: Stewart, Tabori & Chang, 2000.

Wheaton, Barbara Ketcham. *Savoring the Past: The French Kitchen and Table from 1300 to 1789.* New York: Touchstone Books, 1996.

Whelan, Jack. *Smoking Salmon and Trout: Plus Pickling, Salting, Sausaging, and Care.* Bowser, B.C.: Aerie Publishing, 1982.

Wilson, C. Anne. *Food and Drink in Britain: From Stone Age to Recent Times.* London: Constable and Company, 1973.

Winker, Mac, and Claire Winkler. *Ice Sculpture: The Art of Ice Carving in Twelve Systematic Steps.* Memphis, Tenn.: Duende Publications, 1989.

Wright, Clifford A. *A Mediterranean Feast.* New York: William Morrow and Co., 1999.

Yudd, Ronald A. *Successful Buffet Management.* New York: Van Nostrand Reinhold, c1990.

# Recipe Index

Tomato, Corn Salad with Aged
Cheddar and Chipotle-Sherry
Vinaigrette, 132

# B

Baba Ghanoush (Roasted Eggplant
Dip with Mint), 52
Bacon. *See also* Pancetta; Smoked
Bacon
in Braunschweiger, 284
in Cobb Salad, 134
on Croissant, with Avocado, Brie,
Sprouts, 183
and Shrimp, Barbecued, 455
in Shrimp, Wrapped, with Asian
Barbecue Sauce, 478
in Turkey Club, 165
Vinaigrette, Warm, Wilted Spinach
Salad with, 142
Baguette. *See also* Bruschetta;
Crostini
Bahn Saigon (Saigon Subs) with,
169
Chicken Salad, Curried, Open-Faced
Sandwich, 173
Duck Confit, with Apples and Brie,
162
Shrimp, Open-Faced Sandwich, 172
Bahn Saigon (Saigon Subs), 169
Balsamic Vinaigrette, 28, 344
Grilled Vegetable Appetizer with,
418
Port Wine, 28
Bananas, in Ambrosia Salad, 124
Barbecue(d)
Dry Rub, 226
Pork, Pulled Sandwich, 156
Pork Butt, Carolina, 226
Serrano-Wrapped Shrimp, 455
Shrimp and Bacon, 455
Spice Mix, 588
Terrine with Apricot Barbecue
Sauce, Carolina, 331
Barbecue Sauce, 156
Apricot, Carolina Barbecue Terrine
with, 331
Apricot-Ancho, 56

Asian, 478
Asian, Wrapped Shrimp with, 478
Southwestern, 57
Barquettes
with Fois Gras Mousse and
Rhubarb Compote, 503
Smoked Salmon Mousse, 450
Basil
Corona Bean Salad with, 123
Oil, 546
Oil, Tomato Dome Stuffed with Tofu
with Mozzarella and, 438
in Pâté Spice, 590
in Pesto, 48
in Sun-Dried Tomato Pesto, 49
-Tomato Sorbet, 440
and Tomato Soup, Cold Roasted,
62
Bay Leaf
in Bouquet Garni, Standard, 586
in Court Bouillon, 594
in Herbes de Provence, 591
in Sachet d' Épices, Standard, 587
Bean(s). *See also* Bean Salad;
Chickpeas; Haricots Verts;
Lentil(s)
Hash Cake, White Bean, Duck
Confit with Cippolini Onion
Marmalade, 448–449
Papaya and Black Bean Salsa, 44
Bean Salad
Black, 122
Corona, with Basil, 123
Corona, with Grilled Baby Octopus,
136
Mixed Bean and Grain, 116
Red Borlotti with Rosemary, 123
Shrimp and, 135
Beef
Air-Dried, Roman Style, 228
Bologna, 278
Canapés, Steak Tartare, 451
Carpaccio, 408
Corned, 206
Corned, in Reuben Sandwich, 157
Frankfurter, 277
Frankfurter, Reduced-Fat, 277
Jerky, 213
Landjäger, 272

Negimaki, 458
Pastrami, 207
Roast, on a Roll, 168
Saté, 462
Sausage, Southwest Dry, 290
Sausage, Summer, 271
Smoke-Roasted Sirloin, 225
Stock, White, 592
Tenderloin, Chile-Rubbed, 214
Beet(s)
Borscht, Clear Chilled, 72
Chutney, 527
and Horseradish Cure, Norwegian,
for Salmin, 204
Salad, Roasted, 102
Salad, Roasted, Foie Gras Roulade
with Smoked Duck Breast
and, 436
Vegetable Chips, 541
Vinaigrette, 33
Bell Pepper(s). *See* Pepper(s); Red
Peppers; Yellow Peppers
Black Bean
and Papaya Salsa, 44
Salad, 122
Black Pepper Dressing, Creamy, 40
Blitz Puff Pastry, 601
Blood Sausage with Apples, 285
Blue Cheese
in Cobb Salad, 134
Crackers, and Pecan, 544
Dressing, Maytag (Reduced-Fat), 41
Grapes Rolled in Blue de Bresse,
484
Mousse, 456
Tart, 387
Tart, Pear and, 390
Bocconcini, Marinated, 384
Bok Choy, Dim Sum with Chili Sauce,
496
Bologna, 278
Ham, 278
Borscht, Clear Chilled, 72
Boudin, Cajun, 266
Bouquet Garni, Standard, 586
Bratwurst
Chipolata, 281
German, 259
Smoked, 259, 281

# Subject Index

Encapsulations, savory, 404

Endive, 80–81

Enzymes
 in fermenation process, 191
 starter, cheese-making, 361, 376

Epoisses cheese, 365–366

Equipment/tools. *See also* Molds
 brine pumps/syringes, 196
 for cheese-making, 361, 376
 for forcemeats, 302
 garde manger knowledge of, 8
 for ice carving, 577–579
 management of, 10
 meat grinders, 239
 and menu planning, 11
 for omelet station, 561
 for raw bar, 559
 for sausage making, 238–239, 251, 272
 smokers, 198–199
 storage/placement of, 8, 11

Escarole, 80–81

Escoffier, Auguste, 21, 319

European flat oyster, 556

Explorateur cheese, 365–366

Eyes, of cheeses, 371

# F

Farmer's cheese, 363–364

Fats
 in confits/rillettes, 202
 duck, 202, 230–231
 in forcemeats, 237, 298
 oils, infused, 518–519
 rendering, 611
 in sausages, 237, 244

Fermentation
 in food preservation, 191
 sausages, dry/semi-dry, 241–243

Fern leaf dill, 83

Feta cheese, 363–364

Finger sandwiches, 148

Fish. *See also* Shellfish
 dried, history of, 2
 mousseline, 298
 smoking, 198, 208–209

Fish roe. *See* Caviar

5-4-3 mixture, for emulsion sausages, 244

Flatware, in buffet service, 565

Flavor profiles, 556

Flight of cheese, 374

Flowers, edible, in green salad, 87–88

Foams, savory, 403

Focal point, buffet presentation, 571–572

Foie gras, 318–320
 cleaning/preparation, 319–320, 343
 as forcemeat garnish, 300
 grades of, 319
 history of, 318–319
 marinating, 320
 mousse, 320
 presentation, 320, 342
 smoked, 324
 terrine of, 342–343

Fontina cheese, 367–368

Food allergies

Food costing, for buffets, 554

Food presentation. *See* Presentation

Food processor, forcemeat mixing, 302

Food safety. *See also storage* under individual foods
 buffet service, 562, 566, 575
 in cheese-making, 360, 376
 cross-contamination, 239
 eggs in mayonnaise, 19
 nitrosamines, in cured foods, 192
 oils/vinegars, infused, 519
 pork, certified, 236, 241, 272
 shellfish, raw bar, 556, 559

Forcemeats
 binders, 298, 300, 304
 common problems/solutions, 302
 country-style, 304
 defined, 298
 equipment/tools, 302
 fat, 237, 298
 5-4-3 mixture, for emulsion sausages, 244
 foie gras, 318–320
 galantines, 316–318
 garnishes, 246, 300–301, 316–317
 gratin, 304–305
 ingredients, main, 298

 making, 244–245
 mousseline, 305–306
 pâté en croûte, 313–315
 roulades, 316–318
 seasonings, 300
 straight/basic, 303
 terrines, 308–313
 testing, 302

Free water, 191

French country cooking, 75

French Revolution, 4

Fresh sausages, 240

Frisée, 80–81

Fromage blanc, 364

Fruits
 with cheese service, 375
 chips, 521
 chutneys, 517
 cold smoking, 199
 compote, 21, 149, 517
 for foams and encapsulations, 404
 purées, in vinaigrette, 19
 salads, 93
 salsas, 21
 soups, cold, 26–27

# G

Galantines
 on appetizer plates, 398
 compared to roulades, 316
 making, 316–318

Game meats, forcemeats, 298

Garde manger
 and buffets, 552–555
 as businessperson, 10–12
 career development, 6–7
 career opportunities, 5
 defined, 3
 education/training for, 7–9
 history of, 2–4
 professional, qualities of, 12–13
 skills/responsibilities of, 5–6

Garlic
 mayonnaise, 20
 roasting, 606

Garnishes
 in buffet service, 566, 571

Leeks, cleaning/trimming, 610
Legume salads, 93
Lemongrass, 86
Lettuces. *See also* Greens
    mild, 79–81
Liederkranz cheese, 366
Limburger cheese, 359, 366
Linens, for buffet service, 565
Liner, terrine molds, 310–311
Lines, buffets, 563–564
Littleneck clams, 558
Lucanica sausages, 236
Lumpfish roe, 406

## M

Mâche, 80–81
Malossol, 404
Management skills, of garde manger,
    10–12
Manchego cheese, 371–372
Mandoline, 520
Mango chutney, 517
Maple syrup, in cured foods, 193
Marinade, for foie gras, 320
Marjoram, 85–86
Mascarpone cheese, 363–364, 377
Mayonnaise, 19–21
    Aïoli, 20
    breaks, correcting, 20
    colée, 19, 22
    emulsion process, 19–20
    flavorings/garnishes, 20
    making, 19–20
    in mousses, 400
    as sandwich spread, 149
    storage of, 21
Maytag blue cheese, 370
Meats. *See also* specific meats
    as appetizer, 398
    curing. *See* Cured foods
    grain and slicing, 206
    grinders/grinding, 240–241
Menus
    appetizers on, 397–398
    buffet, 553
Mesclun mix, 83–84
Meze, 398

Micro greens, 89–90
Middle Ages, food guilds in, 3–4
Mie de pain, 612
Milk
    in cheese-making, 360–361, 376
    pasteurized/homogenized, 360
Mint, 85
Mise en place, in buffet service,
    561–563
Mizuna, 82
Mold
    blue-veined cheese, 368–369
    cheese, trimming, 376
    on dried sausages, 242
Molds
    for barquettes/tartlets, 395–396
    for cheese-making, 362
    for ice carving, 577
    for mousses, 402
    for pâté en croûte, 313, 315
    for terrines, 308–309
Montadito, 151
Monterey Jack cheese, 359, 367–368,
    373
Morbier cheeses, 367–368
Moulard duck, 319
Mousse
    foie gras, 320
    in hors d' oeuvres, 399–400
    preparing, 399–402
    in profiteroles, 396
Mousseline, 305–306
    ingredients, proportions, 305
    light, mixing technique, 306
    making, 305–306
Mozzarella cheese, 364, 374, 376
    making, 384–385
Muenster cheese, 366, 366, 367–368
Mullet roe, 406
Multiple needle pumps, 196
Mussles, steamed, for raw bar, 558
Mustard, 18, 517
Mustard flower, 88
Mustard greens, 82, 90
    red giant, 83

## N

National Shellfish Sanitation Program,
    556
Networking, professional, 9
Nitrates/nitrites, in cured foods,
    191–192
Nitrosamines, in cured foods, 192
Nitrous oxide, foams and
    encapsulations, 403–404
Nonreactive materials, 376
Nut(s)
    as forcemeat garnish, 300–301
    as hors d' oeuvre, 394
Nut butters, as sandwich spread, 149

## O

Oak leaf lettuce, 79
*Odyssey* (Homer), 235
Officier de bouche, 3
Oils
    emulsions, 16–17
    infused, 518–519
    as sandwich spread, 149
Olives, tapas menu, 397
Omelet station, 560–561
Onions
    aromatic, in sausages, 238
    red onion confit, 202
Open-faced sandwiches, 150
Orach, 90
Oregano/wild marjoram, 85–86, 88
Oriental greens mix, 84
Osetra caviar, 405
Osmosis, in food preservation, 190
Overhauling, in dry cure, 194
Overripe cheese, 365
Oxidization, discoloration, preventing,
    109
Oysters, in raw bar, 556

## P

Pacific oyster, 556
Pajusnay, 405
Panadas, in forcemeats, 300, 304
*Pan bagnat*, 148